AF847572

THE CAMBRIDGE HANDBOOK ON THE MATERIAL CONSTITUTION

Despite a long and venerable tradition, the material constitution almost disappeared from constitutional scholarship after the Second World War. Its marginalisation saw the rise of a normative and legalistic style in constitutional law that neglected the role of social reality and political economy. This collection not only retrieves the history and development of the concept of the material constitution, but it tests its theoretical and practical relevance in the contemporary world. With essays from a diverse range of contributors, the collection demonstrates that the material constitution speaks to several pressing issues, from the significance of economic development in constitutional orders to questions of constitutional identity. Offering original analyses supported by international case studies, this book develops a new model of constitutional reality, one that informs our understanding of the world in profound ways.

Marco Goldoni is Senior Lecturer in Legal Theory at Glasgow University. He is the author of *The Legacy of Pluralism* (2020, with M. Croce) and *The Materiality of the Legal Order* (2022). He is joint general editor of the journal *Jurisprudence* and co-editor of Law and Politics: Continental Perspectives (Routledge).

Michael A. Wilkinson is Professor of Law at the London School of Economics and Political Science (LSE). He is the author of *Authoritarian Liberalism and the Transformation of Modern Europe* (2021). He has held visiting professorships at Cornell, Paris II, the National University of Singapore and Keio University. His work has been translated into Portuguese, Italian, Spanish and Turkish.

The Cambridge Handbook on the Material Constitution

Edited by

MARCO GOLDONI
University of Glasgow

MICHAEL A. WILKINSON
London School of Economics and Political Science

CAMBRIDGE
UNIVERSITY PRESS

CAMBRIDGE
UNIVERSITY PRESS

Shaftesbury Road, Cambridge CB2 8EA, United Kingdom

One Liberty Plaza, 20th Floor, New York, NY 10006, USA

477 Williamstown Road, Port Melbourne, VIC 3207, Australia

314–321, 3rd Floor, Plot 3, Splendor Forum, Jasola District Centre, New Delhi – 110025, India

103 Penang Road, #05–06/07, Visioncrest Commercial, Singapore 238467

Cambridge University Press is part of Cambridge University Press & Assessment, a department of the University of Cambridge.

We share the University's mission to contribute to society through the pursuit of education, learning and research at the highest international levels of excellence.

www.cambridge.org
Information on this title: www.cambridge.org/9781316519462

DOI: 10.1017/9781009023764

© Cambridge University Press & Assessment 2023

This publication is in copyright. Subject to statutory exception and to the provisions of relevant collective licensing agreements, no reproduction of any part may take place without the written permission of Cambridge University Press & Assessment.

First published 2023

A catalogue record for this publication is available from the British Library.

Library of Congress Cataloging-in-Publication Data
NAMES: Workshop on The Material Constitution (2019 : University of Glasgow) | Goldoni, Marco, editor. | Wilkinson, Michael A., editor. | University of Glasgow. School of Law, host institution.
TITLE: The Cambridge handbook on the material constitution / edited by Marco Goldoni, University of Glasgow; Michael A. Wilkinson, London School of Economics and Political Science.
DESCRIPTION: Cambridge, United Kingdom ; New York, NY : Cambridge University Press, 2022. | Series: Cambridge law handbooks | Includes bibliographical references and index.
IDENTIFIERS: LCCN 2022029372 (print) | LCCN 2022029373 (ebook) | ISBN 9781316519462 (hardback) | ISBN 9781009023764 (epub)
SUBJECTS: LCSH: Constitutional law–Philosophy–Congresses. | LCGFT: Conference papers and proceedings.
CLASSIFICATION: LCC K3165.A6 W67 2019 (print) | LCC K3165.A6 (ebook) | DDC 342.001–dc23/eng/20220831
LC record available at https://lccn.loc.gov/2022029372
LC ebook record available at https://lccn.loc.gov/2022029373

ISBN 978-1-316-51946-2 Hardback

Cambridge University Press & Assessment has no responsibility for the persistence or accuracy of URLs for external or third-party internet websites referred to in this publication and does not guarantee that any content on such websites is, or will remain, accurate or appropriate.

Contents

Contributors

Denis Baranger is Professor of Public Law at Paris 2 – Panthéon-Assas University and Director of the Institut Michel Villey. He is co-editor of http://juspoliticum.com/la-revue and www.droitphilosophie.com. He teaches and publishes in several fields: constitutional law, history of ideas, jurisprudence. He has recently published *Penser la Loi* (Gallimard, 2018) and *La constitution: sources, interprétations, raisonnements* (Dalloz, 2022). He has received several awards (Prix François Furet, Grand Prix Charles Aubert de l'Académie des Sciences Morales et Politiques) and is an honorary member of the Institut Universitaire de France.

Francesco Bilancia is Professor of Public Law and Deputy-Director of the Department of Legal and Social Studies at the University of Chieti-Pescara (Italy). His research interests stretch from public and constitutional law, theory of law, fundamental rights, market regulation and social welfare law to EU law and the European integration process. Among his publications are *La crisi dell'ordinamento giuridico dello stato rappresentativo* (Padua, 2000), *I diritti fondamentali come conquiste sovrastatali di civiltà. Il diritto di proprietà nella CEDU* (Giappichelli, 2002; with S. Civitarese Matteucci) and 'The Material Constitutional Arrangement of the European Union', in M. Belov (ed.), *Peace, Discontent and Constitutional Law: Challenges to Constitutional Order and Democracy* (Routledge, 2021).

Ngoc Son Bui is Associate Professor of Asian laws at the Faculty of Law, University of Oxford. He works on comparative and constitutional law in Asia, with a focus on the socialist and Confucian culture-influenced jurisdictions. He is the author of *Constitutional Change in the Contemporary Socialist World* (Oxford University Press, 2020) and *Confucian Constitutionalism in East Asia* (Routledge, 2016).

Emilios Christodoulidis holds the Chair of Jurisprudence at the University of Glasgow. He is author of many articles on constitutional theory, democratic theory, critical legal theory and transitional justice, as well as author of *Law and Reflexive Politics* (Springer, 1998) and, more recently, *The Redress of Law* (Cambridge University Press, 2021). His work has appeared in English, Greek, French, Japanese and Spanish. He is an editor of the series Critical Studies in Jurisprudence (Routledge) and serves as a managing editor of the journal *Law & Critique*.

Stefano Civitarese Matteucci is Professor (chair) of Public Law in the Department of Legal and Social Studies, University of Chieti-Pescara and Honorary Visiting Professor, 2021–2026, at York Law School. His research interests range from constitutional law to theory of law, administrative law, social welfare law and EU law. Among his most recent publications are *Social Rights in Europe in an Age of Austerity* (Critical Studies in Jurisprudence, Routledge, 2017) and 'Public Administration Algorithm Decision-Making and the Rule of Law', *European Public Law* (2021).

Joel Colón-Ríos is Professor of Law at Victoria University of Wellington and Director of the New Zealand Centre for Public Law. His areas of interest include constitutional theory and comparative constitutional law. He has recently published *Constituent Power and Law* (Oxford University Press, 2020).

Mariano Croce is Associate Professor of Political Philosophy at Sapienza University of Rome. His research interests lie in the areas of institutionalism, legal pluralism and LGBTQI+ studies. His books include *The Legacy of Pluralism: The Continental Jurisprudence of Santi Romano, Carl Schmitt, and Costantino Mortati* (Stanford University Press, 2020, with Marco Goldoni) and *Carl Schmitt's Institutional Theory: The Political Power of Normality* (Cambridge University Press, 2022, with Andrea Salvatore).

Sandipto Dasgupta is Assistant Professor of Politics at the New School for Social Research. He is the author of the book *Legalizing the Revolution: India and the Constitution of the Postcolony* (Cambridge University Press, forthcoming) along with several articles on the topic of decolonisation, postcolonial political thought and constitutional theory.

Tom Flynn is a lecturer at the School of Law, University of Essex. His research deals with constitutionalism in the broadest sense, from the sub national to the supra-national. His monograph *The Triangular Constitution* was published by Hart in 2019, and his most recent article is 'Constitutional Pluralism and Loyal Opposition', *International Journal of Constitutional Law* (2021).

Marco Goldoni is Senior Lecturer in Legal Theory at the School of Law, University of Glasgow. Among his most recent publications are *The Legacy of Pluralism* (Stanford University Press, 2020, with M. Croce) and *The Materiality of the Legal Order* (Cambridge University Press, 2022). He is joint general editor of the journal *Jurisprudence* and co-editor of the Routledge series Law and Politics.

Rob Hunter holds a PhD in politics from Princeton University. He has written on the critique of political economy, state theory and constitutional theory. His recent publications include 'Marx's Critique and the Constitution of the Capitalist State', in Paul O'Connell and Umut Özsu (eds.), *Research Handbook on Law and Marxism* (Edward Elgar, 2021) and 'Critical Legal Studies and Marx's Critique: A Reappraisal', *Yale Journal of Law and the Humanities* (2021).

Jennifer Lander is Visiting Research Fellow in the School of Law at De Montfort University, working at the intersection of constitutional theory and political economy. She is the author of *Transnational Law and State Transformation: The Case of Extractive Development in Mongolia* (Routledge, 2020).

Signe Rehling Larsen is Fellow by Examination in Law at Magdalen College. Signe's research is concerned with the study of constitutions in a theoretical, historical and comparative perspective. Recent publications are *The Constitutional Theory of the Federation and the European Union* (Oxford University Press, 2021), 'Varieties of Constitutionalism in the European Union', *Modern Law Review* (2021), and 'European Public Law after Empires', *European Law Open* (2022).

Jessica Lawrence is Senior Lecturer at the School of Law, University of Essex. Her research focuses on international economic law and its impacts on human rights, environmental protection, and social norms. Her monograph *Governmentality in EU External Trade and Environment Policy: Between Rights and Market* was published by Routledge in 2018, and co-edited volume *The Politics of European Legal Research: Behind the Method* was released by Edward Elgar in 2022.

Martin Loughlin is Professor of Public Law at the London School of Economics & Political Science. His publications include *The Idea of Public Law* (Oxford University Press, 2003), *Foundations of Public Law* (Oxford University Press, 2010), *Political Jurisprudence* (Oxford University Press, 2017) and *Against Constitutionalism* (Harvard University Press, 2022). With Jens Meierhenrich, he co-edited *The Cambridge Companion to the Rule of Law* (Cambridge University Press, 2021).

Jens Meierhenrich is Professor of International Relations at the London School of Economics and Political Science. He previously taught for a decade at Harvard University and is the author, among other titles, of *The Legacies of Law* (Cambridge University Press, 2009) and *The Remnants of the Rechtsstaat* (Oxford University Press, 2018). His edited collections include *The Oxford Handbook of Carl Schmitt* (Oxford University Press, 2017) and *The Cambridge Companion to the Rule of Law* (Cambridge University Press, 2021).

Agustín José Menéndez is Associate Professor of Political Philosophy at the Department of Philosophy and Society, Universidad Complutense. He is the author of *Justifying Taxes* (Springer, 2001), *The Constitution's Gift* (Rowman & Littlefield, 2011, with J. E. Fossum) and *Challenging European Citizenship* (Springer, 2020, with E. D. Olsen). He was Editor in Chief of the *European Law Journal* and is now one of the managing editors of *European Law Open*.

Kolja Möller is Researcher at the Institute of Political Science, TU Dresden. His research interests are constitutionalism, political theory, and populism studies. Recent publications include 'Transnational Populism in Context: The UN, the EU and Beyond', in Paul Blokker (ed.), *Imagining Europe: Transnational Contestation and Civic Populism* (Palgrave Macmillan, 2021) and 'From Constituent to Destituent Power beyond the State', *Transnational Legal Theory* (2018).

Eva Nanopoulos is Senior Lecturer in Law at Queen Mary University of London. She is author of the *Juridification of Individual Sanctions and the Politics of EU Law* (Hart, 2020), co-editor of *The Crisis Behind the Euro-Crisis* (Cambridge University Press, 2019) and is currently working on a new book project, *Decolonizing Sanctions: A Legal History and Theory*. More generally, she is interested in critical approaches to the fields of international, EU and constitutional legal theory and history.

Tarik Olcay is Lecturer in Law at the University of Dundee where he teaches UK public law and comparative constitutional law. He holds a PhD from the University of Glasgow and his main research interests lie generally in the fields of comparative constitutional law and constitutional theory. His research particularly focusses on constitutional change, judiciary in illiberal regimes and the relationship between peace-making and constitutional reform processes. His research to date has been published in outlets including the *International Journal of Constitutional Law*, *Hastings Law Journal*, *European Constitutional Law Review* and *Public Law*.

Graziella Romeo is Associate Professor of Comparative Constitutional Law at Bocconi University in Milan, where she is the stream lead of the Bocconi Lab for European Studies. She writes on constitutional theory, also from a comparative perspective. Her most recent publications include 'The Conceptualization of Constitutional Supremacy: Global Discourse and Legal Tradition', *German Law Journal* (2020), and (with P. Cavaliere) 'From Poisons to Antidotes: Algorithms as Democracy Boosters?', *European Journal of Risk Regulation* (2022).

Lucia Rubinelli is Assistant Professor in Political Science at Yale University. Her research interests lie in the history of nineteenth and twentieth century political ideas, with a special focus on how democracy was theorised in debates about plebiscites and referenda in Europe. Her first book was *Constituent Power: A History* (Cambridge University Press, 2020).

Gunther Teubner is Professor Emeritus of Private Law and Legal Sociology at Goethe-University Frankfurt, and a former Otto Kahn Freund Professor at the London School of Economics. He is a member of the British Academy, Accademia Nazionale dei Lincei, Italy and Academia Europaea. Among his recent books are *Three Liability Regimes for Artificial Intelligence: Algorithmic Actants, Hybrids, Matrices* (Hart, 2021), *Critical Theory and Legal Autopoiesis: The Case for Societal Constitutionalism* (Manchester University Press, 2019) and *Constitutional Fragments: Societal Constitutionalism in the Globalization* (Oxford University Press, 2012).

Nikolas Vagdoutis is Postdoctoral Researcher at the University of Luxembourg (Department of Law). He holds a PhD from the University of Glasgow and an LLM from the London School of Economics (LSE). His research interests lie primarily in legal theory, political theory and public and EU law (especially on the economic and monetary governance of the European Economic and Monetary Union).

Mariana Velasco-Rivera is Lecturer at the School of Law and Criminology at Maynooth University. Her research interests are in the field of public law, specifically, constitutional law, comparative constitutional law and constitutional theory.

Lars Vinx is Associate Professor in the Faculty of Law at the University of Cambridge and a governing body fellow at Hughes Hall. Before coming to Cambridge, Lars was a Max Weber fellow at the European University Institute in Florence and then taught in the Department of Philosophy at Bilkent University in Ankara. He received his PhD in philosophy from the University of Toronto.

Neil Walker has been the Regius Professor of Public Law at the University of Edinburgh since 2008. He has written extensively on questions of subnational, national and transnational constitutional theory. His recent work includes *Sovereignty in Action* (ed.) (Cambridge University Press, 2019).

Tim Wihl is Professor (interim) of Public Law and Modern Legal History at Erfurt University, Germany in 2022–23. Before that, he was a visiting professor of constitutional theory at Humboldt University, Berlin. His publications include *Aufhebungsrechte* (Velbrueck, 2019).

Michael A. Wilkinson is Professor of Law at LSE. He has held visiting professorships at Cornell, Paris II, the National University of Singapore and Keio University. He is the author of *Authoritarian Liberalism and the Transformation of Modern Europe* (Oxford University Press, 2021). His work has been translated into Portuguese, Italian, Spanish and Turkish.

Introduction

The Return of the Material Constitution

Marco Goldoni and Michael A. Wilkinson

I.1 INFORMAL CONCEPTIONS OF THE CONSTITUTIONAL ORDER

The aim of this handbook is twofold: to introduce a concept – the material constitution – largely neglected in anglophone constitutional studies, and to provide an extended analysis of its use and application. Before we get going, a brief and abstract working definition can be offered. The material constitution is the set of concrete ordering forces, namely political unity, bearing institutions, social relations and fundamental political objectives, which make up the constitutional order.[1] In other words, it is the material that constitutes, and is constituted by, the formal process of constitutional law and the relation between them.

Analysis of this concept is comprised in this handbook of three different types of inquiry: historical reconstruction of the concept, criticism and specification of the concept, and contemporary applications in multiple legal and constitutional fields. These three focal points are reflected in the structure of the volume and they respond to different needs.

First, given the neglect of the tradition of the material constitution in the anglophone world, it is necessary to provide an historical reconstruction that tracks the most important theoretical reflections on the concept and their development over time in various historical periods. As might be imagined, the materiality that underlies this conception of the constitutional order can be the object of quite different takes and Part I tries to capture that diversity and the richness of conceptions.

Second, and in light of this diversity, the relevance of the notion for contemporary constitutional studies has to be tested and subjected to critical analysis. Part II will present a number of criticisms of the epistemic quality of the material constitution and associated methodology.

Finally, applications of what it means to understand constitutional issues from the perspective of the material constitution are developed. This is the task of the third Part of the handbook, where specific and concrete constitutional issues are addressed from the point of view of the material constitution with a view to show the solidity and utility of the concept as an interpretive device for grasping constitutional reality and its changes over time.

But before illustrating the main contributions of each part of the handbook, we have to answer an obvious but pressing question: why do we need yet another conception of the constitution? Don't we have enough already? After all, in anglophone constitutional theory, there are already a

We acknowledge the support of the Modern Law Review's Seminar Funding that made possible the international workshop organised in May 2019 at the University of Glasgow, out of which this Handbook emerges.

[1] See further M. Goldoni and M. Wilkinson, 'The Material Constitution' (2018) 81 *Modern Law Review* 567.

number of conceptions, including informal ones, of the constitutional order, juxtaposed to the standard view of the constitution as a rigid legal instrument codified in a document whose interpretation is mostly left to a specialised body of legal officials.[2] What is the difference between the material constitution and these informal conceptions? And what is the epistemic value of referring to the material constitution for constitutional studies?[3]

To speak of informal conceptions should not suggest a lack of interest in the juristic aspect of constitutional law; rather, it is to identify the engine of constitutional development in political and social vectors rather than formal legal (and primarily judicial) institutions. Three informal conceptions of the constitutional order can be outlined here and distinguished from the material constitution: the political constitution, the living constitution and the mixed constitution. Though it is possible to track resemblances, none of these conceptions overlap fully with the material constitution for reasons which we will explain. In identifying commonalities as well as differences, we will also be able to gain insight into the nature of the material constitution itself.

I.1.1 *The Political Constitution*

Perhaps the most influential informal conception of the constitution, at least in Commonwealth jurisdictions, is the 'political constitution'. This expression usually signifies experiences of Commonwealth countries (the UK, but also Australia and New Zealand) which do not have a rigid legal constitution, but one that is ultimately based on the political system and the interplay among political parties.[4] As famously illustrated by John Griffith in his seminal article,[5] the political constitution is a flexible order in which all major constitutional questions are answered politically. In Griffith's piercing analysis, this means that constitutional issues are political conflicts, sometimes masked in the guise of legal and judicial debates, but always ultimately political in nature. Griffith's notion retained a link with societal organisation and social conflict and, as we shall see in Section I.1.3, it has echoes of a more ancient informal notion of the constitution.

From the perspective of a normative or functionalist reading, a crucial tenet of constitutional ordering is that the political constitution is an ordinary process whose flexibility is better suited for democratic politics. When it works in a non-pathological way, the political constitution provides a channel for staging social conflict across the most important societal cleavages. For this reason, the notion was given a normative twist at the beginning of the twenty-first century, offered as an argument to defend a political (rather than a legal) conception of democracy and accountability.[6] Ultimately, the political constitution is either an answer to the question of the nature of the constitutional order (irrespective of whether constitutional questions *should* be answered in a legal or political way) or a normative argument in support of the centrality of parliamentary politics in maintaining the constitution.

[2] For an in-depth statement in support of this conception, see A. Sajo and R. Uitz, *The Constitution of Freedom: An Introduction to Legal Constitutionalism* (Oxford University Press, 2017).

[3] In a passing reference, Martin Loughlin implies that informal conceptions share the same realist (as in, political realism) assumptions: see M. Loughlin, *Foundations of Public Law* (Oxford University Press, 2010), 404.

[4] The canonisation of this understanding of the political constitution is J. Griffith, 'The Political Constitution' (1979) 42 *Modern Law Review* 1. See, on more recent developments, S. Gardbaum, *The New Commonwealth Model of Constitutionalism* (Cambridge University Press, 2013).

[5] Griffith, 'The Political Constitution'.

[6] The obvious references are J. Waldron, *Law and Disagreement* (Oxford University Press, 1999); R. Bellamy, *Political Constitutionalism* (Cambridge University Press, 2007) and G. Gee and G. Webber, 'What Is the Political Constitution?' (2010) 30 *Oxford Journal of Legal Studies* 273.

I.1.2 The Living Constitution

A second alternative conception is instantiated in the notion of the 'living constitution'. Though this is a prominent notion in anglophone jurisdictions, it is also well known in other Western constitutional traditions.[7] The notion emerged as soon as constitutions became rigid and codified. The living constitution represented from the beginning an answer to the issue of ossification of constitutional structures and meaning in contexts where constitutional interpretation would be subject to a degree of juridification and constitutional change would be overly demanding. It is not surprising that the living constitution has been a recurrent theme in US constitutional scholarship and judicial practice, understood as an alternative to the other dominant methods of constitutional interpretation, namely textualism and originalism.[8]

According to the living constitution doctrine, the meaning of the constitution constantly evolves in a way that remains at least partially independent from the formal translation of constitutional change into explicit written norms. In most cases, the living constitution allows legal officials to consider signals coming from society. In the case of US constitutionalism, these signals are inputs sent by political parties, social movements, or other social groups concerning a crucial but delimited and circumscribed topic (e.g., racial desegregation, women's rights). The living constitution allows legal institutions to 'catch up' with evolving social meanings of key aspects of community life.

I.1.3 The Mixed Constitution

A third conception – less visible in contemporary debates – is the mixed constitution, which is also the most ancient of the informal conceptions of the constitutional order. The mixed constitution sees the constitutional order as a balance (albeit not necessarily a peaceful one) among different social classes. Its most famous ancient theorists are Aristotle and Polybius, formulating the idea of 'mixed government', and its most famous modern formulation belongs to James Madison.[9] But, strictly speaking, the mixed constitution is not a legal notion but an ideal one.

In its ancient versions, the aim of the mixed constitution is to approximate a synthesis among the major forms of government: monarchy, aristocracy and democracy. Its virtue is meant to lie in the fact that, in achieving a balance of forces, the constitution avoids one of the forms prevailing over the others. In this way, the mixed constitution would provide an economy of the virtues intrinsic to each form of government while limiting the effect of their vices. As such, the 'mixed constitution' represents a harmonious form of constitutional order, but only on the premodern assumption that various constitutional authorities and virtues, as well as powers and vices, derive from particular groups or estates. Stripped of this assumption we are left with the mere idea of the separation of powers, vague hopes around checks and balances, and the uncertain legacy of the 'fear of the majority', as the various powers are merged into one sovereign power in the modern constitutional imagination.

[7] E.g., S. Bartole, *Interpretazioni e trasformazioni della costituzione italiana* (Il Mulino, 2004).

[8] See B. Ackerman, 'The Living Constitution' (2007) 120 *Harvard Law Review* 1737. In more recent times, there have been syncretic attempts at mixing the two approaches: J. Balkin, *Living Originalism* (Harvard University Press, 2011).

[9] Federalist, no 40 and no 51 (which mentions Polybius). On the 'mixed constitution', see further A. Somek, *The Cosmopolitan Constitution* (Oxford University Press, 2013), 76–77.

I.1.4 *The Material Constitution*

The importance placed by the political constitution on the modern political system and its organisation into political parties continues to resonate with many recent analyses of the material constitution. The same can be said of the role of social movements in constitutional change. The idea that constitutional change does not need to be an outcome of a formal process of amendment is in fact common to all three informal conceptions.

But in the case of the political constitution, the autonomy of politics is the condition of the formation and development of the constitutional order, and each profound societal change can be registered as a fundamental constitutional change only if it passes through institutional political channels. Though in the canon of the material constitution the centrality of the political system is far from ignored, the relationship with societal organisation is foregrounded and thematised in a distinct way.

There is a formalist remnant in all theories of the political constitution in the sense that they postulate political action predominantly – or even exclusively – within the space of established institutions.[10] There is no room for politics outside of parliamentary or other institutionalised forms. Ultimately, political representation is taken to be the alpha and the omega of legitimate constitutional space. This entails that the material aspect of the constitutional order cannot be seriously *politicised*; instead, it is bracketed or ignored. It also means that the concept of constituent power, the generation of social power into constitutional power, cannot be theoretically treated. The price to pay for the cordoning off of social relations from political activity is rather high for constitutional studies. Political conflict is analysed only in the form of parliamentary debate or in the relation between parliament and government. Political autonomy takes a very thin form: it is a party-based political system, divorced from its relation to society, let alone class interests and class relations.

There are other crucial elements of differentiation which justify the adoption of the material constitution as a framing device for constitutional analysis. First, both the political and the living constitution takes the question of political unity (its establishment and its material underpinnings) for granted. To put it in more straightforward terms: the approaches advocated by political and living constitutionalists are uninterested in questioning the terms of the formation of political unity. Living constitutionalism does not even register as a constitutional question until – perhaps – secessionist movements become visible and electorally salient. This is not the case for the notion of the material constitution as the conditions of formation and maintenance of political unity are crucial for ordering purposes and the study of them essential for understanding the constitution.

A second crucial question concerns the materiality of constitutional order. At best, the political and living constitutions can build a bridge with societal formations by taking into account the role of social movements as active and influential components of constitutional interpretation.[11] But the internal link between societal organisation and the constitutional order

[10] Martin Loughlin rightly identifies in this version of the political constitution the swan song of a utilitarian tradition which sees legislative law-making as a means for implementing policy objectives and achieving social outcomes: M. Loughlin, 'The Political Constitution Revisited' (2019) 30 *King's Law Journal* 5. Loughlin's critique is also relevant because it spots an essential missing feature in the analysis of the political constitution: the conditions which allow for the emergence of the 'political' are left outside of the scope of analysis and for reasons that have to do with the way politics is understood by Griffith and his heirs.

[11] See, for example, the study of the impact of social movements on the interpretation of the US constitution by R. Siegel and J. Balkin, 'Principles, Practices, and Social Movements' (2006) 154 *University of Pennsylvania Law Review* 827.

is not thematised by either of these informal approaches. The economic and social conditions which enable a certain constitutional order are left invisible or at best mentioned as an aside. In contrast, the material constitution offers an epistemic advantage compared to the political and the living constitution: it thematises the law inherent to the organisation of a society's political economy and other fundamental social relations. In other words, from the viewpoint of these two informal approaches, we could say that the nature of the *relation* between social organisation and constitutional order is not problematised for the understanding of the modern constitution.

In avoiding the question of the ordering force of societal organisation, both political and living constitutionalists elide the political aims of modern societies. As the fact of social and political organisation is excised from the analysis, both informal conceptions end up, once again, in an impasse about which institution represents the privileged site of constitutional development. And because of the rather thin material understanding of the constitutional order, even this last choice is presented in rather reductive terms: either the legislature or the judiciary.

The emergence of the material constitution is embedded in modern processes of social differentiation and specialisation.[12] This entails both a differentiation between those who govern and those who are governed (which should not be limited to the establishment of the political system), *and* a concrete political economy whose organisation requires the establishment of modes and relations of production as well as the regulation and protection of the market economy.

The regime represented by the material constitution is a network of differentiated and conflictual elements which dominant subjects try to mould and steer toward the realisation of fundamental political aims. The material constitution is, thus, dynamic and concrete. Concrete because it is founded on the material conditions of social existence and reproduction. Dynamic because in the formation, separation, and conflict between social classes the gravitational aggregation of interests always leaves space for fundamental material change. In other words, what makes the emergence of social differentiation possible has a direct impact on the constitutional order.

Unlike the normative thrust of the mixed constitution, the material constitution does not identify the balance of forces as a desirable state of things, necessarily conducive to virtuous development.[13] The enquiry inspired by the material constitution is not interested in purely normative questions. Neither, however, is the constitutional order collapsed into political economy; it contains the structuring forces that make solid what would otherwise melt into the air of sheer social relations. The formation of the constitutional order is internal to that of modern society, but of course these two poles do not entirely overlap.

In order to grasp this fully, it is necessary to track the different origins of the notion of the material constitution and how they have evolved in various eras. This handbook documents an historic arc that spans from the second half of the nineteenth century to current times. The temporal starting point is far from arbitrary, the connection between Marx and materialist philosophy is unquestionable. But it is only after the First World War, and especially during the Interwar period, that the notion of the material constitution was developed in a systematic way.[14]

[12] For a recent overview of the topic: E. Christodoulidis, *The Differentiation and Autonomy of Law* (Cambridge University Press, 2022).

[13] For an open plea in favour of a Machiavellian mixed constitution, see J. McCormick, *Machiavellian Democracy* (Cambridge University Press, 2011).

[14] For a detailed analysis, see M. Wilkinson, *Authoritarian Liberalism and the Transformation of Modern Europe* (Oxford University Press, 2021).

1.2 THE MATERIAL CONSTITUTION IN HISTORICAL PERSPECTIVE

The origins of the material constitution lie with Marx, Lassalle and the generation of classical Marxist scholars who followed. 'Origins' here of course is only relative; there is no *creatio ex nihilo*. Marx and Marxists were developing ideas of previous epochs and building on political events, as represented by dates such as 1789 and 1848, as well as the philosophers that inspired them, notably Rousseau and Hegel. As Marxism is a resolutely historical as well as materialist philosophy, it would only be expected that, as history changes, with the gains and losses of revolutionary class struggle, so too would Marxist conceptions of the material constitution. In Chapter 1, we outline the origins as well as various transformations of the Marxist tradition as it evolves, in ebbs and flows, across decisive periods. We track a trajectory that starts with Marx and his focus on modes and relations of production, and is then transformed in sync with crucial socio-economic and political changes: the Russian revolutions and First World War (Lenin and Luxemburg), interwar turbulence and the rise of Fascism (Gramsci) and the emergence of a new financialised political economy within the framework of supranational and global institutions (Balibar, Negri).

What is left of the Marxist material constitution? It is an open question. The main claim of our chapter is that there is still a latent potential that is extremely useful for constitutional analysis in the twenty-first century. But this can be appreciated only by abandoning a determinist philosophy of history that underlies certain Marxisms and by retaining the intuition concerning the centrality of class struggle and the dynamics of the market economy. In Chapter 13, Emilios Christodoulidis adds an important qualification, suggesting that the relation between the institutional and the material levels cannot be treated in structural or functional terms. His contribution addresses directly the question posed here and the answer is clear: a Marxist–structuralist understanding of the material constitution cannot disentangle the institutional from the material if it neglects the 'gap' or 'slack' between these domains. Christodoulidis suggests redeeming an earlier Marx, more attentive to immanent critique which tracks constitutional formation as a question (at the same time) of ordering and disruption. In Chapter 8, Nikolas Vagoudtis presents another important and influential variation on contemporary Marxism as embodied in the work of Greek Marxist theorist Nico Poulantzas. Vagdoutis highlights the relevance for a theory of the material constitution of Poulantzas' conception of the State as the 'condensation of social forces'. Navigating a middle ground between structuralist and humanist conceptions of the legal order, Vagoudtis puts the emphasis on Poulantzas' understanding of the State and its law as relatively autonomous.

The legacy of Marx will remain contested. But Marxism itself retained a significant if often invisible influence even on non-Marxist theories, and perhaps especially on anti-Marxists theorists, forced to contend with the power of Marx's ideas in practice and the political movements that sought to translate his legacy into concrete social change. This was so especially of the writing of the early twentieth century, when reactionary conservatism emerges with such force, partly in response to liberalism's own confrontation with Marxism and socialism. As the handbook illustrates, there are important historical and epistemic reasons behind the development of the concept precisely in the interwar period: the disconnect between liberal constitutional orders and the changes affecting both the political and the economic systems (from the extension of the franchise to the dramatic 1929 crisis) pushed constitutional scholars to think about constitutional orders in more substantive terms, particularly as political parties organised and governed around a set of principles, values and aims.

I.2.1 The Transformation of the Material Constitution in the Interwar Era

The decline of the revolutionary socialism of the era of Lenin and Luxemburg, outlined in Chapter 1, with ossification in the East and defeat in the West, did not mean the decline of the material constitution per se. On the contrary, in significant respects, it gave it renewed impetus, as scholars from other traditions picked up its conceptual toolkit. As the unitary fate of the material constitution in terms of its connection with Marxism was splintered, certain new commonalities with very different politics would thus emerge, partly due to the sense of exhaustion of the energies of classical liberalism, after its domination in the nineteenth century. To put it crudely, if revolutionary Marxism had failed, liberalism had not triumphed, leaving a space for new constitutional ideas and politics to emerge.

For one thing, the hopes and fears of a parliamentary path to socialism remained alive with the political representation of the working-class in conditions of parliamentary supremacy. How concrete this prospect actually was may be debated, but there was a deep conservative political and cultural concern over the fragility of established institutions in conditions of increasing inequality and plurality. Thus, to add to the sense of transition after the First World War, of the decline of prevailing structures of power, there was a growing sense of the inability of liberalism to retain its constitutional hegemony. With the interwar writings of a range of constitutional theorists, notably including Carl Schmitt, Hermann Heller, and Constantino Mortati, a distinct kind of critique of liberal formalism begins to emerge, which doesn't depend on Marx or the prospect of revolutionary socialism.

Rather than tackle the Marxist critique of liberal political economy directly, these theorists, whether conservative or social democratic, often proceeded by underscoring the cultural brittleness of liberalism. In each case there was a critique, whether deep or shallow, of the philosophical–political orientation of liberalism, but not necessarily of its economic assumptions. For the new philosophers of the conservative right, liberal philosophy and politics was simply not up to the task of maintaining an order of private property rights against its socialist opponents. For the new generation of social democrats such as Hermann Heller, the inequalities resulting from a liberal economy would undermine institutions of liberal democracy itself.[15]

This transformation in the practice and grammar of the material constitution, fomented by a concern with liberalism's political weakness, thus assumes different forms. Material constitutional analysis for those in the socialist tradition tends to remain concentrated around issues of societal reproduction, material inequality and class conflict; for conservative scholars, around issues of culture, collective identity and the potential collapse of the security guaranteed by existing liberal institutions. As Vagdoutis further notes in his chapter on materialist thought in Greek constitutionalism, the impact of German conservative scholars such as Rudolph Smend and Carl Schmitt, who to some extent blended left and right critiques of liberal formalism, extended far beyond central Europe. Their work had a profound influence on the social logic of integration pursued by social democratic scholars in their attempt to go beyond classical liberal individualism and remedy its weakness.

Yet as the pillars of the material constitution of liberalism come under more serious political and economic pressure, domestically as well as in the context of contractionary effects of the decline of European imperial powers, a very different set of alternatives to liberalism emerges with the advent of fascism, namely of a material constitution constructed around ideas of racial

[15] See H. Heller, *Sovereignty [1927]* (Oxford University Press, 2019).

identity and a cult of violence. Although novel in important respects, this new movement displays both continuities and discontinuities with the previous constitutional order.[16]

In this new era, Schmitt and Mortati become the standard-bearers for a distinct type of material constitutional analysis and it is no surprise that they so deeply influence a range of contributions to this volume, leaving a profound imprint on twentieth century constitutional scholarship across the political spectrum and in a variety of sub-domains and jurisdictions. As reflected by their scholarship, a new conservative liberalism gains ascendency as the bourgeoise becomes unsure of its own position and of its capacity to maintain political domination. Law itself is not enough to guarantee the material reproduction of the legal regime; in particular the threat of strikes, expropriation of property, loss of asset value through hyperinflation and growing power of trade unions all threaten to undermine the economic and political hegemony of the bourgeoise bloc. As Karl Polanyi explains, this liberal turn to authoritarian structures of power in an attempt to maintain order, against growing counter-movements in defence of society and the increasing commodification of the uncommodifiable (labour, land and money), were widespread in Europe and beyond.[17]

Mortati, like Schmitt, constructs a new version of the material constitution, not only against Marxism but against liberal formalism and the perception of its insufficiently robust political character. As Lucia Rubinelli outlines in Chapter 5, Mortati's project is a reaction to positivism and formalism, as well as the liberal–legalist attempts to separate law from politics. In Mortati's version the constitution is given concrete meaning and social stabilisation by dominant groups in society and through the dominance of their political objectives, albeit not in any decisionistic manner (as Schmitt had proclaimed). Instead, Mortati, like Heller, highlighted the significance of the role of political parties in forging social and political unity over time, acting as 'the institutional arm of intermediate communities'. In the concrete situation of interwar Italy it was for the fascist party to be the bearer of the fundamental political objectives of the bourgeoise state, often with the support of liberals and centrists.

I.2.2 *Weimar's Material Schisms*

The jurisprudence of Weimar Germany contributed in a significant way to the debate on the material constitution. It is important here to exercise some degree of caution in explaining the orientation of Weimar's jurists, and in generalising from it, given the peculiarities of the situation in Germany after First World War. Yet the influence of the Weimar experience, the schisms it created on the left, as well as between left and right, and the meaning given to it by constitutional theorists and political commentators in the post-war era, not only in Germany, but in Europe and beyond, is undeniable.[18]

The Weimar republic was built on a constitutional compromise but the German working class was now fully emancipated as a matter of universal suffrage and had a mass party to lead it toward material social change, including, at least on some accounts, toward a socialist state within the terms of the constitution itself. In the early stages of the Republic there were those on the left, including notably a group of Weimar labour lawyers, who believed in the possibility of

[16] See Wilkinson, Authoritarian Liberalism, ch. 1. Also I. Lander, *Apprentice's Sorcerer: Liberal Tradition and Fascism* (Haymarket Books, 2012).

[17] K. Polanyi, *The Great Transformation [1944]* (Beacon Press, 2001).

[18] See, e.g., U. Greenberg, *Weimar's Century: German Emigres and the Ideological Foundations of the Cold War* (Princeton University Press, 2015).

radical change through utilising the economic parts of the Weimar constitution.[19] What was clear was that social inequality had become a *constitutional question*, a question over the basic rules governing the interrelation between state and society.

Conservative jurists such as Schmitt first turned to the resources offered by the Weimar constitution to shore up the protection of the economically liberal parts of the constitutional order. But it soon became clear that this would not suffice and a more authoritarian turn would be necessary, first with the cabinets of authoritarian liberalism and then with the rise of National socialism. Questions concerning the material constitution and its relationship with constitutional form would quickly multiply.

In the mid-Weimar period, when Schmitt penned his major contribution to constitutional theory, *Verfassungslehre*, his trick was to identify a substantive constitutional order that stood over and above the formal text. This created a concrete difficulty, however, first because of the vast array of provisions, liberal and social, that were covered in the Weimar constitution, and second in the absence of any consensus over or support for the form of the Weimar state, its new Republic still perceived as illegitimate by monarchists, as well as Communists. Politically polarising issues became constitutional questions against a backdrop of increasing distrust toward the Republic and little loyalty toward the background state.

Schmitt's response was, in part, to bracket the question of state theory and collapse the idea of the state into the constitution, as the 'soul of the state', providing its own unity and order. By this, Schmitt did not mean the positive law of the constitution, but a constitutional *identity*. The notion of constitutional identity, the big 'C' or Absolute Constitution, could then be raised above the written text and defended by a decisionistic organ of power. In the immediate context, this meant the use of Article 48 of the Weimar Constitution to rule by presidential diktat and decree, which was later used from 1930–33 in a series of cabinets that bypassed parliament entirely.

In Chapter 2, Jens Meierhenrich recounts Schmitt's attempt to wrest material analysis away from Marxism as a call for an 'affective constitutionalism'. This was, in his view, inspired by the phenomenological tradition as well as German historicism, which he traces back to Herder's eighteenth century 'community of language'. In Meierhenrich's reading, Schmitt's material constitution was pursued predominantly as a collective existentialist project pitted against liberal technologies of rule. Although it eventually became a violent, militaristic and ethnically exclusionary project built on racial identity, this was not intrinsic to its logic. Meierhenrich argues that it would be more appropriate to describe Schmitt's theory, as least in 1928 when he published *Verfassungslehre*, as substituting *nomos*, rather than ethnos, for the concept of *demos*. In this way Meierhenrich even suggests affinities with later work by critical legal scholars such as Robert Cover and Marxist scholar Raymond Williams, for whom the material world was irreducibly cultural as much as economic. Schmitt's material constitutionalism, then, in Meierhenrich's view, was reactionary, but not (yet) racial, militant only in its opposition to the rise of machine politics and to constitutional engineering, in defence of constitutional sentiment and '*Volkish*' feeling.

National socialism had a profound impact on material constitutional theorising. Ernst Fraenkel's *Dual State* makes the case for a historical continuation of a residual normative system in the private economy in combination with the dictatorial prerogative powers of the Nazi regime. Yet, in Lars Vinx's view, outlined in Chapter 6, this dual state, although presenting some aspects of legal continuity with the Weimar constitution, could not be characterised as

[19] See R. Dukes, *The Labour Constitution* (Oxford University Press, 2014).

having a material constitution at all, at least in the normative sense employed by Vinx, who suggests that Nazi Germany also failed to qualify as a state. Vinx argues that the attempt to rest the Nazi regime on the foundations of a 'concrete order' (Schmitt's third type of juristic thought alongside normativism and decisionism) fails because there was no such pre-existing order; one would inevitably have to be determined in an authoritarian fashion, undercutting the plurality of the social order and inevitably returning to a decisionistic frame.

Whatever the correct view of the Nationalist Socialist transition, Schmitt's work would continue to resonate in and influence jurisdictions far and wide, particularly his view that amendments to the constitution must not assail the 'Constitution as a basic decision'. This doctrine would be brought to fruition by many liberal scholars in the post-war period, often with little understanding of its pedigree.

In Chapter 19, Velasco-Rivera and Colón-Ríos show how, in certain Latin American Courts, the concept of the material constitution, lacking the certainty of ordinary legal rules, 'can be deployed by jurists to defend opposite positions about the limits of constitutional reform'. They show that 'judges have applied the concept of the material constitution in order to argue *against* the doctrine of unconstitutional constitutional amendments', quite contrary to Schmitt's intention. In their view the older doctrine of the 'historical constitution', representing the 'fundamental laws' of the nation as a historical community, is the more robust concept in terms of attempts to limit the amending power in favour of an established constitutional identity and more generally in rejection of the notion of constituent power to radically change the constitutional order. This gives it a more solid foundation, based on a doctrine derived from eighteenth and nineteenth century Spanish jurisprudence. They also note its continuing relevance, notably in Hungary, even though largely now replaced by the concept of the constitution in the material sense.

I.2.3 From Legal Positivism to the Sociology of Law: The Institutionalists and Beyond

Outside the extraordinary turbulence of the Weimar republic, other comparable shifts in constitutional approach if not in political temperature can be identified. Even in the context of its more moderate simulacrum in the British constitutional scene, which faced its own crises of authority after the First World War but didn't witness anything like the degree of turmoil experienced in continental Europe, there would be a turn away from the liberalism, positivism and formalism that emerged out of the long nineteenth century.

In Chapter 3, Martin Loughlin argues that Harold Laski's late materialist turn unfolds *in response to* the interwar crisis of parliamentary democracy and the decline of liberal constitutionalism. Laski eventually comes to view the state as a capitalist formation expressing class relations in a rigidly deterministic manner; it was not from any belief in working class emancipation but his realisation of the concrete nature of ruling class power that turns Laski toward Marxism. With the end of the Victorian compromise, and capital ending its period of imperial expansion, crisis was bound to follow. But it was not to result in any socialist solution. The failure of the general strike of 1926, followed by the collapse of Labour party representation in the General Election of 1931, had 'shattered Laski's belief in the parliamentary road to socialism'. And he rejected the revolutionary road as leading 'invariably to dictatorship'. The marriage between democracy and capitalism had ended but there was no new alliance in sight, and Laski ends, in Loughlin's verdict on his last book published in 1950, in a mood of complacency over the status of parliamentary government and a retreat 'from any serious examination of the issues confronting postwar society'.

Although Laski's positions oscillated in response to the changing British political scene, there was a clear and stable conceptual critique undergirding his work as a whole. Legal relations, as well as the state itself, were, for Laski, an expression of class relations, not of the inner logic of a normative system. This diagnosis was combined with a rejection of the dominant legal positivism of the period, which had been taken to its logical conclusion in Kelsen's 'pure theory of law' and associated political relativism.[20]

The constitutional implications of the move away from positivism and formalism were repeated elsewhere and among a range of scholars who didn't share Laski's political trajectory, or Schmitt's for that matter. The new materialist jurisprudence that emerges in the early twentieth century, consolidated in the interwar period, constitutes a broad church, encompassing French institutionalists such as Maurice Hauriou and Léon Duguit (who was a significant influence on Laski), Austrian pluralists like Eugen Ehrlich, the Italian constitutional theory of Santi Romano and socialist state thinkers such as Heller.[21]

This type of sociological institutionalism had its cradle in Europe, but it reached, although in variation, the United States as well, as documented by Rob Hunter in Chapter 7, on the doctrine of the material constitution in the United States. Hunter discusses the limits of the contributions of Charles Beard, Karl Llewellyn and Louis Hartz. In particular, he exposes the crude and disappointing materialism of Beard, which cannot register crucial phenomena like racism in constitution-making and, more predictably, of Hartz's monochromatic account of the dominant liberalism of the Founding Fathers. Llewellyn's approach to the constitution, as Hunter shows, although lacking a proper materialist basis and fetishing the juristic dimension, provides an interesting variation on a material legal institutionalism by recognising the continuous reproduction of institutions through conflict and antagonism.

I.3 THE MATERIAL CONSTITUTION AT THE END OF HISTORY

In Giorgio Agamben's evocative formulation, Schmitt had argued 'without reservation' for the 'involvement of the jurist in the material constitution of [his] times'.[22] But Schmitt also perceived himself to be the 'final representative' of the *jus publicum Europaeum*, with the material constitution of Europe's long nineteenth century coming to an end in the sea of concrete disorder and lawlessness. This, above all, is what Schmitt feared in the interwar conjuncture. And it was a fate, he was convinced, that legal positivism and the technical turn of liberal politics was impotent to defend against.

Schmitt may have been wrong about the ascendance of legal positivism, his own theory ironically being later picked up, often without acknowledgement or even by those in rhetorical opposition to it, to advance all manner of militant and authoritarian positions, notably around the theme of constitutional identity. But he was to some extent correct about the second point, the category of 'the political' eroded or lost (with some important exceptions) through the dominance of behaviouralist, technical, empiricist and systems-theoretical analyses.

[20] See the reconstruction of Kelsen's proceduralist understanding offered in L. Vinx, 'Hans Kelsen and the Material Constitution of Democracy' (2021) 11 *Jurisprudence* 466.

[21] See further, M. Loughlin, *Political Jurisprudence* (Oxford University Press, 2017).

[22] G. Agamben, 'A Jurist Confronting Himself', in J. Meierhenrich and O. Simons (eds.), *The Oxford Handbook of Carl Schmitt* (Oxford University Press, 2017), 458.

I.3.1 The Post-War Material Constitution

The new compromise represented by the New Deal and, slightly later, the rise of the Welfare States across Western European countries, changed the material constitution in profound ways. Roughly, with the rise of the new Fordist organisation of industrial production came a re-organisation of the social security system and an increased involvement of the State in the political economy. Inevitably, these changes would have an impact on the constitutional order of a magnitude which would reverbarate across disciplines and domains.

Constitutional thought registered this change. Buoyed by the pervasiveness of the myth of Weimar's decline as a crisis of democracy, and a related counter-majoritarianism that found support on both sides of the Atlantic, a re-energised liberalism would abandon Kelsenian relativism and embrace its own form of Schmittian militancy. Laissez-faire was buried, and liberalism was resurrected on a new, firmer foundation, ideologically due to the pronounced anti-communism of Western intellectuals and institutions and, materially, due to the gradual ascendance and eventual supremacy of US capitalism and its military–industrial and neo-imperial complex.[23]

In terms of the broader post-war trajectory, two mutually reinforcing trends combine to de-politicise the constitution: the symbiosis of European cultural conservatism with a new moralistic liberalism, particularly as exported and re-imported in the links between German emigres and American scholars, networks and institutions and a de-radicalisation of critical theory under the guise of an ideological Europeanism, retreat from class politics and turn to identity, discourse and culture.

I.3.2 A Symbiosis of Cultural Conservatism and Moralistic Liberalism

On the side of conservativism and liberalism, the anti-Marxist preoccupation of scholars in the 1920s could now count on the material and ideological support of the dominant global superpower. As Udi Greenberg has recently documented, there was a mutual symbiosis between West German and US academic, political and economic elites underpinned by a shared hostility to Communism. 'Ideas from Weimar', Greenberg argues, 'not only enabled democratic revolutions' in the post-war era; they also 'constrained postwar democracy by their anti-communism'.[24] Claims to a new era of free political competition would be undercut by the rigid constraining devices of post-war Europe, narrowing the range of possibilities in the constitutional imagination, as well as the constitutional reality in the case of the Bonn republic and its curtailing of political freedom to those considered 'enemies'. The upshot was an unequivocal rejection of Kelsen's open relativism and embrace of a militant democracy, but recast as a normative, formal liberal constitutionalism.

This new post-war liberalism would turn to judicial guarantees of fundamental rights and dignity and a robust ideological anti-positivism rather than look to presidentialism or dictatorship as a means of constitutional defence as it had in the interwar period.[25] And in terms of constitutional scholarship it would pivot away from institutionalism and positivism, presenting itself in the moralistic tones of normative discourse and even natural law. With the eclipse of the demos,

[23] See L. Panitch and S. Gindin, *The Making of Global Capitalism* (Verso, 2013).

[24] Greenberg, *Weimar's Century*, 17.

[25] This post-war turn is closely associated with both US and West German post-war constitutional discourse. See M. Hailbronner, *Tradition and Transformations: The Rise of German Constitutionalism* (Oxford University Press, 2015) and on the synergies between them, J. Bomhoff, *Balancing Constitutional Rights* (Cambridge University Press, 2013).

and the erosion of sovereignty, state theory itself largely disappeared into normative constitutionalism.[26]

As Tim Wihl notes in Chapter 4, the conservative cultural–materialist turn in interwar Europe constituted a broad alliance, ranged not only against socialism but against positivism as a legal and constitutional method. In the post-war era, not only Schmitt but other conservative scholars such as Rudolf Smend would be rehabilitated as a new legal constitutionalism emerged. Smend belonged to the cohort of conservative scholars who had feared the dominance of the left over 'bourgeois' forces in the interwar era, drawing on various humanist and organicist currents of thought to bolster the judiciary as a 'state power with a mandate to do justice', meaning to defend property rights against mass democracy. The post-war legacy of Smend would be clearly pronounced in the German Constitutional Court's Lüth decision, articulating an 'objective value order', allowing the 'application of fundamental rights in far-reaching abstraction from their textual formulation'.

This new form of judicial interpretivism would attract liberals and social democrats as well as conservatives. In Wihl's account, German constitutional lawyer Konrad Hesse, continuing the integrationist logic but turning Smend upside down, sought an ultimate 'unity of the constitutional and legal order', eliminating contradictions and contrasts, and replacing a statist theory of integration with a functional sociological rationality, now with an individualist inflection.

A parallel trajectory affected a certain reception of the material constitution elsewhere in Europe. Graziella Romeo, in Chapter 18, on the doctrines of constitutional maintenance, investigates the legacy of Mortati's conception of the material constitution by looking at two post-authoritarian experiences with written codified texts: Italy and Portugal. In both cases, the more general question of the gap between the material constitution and the written text acquired growing importance in a manner proportional to the temporal distance from the redaction of the original text. Romeo helpfully identifies the importance of the material constitution during the original enactment and its role in following constitutional developments. The constitutional discourse, by both political actors and academics, has often focussed, in Italy and Portugal, on the need of updating the formal constitution in order to make it congruent with the material constitution. Romeo's insight is important for the study of the material constitution in noting that absorption of the material constitution into the written document is based on a profound misunderstanding of the relation between the material and the formal. The latter is one of the manifestations of the original material constitution, but not the exclusive one. Indeed, the normativity of the material constitution is more foundational and, therefore, there is no logical need to constantly update the (as she calls it) master-text.

I.3.3 The Post-War Inflection of the Material Constitution in Western Marxism

The project of radical social transformation via political action and revolution, so central to the classical Marxist account, is effectively abandoned in post-war Europe. What emerges instead is support for constitutionalism itself, systems of checks and balances, increased veto points, and institutional fragmentation, in an attempt to stabilise liberal democracy. This is materially propped up through class compromises and an oscillating welfarism (expanding in times of growth and contracting through periods of austerity). Critical theory largely acquiesces in this

[26] See K. Son, *The Eclipse of the Demos: The Cold War and the Crisis of Democracy before Neoliberalism* (University of Kansas Press, 2020).

great moderation, accommodating a de-politicisation of basic social goods and objectives, based on its own fear of democratic instability.

As Kolja Möller outlines in Chapter 9, there was initially some hope among socialists that the new West German constitution could represent a class compromise and even 'balance of class forces', recalling the earlier Austrian–Marxist theorist Otto Bauer, who had argued that neither the bourgeoisie nor the proletariat could dominate the state. He focuses on German Marxist theoretician (and tutor of Jürgen Habermas) Wolfgang Abendroth, who had been active in Weimar debates first as a member of the Kommunistiche Partei Deutschlands (KPD), and then KPO (the Communist Party Opposition which tried to initiate broad coalitions between social democrats, communists and the trade-unions). Abendroth initially pushed for a social reading of the Bonn constitution. But in terms of his theoretical contribution, he is notable in maintaining the notion of constituent power, not only to correct constituted powers and, thereby, to conserve the social compromise; he also hinted 'at the possibility of an encompassing social transformation'. Möller identifies some latent possibilities in this conceptualisation, in light of social struggles of the 1970s, particularly in the subaltern forces and anti-colonial movements. But constituent power ultimately takes up a normative and systemic role, representing the self-constitution of society rather than a radical political dynamic of rupture.

In any case, as Möller notes, Abendroth was soon marginalised by the conservative academy. And in terms of his diagnosis of material struggle as a concrete phenomenon, Abendroth elsewhere documents in detail the post-war weakening and fragmentation of the working class, and the parties meant to represent them, right across the continent. In the mid-1950s, the German SPD (Sozialdemokratische Partei Deutschlands) became, in Abendroth's view, 'an instrument for consolidating the influence of the ruling class on the workers' and in most European countries, by the 1960s, social democracy had given up the notion of representing class interests and abandoned the idea of social ownership.[27] This, Abendroth notes, would be reinforced through the European project; whereas the integration of Europe enabled increasing connections between large transnational corporations, the interests and organisation of workers could not be so easily upscaled.

Ideologically, what was left of Marxian materialism was also disarmed in the move away from political economy, and toward philosophy and culture, and then toward a wider consensus around liberal values as underpinning the constitutional paradigm. In Chapter 14, Neil Walker identifies the constitution's own 'meta-political values', which 'as the constitutional state consolidated over the late 19th and 20th century' can be summarised as the 'trinity' of 'democracy, human rights and the rule of law'. This holy trinity of values is defended at a high degree of abstraction, often without reference even to the formal aspects of economic organisation that are codified through constitutional texts, treaty law and extended through their judicial interpretation. In Walker's recounting, this stems from a traditional 'indifference' of constitutional authority toward economic power, enabling it to 'accommodate any sort of economic model, whether or not capitalist'.[28] There was no need, therefore, for any 'explicit reference to the "e" word in the constitutional text'.

[27] W. Abendroth, *Short History of the European Working Class* (Verso, 1972), 151.
[28] Citing G. Gerapetritis, *New Economic Constitutionalism in Europe* (Hart, 2019), 6.

I.4 THE END OF THE END OF HISTORY AND THE RETURN OF THE MATERIAL CONSTITUTION

The left-liberal forgetting of the material constitution, however, can be re-historicised and denaturalised in a way which not only provides explanatory power, but opens up the possibility for exploring possible alternatives. Prominent in recent scholarship is the way the 'holy trinity' of democracy, human rights and the rule of law, and its detachment from material developments, far from conventional, is in fact highly constructed.

Key here is a huge array of scholarship that began to deconstruct the decades of neoliberalism beginning in the 1970s, prominent among which is the work of Marxist geographer, David Harvey.[29] It would then appear that the neoliberal transition, symbolised by the award of the Nobel Prize in 1976 to Milton Friedman, and intellectually spearheaded by a second generation of Chicago-influenced thinkers, was pushed by a combination of concrete political and material forces. Neoliberalism incorporated an added 'myth', of economics occurring outside the control of national governments, or at least many among them. As such, it emphasised that the capacity for control was always already constrained by the conditions of the world market.[30] But this sense of a loss of control accompanied a number of significant constitutional changes, specifically the turn to 'external' constraints. This would be a feature of the 'new constitutionalism' emerging in the 1990s, introduced by international relations scholars who followed the lead of Antonio Gramsci.[31]

Deconstruction of liberal constitutional ideology also returned to the fore. The impact of Cold War liberalism, American legalism and multiple waves of juridification, as well as the turn to human rights as a surrogate for socialism was famously said to represent the 'last utopia' of a defeated left in the 1970s.[32] This turn to abstract values enabled a liberal-left to achieve a wide degree of ideological consensus, cemented in various ways by the hegemony of the French anti-totalitarian turn in the wake of the bicentenary of the French revolution, and the transformation of German critical theory in the hands of Jürgen Habermas and his followers.

In Chapter 10, Gunther Teubner interrogates one of the few authors who did not follow the path toward an immaterial critical theory: Rudolf Wiethölter. Unsatisfied with the communicative turn of critical constitutional theory, Wiethölter thematised the material constitution by placing political economy at the forefront of his concerns, but he did so in a highly original and idiosyncratic way. His main source of inspiration is system theory and he develops his constitutional analysis in a critical dialogue with Luhmann. Wiethölter theorises the radical autonomy of law (and not the relative autonomy typical of sociological or Gramscian conceptions of the material constitution) but gives it a peculiar spin. As all social sub-systems, if the autonomy of the system (and law is no exception) does not maintain a solid connection with society, it degenerates into a pathology. His prescription is for the law itself to 'actively see new, resilient ties back to society precisely because it has gained such a high degree of autonomy'. However, Wiethölter does not suggest resolving the pathologies of social differentiation by reconstructing an integration of systems via the State or any other functional equivalent. Instead, Teubner recounts Wiethölter's kind of material constitutional pluralism: no comprehensive constitution for

[29] See, e.g., D. Harvey, *A Brief History of Neoliberalism* (Oxford University Press, 2005).

[30] For a powerful counter-narrative, see W. Streeck, *Buying Time: The Delayed Crisis of Democratic Capitalism* (Verso, 2014).

[31] S. Gill and C. Cutler, *New Constitutionalism and World Order* (Cambridge University Press, 2014).

[32] S. Moyn, *Last Utopia* (Harvard University Press, 2012).

society, but a multitude of constitutional sites each with its own material constitution connected to social needs.

Wiethölter's vision of the material constitution was not typical. At that point in time, that is, after the collapse of the Soviet Union and the supposed 'end of history', the material constitution disappeared almost entirely from mainstream scholarship, the dominance of the TINA narrative (There Is No Alternative to neoliberalism) rendering it superfluous in many analyses. Perhaps, however, in reality it was the suppression of political autonomy, its 'hollowing out' through decades of democratic disconnect that had merely facilitated the *appearance* of a seamless trinity of values. The role of international and supranational structures of power in this formation was becoming more evident and, when the euro crisis struck, ever more conspicuous.

In Chapter 25, Agustin Menéndez illustrates how the formation of the material constitution of the EU – especially post-Maastricht – is based on a different trinity of fundamental principles: free competition, fundamental freedoms and sound money. His analysis shows precisely how social relations, and an institutional division of labour between centre and periphery and between supranational and national levels, coalesce in pursuit of the primary value of the European Union: the protection of private property *qua* economic wealth. The impact of these operations on the Welfare State is conspicuous and Menéndez identifies in it a specific constitutional function of external constraint. Therefore, the material constitution of the EU tends to become autonomous by pursuing its own fundamental political goals but in the process is transformative of the domestic constitution of the member States. This chapter, together with those dedicated to the federation (Chapter 12) and the empire (Chapter 11), reminds us that the material constitution is not tied to the State form as a matter of conceptual necessity. On the contrary, material analysis reveals the contingency of state formation in the inter-state system. Political unity can take other constitutional forms.

I.4.1 *The Material Constitution beyond Europe*

As Europe was stabilised after the Second World War, partly under the auspices of US power, analysis of the material constitution would be displaced to new contexts, notably Latin America, China and India, partly due to the *destabilising* external effects of that very same power. Indeed, for those interested in the analysis of the material constitution there is much to learn by observing non-European cases. As the original conception of the material constitution was deeply tied to European modernity, the different developments taken by other jurisdictions through decolonisation and processes of staggered modernisation show the limits of a Euro-centric understanding of the concept.

As Sandipto Dasgupta notes in Chapter 20, the tradition of the material constitution stands as critique of the assumption of a 'globally shared mode of organising social-political formations', an assumption which 'erases the socio-historical specificity of the postcolonial transitional moment'. Dasgupta also notes that this was not merely accidental, but an aspect of the 'formal, normative view of constitutions' pushed by Cold War intellectual movements and unipolar economic globalisation.

The example of India, although unique in many ways, brought to independence by the 'largest mass movement of its kinds anywhere in the world', represents one of the projects of state-led transformation in the periphery that pushed against global constitutionalism, attempting to respond to the social question in an underdeveloped and highly unequal society by re-establishing sovereignty over property and autonomy from global capital. The capitalist class in India, due to its historic weakness, had to share power with other dominant classes, notably the rural landowners and professional elites, who were significant in possessing the skill in managing the state and administering the constitution, adopting a functionalist view of public law.

However, the ordering principles of the post-colonial regime were eventually delinked from the anticolonial struggle with the government administration using the 'very same bureaucracy, police and army that was used to suppress the anticolonial movement'. Over time, with the Indian elite facing a crisis of hegemony, parliament in decline and planning subdued as the Third World became liberalised, lawyers and judges would come to supplant administrators, and the rule of law and its institutional expression came to play a more prominent role in the constitutional life of the nation. As Dasgupta concludes, this can best be understood as a change in the material constitution: 'lawyers replacing administrators as the custodian of the Constitution was not just a change in style – from functionalist to legal. It was the result of a major change in the social basis of the transformational project, and hence by extension, the Constitution.' This would also face *reaction*, often conducted in 'extra-legal terms' and 'extra-constitutional' terms, as the social question remained 'the central issue of Indian political life', and one which the formal constitution would be powerless to address.

Animated by this insight about the role of decolonising processes and relations between centre and periphery, Part III contains other non-European 'case studies'. In Chapter 21, Ngoc Son Bui distils the ordering factors of the Chinese constitutional order. The bearing subject here is the party-State, that is, the Communist party and its organisation, which cannot be fully disentangled from State apparatuses. Son shows that the material constitution of China is based on this interpenetration of a monoparty political system that is deeply involved in all State structures. This is a crucial difference with the role of the political system in Western States, which is by now more based on the construction of electoral consent. The Chinese Communist Party musters the political energy for carrying forward the fundamental political objectives of the Chinese state. According to Son, the main objectives of the constitutional order are economic development and socialist politics. The combination of these elements allows Son to identify the material constitution of China as one of a 'socialist developmental state': the governing activity of the Chinese Communist party is directed toward the synthesis of economic development and the main features of a socialist constitution. Moreover, the framework of the material constitution provides an instrument for assessing the role of the 1982 written constitution, which Son notes is not a sham document, but an integral part of the constitutional order, performing important functions. Among these, Son emphasises the formalisation of the fundamental objectives and the clarification of the structure and operations of the party-State.[33]

Tarik Olcay, in Chapter 23, on the role of the military in the material constitution of Turkey, offers an attentive analysis of how a concrete force within the Turkish constitutional order has acted both as a constituent and a protecting factor on several occasions. The advantage of the framework of the material constitution here is to be able to track the constitutional role of an institution, in this case the army, that does not occupy a central position in written constitutional documents, yet does shape the constitutional order in decisive ways. Olcay's claim is basically that it is impossible to understand the dynamics of the Turkish constitutional order without focusing on its army. The dividends of this analysis are illustrated by Olcay with simple efficacy: through an overview of the 1962 and 1982 constitutions, the ongoing authority and

[33] Son has extended the frame of the material constitution to comparative studies in other Asian countries in: Ngoc Son Bui, *Constitutional Change in the Contemporary Socialist World* (Oxford University Press, 2020).

crucial constitutional potestas of the army are tracked and their essential part in the constitution illustrated.

At the beginning of Part II, in Chapter 11, Eva Nanopoulos introduces a largely neglected topic in the debate on the material constitution: imperialism and its function in the formation of modern constitutional orders. Nanopoulos' starting point is the recognition that modern domestic constitutional orders were always shaped in relation to non-European contexts. The chapter takes up two paradigmatic cases: the constitutions of imperial Britain and France. Nanopoulos maintains that the imperial ambitions of both countries were an ordering force of their own material constitution. The organisation of labour and property in the colonies would not only deeply shape the colonies' legal orders; they would have a feedback effect on their domestic constitutions. Pitching the analysis at the level of the material ordering of imperialism allows Nanopoulos to identify important differences in the nature of the constitutional order (for example, the French move from an imperial constitution in 1795 to a colonial constitution in 1799), where constitutional dualism triggers a differentiated set of arrangements for France and its colonies. But the analysis of imperialism's impact on domestic constitutions is not limited to historical reconstruction. Nanopoulos lays down a research programme for decolonising constitutional law which uncovers how contemporary forms of imperialism, without resorting to coercive and violent expropriation or occupation, still mould the material constitution. Racial capitalist imperialism, organisation of the value chain and global financialisation are at the forefront of a decolonising approach to the material constitution.

In Chapter 22, on the constitutional transformation of Mongolia, Jennifer Lander sheds light on the material factors that have shaped its constitutional order over the last 30 years. Of great relevance for a reappraisal of the material constitution in the twenty-first century is the reconstruction of the coupling between the decision to transform the political economy of Mongolia into an extractivist one and the network of transnational norms and rules that the constitutional order of Mongolia had to adapt to in pursuing that objective. The chapter identifies in those objectives – recentring the economy around mining with, crucially, an opening to international investors – the main constitutional conflict and how it has unfolded. This history tracks a profound constitutional change without constitutional formalisation: looking at the Mongolian constitutional order without considering the principles of its political economy and the international actors involved would miss a foundational aspect of constitutional reality.

The constitutional role of the political economy (in this case, international political economy) occupies centre stage in Chapter 24, by Jessica Lawrence and Tom Flynn, on the material constitution of international investment law (IIL). Lawrence and Flynn push the analysis toward the idea that specific subsystems of transnational law might have their own material constitution, though perhaps still dependent, for their existence, on state-based material constitutions. They find particularly frustrating that, despite large criticism of the field, the majority of proposals for reform address (or tweak with) procedures and changes to the formal constitutional rules, but do not engage with the substantial social relations that ground international investment law. In an insightful overview, Lawrence and Flynn recognise the constitutionalist discourse that has been used in IIL during the last years, but they note that it is more of a distraction. They then illustrate the main tenets of the material constitution of IIL: A political unity which is organised around an international space of circulation of capitals, the capacity of pursuing transnational political objectives and a set of subjects – investors – whose interests are driven by entrenching the security of their investments through modification of national constitutional and ordinary law. As well as analysis this also gives the authors an entry point for articulating a strategy for transformation of transnational regimes.

I.4.2 The Material Constitution in the Twenty-First Century: Theoretical Challenges

With the return of the material constitution in contemporary constitutional discourse, many theoretical issues (new and old) remain to be addressed.

To begin, one might wonder whether the material constitution does actually preclude legal positivism, as our historical narrative implies. If the material aspect is taken to signify merely the laws of law-making (written or unwritten, codified or uncodified), that is, the 'positive norms which regulate the creation of legal norms', then perhaps not. But legal positivism assumes precisely what material analysis problematises, namely the material construction, maintenance or breakdown of political authority. In that way, the material constitution shares a great deal with political jurisprudence,[34] albeit casting a more sceptical eye on the symbolic representation of power central to that tradition and foregrounding the material dynamic of constitutional order and disorder. For that reason, the sociology of law may provide a helpful bridge between political jurisprudence and the material constitution, explaining the links between the symbolic and the material.

In Chapter 16, Francesco Bilancia and Stefano Civitarese Matteucci bracket this question, and take the positivisation of the constitution seriously, by presenting a conception of the material constitution as a Hartian rule of recognition, 'rooted in common sense and ordinary language', specifically linking it to a normative belief in the open procedures of a deliberative democracy. But as they note, this holds only under certain normative conditions, requiring a high degree of convergence around democratic procedure, the absence of specific substantive political goals, and the absence of polarising social or political movements.

Another crucial issue that will have to be re-articulated by a contemporary theory of the material constitution, argues Denis Baranger in Chapter 17, is the relation between 'matter' and form. Baranger's chapter puts forward a criticism of the way the interwar theorists of the material constitution assumed as a starting point a stark distinction between two constitutional levels. Baranger warns that the return of the concept in the twenty-first century might introduce more confusion than clarity. In his view, the articulation of the two levels is ontologically controversial and does not have any added value. His proposal is basically to abandon the distinction between formal and material in favour of an honest and for him more accurate dyad: legal and political. The dynamic element of the material constitution is reconnected to a political dynamic while the legal dimension is tied to the unavoidable truth that law always has to take up a formal aspect.

Following the same line of criticism, in Chapter 15, Mariano Croce insists on the necessity to move away from a substantive conception of the material constitution, that is, to shift from structure to process. Croce's argument is that the material constitution was treated, in the twentieth century, as a shortcut for 'social order'. This exposed the notion to two devastating shortcomings: first, the determination of the concept was left to a *regressio ad infinitum* as no one could define what society is; second, no explanation of how the material constitution would mould the legal form was offered. In a move that goes beyond the two classic understandings of the material constitution (as structure and as constitutional identity), Croce maintains that it is still useful to use the framework of the material constitution, but only if it is conceived as a

[34] Loughlin, *Political Jurisprudence*.

process, and not as a substance made of specific norms, values or principles. This entails conceiving the legal order as a set of organisational practices that take place within every social group. There is an inherent pluralism in this latter conception of the material constitution. Indeed, to illustrate the point, Croce contrasts this process-based view with Schmitt's theory of the concrete order[35] and concludes that the latter cannot function anymore as a blueprint for understanding the material constitution.

Another crucial question for future investigations into the material constitution is the study of forms of political unity that go beyond the State and the empire. In Chapter 12, dedicated to this question, Signe Larsen broaches the notion of federation as a form of political unity from the perspective of the material constitution. The starting point of her chapter is that the federation is not a species of the genus 'State', but it is an altogether different political form. The material constitution of the federation diverges from the State primarily because it has a double telos that is the distinctive mark of its constitutional life. Federations pursue two types of fundamental goals: preserving the existence of the member States and pursuing its own autonomous goals (usually related to welfare and/or warfare). The peculiar trait of the federations' material constitution is that a tension lies at its core and, instead of being resolved by a dominant political force or state, it has to be managed (often through a balance of powers). This is an important insight for scholars of the material constitution: the sense of unity and the clarity of the fundamental goals may in this case be lacking. Larsen's chapter is an invitation to examine other forms of political unity and to even question whether, in conditions of contemporary political economy, the unity necessary for maintaining a material constitution can be political at all.

I.5 CONCLUSION

It is possible to see three different lines of interpretation across the chapters of this Handbook. They identify the most frequent conceptions of the material constitution: (1) the material constitution as the set of material conditions of production and reproduction of the social order (the materialist conception); (2) the material constitution as the law of law-making (the positivist conception) and (3) the material constitution as the constellation of principles and values that ground the constitutional order (the institutionalist conception). In many jurisdictions post-Second World War the latter version became dominant; it became formalised as a discourse around value-based constitutional orders and, more recently, as constitutional identity. Although this is still the predominant version of the material constitution (though it is not formalised in these terms), the relation with the social order has been developed in thin ways and the discourse around it has often been pitched in fully-fledged normative tones.

However, as occurred during the interwar period, the currently hegemonic normative model of the constitutional order is losing explanatory strength because context makes it no longer tenable. Is this a misplaced conclusion? After all, ideal normative constitutional theory starts from first principles and only then moves to non-ideal theory.[36] Indeed, our claim is not that normative constitutional theory is by itself irrelevant or useless. Rather, it is not the way to attain constitutional knowledge and understanding. As the widened gap between normative constitutional theory and a constitutional reality is increasingly shaped by one crisis after the other, the

[35] Croce investigates Schmitt's institutionalist turn at length with Andrea Salvatore in A. Salvatore and M. Croce, *Carl Schmitt's Institutional Theory* (Cambridge University Press, 2022).

[36] The classic two-step move is exemplified by J. Rawls, *A Theory of Justice* (Harvard University Press, 1971).

tendency is to merely moralise constitutional phenomena, as is the case with much recent analyses of populism.[37]

There is, to be sure, much work that remains to be done in developing a conception of the material constitution. In that respect, this Handbook does not intend to advance an exhaustive analysis. It offers an overview of the history of the concept, the state of affairs of the current debate and a series of case studies. We hope that it provides fertile ground for further study.

[37] For an exception, see recently M. Tushnet and B. Bugaric, *Power to the People: Constitutionalism in the Age of Populism* (Oxford University Press, 2022).

PART I

History

1

The Tradition of the Material Constitution in Western Marxism

Marco Goldoni and Michael A. Wilkinson

1.1 INTRODUCTION

In this chapter, we provide an overview of Marxist contributions to the concept of the material constitution. Marx was the first philosopher to place the political economy of modern production at the core of his analysis of the social order. Although he did not formally articulate the idea of the material constitution, his thought remains indispensable to a materialist constitutional theory. This chapter covers several key episodes of Marxist contribution to the material constitution following multiple waves of materialist thought since Marx. But it cannot be anything close to exhaustive and will focus on the tradition of Western Marxism.

The chapter traces the historical arc of Marxist influence, beginning with its origins in the work of Marx and Lassalle (Section 1.2), continuing to a peak in the revolutionary era of Lenin and Luxembourg, followed by a swift turn to reformism in the interwar period (Section 1.3). It then examines an important exception to this decline in the work of Gramsci and his concept of hegemony (Section 1.4). After the Second World War, 'post-Marxist' critical theory detaches itself from political practice and working-class struggle, and leaves aside material analysis, particularly under the auspices of the Frankfurt school (Section 1.5). The chapter then examines two exceptions to the recent marginalisation of the materialist canon in the work of Balibar (Section 1.6) and Negri (Section 1.7). We conclude by arguing that this diminution of influence is regrettable as there remains much to learn from the Marxist tradition for understanding the material constitution of the twenty-first century.

1.2 ORIGINS OF THE MATERIAL CONSTITUTION: MARX AND LASSALLE

In the history of constitutional and political ideas, there is no common agreement on the first formulation of the material constitution, which might be said to date as far back as Aristotle's *Politeia*. But it is undisputable that the origins of a modern materialist understanding of political society can be traced to the work of Karl Marx. To avoid any misunderstanding, Marx did not directly use the term 'material constitution'. And Marx's discussion of constitutional questions is often marginal or a pretext to address other issues, such as social and political emancipation. More generally, Marx's approach to constitutions is epitomised by his famous comment on Hegel's doctrine of the State (in what was his first lengthy work, although published only posthumously) that constitutions are riddled by contradictions and the only way to solve those is by resorting to a purely democratic form of government.[1] Only by redefining popular power in terms of constitutive power (a permanent constituent activity) is it possible to avoid the constitutional fetishism of liberal thought, that elevates the constitution above the people as an external constraint on their power.[2]

It is in fact, for Marx, the specialisation of the political constitution that sets up the main contradiction afflicting modern constitutionalism.[3] This is at the centre of *On The Jewish Question*, where the displacement of social emancipation by the political constitution and the rights of man plays a pivotal role in his critique of the limits of modern liberalism and republicanism.[4]

Although Marx's early writings contain only an embryonic vision of the material constitution, clearer outlines can be found in a number of later works on the critique of political economy. In these more mature works, Marx presents two crucial insights. First is the materialist understanding of capitalism, reflected in the core idea that capital is a social relation which shapes productive activities by organising the forces and relations of production. A crucial text is the *Preface to the Critique of Political Economy*, where Marx famously notes that 'the mode of production of material life conditions the general process of social, political and intellectual life. It is not the consciousness of men that determines their existence, but their social existence that determines their consciousness'.[5] Accordingly, production is a fundamental social activity through which labour (as the essence of the human being and the process through which man transforms nature) comes to be organised and transformed into a commodity and it is the organisation of the mode of production that drives historical development. Law is portrayed as a result of such development, as if it were a mere reflection of the underlying dynamics of the productive process.

According to this classical Marxist view, private property and other legal institutions (e.g., the modern family) are thus seen as reflexes determined by underlying structures of production. The *German Ideology* may be read as representative, with Marx directly attacking a certain way of understanding the law as the product of an act of pure will, which he denounces as 'the legal illusion', and which raises suspicion of any purely positivist conception of the constitutional order. In a nutshell, this background reveals the material constitution as a structure embedded in the modern division of labour typical of capitalist relations. In this economy, the written constitution can play one of only two roles: either it consolidates the underlying capitalist relations as instruments for harnessing wage labour to the command of capital or it serves an ideological function by providing a veneer of legitimacy to an otherwise exploitative structure. Be that as it may, the fundamental lesson is the following: society forms around productive structures whose point is to organise the relation between man and nature.

This last observation allows us to introduce the second fundamental insight offered by Marx. Once the connection between social reality and the formal constitution is questioned, a methodological issue arises. As Marx is concerned with the scientific status of his analysis, he

[1] If one had to point to a 'constitutional model' which Marx looked to with favour, it would probably be the short-lived experience of the Paris Commune, as eulogised in *Civil War in France*. On this point, see, from the perspective of constitutional law, N. Sultany, 'Marx and Critical Constitutional Theory', in P. O'Connell and U. Özsu (eds.), *Research Handbook on Marxism and Law* (Edward Elgar, 2021), 235–39.

[2] S. Kouvelakis, *Philosophy and Revolution* (Verso, 2018), 297.

[3] For an exploration of these contradictions, see R. Hunter, 'Marx's Critique and the Constitution of the Capitalist State', in P. O'Connell and U. Özsu (eds.), *Research Handbook on Marxism and Law* (Edward Elgar, 2021), 190–217.

[4] A similar issue affects Hegel's separation between political and civil society, as remarked in K. Marx, 'Critique of Hegel's Philosophy of Right', in *Early Writings* (Penguin, 1991), 72–74.

[5] K. Marx, *Capital*, vol. 1 (Penguin, 1991), 426.

believes it is necessary to present a methodology that allows the observer to grasp the structural components of reality without being distracted by the sparkling lights of ideology or the deceptive objectivity of the legal form. Again, the constitutional observer can benefit: the reality of the constitutional order is not exhausted by the legal form; it should be sought first and foremost in the political economy of modern capitalism, coupled with a secondary interest in constitutional appearances.

In the third volume of *Capital*, this methodology is summarised: 'But all science would be superfluous if the outward appearance and the essence of things directly coincided'.[6] This statement sums up in an elegant way both how Marx addresses the relation between the material and the phenomenal (matter and appearance) and how he tries to overcome Hegel's idealist approach to the historical development of the constitution. The distinction between reality and appearance is a precondition for having proper science, constitutional science included. This critique highlights Hegel's mystification of the equivalence between being and thought, the real and the rational, which entails a double inversion. At one level, being is reduced to thought and so what is concrete is denied autonomous reality. At another level, reason becomes an absolute and self-sufficient reality.[7] Hegel's 'mystical' approach to reality fundamentally denies its material existence or makes it invisible. Marx's approach invites a reversal of the order of the constitutive factors of reality, paving the way for a materialist understanding of the constitution.

The second major mystification concerns Hegel's idealised concept of the State. This is important because the State provides the form of political unity and annexes the functions of creating legal entitlements and effective protection. While, according to Hegel, the State is an achievement as much as it is a synthesis of ethics (*Sittlichkeit*) and morality beyond civil society, that is, a rational expression of the Spirit, Marx (whose conception of the State remained notoriously underdeveloped) takes it to be a complex field whose formation and growth are intimately linked to the development of the capitalist economy. Although later described as the political agent of the bourgeoisie, Marx's concept of the State hints at its constitutive role in both allowing capitalism to flourish and in serving as an internal limit to certain forms of accumulation.[8] At this stage, one could track the first sketch of the material constitution in the condensation of capitalist relations within the political unity of the State form. The State and its political regimes are described as concrete forms whose functions are driven by capitalist development and whose status can be defined, at most, as relatively autonomous.[9]

With these intuitions, we can begin to discern a constellation of ordering factors that hint at a rudimentary notion of the material constitution: a set of forces and relations of production organised around a division of labour (understood as wage labour)[10] and the conditions for class struggle in the development of the constitutional order, tracking the conflict between capital and labour. Two underdeveloped propositions can be offered: the mode of production defines basic aspects of societal organisation and political agency exists not in the political system, but in the class struggle itself.

6 K. Marx, *Capital*, vol. 3 (Penguin, 1991), 897.

7 Commenting on §279 of the *Philosophy of Right*, Marx notes: 'Hegel makes the predicates, the objects, autonomous, but he does this by separating them from their real autonomy, *viz*, their subject. The real subject subsequently appears as a result whereas the correct approach would be to start with the real subject and then consider its objectification.' Marx, 'Critique of Hegel's Philosophy of Right', 78.

8 For a classic analysis, see B. Jessop, *The State* (Polity, 2015).

9 N. Poulantzas, *State, Power, Socialism* (Verso, 2013), 82ff; cf. C. Tomlins, 'How Autonomous Is Law?' (2007) 3 *Annual Review of Law and Social Science* 45.

10 Marx's major focus on wage labour is a constant element of critique from feminist materialism: see, e.g., S. Federici, *Caliban and the Witch* (Penguin, 2021); C. Delphy, 'A Materialist Feminism Is Possible' (1980) 4 *Feminist Review* 79.

Marx's intimations on the material constitution can thus be developed in two directions. One is toward a strict economic structuralism, in which the economy determines the laws of constitutional development. In the twentieth century, a version of structuralism was expounded in the most sophisticated and systematic way by Louis Althusser.[11] Objective conditions of capitalist development theoretically determine the structure of the material constitution (the 'social formation') in its totality, even if only 'in the last instance', *and* provide the conditions for overcoming the same capitalist constitution. A different direction for Marx's materialist understanding of the social order is taken by insisting on a genuine political element in class struggle and on the potential strategic role played by political, institutional and constitutional means.[12] In this direction, the notion of constituent power as revolutionary activity is crucial.

In both versions, social relations are shaped by the struggle between capital and labour. In both versions, the material constitution qualifies as the 'real constitution', meaning either as the basic structure of societal organisation or as the fundamental conflict around which political society develops. The constitutional order is more than a system of rules; it is moulded in a fundamental way by the organisation of relations and modes of production. The particular concrete organisation of the terms of the capitalist relation results in the various material constitutions of modern capitalist States. However, the juridical status of the material constitution remains ambiguous and the added value of this notion for constitutional analysis is unclear.

To pursue this, we can turn to another nineteenth century socialist figure, Ferdinand Lassalle, who did not fully share Marx's approach to capitalism. In two famous and seminal conferences given in 1862 (five years before the publication of the first volume of *Das Kapital*), Lassalle introduced a distinction between the 'real constitution' – basically a synonym for the essentials of societal organisation – and the written constitution (sometimes pejoratively defined as a 'piece of paper'). Lassalle postulated that the former would completely determine the latter.[13] More specifically, Lassalle implies an equivalence between the constitutional text and norms but denies that they are part of social reality. To the question 'what is the nature of the constitution?', Lassalle replied with the following definition: 'a constitution is the fundamental law proclaimed in a country which disciplines the organization of public rights in that nation'.[14] This is because, fundamentally, Lassalle thought that 'constitutional questions are not primordially legal questions, but a matter of relations of force'. By stating that the constitution is the fundamental law of the country, Lassalle assumed that it has higher value than ordinary law. The basis of the legal order has to be found in the material organisation of society, that is, 'always and exclusively in the real effective relations among social forces in a given society'. What remains unclear is whether the real constitution, that is, the organisation of the dominant forces within a society, is also a juridical constitution or only a deeply entrenched state of affairs.

Lassalle adopts an imperativist conception of law: legal norms are enforceable commands. This conception of the law makes the relation between the real constitution and the written constitution ambiguous. It is not clear how the written constitution becomes only a cover or a

[11] L. Althusser, É. Balibar, R. Establet, P. Macherey and J. Rancière, *Reading Capital* (Verso, 2016).

[12] See, further, E. Meiksins Wood, *Democracy against Capitalism: Renewing Historical Materialism* (Cambridge University Press, 1995).

[13] For a similar type of constitutional analysis, see Engels' comments on the British Constitution: The Position of England. The British Constitution, in K. Marx and F. Engels, *Articles on Britain* (Progress Publishers, 1975), 32–58.

[14] F. Lassalle, 'On the Essence of Constitutions' (1942) 3 *Fourth International* 25 (all the quotes are available at: www.marxists.org/history/etol/newspape/fi/vol03/no01/lassalle.htm, last accessed 19 July 2022).

patina for the social organisation of economic power. In fact, it seems that the real constitution becomes law only when codified in written form and with the introduction of explicit sanctions: 'these actual relations of force are put down on paper, are given written form, and after they have been thus put down, they are no longer simply actual relations of force but have now become *laws*, judicial institutions, and whoever opposes them is punished' (original emphasis). Under this description, the formal constitution represents the juridification of the 'real' relations of power or, in the most trivial sense, the registration or codification of the real constitution.

Lassalle is adamant in stating that the formal constitution is stable and lasting 'only when it corresponds [. . .] to the real constitution, that is, to the real relations among social forces'. When this is not the case, what one is observing is just a sham constitution. When there is a gap between the material and the written constitution, then the latter is simply the ideological mask covering the underlying relationships of power or, at best, providing a veneer of legitimacy. In other words, Lassalle maintains that the social order of production is already shaped pre-politically and pre-constitutionally. At most, the formal constitution operates as part of the justificatory ideological apparatus of the dominant social forces.

The limit of such a rigid materialism is that it reduces the legal order to an effect of other social processes, that is, the legal order remains in an external relation to societal organisation. Relations of production are put at the centre of the analysis, but how those relations came to take up those particular *modes* and *forms* of production is left unaddressed. Representing the relation between political economy and the formal constitution in this way prevents a fuller understanding of the normative underpinning of the hegemony of dominant forces.

This reductionist materialism suggests, at the epistemic level, that there is an apparent reality and a deeper one, not immediately visible, but structurally essential. The task for the constitutional observer is to avoid the superficial and retrieve the undergirding structural reality, which is what really matters. Marx's and Lassalle's versions of the material constitution identify the latter as essentially located in a dedicated sphere, that of modern political economy with its patterns and motives of social organisation. The value of this intuition should not be underestimated. Social power, as generated by capitalism's determination of economic activity, is conveyed through legal channels with the aim of strengthening the stability of the social order. But from the perspective of constitutional theory, what is problematic about this intuition is the driving distinction between what is structural (or fundamental) and what is epiphenomenal or supra-structural. Although to different degrees, Marx and Lassalle identify in political economy not only the source of the constitutional order, but the genesis of the social bond (based on domination and exploitation). Almost all institutions of the constitutional order are presented as emanations of political economy, or at least compatible with the rising capitalist legal order. Law, religion, science and, politics are supra-structural.

Economic structuralism obscures other fundamental aspects of society such as political and legal institutions, collective symbols, cultural reality and the experience of political action. Even from within materialist philosophy, discontent with a reductionist representation of the status and role of each system in societal formation grows during the twentieth century. In particular, the representation of the status of culture (and its role in shaping constitutional imagination) as an ideological construction is judged to be excessively reductive if explained in economically causal terms. These concerns would be addressed, in the interwar era, by Antonio Gramsci. But first it is necessary to look at a second generation of Marxist thinkers who, in the years around First World War and the Russian revolution, expanded the analysis of the material constitution of capitalism in revolutionary political directions.

1.3 THE REVOLUTIONARY GENERATION AND ITS DEMISE: LENIN, LUXEMBOURG AND THE TURN TO SOCIAL DEMOCRATIC REFORMISM

In the Marxist tradition, the fortune of the generation of Marxist scholars after Marx and Lassalle was a unity of theory and practice that Marx and Engels had not been able to enjoy due to their distance from national organisations of the working class. Under the direction of Vladimir Lenin, classical Marxism, until then lacking a clear political theory and strategy, would develop in synergy with the revolutionary actions of the Russian masses, from the first Russian revolution of 1905 through to the overthrow of the regime of Tsarist absolutism in 1917. This epochal meeting of constituent power with Lenin's revolutionary practice showed both the promise and the limits of a classical Marxist approach to the material constitution.

The council experience of the Soviets in the first revolution of 1905 (with antecedents in earlier Russian proletarian movements) had presented the direct self-organisation of the working class in the revolutionary struggle, targeting the Russian imperial regime with a series of industrial, political and military strikes.[15] The events of 1905, transforming a 'dormant Russia into a Russia of revolutionary proletariat and a revolutionary people' were, in Lenin's view, bourgeoise-democratic in aim but proletarian in method, principally the use of the mass strike.[16] This was essential preparation for the October revolution of 1917. In the previous year in exile in Switzerland, in 'State and Revolution', Lenin had set out his Marxist theory of the state as an organ of class rule and class oppression. The bourgeoise state needed to be overthrown by a worker's revolution, establishing the transitionary 'dictatorship of the proletariat', a worker's state which would then 'wither away' as material conditions were transformed.[17]

Yet the relationship between the self-organising power of the soviets and the ultimate direction of the Bolshevik party that Lenin had founded was ambiguous. Lenin saw the soviets as a necessary and spontaneous product of class struggle and class consciousness and even as an 'embryo' of a future worker's government,[18] but ultimately as insufficient for organising and fighting a revolutionary insurrection in the concrete conditions of Russia in 1918. For that to succeed, new organs of revolutionary struggle against the bourgeoise would have to arise, since the soviets were in danger of becoming co-opted or outmoded. Lenin's Bolshevik strategy after the assumption of dual power in the first phase of the Russian Revolution in February 1917 was to insist on 'a decisive struggle against the real holders of power',[19] re-establishing the correct relation between the soviets and the revolutionary class through organised leadership. The successful dictatorship of the proletariat required a professional revolutionary outfit to organise class autonomy, and an avant-garde party to ensure the conquest of state power and the success of the proletarian movements. Given the increasingly hostile international context, strong centralised control would be necessary to defend the revolutionary gains of 1917.[20]

[15] Negri identifies in the council tradition simultaneously the directive organs of the revolutionary struggle, the representative of the interests of the working class in the structure of bourgeois power, and the class organised in state power: A. Negri, *Insurgencies* (University of Minnesota Press, 2006), 267.

[16] V. Lenin, 'Lecture on the 1905 Revolution', available at: www.marxists.org/archive/lenin/works/1917/jan/09.htm, last accessed 19 July 2022.

[17] V. Lenin, *The State and Revolution*, available at: www.marxists.org/archive/lenin/works/1917/staterev/, last accessed 19 July 2022.

[18] Lenin, describing the Petrograd Soviet of Worker's Deputies, 'first letter from afar', available at: www.marxists.org/archive/lenin/works/1917/lfafar/index.htm, last accessed 19 July 2022.

[19] V. Lenin, 'On Slogans', available at: www.marxists.org/archive/lenin/works/1917/jul/15.htm, last accessed 19 July 2022.

[20] A. Callinicos, S. Kouvelakis and L. Pradella (eds.), *Routledge Handbook of Marxism and Post-Marxism* (Routledge, 2021), 9.

Over the course of a few years after the events of October 1917, amidst imperial aggression and civil war, Lenin's practical focus changed from a geographic extension of the revolution, particularly in Germany, to the defence of the Soviet Union itself. The soviets, from constituting 'the organs of proletarian dictatorship' would end up as an organ of the state administration, first and foremost with the task of organising social production and increasing productivity.[21] Despite or because of Lenin's equivocation on the role of the soviets, the party would end as the sole bearer of constituent power, displacing the radical mass movements of collective self-organisation.[22]

After the death of Lenin, Marxism–Leninism would be transformed into a state ideology, economic and political power consolidated and concentrated in the centralised bureaucracy of the Communist Party of the Soviet Union under Joseph Stalin. The material constitutional dynamic of the soviets and their collective self-organisation would end, *Leninism* in retrospect 'blocking for half a century any development or renewal of the extraordinary revolutionary experience embodied in Lenin's theoretical work',[23] although it would continue to resonate in the context of national liberation movements against the colonisation of the developing world.[24]

The Russian example was of a revolutionary experience that occurred in conditions of relative backwardness compared with the nineteenth century hubs of imperialist capital expansion in Western Europe, both in terms of objective economic development and subjective working-class consciousness. Lenin's analysis and methods could not be straightforwardly applied in the very different constitutional settings of Central and Western Europe. There, Rosa Luxemburg, attached to the Polish and then German workers' movements, took a related but distinct route, advocating the self-emancipation of the working class under the auspices of the revolutionary councils that had followed those in Tsarist Russia. In the soviets, Luxemburg had seen 'the real embodiment of Marxism among the masses'.[25] This led her to depart from what she perceived as excessive centralism in Leninism, even before its mutation under Stalin. For Luxemburg the elimination of democratic spontaneity was fatal to the ultimate goal of socialism.[26]

Luxemburg also strenuously rejected the social democratic reformism that was coming to dominate parties across Europe, specifically denouncing the German SPD after its support for the War in 1914. Her opposition included a rejection of the constitutive assembly convened after the November revolution in Germany in 1918. There could, in her view, be no negotiated transition to socialism achieved through the compromises between capital and labour that might occur within the framework of the bourgeois state. Instead, it would be necessary to harness the radical, creative energies of the masses through the development of a democratic proletarian class consciousness, based on immediate collective action.

[21] Negri, *Insurgencies*, 290. Negri concludes that 'the compromise of the soviet and the party is a compromise between living labour and a perspective of a new originary accumulation, which should result in the determination of the conditions of communism'.

[22] An alternative to Lenin's and the Bolshevik's centralised conception of the bearing subject of the communist material constitution – the party – was offered by Alexander Bogdanov, an eclectic intellectual and political figure whose philosophy was heavily criticised by Lenin in his *Materialism and Empiriocriticism* (1909). Lenin accused Bogdanov of idealism because of the emphasis put on the importance of an autonomous proletarian culture which – according to Lenin – would imply that reality exists only in the mind of the people. Bogdanov proposed a relational conception of social reality and was strongly opposed to the idea of a political avantgarde. On Bogdanov's theory of physics (strictly related to his conception of the social order) see, most recently, C. Rovelli, *Heligoland* (Allen Lane, 2021), 80–84.

[23] V. Gerratana, cited in Callinicos et al. (eds.), *Handbook of Marxism*, 10.

[24] See Chapter 11, by Nanopoulos.

[25] Negri, *Insurgencies*, 280.

[26] See P. Hudis, 'Rosa Luxemburg', in A. Callinicos, S. Kouvelakis and L. Pradella (eds.), *Routledge Handbook of Marxism and Post-Marxism* (Routledge, 2021), 75–85.

In Luxemburg's materialism, social reform from the top-down was not, and could not be, up to the task of creating a democratic socialist society, not least due to the violence with which the capitalist class would defend its material position. What was required was social and political constitutional change from the bottom-up, through spontaneous revolutionary activity and mass strikes. This task would be performed by worker's councils exercising radical constituent power. Radical democratic socialism would advance by adding new autonomous institutions in a transitional constitutional structure, which would then compete for authority with the institutions of liberal bourgeoise rule.

Interpreting Luxemburg through a constitutional theory lens and reconnecting it with Machiavelli's early modern republicanism, Camila Vergara has recently argued that Luxemburg's work offers a plebeian materialist strand of thought, which 'embraces conflict as productive of liberty, and sees the institutionalisation of popular power as a necessary condition for emancipation'.[27] Vergara even renews the links between Luxemburg and Hannah Arendt, who, inspired by Luxemburg, had also seen the council systems to represent an instantiation of political freedom as action, a political structure neglected (in Arendt's view) by Marxism in its obsession with the 'social question'.[28]

As a matter of historical record, however, Luxemburg's hopes for a spontaneous democratic socialism would be destroyed, the Spartacist uprising ruthlessly crushed and Luxemburg and her co-founder Karl Liebknecht murdered by the Freikorps, under the direction of the social democratic government led by Friedrich Ebert. The worker's council system that promised much in the early interwar conjuncture was rendered ineffective by the end of the 1920s and the German social democratic party and the trade unions had turned into centralised bureaucratic structures pursing economistic strategies in attempts to de-politicise conflicts between labour and capital.[29] Right across Europe, the prospects for revolutionary socialism or a Bolshevik style-takeover were becoming limited or non-existent in the radically different circumstances faced by the left in comparison with Russia. The prospect of a radical democratic exercise of constituent power to overturn the bourgeoise order of the 'long nineteenth century' was receding.

The First World War had proven fateful for any international unity in the cause of social democracy, with the insurgent classes themselves divided due to the scissions created by the war. '1914' had parted the ranks of Marxist theory in Europe 'as radically as it split the working-class movement itself', rapidly destroying the Second International (of socialist and labour parties).[30] After the end of the First World War, socialist uprisings would either be defeated, as in Germany and Italy, or assume reformist postures, seen off by the strength of the capitalist state in Western and Central Europe and the willingness of liberals and social democrats to turn to authoritarian means to frustrate material change.

Belief in the gradual reform of the state on the basis of the constitutional compromise and an 'equilibrium of class strengths' would become a dominant position, represented by Eduard Bernstein's 'evolutionary path to socialism' as well as the work of Austro-Marxists Karl Renner and Otto Bauer.[31] Bernstein in particular had a 'decisive influence' on the SPD.[32] Some in the

[27] C. Vergara, *Systemic Corruption* (Princeton University Press, 2020), 169.

[28] Ibid., ch. 7.

[29] R. Dukes, *The Labour Constitution* (Oxford University Press, 2014).

[30] P. Anderson, *Considerations on Western Marxism* (Verso, 1979), 13.

[31] See, e.g., O. Bauer, 'The Equilibrium of Class Strengths', in M. Blum and W. Smaldone (eds.), *Austro-Marxism: The Ideology of Unity: Austro-Marxist Theory and Strategy [1924]* (Brill, 2015), vol. I., 323–33.

[32] See P. Gay, *The Dilemma of Democratic Socialism: Eduard Bernstein's Challenge to Marx* [1952], 2nd ed. (Collier Books, 1970), 252.

German socialist camp would commit to the promise of economic democracy and the role of workers councils, which was given constitutional recognition in the Weimar Republic.[33] But it was a revisionist and reformist tradition, assuming socialism to be the 'legitimate heir' to the liberal order, that socialist state theorists such as Hermann Heller continued in the German public law academy.[34]

The German social democratic position of constitutional compromise proved to be politically disastrous, as economic democracy was marginalised and even the parliamentary route to socialism was abandoned in the strategy of toleration of authoritarian liberalism for fear of the greater evils of National Socialism.[35] In an intriguing compare and contrast of Heller and the British socialist academic and activist Harold Laski, Franz Neumann insisted that Heller (to his detriment) had rejected the Marxist theory of the state; he rejected the position that the state was, in an important sense, a 'class state' or, put differently, a capitalist state.[36] As a result, Heller failed to transcend the liberal view, which saw the state as standing above or apart from the interests of civil society and the social relations pertaining to the economy. Heller's aim was to construct (and reconstruct) the state as precisely such a unity in contradistinction to the conflict that characterised civil society, as a structure independent of the class struggle. Heller saw the difficulties of maintaining this unity in a society riddled by social inequality but retained faith in a state that was in principle neutral and autonomous. Like Hegel before him, Heller saw inequality and class conflict as merely an irritant rather than as constitutive of the modern capitalist state and one that could be managed by a sufficiently enlightened ruling class. Neumann adds, dismissively, that 'in Heller's book one can read on every page the German idealistic philosophy which constitutes its origins'.[37]

Neumann argued that Heller in effect worked backwards from his rejection of the Marxist utopia of the withering away of the state. Since, in Heller's view, the Marxist theory erroneously supposes the possibility (even inevitability) of the classless society-to-come, it must also be in error to suppose the current political society to be essentially defined by class forces, and the state to be determined by class rule. Neumann refutes Heller's 'radical anti-Marxist conclusions' in the obvious way: 'even if one is convinced that a classless society is an unrealisable objective, this does not contradict the Marxist analysis of the class nature of the actual state'.[38] Marxism without utopia might lead to a deeply pessimistic position, but not necessarily to a false one.

1.4 KEEPING THE FLAME ALIVE: GRAMSCI AND THE CONCEPT OF HEGEMONY

Even within the confines of 'Western Marxism', interwar Marxist theory lost any unity of theory and practice that it had in the era of the birth of organised socialist parties after Lassalle. In conjunction with the isolation of the USSR and its turn under Stalin to the active suppression of revolutionary thought and practice by a harsh bureaucratic apparatus, the fertile seeds of Marxist

[33] Dukes, *Labour Constitution*, 40.

[34] The SPD grew out of the Socialist Worker's Party of Germany, established when Lassalle, Bebel, Liebknecht and others came together at Gotha in 1875, but soon banned under Bismarck's anti-socialist laws until 1890 (and later splitting with the Independent Socialists in 1917). On Heller's relation with the tradition of Lassalle, see H. Heller, 'The Nature and Structure of the State' (1996) 18 *Cardozo Law Review* 1139 (translated by David Dyzenhaus).

[35] M. Wilkinson, *Authoritarian Liberalism and the Transformation of Modern Europe* (Oxford University Press, 2021).

[36] F. Neumann, 'On the Marxist Theory of the State', in K. Tribe (ed.), *Social Democracy and the Rule of Law* (Allen & Unwin, 1987), ch. 4.

[37] Ibid., 76.

[38] Ibid.

praxis were scattered or buried. The era of the classical tradition of Marx and Engels, Lenin and Luxembourg, had come to an end, and with it the exclusively Marxist cast of the material constitution. It would be for new political and social forces to cultivate the material constitution, including conservative and anti-Marxist forces.[39]

The interwar period signalled the beginning of a transformative period for the material constitution and the gradual abandonment of Marxian materialism as its philosophical point of departure. There were, however, exceptions, and one stands out for the scope and originality of its contribution, the work of Antonio Gramsci. Once again, it should be highlighted that Gramsci offered no straightforward formulation of the material constitution. Yet, Gramsci's work contains an indispensable toolkit, which extends beyond the productive dimension of social organisation. In fact, for obvious contextual reasons, Gramsci – while writing in prison – was observing a set of problems very similar to the legal institutionalists of the interwar era.[40] But in contrast, Gramsci would firmly ground his interpretation in a materialist base and would not be attracted by notions of the autonomy of the political.

Gramsci considered economic processes a necessary starting point but not sufficient for understanding the formation of society and put more emphasis (compared to previous Marxists) on the importance of political organisation and especially culture, in its political and popular dimensions. Although he did not leave behind any systematic writing on legal orders, he considered law as more than a mere epiphenomenon of the productive structure. And his idea of a struggle for hegemony as a necessary staple of the material constitution makes it an essential reference point.[41]

A starting point for understanding Gramsci's contribution to the theory of the material constitution is his re-visitation of the relation between State and civil society which is driven by the recognition of the rise of the integral State (*lo Stato integrale*). As such, the integral State provides a more nuanced definition of political unity (and the role of the political party) than advanced by Lenin. The integral State that Gramsci envisages is not the outcome of the suppression of diversity, but the articulation and homogenisation of differences in a manner that is conducive to a specific capitalist form of the productive process. In other words, the integral State is for Gramsci the form in which contemporary modes of productive organisation achieve and maintain political unity. The interest for a theory of the material constitution is Gramsci's rejection of the idea that the State and its constitutional order are exogenous and simply applied 'over' a structure of production. As we shall see, Gramsci postulates (in a way that speaks directly to the theorists of the material constitution) the socialisation of the political and the legal system.

The formation of the integral State certainly entails repression, but this is far from exhaustive of the State–civil society nexus. To understand what is at stake in the relation between State and civil society it is better to start by tracking the function of differentiation. Societal differentiation and the specification of which class manages which function are fundamental dynamics of civil society, and they already contain seeds of statehood. In this respect, the political order emerges out of civil society, although it always remains embedded in it. But this means that social

[39] In particular, Carl Schmitt.

[40] On this, see the following pages and Chapter 2, by Meierhenrich on Schmitt, Chapter 4, by Wihl on Smend and Chapter 5, by Rubinelli on Mortati.

[41] For a recent reconstruction of Gramsci's ideas about law, see P. Ciocchini and S. Khoury, 'Thinking in a Gramscian Way: Reflections on Gramsci and Law', in O'Connell and U. Osuz (eds.), *Research Handbook on Law and Marxism* (Edward Elgar, 2021), 139–55. See also D. Litowitz, 'Gramsci, Hegemony and the Law' (2000) 2 *Brigham Young University Law Review* 515.

differentiation makes it impossible for the political and the legal system to become full expressions of society. Tracking of the formation of the integral State allows Gramsci to identify a space for hegemony, possibly the core concept of Gramsci's philosophy and one of the most important insights offered by his analysis.

The State as political unity is defined as 'political society + civil society, in other words hegemony protected by the armour of coercion'.[42] While Gramsci acknowledges that coercion is still a fundamental component of the modern State, the complexity of modern society means that cultural hegemony has to be generated for the concretisation of political unity. This is possible only if a certain social group musters enough political and cultural strength to be able to integrate societal energies into a political order by acting as a leader: 'A social group can, and indeed must, already exercise "leadership" before winning governmental power (this indeed is one of the principal conditions for the winning of such power); it subsequently becomes dominant when it exercises power, but even if it holds it firmly in its grasp, it must continue to "lead" as well'.[43]

In contrast to Lassalle, Gramsci understands that, in order to forge a material constitution, a leading social group cannot simply resort to oppression and coercion; it also has to inculcate particular values and beliefs. This is a well-rounded integrative strategy: the material constitution is organised not only through force and coercion, but also through intellectual hegemony. Gramsci maintains that it is impossible to eradicate social conflict from the polity; hegemonic forces are thus called to manage it by considering not only their social interests, but those of the wider society. Hence, the material constitution that is shaped by hegemonic forces is always a precarious achievement and needs to be constantly maintained, primarily by persuasion and negotiation among conflicting interests.

Unsurprisingly, the question of political organisation is one of the most pressing concerns for Gramsci. Although the organisation of fragments of civil society can be the outcome of spontaneous initiative, there is always a reminder of distribution of roles and the creation of a leading group that cannot be obtained in a fully 'horizontal' way. It is at this level that Gramsci thematises the importance of a 'new Prince' as a dynamic factor of unification, and the political party is indicated as the subject with the task of coordinating and leading the social groups to maintain political unity. Gramsci did not believe in the purely spontaneous formation of political subjects: an element of verticality is unavoidable in any political and social organisation. For the formation of a material constitution, Gramsci believes that a 'historical bloc' has to be formed (by a political subject),[44] as the first cell which contains the instructions for the development of the social order. But even the historical bloc (the groups whose interests can converge and produce a political alliance) does not aggregate spontaneously around its fundamental interests, as the latter might need to be composed and recomposed in a political formula.[45]

We are now in a position to see that hegemony and the figure of the 'dominant political party' are, according to Gramsci, intrinsic elements of the new material constitution of the twentieth century. Along with institutionalists such as Mortati, the political party is seen as the bearer of

[42] A. Gramsci, *Quaderni dal carcere* (Einaudi, 2014), 263.

[43] A. Gramsci, *Selections from the Prison Notebooks* (International Publishers, 1971), 57–58.

[44] See the still relevant analysis by L. Paggi, *Antonio Gramsci e il moderno principe* (Editori Riuniti, 1970), 125ff.

[45] It should be noted that it is not clear whether the concept of historical bloc is descriptive of the main bearer of the material constitution, or it is a strategic notion. In the latter sense, a historical bloc would be formed in the struggle for achieving hegemony. For this interpretation, see P. Sotiris, 'Gramsci and the Challenges for the Left: The Historical Bloc as a Strategic Concept' (2018) 82 *Science and Society* 94, 95.

the material constitution as it is the only modern entity capable of uniting different social components while keeping them differentiated in the emerging mass society. The political party is the concrete force which takes up the role of Machiavelli's prince, but it has the daunting task of producing order materially from below and symbolically from above. According to Gramsci, mass society has to find within itself its own ordering principle. In order to achieve its integrative functions, the political party ought to become a 'total party' while avoiding ossification in a pernicious bureaucratic centralism where it would have only 'functions of propaganda and police'.[46]

Differentiation and hierarchy remain distinctive but necessary moments in the articulation of the material constitution of mass society. Law is an important aspect of this and its function runs parallel to that of hegemony, addressing a similar problem: how can the masses be persuaded to adopt the values and beliefs of the dominant class? As already noted, the legal order is for Gramsci a human artifice which does not lie outside of social organisation and is ultimately linked to political and social will. The role of law is, thus, ambiguous but functional to the formation and maintenance of the material constitution. The 'juridical question' is for Gramsci one of assimilation of the entire society to its most advanced fraction:

> it is a problem of education of the masses, of their 'adaptation' in accordance with the requirements of the goal to be achieved. This is precisely the function of law in the State in society; through 'law' the State renders the ruling group 'homogenous', and tends to create a social conformism which is useful to the ruling group's line of development.[47]

Accordingly, the legal order assumes a double task. It operates at the level of coercion in the sphere of positive law, which is associated with 'order' and 'violence'. But the legal order also operates as a pedagogical tool, nudging 'education' and 'conformism'. Although Gramsci notes that the ethical dimension of the 'legal question' pertains more to civil society than the government,[48] it is undeniable that positive legal norms as approved by State apparatuses perform a formative task as well. It is coherent with this approach that Gramsci, in another passage, talks of the law as a hegemonic instrument for the selection of certain customs and attitudes, and the elimination of others. The main parallel may be with the school system as a producer of homogeneity. Gramsci thus offers an original variation on the material constitution, one which not only indicates the political party as the main actor, but which identifies in the struggle for political and cultural hegemony a crucial factor of constitutional ordering.

1.5 POST-WAR EUROPE, POST-MARXISM

The effect of the interwar economic, political and constitutional crises of the 1920s and early 1930s had been a deep demoralisation of the left, particularly in Germany. There had been a tremendous diachronic shift in the interwar era from the high optimism about the prospect of progressive social change in the aftermath of the First World War, with the arrival of universal suffrage, working class consciousness and political parties connected to the social masses, to the

[46] Gramsci, *Quaderni dal carcere*, Notebook 17, vol. III, 1939. Notoriously, Gramsci advocated a form of democratic centralism where the political party maintain an opening toward social energies ('the real movement') by maintaining, as already noted, a dynamic of 'push from below, command from above': Gramsci, *Quaderni dal carcere*, Notebook 13, vol. III, 1634.

[47] Gramsci, *Selections from the Prison Notebooks*, 195.

[48] Gramsci notes that '[t]he general activity of law (which is wider than purely State and governmental activity and also includes the activity involved in directing civil society [...]) serves to understand the ethical problem better': *Selections from the Prison Notebooks*, 195.

terrible darkness of the 1930s, with the failure of parliamentary democracy, growth of violent fascism in the West, and the brutal rule of Stalin in the East.

The generation of Marxist thought that takes root in the interwar conjuncture would be deeply pessimistic. As Perry Anderson notes, all the most significant works of 'Western Marxism' in the period between the mid-1920s and 1968 – from Lukacs to Gramsci, Adorno to Sartre – were the product of political failure, of the defeat of working-class struggle or of socialism.[49] With the Stalinisation of the Soviet Union, and the discipline exercised by Communist parties and their dogmatic orthodoxy, the choice for Marxist intellectuals and workers was often either to remain party members and renounce intellectual independence, or leave and risk losing connection with the class struggle. 'The consequence of this impasse' Anderson notes, 'was to be the studied silence of Western Marxism in those areas most central to the classical traditions of historical materialism: scrutiny of the economic laws of motion of capitalism as a mode of production, analysis of the political machinery of the bourgeois state, strategy of the class struggle necessary to overthrow it'.[50] And, we can add, of the material constitution of society and its relationship with formal constitutional norms.

Critical theory after the Second World War would become structurally divorced from political practice and working-class struggle, particularly under the auspices of the Frankfurt school. The post-Marxist turn of the Frankfurt school would generally abandon material constitutional analysis, and particularly the issue of class relations and the political objectives of the state. Neumann himself would turn to the significance of political freedom and a diagnostics of its contemporary loss before his untimely death in 1954. His associate, Ernst Fraenkel would undertake normative work on democratic pluralism on his return from the United States to the Federal Republic of Germany.[51] Along with many of its leading thinkers, the transfer of Frankfurt school theorists to the United States in 1934 had not only wrenched it from European movements of socialism and parties of social democracy but also then installed it in a place with no discernible Marxist tradition, and in fact one which was to become actively hostile to those suspected of sympathising with Marxism in the heat of post-war MacCarthyism. The Frankfurt school brand of post-Marxism turned to philosophy, cultural analyses and increasingly specialised disciplines, often indebted more to Freud than to Marx.[52]

The post-war de-politicisation of the left would also have a profound impact, with leading scholars not only pursuing class collaborationist projects in Germany and urging a pragmatic politics of compromise on the SPD, but also helping to conduct the anti-Soviet international strategy of the United States.[53] In the post-war fate of Marxism and critical theory there were thus deeper continuities with the interwar schisms on the left, particularly in the anti-Communist stance of the social democrats, captured by Hilferding's claim on the eve of National Socialist takeover that the primary fight of the SPD was against communism.

In a significant inflection of material constitutional thought, a new moralistic direction in social democracy took root, building on Heller's ethical notion of the *sozial Rechtsstaat*. Fraenkel, for example, urged workers to unite with the bourgeoisie in pursuit of a 'rational

49 Anderson, *Considerations*, 42–43.

50 Ibid.

51 For a recent reassessment of Fraenkel's legacy, see W. Scheuermann, 'Recalling and/or Repressing German Marxism? The case of Ernst Fraenkel' (2021) 18 *Modern Intellectual History* 1.

52 For an overview, see A. Honneth, 'A Social Pathology of Reason: The Intellectual Legacy of Critical Theory', in F. Rush (ed.), *The Cambridge Companion to Critical Theory* (Cambridge University Press, 2004), 336–61.

53 U. Greenberg, *The Weimar Century* (Princeton University Press, 2014), 78.

natural law' and to leave behind notions of 'power relations' and 'class interests'.[54] This reflected a broader phenomenon, namely a turn by social democrats to the courts to defend social equality and workers' rights, foreshadowing the 'social rights' discourse that would dominate among later generations of constitutional scholars. Social democratic conceptions of democracy were designed, in line with other elitist scholars and emigres such as Carl Joachim Friedrich, if, by different means, 'to foster consensus about state institutions'.[55]

There was, to be sure, a brief resurgence of the radical left toward the end of the Second World War, buoyed by its key part in the Resistance movements, the prestige acquired by the Soviet Union and its Red Army in its victories over Hitler's armies, and the reuniting of social democracy and Communism in broad coalitions and united fronts in the fight against the violence of fascism and national socialism.[56] This briefly opened up a space for new democratic forms of communism and solidarity to flourish, a 'rare moment of European history – the moment of antifascist unity – whose opportunities compared with 1917–18'.[57] The upshot of this moment would be a brief 'wave of communisation',[58] but the opportunities for radical transformation this created would be generally squandered.

Socialist renewal did have a significant impact on post-war political society, legitimising the pursuit of comprehensive welfare states, reduction of unemployment, and rational planning through the involvement of left forces in constituent assemblies, notably in post-war Italy. But in conjunction with a fairly rapid pivot to cold war anti-communism on the socialist left, communist parties themselves would soon disavow any revolutionary constituent ambitions. With the dismantling of Resistance groups, the potential of dual power exercised by Resistance committees was abandoned, backing governments of broad national unity. The Italian Communist Party (PCI) soon settled into the 'centre ground of postwar Italian culture',[59] its prospects anyway dimmed by the US threat to withdraw Marshall aid if it were successfully elected to government. Togliatti's turn had already moved the PCI to the centre, disbanding and disarming the local Resistance, and enabling the path to the historic compromise of the 1970s.

Marxism's classical focus on class conflict would also be displaced from political and constitutional enquiry. In practice, the political element of class struggle declined with the quietening of the working class of Europe, even though they were the 'incontrovertible social victims of the war'.[60] The language of class struggle was thus disappearing not only from intellectual discourse but from party politics, subdued by the security of the bureaucratic 'iron cage' and a paternalistic elite-led system. The founding period of post-war resettlement was characterised by a growing de-politicisation of state–society relations: a combination of class compromise, the de-radicalisation of the trade union movement and the rise of the national corporatist state.

Both the unions and the social democrats across Europe (as well eventually as the communist parties) would attach their flag to the mast of European integration and its modernising agenda. In some ways, this too would be a continuation of interwar strategies of economism, de-

[54] Ibid., 83.
[55] Ibid., 88.
[56] See G. Eley, *Forging Democracy* (Oxford University Press, 2002), 287–91.
[57] Ibid., 288.
[58] Particularly in Eastern and Central Europe, with Communist parties becoming leading national forces in Yugoslavia, Albania, Greece, and Czechoslovakia, major electoral players in France and Italy and even making significant gains in the Benelux countries and Scandinavia, along with a renewal of socialist parties in France, Belgium and the Netherlands.
[59] Eley, *Forging Democracy*, 293.
[60] M. Conway, 'Democracy in Postwar Europe: The Triumph of a Political Model' (2002) 32 *European History Quarterly* 76.

politicisation and consensus-seeking as well as strongly supported in the symbiosis between European and US intellectuals. The turn to modernisation and liberalisation which reflected 'one of the major thrusts of American policy' would be strongly supported by the French socialist party (SFIO) as well as the German SPD, whose programme, announced at Bad Godesberg in 1959, offered a renunciation of Marxist class struggle, an embrace of Christian ethics and acceptance of free market principles and the EEC. It reflected a more general revisionism of social democratic parties across Europe, with the discarding of working-class allegiance, and dilution of any commitment to revolutionary anti-capitalism. The factors considered as central to the moderation of the post-war settlement – the circumstances of global economic growth, and relative equalising of conditions between capital and labour – were conducive to a deradicalised left.

Reinforcing the tendency of conservatism to reinvent itself as a hardened form of Cold War liberalism was the tendency of critical theorists to turn away from material issues and into discourse theory and identity politics. The constitutional fetishism that begins in the Bonn Republic becomes more generally hegemonic in Europe, particularly through the process of European integration. Constitutional patriotism and ideological Europeanism become substitutes for any projects of social emancipation. By 1989, the standard bearer of what is left of the Frankfurt school of critical theory has declared the era of revolution over, the only avenue left to tame capitalism from within, Jurgen Habermas leading the turn away from material analysis in his twin *magnus opi*, *Theory of Communicative Action* and *Between Facts and Norms*. By that stage, the socialist and communist parties of Europe had embraced their own de-radicalisation and Europeanisation. The revolutionary era was decisively over. But the gap between political elites and the populations, aggravated through constitutionalist projects of an international and supranational type, were about to gain more traction even as history had been declared at an end.

1.6 THE FRENCH EXCEPTION?

One strand of contemporary heirs of the materialist tradition in France were theorists of *le politique* and of disagreement and dissensus such as Jacques Rancière. This initially appeared distant from the discourse ethics and rational consensus of Habermasian philosophy. But much of Rancière's own analysis remained at the level of a counter-discourse, uncomfortable with the aesthetics of modern liberal consensus-politics but lacking the resources to tackle its materiality – its political economy, social relations and political teleology. In this respect it shared the tone and temperament, as well as normative and methodological assumptions of Frankfurt school post-Marxism.[61] Although Rancière identified politics as a process with a reflexive quality and not as an outcome,[62] his celebration of the theatrical quality of political action risked emphasising in a rather sterile way the performative nature of dissensus, putting a premium over its symbolic and linguistic achievements at the expense of the material context of its staging.

From a materialist perspective, the problem affecting this kind of post-Marxist analysis is typical of a 'political jurisprudence', which, as Loughlin argues (in the course of defending it), emphasises symbolic over material power, and prioritises abstract over concrete reasoning. In that respect, its contemporary theorists of note are philosophers such as Claude Lefort, Marcel

[61] S. Kouvelakis, 'The Crisis of Marxism and the Post-Marxist Moment', in A. Callinicos, S. Kouvelakis and L. Pradella (eds.), *Routledge Handbook of Marxism and Post-Marxism* (Routledge, 2021), 337–50.

[62] J. Rancière, *Aux bords du politique* (Folio, 2004), ch. 1.

Gauchet and Pierre Rosanvallon.[63] Lefort insists on the 'empty place of power' as the symbolic feature of the democratic state, which, from a materialist perspective, is sheer illusion as an analysis of the modern state or meer utopianism if a projection of a future shorn of revolutionary intent. In this French revival of political jurisprudence, the symbolic order of the state is structured through abstract principles of 'sovereignty, equality and rights'; these principles of *droit politique* 'fulfil the role of maintaining unity while containing social tensions'.[64] This not only leaves behind political economy and class struggle; it can also appear apologetic of liberal expert governance as a legitimate constraint on parliamentary majoritarianism.[65] It is thus no coincidence, for example, that these theorists of *le politique* pay little regard to the material constraints on political sovereignty in the concrete context of the evolving European Union.

Etienne Balibar, a student of French Marxist philosopher Louis Althusser, is something of an exception, maintaining a closer connection with materialist philosophy and the classical Marxist tradition. Balibar neatly captured the necessary relation *between* the political and the material realms, highlighting the materiality of modern political action by noting that the truth of politics 'is to be sought not in its own self-consciousness or its constituent activity, but in the relationship it maintains with conditions and objects which form its "material", and constitute it as a material activity'.[66] This echoes the famous insight of Marx, that 'human beings make their own history, but they do not make it as they please; they do not make it under self-selected circumstances, but under circumstances existing already, given and transmitted from the past'.[67] Material conditions and relations are thus both constituted by politics and constitutive of politics, a dynamic that is intrinsic to constitutional ordering.

Balibar's concept of 'equaliberty' presents the autonomy of the political as a *material struggle*, not merely – or not even primarily for – secularisation, but for equality, set against the pre-modern fusion of political and economic power.[68] This immediately illuminates the path of modern constitutional development in contrast to the theorists of *le politique* who present it as a symbolic rupture from a theological worldview. It enables a foregrounding of the continuous, if uneven, struggle for equality, including over universal suffrage, industrial rights, women's movements, workers' movements, and – broadening the horizon – anti-colonial movements.

Close attention to the evolving relationship between politics and the economy as a concrete and dynamic phenomenon also brought Balibar closer than his peers to the material and constitutional implications of European integration. Surveying the Union at the beginning of the new millennium he argued that the 'impasse' of sovereignty in Europe referred 'to the absolute blockage of the question of "the people" understood … as *demos* or constituent political power'.[69] The absence of 'the people' in Europe, he continued, was not only 'symbolic'; there was an absence of any of 'real control' over the constitutional order that was imposed on their behalf. His diagnosis, accordingly, was nothing less than 'the disappearance of the dialectic of constituent and constituted power … [which] goes beyond the 'bureaucratisation' and

[63] M. Loughlin, *Political Jurisprudence* (Oxford University Press, 2017) 104–7.

[64] Ibid., 106.

[65] As, for example, in Pierre Rosanvallon's suggestion that the supposed impartiality of independent technocratic institutions could be equated with new conceptions of democratic legitimacy, see Pierre Rosanvallon, *Democratic Legitimacy: Impartiality, Reflexivity, Proximity* (Princeton University Press, 2011).

[66] É. Balibar, *Politics and the Other Scene* (Verso, 2002), 10–11.

[67] From Marx's, *The Eighteenth Brumaire of Louis Napoleon*, available at: www.marxists.org/archive/marx/works/1852/18th-brumaire/, last accessed 19 July 2022.

[68] É. Balibar, *Equaliberty: Political Essays* (Duke University Press, 2014).

[69] É. Balibar, *We, the People of Europe: Reflections on Transnational Citizenship* (Princeton University Press, 2004), 157.

'professionalisation' of politics, and the 'political apathy of the masses'. It implied, Balibar lamented, 'the return to a technical, reglementary status of the law'.[70]

It was at this point in time (that is, during the first decade of this century) that Balibar retrieved the notion of the material constitution as an essential device for understanding the political regime of the European Union. Elaborating on some traits of the Marxist conception, he defined the material constitution as the codification of fundamental political practices understood in terms of a substantive (i.e., not formal) organisation of powers (political and economic).[71] The material constitution would serve the purpose of grasping the logic of differentiation within EU law: in the absence of a proper normative and written constitution, Balibar stated that the EU had a material constitution which comprised not only certain EU institutions and national governments, but also provisions whose formal status is not constitutional, such as (his example) the Schengen agreement.[72] If differentiation is consolidated through political practices, then sufficient political unity is obtained to stabilise a machine with certain political objectives.

This diagnosis would be sharpened in the Euro crisis phase. Balibar had by then described the Treaty of Maastricht as having put an end to the long European 'civil war' between economic liberalism and social democracy that took place across the twentieth century. It signalled the decisive triumph of economic liberalism and even the complete victory of capitalism in the constitutional ordering of Europe. Reflecting on the (re-) birth of the EU at the Treaty of Maastricht, he noted how extraordinary it was to set its liberal political–economic goals into explicit, detailed and rigid constitutional guarantees, meaning that

> for the first time in this part of the world a principle of political economy deriving from a specific ideological discourse (namely neo-liberal deregulation and unrestricted competition, believed to produce 'optimal allocation of resources' and spontaneously 'just' redistribution) was presented as the sovereign rule which all member states ought to implement in their national policies under close surveillance of the federal (or quasi-federal) organs of the Union.[73]

As the Euro-crisis progressed, Balibar identified a potential 'revolution from above', a transformation of Europe by the leaders of dominant nations 'and the Brussels and Frankfurt technostructure' using the language of 'necessity'.[74] Invented by Bismarck in the nineteenth century, the notion of a revolution from above designated 'a change to the structure of the *material constitution*' on the part of the ruling classes, altering the 'balance of power between society and state, economics and politics'. Balibar speculated that this process was underway with the European Union's 'neutralisation' of parliamentary democracy, and its institutionalisation of budgetary and fiscal controls, all pushed forward 'in the name of neo-liberal orthodoxy'. Although these changes had been germinating for some time, they were for the first time being demanded as part of a new configuration of political power.[75]

In the new configurations of rule, constraints on democratic self-determination were not predominantly 'constitutional' in the orthodox sense of the term but were relayed by global capital markets and credit rating agencies, which, along with banks that were considered 'too big

70 Ibid., 169.

71 See É. Balibar, *Cittadinanza* (Bollati Boringhieri, 2012), 80–81.

72 É. Balibar, 'Europe as Borderland' (2009) 27 *Environment and Planning* 190, 202.

73 É. Balibar, 'The Rise and Fall of the European Union: Temporalities and Teleologies' (2014) 21 *Constellations* 202.

74 É. Balibar, 'Europe's revolution from above', The Guardian (23 November 2011). Available at: www.theguardian.com/commentisfree/2011/nov/23/europe-revolution-from-above, last accessed 25 September 2020.

75 Ibid. See, in a different context but in analogous manner, S. Wolin, *Politics and Vision: Continuity and Innovation in Western Political Thought* (Princeton University Press, 2004), 605.

to fail', had become constitutional actors for material purposes. These material constraints would then be formally entrenched at the EU level through the provisions of the Fiscal Compact and the European Stability Mechanism, and reinforced by political actors as well as interpretations of the European Court in its rulings on the programmes of the European Central Bank.[76] Marxian material analysis had returned in line with political constitutional events but the focus of Balibar's analysis remained 'top-down'.

1.7 THE AUTONOMIST VIEW: ANTONIO NEGRI

Another notable exception to the decline of the Marxist material constitution is represented by Antonio Negri, especially in his works from the 1970s.[77] Negri openly recognises the intellectual debt to legal institutionalism and especially the constitutional theories of Carl Schmitt and Costantino Mortati, whose notions of the material constitution are embedded in social reality and capable of making sense of the unity of the constitutional order. But Negri's materialist philosophy allows him to circumvent the existentialist (Schmitt) or sociological (Mortati) underpinning of their versions of the material constitution. Negri considers their emphasis on the sovereign or the dominant political force to ultimately betray a circularity that impedes grasping the dynamics of the material constitution.

In a nutshell, the problem with Schmitt and Mortati is their postulation that the material constitution is a fundamental political fact supported by the dominant political force and their simultaneous assumption that the dominant political force is the only one capable of moulding the material constitution. In terms of constitutional science, the risk is not only to fall prey to a form of circular reasoning, but also to a vulgar version of relativism. Whoever manages to impose its will on the fundamental objectives of the polity is the sovereign or the dominant political force. Negri's original contribution lies in the philosophical methodology that allows him to read the development of a capitalist political economy as an ontology of labour. Against a dialectical conception of materialism (still inspired by the looming presence of Hegel), Negri postulates that it is labour (and living labour more specifically) that 'makes' capital as a social relation. In other words, labour is the essential component of the capitalist social relation and capital is parasitical on that relation. Famously, on the basis of this assumption, Negri inaugurated the intellectually fertile workerist approach.[78] Labour is described as an autonomous force and the basis of any political economy. Labour is the substance of productive processes and, for this reason, is constitutive in its relationship with capital. The importance of this move is recognition of the political capacity and agency of labour movements including the potential autonomy of non-wage-based labour.

Against a formalist reading of the constitutional order, Negri recognises that there are two engines driving the development of the constitution: the organisation of the productive process and the conflictual dynamic which lies at the core of the capitalist social relation (i.e., class struggle). Only a Marxist–materialist conception of the material constitution allows us to grasp the constitutional relevance of these intuitions. With an incisive but rather abstract turn of phrase, the material constitution is defined by Negri as 'the level of *political agreement of the*

[76] See Chapter 25, by Agustin Menéndez.

[77] Negri discusses the notion of the material constitution at length in the following publications: A. Negri, *Il lavoro nella costituzione* [1977] (Verona, 2009), 12–16; A. Negri, 'Toward a Critique of the Material Constitution', in *Books for Burning* (Verso, 2005), 180–220.

[78] Cf. S. Wright, *Storming Heaven* (Pluto Press, 2017).

regime that establishes the tendency toward unity of the constitutional project'.[79] This captures the most salient aspects of the constitutional order as a necessary component of a capitalist political economy: (1) a tendency toward political unity of the constitutional order; (2) the purposive character of the constitutional order ('project') as it strives toward the realisation of its potential, which is latent in the idea of tendency;[80] (3) the layered composition of class which affects both the capitalist and the working class, and the evolution of the composition in a way which directly affects the formation of the material constitution and (4) the resort to command by capital, which is not only exercised by forcing workers into a state of necessity, but also with the coercion and management exercised by the State. While capital command is driven by the law of value, labour's political activity is inspired by what Negri defines as self-valorisation, that is, the struggle for supplanting the needs and values imposed upon workers by capitalist command with self-determined needs and values.

From an epistemic perspective, Negri's view is productive for understanding the material constitution. It avoids a strict form of economism as it allows for a certain slack between capital's capacity of command and the political autonomy of labour. It makes social classes the subjective bearers of the material constitution without providing a static account of their composition. In this way, the classic ruling relation – the governing and the governed classes – which is at the centre of political jurisprudence, is reframed in terms of commanding and resisting classes. It also identifies class struggle as the driver of the constitution's material development: it is an antagonistic process of valorisation that determines the material constitution, based upon the primacy of production as the key organising moment of social reality. For this reason, Negri adopts an ontological approach not only to the notion of labour, but also to politics. But – crucially – it is an ontology of labour that makes sense of class struggle and of the engine of constitutional development. By postulating that labour is ontologically autonomous and independent from capital, Negri suggests that political autonomy is not an abstract objective to be pursued, but is embedded in the ontological condition of labour.

As insightful and powerful as this is,[81] the risk of an ontological approach is to elide constitutional reality in terms of the objective dimension of power relations. Moreover, it underestimates capital's capacity for political initiative by reducing its activities to processes of real subsumption and technological reorganisation. In more recent iterations of his theory, Negri has pushed his concept of labour further, to the point of covering almost every aspect of society. This expansion tracks a long trajectory which is described as a move from, first, the professional worker to, second, the mass worker and, finally, the socialised worker. With the latter instantiation, a new class composition emerges as a result of the restructuring and decentralisation of production. The new class composition, based on the communication and sociability made

[79] Negri, 'Toward a Critique of the Material Constitution', 187 (original emphasis). More recently, Negri and Hardt will define the material constitution as the 'continuous formation and reformation of the composition of social classes': M. Hardt and A. Negri, *Empire* (Harvard University Press, 2000), v.

[80] Tendency is a technical word in Negri's work; it refers to the trends and potentialities within the development of capital and the working class that might materialise in the near future. The identification of a tendency is important for two reasons: it allows the observer to understand the dynamics of constitutional development and it provides important information for the formulation of organisational, strategical, and tactical activities.

[81] Think of the intimate connection between class composition and the form of political institutions: to each class composition corresponds a political subject and a form of government (e.g., to the mass worker corresponds the Welfare State, the national trade union and the reformist political party).

possible by new technologies, brings about a profound transformation of the material constitution. Accordingly, the key bearing subject of the new material constitution is the multitude.[82]

The notion of the 'multitude' fails to convince for two reasons: it pushes the notion of material constitution to a limit where it becomes almost entirely congruent with the notion of a globalised societal organisation (and in this way, it loses analytical purchase); or the composition of the multitude is so broad that it is difficult to identify any inner class dynamics. Although the intuition behind this conception of the contemporary material constitution is powerful (i.e., the idea that the political is not a separate and autonomous sphere, but penetrates all social systems),[83] it is doubtful that this new understanding of the material constitution of the empire (as the political form associated with the rise of the socialised worker) is tenable in light of the increased relevance of processes of differentiation along multiple lines (race, gender, sex, territory, to name a few). The price to be paid for the primacy of ontology over politics is, as a constitutional matter, quite high.

1.8 CONCLUSION

Marxist political thought has been the cradle of the material constitution. In this chapter, we have provided an overview of the implicit notion of the material constitution that can be retrieved from Marx's critique of political economy. We then tracked the development of this approach to the material constitution in the first work that explicitly discusses the material constitution (Lassalle) and in some of the most influential followers of Marx (Lenin and Luxembourg). The limits of a determinist conception of the material constitution have led authors to investigate other ordering factors: this expansion beyond economic determinism was central to the innovative thought of Antonio Gramsci and of other (non-Marxist) political thinkers of the interwar period. Finally, we tracked the marginalisation of the materialist approach after the Second World War but singled out two notable exceptions emerging out of the social movements of the 1960s and 70s (Balibar and Negri). Ultimately, the work of these two authors shows that, by avoiding reductionist shortcomings, the critique of political economy still provides essential and fresh insights into the material constitution. Conversely, Marxist thought itself has much to gain by engaging with constitutional phenomena.

82 For the most recent formulation, see M. Hardt and A. Negri, *Assembly* (Oxford University Press, 2016). For a reconstruction of Negri's intellectual trajectory see T. Murphy, *Negri* (Routledge, 2012).

83 There is some affinity between the last version of Negri's political thought and societal constitutionalism: see the interesting exchange between Gunther Teubner and Negri in 'Law, Property, and New Horizons' (2010) 21 *Finnish Yearbook of International Law* 1.

2

The Soul of the State

The Question of Constitutional Identity in Carl Schmitt's *Verfassungslehre*

Jens Meierhenrich

The state *is* constitution, in other words, an actually present condition, a *status* of unity and order. The state would cease to exist if this constitution, more specifically, this unity and order, ceased to exist. The constitution is its 'soul,' its concrete life, and its individual existence.

Carl Schmitt[1]

2.1 INTRODUCTION

In this chapter I seek to contribute to the material study of constitutions by revisiting Schmitt's argument about constitutional identity – which he developed in *Verfassungslehre*. In his magnum opus, published in 1928, Schmitt took issue with liberalism's failure to take seriously the social requisites of constitutional democracy. His was a constitutional theory concerned with the 'soul' of the state. Like Hermann Heller on the left, Schmitt was keen to revive in Weimar Germany a tradition of political thought in which arguments from *sensus communis* were the constitutional norm. His was an attempt to stop the influx of 'mechanical and corpuscularian philosophies' into the theory and practice of law, a development that the publication, in 1637, of René Descartes's *Discourse on the Method of Rightly Conducting One's Reason and Seeking Truth in the Sciences*, had set off.[2]

By addressing the question of constitutional identity in Schmitt's political jurisprudence, I chart what I call *affective constitutionalism*. In my effort to relate mind to matter, I rely on Raymond Williams, the literary theorist, and develop an argument about constitutions as 'structures of feeling'.[3] Williams introduced this concept in *Marxism and Literature*. There, he laid the intellectual foundations for a cultural materialism by way of a trenchant critique of Karl Marx's theory of history.[4] By making this approach to materiality usable for constitutional theory, I hope to bring phenomenology – the philosophy of experience – to the study of constitutional law.[5]

[1] C. Schmitt, *Constitutional Theory*, J. Seitzer, trans. and ed. (Duke University Press, 2008), 60.

[2] R. Serjeantson, 'The Soul', in D. M. Clarke and C. Wilson (eds.), *The Oxford Handbook of Philosophy in Early Modern Europe* (Oxford University Press, 2011), 129.

[3] R. Williams, *Marxism and Literature* (Oxford University Press, 1977), 128–35.

[4] Ibid., 5.

[5] For a broader argument about the phenomenology of the rule of law, see J. Meierhenrich, 'What the Rule of Law Is … and Is Not', in J. Meierhenrich and M. Loughlin (eds.), *The Cambridge Companion to the Rule of Law* (Cambridge University Press, 2021), 569–621.

2.2 AFFECTIVE CONSTITUTIONALISM

'To Schmitt's mind', as John McCormick writes, 'the formalism of liberalism' was a technology of rule.[6] The way Schmitt saw it, the procedural constitutionalists in Weimar Germany were devaluing the 'concept' ('*Begriff*') of the constitution. He faulted them, among other things, for avoiding the question of constitutional identity. By running roughshod over its soul, he was certain, they were failing the state.

Schmitt was a political existentialist par excellence. He had no patience for the excessive legalism en vouge in the 1920s. Everything was a question of identity for Schmitt. Constitutional life was about belonging – or not. In the dying days of the Weimar Republic, Schmitt's constitutional theory, like his institutional theory more generally, was subject to a cumulative radicalisation. It became ever more exclusionary – and divisive.[7] Schmitt's thought in the interwar period combined 'existentialism's "intensity" with militarism's "struggle"'.[8] Because the *telos* of politics for Schmitt was the pursuit of an 'intensive life' ('*intensives Leben*'), any *Verfassungslehre* worthy of the name, or so he felt, had to be vitalist.[9] By flying the flag for facticity in Weimar Germany's *Methodenstreit*, the jurisprudential debate in the 1920s among constitutional theorists over the separation of law and morals, Schmitt outed himself as a constitutional materialist, as Marco Goldoni and Michael Wilkinson use the term.[10]

In drawing our attention to 'the underlying material context', Goldoni and Wilkinson foreground 'the basic political and social conditions of possibility of constitutionalism' as well as 'the dynamics of constitutional change'.[11] The material determinants of constitutions are various. Taking materiality seriously is *not* the same as being wise to the politics of constitutionalism, however. It requires *more* than 'merely supplementing judicial with political analysis'.[12] Not *all* materialist critiques treat the political 'as a superstructural phenomenon determined by productive relations'.[13] Goldoni and Wilkinson insist, as I do, that the study of the material constitution must not be reduced 'to the study of the underlying economic base'.[14]

2.2.1 *The Concept of the Material*

That it is possible to reclaim the idea of materiality from Marxists – to think materially *without* reference to base and superstructure – Costantino Mortati showed in his constitutional thought. Inspired by Paul Laband's disaggregation of the concept of law (*Gesetz*) in the nineteenth century, Mortati, in the 1930s, began to think about 'the long arc of legality' by bringing sociality

[6] J. P. McCormick, 'Three Ways of Thinking "Critically" about the Law' (1999) 93 *American Political Science Review* 413, 415.

[7] On the transformation of his institutional thought from 'pragmatist institutionalism' to 'racial constitutionalism' to 'extremist institutionalism', see J. Meierhenrich, 'Fearing the Disorder of Things', in J. Meierhenrich and O. Simons (eds.), *The Oxford Handbook of Carl Schmitt* (Oxford University Press, 2016), 171–216.

[8] R. Slagstadt, 'Liberal Constitutionalism and Its Critics: Carl Schmitt and Max Weber', in J. Elster and R. Slagstadt (eds.), *Constitutionalism and Democracy* (Cambridge University Press, 1988), 115–16.

[9] C. Schmitt, *Positionen und Begriffe im Kampf mit Weimar – Genf – Versailles* 1923–1939 [1933] (Duncker & Humblot, 1994), 226.

[10] M. Goldoni and M. Wilkinson, 'The Material Constitution' (2018) 81 *Modern Law Review* 567. I hasten to add that Schmitt's understanding of facticity was hardly straightforward. For an insightful discussion, see G. Meuter, 'Zum Begriff der Transzendenz bei Carl Schmitt' (1991) 30 *Der Staat* 483.

[11] Goldoni and Wilkinson, 'The Material Constitution', 568.

[12] Ibid., 569.

[13] Chapter 3 from this handbook, 75.

[14] Goldoni and Wilkinson, 'The Material Constitution', 587.

into play.[15] Intrigued by Laband's idea of law 'in a material sense' (*'im materiellen Sinne'*), especially the German thinker's verbiage, he began to contemplate the analytical possibilities of this neologism – of theorising the interplay between formality and materiality. In 1940, Mortati shared the product of his intellectual labour. He called it *'la costituzione in senso materiale'*.[16]

With his theory of the material constitution, Mortati stood Laband on his head. He subverted the latter's quest for a *Staatsrechtswissenschaft*, a science of constitutional law. With Italy's constitutional order as his reference, Mortati argued *against* Labandian legal positivism – and that of like-minded theorists of public law such as Carl Friedrich von Gerber. The so-called Gerber–Laband School was intent on purging from the theory and practice of constitutional law 'all extraneous matters – history, politics, and ideas from private law'.[17] The ideology of its legalism was anti-materialist, which is what irked Mortati.

Laband and Gerber, not unlike Mary Wollstonecraft in England, imagined that the wheels of government – including the wheel of law – were turning 'like the wheels of any other machine', that is, autonomously.[18] This constitutional imagination did not convince Mortati. To him the imaginary constitutions it conjured were a little too perfect. They had little to do with the life of constitutional law he knew. Not unlike Eugen Ehrlich, whose 1913 treatise on the sociology of 'living law' (*'lebendes Recht'*) a few decades earlier had shaken up pure theorists in the Kelsenian mould, Mortati wanted to explore the 'grey area of constitutional law'.[19] Like Schmitt and Heller, who – along with Rudolf Smend – provided the inspiration, Mortati felt that the value-free, logical method of jurisprudence was wanting. Constitutional law was not machine learning, he averred.

On Mortati's political conception of constitutional law, 'the *nomic* is intrinsic to the material', in the sense of 'a peculiar conformation of the latter that triggers the former'.[20] On this reading of Mortati's constitutional thought, 'a certain aggregate of social forces' created the conditions for constitutional law 'to emerge and work effectively'.[21] The 'social forces' Mortati had in mind, however, were not just – or even primarily – the productive forces so central to Marx's theory of history. Mortati was more realistic, in all senses of the term, about the material foundations of life – and so was Raymond Williams.

For Williams, culture *was* matter. He thought of it as 'practical consciousness', as 'a kind of feeling and thinking' that, rooted in everyday life, was 'social and material'.[22] Taking a leaf from Williams, I argue that constitutions, for Schmitt, were 'structures of feeling', affective parameters to choice:

> The term is difficult, but 'feeling' is chosen to emphasize a distinction from more formal concepts of 'world-view' or 'ideology'. It is not only that we must go beyond formally held and

[15] Related, see D. Dyzenhaus, *The Long Arm of Legality: Hobbes, Kelsen, Hart* (Cambridge University Press, 2021), whose phrase I have borrowed.

[16] P. Laband, *Das Staatsrecht des Deutschen Reiches* (Laupp, 1878), vol. II, 1; C. Mortati, *La costituzione in senso materiale* (Giuffrè, 1940).

[17] M. Loughlin, *Foundations of Public Law* (Oxford University Press, 2010), 191.

[18] M. Wollstonecraft, *An Historical and Moral View of the Origin and Progress of the French Revolution and the Effect It Has Produced in Europe* (J. Johnson, 1794), 404.

[19] E. Ehrlich, *Grundlegung der Soziologie des Rechts*, M. Rehbinder, ed. [1913], 4th ed. (Duncker & Humblot, 1989); L. Rubinelli, 'Costantino Mortati and the Idea of Material Constitution' (2019) 40 *History of Political Thought* 515, 516. The Kelsenian mould was still new at the time. Kelsen had only just presented it in H. Kelsen, *Hauptprobleme der Staatsrechtslehre* (Mohr, 1911). But, as Stanley Paulson has shown, Kelsen's early constructivism is indebted to the 'juridico-scientific' tradition of the Gerber-Laband School. S. L. Paulson, 'Hans Kelsen's Earliest Legal Theory: Critical Constructivism' (1996) 59 *Modern Law Review* 797, 798, 799–80.

[20] M. Croce and M. Goldoni, *The Legacy of Pluralism: The Continental Jurisprudence of Santi Romano, Carl Schmitt, and Costantino Mortati* (Stanford University Press, 2020), 6. Emphasis added.

[21] Ibid., 6.

[22] Williams, *Marxism and Literature*, 130, 131.

systematic beliefs, though of course we have always to include them. It is that we are concerned with meanings and values as they are actively lived and felt, and the relations between these and formal or systematic beliefs [...].[23]

The question of constitutional identity was a material concern for Schmitt.[24] By reconstructing his cultural materialism, I lay bare the constitutional sentiments in *Verfassungslehre*.[25]

Throughout the 1920s, Schmitt was seized by the task of understanding the affective life of constitutions – of interpreting, to borrow from Oliver Wendell Holmes, Jr., 'the feelings which make the content of logic'.[26] Whatever we make of Schmitt's dangerous mind, he made great strides in studying constitutional sentiments. *Verfassungslehre* is a manifestation of cultural materialism *avant la lettre*. His constitutional thought is relevant to thinking about the material constitution in the twenty-first century. Why? Because arguments for – and from – affective constitutionalism shed light on the social origins of dictatorship and democracy. The illumination of material relations is apposite at a time when, as Goldoni and Wilkinson write, 'formal constitutionalism is beginning to look divorced from constitutional reality, and constitutional order is, once again, threatened by radical change'.[27] By approaching constitutionalism phenomenologically – from the direction of culture – mine is a contribution to the debate over the state of constitutional democracy.

2.3 HERDER'S *VOLK*

Schmitt recognised that, for constitutional democracy to thrive and survive, it needed to be meaningful. Effective constitutions were *affective* constitutions. They required substance, not just form, as he insisted in *Verfassungslehre*. They needed to be vitalist, not voluntarist. Constitutions, to him, were life-affirming institutions. His was an argument for vernacular constitutionalism.[28] Pulsating with the lifeblood of a people, Schmitt thought of a constitution as the autochthonous product of an imagined community – and also its social glue. In his hopeful vision, constitutions turned citizens into soulmates.

Schmitt's *Verfassungslehre* – like Hermann Heller's *Staatslehre* – can be traced to the organicist tradition Johann Gottfried Herder established in the eighteenth century.[29] As Isaiah Berlin once put it, as if writing with our two protagonists in mind,

> all defenders of the local against the universal, all champions of deeply rooted forms of life, both reactionary and progressive, both genuine humanists and obscurantist opponents of scientific advance, owe something, whether they know it or not, to the doctrines which Herder [...] introduced into European thought.[30]

[23] Ibid., 132.
[24] Goldoni and Wilkinson, 'The Material Constitution', 568.
[25] Space constraints disallow a closer engagement with Williams. For a comprehensive analysis, with particular reference to German history, see J. Meierhenrich, *The Sentimental Constitution*, Unpublished book manuscript, LSE, December 2021. For a different approach, see A. Sajó, *Constitutional Sentiments* (Yale University Press, 2011).
[26] Holmes's formulation appeared in a critique of Christopher Columbus Langdell, the dean of Harvard Law School, whose formalism he regarded with disdain.
[27] Goldoni and Wilkinson, 'The Material Constitution', 597.
[28] On vernacular constitutionalism, see J. Meierhenrich, *The Legacies of Law: Long-Run Consequences of Legal Development in South Africa, 1652–2000* (Cambridge University Press, 2008), 249–64.
[29] On Heller's *Staatslehre*, see Meierhenrich, *Sentimental Constitution*.
[30] I. Berlin, *Three Critics of the Enlightenment: Vico, Hamann, Herder*, H. Hardy, ed. [1976] (Princeton University Press, 2000), 201.

2.3.1 *The Constitution of Peoples*

The *Volk* makes the constitution, and the constitution makes the *Volk*, or so Schmitt's constitutional theory seemed to imply. His conception of constitutional democracy was exclusionary. It rested on the quality of belonging to a *particular* people ('*zu einem bestimmten Volk*').[31] What precisely facilitated belonging to this *Volk* – and thus the constitution of peoples – was, according to Schmitt, the stuff of culture, notably 'ideas of common race, belief, common destiny, and tradition'.[32] Schmitt was not the first thinker to draw attention to the matter of constitutional identity – and to its cultural determinants. We would also do well to remember that the concept of the *Volk* in German constitutional thought did not always have the racial connotations it took on during the Nazi debate about the *Rechtsstaat*.[33] It has been as fiercely contested as other essentially contested concepts. Indeed, Herder, who invented the *Volk* theorem, was 'an eighteenth-century humanitarian and liberal'.[34]

Schmitt's organicism – like Heller's and that of other thinkers who were disillusioned by the rise of formalism in the theory and practice of nineteenth-century constitutionalism – can be traced back to Herder, and to the German historicist tradition more generally. In Herder's Germany, there existed 'little evidence of a collective sense of national identity'.[35] Germans were still a proto-nation in the eighteenth century. Dispersed across 300 odd states – most of them micro-states, or *Kleinstaaten*, that belonged to the Holy Roman Empire – they did not think of themselves as possessed of a common identity.[36] A we-feeling, they did not have. Schmitt's 'status of unity and order' was inconceivable.

It was Herder, more than anyone else, who ushered in 'a new period of political consciousness'.[37] In thinking about the constitution of peoples, he turned the '*Volk*' into a social imaginary. While it was Ferdinand Tönnies who, in 1887, made the idea of community famous, it was Herder who first made it conceivable.[38] This involved an analytical two-step. The first step he took was theoretical, the second conceptual. Herder, as F. M. Barnard has shown, first 'established the principle that language was the most natural and hence indispensable basis of socio-political association'.[39] For him, a community of language was a major organ in the body politic. 'The organ of thought' is what he called it.[40] *Auch eine Philosophie der Geschichte*, Herder's 1774 tract, anticipated many of historicism's key themes: 'that we should not judge the

31 C. Schmitt, *Verfassungslehre* (Duncker & Humblot, 1928), 227. Emphases omitted.

32 Schmitt, *Constitutional Theory*, 258.

33 On this little-known – but highly consequential – debate in Nazi jurisprudence, see J. Meierhenrich, *The Remnants of the Rechtsstaat: An Ethnography of Nazi Law* (Oxford University Press, 2018), 95–158. On the *Volk* discourse more generally, see J. Retterath, *"Was ist das Volk?" Volks- und Gemeinschaftskonzepte der politischen Mitte in Deutschland 1917–1924* (de Gruyter, 2016).

34 C. J. H. Hayes, 'Contributions of Herder to the Doctrine of Nationalism' (1927) 32 *American Historical Review* 719, 734. On this point, see also I. Berlin, *Three Critics of the Enlightenment: Vico, Hamann, Herder* (Princeton University Press, 2013), 179–82; and, more specifically, F. M. Barnard, 'The Hebrews and Herder's Political Creed' (1959) 54 *Modern Language Review* 533.

35 F. M. Barnard, *Herder's Social and Political Thought: From Enlightenment to Nationalism* (Clarendon Press, 1965), 29.

36 On the institutional design of this sprawling empire, with particular reference to its German-speaking population, see, most recently, B. Stollberg-Rilinger, *The Holy Roman Empire: A Short History*, Y. Mintzker, trans. (Princeton University Press, 2018).

37 Barnard, *Herder's Social and Political Thought*, 30.

38 F. Tönnies, *Gemeinschaft und Gesellschaft: Grundbegriffe der reinen Soziologie* [1887] (Wissenschaftliche Buchgesellschaft, 1979).

39 Barnard, *Herder's Social and Political Thought*, 30.

40 Ibid.

past by the standards of the present; that each culture is an individual and unique whole; that each age has its own standards of happiness and virtue; that the past should be relived and *felt* rather than just described and explained'.[41]

Schmitt's variations on these themes make an appearance in many of his writings, also in his *Verfassungslehre*. Notwithstanding his moody critique, in *Political Romanticism*, of the oeuvres of Friedrich Schlegel and Adam Müller, Schmitt's debt to Herder and the organicist tradition is undeniable. We must not take Schmitt's dismissal of 'configurations of affect' at face value.[42] As so often, his polemic was rash and the analysis on which he based it perfunctory. As Guy Oakes, his translator, remarked about *Political Romanticism*, 'it is the most contentious of all Schmitt's books, the work in which he embraces the *j'accuse* role with an unqualified enthusiasm'.[43] The charge that Schlegel and Müller 'clothe affect with philosophical and scientific raiments and words rich in associations' applies equally to Schmitt.[44] He was no less guilty than Schlegel and Müller, to the extent that they were, of clothing affect, notably in his constitutional theory.

Herder was adamant that 'to empathize with the entire nature of a soul', one must 'enter into the age itself, follow the compass'.[45] To understand the constitution of peoples, he told his readers, 'feel your way into everything – only then will you be on your way to understanding the word' – and the world.[46] Herder's philosophy was of a subjective variety. It stressed the contingent influence of physical and historical circumstances upon national development. His cultural nationalism, in this sense, was a cultural materialism. For him, a *Volk* was made of mind *and* matter. '[S]o transfiguring the word *Volk* that it became the radiation-point in the nineteenth century for the new gospel of nationalism', as one of Schmitt's contemporaries put it just before the publication of *Verfassungslehre*, was Herder's 'most impressive contribution'.[47] It was also his most lasting. Of particular relevance to Schmitt's constitutional theory, however, is another aspect of Herder's cultural materialism: its exclusionary thrust. 'In clear antithesis to the patriotism of the Enlightenment, which on principle kept its borders open for communication, the Romantic concept of the nation', as Bernhard Giesen writes, closed 'the borders to outsiders. Here membership in a nation approaches a primordial significance'.[48]

2.4 SCHMITT'S *VERFASSUNG*

When Herder called his imagined community a *Volk*, he attributed to language the power of affect – the ability to constitute a people. By so doing, he laid 'the ideological foundations of a new dogma in the dialectic of argumentation', a dogma that Schmitt and Heller sought to better in the twentieth century. Both thought highly of the *Volk*, albeit in different ways. In his constitutional theory, Schmitt came at it from the right, Heller took a stab at the question of constitutional identity from the left.

41 F. C. Beiser, *The German Historicist Tradition* (Oxford University Press, 2011), 132. Emphasis added.

42 C. Schmitt, *Political Romanticism*, G. Oakes, trans. [1919] (MIT Press, 1986), 107.

43 G. Oakes, 'Translator's Introduction', in Schmitt, *Political Romanticism*, xiii.

44 Schmitt, *Political Romanticism*, 107. For a discussion, see J. Meierhenrich and O. Simons, '"A Fanatic of Order in an Epoch of Confusing Turmoil": The Political, Legal, and Cultural Thought of Carl Schmitt', in J. Meierhenrich and O. Simons (eds.), *The Oxford Handbook of Carl Schmitt* (Oxford University Press, 2016), 3–70.

45 J. G. Herder, 'Another Philosophy of History for the Education of Mankind', in *Another Philosophy of History and Selected Political Writings*, I. D. Evrigenis and D. Pellerin, trans. [1774] (Hackett, 2004), 24. Emphases omitted.

46 Ibid., 24. See also J. G. Herder, *On World History: An Anthology*, H. Adler and E. A. Menze, eds. (Routledge, 1997).

47 Hayes, 'Contributions of Herder to the Doctrine of Nationalism', 722.

48 B. Giesen, *Intellectuals and the Nation: Collective Identity in a German Axial Age*, N. Levis and A. Weisz, trans. (Cambridge University Press, 1998), 96.

What galvanised them both was the crisis of parliamentary democracy. Then, as now, constitutional faith was on the wane.[49] However, during the 'twenty years' crisis' of the twentieth century, the situation was more dire, certainly in Europe, than it is today, haunted as the continent was by all kinds of collective violence, certainly in Germany.[50] The spectre of democratic breakdown hung in the air – and Schmitt was smelling constitutional rot.[51] By 1932, he recalled years later, this crisis 'already involved the concept of the constitution itself'.[52] His publication in that year of *Legality and Legitimacy*, Schmitt insisted after the war, 'was a despairing attempt to safeguard the last hope of the Weimar Constitution, the presidential system, from a form of jurisprudence that refused to pose the question of friend and enemy of the constitution'.[53] Although most of his contemporaries dismissed his argument from affective constitutionalism as 'political fantasy law', he still believed, in the 1950s, that his early constitutional writings possessed a desperately needed 'intensity' which they communicated 'in a constitutional history sense'.[54] This reminiscence is indicative, I believe, of Schmitt's preoccupation with constitutional affect. He remained convinced that constitutional effectiveness hinged on constitutional sentiments.

This conviction, this constitutional faith, Schmitt felt, had been lost in the nineteenth century. As always with Schmitt, legal positivism was the culprit. In the interwar period, '[t]his thoroughly dominant theory was no longer conscious of its own historical and theoretical presuppositions'.[55] To remedy this supposed failing, Schmitt's constitutional theory conceived of the constitution as 'a special type of political and social order'.[56] The adjectives are telling: 'special', 'political', 'social'. To repair the constitutional framework of Weimar's *Reichsverfassung*, and to reclaim the concept of the constitution from Kelsen in particular, he 're-mystifies the state as a polity that is instilled with the autonomous will of the people', the *Volk*.[57] Schmitt did 'not accept', as Jo Murkens shows, 'Kelsen's equation of the constitution with the normative legal order of the state, which ignores its factual, sociological side', which is to say: its materiality.[58] For Schmitt, 'all constitutional aspects, such as union, order, goals (*telos*), life, soul, are factual'.[59] This is the reason why, for Mortati 'Schmitt's institutional theory was the cradle of a compelling notion of materiality'.[60]

Re-enter Herder. In language that reminds of Schmitt's verbal fusillades in the twentieth century, Herder had in eighteenth-century Prussia complained about the 'dullness' and 'mechanical regimentation' of life.[61] In *Political Theology*, Schmitt took a leaf from Herder's book. This early treatise gives a clear indication of the nature – and the radicality – of Schmitt's

49 M. A. Graber, S. Levinson and M. Tushnet (eds.), *Constitutional Democracy in Crisis?* (Oxford University Press, 2018).

50 For a recent account, see M. Jones, *Founding Weimar: Violence and the German Revolution of 1918–1919* (Cambridge University Press, 2016).

51 The term is J. M. Balkin's. See J. M. Balkin, *The Cycles of Constitutional Time* (Oxford University Press, 2020).

52 C. Schmitt, 'Afterword (1958)', in *Legality and Legitimacy*, J. Seitzer trans. and ed. [1932] (Duke University Press, 2004), 95.

53 Ibid.

54 Ibid.

55 Ibid.

56 Schmitt. *Constitutional Theory*, 60.

57 J. E. K. Murkens, *From Empire to Union: Conceptions of German Constitutional Law since 1871* (Oxford University Press, 2013), 41.

58 Ibid., 45.

59 Ibid. Emphasis added.

60 Chapter 15 by M. Croce, 224.

61 Barnard, *Herder's Social and Political Thought*, xii.

approach to materiality. Although his argument from constitutional identity found its most cogent expression in *Verfassungslehre*, his earlier book already foreshadowed Schmitt's affective constitutionalism. Already in 1922, he was romanticising 'the power of real life', an affective force so potent that it 'breaks through', as he put it, 'the crust of a mechanism that has become torpid by repetition', by which he meant the 'liberal constitutionalism' of Kelsen and other misguided 'neo-Kantians' with their 'juristic rationalism'.[62] He saw himself as a philosopher of 'concrete life'.[63] The reference to life in *Political Theology* is 'absolutely critical', according to David Bates.[64] It makes plain that, for Schmitt, a political community 'was very much like the organism in its self-justifying, purely existential orientation'.[65] We can take Schmitt's reference to Søren Kierkegaard as further evidence of the proposition that he was on a mission to make affect safe for constitutionalism.[66] 'Endless talk about the general becomes boring', Schmitt opined, in a swipe at Kelsen.[67] Why? '[B]ecause the general is not thought about with passion but with a comfortable superficiality'.[68] Kierkegaard, as is sometimes forgotten, was not just an existentialist, he was also a social realist – and a cultural materialist. And so, if my argument is correct, was Schmitt.

Schmitt's concept of the constitution is *both* ideational *and* material. It is rooted, as Murkens writes, in a sphere 'that lies beyond the positive, written constitutional text'.[69] In the year following the publication of *Verfassungslehre*, Schmitt inveighed against 'the age of neutralizations and depoliticizations'.[70] In hyperbolic prose, he elaborated an argument from cultural materialism. Invoking Oswald Spengler's dystopian account of *The Decline of the West*, Schmitt lamented that the interwar period was 'a soulless age of technology in which the soul is helpless and powerless'.[71] He blamed this state of affairs on the 'torpid religion of technicity'.[72] As he put it, 'Once everything had been abstracted from religion and theology, then from metaphysics and the state, everything appeared to have been abstracted above all from culture, ending in the neutrality of cultural death'.[73] This diagnosis of 'cultural decline' is one of many material traces in Schmitt's constitutional theory, another example of the attention he paid – in *Verfassungslehre* and beyond – to what Goldoni and Wilkinson think of as 'the underlying material context'.[74]

2.4.1 *The Materiality of Identity*

Inspired by Herder, but also by Rousseau and especially Emmanuel Joseph Sieyès, Schmitt assumed that the people – the *Volk* – existed 'before and above the constitution'.[75] He regarded

[62] C. Schmitt, *Political Theology: Four Chapters on the Concept of Sovereignty*, G. Schwab, trans. [1922] (MIT Press, 1986), 14, 15.
[63] Ibid., 15.
[64] D. Bates, 'The Political Theology of Entropy: A Katechon for the Cybernetic Age' (2020) 30 *History of the Human Sciences* 109, 113.
[65] Ibid., 113.
[66] Related, see P. Markell, 'Making Affect Safe for Democracy? On "Constitutional Patriotism"' (2000) 28 *Political Theory* 38.
[67] Schmitt, *Political Theology*, 15.
[68] Ibid.
[69] Murkens, *From Empire to Union*, 45.
[70] C. Schmitt, *The Concept of the Political*, G. Schwab, trans. and ed. [1929] (University of Chicago Press, 2007), 80–96.
[71] C. Schmitt, 'The Age of Neutralizations and Depoliticizations', in *The Concept of the Political*, G. Schwab, trans. and ed. [1929] (University of Chicago Press, 2007), 93.
[72] Ibid., 95.
[73] Ibid., 93.
[74] Ibid., 92; Goldoni and Wilkinson, 'The Material Constitution', 568.
[75] Murkens, *From Empire to Union*, 107.

the *demos* 'in romantic and organic terms' as the prerequisite of the nation-state.[76] This '*Volk*-centric, monist reading' of constitutional democracy is further evidence that the Germanic discipline of *Staatsrecht* – which Schmitt hoped to reimagine with his *Verfassungslehre* and Heller to standardise with his *Staatslehre* – stood for a distinctly socio-legal habitus, one that 'searches for and finds answers also outside the discipline of law'.[77] This habitus, to be sure, was *neither* the sole preserve of the right *nor* of the left. In the early twentieth century, the question of constitutional identity, rather, was a concern common to many of Germany's public lawyers. More than a few were ready to break with *Staatsrechtslehre*, that is, the scientific approach to law they felt was a burdensome legacy of 'Labandism'.[78]

As per the quote from *Verfassungslehre* with which I opened this chapter, the state, according to Schmitt, does not 'have' a constitution; the state 'is' the constitution.[79] He held the unity of people, state and constitution to be indivisible. The constitution was the state's 'soul', the people its body politic, the embodiment of Sieyès's *pouvoir constituant*. Schmitt accused statutory positivists of destroying this soul. It was impossible to think about constitutional matters scientifically, he argued. Abstraction, for him, was no substitute for concreteness. As far as the meaning of the constitution was concerned, Schmitt deemed it important to think about the concept phenomenologically. For him a constitution, to count as a constitution, had to have a material existence, it had to be 'actually present in the world', as McCormick puts it.[80] According to Schmitt, a constitution, properly defined, derived from the will of a *pouvoir constituant*. This will, because it is 'existentially present' ('*existentiell vorhanden*'), he regarded as a material fact.[81] Its materiality lies in its 'being' ('*Sein*'), which, for Schmitt, was the source of sovereign authority.[82]

Schmitt's *Verfassungslehre* was, he proclaimed, 'an attempt at a *system*'.[83] It was an exercise in 'categorical ordering', one of many.[84] Any constitution to be deserving of the name, Schmitt maintained, had to achieve a structural unity of people, state and constitution. 'The concept of the constitution is *absolute* because it expresses a (real or reflective) *whole*', he wrote.[85] The cohesiveness and coherence of a legal order, in Schmitt's argument, derived from a constitutional existence, 'an actually present condition, a *status* of unity and order', as he put it.[86] This supposition is a material claim. Schmitt's second claim, which he tied to the first, was cultural. It adds a twist to his argument about constitutional identity and speaks to his idea of the state: 'The constitution is its "soul," its concrete life, and its individual existence'.[87] This aphorism cuts to the heart of Schmitt's constitutional theory, summing it up succinctly – all the while leaving much to the imagination, as was his wont.

Ellen Kennedy is right: *Verfassungslehre* was 'unlike any contemporary work on the Weimar constitution'.[88] It was not 'an interpretation of that one constitution, nor was it a general theory

[76] Ibid.
[77] Ibid., 108.
[78] H. Heller, *Gesammelte Schriften*, vol II. [1926], 2nd ed. (Mohr, 1992), 16.
[79] Schmitt, *Constitutional Theory*, 60. Emphases omitted.
[80] J. P. McCormick, *Carl Schmitt's Critique of Liberalism: Against Politics as Technology* (Cambridge University Press, 1997), 231.
[81] Schmitt, *Constitutional Theory*, 64; Schmitt, *Verfassungslehre*, 9.
[82] Schmitt, *Verfassungslehre*, 9.
[83] Schmitt, *Constitutional Theory*, 53.
[84] Meierhenrich and Simons, 'A Fanatic of Order in an Epoch of Confusing Turmoil', esp. 12–21.
[85] Schmitt, *Constitutional Theory*, 59.
[86] Ibid., 60.
[87] Ibid.
[88] E. Kennedy, *Constitutional Failure: Carl Schmitt in Weimar* (Duke University Press, 2004), 119.

of the state'.[89] Schmitt's take on the material constitution, which is what I believe it was, upended conventional wisdom about the question of constitutional design. Indeed, by mobilising the substance of the constitution 'against its functional elements', as Ulrich Preuß once put it, Schmitt's was an argument *against* constitutionalism, conventionally understood.[90] Schmitt's *Verfassungslehre* was a genre-bending publication, one entirely in keeping with the 'trinity' of his thought, which is why it is entirely fitting to bring phenomenology to legality.[91] An awareness of the interplay of Schmitt's political, legal and cultural thought is useful, and perhaps indispensable, for grasping what the materiality of identity was all about in Schmitt's constitutional theory – where it came from and what it meant.

Schmitt's *Verfassungslehre* is an argument for, and from, 'communitarian existentialism'.[92] Conventional wisdom has it that he conceived constitutional identity in ethnic terms. Many, Jürgen Habermas foremost among them, have portrayed *Verfassungslehre* as an outgrowth and manifestation of Schmitt's 'militant ethnonationalism'.[93] Andreas Kalyvas begs to differ, as do I. Habermas's interpretation of Schmitt's constitutional theory is clouded by outcome knowledge. As are similar interpretations by Ulrich Preuß and Michel Rosenfeld, who influenced the reception of Schmitt's constitutional thought in the English-speaking world early on. In the process, they distorted Schmitt's argument about the question of constitutional identity. Schmitt may well have been 'the most influential theoretical antipode' of liberal constitutionalism in the early twentieth-century, but neither was he the only constitutional theorist to think phenomenologically about the *pouvoir constituant*, nor did he reinterpret the concept of the constitution 'in an ethnicist manner'.[94] It is inaccurate to claim, as Preuß has, that Schmitt regarded 'ethnic and national sameness' as the *sine qua non* of a 'constitutionally unalienated people'.[95] Schmitt may well have *thought* as much, but he did not say so in *Verfassungslehre*.

To be sure, Schmitt *was* a lifelong anti-Semite, and he *did* play handmaiden to dictatorship. Indeed, he was a voluble advocate of 'racial legalism'.[96] This notwithstanding, in 1928, Schmitt's constitutional theory, like Heller's, was *völkisch*, but not yet racial. The radicalisation of his institutional theory was in the offing – but not complete.[97] Homogeneity mattered to Schmitt; it was meaningful to him. But there is no evidence that he, prior to 1933, glorified ethnic identity, neither in *Verfassungslehre* nor in his other writings. As William Scheuerman writes, Schmitt, in what was a liminal period for self and country, 'does leave open the possibility that homogeneity can take distinct forms'.[98] Kalyvas goes even further. On his interpretation, Schmitt 'did not posit ethnicity or race as the fixed essence of identity. On the contrary, political identities and shared conceptions of the "we" are constituted through struggles, antagonisms, and differential relations

89 Ibid.

90 U. K. Preuß, 'The Critique of German Liberalism: Reply to Kennedy' (1987) 71 *Telos* 97, 99; see also U. K. Preuß, 'Carl Schmitt and the Weimar Constitution', in J. Meierhenrich and O. Simons (eds.), *The Oxford Handbook of Carl Schmitt* (Oxford University Press, 2016), 471–89.

91 Meierhenrich and Simons, 'A Fanatic of Order in an Epoch of Confusing Turmoil'.

92 I borrow the moniker from D. Dyzenhaus, *Legality and Legitimacy* (Oxford University Press, 1999) 2.

93 J. Habermas, 'On the Relation between the Nation, the Rule of Law, and Democracy', in J. Habermas, *The Inclusion of the Other: Studies in Political Theory*, C. Cronin and P. de Greiff ed. (MIT Press, 1998), 148.

94 U. Preuß, 'Constitutional Powermaking for the New Polity', in R. Bellamy (ed.), *Constitutionalism and Democracy* (Routledge, 2017), 153.

95 Ibid., 154.

96 See J. Meierhenrich, 'Racial Legalism' (2023) 19 *Annual Review of Law and Social Science* (forthcoming).

97 On the temporal dimensions of this radicalisation, see Meierhenrich, 'Fearing the Disorder of Things'.

98 W. E. Scheuerman, *Carl Schmitt: The End of Law* (Rowman and Littlefield, 1999), 280, fn. 30.

among groups'.[99] Kalyvas has a point. A close reading of *Verfassungslehre* reveals a thinker who cared passionately about preserving the sanctity of the *pouvoir constituant*, but one who was not yet hung up on the essence of constitutional identity. The 'alternative constitutional theory' Schmitt presented in the late 1920s was about preventing the decline of the constituent power of the sovereign *Volk*, whatever its make-up.[100] It is a misreading of *Verfassungslehre* to suggest, as Preuss and others have done, that it contains an argument for substituting 'the *ethnos* for the *demos*' as a category of constitutional theory and practice, for it does not.[101] What it *does* contain, to stay with the Greek nomenclature, is an argument for the *nomos* taking the place of the *demos*. This brings us back to the question of cultural materialism.

Robert Cover, to invoke another genre-bending constitutional theorist, used the concept of *nomos* as a shorthand for the normative universe from which 'legal worlds' derive their meaning. The creation of legal meaning – what he called 'jurisgenesis' – was for Cover 'an essentially cultural' process.[102] According to him, a *nomos* was ideational *and* material, 'a present world constituted by a system of tension between reality and vision'.[103] This normative universe, Cover argued, was 'as much' of our world as 'the physical universe of mass, energy, and momentum'.[104] Schmitt thought similarly, though not identically, about the constitution of constitutional law. In *Verfassungslehre*, he presented a case for taking the *nomoi* of constitutions seriously, both theoretically *and* practically. Schmitt's was a normative case for doing justice to material culture, viz., the 'pre-political identity' of a *pouvoir constituant*.[105] His concept of constitutional identity, at this point in his life at least, was still permissive. He was agnostic regarding its substance, as long as this constitutional substance was organically grown. Schmitt was an existentialist in 1928, not yet the institutional extremist he would become. For him even an economically-stratified 'class' ('*Klasse*') was, theoretically speaking, capable of growing into a *Volk* as long as it behaved like a 'genuine friend-and-enemy grouping' ('*echte Freund- und Feindgruppierung*').[106]

Schmitt was a prophet of extremity, but his constitutional thought in *Verfassungslehre* was reactionary – not yet racial. His break from previous thought was less radical – and far less original – than it is often made out to be. We may want to think of Schmitt as one of several 'reactionary modernists', as a sharp-tongued intellectual who, in law and in life, detested the rise of machine politics, regarding it 'as a threat to the German soul'.[107] However, these 'romantic anticapitalists', as Jeffrey Herf has shown, were 'no less hostile to reason' than 'their contemporaries in the political Center and Left'.[108] What set them apart was an uncanny ability 'to articulate a set of cultural symbols', to which the constitutional sentiments that Schmitt conjured in *Verfassungslehre* belonged, 'in which technology', including constitutional engineering, 'became an expression of that soul, and thus of German *Kultur*'.[109] That Weimar's

[99] A. Kalyvas, *Democracy and the Politics of the Extraordinary: Max Weber, Carl Schmitt, and Hannah Arendt* (Cambridge University Press, 2008), 122.

[100] Ibid., 129.

[101] Preuss, 'Constitutional Powermaking for the New Polity', 153.

[102] R. M. Cover, '*Nomos* and Narrative' (1983) 97 *Harvard Law Review*, 1, 11.

[103] Ibid., 9.

[104] Ibid., 5.

[105] M. Rosenfeld, *The Identity of the Constitutional Subject: Selfhood, Citizenship, Culture, and Community* (Routledge, 2010), 153.

[106] Schmitt, *Verfassungslehre*, 234.

[107] J. Herf, *Reactionary Modernism: Technology, Culture, and Politics in Weimar and the Third Reich* (Cambridge University Press, 1984), 46.

[108] Ibid.

[109] Ibid.

republicans failed to do the same – that they neglected the question of constitutional affect – was one of Heller's major regrets.

2.4.2 Völkisch *Materialism*

Schmitt's argument from cultural materialism, as I have presented it here, differed from comparable arguments on the left. For all his talk of cultural homogeneity, Heller, for example, was a prophet of solidarity. His progressive constitutionalism was about the supply of dignity.[110] By contrast, Schmitt's *reactionary constitutionalism*, to coin a phrase, was about the demand for difference. Consider the following passage from *Verfassungslehre* in which Schmitt articulated the meaning of representation as a constitutional principle, a recurring theme in his 1928 book. In this instance, he repudiated liberal constitutional theory by insisting that the act of representation was 'something existential' ('*etwas Existentielles*'), which is why, he argued, it could not be reduced to a procedure.[111] Schmitt maintained that it only made sense to speak of representation in relation to a *Volk* already possessed of 'political unity' ('*politische Einheit*').[112] Only an existential community could be represented, a random group of individuals ('*eine irgendwie zusammenlebende Menschengruppe*') could not.[113] A community worthy of representation, as far as Schmitt was concerned, had to meet certain requirements: 'Anything dead, anything worthless (*Minderwertiges*) or of little value, anything lowly (*Niedriges*)' could not be represented, he was certain, because such an inferior kind of being was inherently incapable of a political existence.[114] This Schmittian standard of civilization recalls Herder. Yet Schmitt's variation on Herder's theme has a ruthless ring to it that was largely absent from the *völkisch* materialism – this peculiar brand of German nationalism – that preceded it. Given Schmitt's penchant for verbal harshness, and his willingness to countenance constitutional violence, it is easy to see why Habermas and others likened *Verfassungslehre* to the 'steel-like romanticism' ('*stählerne Romantik*') of which Joseph Goebbels dreamt.[115]

Weimar constitutionalism, according to Schmitt, was order-producing, but not in a constitutive sense, only in a regulatory sense. The constitutional design of 1919, he repeatedly opined, was soul-destroying: mechanical, not meaningful. This constitutional effect he diagnosed as a pathology of liberal constitutionalism. Schmitt reasoned that it presented whenever the *pouvoir constituent* becomes the *pouvoir constitué*. When the constituting people in a constitutional founding becomes the constituted people, it loses a part of itself – its sovereign visibility, or so he argued. 'With the creation of a stable constitution, the sovereign moves from a situation of concrete and physical public prominence to a state of invisibility. It exits the political and retreats to the social'.[116] A constitutional founding makes the people invisible – the very people without whose existence the constitution would not have been conceivable. For Schmitt, this transformation of sovereignty was to be expected – and a wellspring of apathy.

[110] More recently, see also D. Cornell and N. Friedman, *The Mandate of Dignity: Ronald Dworkin, Revolutionary Constitutionalism, and the Claims of Justice* (Fordham University Press, 2016).
[111] Schmitt, *Verfassungslehre*, 209.
[112] Ibid., 210.
[113] Ibid.
[114] Ibid.
[115] As quoted in Herf, *Reactionary Modernism*, 47.
[116] Kalyvas, *Democracy and the Politics of the Extraordinary*, 133.

Schmitt worried about the proportion of 'fundamental' to 'circumstantial' elements of a constitution.[117] The more oblique the references to the constitutional sentiments of the *pouvoir constituant* – its constituent will and values – the less expressive of 'the identity and *eidos* of a political community' a given constitution will be.[118] As Schmitt wrote, the 'constituent will of the people' (*'verfassungsgebende Wille des Volkes'*) is an 'unmediated will' (*'unmittelbarer Wille'*), one that exists 'prior to and above' constitutional law.[119] Constitutional democracy, according to Schmitt's *völkisch* materialism, is a non-starter without constitutional ethics (*Verfassungsethik*').[120] The substantiality (*Substantialität*'), univocity (*Eindeutigkeit*) and the authority (*Autorität*) of this affective code of ethics will determine whether constitutionalism is meaningful (and thus potentially democratic) or mechanistic (and thus merely liberal).[121] Schmitt was *for* constitutionalism as long as the crafting of a constitutional framework proved capable of stirring *feelings*, the kind that inspired what John Adams, the world's most famous constitution-builder, in his marginalia of Wollstonecraft's 1794 treatise, called 'attachment'.[122]

Schmitt detested, and viscerally so, the kind of constitutionalism that cared more about creating contractual obligations than achieving constitutive identifications. In *Verfassungslehre*, he put it thus: '[O]ne must insist that a constitution, which rests on an act of the constitution-making power of the people, must be something *essentially different* than a social contract'.[123] If constitutionalism is about nothing more than codifying rules of the game, an understanding that Schmitt dismissed as *'Ethik des fair play'*, he thought it of no use to democracy, as he used that term.[124] 'A constitutional contract', he maintained, 'does not establish the political unity' of a people.[125] 'It presupposes this unity'.[126]

Schmitt's was an argument from the logic of appropriateness. For him, an effective *Verfassungsethik* was affective: it inspired constitutional sentiments. Yet, prior to 1933, to reiterate an earlier point, Schmitt did not call for 'an attachment to any particular country, state, or *ethnos*'.[127] Although Germany was foremost on his mind when he wrote *Verfassungslehre*, his references to, say, '[t]he constitution of the American state of Massachusetts, drafted by John Adams', suggest that Schmitt, prior to throwing his lot in with the Nazis upon their seizure of power, had not yet embraced the 'racial institutionalism' that almost immediately became a hallmark of his scholarship.[128] In his Weimar years, Schmitt still reasoned – and sounded – like a run of the mill anti-positivist. He argued that 'a constitution is stable and efficient when it depends on a population's conscious affection for a set of higher political values, when the citizens recognize the constitution as their constitution – that is, when through the constitution,

[117] C. J. Friedrich, *Constitutional Government and Democracy: Theory and Practice in Europe and America* (Little, Brown, 1941), 144.

[118] Kalyvas, *Democracy and the Politics of the Extraordinary*, 131.

[119] Schmitt, *Verfassungslehre*, 84; Schmitt, *Constitutional Theory*, 132.

[120] C. Schmitt, 'Staatsethik und pluralistischer Staat', in *Positionen und Begriffe im Kampf mit Weimar – Genf – Versailles* 1923–1939 [1930], 3rd ed. (Duncker & Humblot, 1994), 151–65.

[121] Schmitt, 'Staatsethik und pluralistischer Staat', 164.

[122] John Adams, *Marginalia in Mary Wollstonecraft, an Historical and Moral View of the Origin and Progress of the French Revolution; and the Effect It Has Produced in Europe* (J. Johnson, 1794), 404, available at: https://archive.org/details/historicalmoralvoowoll/mode/1up?q=constitution&view=theater, last accessed 20 July 2022.

[123] Schmitt, *Constitutional Theory*, 112. Emphasis added.

[124] Schmitt, 'Staatsethik und pluralistischer Staat', 164.

[125] Schmitt, *Constitutional Theory*, 113. Emphases omitted.

[126] Ibid.

[127] Kalyvas, *Democracy and the Politics of the Extraordinary*, 161.

[128] Schmitt, *Constitutional Theory*, 113; Meierhenrich, 'Fearing the Disorder of Things', esp. 192–98.

as through a mirror, they see themselves as the constituent power'.[129] Although Schmitt was *primus inter pares* among constitutional materialists in Weimar Germany, Heller started from the same assumption.

To tackle the question of constitutional identity, in other words, was unusual – but innocuous. In many respects, Schmitt, Heller and Mortati thought alike. *Unlike* Heller and Mortati, Schmitt was an anti-humanist, however.[130] Hastened by the rise of constitutional dictatorship in the Weimar Republic – and the breakdown of democracy that it facilitated – Schmitt's affective constitutionalism eventually turned sinister.[131] His constitutional sentiments became violent sentiments.

2.5 VIOLENT SENTIMENTS

As I have previously shown, in his 1933 pamphlet *Staat, Bewegung, Volk*, Schmitt

> imbued the idea of the emergent racial state with *völkisch*, that is, racial values. What previously had been 'just' an example of extremist institutionalism he retrofitted with the trappings of National Socialism, including some of the ideological tenets that combined with the regime's 'eliminationist racism.' This was easily done because Schmitt's institutional theory was largely agnostic about the content of the form.[132]

Whereas Schmitt, in 1928, was still agnostic about the *kind* of identity that was required for making constitutional democracy work, in *Staat, Bewegung, Volk* he let rip.[133] In his theory of racial sentiments, he insisted that '*Artgleichheit*', or racial equality, was essential for bringing Hitler's constitutional revolution to fruition.[134] The cultural materialism – the affective interplay of legality and materiality – in Schmitt's constitutionalism was front and centre. 'National Socialism does not think abstractly and rigidly (*schablonenhaft*)', Schmitt declared with evident pride.[135] National Socialism, he predicted, would tend to the *Volk*'s 'real' substance wherever the movement encountered it, whether in 'landscape, tribe, or guild' ('*Landschaft, Stamm, oder Stand*').[136] A year later, in the Nazi mouthpiece *Völkischer Beobachter*, Schmitt marvelled at the latest 'new constitutional law' the dictatorship had given itself.[137] Taking stock of the constitutional revolution that ushered it in, he congratulated the movement for having dispensed with a constitutional document ('*Verfassungsurkunde*') *à la* Weimar and Philadelphia in constitutionalising the *Führerstaat* and for having adopted instead, in rapid succession, 'grand constitutional laws' ('*große Verfassungsgesetze*').[138] Their passage, Schmitt gloated, had laid a new

129 Kalyvas, *Democracy and the Politics of the Extraordinary*, 161.

130 For a recent discussion, see J. Meierhenrich, 'Thinking against Humanity: Carl Schmitt's Critique of Human Rights', in D. Gosewinkel and A. Weinke (eds.), *Menschenrechte und ihre Kritiker: Ideologien, Argumente, Wirkungen* (Wallstein, 2019), 67–95.

131 See, e.g., F. M. Watkins, *The Failure of Constitutional Emergency Powers under the German Republic* (Harvard University Press, 1939). I have traced the cumulative radicalisation of Schmitt's institutional thought in Meierhenrich, 'Fearing the Disorder of Things'.

132 Meierhenrich, 'Fearing the Disorder of Things', 194.

133 C. Schmitt, *Staat, Bewegung, Volk: Die Dreigliederung der politischen Einheit* [1933], reprinted in C. Schmitt, *Gesammelte Schriften 1933–1936 mit ergänzenden Beiträgen aus der Zeit des Zweiten Weltkriegs* (Duncker & Humblot, 2021), 67–115.

134 Ibid., 115.

135 Ibid., 103.

136 Ibid.

137 The constitutional law in question was the *Gesetz über den Neuaufbau des Reiches vom 30. Januar 1934*. C. Schmitt, 'Das Neue Verfassungsgesetz' [1934], in C. Schmitt, *Gesammelte Schriften 1933–1936 mit ergänzenden Beiträgen aus der Zeit des Zweiten Weltkriegs* (Duncker & Humblot, 2021), 127–30.

138 Ibid., 130.

'*Verfassungsboden*'.[139] It was an evocative, carefully chosen term. Although its deeper meaning is lost in translation, the composite noun smacked of cultural materialism. To Schmitt, the laying of new constitutional soil represented the beginning of the end of the 'groundless existence' he – and his country's constitution – had led during the Weimar years.[140]

2.5.1 *Blood and Soil*

The new constitutional order was extraordinarily meaningful for Schmitt, which may explain his odious defence of the indefensible. A few months before the Nazi revolution, Schmitt, in a lecture to chemical industry executives, had complained that 'all fundamental institutions of the Weimar Constitution' were 'completely denatured'.[141] The successful *re*politicisation of the Nazi constitution therefore represented a substantive turnaround – a *volte face* that he greeted with racial fanfare.

It stands to reason that the arrival of sovereign dictatorship also assuaged, at least initially, Schmitt's personal fear of disorder. This may account for the radicalisation of his constitutional sentiments, especially the *speed* of their racialisation. Be that as it may, Schmitt's version of racial legalism bears out Robert Cover's observation that '[r]evolutionary constitutional understandings are commonly staked in blood', that in them 'the violence of law takes its most blatant form'.[142] *Staat, Bewegung, Volk* was full of violent sentiments. And it was one of *many* writings in which Schmitt advocated, justified, or otherwise legitimated constitutional violence to help establish the Nazi *Volksgemeinschaft*.[143] We know, and not only from his diaries and *Glossarium*, that Schmitt welcomed the death of *parliamentary* representation that Nazi rule brought. The arrival of Germany's racial order, he reckoned, would usher in a living constitution, one staked in blood *and* soil. The material constitution, he prophesised, would be *truly* representative.

Already in *Verfassungslehre*, Schmitt had bemoaned the limits of representation – as liberals were using the term. For Schmitt, delegation was *not* a form of representation. Sending representatives to assemblies was anathema to his understanding of politics. Representation, for Schmitt, was an inherently political act – and thus not one that could be regulated by 'general norms' ('*generelle Normen*'), electoral and otherwise.[144] Representation, he wrote in *Verfassungslehre*, was 'something existential' ('*etwas Existentielles*').[145] Schmitt's problem with liberal understandings of representation related to their conception of the *Volk* as an aggregate phenomenon of loosely associated individuals ('*einer irgendwie zusammenlebenden Menschengruppe*').[146] For him, a *Volk* was represented only to the extent that its 'political unity as a whole' ('*politische Einheit als Ganzes*') was expressed.[147] A representation merely of its members, Schmitt implied, was not enough. He wanted to see the *Volk* represented as a unitary

139 Ibid.

140 For the background of my argument, see also M. Marder, *Groundless Existence: The Political Ontology of Carl Schmitt* (Continuum, 2010).

141 C. Schmitt, *Konstruktive Verfassungsprobleme: Rede des Professors Dr. Carl Schmitt gehalten auf der Hauptversammlung des Vereins zur Wahrung der Interessen der chemischen Industrie Deutschlands e.V. am 4. November 1932* (Maurer & Dimmick, 1932), 5.

142 R. M. Cover, 'Violence and the Word' (1986) 95 *Yale Law Journal*, 1601, 1607.

143 Sixty-five others are collected in Schmitt, *Gesammelte Schriften 1933–1936 mit ergänzenden Beiträgen aus der Zeit des Zweiten Weltkriegs*.

144 Schmitt, *Verfassungslehre*, 211–12.

145 Ibid., 211.

146 Ibid., 210.

147 Ibid., 212. To get across the importance of this point, Schmitt rendered the formulation in italics.

phenomenon. Paradoxically, for someone who railed so much against abstraction, an author who fetishised the virtue of concreteness, the object of representation, for Schmitt, was about the idea of the *Volk*, not its grubby reality. He saw no upside in representing the *Volk* 'in its natural state' ('*in seinem natürlichen Vorhandensein*').[148] The locus of representation was the ideal, not the real.

Schmitt thought a great deal about the principle of representation in the 1920s, first in *Römischer Katholizismus und politische Form*, one of his least-read contributions to institutional theory. In it, he warned that 'the capacity for representation' ('*das repräsentative Vermögen*') was becoming extinct.[149] The Catholic Church, Schmitt suggested, was the only truly representative figure still standing. All others, from *Kaiser* to *Ritter*, from emperor to knight, no longer commanded authority. That sovereignty only existed in fragments, Schmitt blamed on liberals and libertarians, on savants and merchants. The way he saw it, the rise of 'economic thought' ('*ökonomische[s] Denken*') spelled the death of representation because it was causing individuals to care more about themselves than the imagined communities to which they belonged.[150] The logic of instrumental choice, Schmitt lamented, was prioritising costs and benefits, not norms and values. For him, nothing could be further removed from the idea of representation ('*des Prinzips der Repräsentation*') than what constitutional theorists in the second half of the twentieth century called 'the calculus of consent'.[151]

For Schmitt, the life of the law was experience. He believed that 'the economical' ('*das Ökonomische*'), especially in combination with 'the technical' ('*dem Technischen*'), demanded a 'real presence of things' ('*Realpräsenz der Dinge*').[152] Such a materialism was anathema to his cultural materialism, however. Bodily representation was not what he thought desirable. For Schmitt, the translation of votes into seats – this central conceit of parliamentary democracy – was not the highest form of representation but its nadir. He wrote dismissively of '*Stellvertretung*', or deputising, in castigating the practice.[153] As far as he was concerned, the mechanisation of politics had turned the principle of representation into a technology of rule. Schmitt regarded the institutions of liberalism – Weimar's parliamentary assembly, the *Reichstag*, foremost among them – as inorganic, inauthentic and immaterial. He derided them as 'automata and machines', inherently incapable of facilitating representation: '*Vor Automaten und Maschinen kann man nicht repräsentieren, so wenig wie sie selber repräsentieren oder repräsentiert werden können*'.[154] Schmitt was not, in any meaningful sense, interested in the political economy of constitutions, which is why *Verfassungslehre* was an argument for a moral economy of constitutions – one that foregrounded the question of constitutional identity. What he delivered was a sentimental manifesto.

2.5.2 *A Sentimental Manifesto*

The spectre of individualism with which Schmitt found fault in *Römischer Katholizismus und politische Form* was also the target of his constitutional theory. In *Verfassungslehre*, Schmitt

148 Ibid., 212.
149 C. Schmitt, *Römischer Katholizismus und politische Form* [1923], 5th ed. (Klett-Cotta, 2008), 32.
150 Ibid., 34.
151 Ibid., 14. Cf. J. M. Buchanan and G. Tullock, *The Calculus of Consent: Logical Foundations of Constitutional Democracy* (University of Michigan Press, 1962).
152 Schmitt, *Römischer Katholizismus und politische Form*, 35.
153 Ibid., 36.
154 Ibid.

returned to the concept of representation. He was convinced that the principle, liberally understood, 'endangered' all affective attachments – that it stood in the way of an organic order of equals.[155] Schmitt longed for an age of *de*neutralisations and *re*politicisations, a cultural materialism that would restore in Germany an affective way of law.

Verfassungslehre was a blueprint for affective constitutionalism. For Schmitt, commonality was a *sine qua non* of equality. He reimagined the ideal of equality as a 'political' concept – and thus in existential terms.[156] 'The equality that is part of the essence of democracy', he wrote, 'orients itself *internally* and not externally'.[157] Equality stops, he suggested, at democracy's edges – on the border of order. On a state's territory, within a democratic body politic ('*Staatswesen*'), all citizens ('*Staatsangehörige*') are equal.[158] Whoever did not belong to this imagined community, however, was out of luck. Schmitt was adamant: 'the other, the stranger' was not entitled to partake of democratic equality.[159] 'A form of equality without the possibility of an inequality, an equality that one has exclusively and that cannot be at all lost, is without value or significance'.[160] For Schmitt, who craved 'intensity', it was precisely the possibility of exclusion that made constitutionalism affective and democracy meaningful.[161] In Schmitt's existentialism, 'the devaluation of all traditional values meant that human existence, in its brute factivity [sic], became a value in and of itself'.[162]

This marks the spot where the cultural and the material in Schmitt's constitutional thought are enjoined. As a founding authority, the *pouvoir constituant*, according to Schmitt, becomes invisible in the course of constitutional democracy, but *not* immaterial. It continues to exist and 'is no mere conceptual fiction'.[163] Schmitt believed, as William Scheuerman writes, that 'we need to take the idea of the inalienability, indivisibility, and absoluteness of the *pouvoir constituant* seriously'.[164] At the same time, Schmitt insisted that a *real* representative was needed to ensure the sanctity of the political unity of the *Volk*. To him the personification of sovereignty – its embodiment – mattered. Schmitt's constitutionalism was always katechontic.[165] For he was, as Hans-Ulrich Wehler, the eminent historian, once put it, 'a fanatic of order in an epoch of confusing turmoil' ('*ein Ordnungsfanatiker in einer Epoche turbulenter Wirren*').[166] However misguided Schmitt's prescriptions, staving off chaos was the *telos* of his constitutional theory – and of his practice.[167]

Faith in constitutional law, which Schmitt took to mean 'a multitude of individual constitutional laws' ('*eine Vielheit von einzelnen Verfassungsgesetzen*'), he deemed insufficient.[168] As he noted in his *Glossarium*, on 3 October 1947, faith in law (*Gesetzesglaube*) was a sign of the

155 Schmitt, 'The Age of Neutralizations and Depoliticizations', 94.
156 Schmitt, *Constitutional Theory*, 258; Schmitt, *The Concept of the Political*, 27.
157 Schmitt, *Constitutional Theory*, 258.
158 Schmitt, *Verfassungslehre*, 227. The translation of '*Staatswesen*' as 'state system' in the English edition of *Verfassungslehre* does not do justice to the vitalist and organicist connotation in the German original. As a result, it conceals Schmitt's anthropomorphisation of the state. Cf. Schmitt, *Constitutional Theory*, 258.
159 Schmitt, *The Concept of the Political*, 27.
160 Schmitt, *Constitutional Theory*, 258.
161 See, for example, Schmitt, *Political Theology*, 15; Schmitt, *The Concept of the Political*, 26.
162 R. Wolin, 'Carl Schmitt, Political Existentialism, and the Total State' (1990) 19 *Theory and Society*, 389, 394. Emphasis omitted.
163 Scheuerman, *Carl Schmitt*, 70.
164 Ibid.
165 See also J. Meierhenrich, 'The Dictatorship of the *Kaiser*: Carl Schmitt's Theory of Monarchy', in C. Armenteros and I. Zarikos (eds.), *The Making of Modern Atlantic Monarchy* (Bloomsbury, forthcoming), vol. II.
166 H. Wehler, *Deutsche Gesellschaftsgeschichte* (C. H. Beck, 2003), vol. IV, 491.
167 Meierhenrich, 'Fearing the Disorder of Things'.
168 Schmitt, *Verfassungslehre*, 20.

'instinctlessness of a life-form condemned to decline' ('*Instinktlosigkeit der zum Untergang verurteilten Lebewesen*').[169] Schmitt contrasted this unsentimental approach to law, the kind he abhorred, with that of Hitler, which he still, even after war's end, endorsed. Paraphrasing Seneca's *De Providentia*, Schmitt recalled reverentially the Nazi dictator's 'method of legality oaths' ('*Methode der Legalitätseide*'), the legal performances that, starting in September 1930, put paid to the idea of law's sovereignty.[170] Schmitt implied that Hitler's deception deserved not revulsion but respect – for the cunning with which the wannabe dictator had exposed the degenerate law of the Weimar Republic.

The two entries in the *Glossarium* speak to my argument about affective constitutionalism. They attest to Schmitt's 'visceral reaction to "the law"', as Helmuth Lethen put it.[171] Or, as Schmitt himself wrote, on 19 January 1948, 'the word' and 'the concept' of law caused in him 'shudder and outrage' ('*Schauder und Entsetzen*').[172] Appreciating Schmitt's visceral reaction to the law is key to seeing *Verfassungslehre* for what it was – a sentimental manifesto. Schmitt's was an argument for nurturing the soul of the state. In his moral economy, the cultural production of value mattered more than anything else. Schmitt wrote more passionately than most about the affective life of constitutions, which is one of the reasons why his constitutional theory remains a touchstone in the twenty-first century.

The spectre of violence was key to Schmitt's understanding of constitutional identity. Schmitt stated his position especially bluntly in 1926, in his preface to the second edition of *The Crisis of Parliamentary Democracy*. Several of his observations about 'the substance of equality' in that monograph resurfaced almost verbatim in *Verfassungslehre* two years later.[173] One passage I want to single out goes like this: 'Democracy requires', according to Schmitt, 'first homogeneity and second – if the need arises – elimination or eradication of heterogeneity'.[174] To illustrate his principle of constitutional identity, Schmitt invoked the case of Turkey, 'with its radical expulsion of the Greeks', as an example of a 'modern democracy' and a nation that knows how to 'keep at bay something foreign' which 'threatens its homogeneity'.[175] The passage recalls twenty-first century debates about the crisis of constitutional democracy which also revolve around the accommodation – and annihilation – of difference. The passage is also testament to the radicalisation of Schmitt's constitutional thought in the years 1933–36, when the material requirement of racial equality replaced political equality as the constitutional *eidos* for which he advocated.

2.6 CONCLUSION

Verfassungslehre, for all its flaws, was a pioneering achievement. In 1931, Eric Voegelin had mostly praise:

> Those who move within the circle of ideas of modern constitutions of the Weimar type find there such concepts as: constitution, constitutional law, constitution-giving power, bearer of constitution-giving power, continuity of state and constitution, validity of the constitution, constitutional changes, constitutional breach, and so on. And, if it can be done, it is doubtless

[169] C. Schmitt, *Glossarium: Aufzeichnungen der Jahre 1947–1951*, E. F. von Medem, ed. (Duncker & Humblot, 1991), 23.
[170] Ibid., 23.
[171] H. Lethen, *Cool Conduct: The Culture of Distance in Weimar Germany*, D. Reneau, trans. (University of California Press, 2002), 179.
[172] Schmitt, *Glossarium*, 85.
[173] C. Schmitt, *The Crisis of Parliamentary Democracy*, E. Kennedy, trans. [1926] (MIT Press, 1988), 9.
[174] Ibid.
[175] Ibid.

a task of extraordinary importance to order this conceptual world according to its immanent sense. Only one scholar has risen to the task [. . .].[176]

Voegelin lauded Schmitt's phenomenological approach, especially the 'perspective on the totality of the experience of the state' that *Verfassungslehre* afforded. But he was not persuaded by the universalising claims that it also contained.[177] 'Throughout the whole book', complained Voegelin, Schmitt let it be known 'that the world of ideas is itself politics, yet he makes statements about the reality of the state as though politically immanent concepts were at the same time scientifically transcendent ones'.[178] That Schmitt advanced his opinions 'in the tone of scientifically objective statements' Voegelin found problematic, and rightly so.[179] For all its erudition, *Verfassungslehre* is less learned than it appears to be. Like all of Schmitt's books, it 'provides little more than formulas'.[180] Nonetheless, Schmitt's sentimental manifesto has stood the test of time.

I presented Schmitt in this chapter as a protagonist of *affective constitutionalism*. I took the term to refer to a quest for a constitutional order – a constitutional ideology – that eschews, in Schmitt's parlance, the 'dead hand of abstraction'.[181] Because *Verfassungslehre* addresses the sentimental life of constitutional law, it is uniquely capable of informing the debate about the crisis of constitutional democracy in our time – a debate in which the expressive function of constitutional law has taken a backseat to its instrumental function. Constitutionalism today, as it did then, turns 'on the contradiction between representation and identity'.[182] In the 1920s, Schmitt, alongside Heller, recognised the importance of thinking about the affective life of constitutions – of toning down the neo-Kantian rhetoric of rationality. His was an argument *against* constitutionalism as technology, an argument that resonates in the 2020s.[183]

Like Heller on the left, Schmitt regarded the constitution as the 'soul' ('*Seele*') of the state.[184] Both thought about the constitution of peoples, specifically about the constitutional embodiment of the German *Volk*. Both raised the question of constitutional identity as a practical response to the crisis of parliamentary democracy in Weimar Germany. Both developed answers from cultural materialism. And both gave pride of place to constitutional affect. The key difference between Schmitt and Heller was *where* they located the soul of the state. Schmitt was convinced it lay in the purity of the *Volk*, Heller that it revealed itself in the solidarity of the *Volk*. Heller was consumed by 'civil passions', especially the integration of marginalised groups, and thus the eradication of difference.[185] Schmitt's 'sentiments and desires' revolved around the intensification of difference. This decidedly uncivil passion will forever be a stain on his constitutional theory.[186]

176 E. Voegelin, 'Die *Verfassungslehre* von Carl Schmitt', in *The Collected Works of Eric Voegelin, vol. XIII: Selected Book Reviews*, J. Cockerill and B. Cooper, trans. and ed. [1931] (University of Missouri Press, 2000), 63.
177 Ibid., 66.
178 Ibid., 65.
179 Ibid.
180 Ibid., 50.
181 As quoted in Kennedy, *Constitutional Failure*, 96.
182 Ibid., 98.
183 More generally, see McCormick, *Carl Schmitt's Critique of Liberalism*. For a neo-Schmittian critique of liberal constitutionalism, see M. Loughlin, *Against Constitutionalism* (Harvard University Press, 2022).
184 Schmitt, *Verfassungslehre*, 4.
185 Sharon R. Krause, *Civil Passions: Moral Sentiment and Democratic Deliberation* (Princeton University Press, 2008).
186 The stain became indelible when Schmitt put his argument about the material constitution in the service of an authoritarian regime intent on the annihilation of difference.

3

Laski's Materialist Analysis of the British Constitution

Martin Loughlin

3.1 INTRODUCTION

Over the first decade of his academic life, Harold Laski pursued an ambitious intellectual and political project whose objective was to present a compelling account of the principles and practices needed to legitimate the new social order of democracy that was emerging. Beginning with critical analysis of orthodox conceptions of state, sovereignty and authority, this project culminated in the publication in 1925 of *A Grammar of Politics*. This, he stated, 'completes an effort, begun in 1915, to construct a theory of the place of the State in the great society'.[1] By the end of the 1920s, his intellectual achievements were widely admired and his influence on public affairs universally recognised.[2]

During the 1930s, however, the orientation of Laski's work changed. Political developments led him to doubt the efficacy of the pluralism and gradualism he had previously so vigorously advocated and to adhere instead to an economic determinism that saw the state as the executive instrument of the class that controlled the means of production. Accordingly, he developed a materialist analysis of British constitutional arrangements. This chapter examines this later development of his thought.

By 1930, Laski recognised that the prospects for continued social progress were receding and across Europe 'a widespread dissent from the principles of constitutionalism' was spreading. The reforms of the nineteenth century, bringing religious equality, universal suffrage and popular education, had been conceded gradually and without huge sacrifice. But there were now more formidable barriers facing the newly enfranchised who were seeking greater social and economic equality. This type of reform encountered stiff resistance, he argued, because it threatened the entrenched order of property.[3] Throughout the 1920s, he had continued to hope that, with determined political will, the barriers to realising a democratic society could be overcome. But during the 1930s that optimism quickly evaporated.

By 1932, we find him arguing that nineteenth century reforms had only been made possible by the opening up of capital investment through colonialisation alongside the 'vast expansion of material well-being which scientific discovery effected'. In the twentieth century these material conditions were disappearing and political conditions were accordingly changing. The growth of administrative government had transferred power to the executive, leading to Parliament

[1] H. J. Laski, 'Preface', *A Grammar of Politics* (Allen & Unwin, 1925).
[2] See M. Loughlin, 'The Political Jurisprudence of Harold J. Laski' (2021) 50 *Quaderni fiorentini* 251.
[3] H. J. Laski, 'The Prospects of Constitutional Government' (1930) 1 *Political Quarterly* 307, 307.

becoming 'little more than an organ of registration'. The technicality of legislation had rendered its meaning 'unintelligible to the multitude'. Colonies were 'in revolt against tutelage'. The idea of national economic self-sufficiency was finished. And the Victorian spirit of liberty '[was] everywhere at a discount'. Representative democracy, in short, had reached a cul-de-sac in political purpose.[4]

The system of representative democracy was not working effectively, he surmised, because no agreement could be reached on the fundamental principles necessary for the common good. A programme of institutional reforms could be listed but, without political will, they would just be words on paper. With guidance from Alexis de Tocqueville, he identified the problem. What holds society together, Tocqueville had argued, 'was not the constitution of the government, but the unalterable laws that constitute society itself'.[5] This insight led Laski to conclude that the malaise of representative democracy had arisen because the governing classes were either unwilling or unable to alter the essential characteristics of capitalist society.[6]

Confronted with this realisation, he turned to Marxism as an explanatory tool. Laski was never a Marxist in the sense of someone who accepted 'the vast all-embracing structure known as dialectical materialism'.[7] He could never fully accept Marxist determinism because of his liberal belief in the emancipatory potential of the individual, but what he did take from it was the materialist conception of history.[8] During the 1930s this materialist method came to dominate his work. The implications for his understanding of the character of parliamentary government, the nature of the state and the constitution will be examined later, but what were the reasons for this shift in thought?

3.2 ACCOUNTING FOR THE MATERIALIST TURN

The significance of Laski's shift is gleaned from the fourth edition of *A Grammar of Politics*, published in 1938. The main text remained unaltered but it was accompanied by a new introductory chapter, the tenor of which was very different from the self-assurance behind his account of the 'new philosophy' of the 'new world' written in 1925. When the book was first published, Laski accepted that democracy could only be realised by promoting an equality of conditions. But he was then confident that such conditions could be met by political reforms and that Britain was capable of evolutionary transition from capitalism to socialism. By the mid-1930s, his mood had changed.

The announcement that 'no theory of the state is ever intelligible save in the context of its time' was a direct comment on his own book. He now argued that the state 'expresses a will to maintain a given system of class relations' and that, although democratisation might give those without privileges the power to bring about change, those with the privileges of ownership would actively work to maintain them. This leads to a crisis in understanding that only the Marxian

4 H. J. Laski, 'The Present Position of Representative Democracy' (1932) 26 *American Political Science Review* 629, 629–30, 631.

5 A. de Tocqueville, *Recollections*, trans. G. Lawrence (Doubleday, 1971), 95.

6 Laski, 'Representative Democracy', 639.

7 R. Miliband, 'Harold Laski's Socialism' (1995) 31 *Socialist Register* 239, 240.

8 H. J. Laski, *Communism* (Thornton Butterworth, 1927), 90: 'We conclude, then, that the materialist interpretation of history is, as a general doctrine, undeniable. In the context of communism, there is no necessary connection between its theses and the inferences and predictions made by Marx. A necessary connection may, however, be made. The only way to avoid its coming is to prove by social policy that it is unnecessary.'

theory of the state could meet. 'As an index to the problems of our age', Laski asserted, 'it decisively ... holds the field'.[9]

Just as there was a crisis in the theory of the state, so too was there a crisis in legal thought. Kelsen's pure theory of law might provide a cogent account of positive law but 'its substance is an exercise in logic and not in life'. Only the Marxian interpretation could explain the substance of law. A true sociological conception of law must therefore acknowledge that 'legal relations are rooted in class relations'. As such they could not be transcended because their postulates 'are never self-determined, but given to it by the economic system of which it is the expression'. His earlier legal pluralism, he acknowledged, 'did not sufficiently realise the nature of the state as an expression of class-relations'.[10]

In his 1938 account, Laski conceded that his earlier pluralism was merely a stage in the process of accepting the Marxian method. This pluralism, he now recognised, could only be realised when society attained an approximate social and economic equality. Only when a class-society is destroyed can 'both the nature of authority and the law it ordains undergo a fundamental transformation'.[11] What caused Laski to amend his accounts of law and state?

The failure of the General Strike of 1926, followed by the enactment in 1927 of a Trades Disputes Act that made sympathy strikes unlawful, were undoubtedly significant factors. At the time, Laski reaffirmed his position of maintaining a class analysis of the social order while rejecting economic determinism, but his confidence in the ability of parliamentary methods to achieve socialism was already being strained.[12]

The crunch came in 1931. In the 1929 election, Labour was returned as the largest party and formed a minority government. Two years after the stock market crash and under pressure to make cuts, the Labour cabinet refused to include cuts in unemployment benefits in a package to resolve the budget crisis. But, rather than resigning as prime minister, Ramsay MacDonald split the party by agreeing to form a National government and, in the general election that followed, Labour's representation was reduced from 287 to 52 MPs.[13] These events shattered Laski's belief in the parliamentary road to socialism. He claimed that both the king and MacDonald had acted unconstitutionally and the crisis strengthened his belief that 'effective authority lies in the hands of a small knot of financiers, responsible ... to no one'. It also caused him to question whether evolutionary socialism had 'deceived itself into believing that it can establish itself by peaceful means within the ambit of the capitalist system'.[14]

The 1931 crisis was the most important single event in his 'swing to the left',[15] but it was strengthened by other factors. In a later statement of his beliefs he explained:

[9] Laski, *Grammar*, i, iii, v.

[10] Ibid., vii–viii, ix–x, xxii, xi.

[11] Ibid., xiii.

[12] Laski, *Communism*, 83: 'To accept the materialist conception is not, of course, to say that it explains all historical phenomena. There are passages in Marx's works in which this claim seems to have been made ...'. H. J. Laski, *Karl Marx: An Essay* (Allen & Unwin, 1922), 33–34: 'No economic conditions can explain the suicidal nationalism of the Balkans ... Historically, too, the part played by religion in the determination of social outlook was, until at least the peace of Westphalia, as important as that played by material conditions ... The impulses of men, in fact, are never referable to any single source. The love of power, herd-instinct, rivalry, the desire of display, all these are hardly less vital than the acquisitiveness which explains the strength of material environment.'

[13] See R. Skidelsky, *Politicians and the Slump: The Labour Government 1929–1931* (Macmillan, 1994).

[14] H. J. Laski, *The Crisis and the Constitution: 1931 and after* (Hogarth Press, 1932), 9, 34, 49.

[15] N. Riddell, *Labour in Crisis: The Second Labour Government 1929–1931* (Manchester University Press, 1999), 213: 'For Harold Laski, the 1931 crisis was the catalyst for his swing to the left, both ideologically and in factional terms.'

> The experience of Russia, the advent of Fascism in central and south-eastern Europe, the attitude of the owning class in Spain and France and the United States to all serious attempts at social reform, the general strike of 1926 and the betrayal of 1931 in England, the new imperialisms of Japan and Italy, have all convinced me that, in large outline, there is no answer to the philosophy of Marx.[16]

Similarly, in his 1938 introduction to *Grammar*, he stated that the 'union of economic oligarchy and political democracy worked well enough so long as capitalism was in its phase of expansion', but at the end of the First World War capitalism entered into a period of contraction. In the expansionary phase, it could make concessions, but during contraction resistance mounted. The state could present itself as a regime of toleration and pluralism only on the implicit condition that these values 'did not threaten the economic foundations of the regime itself'.[17]

3.3 THE CRISIS OF PARLIAMENTARY DEMOCRACY

Laski's first task was to address the implications of these developments on the standing of parliamentary democracy. This he did in *Democracy in Crisis*, published in 1933 and based on lectures he had given in the United States.

His first lecture, on 'the illusion of security', advanced the thesis that the present generation has 'lost its scheme of values'. Conditions in advanced societies undoubtedly differed from those that brought about the Russian revolution: 'our administrative mechanism is not in decay', 'our middle class ... remains strong', the armed forces 'have shown no signs of serious disloyalty to the civil government' and 'strike after strike ... has been met and broken without exceptional loss'. Nevertheless, the general state of affairs was one of disillusion: 'certainty has been replaced by cynicism', 'the war dealt a mortal blow at religious belief' and the victory of individualism and triumph of the acquisitive society is a merely Pyrrhic one since we have learned 'the arts of production' but have 'no clue to the problem of justice in distribution'.[18] The evolving British parliamentary system had avoided revolutionary overthrow because it could consolidate in a period of continuous economic expansion and at a time when the two main parliamentary parties were agreed on political fundamentals. But, having ended the Victorian compromise, the rise of the Labour party has brought about a crisis, as it sought to achieve a social revolution through the redistribution of economic power.

The political crisis was taken up in his second lecture on the 'decay of representative institutions'. Laski explained that legislatures are in an unsatisfactory condition because they are overwhelmed with work, controlled by parties, and have ceded initiative to governments. Two traditional institutions in particular need of fundamental reform were highlighted: the monarchy and the judiciary. Although the monarchy appeared to be a merely decorative part of the constitution, this was deceptive. Since a king implies a court and a court implies an aristocracy, 'all its effective social relationships are a denial of the hypothesis of equality'. And although law requires impartiality, there can be no true equality before the law without social and economic equality. This is unattainable 'so long as the assumptions of capitalist philosophy dominate the practice of the courts'.[19]

16 H. J. Laski, 'I Believe', in W. H. Auden et al. (eds.), *I Believe: The Personal Philosophies of Twenty-Three Eminent Men and Women of Our Time* (Allen & Unwin, 1940), 163–68, 168.

17 Laski, *Grammar*, xiv, xxiv.

18 H. J. Laski, *Democracy in Crisis* (Allen & Unwin, 1933), 14, 16–17, 19.

19 Ibid., 125, 129, 133.

Fundamental reform, Laski maintained, requires either a period of dictatorship or a gradual change in which expectations are slowly altered. The dilemma is that parliamentary democracy precludes the former but, when the main levers of leadership (access to education, the professions, the media) remain under capitalist control, the electorate will not be allowed 'to stumble into socialism by the accident of a verdict at the polls'. From this he concluded that a Labour government must bring about 'a radical transformation of parliamentary government', requiring them to adopt new procedures, 'take vast powers, and legislate under them by ordinance and decree'.[20]

Radical though that argument may be, in the next lecture, on 'authority and discipline in capitalist democracy', Laski contended that 'no mere changes in political machinery are adequate to the proportions of the problem'. Since institutions have value only by virtue of the spirit that energises them, the question is whether socialism can transform their meaning. Having previously thought that socialism could reach a compromise with capitalist democracy, he now admitted that a 'society can no more make peace between the motives of private profit and public service than it can continue half-slave and half-free'. The critical question was whether such fundamental reforms could be achieved without violence. Laski acknowledged the primacy of reason as a method of resolving social differences but doubted the prospect of finding the conditions of maintaining that temperament. Critics might see in democratic socialism the destruction of liberty, but this was because, for them, liberty is a function of possession of property. It is a name 'of noble sound and squalid result'.[21] Liberty can only have value on the basis of equality.

In his final lecture, Laski assessed the merits of 'the revolutionary claim', the argument that nothing can be gained in seeking to realise socialism by constitutional means since the capitalist class 'is likely to defend with violence the injustice for which it is responsible'. Acknowledging its force, he emphasised its pitfalls. First, revolution is an art: 'nothing is gained by embarking upon it except under conditions which maximise the prospects of success', and the 'environment in which Lenin was successful is of extreme rarity in history'. Secondly, revolutions lead invariably to dictatorship, the conditions of which vary. The proletarian dictatorship imposed in Russia was founded on the specific conditions of a collapsed autocracy. In Britain, by contrast, where there is 'a large middle class habituated to domination and privilege', the dictatorship – like that in fascist Italy – would be that of the middle class. Laski recognised, thirdly, that revolution is 'infinite tragedy, since, in its very nature, it means pain and suffering and the tragic confusion of means and ends'. And, finally, it is 'the enemy of Reason and Freedom – the twin goddesses whose triumph gives what of beauty there is in the ultimate texture of men's lives'.[22]

The crisis of parliamentary democracy thus arises from the fact that, although capitalism and democracy arrived at the same point in history through a common need to destroy hereditary aristocracy, they could no longer work together. The dilemma facing a capitalist society is that the logic of universal suffrage leads to a continuous expansion of welfare which not only reduces the contrast between rich and poor but also undermines capitalism's profit-making motive. The challenge is great indeed but, having rejected the revolutionary option, Laski accepted there was no serious alternative to promoting radical reforms through constitutional methods.

[20] Ibid., 77, 87.
[21] Ibid., 149, 164, 189, 207.
[22] Ibid., 233, 234, 236, 256–57, 266.

3.4 THE NATURE OF THE MODERN STATE

In *Democracy in Crisis,* Laski resiled from his earlier pluralism. He also abandoned his earlier critique of state sovereignty, now presenting the state as the supreme coercive organisation of society. It is to this institution that Laski next turned. The aim of his 1935 work, *The State in Theory and Practice,* was 'to discover the nature of the modern state'.[23] He pursued the inquiry by offering answers to three questions. What should be the basic purpose of the state? To what extent is that purpose actually being served? And, in the light of actual practice, what is to be done?

Laski first defined his key terms. By society is meant 'a group of human beings living together for the satisfaction of their mutual wants' and a state is 'a society of this kind which is integrated by possessing a coercive authority legally supreme over any individual or group which is part of that society'. The supreme coercive power exercised by the state is called sovereignty and, once the idea of sovereign state is accepted, 'law can be no other thing than the will of the state'.[24] These definitions are the basis for the critique that followed.

Law, Laski argued, must be founded on something more than coercive power because otherwise law cannot provide an adequate justification for demanding obedience. Idealist political philosophers maintain that the basis for obedience is that only within the state can our real will be expressed. The spirit informing this idealist argument, Laski asserted, is equality: 'It is to protect equality that law, to be law, must always be general' and 'it is to protect equality . . . that a civil religion is established, that men may be trained passionately to safeguard the spirit of the constitution'. The problem with idealism, he maintained, is that it tends to confuse the ideal purposes of the state with the actual policies of the government. He avoids this conflation, arguing that the state's legitimacy depends on the extent to which it is able to satisfy the equality claims of its citizens. Law must therefore find its 'title to consent' in the individual citizen's judgment.[25]

In answer to the second question, on whether the state's purpose is actually being served, Laski argued that, although it is natural to infer that the state seeks to realise the common good, in reality it cannot transcend particular interests. The modern struggle for control of the state has always been between economic classes and it is a struggle in which the state itself is never neutral. This has left the disadvantaged class doubting the validity of the existing order, demanding change and developing hostility to the dominant ideology. But since the will of the state is enforced through its government and the will of the government is 'determined by the character of the class-relations in society', this will also determines 'the end for which law and order are preserved'.[26]

This brings us to Laski's last question: if unity in the state is actually based not on consent but on coercion and if its essential feature is not common welfare but its power to compel the acceptance of class-relationships, what is to be done? There is, he states, no reason to suppose that 'we can transform the foundations of bourgeois society without heavy fighting'. To assume otherwise 'is an illusion born of special historical circumstances . . . now fading before our eyes'. Capitalist democracy 'had conferred political power upon the masses; but it was on the saving condition that political power should not be utilised to cut at the root of capitalist postulates'.

[23] H. J. Laski, *The State in Theory and Practice* (Allen & Unwin, 1935), 9.

[24] Ibid., 20–21, 31.

[25] Ibid., 62, 69, 76, 95.

[26] Ibid., 198, 199.

And today class relations 'have become incompatible with the maintenance of social peace'.[27] Returning to the issue that closes *Democracy in Crisis*, Laski here comes much closer to abandoning faith in the prospect of reform through constitutional methods.

Laski concluded his book on the state on a highly ambivalent note. His argument runs as follows: (i) in order to realise the true ends of the state, it is necessary to change the existing system of class relations, (ii) 'it is the duty of the citizen to exhaust the means placed at his disposal by the constitution of the state before resorting to revolution', (iii) 'the nature of capitalist society weighs the scales unduly against him', (iv) nevertheless 'the gains which are inherent in the technique of constitutionalism are profounder, even though they are more slow, than those which are implicit in the revolutionary alternative' and (v) that, since 'changes in the class-structure of society have rarely been made without revolutionary means', those who make preparation for it 'have a case that has not been answered by the proponents of peaceful change'.[28] *The State in Theory and Practice* is Laski's most pessimistic work. It closes with the prediction that it is unlikely Britain can be transformed through violent revolution and equally unlikely that radical reform can be effected through constitutional means.

3.5 THE MATERIAL CONSTITUTION

The impact of Laski's analysis of the crisis of democracy and the nature of the modern state on his materialist understanding of the British constitution is clarified in his 1938 book, *Parliamentary Government in England*.[29] The book follows the conventional format of examining sequentially the main institutional arrangements of the British system: the party system, the House of Lords, the House of Commons, the Cabinet, the Civil Service, the Judiciary and the Monarchy. But his objective was not to explain the basic machinery of British government; it was to expose the underpinning ideology enabling that machinery to work. This led him to critically examine the limits to the British constitution's feted flexibility. If the ambition of Bagehot's classic analysis of the constitution had been to explain its workings to a mid-Victorian liberal audience, 'the upper ten thousand', Laski's was to offer a socialist analysis for the newly-enfranchised citizens of Britain's parliamentary democracy, the multitude.

His account of the workings of these institutions is similarly conventional. What is innovative is its basic thesis, which runs as follows. The British constitution may have been 'the deposit of a grim civil war', but for a period of 250 years, when other states have been reshaped by violent revolutions, all of its fundamental changes have since been effected by peaceful compromise. This achievement was not due to 'some special British genius for the difficult art of self-government' but because certain pre-requisites enabled contending political factions to reach settled agreement on fundamentals. These fundamentals bolster the basic principles of capitalism and it was this settlement, emerging from the protection of property rights and reinforced by successes in war and empire-building, that enabled Arthur Balfour in 1928 to claim that 'our whole political machinery presupposes a people so fundamentally at one that they can safely afford to bicker; and so sure of their own moderation that they are not dangerously disturbed by the never-ending din of political conflict'.[30]

[27] Ibid., 271, 272, 274.

[28] Ibid., 213, 214–15.

[29] H. J. Laski, *Parliamentary Government in England* (Allen & Unwin, 1938).

[30] Ibid., 13, 18. The Balfour quotation is from A. J. Balfour, 'Introduction', in W. Bagehot, *The English Constitution* (Oxford University Press, 1928), xxiv.

It was this underlying sense of unity that enabled Ministries to be formed and overthrown with relative equanimity.[31] And it was the growing wealth that flowed from this settlement that permitted concessions to social reform. These developments led many British socialists to regard the state as 'a neutral force which responded objectively to the will of an electoral majority'. But although the evolving political constitution placed governmental power at the disposal of the party that commanded a majority in the House of Commons, Laski emphasised that the pivotal positions in the judiciary, the civil service, the defence forces, and the police remain commandeered by members of the governing class, whose 'rules and habits ... are those which do not disturb the social order they dominate'.[32]

The critical question was whether these constitutional arrangements could still work when one of the two major parliamentary parties advocated radical reform of the economic foundations of society. The question, in other words, was whether the constitution 'not seen abstractly, but in terms of the social order, of which it is the protective envelope, is elastic enough to admit changes which seek its basic transformation'.[33] In its form, the constitution provides 'all the necessary avenues to achieve this transformation peacefully' but in its material reality 'every political democracy that is based on the principle of inequality in matters of social and economic constitution encounters a difficulty here from which Great Britain is no more free than any other country'.[34]

Having expounded his thesis, Laski sought to vindicate it through an examination of constitutional practice. All of his proposed reforms had previously been canvassed in the *Grammar*, but his objective now was to explain the workings of these constitutional arrangements from this materialist perspective.

Laski began with the party system. Despite its lack of legal recognition, the system is a vital component of the constitution and is expressed through the division between government and opposition. The 'mimic warfare' it generates has many advantages, not least in ensuring the control of the Commons by the Cabinet. But its most striking feature is that 'it maintains (or has so far maintained) the peace'. Continuity of policy had been possible because, since 1689, 'disputes between political parties tended ... to conceal their unity of essential purpose and emphasise their inessential differences'. In reality, a single party has been in continuous control of the state and, though it might have been divided into two wings, its quarrels were essentially family quarrels. This is the great change that occurs with the coming of democracy and the emergence of the Labour party. A political democracy 'seeks, by its own inner impulses, to become a social and economic democracy' and, embarking on that trajectory, it 'finds the road barred by the capitalist foundations upon which the political democracy is built'.[35]

[31] Laski, *Parliamentary Government in England*, 94: 'Since 1689 ... neither [party] has ever moved so far from each other upon any vital question as to bring an ultimate disharmony into view. Each has always remained convinced that the private ownership of the means of production could not legitimately be called into question. The men who directed the destinies of both circles came, broadly, from the same social environments; they spoke the same language; they moved in the same circles; they depended upon the same common stock of ideas. They thought in the same way because they lived in the same way. Members of either wing could cross to the other without any alteration of fundamental doctrine. A Tory democrat like Disraeli could be more advanced in matters of social legislation than a Liberal like Gladstone or a Radical like John Bright. A Conservative aristocrat like Lord Cecil could have more cosmopolitan conceptions of foreign policy than a Radical "man of the people" like Mr. Lloyd George. A Liberal like Sir Herbert Samuel could take the same view of the problems of Indian self-government as a high Tory like Sir Samuel Hoare.'

[32] Ibid., 19, 23.

[33] Ibid., 24.

[34] Ibid., 26, 35, 48.

[35] Ibid., 72, 90, 89.

This material reality of the constitution, he explained, was hidden even from the Labour Party 'because it has accepted traditional economics and the traditional theory of the State'. Labour too readily accepted the state as a neutral institution available to any party obtaining a parliamentary majority, failing to appreciate that 'the neutrality of the State between Liberals and Conservatives was because both had the same fundamental ends in view'. Whichever party was in power, both upheld the principles and policies of a capitalist society.[36]

This was the challenge of the parliamentary road to socialism. The institutional barriers were immense. The House of Lords, as the second chamber of a political democracy, was 'an indefensible anachronism ... responsible to no one but themselves'. Expressing a fusion of aristocracy and wealth, its delaying power was simply 'a bulwark against the will of the masses'.[37] The great extension of governmental business required the minister 'to leave to his officials all but the largest decisions on major policy' and, although the abolition of patronage resulted in a civil service with high standards of competence and conduct, its leaders still came from the traditional governing class: 'they go to the same schools and universities ... belong to the same clubs ... [and] the assumptions upon which their ideas rest are the same as those of the men who own the instruments of production in our society'. This is why civil servants could maintain neutrality and why 'the measures they have recommended have proved equally acceptable to Cabinets of either party'.[38] The judiciary acted as the guardian of a common law tradition which 'has been predominantly shaped by the need to serve the wants of a business civilization' and whose individualism is unsuited to a collectivist age.[39] And the monarchy 'has been sold to the democracy as a symbol of itself'.[40]

In *Parliamentary Government*, Laski departed radically from classical commentaries on the glory of the British constitution. From Montesquieu and Burke to Dicey and Bagehot the standard refrain had been that its virtue was its ability to maintain flexibility in its governing apparatus while continuing to protect life, liberty and property from governmental interference. In one sense, Laski does not disagree. But in explaining how this flexible constitution was settled by those material interests its fixed policy was to protect, he raised profound questions for those who sought political equality as a stage in realising social and economic equality. For those seeking to advance the common good, the institutions that made British parliamentary government such a success story had become major obstacles to continuing innovation.

3.6 THE MATERIAL CONSTITUTION REVISITED

Laski's last book was published posthumously as *Reflections on the Constitution*. Based on the Simons Lectures delivered at the University of Manchester in 1950, it reviewed the performance of political institutions in an age of 'turbulence and confusion'. Adopting a very different tone to that of *Parliamentary Government in England* written 13 years earlier, the book is something of a puzzle. Not only is his account of the institutions of government thoroughly orthodox, it also diverges from the radical criticisms of the earlier work. Indeed, the only allusion to the earlier book was his suggestion that, if there is a threat to the system, 'it seems to me to lie in the use of great financial and industrial power to prevent the will of the electorate being made effective by the government of its choice'. But even this was tempered by his claims that there is 'no reason to

36 Ibid., 186.
37 Ibid., 111, 130.
38 Ibid., 309, 316, 317.
39 Ibid., 363, 370.
40 Ibid., 392.

suppose that the status of the House of Commons has deteriorated in the last 50 years' and that 'I see no decline in its greatness, nor any ultimate danger that it should be by-passed in its fundamental purposes'. He further asserted that the 'growth of cabinet power has not meant the reduction of the House of Commons to what may be termed colonial status'.[41]

What explains such complacency and the change from his fears for parliamentary government expressed in 1938? One commonly touted explanation is that the experience of the war and the delivery of the post-war Labour government's programme changed his views of possibilities in unexpected ways. In the social and economic conditions of the post-war period, the great gulf between the major parties he foresaw and which he believed would lead not only to the sabotage of Labour's nationalisation and welfare programme but even to the breakdown of parliamentary government, did not materialise. Major differences between the parties remained, but there was also a much greater degree of cross-party support on such issues as the Beveridge Report, the National Health Service, the Butler Education Act and the White Paper on Employment than Laski might have expected. Neither was there much evidence that the capitalist class had managed to subvert the significant change in property relations brought about by these and related reforms.

Yet another explanation for dissonance between the texts is simply that Laski had misread the constitutional crisis of the period. Laski had convinced himself that the Labour party was a militant force determined to use Parliament to overthrow the citadel of capitalism. This led him to believe that, should this programme be frustrated by the establishment, direct revolutionary conflict was likely to follow. As Robert Mackenzie commented, this 'surely was almost pathetic romanticizing on Laski's part'. Laski had exaggerated the ideological gap between the two parties: 'Labour was less militant than Professor Laski hoped; the Conservatives, for whatever motive, have been nothing like as reactionary as he feared'. In reality, Mackenzie concluded, 'both parties when in power have had to operate in a set of circumstances which have drawn them very close together indeed'.[42]

Laski remained thoroughly ambivalent about the post-war achievements. In his last recorded notes, he recognised that:

> The history of law in the last eighty years has been, very largely, the history of an importation into freedom of contract of limitations and conditions which are less and less the result of agreements of the parties to the contract, and more and more the result of the intervention of society which uses the authority of the state-power to deprive the owner of property of the economic sovereignty his possession of which seemed 'natural'.[43]

But he then reflected on actual achievements. This development may have improved the lot of the agricultural worker but it 'has not involved any serious change in the relations of production in agriculture'. Although the national health service, social welfare and education reforms 'are all of them big and impressive gains' nonetheless 'it must be remembered that there still remain two systems of education in Great Britain, one for the rich and one for the poor'. And, although a 'brave effort' had been made to deal with the housing problem, 'there is nothing yet which permits us to say that a still predominantly capitalist society can solve the housing problem'.[44]

[41] H. J. Laski, *Reflections on the Constitution* (Manchester University Press, 1951), 2, 104, 34, 103, 107.

[42] R. T. Mackenzie, 'Laski and the Social Bases of the Constitution' (1952) 3 *British Journal of Sociology* 260, 262, 263.

[43] H. J. Laski, *The Dilemma of Our Times: An Historical Essay* (Allen & Unwin, 1952), 79–80. (This is a draft of a proposed updated version of his work, *Faith, Reason and Civilization* (1944); it remained incomplete but was prepared posthumously for publication by R. T. Clark.)

[44] Ibid., 105.

This type of argument led Laski to characterise those aiming to 'transform capitalist democracy into socialist democracy by peaceful means' as 'radical bourgeois'. They differ in degree but not in kind from the 'conservative bourgeois' in that they 'assume that as the relations of production change in a political democracy the values of the class which has hitherto owned the instruments of production will change also' and so far 'all the evidence is against this assumption'.[45] Analysis here is replaced by labelling. Abandoning historical realism, Laski ends up employing a kind of argument that signifies retreat from any serious examination of the issues confronting post-war society.

3.7 CONCLUSION

Harold Laski was a remarkably astute constitutional analyst of the inter-war period. The range of his learning was immense, his eye for detail outstanding, and he had a talent for coining biting epigrams that exposed the hypocrisy of so much writing about the British constitution. Laying bare many of the orthodox assumptions about the subject, he revealed how the modern settlement depended on the entrenched order of property and directly addressed the challenges facing political movements seeking radical social change through inherited parliamentary arrangements. In these respects, his was a penetrating critique of the modern constitution.

But Laski was also a political activist and his growing frustration with the labour movement's failure to deliver transformative change and bring about a socialist society led him into a type of economic determinism that seemed increasingly dogmatic and formulaic, and which ultimately dulled his analytical insights. 'No theory of the state is ever intelligible', he had declared, 'save in the context of its time'. In the 1930s, this led him to amend the theory of the state he had advanced in the 1920s. But despite the fact that his prediction that social peace would not be maintained without radical change not being realised in the post-war period, Laski was incapable of further revisions during his last years.

One reason is that he still believed that the march of history was on his side. In his 1943 *Reflections on the Revolution of Our Time* he acknowledged that, being in a period of reaction from its ideology, it was difficult to judge the Russian Revolution. But he went on to assert that we should recognise it as 'the first stage in a fundamental transformation of the social principles of Western civilization'. Maintaining that we must 'build an equal society in the next generation or we must abandon the democratic experiment', he argued that the fight must be won not just against reactionaries but also against counter-revolutionaries. The counter-revolutionaries most surely recognised the impossibility of returning to the world of laissez-faire and an aristocracy of birth, but their aim 'is to adapt capitalist society to the conditions of modern technology, of a world market, of a division of labour which has made the collectivist organization of social relationships inevitable'.[46]

The counter-revolutionary movement he had in mind here was fascism. But in the post-war period, things turned out rather differently. Fascism was defeated and much later the experiment of the Soviet Union imploded. Managed capitalism organised through a regulatory welfare state became the western model. Towards the end of the twentieth century, however, it was increasingly apparent that we were facing a different type of counter-revolution, that of neo-liberalism. Neo-liberalism marked a radical shift from social democracy, managed capitalism, or what Laski

[45] Ibid., 65, 66.
[46] H. J. Laski, *Reflections on the Revolution of Our Time* (Allen & Unwin, 1943), 42, 203, 252.

called a radical bourgeois politics. Its extending influence might lead us to further reflections on the material bases of constitutional orders, though with a rather different inflection to Laski's.

Laski's world is no longer ours. But does his materialist method still have something to offer? The fundamental problem of Laski's constitutional analysis is that he presented the two conceptions of constitution – the ideal and the material – as a chasm, one being romantic and the other real. Yet, far from being polar opposites, they most surely express a tension that is inherent in the nature of the modern state. The two aspects do not express, as Laski seems to believe, the ideal version he presented in the 1920s and the material emphasised in the 1930s. Laski conceives them almost as the normal and the pathological. But as so many scholars have demonstrated, the two aspects inhere in the very idea of the state.[47] There is, as Pierre Bourdieu noted, a fundamental ambiguity about the state: 'The state is a Janus about which it is impossible to state a positive property without simultaneously stating a negative property, a Hegelian property without a Marxist property, a progressive property without a regressive or oppressive property'.[48]

The flaw in Laski's analysis – and perhaps in all theories founded on the idea of 'the material constitution' – is its tendency to one-sidedness. For the Laski of the 1930s, the state is presented as a mechanism which bourgeois capitalists, conscious of their own class interests, have devised and continue to operate for their own ends. There are elements of truth in this, but as an analysis of the state and its constitution it leads ultimately to a reductive account of excessive abstraction and simplification. Bourdieu had suggested that the two-sided character of the state 'is troubling for those who like to think that everything will turn out rosy'.[49] It is equally troubling for those who, like Laski, veer between an inflated ideal and a depressed hyper-reality. The nature of the state can be adequately explained only once the autonomy of the political is taken seriously and this requires recognising that the political is concerned with a set of human relations that is not reducible to class conflict or socio-economic tensions.

Unless the political is accepted as a distinct domain in which this tension between ideal and reality, state and government, sovereignty and sovereign, is played out, then one cannot explain the hypocrisy of using legality as a cloak for exploitation. If there is no symbolic representation, there is no concept of state; there is only despotic power. The materialist critique highlights the gulf between ideal and reality but, once it treats the political as a superstructural phenomenon determined by productive relations rather than being itself a constitutive element of human experience, this materialist analysis fails to offer an adequate account of power dynamics in contemporary society.

[47] See M. Loughlin, *Foundations of Public Law* (Oxford University Press, 2010), 163–64.
[48] P. Bourdieu, *On the State: Lectures at the Collège de France, 1989–1992*, D. Fernbach, trans. (Polity, 2014), 98.
[49] Ibid., 98.

4

Rudolf Smend's Legacy in German Constitutional Theory

Tim Wihl

4.1 INTRODUCTION

Compared to figures like Hermann Heller or Carl Schmitt, Rudolf Smend's heritage in German constitutional law seems to be at the same time more evident and more obscure. More evident, because powerful constitutional lawyers like Konrad Hesse, Horst Ehmke and Peter Häberle were heavily influenced by Smend and because, last but not least, the German Federal Constitutional Court took up several parts of Smend's doctrine in its judgments – mostly in the area of fundamental rights, as in its famous *Lüth* decision on the 'objective value' of rights in the entire legal order. More obscure, because it is highly debatable not only whether Smend's legal thought is actually still alive in dominant constitutional doctrines like the proportionality test, the balancing of constitutional goods, cooperative federalism or even fundamentals of immigration and citizenship law – but also whether Smend's influence on Germany's material constitution has been, on the whole, advantageous for post-war legal development. Germany's collision model of constitutional rights, an apparent heir to Smend's obsession with *Abwägung* (balancing) *avant la lettre*, is coming under stress as more and more conflicts arise between opposing rights claims, for instance.

Yet Smend's success in established constitutional doctrine is striking. Rights are no longer understood primarily as subjective claims, but rather as objective principles. Society and the state are no longer diametrically opposed in constitutional theory. Furthermore, the success of the concept of integration in German political culture is evident. Rarely a politician forgoes an opportunity to remind German citizens of the value of integration, first of all in debates on immigration law. It is however unclear whether this idea of cultural integration – as opposed to assimilation or multiculturalism – can be traced back to Smend's *Integrationslehre*.[1] In any case, its hegemonic position in German political discourse renders it necessary to analyse whether integration in the Smendian sense amounts to an overarching model of societal harmony and internal peace that is, in turn, concretely reflected in constitutional and legal doctrine. Beyond that, it is worthwhile looking at how Smend's ideas were assimilated, but also transformed in important ways in highly influential casebooks and monographs such as Konrad Hesse's *Grundzüge des Verfassungsrechts der Bundesrepublik Deutschland*, a milestone in shifting the generally conservative legal discourse in West Germany after 1949 toward more pluralist and

[1] On the concept of integration in German immigration law, cf. J. Eichenhofer, *Begriff und Konzept der Integration im Aufenthaltsgesetz* (Nomos, 2013).

liberal positions. At first sight, it seems odd that Smend's integration thesis inspired pluralist conceptions like Hesse's. This powerful path of renewed constitutional thought in post-war Germany therefore merits special attention.

4.2 FROM ANTI-POSITIVISM IN WEIMAR GERMANY TO INTEGRATION THEORY

Smend belonged to the important anti-positivist current in the constitutional law of the Weimar Republic, which was formed against the positivism inherited from the pre-war Empire, such as that represented by Gerhard Anschütz and Richard Thoma. In this context, his lecture at the German conference of constitutional law teachers on freedom of opinion on the one hand, and his monograph '*Verfassung und Verfassungsrecht*' (Constitution and Constitutional Law) on the other hand, were trend-setting. Smend was part of a cohort that was rather sceptical of the first German democracy and feared in particular a dominance of the political left over 'bourgeois' forces. The discovery of legal 'substances' indispensable for democratic law can therefore be interpreted in terms of social history: these substances were intended to help secure a continuity of the state and its apparatuses as well as defend a certain bourgeois social order.

An essential role in this process was played by the reception of traditional currents of legal philosophy – after all, the representatives of anti-positivism describe themselves as a 'humanistic' school. This insinuates that positivism is bound to an ideal of science that is actually natural-scientific and somehow under-complex. Humanists, on the other hand, allegedly 'understand' life in its entirety and complexity. Positivists 'only' describe and explain causalities, and when applying the law, they work like 'subsumption machines'. Humanists try to dig deeper and 'comprehend' what the law as a living phenomenon is all about. Often, Smend's references to Theodor Litt's philosophy of 'life' are pointed out, which are indeed very numerous, but philosophically doubtful. It is unclear whether Litt (and Smend, as his supposed follower) succeeded in overcoming the contradictions of 'individual' and 'community', 'man' and 'world'. Nevertheless, such rather vague philosophies of life played a not insignificant role as an intellectual fashion at the time.

Another deep current of Smend's teaching was the influence of the Prussian 'state philosopher' Friedrich Julius Stahl with his organic conception of the state. Although it would be quite erroneous to draw a line from Hegel to Smend just because both share a certain meta-theoretical tendency (Smend cannot even come close to the conceptual strength and intellectual substance of Hegelianism), Smend describes Stahl's definition of the state – a 'dialectical vitality with the moral goal of a constantly re-established, preferably harmonious balance of conflicting political forces' – as exemplary for his theory of integration.[2] Furthermore, Smend shared Stahl's fundamental view that the law only has the 'justice value' of a negative barrier for the executive and the legislature, while the justice value of the law for the judiciary is to be a 'positive goal'.[3] This not only expresses a political position in the dispute over the role of the judiciary in Weimar, but also a privileging of the judiciary as a state power with a mandate

[2] H. Wiegand, *Das Vermächtnis Friedrich Julius Stahls* (Müller, 1980), p. 19, with reference to R. Smend, 'Verfassung und Verfassungsrecht', in *Staatsrechtliche Abhandlungen* (Duncker, 1968), 119 ff., 183. (All translations from German literature are mine.)

[3] Wiegand, Vermächtnis, 77, fn. 31 with reference to Smend, 'Verfassung und Verfassungsrecht', 210.

to do *justice*, which was an influential current in Germany – especially after National Socialism.

In terms of fundamental rights theory, Smend elaborates on the 'integration thesis' in his '*Staatsrechtslehrerreferat*' on freedom of speech (more extensively than in 'Constitution and Constitutional Law'), which emphasises the freedom of university professors in comparison to the *Kaiserreich*, but (ironically) further relativises liberal rights (such as freedom of opinion) that are not specific to the status of a state academic.[4] Smend sums up the role of fundamental rights very clearly and reminiscent of Stahl: 'For today's fundamental rights . . . the principle of human rights determines that these rights should not be barriers but reinforcements of the state and state power, whose acts, as executed within the framework of these rights, should therefore be all the more effective.'[5]

Although neither Stahl nor Smend present a sophisticated balancing theory of rights, they do provide arguments for *relativising* liberal and political rights in particular, especially on the basis of common or 'state welfare' interests.[6] At first glance, this statist, legalist, and positivist line seems to have little in common with Weimar anti-positivism. And indeed, legalism and positivism are refined. But both are united by the statist rejection of rationalist natural law and thus of the idea of a juridical, subjective fundamental right that is conceptually directed against state rule instead of being 'granted' by the state in an objectively reflexive way. Laws, in this line of continuity, are neither expressions of rights nor their potential opponents. The purpose of such a conception of the state as a 'real-dialectical unit of action' is the 'reintegration of divergent political and intellectual forces into a unified sphere of rule'.[7]

Smend himself distinguished between three different types of 'integration' – all of them are state-centred instead of fundamentally democratic. The individual is entirely functionalised for 'greater ends'. Personal integration means active participation in the integration process, which is always thought of in terms of the state. Functional integration, on the other hand, refers to institutional participation in elections, for example. Finally, the paths of material integration are very heterogeneous: They include flags or other state symbols as well as other 'state values'. The assignment of fundamental rights to the domain of material integration is of particular legal significance. As a result, they appear first and foremost as state-related 'values' and not, for example, as strict concepts with clear boundaries and an initial power-framing character or as substances with clearly defined qualities that would correspond to normative individualism. Rather, fundamental rights appear in a serving function and come 'from above' in a rather diffuse way, instead of being primarily an expression of personal autonomy. Moreover, their functionalisation in favour of the state dictates that they are to serve the strengthening, not the weakening, of the monopoly on the use of force.

4.3 SMEND'S LEGACY IN THE FEDERAL REPUBLIC AFTER 1949

After the Second World War, the doctrine of integration was dogmatised; Smend attempted to make it digestible for constitutional law, which was now to be democratic again, in concise,

[4] *Veröffentlichungen der Vereinigung der deutschen Staatsrechtslehrer* (*VVDStRL*) 4 (1928) 44 ff.

[5] R. Smend, 'Das Recht der freien Meinungsäußerung' (1927) 4 *VVDStRL* 44, 48.

[6] On Stahl's theory of political rights in F. J. Stahl, *Philosophie des Rechts*, vol. II, 2nd ed. [1837] (Heidelberg, 1846), 266, cf. H.-J. Böhme, *Politische Rechte des einzelnen in der Naturrechtslehre des 18. Jahrhunderts und in der Staatstheorie des Frühkonstitutionalismus* (Duncker 1993), 77.

[7] Wiegand, *Vermächtnis*, 39.

sober statements. From the outset, many constitutional lawyers feared that, in Smendianism, the Hegelian dualism of state and civil (bourgeois) society would be resolved in a conceptually blurred manner and that the intrinsic liberal value of individual rights, and indeed the legal form as a whole, would be eclipsed by state-defined goals. Admittedly, the weak side of West German constitutional law does not tend to consist in excessive republicanism. That would be a misunderstanding of Smend's teaching. Despite his proclaimed sympathy for the *citoyen* and therefore certain Rousseavian echoes, for instance, in his opposition of 'citizen' and 'bourgeois' – he even goes so far as to interpret his principle of integration as a *volonté générale* conceived in a dynamised way – neither the popular sovereigntist pathos nor the main goal of preserving freedom precisely through republican association is present in Smend's work.

Konrad Hesse, Horst Ehmke and Peter Häberle took up the thread as Smendians[8] and quite soon asserted themselves through the Basic Law[9] against Schmittians who were sceptical of balancing, and above all against the 'Ridder school'[10] (which proclaimed: The Basic Law is 'to the left of social reality').[11] The point of attack of the latter was the vicious dialectic of German statism: either to overcome pre-state 'chaotic nature' as a unity or to reconstruct a given order as a unity.

According to a common narrative, in the early days of West German constitutional law doctrine in the post-war period, there were essentially two major currents opposing each other, each of which felt more or less strongly connected to the work of Carl Schmitt or Rudolf Smend.[12] Indeed, for the debate on fundamental rights in particular, a clear frontline can be discerned, related to Ernst Forsthoff's and Carl Schmitt's invective against the 'tyranny of values'.[13] On the other hand, large sections of legal academia used to encourage the Federal Constitutional Court (FCC) to continue following the 'Smendian' line it had taken in its epochal '*Lüth*' decision.

[8] Cf. R. Camilo de Oliveira, *Zur Kritik der Abwägung in der Grundrechtsdogmatik* (Duncker, 2013), 19, 144 f. on the 'genealogical' connection of Smend, Häberle and Alexy in 'Abwägungs- und Wertdenken' as a special case of moral discourse; specifically on Häberle's Smend-translations, pp. 154 f.

[9] The formulations in the Basic Law may follow stylistic principles in detail, cf. C. Bumke, *Der Grundrechtsvorbehalt* (Nomos, 1998), 124. However, the 'subjective' considerations of the Parliamentary Council on stronger specification hardly succeeded in shaping the 'objective' practice of jurisprudence, as it prevailed from 1958 onward (Lüth, Apotheken).

[10] K. Hesse, *Grundzüge des Verfassungsrechts der Bundesrepublik Deutschland* (Müller, 1967); P. Häberle, *Die Wesensgehaltsgarantie des Art. 19 Abs. 2 Grundgesetz* (Müller, 1962). In case law as a 'collision theory' based on what is misleadingly (and rather rarely) called 'optimization imperatives', see Bumke, *Grundrechtsvorbehalt*, 157 ff, 226. Richard Thoma had intended the optimisation of effectiveness to refer to nothing other than the legally binding character of fundamental rights, see P. Lerche, Die Verfassung als Quelle von Optimierungsgeboten?, in *Ausgewählte Abhandlungen* (Duncker, 2004), 72 ff., 75.

[11] H. Ridder, *Die soziale Ordnung des Grundgesetzes* (Westdeutscher Verlag, 1975), 17.

[12] More nuanced: C. Möllers, *Der vermisste Leviathan* (Suhrkamp, 2008); F. Günther, *Denken vom Staat her* (Oldenbourg, 2004).

[13] Carl Schmitt, *Die Tyrannei der Werte* (Duncker, 2011); E. Forsthoff, Die Umbildung des Verfassungsgesetzes, in: M. Tohidipur (ed.), *Der bürgerliche Rechtsstaat* (Suhrkamp, 1978), vol. I, 177 ff. On this point, see the account in F. Meinel, *Der Jurist in der industriellen Gesellschaft* (Akademie, 2011), 410 ff. Meinel points out that the attack on the value-material understanding of the constitution cannot be understood as a mere school dispute (p. 412). Nevertheless, it must be objected that the 'German' formal type of fundamental right of the *Lüth* judgment has been conceptually captured in an almost 'ideal-typical' way precisely by Smend's teachings. But Smend was not alone, Hesse has strongly modified his theory (pp. 414 f.), and the doctrinal power of FCC case law is undisputed (p. 413). Forsthoff, in addition to the Smendians, also opposed a welfare-state line, for example, in Jürgen Habermas (pp. 415 f.), which one cannot deny having an increasing influence on jurisprudence. This is one of the initially latent, then emerging tendencies of German constitutional theory.

For the FCC, the tendency to enrich rights with 'objective' content[14] culminated for the time being in the court's 'NC' ruling,[15] which established the idea of a derivative right of participation, as well as in the first abortion decision,[16] which introduced the so-called duty to protect. For scholars, this tendency culminated in Peter Häberle's dialectical sublation of rights between their subjective definition and their objective institution,[17] from the 'status activus processualis' to the interpretive sovereignty of the holders of fundamental rights to their social participation dimension.[18] The opening up of the definition of the scope of protection for those entitled to fundamental rights[19] and the opening up of new 'dimensions' (private law effect, participation, social welfare, protection) makes rights more *global*, in that both greatly expand the areas of life covered by rights, though they remain unchanged in their formulation; the internal normative sphere of rights therefore becomes more *abstract* in the overall view, without the formulations of the articles of fundamental rights necessarily having to change, because more abstract rights come to the fore in the case law, such as the general principle of equality and the 'connection' of fundamental rights with the principle of equality[20] or (later) even, marginally, the article on human dignity.[21] Finally, the *relativity* of the external normative sphere of rights becomes quite dominant, as rights constantly have to assert themselves against each other and against further, ever more numerous 'constitutional goods' (*Verfassungsgüter*, a very Smendian vocabulary!).[22]

The expression of this movement in constitutional theory, which was able to assert itself in the long-term, not least in Court decisions, was the integration-theoretical concept of fundamental rights as 'objective values' of the 'state community', which was continuously developed by the 'Smendians' and in which the constitutional dualism of state and society – the central dilemma for (right-wing as well as left-wing) Hegelianism – could be resolved. It is nevertheless open to questions as to which part of those conceptions of objective fundamental rights was actually inferred from Smend's teachings. For Smend's theory of integration, which was only sketchily modified after the war,[23] does not say much more about fundamental rights than that they are a means to the higher end of (objective) state integration.[24] In the interpretation of positive fundamental rights, Smend himself was rather erratic, as demonstrated by his remarkably contradictory *Staatsrechtslehrervortrag* which he gave briefly on freedom of speech, but then mainly on freedom of science as the freedom right of his guild.[25]

'Smendianism' allowed the application of fundamental rights in far-reaching abstraction from their textual formulations, especially regarding the limitation clauses of fundamental

[14] W. Schmidt, 'Grundrechte – Theorie und Dogmatik seit 1946 in Westdeutschland', in Dieter Simon (ed.), *Rechtswissenschaft in der Bonner Republik* (Suhrkamp, 1994), 188 ff., 202 ff.

[15] BVerfGE 33, 303, 338 – NC.

[16] BVerfGE 39, 1, 42 ff. – Abortion I.

[17] Häberle, *Wesensgehaltsgarantie*.

[18] P. Häberle, 'Grundrechte im Leistungsstaat' (1972) 30 *VVDStRL* 43. For an analysis, see A. Voßkuhle and T. Wischmeyer, 'Der Jurist im Kontext. Peter Häberle zum 80. Geburtstag' (2015) 63 *Jahrbuch des öffentlichen Rechts der Gegenwart* (*JöR*) 401.

[19] P. Häberle, 'Die offene Gesellschaft der Verfassungsinterpreten' (1975) 30 *Juristenzeitung* (*JZ*) 297–305.

[20] BVerfGE 33, 303, 338 – NC.

[21] BVerfGE 45, 187, 228 f. – Life imprisonment.

[22] Pioneering, esp. BVerfGE 28, 175 ff., 185 ff. (military security); BVerfGE 28, 191 ff., 200 ff. (state administration). Concise critique in K. Kröger, *Grundrechtstheorie als Verfassungsproblem* (Nomos, 1978), 22.

[23] R. Smend, 'Art. Integrationslehre', in *Staatsrechtliche Abhandlungen* (Duncker, 1968), 475–81. Smend concedes here, after all, an overly strong harmony and totality orientation of integration theory.

[24] R. Smend, 'Verfassung und Verfassungsrecht', 119 ff., 260 ff., 264: '(the catalog of fundamental rights) intends to standardize an objective series of a certain unity, i.e. a system of values or goods, a system of culture'. They are at least 'rules of interpretation' (p. 265).

[25] Smend, 'Meinungsäußerung', 44 ff.

rights, and thus their mutual blunting through 'practical concordance'[26] and balancing, in other words.[27]

Smend's impact must therefore be seen primarily in the doctrine of balancing. In German fundamental rights jurisprudence, the balancing doctrine combined with the proportionality test has dominated to this day.[28]

In contrast to this rather moralistic resolution of rights conflicts, which seeks to rely on the Aristotelian epikeia (equity) as a universal demand on the law,[29] classical 'conceptual' solutions – which include, for example, the *Sonderrecht* doctrine in freedom of speech (no viewpoint discrimination and no discrimination against speech per se) – seek to avoid balancing as well as rhetorically affirmed ad hoc solutions without denying the necessary mediation with the case material. Indeed, it is one of the concomitants of the Smendian compulsion to clarify that fundamental rights are no longer understood as concepts (in a strong sense) and thus in their full ideational depth.

The FCC's 'objective value order' (*objektive Wertordnung*) was the door-opener for universal balancing and can be traced back to Weimar, but, contrary to common wisdom, not to the 'value philosophy' according to Hartmann or Scheler,[30] but to Albert Hensel,[31] among others. Finally, balancing ideology reached its theoretical climax in Robert Alexy's so-called legal principles theory, which is firmly grounded in FCC case law.[32]

The ambivalence of the German tradition, which is expressed up to the present day as a juxtaposition of balancing and severe doctrinal criticism of it, especially in the variant of the 'middle way' as a constant attempt to rationalise balancing at the court itself and even more in doctrine,[33] nevertheless allows relativity – which is also disposability – of rights to become ubiquitous.

[26] Thus, originally Richard Bäumlin, cf. critically, also on the historical references to Gratian's 'Concordia discordantium canonum' rather than to Nicolaus of Cusa's 'De concordantia catholica': A. Fischer-Lescano, 'Kritik der praktischen Konkordanz' (2008) 41 *Kritische Justiz* (*KJ*) 166, 170. Bäumlin later explained in his *Staatsrechtslehrerreferat* how this concordance technique is able to valorise community tasks such as school, military and administration because these are precisely not to be subordinated to fundamental rights. As a result, freedom of conscience in particular runs largely empty in terms of fundamental rights. R. Bäumlin, 'Das Grundrecht der Gewissensfreiheit' (1970) 28 *VVDStRL* 3. For an account of Hesse's method, see, more precisely, T. Marauhn and N. Ruppel, 'Balancing Conflicting Human Rights: Konrad Hesse's Notion of "Practical Concordance" and the German Federal Constitutional Court', in E. Brems (ed.), *Conflicts between Fundamental Rights* (Intersentia, 2008), 273 ff., 279 ff. Marauhn and Ruppel emphasise the ultima-ratio character that underlines the centrality of the method, however, the value-levelling premise of the method and its anchoring in Kantian practical reason. One can then hardly avoid registering the proximity to the 'community reservation' of fundamental rights advocated earlier by the Federal Administrative Court (p. 282). For a decided demarcation of (dogmatically secured) practical concordance from situational value considerations, see F. Müller, *Die Positivität der Grundrechte* (Duncker, 1969), 49, 53, 89, et seq. Dogmatic consolidation, however, does not contradict the relativity thesis.

[27] Hesse, *Grundzüge*. Cf. on genealogy likewise (by proxy) Camilo de Oliveira, *Abwägung*, 144.

[28] See BVerfGE 7, 198, 209 f. – Lüth (private effect) for a fundamental discussion of the balancing of interests. Further essential stations: BVerfGE 28, 243, 261 – Dienstpflichtverweigerung (unconditional fundamental rights); BVerfGE 30, 173, 195 f. – Mephisto (collisions of fundamental rights). On the genealogy, Camilo de Oliveira, *Abwägung*, 150, following B. Schlink, *Abwägung im Verfassungsrecht* (Duncker, 1976), 22, and Kröger, *Grundrechtstheorie*, 17 ff.

[29] Aristotle, *Nicomachean Ethics* V, 15; 1137b26.

[30] G. Lübbe-Wolff, *Grundrechte als Eingriffsabwehrrechte* (Nomos, 1988), 283, 289, fn. 225

[31] Cf. Kröger, *Grundrechtsentwicklung*, 65: Aim of the contradiction-free unity of the legal order based on fundamental rights.

[32] R. Alexy, *Theorie der Grundrechte* (Suhrkamp, 1994).

[33] In particular: P. Lerche, *Übermaß und Verfassungsrecht* (Heymann, 1961); with an effort to avoid 'overstretching', according to the ed. in: 'Übermaß und Verfassungsrecht. Bemerkungen zur Wiederauflage', in *Ausgewählte Abhandlungen* (Duncker, 2004), 244, 252.

As a result, an ordered competition of rights does not open up 'community-damaging', but only state-approved spheres of freedom on the basis of relative societal homogenisation, for example in the case of the Basic Law's freedom of opinion, which can be restricted according to Smend's 'theory of balancing' and which may thus serve as a kind of paradigm.

4.4 KONRAD HESSE: TURNING SMEND UPSIDE DOWN

Konrad Hesse is the most influential student of Smend's in the Federal Republic. In particular, he served as a judge on the Federal Constitutional Court and also wrote the most important textbook of constitutional law under the Basic Law to date. At the same time, he departs from his academic teacher in many, if not most, respects. His ability to learn and his intellectual suppleness are evident in numerous gradual changes of position that can be seen in the various editions of his textbook (for example, on the private law effect of fundamental rights or on general freedom of action).

Personally, he is portrayed as a man of balance and this temperament was reflected precisely in his legal convictions and judicial practice. In this way, he may have played his part in shifting the Basic Law to the social 'center/middle ground' so overly valued in post-1949 Germany.[34] The FCC judgment on co-determination in companies then appears as an expression of 'balance',[35] the judgments on public broadcasting as 'reality-based'[36] (the latter because Hesse laid the foundation for the typically German dual broadcasting system, in which private broadcasting is not given priority as neither publicly nor privately organised media guarantee sufficient diversity on their own. Instead, they both require a constitutional framework in order to be able to develop in the spirit of pluralism of opinions). The Court has stuck to this convincing, 'realist' line, arguably performing an invaluable service to German democracy to this day.

The constitutionalisation of the entire legal order, that is, in particular, the radiation effect of fundamental rights on private law as a typical part of a strongly substantive concept of the constitution, became a focus of Hesse's influence on the Court. This was ironic because Hesse was initially rather cautious about this tendency.[37] He had himself advocated tying the private law effect of fundamental rights to the criterion of social and economic power. Later, however, he spoke of 'protective, guideline, and impulse functions' of constitutional law vis-à-vis private law.[38] He continued to emphasise the importance of private law for human self-determination, but now saw the main problem not so much in substantive constitutionalisation as in overtaxing the constitutional court. From his point of view, it was the legislature that should act.

From a theoretical-scientific, rather than a constitutional-court perspective, Hesse's greatest legacy probably remains the methodological figure of 'practical concordance', even if it originates from Richard Bäumlin. At its core, it involves the balancing of conflicting fundamental rights positions. Constitutionally protected legal interests must be harmonised with each other in such a way that each of them gains reality, and limits must be set to both goods so that both can achieve optimal effectiveness. This only makes sense if the entire constitution is regarded as a totality of legal 'values' that (reciprocally) limit each other – a highly dubious claim because it

34 A. Voßkuhle and J. Schemmel, 'Der Staatsrechtslehrer Konrad Hesse als Richter des Bundesverfassungsgerichts' (2019) 144 *Archiv des öffentlichen Rechts (AöR)* 425, 432.
35 Ibid.
36 Ibid., 433.
37 Ibid., 438.
38 Ibid., 439.

reifies the legal constitution into a 'superstructure' in the realm of (Schmittian) political legitimacy.

In his lecture 'The Normative Power of the Constitution',[39] Hesse spells out the constitution's reference to reality. This is not an independent world of ideas, but always demands its final realisation in the real world. In doing so, Hesse adopts Smend's process thinking. The claim to validity cannot be detached from the historical conditions of its realisation:[40] 'Reality-conditionality and normativity of the constitution can only be distinguished; they can neither be separated from each other nor identified with each other.'[41] Obviously, this conception of normativity is directed both against a Lassallean rash (supposedly materialistic) identification of the constitution with actual conditions and against an overly idealistic opposition of the constitutional ideal and a bad reality. Both positions were constitutionally useless, Hesse believed. Admittedly, this meant a defence of the Basic Law against its numerous detractors at the time, but perhaps somewhat underestimated the polemical–provocative potential of a 'raw', young constitution, which was also directed or had to be directed head-on against restorative tendencies in society. This aspect was later emphasised by Wolfgang Abendroth, Helmut Ridder and Jürgen Seifert with their normatively more demanding interpretations of the Basic Law. Hesse, on the other hand, wrote that no one could hope 'that the tensions indicated here between constitutional standardization and political and social reality would lead to a serious conflict between the two. The outcome of such a conflict would by no means be certain (. . .)'.[42]

Possibly clairvoyantly, Hesse saw the most important challenge in strengthening the 'will to the constitution', that is, popular identification with its commands, which was not and is not always self-evident at the time or even today. After all, the federal government at the time was more inclined to abuse the court (e.g., in the proceedings against the Communist Party), and the after-effects of the fascist dictatorship were evident everywhere, for example in the prominent role of National Socialist functionaries in key positions in West German society and in the relentless persecution of communists or homosexuals. Both of these groups suffered from continuing criminalisation, and thousands of them got convicted under the 1951 political crimes law and the infamous §175 (male homosexuality), respectively, until the end of the 1960s.

Smend's legacy lives on in Hesse's work, above all in the postulated openness of the constitution to historical change. This is somewhat surprising in that Smend himself had pursued more conservative intentions with his doctrine of integration. However, the processual character of integration could be perfectly suited to the needs of post-war democracy for a theory of the evolving constitution, which is still part of constitutional self-understanding today. Originalism has never had a real chance in the constitutional interpretation of the Federal Republic. One may regret this insofar as the spirit of constitution-making in a post-totalitarian 1948 Constitution was, after all, quite different from that of the US founding in the eighteenth century. The progressive potential of a short-lived anti-fascist consensus was thus possibly wasted.

Later on, the true dialecticians of German constitutional theory, such as Ridder, were to remind us of this again and again: dialectics in the doctrine of the normativity of the constitution means pushing it to the extreme and, in constructing the case, also engaging with the facts unconditionally, and that often means materialistically – by looking for all the material interests

[39] K. Hesse, *Die normative Kraft der Verfassung* (Tübingen: Mohr, 1959).
[40] D. Grimm, 'Offenheit als Leitmotiv im Verfassungsverständnis von Konrad Hesse' (2019) 144 *AöR* 457.
[41] Hesse, *Kraft*, 8.
[42] Ibid., 24.

involved. However, rudiments of this dialectical thinking can also be found in Hesse, not only in his aforementioned lecture, but also in his magnum opus, the textbook on constitutional law.

The '*Grundzüge*' (the title of Hesse's famous textbook) work their way consistently from the politics to the theory to the dogmatics of the constitution. In doing so, the entire enterprise can be characterised as Hesse's 'turning Smend from his head to his feet', with set pieces ranging from Hermann Heller to modern political science. Smendian set pieces generally remain purely rhetorical. Throughout, even against Smend and the anti-positivists, Hesse rejects a norm-theoretical special status of the constitution vis-à-vis statutory law. He goes so far as to discuss a 'constitutional interpretation in conformity with the law'.[43] This is the flip side of the constitutional interpretation of sub-constitutional law and, for Hesse, simply an expression of the strong interrelatedness of ordinary law and the constitution, ultimately even of the 'unity of the constitutional and legal order'. For Hesse, this unity is virtually a fetish of constitutional interpretation: the individual norms of the constitution are not to be read in isolation, but always in their logical context. Hesse extends the idea to the entire legal order: This must – above all – be free of contradictions.

At this point, the undialectical trait of Hesse's thought perhaps comes to the fore most clearly. Ideas of continuum and process may dominate the entire textbook, but these are largely not of the type of sharply contoured contradictions and conceptual contrasts, but rather animated by the will to harmonise. Thus, although the constitution shapes the entire legal order, it is also for its part concretised by laws, and requires, moreover, the 'will to it' in the everyday application of the law, and remains itself determined by contradictory norms that are never resolved, but are to be defused by balancing them. Moreover, unity is understood as the 'political unity to be constantly won anew ... made possible and brought about by agreement or compromise, by tacit consent or mere acceptance and respect, under certain circumstances even by successfully exercised coercion, that is, a unity of a functional kind.'[44] Here, Hesse skilfully avoids the shoals of the concept of the political unity of the state, as they had burdened the Weimar and fascist discussions. Nevertheless, the orientation toward unity as the overriding goal of Germany's historical development from 1800 to 1990 (and today?) remains. This definition of direction is not necessarily emancipatory, but it is certainly taken over in essence from Smend and others. The insertion of the functional aspect is quite typical for Hesse, who likes to rely on a sociologically sober theory of the state, which largely replaces Smend's theory of integration's statist surplus with sociological rationality.

4.5 DE-DIFFERENTIATION OF STATE AND SOCIETY

The Constitution is the 'basic legal order of the polity'. This formulation is important[45] because it refers not only to the state, but it can also potentially shape social life. In general, Hesse, like Smend, is sceptical of an overly strong separation of 'state and society'. As a leitmotif, the critical questioning of this dualism can be found in the work of other scholars,[46] and, in the Federal Republic in general, it represents an important prerequisite for a materialisation of the constitution and constitutionalisation of the legal order.

[43] K. Hesse, *Grundzüge des Verfassungsrechts der Bundesrepublik Deutschland*, 20th ed. (C. F. Müller, 1995/1999), 33.
[44] Ibid., 6.
[45] Cf. Grimm, 'Offenheit', 461.
[46] For example: H. Ehmke, 'Prinzipien der Verfassungsinterpretation' (1963) 20 *VVDStRL* 61.

Dieter Grimm comments on the problematic balance of rigidity and openness of the constitution in Hesse and Smend: '... the fulfillment of the integration mandate "will often be achieved in ways that are not exactly constitutional." Unlike Hesse, however, Smend does not take offense at this. Deviations from the constitutional trajectories would do better justice to the meaning of the constitution than a "more faithful to the paragraph" constitutional life.'[47]

If Hesse wants to stick to the limits of the constitutional text, this also shows in his interest in rationalisation and a certain sobering up, which is contrary to Smend's more irrationalist inclinations. In case of doubt, rationalisation beats integration for Hesse. In general, Hesse's textbook is characterised by the spirit of an imperfect Westernisation, a primacy of securing freedom on an individualistic basis, but still within the unity of the state.

Hesse also takes some of Smend's claims more seriously than Smend himself. This applies, for example, to his more rational methodology. Hesse realises the dynamics of the constitution, which Smend proclaimed more than he realised, on the basis of the *concretisation*-oriented methodology of his eminent student Friedrich Müller, which aims at a rigorous ('concrete') construction-interpretation of the constitution in view of the facts of the particular case. Instead of being integrated by the 'ethos' of a 'bourgeois' constitutional order, it is thus integrated by rational legal practice.

Democratic politics is accordingly affirmed insofar as the role of the judge is more rationally circumscribed. According to Hesse, it is precisely in order to be able to concretise the constitutional text in a rationally justified way that one must demonstrate one's own prior understanding of constitutional theory in a transparent way. The reflexive rationality that can be achieved in this way takes the place of the meta-constitutional yardstick of the contribution to 'integration'.

Although a spirit of balancing pervades Hesse's unity-regulated constitutional theory, he nevertheless speaks out against any merely abstract balancing of constitutional goods. The best-known doctrine associated with his writing, namely the 'practical concordance' of fundamental rights, works much more concretely than an unstructured balancing.

More concrete, more sober, Hesse's textbook also makes other substitutions, all of which are concessions to a sociological–political enlightenment: Politics instead of the 'political', sociology instead of phenomenology, action instead of the 'integration process'. A pseudo-sublation of opposites (which has absolutely nothing Hegelian about it because of its open disregard for social facts) is displaced by questions of organisation, power and the separation of powers. Pluralistic conflict-orientation moves in. Substantially, a lot is closer to Hermann Heller than to Smend. The contents of the textbook are also substantially different; Hesse talks a lot about political parties, democracy and the *sozialer Rechtsstaat* (Heller). There remains a certain, but now democratically purified, anti-relativism. His remarks on federalism favour stronger centralisation, which Smend had vocally criticised.

Hesse also has an interesting comment to make on the interpretation of fundamental rights as an 'objective value system' by the Federal Constitutional Court,[48] which is so central to the materialisation of the German constitution: instead of working through in detail the fierce criticism of it, especially from the liberal–conservative or Schmittian side, but also from the left, he interprets the invocation of fundamental rights as values primarily as a temporary solution, a stopgap of the Court. Values were invoked because rights as norms had not yet been sufficiently

[47] Grimm, 'Offenheit', 463.

[48] FCC – *Lüth* decision (1958) (s.a.).

concretised and contoured. This also had the advantage of referring to international human rights as a system of values.[49] Hesse probably hits an important point here.

The more fundamental rights have been 'concretised' through case practice, that is, they have gained reality through the development of legal topoi, the more any direct recourse to values is prohibited.[50]

The fact that it is thus also forbidden to resort to abstract trade-offs follows from this concretisation theory of constitutional norms. Once again it becomes clear that Hesse turns Smend upside down by means of his methodological (besides the social-scientific) innovations. Therefore, it would also be mistaken to understand his idea of practical concordance, taken over from Bäumlin, as a simple balancing that tends to be repressive (or repressive-tolerant) because it is abstracting. Hesse writes on practical concordance, which he by no means conceives only as a fundamental rights doctrinal figure and even less only as a collision management mechanism of boundless fundamental rights in reasonableness tests (as suggested in more recent legal textbooks): this requires the 'proportionate' allocation of fundamental rights and legal interests limiting fundamental rights. Both would have to reach optimal effectiveness in the individual case.[51]

Also striking, because they are contrary to Smend, are Hesse's many theoretical statements on democracy as a principle – with which Smend could do nothing, but which Hesse very clearly designs as a necessarily *representative* system on indeterminate 'realistic' grounds and which, like so much else in constitutional law, he understands as an expression of the modern 'rationalisation' of rule. Hesse's conception of rational rule is almost Weberian in kind: the state becomes demystified and lives on as a bureaucratic machine in a society of 'organisations'.

4.6 RICHARD BÄUMLIN

Finally, I would like to add a few words about the Swiss constitutional lawyer Richard Bäumlin, who was certainly Konrad Hesse's equal and whose work also exerted a rather significant, too often overlooked influence in Germany. Regarding Bäumlin, Grimm remarks:

> Bäumlin pushes the idea of the historicity and the consequent objective character of law. In this context he quotes Hesse's inaugural lecture approvingly. But in the course of Bäumlin's investigation, the character of law as a 'concept of stabilizing behavior' recedes more and more behind the processual, until in the end it can only be understood 'from its completion, as an event of the realization of law'. Hesse sees in Bäumlin's conception 'an essential modification of traditional terms and distinctions, insofar as it does not render them irrelevant at all'. Since everything is ultimately only process, Bäumlin is rightly asked by Hesse in the review of his writing whether law, if it depends solely on the respective concretization, does not become 'an all too easily disposable quantity'.[52]

This seems like a rather harsh judgment with regard to Bäumlin's later and more concrete writings, which appear to paint a more diverse picture.

[49] Hesse, *Grundzüge*, 20th ed., 135.

[50] For a summary account of his theory of rights, cf. K. Hesse, 'Grundrechte – Bestand und Bedeutung', in E. Benda, H.-J. Vogel and W. Maihofer (eds.), *Handbuch des Verfassungsrechts* (De Gruyter, 1984), 79.

[51] Hesse, *Grundzüge*, 20th ed., 142.

[52] Grimm, 'Offenheit', 463.

For Bäumlin, freedom of conscience was a concise example to demonstrate that the individual can neither be harshly opposed to the state (for then conscience as a private thing would be irrelevant for law) nor be identified with it (that would be totalitarian). So there remained only one way of mediation:

> The idea of the 'constitutional polity' understands the state from society. The *political society* is the civil society with respect to a certain function: the solution of social conflicts by coping with absolutely necessary (but related to historical utilitas) community tasks. A principled resolution of the conflict between individual conscience and societal-state sanctioned notions of rightness is not sought ('open society'). Rather, it is a matter of establishing optimal concordance, of developing workable solutions to the conflict.[53]

So here it reappears, the leitmotif of 'optimal' or 'practical concordance'. Interestingly, it is not a matter of any liberal notions of the material rule of law, but only of defining the function of the democratic legislative state. The latter must exercise restraint and be tolerant – no less, but above all no more:

> 6.1 The guiding principle is 'tolerance as a legal principle'. Concordance is tolerance in practice.
>
> 6.2 Freedom of conscience imposes limits on the state. However, it also imposes a duty of concretization. It is a matter of shaping the legal order in such a way that the possibilities of conflict are limited as far as possible in advance. Where conflicts can be avoided by alternatives which are acceptable to the community, such alternatives should be provided.
>
> 6.3 The concordance of 'freedom and obligation' (e.g. also the question of the acceptability of an alternative solution) is always a question of case-related balancing of legal interests. However, problem-structuring principles can be developed.[54]

Bäumlin – following the direct-democratic tradition of Switzerland – does not move away from this scepticism towards a hypostasised rule of law ('*Rechtsstaatlichkeit*') even later. This part of Bäumlin's doctrine, which distinguishes him considerably from Smend's doctrine of integration, shows, once again, how little of the authoritarian, statist trait of Smend's doctrine remained among his most important students. Bäumlin's rejection of an excessively 'materialised' interpretation of the constitution in the interest of bourgeois individualism and private-sector actors goes so far that, together with Helmut Ridder, he passes a rather scathing judgment on the original integration doctrine in the 1984 'Alternativkommentar'.[55] Following them, this doctrine was 'decidedly anti-liberal', inspired by Italian fascism, and ultimately wanted to return to a sort of renewed Bismarckian constitutionalism. Very unlike the late jurisprudence of the Federal Constitutional Court, a strongly pronounced constitutionalisation of democratic majority rule is met with the greatest scepticism. This important, de-materialising critique was soon taken up by Ingeborg Maus' radical–democratic constitutional theory and Jürgen Habermas' opus 'Between Facts and Norms'.

Ultimately, the most important Smendians in the Federal Republic no longer agreed on how the deeply materialised constitutional order of the Federal Republic should be judged (*democratically*) with regard to the democratic legitimacy of the Court as a counter-majoritarian body or, rather, substitute/ersatz institution for Parliament when it comes to balancing so-called

[53] Bäumlin, 'Gewissensfreiheit', 28.

[54] Ibid., 31.

[55] R. Bäumlin and H. Ridder, 'Rechtsstaat', in R. Wassermann (ed.), *Alternativkommentar zum Grundgesetz* (Luchterhand, 1984), 1288, 1305.

constitutional values. They remained deeply divided on questions such as the '*Wertordnung*' (value order) of the Basic Law or liberal-democratic separation of powers. For an, in the eyes of many, overly materialised, multi-layered constitutional order increasingly limits the democratic sovereignty of the people. Even the Constitutional Court itself has shown some signs of self-doubt lately. During the COVID-19 Pandemic, the Court has been mostly deferential to all kinds of emergency legislation. Clearly, Smend himself did not provide any useful yardsticks for an answer to the question of how much 'democratic deference' is due by the Courts, which today seems more open than ever.

5

The Constitution in the Material Sense According to Costantino Mortati

Lucia Rubinelli[*]

This chapter will examine the legal and political thought of Costantino Mortati, the Italian constitutional thinker who, more than any other, dedicated time and effort to theorising the material aspects of twentieth century constitutions. Writing during and after the fascist regime and in opposition to Italian and German legal positivism, Mortati was committed to exploring the 'grey area between law and politics'. This space, where law and politics meet and merge into each other, was seen by Mortati as the source of all normativity and had to be studied as such. To do so, he developed the theory of the 'constitution in the material sense', which he juxtaposed to the legalism of those who focused exclusively on the formal aspects of the constitution. This emphasis on the material reality of the constitution led him not only to theorise about it, but also to actively promote means of popular participation suitable to uphold the material constitution and keep its relationship to the formal aspects of law active and dynamic. In what follows, I will first offer a brief overview of Mortati's life and oeuvre, aimed at situating his intellectual commitments within wider debates taking place in Europe, and especially in Italy and Germany, at around the same time. Second, I will provide a detailed discussion of Mortati's concept of the 'constitution in the material sense', in which I will highlight how it differs from the formal constitution and discuss its two fundamental features: the essential content and the normative material elements. Last, I will focus on the political and institutional implications of thinking about the constitution as a by-product of material relations. This, in Mortati's view, demanded committing to extensive forms of popular involvement in the political process which, alone, could guarantee the correct correspondence between the material reality of social relations and the formal positivity of the legal system.

5.1 THE GREY AREA OF POLITICS AND LAW

Throughout his long life, Mortati remained consistently committed to studying the workings of the legal system, with a specific focus on the constitutional order. This, in his view, demanded going beyond the analysis of black-letter law, of the written legal text and of its instantiation in legal procedures and judgments. By contrast, Mortati was firmly convinced that any given constitutional order could only be understood when seen as a socio-political artefact. In other words, he believed that the core meaning of law in general, and constitutional law in particular, had to be found in the 'grey area' where politics and law meet, and where it is possible to identify

[*] A longer version of this article appeared in L. Rubinelli 'Costantino Mortati and the idea of material constitution' (2019) 40 *History of Political Thought* 515–546.

the political will of a given community and retrace its transformation into a set of formalised legal provisions. From early on in his intellectual life, he thus decided to make the relationship between law and politics the centre of his intellectual endeavours. This commitment took the shape of a sustained intellectual engagement with two strands of legal positivism that were popular at the time: that of Austrian jurist Hans Kelsen, and that of Italian constitutional theorist Vittorio Emanuele Orlando.[1]

In brief, Mortati took issue with Kelsen's vision of law as a pure science, as theorised in his *Reine Rechtslehre*, the *Pure theory of law*. What worried Mortati about Kelsen's methodology was the idea that the origins, validity and functioning of the legal system could be ascribed to criteria that are either formal or internal to the law itself. This formalistic approach, also adopted by Orlando, appeared to Mortati like a misguided attempt to free law, and legal science more broadly, from the context in which they operate, which is necessarily much wider and tangled in interactions with other spheres of social life. Mortati's engagement with Kelsen took the form of a long-lasting effort to come to terms with his strand of positivism, as evident in the fact that he often criticised him in his writings. Just to offer an example, when analysing the first article of the Italian constitution for Branca's Commented Edition, Mortati attacked Kelsen for his anti-voluntarism. In this context, he argued that Kelsen's approach reduced the source of legal normativity to a hypothesis, whose necessary implication was that a legal act is willed simply because it is valid. This appeared like a nonsensical conclusion to Mortati, who firmly believed that legal acts were valid only when it was possible to identify a will behind them.[2] In other words, the validity of legal acts derives, according to Mortati, exclusively from the will.

Similarly, Mortati also took issue with Orlando's attempts to separate law from politics, as the following example demonstrates. On 23 April 1947, both Mortati and Orlando were sitting in the Italian Constituent Assembly, which was discussing the desirability of regulating ethical and social relations in the constitutional text. Orlando spoke against this proposal, arguing that all norms that touched on social, political or even moral issues had to be excluded from the constitution, insofar as they were not formal legal problems, and hence had no place in a constitutional text. Mortati responded accusing Orlando of misleadingly trying to separate what cannot be set apart: the purely legal from the social and political context from which it arises. All legal norms, Mortati maintained, directly derive from considerations that are socio-political in nature, and it is precisely their relationship to these socio-political origins that gives them legal validity.[3] The distinction between purely legal and socio-political norms is thus a chimera, all norms are political in Mortati's view.

Although these examples do not do justice to the complexities of both Kelsen and Orlando's thought, they point to the main difference that separated legal positivism from Mortati's approach. While legal positivism portrayed law as an independent and autonomous sphere,

[1] For a detailed discussion of Mortati's relationship to German legal thought see I. Staff, 'Costantino Mortati: Verfassung im materiellen Sinn. Ein Beitrag zur Rechtsentwicklung im faschistischen Italien und im Deutschland der Weimarer Zeit und im Nationalsozialismus' (1994) 23 *Quaderni fiorentini per la storia del pensiero giuridico moderno* 265; I. Staff, *Staatsdenken Im Italien des 20. Jahrhunderts Ein Beitrag Zur Carl Schmitt-Rezeption* (Nomos, 1991). On Italian formalism and Orlando see M. Fioravanti, 'Dottrina dello stato persona e dottrina della costituzione – Costantino Mortati e la tradizione giuspubblicistica italiana', in M. Galizia and P. Grossi (eds.), *Il pensiero giuridico di Costantino Mortati* (Giuffre, 1990), 45–186.

[2] C. Mortati, 'Commento all'art. 1 della Costituzione', in G. Branca (ed.), *Commentario della Costituzione* (Zanichelli, 1975), 1–50. A similar point is raised in C. Mortati, 'Costituzione dello stato', in Cosa-Delib., *Enciclopedia del Diritto* (Giuffrè, 1962), vol. XI, 152. See also C. Mortati, *La volontà e la causa nell'atto amministrativo e nella legge* (De Luca, 1935) and V. Frosini and F. Riccobono, 'Mortati e Kelsen', in M. Galizia (ed.), *Forme di stato e forme di governo: nuovi studi sul pensiero di Costantino Mortati* (Giuffrè, 2007), 407–30.

[3] This exchange between Mortati and Orlando happened on 23 April 1947 and is reported by Fioravanti, 'Dottrina dello stato persona', 168–69.

Mortati believed that the validity of law could only be ascribed to extra-legal sources, which are political and social in origins as well as in nature. This belief explains his life-long commitment to a realist legal methodology, which consisted in identifying 'the reality of the state with the system of social forces organised in such a way as to guarantee their supremacy'.[4] If the reality of the state is reliant on a given hierarchy of social forces, the normative validity of the law cannot be separated from its efficacy, in that both depend on the material reality in which they operate and from which they arise.[5] This material reality, as it will become clear later in the chapter, reflects a specific organisation of social forces, which are capable of expressing a *fine politico*, a 'political goal'. This, in Mortati's words, is 'a political idea, whose working entails a certain degree of political homogeneity, able to create a superior unity comprising the majority and the minority of the population and able to give shape to all the prerequisites necessary for the existence of a consistent and harmonious state's will'.[6] The validity and efficacy of a state's legal system is thus ascribed to the ability that the dominant social forces have to create unity around their specific political project and make it appear like a political goal of general import. This political goal, when successfully established and recognised by the rest of society, becomes the source of both legal and political normativity, giving shape to the unity and coherence of the legal system from the outside. It thus follows that, contrary to legal positivism, this political source of normativity cannot be discovered in the mere working of the legal system, nor can it be recognised in a hypothetical norm that has no relationship to the material and contextual reality of a given state. The only methodology truly apt to investigate the foundation of a legal system is the study of the 'grey area of politics and law', which is where the *fine politico* is first articulated, then translated into legal norms and finally applied to the institutional and constitutional structure of the state. Understanding the workings and logic of a constitutional system thus demanded, according to Mortati, looking at the fundamental political projects and values that inspired its functioning and reconnecting these political values to the social forces that established them as fundamental political goals for the state.

5.2 THE CONSTITUTION IN THE MATERIAL SENSE

The key tool for the study of the 'grey area' between politics and law is the concept of material constitution. This, as will become clear in the following paragraphs, is part of a conceptual pair, whose other pole is the idea of formal constitution. Mortati's reliance on this dichotomy is key to understanding two aspects of his work: on the one hand, it allowed him to explore how the formal legal text relates to the material context in which it operates, by foregrounding the importance of the *fine politico* and of the social forces that maintain it. On the other hand, this shift in focus, away from the formal legal text and toward the socio-political relations that underpin it, allowed Mortati to give institutional and organisational priority to the 'extra-legal' aspects of the constitution. While this second implication will be discussed at length in the Section 5.3, I will now focus on the explanatory power of this dichotomy, and of the concept of material constitution more specifically, for Mortati's realist study of legal theory.

[4] C. Mortati, *Istituzioni di diritto pubblico* [1949] (CEDAM, 1969), 33.

[5] This methodological orientation, it should be noted, is heavily indebted to the work of Santi Romano, one of the most prominent anti-positivist thinkers in Italy, to whom Mortati dedicated his 1940 *La Costituzione in Senso Materiale*. See C. Mortati, *La costituzione in senso materiale* (Milan, 1998 [1940]). Romano not only built upon the French institutionalist tradition, but also argued that the legal system results from the 'spontaneous secretion' of norms from society. Further, Romano's belief that *ubi societas, ibi ius* provided a rich source of methodological inspiration for Mortati. See Santi Romano, *The Legal Order* (Routledge, 2017).

[6] Mortati, *La costituzione in senso materiale*, 55.

To do so, it is necessary to start by what Mortati meant by formal constitution. This, in its more general formulation, is the actual text of the constitution, the legal document. It regulates the workings of state institutions by setting norms and procedures. And yet, it has no normative value in and of itself. This is because, according to Mortati, and differently from (old) positivist thinkers, the core content of the constitution [*il contenuto proprio*] cannot be identified in the text of the constitution. The latter amounts to a list of organisational and technical prescriptions, that say nothing about the political orientation of the constitutional system, its aims and its political goal. It follows that the legal text does not have the force to demand obedience, but its power is limited to describing the mode of existence [*modo d'essere*] of the legal system. Otherwise said, the formal constitution is a photographic description of an existing order which, like all descriptions, has no power to ground the validity of the object it describes, let alone enforce its content and demand obedience for it. As such, the formal constitution is needed to visualise the state's legal system and to organise its organs and their reciprocal relations at institutional level. In turn, the descriptive capacity of the formal constitution makes the legal system intelligible to itself and internally consistent, thus enhancing its applicability and functioning. The main implication of this way of thinking about the legal text of the constitution is that of importantly deflating its role and status in legal theory. It is indeed clear that, for Mortati, it is 'impossible to retrace in the formal elements the defining features of the constitution, as the former, by themselves, can in no way perform the tasks of identification, guarantee and unification that are proper of the constitution'.[7] The role of the formal constitution is thus limited to purely organisational and instrumental tasks. The actual core content of the constitution, what gives it normative power and validity, is to be found elsewhere. Those who 'want to deduce the actual core content [*contenuto proprio*] of the constitution from the constitutional text necessarily lead to absorbing the material determination into the formal, and, eventually, to denying the autonomous function of the constitution'.[8] And the autonomy of the constitution, for Mortati, lies in the fact that it does not merely describe the presence of a legal political order. Rather, it brings it into existence by prescribing its defining features, its core content, and making it valid and binding. This prescriptive power, the *contenuto proprio* of the constitution, can only be found in the material reality of the latter.

The constitution in the material sense is comprised of two distinct elements. The first is what he calls the 'typical and essential content' of the constitution – which Mortati also calls the *fine politico* – and the second is the 'normative material elements' that give shape to the essential content of the constitution. Starting from the normative material elements, it should be noted that these refer to the specific socio-economic relationships that shape a specific political goal, make it emerge and impose it on the general population. It is important to note, at this point, that Mortati never refers to 'society' as a relevant agent in this context. Society is a general term that refers to an abstract entity, which, by definition, is too general and abstract to be able to act in the first place. It thus follows that society at large cannot be considered the normative material element at the origins of a *fine politico*. When taken in its pure pre-state form as a spontaneous general will, society – or 'community', 'nation' and 'people', for that matter – has no direct juridical character. If considered as the sum of citizens, active in an already established state formation, it only refers to passive individual citizens, who have no specific relation to each other

[7] Ibid., 201.

[8] Ibid., 7. Mortati criticises Kelsen in a similar way also in Mortati, 'Costituzione dello stato', vol. XI, 152. There he says that it is unacceptable to 'identify the point of reference of the legal system in a hypothetic norm, detached from the structure in which it is rooted and relegated to the domain of legally unknowable'.

and hence cannot contribute to shaping the political goal of the constitution. If it refers to a collective entity, then it is too general to identify any specific actor and is thus only useful to indicate the recipients of the law, the entity that is organised by the specific vision of politics enshrined in the constitution. It should thus be clear that, for Mortati, the *fine politico* does not come about from the general will of an abstract and undifferentiated social whole.

On the contrary, the agent behind the articulation of the *contenuto proprio* of the constitution is always a complex entity, made up of a number of different social forces that coalesce and unite around 'basic elements of organisation'. As Mortati explained:

> the content of the material constitution that we are looking for here ... cannot be found but in the social community itself, yet no longer considered as an undistinguished whole, but as organised according to a minimum level of organisational elements that are necessary to conceive of society as capable of action.[9]

These organisational elements consist in the specific organisation that given social groups obtain to act collectively and gain power and influence over competing social forces. The organisational elements amount to 'the production, within society, of a certain organisational structure indicating the position of its members whereby some succeed at exercising power over others and obtain their obedience'.[10] It follows that the first feature of the material constitution, its 'normative material elements', amounts to a given configuration of power as reflected in the relative strength and organisation of given social groups. As such, this configuration is always the expression of relations of power, where one or more groups succeed at imposing themselves upon others. The group, or groups, which end up shaping the *fine politico* and giving normative substance to the constitution

> can result from unitary social forces which present themselves as a unique subject, because they share the same interest and represent only one centre of political unity. Alternatively, it can result from a compromise between different forces, which agree, during the constituent phase, to establish a common ground where various interests able to create a solid political order meet, merge and secure their pacific coexistence.[11]

In both cases, there are forces that dominate and forces that remain out of the picture and are, thus, dominated. Yet these forces can either passively accept their condition of domination or actively seek to challenge and contest it. And the movements sparked by competition among dominant and dominated forces explain the changes in meaning, efficacy and normative value of the formal constitutional text.

Alongside the normative material elements, the other feature defining the constitution in the material sense is what Mortati calls the 'essential content'. While the former refers to the material relations that are at the origins of constitutional normativity, the latter points at what the content of this normativity is. This is equivalent to what Mortati calls, in other passages, the *fine politico* or the *contenuto proprio* of the constitution. All three expressions are used to indicate the 'grey area' between politics and law, the space in which a contingent and partial political project, elaborated by a given configuration of socio-economic groups, is transformed into a general principle valid for the entire community. This principle then becomes the foundation of the constitution, which gives meaning and normative purchase to the formal text of the law. The essential content of the constitution thus acts as the 'centre of unification for the

[9] Mortati, *La costituzione in senso materiale.*
[10] Ibid., 75.
[11] Ibid., 25.

life of the community, that distinguishes and protects it from the outside, from other communities living in other territories, and organises from the inside the conflict of contrasting interests through the determination and protection, even through violence, of the interests considered as prevalent.'[12] As the quote makes clear, the 'essential content' of the constitution becomes a principle of unification of the community as well as a tool of organisation of its social and political life. It articulates the identity of the community and posits it as a political will to be realised and obeyed by all members of society. In other words, it gives structure and direction to the whole community and, in so doing, it distinguishes it from other political communities. And yet, Mortati is careful to underline that the 'essential content' should not be mistaken for the expression of the general will: it always and unmistakably relates back to the initial interests of the dominant social groups which, thanks to their relative position vis à vis the rest of society, are able to transform their particular vision of politics into an authoritative power, that becomes the 'stable centre of qualification of social activities, of their diverging relevance vis-à-vis the political goals it presents as necessary'.[13] In short, the dominant social groups succeed when they transform their political vision into the '*idem sentire de repubblica*'.[14] This is what Mortati means by 'essential content' of the constitution, which not only expresses the fundamental principle of order for the political community but also institutionalises the relationship between dominant and dominated social forces. This relationship reflects both sheer asymmetries of power and the relative distance that separates various groups from the *fine politico*. This indeed becomes the reference point against which the legitimacy of competing visions of politics and the social groups that underpin them is assessed. As Mortati argues, the material constitution 'does not contain only the indication of the goals to be achieved, but it also expresses the relevance of the values of the dominant group and creates an organisation aimed at their maintenance'.[15] The material constitution is not indifferent to the reciprocal relation between social forces, but is instead committed to crystallising them in favour of the forces that first expressed the *fine politico*, its 'essential content'. This institutionalisation of social relations is guaranteed by the relative rigidity of the formal constitution, even though Mortati admits that minor changes and revisions are needed to absorb and integrate competing forces and draw them closer to the dominant *fine politico*. The goal is that the 'essential content' of the material constitution, as reflected in its formal text, is 'rigid enough to be a stronghold in the oscillations of forces and their relationships over time, but it is also elastic enough to look over the working of the associate life, thus allowing for the amendments it requires'.[16] As such it harmonises and unifies the static

[12] Ibid., 76.

[13] Ibid.

[14] Ibid., 118.

[15] Ibid., 206. In underlying the tight connection between the legal system and the interests of dominant forces in society, Mortati is unmistakably close to Antonio Gramsci. Not only does Mortati's dominant social force resembles Gramsci's party as the modern prince, but also Mortati seems to echo some aspects of Marxist materialism, that is, the law as expression of the material interests of dominant social forces. Yet, up until 1962, Mortati makes little to no reference to the idea of social classes, nor anything that could suggest that the law is purely super structural (on the contrary, Mortati repeatedly refers to values too). In addition, it is unlikely that, when writing *La costituzione in senso materiale*, Mortati had any knowledge of Gramsci's work. See M. Loughlin, *Foundations of Public Law* (Oxford University Press, 2010), 397 and M. La Torre, 'The German Impact on Fascist Public Law Doctrine – Constantino Mortati's Material Constitution', in C. Joerges and N. Singh Ghaleigh (eds.), *Darker Legacies of Law in Europe: The Shadow of National Socialism and Fascism Over Europe and its Legal Traditions* (Hart, 2003), 340.

[16] Mortati, *La costituzione in senso materiale*, 88.

and dynamic elements of society, making sure that the fundamental *fine politico* remains the unchallenged source of juridical normativity as well as of social stability.

And yet, the material constitution cannot remain permanently stable. Even though its content tends to remain stable over long periods of time, as the social forces that underpin it keep their hold on society, it is eventually destined to change. Mortati offers a long historical perspective, when discussing changes in the material constitution. He is clear that a simple constitutional revision, a mere change in government or a shift in balance amongst parties in parliament, does not add up to a change at the level of the material constitution. These are superficial changes, which touch upon the composition of the ruling elite or minor norms and constitutional procedures. For a change to happen at the level of the material constitution, more is needed. In fact, the single most important signal of such change is a radical shift in the vision of politics underpinning a given political system. For a liberal constitutional state, that would mean abandoning the principles of rule of law, party pluralism and alternation in government in favour of, for example, a fascist dictatorial regime. Another example, Mortati suggests, can be identified in France in the passage from the monarchical system based on the ancien régime to the revolutionary regime based upon the principle of popular sovereignty. This passage reflects a change from a vision of politics based on an aristocratic system to a democratic regime underpinned by the principle of collective self-government. It thus follows that it takes time to change the material constitution, as the new and sufficiently powerful configuration of social groups needs to coalesce behind an alternative political vision. This is necessarily a slow process and one that requires structural changes at the level of the organisation and distribution of power in society. The content of the material constitution is thus certainly open-ended and liable to challenge, but its tight connection to deeply entrenched social relations makes it extremely stable in time. This stability, in turn, points to the fact that the sources of normativity, for Mortati, are never the simple and straightforward outcome of the exercise of power. By contrast, they emerge from the complexity, durability and materiality of social relations.

In this sense, Mortati's account of the material constitution is different from Schmitt's. The German jurist had also introduced a distinction between 'the two meanings of the constitution': the first being relative and the second absolute.[17] The relative constitution refers to the legal text itself, similarly to what Mortati means by formal constitution. The absolute meaning points instead at the decision that creates the constitutional text and gives it validity. This could be interpreted as similar to Mortati's constitution in the material sense, and there certainly exist important points of convergence: both describe the political will that gives normative validity and stability to any given constitutional order. For Schmitt, the absolute meaning of the constitution refers to a political decision, affirming the creation of a new ordering principle, and corresponds, roughly, to Mortati's 'essential content' of the constitution. Yet the difference comes in once we consider the source of the decision in Schmitt. While for Mortati this is found in the complexity of the 'normative material elements', for Schmitt it expresses the unity of the will of the nation and it is best represented by the bearer of the executive power. Schmitt is indeed not particularly interested in investigating the specific relations of power that give rise to the decision. By contrast, once it has been taken, the decision has a normative power of its own. Schmitt's account of the material origins of the constitution is thus not satisfactory for Mortati, as it is not enough to assume that a decision exists to explain the normative, creative and directive power this exercises upon the state and its legal system. It is on the contrary necessary to

[17] See C. Schmitt, *Constitutional Theory [1928]* (Duke University Press, 2008).

investigate where this decision comes from, what configuration of social relationships make it possible and what social context makes it meaningful and valid. In other words, Schmitt's version of the constitution in the material sense – the absolute constitution – importantly misses one of the two elements that are key in Mortati's theory: the role that material relationships have in shaping the essential content of the constitution. By ignoring the complexity and the durability of the social relations behind the political decision, Schmitt assumes the normative validity of the constitution to spring from the unitary will of a fictitiously unitary nation.[18] This, in Mortati's view, is undesirable both as a descriptive account of the origins of the constitution and as a political statement, in that it oversimplifies the relations of power active behind the formal text of the constitution.

But Mortati was not satisfied with attributing the source of the constitution to the *Volk* either.[19] This is because, although Mortati recognised that society is certainly the material basis of all legal and political norms, he refused to see it as a unitary undifferentiated actor, with a unitary national consciousness. The very terms 'society' or 'people' referred, for Mortati, to an overgeneralisation that had no use to explain the relations of power behind the emergence of a given normative constitutional outlook. 'The people' does not exist for Mortati, what exists is only a variety of groups in a constant state of conflict and competition with each other, and it is precisely from this conflict that the collective will arises and is translated into law.

The differences separating Mortati's theory of the constitution from similar accounts developed in Weimar Germany thus signal the main points of originality of Mortati's thought. This lies not only in the distinction between the constitution in the formal and in the material senses but also, and most importantly, in the unpacking of the two elements that comprise the material constitution: its 'essential content' and the 'normative material elements' from which the validity of the constitution arises. These two elements combined have the power to produce and maintain the constitutional structure, while presenting it not just as 'the expression of a purely existential entity, but rather as a deontological one'.[20] The study of the material constitution thus helps Mortati achieve a double objective. On the one hand, it allows him to describe the 'grey area' of politics and law, with a degree of precision that cannot be achieved by the traditional language of constitutional law, which systematically collapses in the term constitution both the fundamental principle organising the state and its legal structure. On the other hand, the idea of the material constitution allowed Mortati to move the attention of legal theory away from the study of purely legal structures, in favour of wider reflections about politics and its relationship to law. The result was a new focus on the social dimension of law, which becomes just one amongst other manifestations of a socially embedded political will. In other words, it shed light on the priority of the 'grey area' over the positive text.

[18] On Mortati's relationship to Schmitt, see Mortati, 'Costituzione dello stato', 17. See also C. Mortati, 'Brevi note sul rapporto fra costituzione e political nel pensiero di Carl Schmitt' (1973) 2 *Quaderni fiorentini per la storia del pensiero giuridico moderno* 511. On Schmitt and Mortati see A. Catania, 'Mortati e Schmitt', in A. Catelani and S. Labriola (eds.), *La costituzione in senso materiale. Percorsi culturali e attualità di un'idea* (Giuffrè, 2001), 109–28.

[19] On Mortati's interpretation of other German jurists, such as Smend and Heller, see Staff, 'Costantino Mortati: Verfassung im materiellen Sinn' and S. Rossi, 'La costituzione in senso materiale e il dibattito Tedesco degli anni 20 e 30', in P. Galizia (ed.), *Forme di stato e forme di governo: nuovi studi sul pensiero di Costantino Mortati* (Giuffre, 2007), 902–3. For an analysis of Heller's account of the material constitution and its socio-economic and democratic basis, see M. Goldoni and M. Wilkinson, 'The Material Constitution' (2018) 81 *Modern Law Review* 576.

[20] Mortati, *La costituzione in senso materiale*, 89. Clearly, it is Kelsen who presented the material elements of the constitution as purely existential and, hence, excluded them from legal considerations.

5.3 THE INTERMEDIATE COMMUNITIES

In assigning a new priority to the extra-legal sphere, the study of the material constitution led Mortati to reflect on the interaction between law and politics. This reflection became particularly urgent and acute once Mortati got involved in politics, at the end of the Second World War. It is indeed in the early 1940s that he became a member of the Christian Democratic party and, as such, was elected to the Italian Constituent Assembly. In this new role, he had the opportunity to test his theory of the material constitution, as well as to apply some of the insights gained from his studies to post-war politics in Italy. More specifically, during his time at the Constituent Assembly and in his later written work about it, Mortati relied on his reflections on the social origins of the constitution to argue for popular involvement in democratic politics, thus turning his realist analysis into an instrument of normative theorising.[21]

The starting point of Mortati's involvement in the constitution-writing process was the realisation that, with the end of the war and the referendum that installed the republic, a new *fine politico* had been established for the Italian state – one he shared and was committed to. This *fine politico* was of a clear democratic nature and represented a clear break from that animating the fascist state. To become the essential content of the new Italian constitution, however, this democratic principle needed further spelling out and qualification, especially when considering the diminished – but nonetheless present – influence of formalist theorists amongst the drafters of the new constitution. He thus committed himself to finding ways to insert extensive popular participation in the very working of the constitution. This is because he believed that, when the political '*fine*' is democracy, 'each single citizen should actively and responsibly contribute to create the totality'.[22] But for this to be possible, 'it is key to put in place the material conditions and the technical instruments necessary to allow every citizen to emerge from the mass and contribute to the common oeuvre with his personal and unique contribution'.[23] As this quote makes clear, two factors are required for popular participation. The first is what he calls 'material conditions' and the second is the 'technical instruments'. I will briefly examine both.

The material conditions intuitively refer to his theory of the material aspects of the constitution. Mortati did not believe that concepts such as 'society', 'nation' or 'people' could point to any real entity capable of breathing life into a constitution. By contrast, he believed them to be empty words. In much the same way, also the abstract and isolated individual did not correspond to any entity capable of action at the level of constitutional politics. As a result, popular participation could not be conceived of as involving either the unorganised and general public, for example via direct self-government, or the individual citizen, through occasional instances of isolated and optional participation. In other words, the material conditions for the expression of the democratic *fine politico* demanded a firm grasp of the actual organisation of society, and not a general and void reference to either society or the individual citizen. This meant, for Mortati, that participation, to be meaningfully integrated in the state's constitutional structure, had to be organised around social groups. The importance of social groups to the realisation of the democratic *fine politico* is evident, for example, in Mortati's endorsement of the institution of a second chamber organised around the principle of 'complex representation'. This was meant to organise political representation around interests and groups, as opposed to atomised

[21] For Mortati's work and reflections following the Constituent Assembly, see C. Mortati, *La teoria del potere costituente*, (Quodlibet, 2020), 1–160.

[22] C. Mortati, *Studi sul potere costituente e sulla riforma costituzionale dello stato* (Giuffrè, 1972), 4.

[23] Ibid.

individuals, and would have reflected the relative strength of organised groups within society. But Mortati went further than that and argued that the fundamental unit of a democratic material constitution was the *comunità intermedia* or 'intermediate community'. These would act as 'intermediary structures between governors and governed',[24] in that they are social groups that establish themselves to satisfy needs that arise in relation to the state. This means that, depending on the relative positioning of the different groups present at any given time, intermediate communities can act to both solidify the grip of certain groups on the state or to challenge it. In a democratic state, the presence and action of these intermediate communities is thus key to channel citizens' personal as well as group preferences into the daily working of state institutions and the resulting policy decisions. Amongst the large number of intermediate communities, the most relevant ones were, for Mortati, the family, religious associations, cultural organisations of all types and inspirations as well as professional associations and labour unions. To these, he also added territorial communities, such as regions, provinces and cities. Citizens would of course be members of a number of different communities at the same time, which would in turn organise their base around shared values, interests and territories. The role of the community is thus that of expanding 'the consciousness of the citizen and their understanding of the progressively more complex requirements of associational life',[25] and thus increasing their capacity to act upon it. In other words, the intermediate communities are the space where the essential content of a constitution is first conceived, elaborated and negotiated. This is because, in Mortati's rather emphatic account, the intermediate communities are

> organised internally in such a way as to encourage each member to contribute his best, within the limits of his capacities; to escape anonymity and acquire a personal voice; to express his own value, that cannot be reduced to a number to be added up to a final count, but that is a soul to be joined by other souls in a process of common elevation.[26]

Not only are intermediate communities the institutionalised version of the social groups Mortati identified as being the actors of the material constitution; their capacity to collectively elevate particular interests into a common will also closely resonates with the process of creation of a *fine politico*.

And yet, the material presence of intermediate communities did not, in itself, guarantee the realisation of the *contenuto proprio* of the Italian constitution: technical instruments had to be put in place to make democratic participation effective and institutionalised. These technical instruments amounted to a series of institutional mechanisms, to be added to the text of the constitution, which would give individuals the practical means to act according to the values and strategies developed in the intermediate communities and, in so doing, shape the orientation and priorities of the state. These can be divided in two groups, the first pertaining to the workings of representative democracy, the second relating to practices inspired by direct democracy.

The technical instruments relying on representation embraced the idea that popular participation had to be mediated by some sort of political expertise. The most important of such institutions was the political party. Mortati dedicated much of his work to the study of the modern party and concluded that it acts as the institutional arm of intermediate communities and, although different from them, is their loudspeaker. For parties to be successful, however,

[24] C. Mortati, *La persona, lo stato e le comunità intermedie* (Edizioni RAI, 1959), 84.
[25] Ibid., 141.
[26] Ibid., 83.

Mortati believed that they should exist in a system of proportional representation. Majoritarian systems would give excessive powers to the relatively larger party, thus debilitating the pluralism that was so fundamental to the representation of all social groups, and the corresponding intermediate communities. To further connect the political party to the relevant social group, Mortati argued in favour of practices of intra-party deliberative democracy, as well as public deliberation in the context of party primaries to elect leaders and set the party's political agenda. In line with Mortati's preference for a proportional system, he campaigned in favour of proportional electoral laws, which would make each single vote count and accurately mirror the composition of society in social groups and intersecting intermediate communities, thus guaranteeing as extensive a representation of the complexity of the material constitution as possible.[27] Amongst the technical instruments inspired by direct democracy, Mortati referred to the right of petition, the right to initiate a law-making process and the right to organise referenda. These, in his view, would have given intermediate communities the possibility of exercising direct influence upon the formation and realisation of the *fine politico*, even beyond or against the work of elected representatives. The referendum, in particular, appeared to Mortati like a truly desirable way of making sure that the formal constitution would be kept up to date with the changing material constitution. Following in the footsteps of Carré de Malberg, Mortati argued that the referendum could create two 'organs of will', one made of the citizens and the other comprising the elected politicians. These instruments, 'far from being a redundant duplication, are suitable means to make people's unmediated participation to supreme political decisions effective'.[28] As a result, all these 'technical instruments' gave citizens, organised through intermediate communities, the means to act upon the direction of the state, to orient it according to their political visions. The existence of these instruments is thus key, according to Mortati, not only to realise the democratic *fine politico* of the new Italian constitution, but also to give space to the forces active in the material constitution, so as to give them the possibility of imprinting their will and political vision upon the formal legal text of the constitution.

5.4 CONCLUSION

The theory of the constitution in the material sense, with its related emphasis on the institutionalisation of popular participation, is the defining feature of Costantino Mortati's legal and political thought. Not only did it give shape to his early intuition that, to understand the source of legal normativity, it is necessary to go beyond the formal text of the constitution and look for the 'grey area' where law and politics meet, it also allowed him to describe and explain the complex set of material relations that underpin the constitution and give meaning to its political orientation. Although not alone, Mortati has certainly been amongst the most influential mid-century European thinkers to reject legal positivism and its formalistic approach to constitutional theory and shift the attention toward the social and political meaning of the constitution. This move, I believe, remains meaningful today, as an inspiration for anyone interested in understanding the sources of constitutional normativity as well as a heuristic tool to make sense of the politics of constitution-making and constitutional change.

[27] It should be noted that, later in his life, Mortati changed his mind and moved his preferences away from proportional representation in favour of majoritarian systems.

[28] Mortati, *Studi sul potere costituente e sulla riforma costituzionale dello stato*, 91. See also C. Mortati, 'Significato del referendum' (1960) I *Rassegna parlamentare* 63.

6

The Material Constitution of the Dual State

Lars Vinx

6.1 INTRODUCTION

The term 'constitution' is ambiguous. We often use it in ways that imply that to have a constitution is a contingent characteristic of a state. Phrases like 'the constitutional state' suggest that a state may or may not be constitutionally ordered. There is another sense of 'constitution', however, according to which it is essential for a state to have a constitution. In any securely established state there must be rules, whether these are merely customary or codified, that confer and delimit the powers of the key institutions of a state. Such rules will determine, for instance, how legislative power can be validly exercised and by whom, how it relates to the executive power of government and to the authority of the courts, and what authority the legislator and the government have over individual members of society.[1]

The German-language public law theory of the nineteenth and early twentieth century originally took the term 'material constitution' to refer to the second of the two senses of the term 'constitution' just distinguished.[2] The material constitution, thus understood, may take the form of a formal constitution, that is, of a set of organisational norms and provisions about individual rights that are laid down in a constitutional document and protected by a rule of constitutional amendment. But a polity's constitution can also be purely material, in cases where those accoutrements of formal constitutionalism are absent.[3]

This paper will discuss the applicability of the notion of material constitution to National Socialist Germany in the 1930s. If every state must have a material constitution, and if Nazi Germany was a state, then Nazi Germany must have had a material constitution. But did Nazi Germany have a material constitution? I will argue that it did not.

My chapter will begin with a discussion of Ernst Fraenkel's famous description of Nazi Germany as a 'dual state', composed of a 'prerogative state' interacting with a 'normative state'.[4]

[1] See J. Gardner, 'Can There Be a Written Constitution?', in J. Gardner (ed.), *Law As a Leap of Faith: Essays on Law in General* (Oxford University Press, 2012), 89.

[2] Compare H. Heller, *Staatslehre*, G. Niemeyer, ed., 6th edn. (Mohr Siebeck, 1983), 309–13 and G. Jellinek, *Allgemeine Staatslehre* (O. Häring, 1914), 505–39.

[3] For the distinction between material and formal constitution see H. Kelsen, *Allgemeine Staatslehre* (Springer, 1925), 251–53. Further discussion in L. Vinx, 'Hans Kelsen and the Material Constitution of Democracy', *Jurisprudence* 12 (2021) 466.

[4] E. Fraenkel, *The Dual State: A Contribution to the Theory of Dictatorship* (Oxford University Press, 1941). On Fraenkel's *Dual State*, see J. Meierhenrich, *The Remnants of the Rechtsstaat: An Ethnography of Nazi Law* (Oxford University Press, 2018); D. G. Morris, *Legal Sabotage: Ernst Fraenkel in Hitler's Germany* (Cambridge University Press,

The dual state thesis suggests, I will argue, that Nazi Germany did not have any constitution at all. It was governed, instead, by a form of permanent dictatorship that relied on remnants of legality for purely prudential reasons but that did not constitute a genuine constitutional order.

I will go on to consider an objection to the claim that Nazi Germany did not have a material constitution. Carl Schmitt claimed that there are three basic types of jurisprudential thought (normativism, decisionism, and concrete order thought) that correspond to three basic elements of legal order (norms, decisions, and concrete or institutional orders).[5] Translated into Schmitt's terminology, Fraenkel's dual state thesis describes Nazi Germany as a combination of a residual normativism (the normative state) with a legally unfettered decisionism (the prerogative state). This analysis, Schmitt would likely have claimed, is deficient since it considers only two of the three basic elements of juristic thought and legal order. The material constitution of Nazi Germany, Schmitt and his followers argued in the 1930s, was neither grounded in a norm nor in a decision. It was an expression, supposedly, of a concrete social order, capable of providing adequate legal justification for the judicial decisions that Fraenkel's *Dual State* denounces as lawless acts of dictatorship.[6]

Fraenkel, having studied Schmitt's relevant works carefully, anticipated this line of reply to his dual state thesis. The second part of *The Dual State* contains an insightful but neglected rebuttal of Schmitt's concrete order thought.[7] This rebuttal, I will argue, helps us to understand the limitations of material constitutionalism.

6.2 THE DUAL STATE

The Nazi takeover of power in Germany in the course of 1933 and 1934 had the appearance of a legal process. The key steps of the *Machtergreifung*, in particular the suspension of fundamental rights in the wake of the *Reichstag* fire and the enactment of the Enabling Act that transferred legislative power to Hitler, were designed to give the impression that they had taken place in accordance with the relevant norms of the Weimar Constitution.[8]

The near-unanimous consensus opinion among legal historians is that the *Machtergreifung* was not legal.[9] Some contemporary commentators had their own misgivings about the apparent legality of the Nazi seizure of power. Carl Schmitt agreed that the *Machtergreifung* had been legal, but he vehemently rejected the hypothesis of legal continuity. Schmitt argued that the *Machtergreifung*, though legal in form, had been revolutionary in substance. The parliamentary elections of March 1933, Schmitt held, had been a plebiscite on the introduction of a new constitution.[10]

Still, as revolutions go, the *Machtergreifung* was a rather peculiar affair. Power had been transferred to the new regime through a small number of carefully constructed legal tweaks.

2020); J. C. Suntrup, 'Between Prerogative Power and Legality – Reading Ernst Fraenkel's *The Dual State* as an Analytical Tool for Present Authoritarian Rule' (2020) 11 *Jurisprudence* 335.

[5] C. Schmitt, *Über die drei Arten des rechtswissenschaftlichen Denkens [1934]* (Duncker & Humblot, 1993).

[6] C. Schmitt, *Staat, Bewegung, Volk. Die Dreigliederung der politischen Einheit* (Hanseatische Verlagsanstalt, 1933). For an attempt to outline the constitutional law of Nazi Germany that followed Schmitt's theoretical lead, see E. R. Huber, *Verfassungsrecht des Grossdeutschen Reiches* (Hanseatische Verlagsanstalt, 1939).

[7] Fraenkel, *Dual State*, 139–49.

[8] K. D. Bracher, W. Sauer and G. Schulz, *Die nationalsozialistische Machtergreifung: Studien zur Errichtung des totalitären Herrschaftssystems in Deutschland 1933–1934* (Springer, 1962), 31–168.

[9] C. Gusy, *Die Weimarer Reichsverfassung* (Mohr Siebeck, 1997), 459–63; H. Dreier, 'Die deutsche Staatsrechtslehre in der Zeit des Nationalsozialismus', in H. Dreier, *Staatsrecht in Demokratie und Diktatur. Studien zur Weimarer Republik und zum Nationalsozialismus*, M. Jestaedt and S. L. Paulson, eds. (Mohr Siebeck, 2016), 197–201.

[10] Schmitt, *Staat, Bewegung, Volk*, 5–11.

Even Schmitt had to concede that this approach had been necessary for the Nazi seizure of power to work. The minimal disruption to established legality in the course of the *Machtergreifung*, he observed, had allowed the bureaucracy to continue to function.[11] The rule of law had nevertheless been put at the disposition of the new regime. The legal constraints on legislative and executive power that had been imposed by the Weimar Constitution did not bind the new regime.

Fraenkel agreed that the Weimar Constitution was no longer in force. He described the *Reichstag* fire decree of 28 February 1933 as the 'constitutional charter of the Third Reich'.[12] The decree had been issued by Hindenburg, who was then still the President of the *Reich*, pursuant to his authority under article 48 of the Weimar Constitution.[13] On its face, the decree might thus have been regarded as deriving its legal force from the Weimar Constitution. To say that the decree had come to function as a constitutional charter was to reject the hypothesis of legal continuity.

Fraenkel's argument against the assumption of continuity is developed, in the first part of *The Dual State*, by way of a painstaking analysis of a large number of judicial decisions in 1930s Nazi Germany that, in upholding administrative decisions of dubious legality, made appeal to the decree of 28 February. The courts, Fraenkel was able to show, interpreted the decree in a way altogether incompatible with the hypothesis of continuity.[14]

The decree of 28 February suspended a number of basic rights protected by the Weimar Constitution (habeas corpus, the freedom of opinion and press, the freedom of association and assembly, the secrecy of postal communication, and the protection against warrantless searches and seizures). According to the constitutional doctrine that had prevailed in the Weimar years, the President's powers of dictatorship under article 48 did not include a power to suspend or to otherwise violate constitutional rights not explicitly listed as suspendable in article 48.[15] Judges in Nazi Germany nevertheless held that the decree licensed infringements of constitutional rights that had not been and could not be suspended.[16]

The courts, for instance, upheld 'the dissolution of the German branch of Jehovah's Witnesses', by decree of the Minister of the Interior, though article 137 of the Weimar Constitution, which guaranteed the freedom of religious belief and practice, had not been and could not be suspended.[17] The minister's decree was held to have the force, under the Enabling Act, to override a constitutional right. The preamble of the decree of 28 February had stated that the purpose of the suspension was to allow the executive to mount a successful defence against 'communist acts of violence endangering the state'. But the decree was routinely invoked to suppress activities that had no relation to communist activity. Members of a Catholic youth group that had gone on hiking trips were punished, for instance, by appeal to the decree of 28 February, for having violated an order issued by a local administrator that had prohibited activities of youth groups not affiliated with the Nazi party.[18] Organisational activity not

11 Ibid., 7–8.
12 Fraenkel, *Dual State*, 3.
13 See Bracher et al., *Die nationalsozialistische Machtergreifung*, 75–88.
14 Fraenkel, *Dual State*, 9–103.
15 R. Grau, 'Die Diktaturgewalt des Reichspräsidenten', in G. Anschütz and R. Thoma (eds.), *Handbuch des Deutschen Staatsrechts* (Mohr Siebeck, 1932), vol. II; G. Anschütz, *Die Verfassung des Deutschen Reichs vom 11. August 1919*, 14 ed. (Georg Stilke, 1933), 275–96.
16 Compare I. Müller, *Furchtbare Juristen. Die unbewältigte Vergangenheit der deutschen Justiz* (Edition Tiamat, 2014), 60–65.
17 Fraenkel, *Dual State*, 15.
18 Ibid., 17–18.

controlled by the party was seen to undermine the integrity of the *Volksgemeinschaft*, the national socialist people's community. The interpretive practice of the courts, in short, treated the decree of 28 February as part and parcel of a new constitutional order.

Fraenkel, however, did not accept Schmitt's view that the *Machtergreifung* had been a revolution, that is, that it had succeeded in founding a new legal order that possessed a legitimacy of its own. According to Fraenkel, the Nazi takeover had been nothing more than an 'illegal coup d'état'.[19] The *Machtergreifung*, Fraenkel surmised, could not have been successful without the veneer of legitimacy provided by the assumption of legal continuity. The Nazis were accordingly concerned, he observed, to maintain the fiction that Germany was still a state governed by the rule of law and to conceal from the wider public that the regime had empowered itself to compromise the operation of the remnants of legality at its legally unfettered discretion.[20]

The powers claimed by the Nazis, then, had no basis in the Weimar Constitution, but no new constitution had been put in place. Instead, constitutional order had come to be replaced by a permanent dictatorship. Fraenkel acknowledged that dictatorship can be legitimate in the defence of an existing constitution. It might be argued, perhaps, that dictatorship, as 'sovereign dictatorship', can also be a legitimate means to establish a new constitution.[21] But the Nazis, Fraenkel pointed out, did not employ the means of dictatorship for the purpose of the conservation or construction of a constitution.

> The National-Socialist coup d'état consisted in the fact that the National-Socialists, as the dominant party in the government, (1) did not prevent but rather caused the infringement of the Rule of Law, (2) abused the state of martial law which they had fraudulently promoted in order to abolish the Constitution, and (3) now maintain a state of martial law despite their assurances that Germany, in the midst of a world corrupt with inner strife, is an 'island of peace'.[22]

The dual state thesis points out that the governance of Nazi Germany still did rely, in large part, on established legality. A normative state, governed by law, continued to exist. But the agents of the Nazi regime, of the prerogative state, were at liberty to disregard that normative order and to intervene by the use of extra-legal, dictatorial measures whenever they saw fit.[23] The resulting dictatorial power, however, was not used to build a new constitutional order but simply to secure the permanent ascendancy of the Nazi party, which was unable or uninterested (or both) in re-establishing the rule of law. The dual state was thus constitutionally groundless. It did not derive any genuine legitimacy from the Weimar Constitution, by whose abuse it had been established, and which it disregarded in practice. Neither, however, did the dual state possess a recognisable legitimating ground of its own. Though the agents of the prerogative state had usurped the *de facto* power to draw the boundary between rule by law and rule by discretion, the prerogative state, as Fraenkel's analysis makes clear, was dependent on what remained of the normative state in at least two crucial ways. It required a sufficiently dependable operation of the law to keep the economy running and it drew a good part of its perceived legitimacy from the appearance of continuing respect for legality.[24]

[19] Ibid., 3–6.
[20] Ibid., 38–40.
[21] C. Schmitt, *Dictatorship. From the Origin of the Modern Concept of Sovereignty to Proletarian Class Struggle*, M. Hoelzl and G. Ward, trans. (Polity Press, 2014), 112–31.
[22] Fraenkel, *Dual State*, 10.
[23] Ibid., 14–46.
[24] Ibid., 171–87.

Did the dual state have a material constitution? Fraenkel's claim that the decree of 28 February was the constitutional charter of the Third Reich might be taken to suggest that the content of the material constitution of Nazi Germany can be identified with the key decrees and acts empowering the Nazi regime that were put in place in 1933 and 1934. The fraudulent use of the decree of 28 February 1933 had given rise, according to Fraenkel, to the duality between the normative and the prerogative state. The Nazi government, led by Hitler, had also been vested, by the Enabling Act, passed on 24 March 1933, with a power to make laws, and the act, which was passed in the form of a constitutional amendment to the Weimar Constitution, explicitly stated that laws made by the new government that contravened the Weimar Constitution were nevertheless to be regarded as valid. Other, later pseudo-legal acts completed the seizure of power, in particular the unification of the offices of Prime Minister and President in Hitler's hands on 2 August 1934.[25]

But did these norms play the role of a material constitution in 1930s Germany? There are at least two reasons, reasons which are implicit in Fraenkel's analysis, to reject that claim. The real powers to which the agents of the prerogative state laid claim, as we have seen, went far beyond the powers conferred by the explicit content of the supposed constitutional laws of Nazi Germany. The decree of 28 February, the supposed constitutional charter of the Third Reich, cannot be said to have offered a legal regulation of the interactions of the normative and the prerogative state. The claim that the Enabling Act was the material constitution of Nazi Germany, or at least a part thereof, is equally problematic.[26] To affirm that claim is to argue not merely that laws or decrees issued by Hitler and his underlings were, in fact, recognised to have the force of law in 1930s Germany. It is to argue that the Enabling Act, which was put in place by the use of the Weimar Constitution's procedures for amendment, authorised Hitler and his underlings, in the first place, to make laws. But that view was rejected by Schmitt and most other Nazi legal theorists, for the obvious reason that it would have suggested the hypothesis of legal continuity and potentially imposed legal limitations on the Führer's authority.

The conclusion to be drawn from these observations is that it would be wrong to say that the decree of 28 February and the Enabling Act (together with other comparable laws or decrees) functioned as the material constitution of 1930s Nazi Germany. The enactments in question did not constitute, regulate, or validate public power in Nazi Germany. At best, they offered a pale, pseudo-legal reflection of the actual distribution of *de facto* authority. Fraenkel's dual state thesis thus leads to the conclusion that Nazi Germany had neither a formal nor a material constitution. That Nazi Germany had no formal constitution follows from the rejection of the hypothesis of legal continuity, given that the Nazis never enacted a new formal constitution.[27] And if norms such as the decree of 28 February and the Enabling Act cannot be regarded as the material constitution of Nazi Germany, we seem forced to concede that Nazi Germany had no constitution at all, either formal or material, and should therefore be considered to have been an a-constitutional entity that failed to qualify as a state, a conclusion that has indeed been drawn by

[25] For a lucid overview from a Nazi perspective see E. Huber, *Verfassungsrecht*, 11–57.

[26] Some authors in Nazi Germany did take the view that the Weimar Constitution was still valid and that Hitler's authority continued to depend on it. The view is discussed (and dismissed) in Huber, *Verfassungsrecht*, 46–52, and it was a minority view among Nazi public lawyers that lost attraction as Nazi dictatorship wore on. See M. Stolleis, *Geschichte des öffentlichen Rechts in Deutschland. Weimarer Republik und Nationalsozialismus* (C. H. Beck, 2002), 316–18.

[27] Compare Huber, *Verfassungsrecht*, 54–55, who argued, accordingly, that the constitution of Nazi Germany was not 'a constitution in the formal sense, as it was characteristic of the 19th century'.

some historians of Nazi Germany, who have argued that the system was held together by nothing more than the shifting ties of persons and competing networks to Hitler.[28]

6.3 THE MATERIAL CONSTITUTION AS CONCRETE ORDER

In 1934, Carl Schmitt published a short monograph entitled *The Three Types of Juristic Thought*.[29] On its face, this text is a contribution to legal theory. It takes up questions that had animated some of Schmitt's earlier legal-theoretical work, in particular in *Statute and Judgment* (1912)[30] and *Political Theology* (2022).[31] In these earlier works, Schmitt had emphasised that the legitimate applicability of a legal norm presupposes a situation of social normality and he had criticised the view, accordingly, that stable and predictable legality can be guaranteed by the existence of a system of general statutory norms alone. Legal practice, Schmitt had argued, cannot provide for the social presuppositions of its own functioning. It is dependent on a sovereign or constitutional guardian endowed with the power to suspend the operation of rule-based legality and to use dictatorial measures to create or restore a situation of social normality.

Schmitt did not abandon this view in *The Three Types of Juristic Thought*. But his renewed presentation of his legal theory in 1934 was characterised by a shift in emphasis, one that was intended to offer a response to the claim that Nazi Germany lacked a legal order. In his earlier jurisprudential essays, Schmitt had been concerned to emphasise the need for a political authority capable to take a decision on the exception. In Weimar, Schmitt had played out a Hobbesian 'decisionism' against the 'normativism' of the nineteenth-century advocates of the liberal notion of the rule of law. A legal order, Schmitt had argued, rests on a decision, not on an ultimate rule. *The Three Types of Juristic Thought* supplements this dualist picture with a third element. A legal order, Schmitt now claims, is composed not merely of norms and decisions. It also contains what Schmitt calls a 'concrete order'.[32]

A concrete order, Schmitt explains, consists of the arrangement of social institutions that must underpin the functioning of the law as a system of general norms. Such institutions include, for instance, marriage and the family, the Church, informal structures of social authority, the social relations that structure the workplace, etc. Appealing to Duguit and Santi Romano, Schmitt now argues that the presupposition of social normality, which he had always argued was a condition

[28] See Peter Hüttenberger, 'Nationalsozialistische Polykratie' (1976) 2 *Geschichte und Gesellschaft* 417. Constitutional theorising was itself drawn into the resulting competition for the Führer's favour and attention. See P. Caldwell, 'National Socialism and Constitutional Law: Carl Schmitt, Otto Koellreutter and the Debate over the Nature of the Nazi State, 1933–1937' (1994) 16 *Cardozo Law Review* 399. I owe this reference to Michael Wilkinson.

[29] Schmitt, *Über die drei Arten*.

[30] C. Schmitt, 'Statute and Judgment', in C. Schmitt, *Carl Schmitt's Early Legal-Theoretical Works*, L. Vinx and S. G. Zeitlin, eds. and trans. (Cambridge University Press, 2021), 39–155.

[31] C. Schmitt, *Political Theology. Four Chapters on the Concept of Sovereignty*, G. Schwab, trans. (University of Chicago Press, 1985).

[32] For further analysis of Schmitt's concrete order thought, see M. Croce and A. Salvatore, *The Legal Theory of Carl Schmitt* (Routledge, 2013); and M. Croce and M. Goldoni, *The Legacy of Pluralism. The Continental Jurisprudence of Santi Romano, Carl Schmitt, and Costantino Mortati* (Stanford University Press, 2020), 99–135. These recent discussions give an incomplete picture of Schmitt's concrete order thought, in portraying it as a disinterested scholarly contribution to an institutionalist jurisprudential tradition. Schmitt's concrete order thought had political intentions that should not go unnoticed. It was meant to provide legitimation for judicial attempts to re-interpret inherited statutory norms so as to bring them into line with Nazi ideology. See B. Rüthers, *Die unbegrenzte Auslegung. Zum Wandel der Privatrechtsordnung im Nationalsozialismus* (Mohr Siebeck, 2017); a shorter summary in B. Rüthers, *Entartetes Recht. Rechtslehren und Kronjuristen im Nationalsozialismus* (C. H. Beck, 1989), 54–98.

of the existence of legal order,[33] ought to be understood in institutional terms. Stable and legitimate legal normativity must be grounded in a framework of established and accepted social practices. Legal rules can serve to concretise such practices by way of formal regulation, and thus facilitate and enhance their operation, but they are ultimately dependent, for their own functioning, on social custom which they cannot themselves create.

The theory of concrete order opens up a novel way to argue that Nazi Germany had a material constitution. According to the theory of concrete order, the legal rules that we hold to be constitutional are dependent on underlying political institutions, that is, on shared and accepted understandings, conventions, and practices that determine the distribution of political authority, at least in broad outline, even before it is given more precise form by constitutional laws. In *The Three Types of Juristic Thought*, Schmitt was concerned to argue that Nazi Germany had a material constitution, so understood.[34]

Schmitt, as has been pointed out already, distinguished between three fundamental forms of juristic thought which he took to correspond to the three basic elements of legal order.[35] There is a form of legal thought, according to Schmitt, that emphasises the centrality of general legal norms and that conceives of the rule of law as compliance, on the part of the state, with pre-announced general rules.[36] This 'normativist' approach contrasts with decisionism, as we have seen, which emphasises the origin of legal order in political decisions. Normativism, Schmitt argued, abstracts from the presupposition of normality that conditions the legitimate applicability of general legal norms. Decisionism, which Schmitt associates with Hobbes, reacts to the problem of anarchy that might ensue from such lack of attention to the presupposition of social normality. A truly sovereign decision, Schmitt avers, responds to a condition of complete anarchy, to a situation where there are no accepted institutional underpinnings for legal order. Pure decisionism presupposes a complete disorder and, to end that all-out disorder, all that matters is that a sovereign decision is taken, not what decision that is.[37]

Schmitt's claim, which echoes the earlier *Political Theology*, that a sovereign decision 'springs from normative nothingness'[38] need not be interpreted as an endorsement of nihilism. A sovereign decision is necessary, Schmitt should be taken to argue, where there is no underlying concrete social order. A sovereign decision decides, in the face of comprehensive anarchy, what concrete order is to be put in place. It cannot, therefore, be portrayed as a decision that draws its legitimacy from the fact that it defends some already existing concrete order. A truly sovereign decision is not an act of constitutional guardianship, not even if the constitution is identified with concrete order. Still, a sovereign decision is always a decision *for* some concrete order or other which is to be established by it. Schmitt's description of sovereign decision, then, does not rule out that such a choice might be guided by ideals and values, a notion of good social order. And Schmitt seems to concede that the early modern absolutist state did succeed in the endeavour, at least for a time, to establish order from comprehensive anarchy.

But Schmitt is wary, in 1934, of the view that the constitutional situation in Germany ought to be addressed from a decisionist point of view. It is noteworthy that Schmitt and his followers

33 Schmitt, *Political Theology*, 13.
34 Schmitt, *Staat, Bewegung, Volk*.
35 Schmitt, *Über die drei Arten*, 7–33.
36 Ibid., 10–13.
37 Ibid., 24.
38 Ibid.

pointedly avoided portraying Hitler as a Hobbesian sovereign.[39] This avoidance made good theoretical sense. The ideological self-presentation of the Führer did not fit into a decisionist mould. Hitler presented himself as the charismatic embodiment of the *Volksgemeinschaft*, the racially defined people's community. Though the powers he claimed were as legally unlimited as those of an absolute sovereign, their legitimating basis lay in the claim that the Führer's decisions were to be regarded as the authentic expression of the substantive character and identity of the German people. Hitler did not present himself as a political demiurge, creating a new social order from scratch. He pretended to be the mere voice, however infallible and providentially ordained, of a social collective that undoubtedly had had its own history before the Führer had taken over.[40] For that claim to make sense it was necessary to at least pretend that the Führer's pronouncements had a communal anchor, that they referred back to German society's existing practices and institutions.

The third fundamental type of juristic thought postulated by Schmitt in 1934 – concrete order thought, that is, an emphasis on the fundamentality of institutional order for the law – therefore appeared to offer a more suitable defence of the legitimacy of Nazi governance than Hobbesian decisionism.[41] Nazi Germany, Schmitt suggested, did not find itself in a state of complete anarchy that might have required a demiurgic sovereign intervention. It already had a concrete order, a material constitution, and the legal constitution of Nazi Germany, as given voice by the Führer's pronouncements, was to be understood as the expression of that concrete order.[42]

Fraenkel's critique of Nazi governance, to recall, argues that the judicial and administrative decision taking, in a dual state, becomes divorced from clear and predictable statutory programming. But why, or so Schmitt might have replied, should such a weakening of the standard of congruence of legal rule and official act be seen to indicate a breakdown of legal order or be held to be undesirable? The statutory rules that were 'read down' in the courts of Nazi Germany, or disregarded by the agents of the prerogative state, had been put in place, after all, by a corrupt parliamentary process that, in Schmitt's view, was to be expected to produce substantively arbitrary norms.[43] For Schmitt, the judicial decisions of the 1930s that Fraenkel denounced as tyrannical for their lack of compliance with statutory norms were attempts to reconnect legal practice to the concrete order of German social life, the true substance of law.

Let me set the stage for Fraenkel's reply to this line of reasoning by offering a short excursus into the work of Ernst Rudolf Huber, one of Schmitt's doctoral students of the Weimar period, who authored a voluminous treatise on the constitutional law of Nazi Germany (the only such work produced in Nazi Germany) that aims to work out the implications of the claim that the constitution of Nazi Germany is to be seen as a concrete order.[44]

Huber agrees with Schmitt's rejection of the hypothesis of legal continuity and insists that the *Machtergreifung* has put in place a new constitution.[45] The view that the Weimar Constitution is no longer in force implies, Huber points out, that there is no longer a constitution in the

[39] In his infamous justification of the murder of Ernst Röhm and his associates, Schmitt portrays Hitler not as sovereign but rather as the supreme judge ('oberster Gerichtsherr') of the German people who realises the pre-existing right of the people. See C. Schmitt, 'Der Führer schützt das Recht', in C. Schmitt, *Positionen und Begriffe im Kampf mit Weimar – Genf – Versailles 1923–1939* (Duncker & Humblot, 1994), 227–32.

[40] Huber, *Verfassungsrecht*, 194–99.

[41] Schmitt, *Über die drei Arten*, 13–20.

[42] Schmitt, *Staat, Bewegung, Volk*, 32–46.

[43] C. Schmitt, *The Crisis of Parliamentary Democracy*, E. Kennedy, trans. (MIT Press, 1985); C. Schmitt, *Legality and Legitimacy*, J. Seitzer, trans. (Duke University Press, 2004).

[44] Huber, *Verfassungsrecht*.

[45] Ibid., 46–52.

formal sense. The constitution of Nazi Germany must be a flexible as opposed to a rigid constitution.[46] It is possible, nevertheless, to develop an account of the constitutional law of Nazi Germany, Huber argues, and altogether wrong to portray Nazi Germany as a permanent dictatorship.[47] The distinction between laws that have constitutional standing and laws that do not, Huber claims, is to be drawn by appeal to the substance of concrete order. The core of the constitution of Nazi Germany consists of a number of fundamental principles which Huber claims are implicit in the political life of German society.[48]

True to the methodology of concrete order thought, Huber then proceeds to show that the material constitution of Nazi Germany grows spontaneously from a number of basic social institutions and practices. But the institutions he describes as forming the material constitution of Nazi Germany cannot be said to be as clearly defined and as securely rooted in history and practice as an appeal to the idea of concrete order would seem to require.

Huber's presentation of the structure of the political order of Nazi Germany, to highlight one prominent instance of the problem, takes the form of an extended discussion of the principle of leadership (*Führerprinzip*).[49] Huber goes to great lengths to argue that the principle of leadership has nothing to do with arbitrary tyranny. Leadership, according to Huber, connotes a trusting relationship between a leader and his follows, characterised by voluntary and unconditional loyalty on the part of the follower, which is reciprocated, on the part of the leader, by responsible governance in the interest of the community.[50] But of course, leadership is to be free from any formal legal control as well as from organised mechanisms of political accountability. Hitler's authority is not to be reduced to the formal constitutional authority of the different political offices of the Weimar Constitution (Prime Minister and President) that he had managed, in the process of the consolidation of Nazi power, to unite in his hands. Hitler, according to Huber, was supreme legislator, head of the executive and highest judge of the land in virtue of his providentially ordained leadership of the German people and not the other way around.[51]

Whatever one may think of Huber's account of the principle of leadership, the institution of leadership was certainly not traditional or widely recognised in German society before the Nazis took power. The observation that the *Machtergreifung* had had to rely on manipulations of existing constitutional legality to succeed strongly suggests that an appeal to the notion of leadership could not, by itself, have legitimated the Nazi's seizure of power. It is difficult, therefore, to credit Huber's claim that the supposed new constitution expressed an existing concrete order of German political life.

Huber, like Schmitt, denied that Hitler was a sovereign. The *Führer*, as the voice or embodiment of a political community that had existed before he came to power, and that was supposed to continue to exist after his demise, did not possess the demiurgic power, for Huber, to put a new concrete order in place. Huber goes so far as to imply fairly openly that the *Führer* lacked the authority to take decisions that contravened the concrete order of German society.[52] But such attempts to construct constitutional limitations on Hitler's leadership were difficult to square with the view, on which Huber insisted equally emphatically, that the leader, in a state

46 Ibid., 56–57.
47 Ibid., 210–11.
48 Ibid., 46–57.
49 Ibid., 194–286.
50 Ibid., 195–99.
51 Ibid., 230–34.
52 Ibid., 56.

based on the principle of leadership, must enjoy all but absolute powers and be free from any kind of formal accountability.[53] For all practical intents and purposes, the material constitution of the German people was what the *Führer* declared it to be.[54]

6.4 FRAENKEL ON CONCRETE ORDER THOUGHT

Fraenkel's assessment of Schmitt's claims about the material constitution of Nazi Germany did not reject the view that the functioning of legal order is dependent on underlying social institutions. The claim that 'the law actually being enforced in a given situation is not found in statutes but in the legal customs practiced' by members of a society, Fraenkel pithily remarked, 'is not especially new in the sociology of law in Germany'.[55] Eugen Ehrlich, to whom Schmitt himself had appealed in one of his early legal-theoretical works, had made the same point a long time ago.[56] What was novel about Schmitt's concrete order thought, in 1934, Fraenkel observed, was 'not the "concrete theory of order" as such but its association with the concept of "community"'.[57]

What Schmitt needed to claim was not merely that social groups and associations tend to spontaneously bring forth their own, inchoate law and at times without the assistance or direction of the legal apparatus of the state. He needed to claim that German society as a whole, the *Volksgemeinschaft*, the people's community, as a community of communities, could lay claim to the status of an autochthonous social institution or concrete order. That claim, Fraenkel argued, was not merely false. It was meant to conceal the decisionist character of Nazi governance:

> A critical analysis of Schmitt's theories reveals that, according to the theory of concrete order, the concrete communities are not the primary sources of law. If they were, then every concrete group, so long as it constitutes an orderly whole, would have to be regarded as equivalent to a concrete community order. But if this were the case, Schmitt's theory would logically imply a liberal theory of group autonomy. But this conclusion does not follow because Schmitt's 'concrete theory of order' really contains a decisionist element connected with the conception of 'community.' Only those groups are to be regarded as bearers of the 'concrete order' to which the character of 'community' is granted by National-Socialism.[58]

National socialist governance did not accord the status of genuine communities, of social groups pregnant with institutional order worth preserving, to all existing associations. Many, perhaps most, of the legal cases analysed by Fraenkel in *The Dual State* concern the repression of social groups, of concrete orders, that were seen not to fit into the supposed material constitution of the Nazi *Volksgemeinschaft*: independent labour unions, religious groups, youth organisations, political parties other than the Nazi party, etc. For the encompassing people's community to amount to a coherent concrete order, German social life had to be coercively homogenised, without regard to the constraints of the rule of law. But this need for coercive homogenisation entails that German society did not have a ready-made concrete order, available to be expressed in acts of leadership embodying a pre-existing shared identity. The concrete order of the

53 Ibid., 230.

54 Legal historians have pointed out that the resulting 'indifference to form' made doctrinal legal analysis next to impossible. See Dreier, 'Die deutsche Staatsrechtslehre', 231–40; Stolleis, *Geschichte des öffentlichen Rechts*, 316–25.

55 Fraenkel, *Dual State*, 142.

56 Schmitt, *Statute and Judgment*, 139, 147–49.

57 Fraenkel, *Dual State*, 142.

58 Ibid., 143.

Volksgemeinschaft, rather, had to be coercively constructed and, for that construction to begin, a choice had to be made between different available visions of proper concrete order.

The Nazis opted to try to turn Germany into a hyper-authoritarian racial ethnocracy. This choice, as Fraenkel points out, was not just morally abhorrent. It had no firm basis in existing concrete social order.[59] The political practices of Nazi Germany, such as they were, rested on an unacknowledged decision, but on one that, unlike the acts of sovereignty performed by the early modern absolute state, could not have been justified by appeal to generalisable interest, like the Hobbesian concern with the provision of the social conditions of individual survival. The terrible disorder that was to be prevented by Schmitt's invocation of concrete order as the basis of Hitler's claim to leadership was not that of a state of nature but the prospect of having to live in a pluralist society.

6.5 MATERIAL CONSTITUTIONALISM?

Nazi Germany lacked a material constitution, whether the notion is understood to refer to a set of rules that establish a clear distribution of political competences or to a 'concrete order' of social life whose institutions underpin the law. Contemporary proponents of material constitutionalism[60] will perhaps shrug their shoulders and reply that this result is of little interest to contemporary efforts to make use of the idea of material constitution. The Nazis, they might argue, made bad use of the idea of material constitution, but the approach can be given a legal pluralist reading that gets civil society out from under the oppressive hand of the state.

This response to Fraenkel's analysis, I would like to suggest by way of conclusion, would be too facile. Fraenkel's critique of concrete order thought gives rise to a general challenge to the notion of a material constitution. Let me conclude by outlining that challenge.

I do not dispute the sociological observation that gives rise to the theory of material constitution – the claim that a formal legal order is dependent, for its predictable functioning, on underlying social practices and institutions. I am happy to concede that the question of the social conditions of stable legal order is an important one, which ought to be carefully investigated by legal sociologists and political scientists. My claim is that attempts to invoke the idea of material constitution in legal argument are bound to face the dilemma that Fraenkel identified in Schmitt's employment of the notion of concrete order.[61]

A society's explicit constitutional law will either be in tune or be out of tune with underlying shared social practices and understandings. In the first case, the material constitution will remain legally invisible, as there is no need to invoke the material constitution to decide how to go on. What is more, tensions between a society's explicit constitutional law and underlying social practices may appear in a benign form. Social institutions may have developed in ways that have made some formal constitutional law obsolete and there may be broad social

[59] Ibid., 188–208.

[60] See M. Goldoni and M. Wilkinson, 'The Material Constitution' (2018) 81 *Modern Law Review* 567. Goldoni's and Wilkinson's use of the term 'material constitution' follows Mortati. See C. Mortati, *La costituzione in senso materiale* (Giuffrè, 1940).

[61] Here is one of countless examples from Nazi Germany of the use of the notion of material constitution in legal argument (see Rüthers, *Die unbegrenzte Auslegung*, 166–68): In 1930s Nazi Germany, Jewish tenants were denied the legal protections against eviction to which they were statutorily entitled and which 'Aryans' continued to enjoy. The Courts argued, in flagrant violation of the statutory law Nazi Germany had inherited from the Weimar Republic, that tenants formed part of a concrete order, the 'community of the house', and Jews, due to their racial otherness, could not belong to that particular concrete order, and were therefore not entitled to the statutory protections against eviction.

agreement as to how to adapt formal law to changes in social circumstances. But tensions between the formal constitution and its material basis need not take this harmless form. It may be, rather, that different and antagonistically opposed forms of social life, competing conceptions of good social order, come to clash with one another, as was the case in 1930s Germany.

In that latter scenario, appeals to a supposed material constitution will turn out to be deeply problematic, at least if they aim to elevate one of the contending conceptions of social order into society's supposed material constitution, with the intent to endow it with a surplus of legitimacy. There are no non-arbitrary grounds to privilege one of the contending understandings of concrete order, at least from the point of view of the theory of material constitutionalism. The theory of the material constitution, after all, does not provide any normative guidance as to how the choice is to be taken. It appears to promise, rather, that a coherent and accepted material constitution is already there, grounded in social fact and waiting to be recognised by the law. The appeal to a material constitution, under circumstances of deep and antagonistic pluralism, will not help us to escape decisionism. It will merely conceal the choices that are taken and shield those who manage to make their choices prevail from having to meet a burden of justification.

Schmitt's response to the absence of a widely accepted concrete order of Germany society was to exclude those who disagreed with him, as internal enemies, from what he took to be the political community of Germans.[62] That is too easy a way of making the claim that one's nation already possesses a coherent material constitution, waiting to be expressed in acts of charismatic leadership, come out true. This is not to say that there may not be valuable descriptive, diagnostic or critical uses of the notion of material constitution. Schmitt, however, invoked the material constitution as the ground of the legitimacy of formal legality. It is this legitimating use of the notion of material constitution that should be rejected.

[62] L. Vinx, 'Carl Schmitt's Defence of Sovereignty', in D. Dyzenhaus and T. Poole (eds.), *Law, Liberty and State: Oakeshott, Hayek and Schmitt on the Rule of Law* (Cambridge University Press, 2015), 96–122.

7

'A Certain Shadowy Totality'

In Search of the Material Constitution of the United States

Rob Hunter

[I]t is precisely the immersion in the concretions that allows us to move beyond the merely factual.[1]

7.1 INTRODUCTION

The study of the constitution of the United States has made little progress since the publication of W. E. B. Du Bois' *Black Reconstruction* in 1935.[2] Analysing the legislative debates leading up to the drafting of the Fourteenth Amendment in the aftermath of the Civil War, Du Bois explicitly critiqued the fetishised 'constitutional metaphysics' that inhibited most participants' capacities for apprehending constitutional reality:[3] 'with incantation and abracadabra, the leaders of a nation tried to peer back into the magic crystal, and out of a bit of paper called the Constitution, find eternal and immutable law laid down for their guidance forever and ever, Amen!'[4] The constitution – manifestly antidemocratic, transparently racist and designed and intended to accommodate slavery and to protect private property – had plainly disintegrated. Four years of industrialised warfare and the collective rebellion of Black slaves had seen to that. And yet virtually all of those who drafted, debated or voted on the Reconstruction Amendments persisted in claiming that the constitutional order had been neither suspended nor disrupted. Du Bois understood, of course, that such performances had a purpose. They ensured that the democratisation of American society was limited, tentative and vulnerable. The constitutional renovation that took place after Appomattox was quickly effaced and smoothed over. The Fourteenth Amendment was even de-fanged by judicial fiat in 1873.[5] What Du Bois dubbed 'abolition-democracy'[6] was suppressed not just through the institutional and social demolition of the fledgling democracies in the southern states, but also through the concerted restoration of many aspects of antebellum constitutionality. The rapid destruction of the first genuine attempt at institutionalising democracy in the United States was carried out under the banner of constitutional continuity – the banner, that is, of the priority of constitutional abstractions over

[1] T. W. Adorno, *Philosophical Elements of a Theory of Society* (Polity Press, 2019), 11.

[2] W. E. B. Du Bois, *Black Reconstruction: An Essay toward a History of the Part Which Black Folk Played in the Attempt to Reconstruct Democracy in America, 1860–1880* (Harcourt, Brace and Company, 1935).

[3] A. Powers, 'Tragedy Made Flesh: Constitutional Lawlessness in Du Bois's Black Reconstruction' (2014) 34 *Comparative Studies of South Asia, Africa and the Middle East* 106.

[4] Du Bois, *Black Reconstruction*, 267.

[5] *Slaughter-House Cases*, 83 U.S. (16 Wall.) 36 (1873).

[6] Du Bois, *Black Reconstruction*, 83 ff.

historical social reality. For neither the first nor the last time, white supremacy draped itself in the garlands of constitutional fidelity.[7]

The slippery divergences among constitutional rhetoric, constitutional myth and constitutional politics during and after Reconstruction suggest that neither constitutional text nor constitutional doctrine can serve as reliable guides to apprehending constitutionalism as a set of historically-specific practices. Du Bois evinced a subtle understanding of this problem in his critique of the revivification of antebellum constitutionality. This cannot be said of many of those who came after him, however. Constitutional metaphysics continues to pervade constitutional culture in the United States today. It is a signal example of the 'reified authority'[8] that is constitutive of the domination and unfreedom characteristic of contemporary society. It naturalises the racialised hierarchies,[9] omnipresent violence[10] and structural (i.e., abstract and impersonal) domination[11] that have been, and still are, constitutive of contemporary society. American constitutional theory is marked by a continued indulgence in constitutional metaphysics, rather than the self-reflexive critique of the social relations that make it possible. Many contemporary theorists treat constitutional norms and meanings as self-subsistent and socially autonomous. They would deny such a characterisation, of course; in Hartian terms, the rules of recognition[12] that they propose are not merely formal but incorporate normative or practical considerations as well. And yet such rules occlude and inhibit the apprehension of constitutionality as an ensemble of practices, concepts, and categories that are mutually constitutive with society as a whole.[13]

US constitutional theory, in other words, is distinguished by a widely-shared commitment to understanding constitutionalism as a 'legal technology for structuring state power',[14] not as a complex of thought and practice that both posits and is manifested in definite social relations. This can be seen in most theorists' inattention to the mutually-constitutive character of the seemingly-distinct spheres of politics and economics; to the violence and domination through which constitutional law is made and reproduced; and to the imbrication of the American constitutional order with the totality of world market relations. If constitutionalism is to be apprehended in its historical specificity – rather than in normative prescriptions for how it should be ordered – then most American constitutional theory will be of little help. Apprehending the constitution as an ensemble of determinate social relations that are the actual content of the forms of historically definite structures and processes is a task best accomplished through recourse to critical theory (understood as a critique of contemporary society's essential determinations or 'social forms'[15]). Such a task does not simply presuppose the adequacy of liberal legality or the anteriority of legal norms.[16] An adequate critique along such lines would

7 Cf Powers, 'Tragedy Made Flesh'.

8 C. O'Kane, 'Reification and the Critical Theory of Contemporary Society' (2021) 8 *Critical Historical Studies* 57.

9 R. M. Smith, 'Beyond Tocqueville, Myrdal, and Hartz: The Multiple Traditions in America' (1993) 87 *The American Political Science Review* 549.

10 R. M. Cover, 'Violence and the Word' (1986) 95 *Yale Law Journal* 1601.

11 T. Smith, *Beyond Liberal Egalitarianism: Marx and Normative Social Theory in the Twenty-First Century* (Brill, 2017), 110–30.

12 H. L. A. Hart, *The Concept of Law*, 2nd ed. (Oxford University Press, 1997), 94–110 and passim.

13 R. Hunter, 'Marx's Critique and the Constitution of the Capitalist State', in P. O'Connell and U. Özsu (eds.), *Research Handbook on Law and Marxism* (Edward Elgar, 2021), 190–208.

14 A. Bâli and A. Rana, 'Constitutionalism and the American Imperial Imagination' (2018) 85 *University of Chicago Law Review* 257.

15 Smith, *Beyond Liberal Egalitarianism*, 73.

16 M. Postone, 'Critique, State, and Economy', in F. Rush (ed.), *The Cambridge Companion to Critical Theory* (Cambridge University Press, 2004), 165–93. Critical theory is concerned with the inverted and antagonistic social

have the potential to destabilise the constitutional metaphysics derided by Du Bois and to open up the possibility of achieving fuller and deeper explanations of the United States as a polity.

This chapter examines several strands of American constitutional theory. Several early attempts – by Charles Beard, Karl Llewellyn and Louis Hartz – provide instructive examples; any attempt to theorise the constitution's historical specificity must begin by examining them. However, the main contenders in contemporary theory – originalism and living constitutionalism – do not illuminate many of the historically specific features of constitutionality in the United States. Moreover, most forms of US constitutional theory succumb to 'constitutional fetishism'[17] and treat constitutional forms, meanings or ideals as self-subsistent, natural or timeless. Those constitutional theories that do acknowledge the irreducibly social character of constitutionalism – specifically, recent contributions to originalism and to living constitutionalism – nevertheless rest on contradictory foundations. The former hypostatises constitutional meanings as trans-historically valid abstractions; the latter is predicated on a claim for the ever-possible perfectibility of the constitution. Neither can fully affirm that constitutional meanings are always mediated by context and theory; both are ill-equipped to confront the determinate features of American constitutionalism without imposing anterior normative frameworks upon them. Despite originalism's emphasis on the purported facts of fixed constitutional meanings and despite living constitutionalism's emphasis on the dynamics of political struggle and public opinion, both accounts remain ensnared by constitutional fetishism.

7.2 THE SOCIAL CONSTITUTION OF THE MATERIAL CONSTITUTION

I propose that the concept of the 'material constitution'[18] is best developed as part of a form-analytic approach to theorising the state. The 'materiality' in question is that of determinate and historically specific relations among social individuals (I do not have in mind a reductive or economistic materialism that treats unmediated 'interests' as brute facts). The recognition of the constitution as an historically specific ensemble of practices, concepts and categories is contrasted with the notion of a constitution consisting of self-subsistent abstractions. Understanding the constitution as it appears in history requires that we refrain from begging questions with respect to its particular content and social appearance.

A polity's actual constitution – consisting of an ensemble of practices, concepts and categories – is an appearance of the form of the state. The state itself is the historically specific politico-juridical form of definite social relations.[19] The constitution is the appearance – that is, the specific historical existence – of that form in particular practices, in actual institutions, and in conceptually-mediated modes of acting, thinking, and knowing. To understand the constitution of a polity is to understand definite social activity, both as it appears in history and as it is mutually constitutive with the particular concepts and categories that mediate it. To understand the constitution is to apprehend real social individuals' thought and action. It is a matter of the

world of modernity, an adequate understanding of which is possible only through the apprehension of its historically specific social forms through the critique of political economy. For the latter, see M. Heinrich, *An Introduction to the Three Volumes of Karl Marx's* Capital (Monthly Review Press, 2012); W. Bonefeld, *Critical Theory and the Critique of Political Economy: On Subversion and Negative Reason* (Bloomsbury, 2014); Smith, *Beyond Liberal Egalitarianism.*

17 F. L. Neumann, *The Democratic and the Authoritarian State: Essays in Political and Legal Theory* (Free Press, 1957), 199.

18 M. Goldoni and M. Wilkinson, 'The Material Constitution' (2018) 81 *Modern Law Review* 567.

19 A. Neupert-Doppler, 'Society and Political Form', in B. Best, W. Bonefeld, and C. O'Kane (eds.), *The SAGE Handbook of Frankfurt School Critical Theory* (SAGE, 2018), vol. III, 816–33; W. Bonefeld, 'On the State as Political Form of Society' (2021) 85 *Science & Society* 177.

critique of contemporary society as it exists, not the normative prescription of society as it might be. In the case of the United States, such a critique must necessarily account for and proceed from the structuration of society through capitalist production and exchange relations, racism and settler-colonialism and integration with the world market.[20] Indeed, it must proceed from the recognition of the observations that Du Bois stated plainly and that most subsequent students of the constitution have ignored.

Constitutions appear in history through the continuous and contingent activity of social constitution. By 'social constitution' I refer to the contradictory and antagonistic processes whereby the reproduction of society 'manifests itself in the form of' fetishised (that is, seemingly natural) social forms and categories that mediate subjects' thought and action; such forms 'assert themselves behind the backs of the acting subjects' who themselves give those forms determinate reality in their own thought and action.[21] (I do not refer to approaches to constitutional theory that treat constituent power as an ongoing and immanent feature of established constitutional orders.[22]) It is with reference to the concept of social constitution that a polity may be understood as an appearance of a social form, the determination of which is found in the activity of real social individuals. To describe a constitution as socially constituted is to refer to the determinate reality of concepts that both mediate and are reproduced by definite and historically-specific social relations. Constitutional documents do not themselves cause the historical specificity of determinate social relations. Instead, constitutionality *qua* categories, concepts, and practices is constituted through a continuous and contradictory 'process of becoming'.[23] It is reproduced through the activity of political subjects along with the simultaneous (and typically depoliticising) mediation of social relations by constitutionality.[24]

In contrast, most American constitutional theory is distinguished by the special attention given to constitutional review of legislation – a judicial prerogative with a central role in the political development of the United States.[25] As such, US constitutional theories tend to be either formalist, textualist or 'normativist'[26] in character. This is in no small part due to the construction of constitutionality as a fundamentally jurisprudential domain. The entrenchment of judicial supremacy – pursued in the defence of the agendas of particular political coalitions, and generally supported by successful national coalitions, especially as they are expressed through presidential politics[27] – is accompanied by the continued gravitational pull of the 'counter-majoritarian difficulty'.[28] An obsession with paradox attends much of the activity of US constitutional theorists who seek to reconcile majoritarian legitimation with the acutely antidemocratic features of the formal constitution.[29]

US constitutional theory does little to investigate or unsettle the reification and hypostatisation that subtend constitutionalism as a cultural practice. It is still as fetishistic as it was in Du Bois's

[20] An adequate understanding of constitutionalism is possible only through attending to the critique of capitalism as abstract social domination. See Hunter, 'Marx's Critique'.

[21] Bonefeld, *Critical Theory*, 21.

[22] P. Blokker and C. Thornhill (eds.), *Sociological Constitutionalism* (Cambridge University Press, 2017).

[23] Goldoni and Wilkinson, 'Material Constitution', 581.

[24] On depoliticisation and the reproduction of constitutionality, see Hunter, 'Marx's Critique'.

[25] K. E. Whittington, *Repugnant Laws: Judicial Review of Acts of Congress from the Founding to the Present* (University Press of Kansas, 2019).

[26] M. Loughlin, 'The Concept of Constituent Power' (2014) 13 *European Journal of Political Theory* 218.

[27] K. E. Whittington, *Political Foundations of Judicial Supremacy: The Presidency, the Supreme Court, and Constitutional Leadership in U.S. History* (Princeton University Press, 2007).

[28] A. M. Bickel, *The Least Dangerous Branch: The Supreme Court at the Bar of Politics* (Bobbs-Merrill, 1962), 16–17.

[29] N. Sultany, 'The State of Progressive Constitutional Theory: The Paradox of Constitutional Democracy and the Project of Political Justification' (2012) 47 *Harvard Civil Rights–Civil Liberties Law Review* 371.

day. It lacks an adequately developed vocabulary for the apprehension of constitutionalism as the activity of real social individuals. To hear the practices and concepts of constitutionalism described in terms of the real appearances of definite social relations may come as a shock to 'those for whom the concepts of the bourgeois social sciences ("society", "norms", "equilibrium", "legitimacy" etc.) are so familiar that their reality is almost tangible'.[30] But the concepts that populate constitutional thought are not autonomous ontological constituents of our world. They are not simply illusory, but they are certainly neither natural nor self-subsistent – as so many constitutional theorists suppose them to be. They may be explained, understood and critiqued only with reference to the broader array of social relations of which they a part. I now turn to the consideration of some early attempts to contribute to such a critical project.

7.3 BEARD, LLEWELLYN AND HARTZ

This section surveys three thinkers from the first half of the twentieth century – Charles Beard,[31] Karl Llewellyn[32] and Louis Hartz[33] – who departed from conventional accounts of American constitutionalism. The objects of their inquiries were neither constitutional provisions nor doctrines. Beard pursued a relatively rare approach to understanding the constitution, viewing it as the product of social conflict rather than deliberation over principles and institutional design. But his analysis was 'materialist' only in the most limited and reductionist sense of the term, as I argue in this section. Llewellyn, in turn, gave a rough-hewn but perceptive articulation to the notion of the 'living constitution'. He remained focused on the pragmatics of judicial review, but he emphasised that the constitution is identical neither with the constitutional text nor the extant body of doctrine. Finally, Hartz placed a greater emphasis on political thought than either Beard or Llewellyn, who were preoccupied with economic interests and judicial decision-making, respectively. Hartz's explanation of American political culture – in terms of an historically invariant liberalism – attended to the articulation of politics through categories and modes of thought, but it did not offer explanations in terms of definite social relations.

'Beard's method was unrefined in details';[34] he focused on the economic and sectional interests of the framers themselves.[35] His account, as well as Hartz's monochromatic portrait of a liberal polity, are inadequate causal accounts of constitutional practice (the creation and the reproduction of constitutionality); Llewellyn's rather more modest argument did not even attempt to provide such an account. Precisely because they sought to offer critical explanations of the constitution, however, all three warrant more attention than is customarily given to them in contemporary constitutional theory.

Beard described the constitution as 'an economic document'[36] rather than as a politico-philosophical document. The interests of the framers determined the drafting and ratification of the constitutional document. For Beard, the political content of that document – and the

[30] S. Clarke, 'Marxism, Sociology, and Poulantzas's Theory of the State', in S. Clarke (ed.), *The State Debate* (Macmillan, 1991), 85.

[31] C. Beard, *An Economic Interpretation of the Constitution of the United States* [1913] (Free Press, 1986).

[32] K. Llewellyn, 'The Constitution as an Institution' (1934) 34 *Columbia Law Review* 1.

[33] L. Hartz, *The Liberal Tradition in America: An Interpretation of American Political Thought since the Revolution* (Houghton Mifflin Harcourt, 1955).

[34] R. Hofstadter, 'Beard and the Constitution: The History of an Idea' (1950) 2 *American Quarterly* 195.

[35] 'Beard occasionally seemed to be charging the Framers with lining their own pockets . . . At other times, however, he suggested only that the Framers advanced the economic interests of the class to which they belonged . . .'. M. J. Klarman, *The Framers' Coup: The Making of the United States Constitution* (Oxford University Press, 2016), 377.

[36] Beard, *Economic Interpretation*, 152 ff.

procedural chicanery through which it was created and ratified[37] – represented a victory for financial and commercial élites. Far from being a principled compromise, the creation and ratification of the constitution amounted to 'a genteel scam'[38] – an anti-democratic measure taken by the holders of specific kinds of wealth in order to secure their property and profits against policies that might threaten them. The framers' fear of democracy was best understood through the lens of 'economic determinism', which Beard considered 'as nearly axiomatic as any proposition in social science can be'.[39] He held that such an analytic frame is a necessary corrective against 'the juristic view' that imagines that the constitution is 'the work of the whole people' and 'bears in it no traces of the party conflict from which it emerged.'[40]

The term 'party conflict' reveals the limits of Beard's argument, which was constrained by his methodological individualism. He averred that 'no movement by a mass of people can be correctly comprehended until that mass is resolved into its component parts'.[41] Moreover, by restricting his focus to a conflict between 'parties', Beard's analysis occluded the broader social conflict of which that particular party conflict was only one particular instance. He indefensibly effaced slavery in his account; by failing to analyse slavery with precision and sustained emphasis, he also failed to provide an adequate account of the creation of the constitution as a victory for the possessors of wealth rather than for the members of sectional parties.[42] Moreover, his critique was limited to the constitutional text, its drafting, and its ratification; he was not concerned with actual historical constitutional practice. But Beard's argument remains valuable as an early example of critical (rather than celebratory) constitutional analysis. It is limited and incomplete; but these limits must be surpassed, rather than used as an excuse for dismissing critical constitutional scholarship.[43] Who will deny that the US constitution is 'based upon the concept that the fundamental private rights of property are anterior to government and morally beyond the reach of popular majorities'?[44] But this is not enough to ground a critique of the constitution, not least because it misses so much of what distinguishes constitutional practice in the United States.

Llewellyn counted Beard among those students of politics and law who were more attentive to their actual practice than their formal specifications.[45] Llewellyn attempted to manifest this attentiveness by distinguishing between constitutionalism in an institutional sense and 'mere working government'; he held that the former is a 'penumbra' of beliefs, understandings, and conventions that accumulates (and may, perhaps, dissipate) over time and through practice.[46] The metaphor of an institution contrasts sharply with the conventional American conception of a constitution as a textually-specified framework or body of rules. Llewellyn advanced a distinct

[37] Ibid., 239–52.
[38] W. Hogeland, *Founding Finance: How Debt, Speculation, Foreclosures, Protests, and Crackdowns Made Us a Nation* (University of Texas Press, 2012), 6.
[39] Beard, *Economic Interpretation*, 15, n. 1.
[40] Ibid., 11.
[41] Ibid., 253.
[42] Cf S. Lynd, 'On Turner, Beard and Slavery' (1963) 48 *Journal of Negro History* 235.
[43] Beard has been the target of 'an aggressive, largely successful effort . . . to discredit and dismiss him'. Hogeland, *Founding Finance*, 6.
[44] Beard, *Economic Interpretation*, 324.
[45] Llewellyn, 'Constitution as an Institution', 2.
[46] Ibid., 26 ff. It is interesting to note that Llewellyn used the term 'penumbra' to denote a relatively determinate ensemble of practices and understanding, while Hart later used the term to describe a region of legal *indeterminacy* outside the perimeter of 'a core of certainty'. Hart, *Concept of Law*, 123. The term has also had a chequered history in judicial decision-making; see L. J. Sirico Jr., 'Failed Constitutional Metaphors: The Wall of Separation and the Penumbra' (2011) 45 *University of Richmond Law Review* 459.

criterion for recognising constitutional content: continuous practice, not textual fidelity or normative prescription, is the modality through which constitutional content is determined. For Llewellyn, the constitution as an institution does not obtain historically in the form of a fixed body of rules or a web of power relations, but rather in 'a certain shadowy totality'[47] – a dynamic yet path-dependent pattern of continually-developing constitutional meaning. This totality may not be identified with any text. It is nevertheless socially determinate and its development exerts a tendential influence on judicial outcomes. In Llewellyn's sketch, such development falls within the penumbra of the living and unwritten constitution that is non-identical with the textual constitution. Our recognition of the actuality of such relations does not necessarily give us interpretive guidance in hard cases, but it does give us good reason to believe that judges do not rely solely on textual materials when making decisions.

Llewellyn may be glossed as saying that a polity is constituted socially, not textually. The social constitution of reality is necessarily antagonistic and contradictory. Institutions may persist, but that persistence is reproduced through conflict and contradiction; the ramifications for the determinacy of constitutional meaning are obvious. But contingency and conflict do not efface determinacy altogether. Llewellyn's penumbra is no less real for having been constituted through conflict. Llewellyn argued that the United States 'have [an unwritten] Constitution, and that nobody can stop their having such a Constitution, and that whether anyone likes that or not, the fact has been there for decades . . .'[48] Llewellyn's narrow focus on the juridical – and *a fortiori* his conception of social constitution as a mere process of institutionalisation – renders his account inadequate as a material theory of constitutionalism. Even so, his insight that constitutionality is made and re-made through contestation and conflict is generative and compelling.

Hartz emphasised the politically-constitutive role of concepts, but he did not understand them to be historically-specific and determinate categories mediating thought and social behaviour. That is, he did not understand them to be constituted through definite historical processes of conflict and antagonism. Instead, he offered a '"single factor" analysis'[49] of the American polity, characterised by an absent feudal past and a pervasively liberal political culture (among its élite, at least, to which his 'single factor' analysis was largely restricted). His argument hypostatises liberalism and effaces political subjects other than normative citizens of the settler-colonial polity: propertied white men. Lacking an account of how liberalism was and is socially constituted, Hartz could not offer an adequate explanation of how and why it came to dominate and define American politics. Unlike Beard, Hartz recognised the centrality of racism and slavery to the American political tradition; but even these are treated primarily as concepts standing to one side of historical conflict. Violence rarely intrudes in Hartz's account, and even when it does it is quickly brushed aside – as, for example, when he describes the antebellum United States as 'a land where liberalism had destroyed nothing, unless it was the society of the Indians'.[50] He even describes the Civil War not in terms of violence and destruction but in terms of 'the strange agonies the Southerners endured trying to break out of the grip of Locke and the way the nation greeted their effort'[51] – a telling contrast with Du Bois's own account of the struggle for abolition.

47 Llewellyn, 'Constitution as an Institution', 8.
48 Ibid., 2.
49 Hartz, *Liberal Tradition*, 20.
50 Ibid., 152.
51 Ibid., 177.

7.4 ORIGINALISM AND ITS DISCONTENTS

Despite their attentiveness to certain aspects of constitutional practice, both strands of contemporary American constitutional theory – originalism and living constitutionalism – have moved further away from Beard's, Llewellyn's or Hartz's attentiveness to constitutionalism as a form taken by definite social relations. Originalism rests on a paradoxically ahistorical conception of constitutional meaning. Meanwhile, living constitutionalism emphasises constitutional practice – but it imposes exogenous normative standards in order to distinguish valid constitutional changes from invalid departures from what Llewellyn called the 'certain shadowy totality' of established practice.

7.4.1 *Originalism*

Originalism is grounded in the contention that constitutional meanings are trans-historically stable and interpretively recoverable. It is intimately linked to conservative efforts to re-shape the contours of the American state (particularly its administrative apparatus) during and beyond the second half of the twentieth century.[52] It is a 'political practice' whose 'ascendancy', according to two prominent critics, 'does not reflect the analytic force of its jurisprudence, but instead depends upon its capacity to fuse aroused citizens, government officials, and judges into a dynamic and broad-based political movement.'[53]

A contemporary cohort of 'new originalists' emphasises public constitutional meaning over the original intentions of constitutional framers or the putative plain meaning of the constitutional text.[54] They focus on the publicity of provisions' original meanings at the moment of their 'fixation' through writing and ratification.[55] The particular intentions of individual framers do not disclose constitutional meanings. Such a task requires investigating historical facts about speakers, utterances, and their political contexts. Many contemporary originalists also acknowledge that '[u]ncertainty and indeterminacy are inherent in the originalist approach to constitutional interpretation'.[56] Accordingly, they distinguish between constitutional interpretation[57] – the discernment of original public meanings – and constitutional construction[58] – the elaboration of constitutional meaning (and its translation into constitutional provisions and institutions) in instances of vagueness or ambiguity. Judicial review should be guided by the canons of interpretation, not the vagaries of construction. Interpretation is neither mechanical nor purely procedural; it is a hermeneutic encounter, the outcome of which must not be imagined to be foreseeable or foreordained. Nevertheless, judicial review takes as its object – so new originalists argue – the relatively fixed, public meaning of the constitutional text. The

52 S. M. Teles, *The Rise of the Conservative Legal Movement: The Battle for Control of the Law* (Princeton University Press, 2012); A. Hollis-Brusky, *Ideas with Consequences: The Federalist Society and the Conservative Counterrevolution* (Oxford University Press, 2015); P. Baumgardner, 'Originalism and the Academy in Exile' (2019) 37 *Law and History Review* 787.

53 R. Post and R. Siegel, 'Originalism as a Political Practice: The Right's Living Constitution' (2006) 75 *Fordham Law Review* 549; cf. C. TerBeek, '"Clocks Must Always Be Turned Back": *Brown v. Board of Education* and the Racial Origins of Constitutional Originalism' (2021) 115 *American Political Science Review* 821.

54 K. E. Whittington, 'The New Originalism' (2004) 2 *Georgetown Journal of Law & Public Policy* 599.

55 L. B. Solum, 'The Interpretation-Construction Distinction' (2010) 27 *Constitutional Commentary* 116.

56 K. E. Whittington, 'Originalism: A Critical Introduction' (2013) 82 *Fordham Law Review* 403.

57 K. E. Whittington, *Constitutional Interpretation: Textual Meaning, Original Intent, and Judicial Review* (University Press of Kansas, 1999).

58 K. E. Whittington, *Constitutional Construction: Divided Powers and Constitutional Meaning* (Harvard University Press, 1999).

normatively defensible role of judicial review involves the interpretive determination of meaning in order to enforce institutional boundaries and protect individual rights.

Originalism does not apprehend constitutional practice as a moment of a social totality that is suffused by violence, domination and subordination. Moreover, originalists have been largely untroubled by historiographical objections to the narrowness of originalism's historical vision.[59] It is true that new originalist theories could only be the products of a post-Realist legal academy in which 'the interpenetration of law and politics' is an accepted fact.[60] Few new originalists would deny 'the truism that judges make law'.[61] Nevertheless, contemporary originalists' acknowledgement of the mutual constitution of law and politics is a thin one; they still abstract institutional conflict from social conflict. Moreover, originalism casts constitutional meanings as autonomous abstractions. As such, it cannot apprehend the constitution as both mediating – and socially constituted through – antagonism and contradiction.

7.4.2 *Living Constitutionalism*

Originalism's opponents insist on recognising 'a living Constitution which completes, alters, aye, and overrides the Document'.[62] Since the advent of the Warren Court,[63] living constitutionalists have engaged in the defensive[64] justification of left-liberal judicial interventionism.[65] They attempt to show that the unwritten constitution supersedes the written constitution but is nevertheless compatible with or presupposed by the values implicit in the written constitution (the enforcement of which is often understood in terms of moral perfectibility or 'redemption', not textual fidelity).[66] It is reasonable to characterise this project as 'a mood and an anxiety', rather than a method.[67] It is not Whiggish, in other words; after all, to describe the constitutional order as living is to acknowledge that it may die.[68]

Living constitutionalism elevates Llewellyn's 'certain shadowy totality' above the documentary constitution. The former must guide interpretive practice, while the latter can neither adequately describe the salient features of contemporary constitutional practice nor explain the histories of struggle and contestation through which it was made. But living constitutionalists lack a fixed interpretive anchor; they can only point to departures from consensuses that are controverted and contested – essentially and necessarily so. They cannot propound consistent methods for distinguishing between those constitutional innovations that are popularly authorised and those that are not. Recourse to contractarian theories of political consent only deepens

59 C. TerBeek, 'The Search for an Anchor: Living Constitutionalism from the Progressives to Trump' (2021) 46 *Law & Social Inquiry* 860. A forceful statement of the historiographical objection may be found in J. N. Rakove, *Original Meanings: Politics and Ideas in the Making of the Constitution* (Vintage Books, 1996).

60 S. M. Griffin, *American Constitutionalism: From Theory to Politics* (Princeton University Press, 1998), 18.

61 N. Duxbury, 'Faith in Reason: The Process Tradition in American Jurisprudence' (1993) 15 *Cardozo Law Review* 636.

62 Llewellyn, 'Constitution as an Institution', 2.

63 Cf L. A. Powe, *The Warren Court and American Politics* (Belknap Press, 2000).

64 J. M. Balkin, *Living Originalism* (Harvard University Press, 2011), 125.

65 Notable contributions to this literature include B. Ackerman, *We the People: Foundations* (Belknap Press, 1991); B. Ackerman, *We the People: Transformations* (Belknap Press, 1998); B. Friedman, *The Will of the People: How Public Opinion Has Influenced the Supreme Court and Shaped the Meaning of the Constitution* (Farrar, Straus and Giroux, 2009); D. A. Strauss, *The Living Constitution* (Oxford University Press, 2010).

66 J. M. Balkin, *Constitutional Redemption: Political Faith in an Unjust World* (Harvard University Press, 2011).

67 E. J. Leib, 'The Perpetual Anxiety of Living Constitutionalism' (2007) 24 *Constitutional Commentary* 370.

68 Cf J. M. Balkin, *The Cycles of Constitutional Time* (Oxford University Press, 2020).

the problem of fetishism.[69] Living constitutionalists must either make recourse to fetishistic patterns of political thought, such as natural law or hypothetical consent, or else abandon the *teloi* of living constitutionalism – in exchange, perhaps, for the commitments of 'popular constitutionalism'[70] or the contemporary 'law and political economy' movement.[71] Originalists simply deny the actuality of any shadowy totality; but living constitutionalists can only gesture at it, rather than isolate its determinate content.

7.5 ORIGINALISM AND LIVING CONSTITUTIONALISM AS CONSTITUTIONAL FETISHISMS

Du Bois would have had little patience with today's dominant theories, which cannot be said to have built upon the contributions of Beard, Llewellyn or Hartz. Both originalism and living constitutionalism, even in their most sophisticated forms, remain theories of constitutional metaphysics. Neither furnishes sufficient theoretical materials for the apprehension of the constitution as a socially constituted ensemble of practices, concepts and categories. Despite its notable gains in sophistication – and tendencies toward convergence or at least complementarity with certain accounts of living constitutionalism[72] – originalism cannot ground an adequate account of the US constitution. The chief objects of originalist theory are not political struggles or settlements themselves, but 'fixed' meanings that are specified – with lesser or greater degrees of determinacy – in the constitutional text and are held to codify the content of political settlements. As such, originalism is necessarily counterposed to the apprehension of constitutionality as the specific form of appearance of definite social relations. It is predicated on the transhistorical recoverability of meanings (either subjective or public); it is ultimately defensible only on the basis of insisting on the adequacy of conceptions of meaning and reference that largely predate the twentieth century[73] (although that would at least be consistent with a constitutional theory that presumes that early modern political theory is adequate for describing the inverted and contradiction-laden contemporary social world).

We are now far from the paths trodden by Beard or Llewellyn – let alone by Du Bois. Originalism is defensible only on the basis of disavowing 'the contribution of society and the contribution of the real world' to 'the determination of reference'.[74] To the extent that it is predicated on the adequacy of the fixation thesis, originalism is a curiously ahistorical – even antihistoricist – theory of the historical translation of meaning.[75] What sincere originalist could affirm Wittgenstein's statement that 'words only have meaning in the stream of life'?[76] Originalists adhere to the claim that at least some meanings – constitutional meanings among them – are essentially untransformed by discursive encounters. As such, they argue for the persistence of specific abstractions even in the absence of their reproduction through socially

69 G. Kay, 'Right and Force: A Marxist Critique of Contract and the State', in M. Williams (ed.), *Value, Social Form and the State* (Macmillan, 1988), 115–33.

70 M. Tushnet, *Taking the Constitution Away from the Courts* (Princeton University Press, 2000); L. D. Kramer, *The People Themselves: Popular Constitutionalism and Judicial Review* (Oxford University Press, 2004).

71 J. Britton-Purdy, D. S. Grewal, A. Kapczynski and K. S. Rahman, 'Building a Law-and-Political-Economy Framework: Beyond the Twentieth-Century Synthesis' (2020) 129 *Yale Law Journal* 1784.

72 Balkin, *Living Originalism*; Whittington, 'Originalism: A Critical Introduction'.

73 Whittington, *Constitutional Interpretation*, 88–109.

74 H. Putnam, 'Meaning and Reference' (1973) 70 *The Journal of Philosophy* 711.

75 J. Gienapp, 'Historicism and Holism: Failures of Originalist Translation' (2015) 84 *Fordham Law Review* 935.

76 L. Wittgenstein, *Last Writings on the Philosophy of Psychology*, G. H. von Wright and H. Nyman, eds., C. G. Luckhardt trans. (University of Chicago Press, 1996), vol. I, §913.

constitutive processes of antagonism and contestation. Moreover, unlike the 'real abstraction' of capital mediating contemporary society, the abstractions that originalism concerns itself with – constitutional meanings – are essentially contested concepts, not socially objective categories.[77] They are not, in other words, historically specific forms of appearance of determinate social relations. Instead, they are normative statements about how social relations ought to be ordered. Any conceivable new originalist synthesis – combining the fixation thesis, on the one hand, and the insistence on the diachronic interpretability of synchronic public meanings, on the other – is unstable and ultimately untenable. Even if it is granted that the indeterminacy of the meaning of legal texts is bounded,[78] the meaning of any particular text cannot serve as an adequate explanation of the struggles that preceded its inscription, nor as a guide to its application to future cases. The originalist conception of the constitutional order abstracts constitutional meanings from their dynamic historical contexts and presents them as anterior to, rather than constituted through, social relations. This is fetishism of the first order.

Living constitutionalism fares no better. New originalists at least attempt to grapple with the social character of meaning. Such an attempt does not ultimately succeed, inhibited as it is by the commitment of originalists (old and new) to the fixity and (relative) determinacy of meaning – such that originalists trade in hypostatised meanings shorn of specific social contexts. Living constitutionalism, by contrast, is always already fetishistic. The notion of the living constitution requires the imposition of particular normative standards – even if they are exogenous to political practice as it actually obtains in history – in order to determine which constitutional changes are democratically authorised and which are ephemeral (and hence non-authoritative or, indeed, invalid). Originalists are more able than living constitutionalists to tell stories about democratic justification for judicial review – within the US context, that is, in which popular sovereignty is the default normative anchor for democratic legitimacy. One need not grant the truth of originalists' premises (particularly regarding meaning and translation, but also regarding the adequacy of popular sovereignty as a theory of political justification) in order to acknowledge that they have presented a coherent (if not convincing) story of how democratic publics authorise constitutional creation and change – that is, by writing things down. Living constitutionalists cannot offer such a parsimonious protocol for institutionalising constituent power. Even so, new originalists are unable to adequately apprehend constitutional reality as a result of their commitment to the absolute anteriority of constitutional norms with respect to social practice. Living constitutionalists are at least motivated by an awareness of 'the entanglement of facts and value'.[79]

Originalists and living constitutionalists both draw pictures of American society that Du Bois would recognise as caricatures. They ask questions that Beard would dismiss as trivial and Llewellyn would regard as distractions. The originalist conception of constitutional meaning cannot serve as an adequate picture of what settlements have been achieved or even what has been struggled over.[80] Living constitutionalists imagine that either settlements are self-justifying and self-enforcing or that their having been achieved is an authoritative reason against contesting

[77] On real abstraction see C. O'Kane, 'The Critique of Real Abstraction: From the Critical Theory of Society to the Critique of Political Economy and Back Again', in A. Oliva, Á. Oliva and I. Novara (eds.), *Marx and Contemporary Critical Theory: The Philosophy of Real Abstraction* (Palgrave Macmillan, 2020), 265–87. On social objectivity, see Bonefeld, *Critical Theory*, 54–60 and passim; P. Mattick, *Theory As Critique: Essays on* Capital (Brill, 2018), 79–85 and passim.

[78] L. B. Solum, 'On the Indeterminacy Crisis: Critiquing Critical Dogma' (1987) 54 *University of Chicago Law Review* 462.

[79] H. Putnam, *The Collapse of the Fact/Value Dichotomy and Other Essays* (Harvard University Press, 2002), 28–45.

[80] B. Ackerman, 'The Living Constitution' (2007) 120 *Harvard Law Review* 1737.

them. In neither instance, however, do we have an adequate account of the US constitution. Originalist fixation and constraint are inevitably poor guides to understanding how or through what processes and antagonisms a polity is actually constituted. Living constitutionalism, meanwhile, is actively at odds with the actual US constitution. It holds some struggles up as discharging authoritative settlements and others as illegitimately threatening constitutional democracy. Originalists trade on a crabbed and exclusionary conception of democracy that posits a singular 'people' (one that is throttled by the dead hand of the past, no less). But living constitutionalists must simply resort to question-begging, contractarian theories of political justification. And both approaches trade on fetishistic understandings of institutions. That is, they tend to treat institutions (formal and non-formal) as self-subsistent or natural, rather than as particular forms of appearance of social reality – the constitutive processes of which cannot be identified with either the formal constitution or the normative constitution.

7.6 CONCLUSION

Critiquing the formal constitution of a polity does not necessarily get us any closer to a critique of the polity itself. What does the formal constitution reveal, and what does it efface, about the make-up of the American polity as an ensemble of material social relations? What were the social relations that made possible, and both mediated and were presupposed by, the constitutional categories and concepts of American constitutionalism? How did they change and develop through the antagonism – the brutality and barbarism – at the heart of the American state-building project? Du Bois's rejection of constitutional metaphysics prompts such questions, but few American constitutional theorists seem interested in answering them. American constitutional theorists have been unable to give definite and coherent shape to Llewellyn's 'certain shadowy totality' of practices, beliefs and understandings. They will remain unable to do so as long as they fail to take seriously and learn from the tentative steps taken by earlier scholars toward an adequate understanding of constitutional reality.

More fundamentally, after almost a century, we are no closer to answering Du Bois's challenge. We can gesture at what an adequate response would look like. The constitution of the United States, considered as an historically specific appearance of the form of the state, is distinguished by, *inter alia*, capitalist relations of production and exchange; anti-indigeneity and settler-coloniality; ascription to racialised and gendered hierarchies of domination, exclusion, and extermination; and the articulation of domestic governance with global relations of circulation and accumulation. But these cannot be explained on the basis of the hegemonic modes of constitutional thought in the contemporary United States. Doing so requires the further development of the critical concept of the material constitution.

8

The Material Constitution in Greek Constitutional Thought

Nikolas Vagdoutis

8.1 INTRODUCTION

The origins of the concept of the material constitution can be traced back to Costantino Mortati. He is the 'founding father' of the term 'constitution in the material sense', used in his monograph *La Costituzione in senso materiale* (1940).[1] With this concept, Mortati distanced himself from a legal formalism that 'is unable to conceive of the legal order as a substantive coherent unity'.[2] On the contrary, his concept of the material constitution aimed at the consolidation of a substantive political unity, and this could not be achieved through a concept of the constitution as a set of norms.[3] This unity was provided by the ruling political party or, in his post–Second World War theory,[4] by the dominant political forces in a multiparty system and their fundamental aims. The 'ruling party' was the 'privileged holder of constitutional values'[5] and guaranteed the unity in the legal order and, therefore, the unity of the state. The aims of the political parties had, therefore, 'an immediate legal value',[6] being the ordering principles of the constitution. Hence, Mortati's material constitution had a legal – and not solely a sociological – character.[7] The material constitution was 'a source of validity' and a 'condition of effective implementation' of the formal constitution.[8] It 'prevails', therefore, over the latter.[9]

Mortati's concept of the material constitution was introduced into Greek constitutional thought in the 1980s. However, material approaches to the constitution were developed in Greek constitutional thought even before this period. This chapter will explore these approaches

This chapter is part of my completed post-doctoral research at the Aristotle University of Thessaloniki (School of Law).

[1] M. La Torre, 'The German Impact on Fascist Public Law Doctrine – Costantino Mortati's Material Constitution', in C. Joerges and N. Singh Ghaleigh (eds.), *Darker Legacies of Law in Europe: The Shadow of National Socialism and Fascism over Europe and its Legal Traditions* (Hart, 2003), 305.

[2] Ibid., 310.

[3] M. Goldoni and M. Wilkinson, 'The Material Constitution' (2018) 81 *Modern Law Review* 576.

[4] M. Croce and M. Goldoni, *The Legacy of Pluralism: The Continental Jurisprudence of Santi Romano, Carl Schmitt, and Costantino Mortati* (Stanford University Press, 2020), 169–70.

[5] La Torre, 'German Impact', 316.

[6] Ibid., 314. As Mortati argued, 'the political parties act . . . as an autonomous source of validity of the legal order, a factor and mechanism necessary to ensuring the order'. Ibid.

[7] Ibid., 327.

[8] Ibid., 314.

[9] Ibid.

by distinguishing three chronological periods: (a) the interwar period in which a sociological concept of the constitution was developed by Alexandros Svolos; (b) the period after the end of the Greek civil war, in which there was no common stance toward a material approach to the constitution among Greek constitutional theorists: George Daskalakis developed a normative approach to the material constitution under the influence of Rudolph Smend and Carl Schmitt, which was criticised by Aristovoulos Manessis and (c) the period after the fall of the dictatorship, in which there was a revival of material understandings of the constitution through the theories of Manessis and Antonis Manitakis. As will be demonstrated, they developed both a sociological and a juristic understanding of the material constitution, influenced more by Nicos Poulantzas' state theory than Mortati's concept of the material constitution. This chapter will follow that division and proceed in three parts.

8.2 THE INTERWAR PERIOD: SVOLOS' SOCIOLOGICAL APPROACH OF THE CONSTITUTION

The Greek constitutional theorist who was the first to develop a material understanding of the constitution was Alexandros Svolos (1892–1956). He was the most significant constitutional theorist in the interwar period,[10] 'with social-democratic political leanings'.[11] Although he did not deploy the term 'material' constitution, he followed a 'sociological approach',[12] exploring the social reality that lies behind the 1927 Greek republican constitution and its principle of popular sovereignty.[13] His approach was influenced by Rudolf Smend's *Integrationslehre* and Smend's idea that the State is not a static entity but is in the constant process of dynamic renewal, living through '*un plebiscite de tous les jours*'.[14] He followed Smend's relation of the state to a dynamic social life because otherwise the nature and the activity of the state would not be understood, and the state would remain a 'dead object'.[15] As a consequence, he delved into a 'research on social forces, mainly regarding representative democracy', which 'is literally a research on polity'.[16]

However, he did not follow Smend's normative aim of integrating the citizens into the state,[17] which was considered as a 'unified experience' and a 'totality of values'.[18] On the contrary, Svolos' theory stood in contrast to Smend's communitarian theory, based on his sociological observation of the absence of a homogeneous people in a society riddled with (predominantly if not exclusively) class conflict.[19] Based on this observation, Svolos argued that behind the constitutional principle of popular sovereignty exists a multi-class society.[20] This led to his

[10] Svolos held the Chair of Constitutional Law at the University of Athens in 1929. However, he only served for a few years because he was fired four times from this position, the last being in 1946. This dismissal had been preceded by the fact that he served in 1944 as a President of the Political Committee of National Liberation [ΠΕΕΑ] which was the government created by the National Liberation Front [EAM] during the resistance.

[11] S. Ploumidis, 'Corporatist Ideas in Inter-war Greece: From Theory to Practice (1922–1940)' (2014) 44 *European History Quarterly* 61.

[12] A. Svolos, *Το νέον Σύνταγμα και αι βάσεις του πολιτεύματος* [1928] (Εκδόσεις Αντ. Σάκκουλα, 2008), e', 88.

[13] According to article 2 of the 1927 Greek constitution 'All the powers derive from the Nation, exist for the Nation ...'.

[14] Svolos, *Το νέον Σύνταγμα*, 103.

[15] Ibid.

[16] Ibid.

[17] S. Korioth, 'Rudolf Smend: Introduction', in A. J. Jacobson and B. Schlink (eds.), *Weimar: A Jurisprudence of Crisis* (University of California Press, 2002), 210.

[18] R. Smend, 'Constitution and Constitutional Law' [1928], in A. J. Jacobson and B. Schlink (eds.), *Weimar: A Jurisprudence of Crisis* (University of California Press, 2002), 230.

[19] Svolos, *Το νέον Σύνταγμα*, 87.

[20] Ibid., 85.

argument that the general will is a 'fiction' and that the ruling power of modern democracies cannot be based on a unity called 'the people' but 'is mostly the will of a [social] group'.[21] This group is 'usually' the one that has 'economic power'.[22] In other words, the economic-social power of capital has a severe impact on the formation of the state will, whereas the masses hold the 'impotent power of universal suffrage'.[23]

This dominance of the 'bourgeoisie' and the lack of social solidarity is one of the main reasons for the crisis of parliamentarism and of democracy in Europe in the early 1930s.[24] Svolos' material understanding of the constitution leads him to stress the necessity of social democracy for overcoming this crisis.[25] His concept of social democracy draws from the tradition of Weimar social democracy. He argues for a 'démocratie socialisante'[26] through the state by referring, among others, to the state theories of Heinrich Cunow, Karl Renner and Hans Kelsen, namely theories according to which the state is considered to be transformable and is deemed as an apparatus that could lead to socialism.[27] According to Svolos, the indication that the state is being transformed in this direction of a 'popular state' [Volksstaat] – that is Ferdinand Lasalle's notion of the state, which inspired the aforementioned theories[28] – could be seen by the electoral rise of the socialist and the communist parties across Europe in this period.[29]

However, the suggested path to social democracy was centred less on parliamentary representation than on 'professional representation'.[30] More concretely, from 1921, Svolos proposed an 'Economic Senate' that would be comprised equally of labour and capital and would have – unlike the predominantly consultative role of the Reich Economic Council in Weimar – a legislative role along with the parliament.[31] He considered this institutional form as necessary to oppose the impact of the bourgeoisie on the democratic state and to express 'in a more honest and authoritative way the wills of the society'.[32] It would dissolve the fiction of the general will and would adjust representation to the existing social reality of interwar organised capitalism that 'made inevitable the absorption of the individual to a social group'.[33] Parliamentary representation was considered as part and parcel of individualism – that is the 'ideological flag of liberalism' – because it was grounded in individual voters and on a free mandate and did not

21 Ibid., 84–88.

22 Ibid., 88.

23 Ibid., 167.

24 A. Svolos, *Η αναθεώρησις του Συντάγματος* (Η Θέμις, 1933), ιθ', κα'.

25 Ibid., κ'–κγ'. Svolos' argumentation seems quite similar to Heller's call for 'social Rechtsstaat' in H. Heller, 'Rechtsstaat oder Diktatur' (1987) 16 *Economy and Society* 141.

26 A. Svolos, *Le travail dans les constitutions contemporaines* (Librairie du Recueil Sirey, société anonyme, 1939), 22.

27 Svolos, *Το νέον Σύνταγμα*, 106–17. Kelsen referred approvingly to Lassalle, Cunow and Renner, among others. He took a favourable view of Renner's analysis according to whom the 'germ of socialism is to be found today in all the institutions of the capitalist state' and that the state is the 'lever to socialism'. H. Kelsen, 'Marx oder Lassalle' (1925) 11 *Archive für die Geschichte des Sozialismus und der Arbeiterbewegung* 261–98, especially 270–75. The affinities between Kelsen's political theory and the reformist side of Weimar social democracy have been demonstrated in N. Vagdoutis, 'Hans Kelsen and Carl Schmitt in Weimar: A Riddle of Political Constitutionalism', PhD thesis, University of Glasgow (2018), 226–32. See also C. Herrera, 'La théorie politique de Kelsen et le socialisme réformiste' (1998) 84 *ARSP: Archiv Für Rechts- Und Sozialphilosophie / Archives for Philosophy of Law and Social Philosophy* 195.

28 Lassalle had conceived the state as 'the big association of the poorer classes'. This phrase was cited approvingly by Kelsen in his 'Marx oder Lassalle', 293 and by Svolos, *Το νέον Σύνταγμα*, 116.

29 Svolos, *Το νέον Σύνταγμα*, 116–17.

30 Ibid., 195–203, 208–10.

31 Ibid.

32 Ibid., 166.

33 As Svolos argued, 'the new form of economic life made inevitable the absorption of the individual to a social group'. This new form comprised of 'trusts', 'cartels', 'professional and economic organizations', etc. Ibid., 128–31, 170.

conform to the existing social reality, which was comprised of 'economic and professional organizations'.[34] So, liberal parliamentarism did not adequately represent the social interests of the various social groups.

Svolos' suggestion for professional representation derived, therefore, from his analysis regarding the multi-class society and the dominance of the bourgeoisie on political representation in conditions of organised capitalism. As a result, he ended up arguing for a 'syndicalism' based on professional representation – under Duguit's influence – because this sort of syndicalism would, first, express in a more democratic way the various social interests that are concealed through the 'fiction' of a general will.[35] So, his argumentation aims at giving political expression to social pluralism. Second, his suggestion also indicated a corporatist–functional dimension since he argued that such an institutional form would achieve a substantive equilibrium among social forces.[36] It was, nevertheless, a 'societal'–democratic type of corporatism and not a 'state'–authoritarian one,[37] given Svolos' emphasis on the independence of unions from state power, on their 'voluntary participation' in the Economic Senate and on 'freedom of assembly'.[38] Hence, he opposed the 'dictatorial' *stato corporativo* that existed in Italy.[39] Moreover, his corporatism cannot be identified with Duguit's 'corporatist syndicalism'[40] because Svolos' notion of substantive equilibrium does not underplay social conflict – as Duguit's concept of social solidarity does.[41] Equilibrium instead emerges out of the prior expression of different class interests.[42] Besides, whereas Duguit despised class struggle, Svolos argued that professional representation is the explicit recognition of class struggle.[43] However, it remains unclear how professional representation – given its composition – could be combined with the aim of socialism that Svolos endorsed.

Finally, the material analysis of Svolos remained mainly at the sociological level, namely at the level of social reality that lies behind the formal democratic constitution, its principle of popular sovereignty and the institutions through which this principle is expressed. He neither discarded the normative character of the formal constitution nor attributed any normative character to social reality. His material understanding of the constitution is an explanatory study of the socio-political forces rather than a method for the interpretation of the constitution. Svolos' material analysis of the constitution was therefore different from those developed by

[34] Ibid.

[35] On this, Svolos followed Kelsen's and Duguit's deconstruction of the general will. Ibid., 83–88, 105.

[36] Ibid., 210, 331. He argued that professional representation would 'create … an entirely different form of democracy, which will be based … on a substantive equilibrium of social forces'.

[37] See Schmitter's typology of corporatism, in P. C. Schmitter, 'Still the Century of Corporatism?' (1974) 36 *The Review of Politics* 103.

[38] Svolos, *Το νέον Σύνταγμα*, 195–97.

[39] Ibid. See also Ploumidis, 'Corporatist Ideas in Inter-war Greece', 61.

[40] As Laborde described Duguit's theory. C. Laborde, *Pluralist Thought and the State in Britain and France, 1900–25* (Palgrave Macmillan, 2000), 101.

[41] As Laborde writes with regards to Duguit's theory, 'social solidarity was an 'efficient fiction' which underplayed social tension'. Ibid., 113.

[42] Svolos' thinking was closer to Duguit's corporatism during the early 1920s. This is visible in his preface to the translation of Duguit's *Le droit social, le droit individuel et la transformation de l'État* (1908), which is a book that Svolos had translated into Greek in 1923. In this preface, Svolos proposed an 'economic representation of the social classes', arguing that the organisation of the social classes should be based 'not on struggle and violence, as the Marxists wish' but 'on social solidarity'. A. Svolos, 'Πρόλογος' [Preface], in L. Duguit, *Το Κοινωνικόν Δίκαιον, το Ατομικόν Δίκαιον και η μεταμόρφωσις του Κράτους* (Ελευθερουδάκης, 1923), ii–iii. See also Ploumidis, 'Corporatist Ideas in Inter-war Greece', 74.

[43] Svolos, *Το νέον Σύνταγμα*, 197.

Smend and Mortati, according to which a normative function of the constitution is to integrate society.[44] In fact, Svolos' sociological approach indicated how the democratic constitution – and its principle of popular sovereignty – turns into a relatively sham constitution to the extent that it does not provide for a pluralist expression of antagonistic social interests. Hence, he argued for a change of the 1927 Greek constitution in the direction of creating an Economic Senate that would be entirely composed of representatives of professional organisations. Although he did not define in detail its competences, he insisted that it should have at least the same legislative role that the Senate already had under the 1927 Greek constitution.[45]

8.3 THE 'GUIDED DEMOCRACY' PERIOD AND ITS DIVERGENCE: FROM THE CRITIQUE OF A MATERIAL APPROACH OF THE CONSTITUTION TO ITS DEFENCE

After the end of the Greek civil war in the late 1940s, there was a regime of 'weak democracy' or 'guided democracy', namely 'the deeply original phenomenon of an authoritarian regime … built under the auspices of a democratically organized parliamentary state'.[46] During this period, and more specifically from 1952 until the colonels' dictatorship in 1967, there was a dual constitutional system. First, formal constitutional legality according to the 1952 Greek constitution. This constitution had a conservative character given that it established monarchical democracy (whereas the 1927 constitution was republican). However, it was not dictatorial and it also included politically liberal features to an extent, even though it is considered as a 'step backwards' from the liberal constitutional tradition that had existed in Greece since the 1864 constitution,[47] due to its 'ethnocentric ideological flavor'.[48] Secondly, there was also a parallel constitutional order in force – the 'para-constitution', as it came to be known.[49]

The para-constitution was comprised of constituent acts and parliamentary resolutions that were promulgated after the occupation and before the 1952 constitution, mostly during the civil war (1946–49).[50] These exceptional measures were imposed by the winners of the civil war and remained in effect after the 1952 constitution came into force due to a parliamentary resolution of 29 April 1952[51]. The significant point is that many of the measures that comprised the 'para-constitution' opposed the formal 1952 constitution. These measures entailed a severe restriction of civil rights and political liberties, such that '… the rights of free speech, free association and so on were enjoyed mainly by the non-communists, and particularly the *ethnikophrones* (those who

44 Smend, 'Constitution and Constitutional Law', 240.

45 Svolos, *Το νέον Σύνταγμα*, 209–10. The 1927 Greek constitution was the only Greek constitution during the twentieth century that established a Senate. However, only 18 out of the 120 Senate members were representatives of professional organisations. On the contrary, Svolos suggested that the Senate should be composed merely of such representatives. Regarding the Senate's competences under the 1927 Greek constitution, it had a legislative role, but the parliament prevailed in cases of disagreement. However, the Senate's consent was essential for a constitutional revision (Article 125). See Ploumidis, 'Corporatist Ideas in Inter-war Greece', 61. See also N. Alivizatos, *Το Σύνταγμα και οι εχθροί του* (Πόλις, 2011), 265

46 C. Tsoukalas, 'The Ideological Impact of the Civil War', in J. O. Iatrides (eds.), *Greece in the 1940s. A Nation in Crisis* (University Press of New England, 1981), 320.

47 This is argued by Alivizatos, *Το Σύνταγμα και οι εχθροί του*, 366–72.

48 I. Tassopoulos, 'The Golden Dawn Case: An Exercise in "Constitutional Dismemberment" and Constitutional Continuity', *Constitutional Change Blog* (2021), available at: www.constitutional-change.com/the-golden-dawn-case-an-exercise-in-constitutional-dismemberment-and-constitutional-continuity/, last accessed 21 July 2022.

49 N. Alivizatos, *Οι πολιτικοί θεσμοί σε κρίση: 1922–1974. Όψεις της ελληνικής εμπειρίας* (Θεμέλιο, 1983), 536–600.

50 Ibid., 536–42.

51 These measures were definitively abolished in 1975 (law 233/1975). Alivizatos, *Το Σύνταγμα και οι εχθροί του*, 499.

think "patriotically", who are "nationally-minded")'.[52] Moreover, thousands of communists were exiled to concentration camps. So, according to this dual constitutional system, there was, on the one hand, the 1952 Constitution and, on the other hand, the para-constitution that applied to the internal enemy, namely to those considered as non-*ethnikofrones*. The fact that the para-constitution was in force – even though it contravened the formal constitution that was supposed to be the source of the legal order – signified the 'dissolution of the distinction between the legal and the political sphere' as Drossos writes.[53]

This political and constitutional context is important in order to grasp the critique of a material understanding of the constitution offered by Aristovoulos Manessis (1922–2000),[54] who was an influential constitutional theorist during the post-civil war period. He criticised those approaches that 'in contrast with the legal definitions that are deemed "static" and … "formalistic" develop "dynamic" theories that define the substantive constitution in a way that will take into account the "living" and ever changing reality'.[55] Manessis' fear was that, through a distinction between formal and substantive constitution, there would be a dissolution of the distinction between the legal and the political sphere. This dissolution would undermine the formal constitution and would be advantageous at a political level for the rulers because they would have the power to interpret constitutional legality according to their own perception of the 'living' reality.[56]

On the basis of this analysis, Manessis opposed Smend's theory, according to which 'the constitution is the legal order of the state, or more precisely, of the life through which the state has its reality – namely of its integration process'.[57] In Smend's definition, the formal constitution is underplayed in favour of a vague 'ontological' concept of the constitution.[58] This is evidently indicated in Smend's phrase that the meaning of the constitution can change without being 'bound by the requirements of the development of a prescriptive law'.[59] Moreover, Manessis rejected Schmitt's 'positive concept' of the constitution as the 'complete decision over the type and form of the political unity'.[60] Schmitt had distinguished this positive concept of the constitution (named as 'Constitution') from the formal one (named as 'individual constitutional laws').[61] The former was based on 'the concrete existence of the politically unified people [and] is prior to every norm',[62] meaning that it prevailed over the latter.

According to Manessis, both Schmitt's and Smend's theories are based on 'ontological',[63] and, therefore, non-legal concepts of the constitution. On the contrary, Manessis argued that there is a 'political importance' in the formal constitution, which is the prevention of the arbitrariness of

[52] N. Mouzelis and G. Pagoulatos, 'Civil Society and Citizenship in Postwar Greece', in F. Birtek and T. Dragonas (eds.), *Citizenship and the Nation-State in Greece and Turkey* (Routledge, 2005), 88–89.

[53] Y. Drossos, *Δοκίμιο Ελληνικής Συνταγματικής Θεωρίας* (Εκδόσεις Αντ. Σάκκουλα, 1996), 371.

[54] Manessis held the chair of Constitutional Law at the Aristotle University of Thessaloniki in 1965. He was fired from his position during the dictatorship. Between 1970 and 1974 he taught Public Law at the University of Amiens in France. After the fall of the dictatorship, he taught again at the Aristotle University. In 1981 he became a Professor of Constitutional Law at the University of Athens.

[55] A. Manessis, *Αι εγγυήσεις τηρήσεως του Συντάγματος, τ. I'* (Το Νομικόν, 1956), 62.

[56] Ibid., 63.

[57] Smend, 'Constitution and Constitutional Law', 240.

[58] Manessis, *Αι εγγυήσεις τηρήσεως του Συντάγματος, τ. I*, 63.

[59] Smend, 'Constitution and Constitutional Law', 240. See Manessis, *Αι εγγυήσεις τηρήσεως του Συντάγματος,τ. I*, 63.

[60] C. Schmitt, *Constitutional Theory* [1928] (Duke University Press, 2008), 75.

[61] Ibid.

[62] Ibid., 166.

[63] Manessis, *Αι εγγυήσεις τηρήσεως του Συντάγματος,τ. I*, 64.

the rulers.[64] The political reason for this approach can be easily deduced: he tries, in this way, to defend constitutional legality as written in the 1952 Constitution against a concept of the constitution that would legitimise the para-constitution.

At the same time, Manessis was opposed to the Greek constitutional theorist George Daskalakis (1912–94), who was influenced by Smend's and Schmitt's concepts of the constitution. Daskalakis was one of the four *Habilitants* of Carl Schmitt during the period 1934–44 at the University of Berlin.[65] After he left Germany, Daskalakis became a Professor of Introduction to Public and Constitutional Law at Panteion University in Athens from 1943–81. Daskalakis developed an understanding of the constitution not solely as a legal text but as the medium of integration. Hence, he agreed with Smend's concept of the constitution as a system of integration,[66] arguing that the constitutional order 'appears as the medium of state and social integration. It tries to harmonize every moment and to adjust various contradictory tendencies and views, ideologies and interests, groups and people in the line of the whole . . .'.[67] Moreover, he suggested a concept of the constitution as 'The Plan of Plans', which would establish the fundamental aims that people will pursue.[68] These aims constitute the 'basic decisions – [this is where Schmitt's influence is also revealed] for the formation of the future social and economic structure of α people . . .'.[69]

Manessis showed that this concept has political ramifications. He emphasised that, for Daskalakis, the 'governmental directions and decisions for drawing up the [1949] long-term economic program for the economic recovery of Greece' – in the context of the 1948 European Recovery Program – had a 'constitutional content' that would bind not only the governments in power but also the parliament.[70] Daskalakis conceived the aims of this economic program as the 'economic constitution' of the country that is in effect for 'all the political parties and social classes'; it is a 'common national aim'.[71] He concludes that this program is the 'sine qua non element of the Constitution-Plan'.[72]

It becomes evident that Daskalakis' conception of the constitution attributes a normative character to a political and economic program. There is an ideological element here in that the conflictual social reality is elided through Daskalakis' argument that this program represents a 'common national aim'. So, through his material conception of the constitution, the people are presented as a homogeneous entity and the governmental plan prevails over the formal constitution (and, therefore, over the parliament's decisions).

In the light of the dual constitutional system that was in effect, Manessis justifiably rejected this concept. He argued that it would render the content of the formal constitution uncertain and, as a consequence, it would be not clear whether the activities of the state organs were in accordance with the constitution or not.[73] In this way, the rights of the ruled would be threatened. As a result, he held fast to his formalist approach.

[64] Ibid., 76–78.

[65] His unpublished Habilitation was examined by Schmitt himself and Emge in 1938. Reinhard Mehring, *Carl Schmitt: A Biography* (Polity Press, 2014), 331, 352.

[66] Smend, 'Constitution and Constitutional Law', 248.

[67] G. Daskalakis, 'Η αναθεώρησις του συντάγματος και το νόημα του συντακτικού έργου', in *Επιστημονική Επετηρίς της Ανωτάτης Σχολής Πολιτικών Επιστημών* 1949–50 (Πάντειος, 1950), 609–709, 687.

[68] Ibid., 681.

[69] Ibid., 682.

[70] Ibid., 683–84; Manessis, *Αι εγγυήσεις τηρήσεως του Συντάγματος,τ. I*, 64.

[71] Daskalakis, 'Η αναθεώρησις του συντάγματος', 684.

[72] Ibid., 684.

[73] Manessis, *Αι εγγυήσεις τηρήσεως του Συντάγματοςτ. I*, 65.

8.4 THE *METAPOLITEFSI* PERIOD: REVIVAL OF MATERIAL APPROACHES OF THE CONSTITUTION UNDER THE INFLUENCE OF POULANTZAS' STATE THEORY

The fall of the dictatorship in 1974 was followed by the *metapolitefsi*, as it came to be known (this term means, literally, regime change). In this period, Greek constitutional theorists explored not only how the constitution could guarantee the rights of the ruled – given that the para-constitution was no longer in effect – but also how the constitution relates to socio-political forces. Hence, there was a development of material approaches to the constitution, influenced by Poulantzas' state theory.

The first to attempt such an approach was Manessis. On the one hand, he continued to level critique against value-laden concepts of the constitution as 'system of values' or as an 'order of values' such as those developed in post-war Germany at a theoretical level and in the case law of *Bundesverfassungsgericht*.[74] He still opposed, therefore, the conflation between 'is' and 'ought' that he considered as the consequence of these value-laden theories to the extent that these values compose a 'value system' that differentiates itself from the formal constitution and prevails over the latter's normative character.[75] He thought that these theories have an 'ideological function' in that they 'attribute a substantive unity' in the constitution beyond its provisions.[76] In this way, they establish a 'transcendental legitimacy' that prevails over formal legality.[77] This undermines the normative character of the formal constitution and puts political liberties in danger.[78]

However, on the other hand, Manessis shifted from his formalist approach (that, as seen in Section 8.3, served a political purpose) to a material understanding of the constitution, without side-lining the formal constitution. This material understanding was developed at two levels: a sociological and a juristic one. Regarding the sociological level, he developed the idea of the constitution as the 'condensed legal expression of the relation of socio-political forces that exists at a given time in a given social formation'.[79] This meant the rejection of an instrumental view of the constitution – namely its conception as an instrument of an 'imposition' of the will of the rulers – and the adoption of a conception of the constitution as a 'field of socio-political antagonisms'.[80]

This materialist approach was influenced by Poulantzas' concept of the state as 'a strategic field' (instead of a 'monolithic bloc').[81] Namely, the state is considered neither as a 'thing–instrument' in the hands of the ruling class nor as an entity that is fully autonomous from class struggle.[82] It is the 'specific material condensation of a relationship of forces among classes and class fractions'.[83] Manessis, like Poulantzas, argued that 'the state will is neither identified necessarily ... with the will of the class that is dominant at the economic level nor ... of the

[74] These were based on the concept of 'free democratic basic order'. A. Manessis, *Συνταγματικό Δίκαιο I* (Σάκκουλας, 1980), 174–75.

[75] Ibid., 175.

[76] Ibid.

[77] Ibid.

[78] Ibid., 175–76.

[79] Ibid., 166.

[80] Ibid., 170.

[81] N. Poulantzas, *State, Power, Socialism* (Verso, 1980), 138.

[82] Ibid., 129.

[83] Ibid.

class that is dominant at the political level'.[84] Based on this, Manessis argued that contemporary constitutions 'usually express a compromise between opposing socio-political forces' and he referred to the Weimar constitution, the 1948 Italian constitution and the 1975 Greek constitution as examples.[85]

In terms of historical context, the 1975 Greek constitution does not seem at first glance to be a compromise constitution, given that, in contrast with the 1948 Italian constitution, it was voted merely by the deputies of New Democracy [Νέα Δημοκρατία], which had obtained 54.37% of the popular vote in the 1974 elections. The entire opposition abstained from voting because of its disagreement with the so-called super-prerogatives that the new Constitution allotted to the President of the Republic (e.g., he had the power to dissolve the parliament under certain circumstances).[86] Although these prerogatives were never used until the 1986 constitutional revision (in which they were significantly curtailed, almost cancelled), there was a widespread fear that they would be a 'hidden para-constitution' that would oppose the popular will.[87]

Despite that, this constitution was also shaped (to an extent) by the suggestions of the opposition parties.[88] This was evident from the fact that it definitely established parliamentary democracy and did not opt for a semi-presidential system, and mainly from its 'social-democratic inspired' section on economy seen especially in article 106 of the Constitution.[89] According to this article, '[par. 1] … the State shall plan and coordinate economic activity in the Country, aiming at safeguarding the economic development of all sectors of the national economy'. Moreover, the state can even nationalise enterprises under certain circumstances (par. 3–6). So, Manessis was not wrong to argue that this constitution was a compromise constitution, at least to an extent, in the sense that it expressed not only the will of New Democracy but a certain balance of forces.

Poulantzas' relational state theory 'allowed' Manessis to analyse the 1975 Greek constitution as a compromise constitution and, conversely, the content of this constitution fitted into his (influenced by Poulantzas) analysis of the constitution. Hence, although Manessis was also influenced by Svolos' theory – according to which the state will is usually determined by the social group that has economic power,[90] (see Section 8.2) – his sociological approach of the constitution is more relational.

At the same time, Manessis' analysis of the constitution captures the *dynamic relationship* between the living political reality and the formal constitution through his concept of 'constitutional reality'.[91] This is where his juristic account of the material constitution becomes visible. Constitutional reality, according to Manessis, is 'the real way in which the constitution is implemented, namely the real meaning that the constitution takes when implemented'.[92] This constitutional reality signifies, therefore, the 'dialectical unity between constitutional provisions and political reality'.[93] However, his material understanding of the constitution is quite reductive at this level in the sense that constitutional reality seems determined merely by

[84] Manessis, *Συνταγματικό Δίκαιο I*, 71–72.
[85] Ibid., 167–68.
[86] Alivizatos, *Το Σύνταγμα και οι εχθροί του*, 500.
[87] N. Alivizatos, 'Greek Constitutionalism and Patterns of Government', in K. Featherstone and D. Sotiropoulos (eds.), *The Oxford Handbook of Modern Greek Politics* (Oxford University Press, 2020), 112.
[88] Alivizatos, *Το Σύνταγμα και οι εχθροί του*, 500.
[89] Ibid., 501.
[90] Manessis, *Συνταγματικό Δίκαιο I*, 66.
[91] Ibid., 181.
[92] Ibid.
[93] Ibid., 182.

those who implement the constitution (legislature, administration, courts). As he writes, constitutional reality is political reality but 'as it functions regulated by the constitutional provisions and by their concretization that is made by the ordinary legislator, the administration and the courts'.[94] So, political parties, social movements and other factors (e.g., ideas) are not considered to be factors that could play a role in constitutional ordering.

The dialectical relation between political reality and constitutional norms is captured in a more developed way by Antonis Manitakis (b. 1944), a student of Manessis and his successor at the Chair of Constitutional Law in Thessaloniki.[95] He was the first to introduce Mortati's concept of the material constitution into Greek constitutional thought.[96] Manitakis himself developed a concept of the material constitution using the term 'real constitution', which is the term used by Ferdinand Lassalle. Lassalle was the first to distinguish between the 'real' and the 'formal' constitution. The real constitution is, according to Lassalle's definition, 'the relation of forces actually existing in the country'.[97] It is based on various forces (such as the head of state, the judiciary, the stock exchange, etc.) and it is clearly superior to the formal constitution that is considered a 'piece of paper'.[98] Lassalle's real constitution does not have any normative character (in contrast with Smend's, Schmitt's and Mortati's concepts); it is merely sociological. Moreover, his account of the constitutional order does not recognise the autonomy of the constitution. This is evident in his phrase that 'constitutional questions are not fundamentally questions of right, but questions of might'.[99] Hence, his concept of the constitution is 'overdetermined by politico-economic forces and dynamics'.[100]

Although Manitakis used the term 'real constitution', he understood the real constitution, on the one hand, in terms close to Mortati in that he conceived it not as an empirical fact but as having a normative force (unlike Lassalle). As he wrote, the real constitution 'expresses a complex of power relations and ideas that contains a normative force and belongs … to the sphere of "ought" and not to the sphere of "is"'.[101] The normative character of the real constitution is seen 'when the acts of the state institutions and of the people meet with the provisions of the formal constitution', producing in this way a 'normative force'.[102] So, Manitakis did not develop a merely sociological account of the material constitution. Moreover, similarly to Mortati, the real constitution is grounded in political forces and in their aims.

However, on the other hand, Manitakis' material understanding is also different in that he conceives Mortati's theory of the material constitution as leaning toward an 'instrumental' concept of the constitution.[103] Manitakis identifies Mortati's concept of the material constitution

[94] Ibid.

[95] Antonis Manitakis was appointed Professor of Constitutional Law at the Aristotle University of Thessaloniki in 1982 and he has been an Emeritus Professor since 2012.

[96] It was firstly introduced in his book A. Manitakis, *Συνταγματικό Δίκαιο, τ. Ι* (Σάκκουλας, 1987), 65–75. However, Manitakis' concept of the real constitution was more developed in his book A. Manitakis, *Ερμηνεία του Συντάγματος και λειτουργία του Πολιτεύματος* (Αντ. Σάκκουλας, 1996), 161–99.

[97] F. Lassalle, *On the Essence of Constitutions* (1862). Available at www.marxists.org/history/etol/newspape/fi/vol03/n001/lassalle.htm, last accessed 21 July 2022.

[98] Ibid.

[99] F. Lassalle, 'The Deliverers of the Constitution', in *Voices of Revolt, Vol. III: Speeches of Ferdinand Lassalle* (International Publishers, 1927), 40.

[100] M. Goldoni, 'Introduction to the Material Constitution: Traditions and Constitutive Elements', Legal Form (2018), available at: https://legalform.blog/2018/02/09/introduction-to-the-material-constitution-traditions-and-constitutive-elements-marco-goldoni/, last accessed 21 July 2022.

[101] Manitakis, *Ερμηνεία του Συντάγματος και λειτουργία του Πολιτεύματος*, 179–80.

[102] Ibid., 180.

[103] Ibid., 184.

with Carl Schmitt's positive concept of the constitution, considering them both as 'instrumental' because they understand the constitution as based on a fundamental will (in Schmitt's case) or on the aims of the dominant political forces[104] (in Mortati's case).[105] On the contrary, Manitakis seems to conceive the real constitution in more relational terms, which is also due to the influence of Poulantzas.

This becomes evident in Manitakis' argument that the real constitution cannot be identified merely with the fundamental aims of the dominant political forces but is also an outcome of social and political forces that are opposed to them. The oppositional forces have an impact both on the original content of constitutional provisions and on their meaning during their implementation.[106] Hence, he defined the real constitution as

> the complex of fundamental principles and rules that, regardless of whether they are explicitly written in the constitutional text or can be deduced from this latter, constitute at a given moment the substantive core of a particular legal order ... expressing aims or values of the dominant political and social forces or reflecting the resultant of values of antagonistic forces. This complex of principles and rules is in effect and is implemented because it conforms to a collective political and social consciousness that ... determines the real meaning of constitutional provisions ...[107]

Manitakis' notion of a collective political and social consciousness – which is central to his concept of the real constitution – is, therefore, not identified with the aims of the dominant political forces but also considers oppositional political forces and, crucially, social forces. These latter seem neglected in Manessis' concept of 'constitutional reality', due to his focus on those who implement the constitution.[108] They also seem marginalised in Mortati's concept of the material constitution due to his emphasis on political parties. Moreover, in contrast with Mortati, Manitakis' concept of the real constitution does not have an 'originalist' perspective, but a 'historical–evolutionary' one.[109] This is because the collective consciousness is not only determined by the aims and values of the political forces that were dominant during the 'constitution-making process' (as in Mortati's theory), but is formed in a dynamic process.[110] The main example that Manitakis gives concerns the inactivation of the presidential prerogatives during the decade 1975–85, due to the fact that the parliamentary forces never invoked these prerogatives, accepting in practice a monistic parliamentary system.[111] The 1986 constitutional revision 'ratified' at a formal level the existing real constitution.[112]

Manitakis' concept of the real constitution is ultimately not far from Lassalle's definition of the real constitution. But it is not limited to Lassalle's sociological conception. For Manitakis, the collective consciousness has an impact on the constitutional order only through the

104 Manitakis does not draw a distinction between Mortati's thought during the fascist period and his post–Second World War thought. In fact, he examined Mortati's post–Second World War version of the material constitution, according to which the material constitution is grounded in the aims of the dominant political forces. Ibid.

105 Ibid.

106 Ibid., 185–86.

107 Ibid., 198.

108 Ibid., 182.

109 C. Anthopoulos, 'Το Σύνταγμα πίσω από το Σύνταγμα: Ιστορία και Κριτική της Έννοιας του Πραγματικού Συντάγματος', in *Το Σύνταγμα εν Εξελίξει. Τιμητικός Τόμος για τον Αντώνη Μανιτάκη* (Σάκκουλας, 2019), 175–209, 188.

110 Ibid.

111 Manitakis, *Ερμηνεία του Συντάγματος και λειτουργία του Πολιτεύματος*, 170.

112 Ibid., 171.

'mediation' of the 'principles and rules of the [formal] constitution'.[113] So, the real constitution is not conceived as fully autonomous from the formal constitution. Otherwise, the normative force of the constitution would be undermined. This differentiates Manitakis' concept of the material constitution from theories that identify the constitution with political reality (such as Griffith's concept of the political constitution).[114]

8.5 CONCLUSION

It has been demonstrated that a material understanding of the constitution has developed in Greek constitutional thought since the interwar period, initially from a sociological perspective but later from a juristic perspective as well, especially during the *metapolitefsi*. Manitakis' concept of the material constitution has been the most sophisticated approach that has adopted such an understanding.[115] Its significance is that it captured as an object of juristic knowledge the dynamic relation between the formal constitution and the socio-political forces without concealing the element of social conflict that exists in modern, capitalist societies. Hence, his theory distinguishes itself from other conceptions of the material constitution that emphasised the consolidation of political unity (namely Smend's, Schmitt's and Mortati's conceptions).[116]

This conflictual element is important because, where it is elided, the material constitution runs the danger of playing an ideological function, concealing social conflict and opposing its political expression as it takes place through formal democratic constitutions (such as the Weimar constitution that guaranteed a certain political expression of social conflict). In this way, it would legitimise authoritarian transformations of the constitutional order by a ruling political force at any moment in the name of a substantive political unity. For instance, Schmitt's theory of the constitution legitimised the transformation of the Weimar constitutional order from a parliamentary to a presidential regime in the early 1930s.[117] This is the main reason why Greek constitutional theory – and notably Manessis, with Manitakis to a lesser extent – has been relatively cautious about a material understanding of the constitution. In light of the para-constitution that was instrumentalised in Greece during the post-civil war period, the fear remains that the concept of the material constitution may be used to justify departure from formal constitutional norms.

[113] As Manitakis argued, the real constitution is 'neither a hyper-constitution . . . nor a para-constitution but [is] the living voice . . . and the condensed expression of the principles and rules that are included anyway in the formal constitution'. Ibid., 180, 188.

[114] Ibid., 181. According to Griffith, 'the constitution is no more and no less than what happens'. See J. A. G. Griffith, 'The Political Constitution' (1979) 42 *Modern Law Review* 1, 19.

[115] During the last years, Manitakis seems to have set aside this concept of the material constitution. Analysing the constitutional aspects of the Greek financial crisis, he has adopted instead the notion of 'adaptability', arguing that the Greek constitutional order proved to be 'resilient' during the crisis due to its 'adaptability to both the multiple demands of the European integration process and the "real" coercive forces of the globalized market economy'. See more in his article Manitakis, 'The Impressive Resilience of the Greek Constitution in the Current Financial Crisis in Europe', in L. Papadopoulou, I. Pernice and J. Weiler (eds.), *Legitimacy Issues of the European Union in the Face of Crisis, Dimitris Tsatsos in Memoriam* (Nomos, 2017), 217–30. See also Anthopoulos, 'Το Σύνταγμα πίσω από το Σύνταγμα', 194.

[116] However, as Loughlin shows, 'Mortati criticized both the decisionist theory of Schmitt and Smend's communitarian theory, in each case claiming that such theories are unable to maintain stability: The former because it highlights the necessity of decision without institutional constraint, and the latter because "the people" as an existential entity are riven by conflict and can never form a homogeneous group'. M. Loughlin, *Foundations of Public Law* (Oxford University Press, 2010), 397. See also La Torre, 'German Impact', 310–11.

[117] Vagdoutis, 'Hans Kelsen and Carl Schmitt in Weimar', 129–212. This is also argued in M. Wilkinson, *Authoritarian Liberalism and the Transformation of Modern Europe* (Oxford University Press, 2021).

9

The Constitution As Social Compromise

Hybrid Constitutionalisation and the Legacy of Wolfgang Abendroth

Kolja Möller

In the post-war era, constitutional theorist Wolfgang Abendroth elaborated a sophisticated approach to the democratic constitution as a social 'compromise'.[1] He argued that the German Basic Law (*Grundgesetz*) did not constitutionalise either a liberal-capitalist or a socialist order but instead transferred these issues to democratic decision-making. Abendroth mainly drew on Articles 20 and 28 which defined the *Bundesrepublik* as a 'democratic and social federal state' and ascribed constituent power to the people ('All state authority is derived from the people'). To Abendroth, these articles represented a clear commitment to the welfare state as a 'structural principle of constitutional law'[2] which emanated from a class compromise between organised labour and the ruling class. The result was an open situation in which the existing social order remained at the disposal of democratic will-formation. In the words of Abendroth, the 'societal and economic order is subjugated to being shaped by those organs which represent the self-determination of the people'.[3] In bringing this interpretation of the Basic Law to the fore, Abendroth participated in foundational constitutional conflicts in post-war Germany.

A left-leaning legal scholar, Abendroth assumed a chair of political science at the University of Marburg in the 1950s. Previously – from the 1920s to the 1940s – he had been a public intellectual and political activist, socialised in the 'middle-currents' of the Weimar republic's workers movement – most notably the 'Communist Party Opposition' (KPO) which aimed at establishing pro-democratic united front policies between the social-democrats and the communists. He was incarcerated from 1937 to 1941 and then, at the end of the Second World War, fought against fascism as a partisan in Greece.

In the 1950s, Abendroth became famous through his controversy with Ernst Forsthoff, a disciple of Carl Schmitt. Forsthoff, in contrast to Abendroth, interpreted the *Grundgesetz* as a liberal rule of law constitution which did not have a 'specific social content'.[4] Forsthoff argued that the 'social norms' should be seen as 'programmatic sentences'. He denied their legal status by arguing that they are located in the 'forecourt of current constitutional law'.[5] Abendroth

[1] W. Abendroth, 'Zum Begriff des demokratischen und sozialen Rechtsstaates im Grundgesetz der Bundesrepublik Deutschland (1954)', in M. Buckmiller, J. Perels and U. Schöler (eds.), *Gesammelte Schriften Band 2* (Offizin, 2008), 354.

[2] Ibid., 339.

[3] Ibid., 341.

[4] E. Forsthoff, 'Begriff und Wesen des sozialen Rechtsstaats (1954)', in E. Forsthoff (ed.), *Rechtsstaatlichkeit und Sozialstaatlichkeit* (Wiss. Buchgesellschaft, 1968), 185.

[5] Ibid., 169.

emerged in a difficult position: though he was initially elected to the board of the *Vereinigung deutscher Staatsrechtslehrer*, the conservative members refused to hear his 1953 report on the 'Concept and essence of the social constitutional state'. While Forsthoff could enter the stage to make his case, Abendroth was subsequently marginalised. However, in the long run, his approach appeared to score some late victories: in recent judgements on social benefits, the Federal Constitutional Courts partly adhered to Abendroth's position. It interpreted the welfare state as a constitutional principle which commits political legislation to guarantee 'material preconditions' for 'participation in societal, cultural and cultural affairs'.[6] And only recently, echoing Abendroth's claim that the economic sphere is open to societal intervention, it obliged the state to safeguard 'life and health' against the 'threats from climate change' and to engage in 'internationally oriented action in favor of global protection of climate' in order to achieve the 1.5°C target of global warming.[7]

In this chapter, the contribution reconstructs Abendroth's approach to the constitution as social compromise, clarifies its historical background and asks for its potential with regard to current challenges of constitutionalisation. In Section 9.1, it will be demonstrated how the concept of 'balance of social forces' was used in the context of the labour movement in Austria and Germany in order to approach constitutional issues. This is expanded in Section 9.2, where the contribution turns to an investigation of Abendroth's theory of social compromise. In Section 9.3, it is argued that this approach can make sense of the subsequent evolution of constitutionalism and international law after the Second World War. However, its main weakness consists in the focus on the central role of industrial labour within social conflicts: the constitutional compromises were often affected or even shifted by unforeseen agents of change which exceeded the sphere of blue-collar workers. Finally, Section 9.4 addresses how Abendroth's approach can be used in order to refine current attempts to re-establish a 'balance of social forces' through either hybrid constitutionalisation (sociological constitutionalism) or counter-institutions (plebeian constitutionalism).

9.1 THE BALANCE OF SOCIAL FORCES

Abendroth's approach relied on long-standing background assumptions about the relationship between constitutional forms and social structures. It is important to recall that the theoretical debates in the labour movement of the 1920s and 1930s foreshadowed his theory of constitutional compromise.[8] In the aftermath of the revolutions in 1918, new constitutions had been established in Germany and Austria. The labour movement participated in the constitution-making processes and was successful in establishing social rights and economic co-determination.[9] However, there was lively discussion about how to make sense of these new arrangements.

In the Austrian case, the social-democrats Hans Kelsen and Karl Renner, who both took part in drafting the constitutional document, interpreted the constitution from a basically proceduralist perspective. To them, the advent of parliamentary legislation provided the framework for a dynamic interplay of government and opposition and this had to be seen as the prime ground for

[6] BVerfG, Urteil des Ersten Senats, 9 February 2010.

[7] BVerfG, Beschluss des Ersten Senats, 24 March 2021.

[8] For a genealogy of the discussion on the *Rechtsstaat*, see C. Maier, 'The Weimar Origins of the Westgerman Rechtsstaat, 1919–1969' (2019) 62 *The Historical Journal* 1069.

[9] For an overview see R. Dukes, *The Labour Constitution: The Enduring Idea of Labour Law* (Oxford University Press, 2014), 36 ff.

social democratic action.[10] The leader of the Austrian Social Democratic Party and intellectual Otto Bauer took a slightly different stance and reconstructed the constitution as emanating from a 'balance of class forces'.[11] Thus, the constitution must be seen as depending on a social substrate, namely the balance between the labour movement and the ruling class in which 'neither the bourgeoisie nor the proletariat is able to dominate the state'.[12] In the Austrian case, the social democrats had renounced the introduction of socialism through civil war and abided by a strategy of defensive violence.[13] According to Bauer, the constitution of 1920 reflected an undecided and open status of societal development which was committed neither to liberal capitalism nor to socialism.

In Germany, critical constitutional thought echoed Bauer's approach with regard to the Weimar constitution: the critical legal theorist Franz L. Neumann, a member of the first generation of the Frankfurt School, used the notion of *soziale Rechtsstaat* in his constitutional interpretation and highlighted its progressive character.[14] Otto Kirchheimer, another important figure of the early *Institut for Sozialforschung*, argued that the 'precondition of formal democracy' consists in 'an approximate balance of classes in their struggle'.[15] He observed that, within the emerging executive of the Weimar Republic, a 'sphere of direction' (attached to the ruling class) confronted 'a sphere of distribution' in the administration of social and economic affairs.[16]

Widespread reliance on the notion of a 'balance of social forces' was not accidental. Friedrich Engels already utilised this notion in his meditations on historical evolution. He modified unidirectional schemes of development by arguing that there are long periods 'when the warring classes are so nearly equal in force that the state power, as apparent mediator, acquires for the moment a certain independence in relation to both'.[17] Admittedly, the transfer of these motifs to constitutional thought, as endorsed by Bauer, Kirchheimer, Neumann and – later – Abendroth, was controversial. It was discussed and attacked both by more formal approaches to the constitution as well as by the radical left, which saw every constitution under the sway of bourgeois rule. However, it was the starting point for a distinct approach to constitutionalism which embraced a decisive strategic option: if the constitution brings a compromise to the fore, a 'double strategy' is plausible which aims at shifting the balance of class forces in the shadow of a consciously endorsed constitutional compromise.[18] The hope was that the compromise could

[10] Karl Renner, who is now mainly known for his path-breaking works on the public dimension of private law, considered state and law to be 'technical means' which could be employed for a vast range of ends, see: K. Renner, 'Probleme des Marxismus (1916)', in H. Sandkühler and R. De La Vega (eds.), *Austromarxismus: Texte zu "Ideologie und Klassenkampf"* (Europäische Verlagsanstalt, 1970), 296; see, in a similar vein, H. Kelsen, *Sozialismus und Staat: Eine Untersuchung der politischen Theorie des Marxismus* [1920] (Wiener Volksbuchhandlung, 1965), 170 ff.

[11] O. Bauer, 'Das Gleichgewicht der Klassenkräfte (1924)', in H. Sandkühler and R. De La Vega (eds.), *Austromarxismus: Texte zu "Ideologie und Klassenkampf"* (Europäische Verlagsanstalt, 1970), 79–97.

[12] Ibid., 79; see also Kelsen's critique of Bauer: H. Kelsen, 'Otto Bauers politische Theorien (1924)', in G. Mozetic (ed.), *Austromarxistische Positionen* (Hermann Böhlaus Nachf., 1983), 212; on the debate in general, A. Scott, 'Introduction to the Kelsen–Bauer Debate on Marxist State Theory and the Equilibrium of Class Forces' (2021) *Thesis Eleven* 72.

[13] See the reflections in O. Bauer, *The Austrian Revolution* (L. Parsons, 1925).

[14] F. L. Neumann, 'Die soziale Bedeutung der Grundrechte in der Weimarer Verfassung (1930)', in F. L. Neumann (ed.), *Wirtschaft, Staat, Demokratie: Aufsätze, 1930–1954* (Suhrkamp, 1978), 68 ff.

[15] O. Kirchheimer, 'Zur Staatslehre von Sozialismus und Bolschewismus', in W. Luthardt (ed.), *Von der Weimerer Republik zum Faschismus: Die Auflösung der demokratischen Rechtsordnung* (Suhrkamp, 1976), 35.

[16] O. Kirchheimer, 'Weimar und was dann? Entstehung und Gegenwart der Weimarer Verfassung (1930)', in O. Kirchheimer (ed.), *Politik und Verfassung* (Suhrkamp, 1964), 47.

[17] F. Engels, 'Der Ursprung der Familie, des Privateigentums und des Staats (1884)', in K. Marx and F. Engels (eds.), *Werke Band 21* (Dietz-Verlag, 1975), 167 f.

[18] See K. Möller, 'The Red Polybius: Otto Bauer's Theory of the Democratic Republic' (2017) 27 *Studies in Social and Political Thought* 76.

foster a 'socialist democracy as a form of organization for a classless socialist society' founded 'on the regulative idea of a society of free-willing humans (. . .)'.[19] Instead of abiding by either purely reformist-institutional or by radical extra-institutional politics, it would be necessary to combine both in an intelligent manner. On these grounds, theorists such as Bauer, Neumann or Kirchheimer could envisage a peaceful transformation of society in the long-run without risking potentially self-destructive civil-war scenarios.[20]

In the late 1920s, this approach was also adopted in order to make sense of the fascist surge. Most prominently, Karl Marx's analysis of French Bonapartism was rediscovered.[21] In his text on the '18th Brumaire of Louis Bonaparte', Marx had investigated how the precarious balance of social classes and power blocs in the revolutionary process in 1848 France opened the window of opportunity for an authoritarian movement under the leadership of Louis Bonaparte, which toppled the parliamentary constitution. Taking up these insights, critical constitutional thought casted fascism as a lingering counter-possibility in the background of democratic constitutions, since the balance of class forces could also be shifted in a regressive direction. Reform need not necessarily pave the way for peaceful transformation, but also for regressive takeover which could – as was the case in Fascism – destroy constitutionality as such.

Initially, Abendroth was having some reservations toward the reformist penchants of the Austro-Marxist movement[22] and became involved in the circles of an oppositional communist current in the late 1920s. He started as a member of the communist party's youth branch and, later, belonged to the current which criticised the ultra-leftist orientation of the party leadership and its endorsement of the so-called theory of social-fascism from 1928 onward.[23] It considered the social-democrats and established trade-unions as opponents. They were not seen as potential partners in a united front strategy anymore. The foundation of the Communist Party Opposition (KPO) in 1928 was a reaction to these tendencies. Subsequently, its adherents were excluded from the party. Being led by influential figures such as Heinrich Brandler and August Thalheimer, the KPO members tried to initiate broad coalitions between social democrats, communists and the trade-unions in the late Weimar Republic.[24] One of the KPO's defining characteristics was the fact that it drew heavily on a reinvigorated variant of Marx's theory of Bonapartism. Accordingly, both a possible socialist transformation as well as the defeat of fascism had to rely on a united front approach of the labour movement. The main task consisted in neutralising the fascist threat, neither through a mild constitutional patriotism which renounced

[19] O. Bauer, 'Demokratie und Sozialismus (1934)', in H. Sandkühler and R. De La Vega (eds.), *Austromarxismus: Texte zu "Ideologie und Klassenkampf"* (Europäische Verlagsanstalt, 1970), 113.

[20] Admittedly, Neumann refrained from his optimism in the early 1930s, see C. Offe, 'The Problem of Social Power in Franz L. Neumann's Thought' (2003) 10 *Constellations* 211.

[21] A. Thalheimer, 'Über den Faschismus (1928)', in W. Abendroth (ed.), *Faschismus und Kapitalismus: Theorie über die sozialen Ursprünge und die Funktion des Faschismus* (Europäische Verlagsanstalt, 1972), 19–38; M. Kitchen, 'August Thalheimer's Theory of Fascism' (1973) 34 *Journal of the History of Ideas* 67; see also Marx's classical text: K. Marx, 'Der 18. Brumaire des Louis Bonaparte (1852)', in K. Marx and F. Engels (eds.), *Werke Band* 8 (Dietz-Verlag, 1972), 111–207.

[22] Cf. the reservations in W. Abendroth, 'Das Programm der Austromarxisten (1926)', in M. Buckmiller, J. Perels and U. Schöler (eds.), *Gesammelte Schriften Band* 1 (Offizin-Verlag, 2008), 37–41.

[23] Cf. Abendroth's autobiographical reflections: W. Abendroth, *Ein Leben in der Arbeiterbewegung* (Suhrkamp, 1976), 78 ff. See also A. Diers, *Arbeiterbewegung – Demokratie – Staat. Wolfgang Abendroth: Leben und Werk 1906–1948* (VSA Verlag, 2006), 209 ff.

[24] Such a split could also be observed in the social-democratic camp: In 1931, a left current with a united front approach split from the SPD and founded the Social Democratic Labour Party (SAPD) – among its members was the later chancellor Willy Brandt.

transformative ambitions, nor through voluntaristic mass action, but by combining the defence of existing achievements with the quest for social transformation.

9.2 ABENDROTH'S THEORY OF CONSTITUTIONAL COMPROMISE

After being imprisoned and then having fought in Greece as partisan, Abendroth returned to Germany and was working as a professor at the Universities of Leipzig and Jena. However, he was critical of the repressive politics of Eastern authorities and finally 'fled' back to Frankfurt in 1948.[25] From 1950 onward, he received a professorship at the University of Marburg and took an active part in the establishment of political and legal sciences in post-war Germany.[26] In order to make sense of the constitutional order of the *Grundgesetz*, he renewed his lines of thought from the 1920s and 1930s. In a systematic sense, his notion of constitutional compromise can be reconstructed as a (1) norm-compromise which relies on specific notions of (2) constituent power and of (3) social transformation.

9.2.1 *Norm-Compromise*

In a first step, Abendroth reconstructed central articles of the *Grundgesetz* as norm-compromises. In his perspective, Article 20, which stipulates that the *Bundesrepublik* is a 'democratic and social federal state', combines liberal rights with welfare state principles. This, again, is emphasised in Article 28 where 'principles of a republican, democratic and social state governed by the rule of law' are invoked. Further, Article 20 ascribes constituent power to the people ('All state authority is derived from the people') and Article 14 allows for legislative interventions in private property relations, even through expropriation: '(2) Property entails obligations. Its use shall also serve the public good. (3) Expropriation shall only be permissible for the public good.' To Abendroth, these norms must be seen as compromises which open up the societal order to re-negotiation. The 'social and economic order' lays at the 'disposition of democratic will-formation of the people'.[27] Further, the norm-compromise extended to the role of mass parties and free trade unions (Art. 21). The constitutional acknowledgement of such mass organisations indicated that the relationship between society and the state should be arranged as vertically, where 'society' assumes constituent power over constituted organs. Abendroth was well aware that this was a counterfactual assumption and one which was regularly undermined; foremost in capitalist societies, where the state performs important functional tasks in safeguarding property relations. However, he saw parties and trade-unions as collective agents which could inhibit these tendencies. In the long run, these counter-powers should be able to transform society from within the constitutional framework: 'The *Grundgesetz* takes a long period into account where existing society is converted to social democracy and has, therefore, opened up the constitutional-legal possibility for continual intervention in the order of property relations.'[28]

[25] Diers, *Arbeiterbewegung – Demokratie – Staat*, 474 ff.

[26] In Marburg, he was the founder of a critical scholarship tradition: cf. L. Peter, *Marx on Campus: A Short History of the Marburg School* (Brill, 2019). Abendroth was *inter alia* the supervisor of Jürgen Habermas 'Habilitations'-thesis 'On the Structural Transformation of the Public Sphere' in 1961. In the Frankfurt circles of the *Institut für Sozialforschung*, Max Horkheimer considered Habermas to be politically too much on the left. This is why Habermas finally transferred his Habilitations-procedure to Marburg.

[27] Abendroth, 'Zum Begriff des demokratischen und sozialen Rechtstaates', 346.

[28] Ibid., 345.

9.2.2 Constituent Power and Background Conditions

The constitutional compromise, however, was not only a norm compromise. It had to be seen as a coupling of social forces and a determination of their respective intercourse in society. One can make sense of it as the coupling of two processes of constitutionalisation. The first is the constitutionalisation of norm-compromise in the written constitution. But it relies on a second process of constitutionalisation in the societal sphere. Here, the self-constitutionalisation of parties and trade-unions is decisive because it creates the conditions of possibility for the compromise and is necessary in order to subsequently maintain it.[29] In that regard, Abendroth's work echoes the theory of Bonapartism mentioned in Section 9.1: as the ruling classes tend to introduce authoritarian answers in response to recurring crises and social inequality, the self-constitutionalisation of subaltern powers is a necessary prerequisite for neutralising these dynamics. Abendroth started from the assumption that 'either the formal democracy of state institutions extends to the social democracy of society (…) or the economic power-holders of partial interests in society strip off the democratic form of political organisation (…) and leave the liberal tradition behind'.[30] Large groups of society will be intrigued by 'irrational actions and movements with a decisionistic character' which are instigated by 'parts of the economic ruling classes'.[31]

Abendroth's approach diverges from corporatist constitutionalism: trade-Unions and labour parties not only advance the particular interests of members and voters related to the economy, they also assume a universalist role in establishing the constitution and defending it against authoritarian takeovers. They must be seen as the 'natural guardians of democracy'.[32] The densest expression of this argument can be identified in Abendroth's thoughts on the right to strike. To him, strike activities do not only revolve around the particular interests of employees, but bring to the fore that the 'workers represent with their interests at the same time the general interest of democracy (…)'.[33] Hence, the 'democratic character' of a 'formally democratised parliamentary system' hinges upon 'forces' which are themselves 'democratic' and are, in particular, 'eager to defend the democratic content and the democratic structural elements of the formal constitution' by 'extra-parliamentary' action.[34]

From the perspective of the distinction between *pouvoir constituant* and *pouvoir constitué*, one has to start from the assumption that constituent power is mainly located in the second process of self-constitutionalisation – it is here that the social substrate can be found which either prevents democracy from being undermined by authoritarian takeovers or induces the social energy which pushes for societal transformation. It is important to note that, in order to play out as constituent power, parties and trade-unions must demonstrate a certain autonomy vis-a-vis the constituted norm-compromise: strikes and autonomous activities which not only address the corporate sphere but the social whole are vital as they set the interplay of constituent and constituted powers in motion. Most importantly, they remind the constituted organs and ruling

[29] W. Abendroth, 'Demokratie als Institution und Aufgabe (1954)', in M. Buckmiller, J. Perels and U. Schöler (eds.), *Gesammelte Schriften Band 2* (Offizin, 2008), 412 ff.

[30] W. Abendroth, 'Zur Funktion der Gewerkschaften in der westdeutschen Demokratie (1952)', in M. Buckmiller, J. Perels and U. Schöler (eds.), *Gesammelte Schriften Band 2* (Offizin, 2008), 222.

[31] W. Abendroth, 'Die politische Wissenschaft unter dem besonderen Gesichtspunkt der Staatslehre (1952)', in M. Buckmiller, J. Perels and U. Schöler (eds.), *Gesammelte Schriften Band 2* (Offizin, 2008), 218.

[32] Abendroth, 'Zur Funktion der Gewerkschaften', 229.

[33] W. Abendroth, 'Der Kampf um das Streikrecht (1953)', in M. Buckmiller, J. Perels and U. Schöler (eds.), *Gesammelte Schriften Band 2* (Offizin, 2008), 310.

[34] Abendroth, 'Demokratie als Institution und Aufgabe (1954)', 413.

classes that not only reformist, but also radical change remains a possibility. Hence, the role of unions and mass parties cannot be restricted to democratic deliberation in society. Their role is also to provide forceful background conditions understood in terms of latent but available courses of action which influence the calculus of decision-making in strategic interaction. Constituent power is not only a matter of democratic legitimation, but also of substantive and transformative options which threaten to disempower the constituted organs and elites.

9.2.3 *Social Transformation*

While in the 1920s the young Abendroth was still hesitant with regard to the Austro-Marxist strategy of peaceful transformation, he revived this tradition in the 1950s. Starting out from the norm-compromise (1) and extending it to a conception of constituent power (2), Abendroth also addressed the pertinent challenge of social transformation (3). The role of constituent power was not restricted in his account merely to correcting constituted powers and, thereby, to conserving the social compromise. He hinted at the possibility of an encompassing social transformation as well. A revolution in the literal sense, which changes power and property relations, can be pursued from within the framework of the constitutional compromise. Accordingly, the hierarchy between constituted powers of the state and constituent powers could be reversed without suspending the constitution:

> In the hands of the workers, political democracy can be expanded to a social democracy through changes in the legal order, through the systematic transmission of the principle of democratic equality and democratic will-formation to economy and society by law, where the state loses its repressive character and transforms itself into the common self-management (*Selbstverwaltung*) of the social process.[35]

In sum, Abendroth's theory of constitutional compromise re-located notions of democracy, constituent power and revolution by connecting them to the structure of capitalist societies. Most importantly, Abendroth argued that state, society and the capitalist economy are constituting different social spheres.[36] Taking up the Marxist legacy, he started from the assumption that these spheres are functionally connected to each other since only their interplay can provide for societal regulation by – at the same time – being crisis-ridden through internal contradictions. Abendroth took a nuanced stance: on the one hand, he was clear that typical affinities between the state apparatus and the ruling class constitute an obstacle to the social transformation he envisaged. However, on the other, he saw the constitutional nexus as a fertile ground for subaltern social forces to re-enter the circuits of rule and to fundamentally transform them.

9.3 THE EVOLUTION OF SOCIAL COMPROMISE: FROM INTERNATIONAL LAW TO NEOLIBERAL CONSTITUTIONALISM

It needs to be acknowledged that Abendroth elaborated his constitutional theory in the age of industrial capitalism. The decisive class divide, for Abendroth, was located in the industrial

[35] This is how Abendroth envisaged the aims of the social democratic party in his alternative proposal to the SPD's Godesberger Programm from 1959: W. Abendroth, *Antagonistische Gesellschaft und politische Demokratie* (Luchterhand, 1967), 414.

[36] Cf. how Abendroth stressed the contradiction between constitutional law and economic powers, in W. Abendroth, 'Aufgaben einer deutschen Linken (1963)', in M. Buckmiller (ed.), *Gesammelte Schriften* (Offizin, 2013), 520 ff.

sphere and was articulated by strong labour parties and trade-unions with mass membership. Though he published selective attempts to transfer his approach to European integration and international law,[37] he took the nation-state as the central unit of constitutionalisation. However, it is possible to generalise some of his assumptions and make fruitful use of them when it comes to reconstructing the evolution of constitutional compromises. In the post-war era, being influenced by Roosevelt's 'New Deal' in the United States and anti-fascist popular front approaches, constitutional orders were committed to both civil *and* social rights and kept the question of whether the societal order is liberal-capitalist or socialist open.[38] This is true for post-war constitutions in Western Europe as well as for international law and the foundation of the United Nations. They were characterised precisely by the compromise that Abendroth investigated.

However, Abendroth's theory tends to be too static to trace the evolution of these compromises because it resurrects an enduring 'war of position' (Gramsci) between organised industrial labour and the ruling classes. As the subsequent development of constitutional compromises demonstrates, the overall approach has to be reformulated in more dynamic terms: modern societies are capitalist societies. But capitalist societies are – as already observed by Marx – functionally differentiated: They establish an interplay of different social systems, most notably the economy, politics and law. In this interplay, each system reproduces itself in a self-referential and dynamic manner. Not least, the political and legal system are formally detached from the economy.[39] However, in this ensemble the capitalist economy exerts a structural dominance as law and the political state are configured in a way that guarantees the self-reinforcing process of capital accumulation. Since social systems (re)-produce their own contradictions between dominant and subaltern social forces, antagonistic conflicts spread beyond the industrial sphere and the capital/labour divide. The 'causal nexus of functional differentiation and class struggle, of functional disorder and legitimization crisis' is not reducible to the economic sphere, rather 'one should take the conflict of capital and labour as a paradigm case for the critical analysis of other functional spheres of modern society'.[40]

Admittedly, the appeal of 'class' as a category stemmed not only from highlighting economic domination, but from determining a societal force which is able to lever the blockades of social evolution through its functional role within industrial production. However, historically, other well-organised social groups and labouring classes established effective alliances which transformed the course of social evolution by drawing on contradictions such as those between the global north and the global south or between men and women. Following these insights, there is a compelling case to re-specify the notion of class in terms of subaltern social forces. This dynamisation can be observed in the subsequent evolution of constitutional compromise from the 1960s onward. In western societies of that period not only blue-collar workers, but civil rights and black power movements, student groups, feminists and new working classes were able to instigate a democratisation of society. They challenged dominating structures in families, schools, companies and political institutions and paved the way for a radical reformism: the

[37] See, for an overview, A. Fischer-Lescano and G. Stuby, 'Wolfgang Abendroth und das Völkerrecht', in A. Fischer-Lescano, J. Perels and S. Thilo (eds.), *Der Staat der Klassengesellschaft: Rechts- und Sozialstaatlichkeit bei Wolfgang Abendroth* (Nomos, 2012), 237–56.

[38] See H. Brunkhorst, *Critical Theory of Legal Revolutions* (Bloomsbury Academic, 2014), 83 ff.; S. Kott, *Organiser le monde: Une autre histoire de la guerre froide* (Seuil, 2021), 35 ff.

[39] See the differentiation of 'organised forms' in law, politics and the economy in Marx early writings: K. Marx, 'Kritik des Hegelschen Staatsrechts (1843)', in *Marx-Engels-Werke Band 1* (Dietz-Verlag, 1972), 232.

[40] Brunkhorst, *Critical Theory of Legal Revolutions*, 76.

balance of forces was not unilaterally changed in favour of industrial labour, as envisaged by Abendroth. Rather, a more pluralistic scenery of social conflict could be observed. Nevertheless, in many countries, substantive shifts toward democratisation in fields such as the educational systems, the family and the economy took place and a strengthened bargaining power of trade-unions was emerging. Even the radical groups could be considered as playing a vital role for this shift. They provided the necessary background scenarios which threatened existing office-holders, and, at least in part, created windows of opportunity for progressive reformers.[41]

It is worth noting that the evolution of constitutional compromises extended to international law as well. The two covenants on civil rights and political rights and economic, social and cultural rights from 1966 reflected the balance between liberalism and socialism. But, again, the compromise was shifted from an unexpected direction. The successes of anti-colonial national liberation movements, which aimed for self-determination at a distance from both western capitalism and real-existing socialism, transformed the scene. Though pursuing different national pathways, the countries of the global south established international coordination with a view to effectuate changes in world politics, most notably against the attempt of powerful nations to exert dominance through foreign military interventions, economic exploitation and neo-colonial dependencies.[42]

Countries in the global south engaged in a constitutional politics in the vein suggested by Abendroth and combined an institutional strategy with a quest for social transformation. The so-called non-aligned countries had established the United Nations Conference on Trade and Development (UNCTAD) in 1964 and organised themselves as the 'Group of 77'. The group was able to constitute a majority in the UN's General Assembly. It pushed the resolution on a 'New Economic International Order' in 1974 which aimed at dissolving the dominance of former colonial powers and establishing more sustainable pathways of economic development.[43] It made constructive use of the UN General Assembly, constructed its own institutions and brought its own interpretation of international law to the fore. However, the Group of 77 conceived of itself as representing the world's masses and dispossessed and, thus, as constituent power against the former colonial countries. The NIEO resolution stated: 'The developing countries which constitute 70 per cent of the world's population, account only for 30 per cent of the world's income. It has proved impossible to achieve an even balanced development of the international community under the existing international economic order.'[44] An influential figure of the non-aligned bloc, the international lawyer Mohammed Bedjaoui, saw the movement as a forerunner of the whole world community by proposing a 'new world-wide legal, economic and political order, based on the integrated development of the whole earth and on the right to progress of all peoples'.[45] The Charter of Economic Rights and Duties of States echoed these ambitions.[46] It was called for 'Joint consideration of and concerted action

[41] See, for example, in the case of Germany how even the progressive circles of the liberal party FDP (which entered a coalition with the social-democrats in 1969) considered themselves as depending on the scene of social movements and reform forces, cf. R. Appel and M. Kleff, *Grundrechte verwirklichen, Freiheit erkämpfen – 100 Jahre Jungdemokrat*innen* (Academia-Nomos, 2019), 137 ff.

[42] J. Bockman, 'Socialist Globalization against Capitalist Neocolonialism: The Economic Ideas behind the New International Economic Order' (2015) 6 *Humanity: An International Journal of Human Rights, Humanitarianism, and Development* 109.

[43] UN Declaration on the Establishment of a New International Economic Order, Res. 3201, 1974.

[44] Ibid.

[45] M. Bedjaoui, *Towards a New International Economic Order* (Presses Universitaires de France, 1979), 13; see also U. Özsu, '"In the Interests of Mankind as a Whole": Mohammed Bedjaoui's New International Economic Order' (2015) 6 *Humanity: An International Journal of Human Rights, Humanitarianism, and Development* 129, 131.

[46] UN Charter of Economic Rights and Duties of States, General Assembly Resolution 3281, 1974.

regarding international economic problems' in order to take steps in the direction of a 'just and rational development of all parts of the world'.[47] This project had already resonated in the speech of Chilean President Salvador Allende before the UNCTAD in 1972. Here, Allende argued that 'our community is not homogeneous, but divided up into peoples that have grown rich and peoples that have remained poor'.[48] In his speech, Allende invoked 'us, the peoples of the third world' and accused the 'affluent countries' of pursuing their selfish interests with 'bulldog tenacity'.[49]

The obstacles faced by the non-aligned bloc also reflected Abendroth's diagnosis of constitutional politics. Starting out from existing international law, the non-aligned bloc achieved new norm-compromises and engaged with the institutional structures of the UN. As an organic intellectual of the international free trade system warned: 'The catalogue of development-political demands as e.g. formulated in the Charter of Algier (1967) and the action program of Lima (1971) by the trade-union-like organized Group of 77 leads to an overall revolutionary revision of traditional international economic law from the viewpoint of development policies.'[50] However, this shift was ultimately thwarted by a counter-revolution from above – a danger that Abendroth already elaborated on in his thoughts about the risk of Bonapartist seizures of power. Once social transformation becomes a possibility, ruling classes are likely to renege on the compromise and establish less democratic modes of political rule. With economic globalisation already under way, neoliberals were able to ally with political forces in different countries such as Chile, the United States, Germany or the United Kingdom and propagate their world-view. In sum, the quest for a 'New Economic International Order' was undermined from the 1980s onward through a distinct constitutional project as meticulously demonstrated in recent studies on the advent of neoliberalism.[51]

The central ambition of the neoliberal turn was to undermine socialist tendencies by shielding central tenets of capitalist society – such as private property and investment – from democratic intervention, and, thereby, destroy the social compromise that Abendroth had reconstructed. In scholarly debates, this turn was investigated as a 'new constitutionalism' which was successful in providing a framework for a transnational neoliberal order by dint of institutions such as the IMF, the WTO and the ICSID.[52] As Agustin Menendez recounts in Chapter 25, neoliberalism also became hegemonic in the EU's constitutional development with the affirmation of private property as the sovereign value of European law, which becomes a powerful *external constraint* that constitutes, disciplines and fragments public power.

9.4 ABENDROTH BEYOND ABENDROTH: NEW DIRECTIONS IN CONSTITUTIONAL THEORY

In the last decade, the pitfalls of the neoliberal project became more and more visible. The constitutional compromise was wrecked, the 'new constitutionalism' was unable to establish societal cohesion and sharp crisis tendencies were constantly revealed, ranging from the

47 Ibid., Preambule.

48 S. Allende, 'Address at the Inaugural Ceremony', in UN Documents, *Proceedings of the United Nations Conference on Trade and Development, Third session Santiago de Chile* (United Nations, 1973), 349.

49 Ibid., 349, 350.

50 E. Petersmann, 'Die Dritte Welt und das Wirtschaftsvölkerrecht' (1976) 36 *Zeitschrift für ausländisches öffentliches Recht und Völkerrecht* 492, 496.

51 Q. Slobodian, *Globalists: The End of Empire and the Birth of Neoliberalism* (Harvard University Press, 2018), 263ff.; see also T. Biebricher, *The Political Theory of Neoliberalism* (Stanford University Press, 2018).

52 S. Gill and C. A. Cutler, *New Constitutionalism and World Order* (Cambridge University Press, 2014).

financial crisis in 2008 and the crisis of democratic representation to the incapacity to mitigate climate change. In constitutional theory, the 'new constitutionalism' was conceived of as taking up to the legacy of 'authoritarian liberalism'; a distinct constitutional approach which was highlighted by conservative and neo-liberal circles in the 1930s and 1940s. It aimed at shielding private property, financial markets and the distribution of wealth from democratic intervention through the use of constitutional constraints and de-parliamentarisation of decision-making.[53] Since its hey-day in the 1990s and 2000s, the authoritarian liberalism of our time, obviously, became more and more crisis-ridden and faced a broad range of reaction patterns: on the one hand, attempts to safeguard its neoliberal kernel from re-negotiation were even exacerbated, for example, in the context of the Euro-Crisis from 2009 to 2013.[54] On the other hand, this kernel was recalibrated or even undermined – not the least in the light of new types of geopolitical conflict and the apparent need for public investment in order to keep the economy running.[55]

Against this backdrop, it is not surprising that new directions in constitutional theory are investigating the potential of compromise and constitutional hybridity.[56] This is an important tendency because it re-orients the debates on overcoming the democratic deficits of the neoliberal era. At least in constitutional theory, the struggles for inter- and transnational constitutionalism largely revolved around issues of procedural legitimation. The questions of whether to distribute competencies at the national, the supra- and/or the transnational level and how to design legitimate procedures were hotly debated.[57] From the perspective of social compromise in the vein of Abendroth, one would take a different starting point and ask not only how to apply democratic procedures in general, but how to embed them in the larger background conditions of societal co-evolution so that they contribute to inhibiting domination and, potentially, transforming constitutional orders.

In the contemporary world, this perspective has recently and compellingly been advanced by variants of 'plebeian' and 'sociological' constitutionalism. Taking its cue from the early modern thought of Niccolò Machiavelli, plebeian constitutionalism draws on a materialism of political power.[58] Accordingly, societies are split between the rulers and the ruled, which are driven by the competing *umori*. While the few who rule are driven by their hunger for domination, Machiavelli observed that the many tend to adhere to a different social psychology – they gather around the opposite affect of not being ruled.[59] Hence, nurtured by the few's hunger for domination, constitutional orders are always characterised by the danger of 'systemic corruption' from above, which can be defined as 'a form of political decay that manifests itself as an

[53] See M. Wilkinson, *Authoritarian Liberalism and the Transformation of Modern Europe* (Oxford University Press, 2021), 25 ff.; G. Chamayou, *The Ungovernable Society: A Genealogy of Authoritarian Liberalism* (Polity Press, 2021), 204 ff.

[54] Wilkinson, *Authoritarian Liberalism*, 215 ff.

[55] See, e.g. for the case of the WTO: E. Petersmann, 'The WTO Legal and Dispute Settlement Systems in Times of Global Governance Crises', in J. Cheng-Chia (ed.), *A New Global Economic Order* (Brill, 2021), 84–118.

[56] G. Teubner, 'Quod Omnes Tangit: Transnational Constitutions without Democracy?' (2018) 45 *Journal of Law and Society* 5; C. Vergara, *Systemic Corruption: Constitutional Ideas for an Anti-Oligarchic Republic* (Princeton University Press, 2020).

[57] See, e.g., A. Peters, 'Dual Democracy', in J. Klabbers, A. Peters and G. Ulfstein (eds.), *The Constitutionalization of International Law* (Oxford University Press, 2009), 263–341; M. Kumm, 'The Cosmopolitan Turn in Constitutionalism. An Integrated Conception of Public Law' (2013) 20 *Indiana Journal of Global Legal Studies* 605.

[58] J. P. McCormick, *Machiavellian Democracy* (Cambridge University Press, 2011).

[59] For the competing *umori*, see N. Machiavelli, *The Prince* [1532] (University of Chicago Press, 1998), 39; N. Machiavelli, *Discourses on Livy* [1532] (University of Chicago Press, 1996), 16.

oligarchization of power in society'.[60] In order to oppose this type of corruption, the plebeian current in constitutional theory stresses the importance of counter-institutions which 'empower common people against the powerful few (...)'.[61] Thus, a hybrid constitutionalisation must be established which allows the many to control the elites through '(...) class-specific popular empowerment, and elite-constraining institutions'.[62] Again, taking up the materialist tradition, these analyses start from a 'complex examination' which 'conceives of the constitution as an embedded set of norms that can be adequately grasped only if we integrate the political, economic, and social spheres into the analyses of forms of higher-law'.[63]

However, the co-evolution of the political, the economic and other social spheres must be addressed. Admittedly, Machiavelli drew on the *umori* of different social classes and, for that reason, has always been considered as a materialist *avant la lettre*.[64] But it needs to be noted that he was a child of early modernity and committed to a cosmological worldview where society is ordered around constant proportions. As analysed, however, from the nineteenth century onward, societies are evolving, leaping forward, regressing backward, overcoming and negating themselves or even breaking down; they are in constant motion. They are not stratified, but functionally differentiated societies. Though Machiavelli's observations may be to some extent timely when it comes to contest clear tendencies of oligarchisation, the overall setup of modern societies does not consist of clearly demarcated class-segments (wealthy versus normal people) which are either repressed or expressed within the constitutional order. Most importantly, it is characterised by a combination of complex social systems and the dominance of the capitalist economy where conflicts between the many and the few are proceeded. Hence, one needs to engage with the paradoxes and contradictions of law, politics and the economy and how they are formally detached from each other while being constitutionalised as a mutually reinforcing systemic set-up of capitalist society.[65]

To overcome a static materialism, what must be investigated is how social conflict is constituted and reproduced through abstraction and dynamism within social systems. Even Marx always stressed the importance of this aspect in his inquiries into the ambivalence of plebeian movements. Though he was a political activist in the 1840s who sympathised with revolutionary circles, he was suspicious of French insurrectionism for exactly this reason: as these movements replicated the symbolic inventory of the French Revolution and confined themselves to an insurrection from 'below', they were not able to take the emerging conflicts of modern society into account and, most prominently, its political economy. Marx feared that 'the proletariat will squander its energies – at least in the initial stages of the movement – in senseless, futile uprisings that will be drowned in blood'.[66] Thus, one has to analyse a complex process of co-evolution which not only revolves around the vital interests of 'normal people', but also

60 Vergara, *Systemic Corruption*, 2.
61 Ibid., ix.
62 McCormick, *Machiavellian Democracy*, 16.
63 Vergara, *Systemic Corruption*, 106.
64 See L. Althusser, *Machiavelli and Us* (Verso, 2011); A. Gramsci, 'Anmerkungen zur Politik Machiavellis', in K. Borchmann and W. F. Haug (eds.), *Gefängnishefte – kritische Gesamtausgabe* (Argument-Verlag, 1991), 1532–622.
65 See, e.g., how critical systems theory conceives of capitalism: 'In such a view, "capitalism" characterizes not only the functioning of the economic system, but a (historic) system formation, a very distinct situation of interdependence between the systems of politics, economy and law in the world's societal ensemble of institutions': A. Fischer-Lescano, 'Critical Systems Theory' (2012) 38 *Philosophy and Social Criticism* 3, 7. See also the approach to capitalism as functionally differentiated society, in: D. Schecter, *Critical Theory and Sociological Theory: On Late Modernity and Social Statehood* (Manchester University Press, 2019).
66 K. Marx, 'Kritische Randglossen zu dem Artikel "Der König von Preußen und die Sozialreform. Von einem Preußen" ("Vorwärts!" Nr. 60) (1844)', in *Marx-Engels-Werke Band 1* (Dietz-Verlag, 1976), 407.

around economic innovation, cultural change, productive forces and administrative and technocratic non-popular passive revolutions and negative externalities. Admittedly, to confront the few in order to overcome the oligarchy can serve as a plausible political strategy. However, it must disclose how the co-evolution of constitutionalism and society actually operates. Therefore, it can encounter practical problems when it comes to identifying transformative potential which does not correspond to the many/few-divide but shifts the balance of class forces from unexpected directions (see Section 9.3).

What still needs to be addressed is how compromises interact with the existing arrangement of social systems. While drawing on hybridity as well, sociological constitutionalism has highlighted this dimension. It takes its cue from systems theory and observes that societies undergo an increased functional differentiation in the passage to transnational constitutionalism.[67] In that perspective, increasingly, global social systems tend to carry out their own particular constitutional regimes in fields such as the world economy, world politics, world health, etc. The call for hybrid constitutionalisation sneaks in because of the lingering tendency of these regimes toward self-referential closure and rationality-maximisation to the detriment of their respective social environment. From that perspective, systemic corruption and elite dominance are not identified as emanating from clearly demarcated social classes. Rather, it is assumed that each regime tends to totalise its rationality and expand its communicative media: this is not only true for the capitalist economy in the transnational economic regime ('money'), but also for the expansionary logic of the sciences ('truth') or of the political system ('power'). The respective rationalities should be domesticated through regime-specific communicative counter-cycles. It is assumed that 'democratization cannot be realized as a guarantee for the identity of rulers and ruled. But it can be realized as a guarantee for forceful organized dissent which challenges the decisions of power-holders effectively (. . .)'.[68]

However, organised dissent must be re-specified in view of the fragmented structure of constitutional regimes and in order to react adequately to the respective expansionary tendencies. It can be seen as a plurality of contestations which calls ossified communicative self-reference into question. In sociological constitutionalism, these counter-cycles mostly stem from civil societal protest movements and transnational governance regimes. But such cycles are limited since they may not revoke functional differentiation which, in that perspective, amounts to a normative conception that allows the emergence of a plurality of social communication spheres. On these grounds, it is assumed that over-politicisation can also trigger a totalising dynamic, no less destructive than the regimes' universalising urge.[69] Though this is a nuanced approach to the co-evolution of constitutionalism and social structure, it aims at taming constituent powers' holistic dimension. Abendroth's approach reminds us, however, that the constitutional compromise relies on holistic threats such as scenarios of revocation and transformation which can be seen as a pre-condition of adequate hybridity.[70] This counts even for a central conception of sociological constitutionalism: the functional differentiation of liberal western societies. From an orthodox systems-theoretical perspective, functional differentiated societies are characterised by the interplay of constituted social systems which do not guarantee for the full inclusion of the individual in all systems but offers inclusionary perspectives through

[67] G. Teubner, *Constitutional Fragments: Societal Constitutionalism and Globalization* (Oxford University Press, 2012); A. Fischer-Lescano and G. Teubner, 'Regime-Collisions: The Vain Search for Legal Unity in the Fragmentation of Global Law' (2004) 25 *Michigan Journal of International Law* 999.

[68] Teubner, '*Quod Omnes Tangit*', 13.

[69] Teubner, *Constitutional Fragments*, 55.

[70] K. Möller, 'From Constituent to Destituent Power Beyond the State' (2018) 9 *Transnational Legal Theory* 32.

the welfare state. Nevertheless, it needs to be noted that this type of embedded liberalism was connected to potentially de-differentiating background conditions.

Taking up insights about the evolution of social compromise (Section 9.3) and new directions in constitutional theory (this section), one could argue that what was true for constitutional compromises in the post-war era may also be true for our contemporary world: the struggle for new compromises hinges upon the re-invigoration of constituent power and background scenarios. As the insights into the evolution of social compromise demonstrated, transformative options which pave the way for hybrid constitutionalisation may emerge in forms which neither correspond directly to the many/few distinction (plebeian constitutionalism) nor mirror functional differentiation (sociological constitutionalism) but emanate from unexpected places. While the quest for new types of transnational constitutional compromise are already under way and the ecological crisis becomes more and more pressing, Abendroth's legacy can be used as a starting point which connects the efforts for a global 'New Deal' to basic tenets of constitutional theory – thereby integrating in the calculus that the challenge cannot be reduced to correct the existing courses of constitutional evolution, but to overcome systemic blockades in order to achieve social transformation.

10

'Self-Justifying Law of Constitutional Law'

The Material Constitution in Rudolf Wiethölter's Critical Systems Theory

Gunther Teubner

10.1 MORTAL SINS

Avaritia, superbia, contentio, curiositas, concupiscentia oculorum – should overcoming these mortal sins of the Middle Ages be a key to Rudolf Wiethölter's concept of a material constitution? Indeed, this is my thesis – but only under the condition that the drastic re-evaluation of the old deadly sins in the process of forming modern constitutionalism is considered consistently.

10.1.1 Re-evaluation

What counted in the Middle Ages as the mortal sins of individuals, which – minded by the pastoral discipline of the Catholic Church – determined the salvation/damnation of souls, was radically re-valued during the Renaissance. For one, mortal sins became admirable individual virtues.[1] More importantly, though, deadly sins were transformed into autonomous social institutions, each seeking to perfect a single *idée directrice*. *Avaritia*, the vice of miserliness and greed for worldly wealth and profit, described by Augustine as the root of all sins,[2] transformed into a praiseworthy virtue, at the latest since the Medici of Florence. Ultimately, *avaritia* became one of the great social institutions: the modern profit-driven economy, touting value maximisation above all.[3] Since Machiavelli, *superbia* has no longer been a mortal sin but rather the princes' primary virtue as the lust for power; meanwhile, it has become the leading motive for actions in the autonomous political system. Galileo's insatiable *curiositas* was still condemned by the Church as hubris, but appreciated by his contemporaries as the privilege of man and had meanwhile become the core of the institution of science as it liberated itself from pope and

Translated from German by Jacob Watson. For their critical, constructive comments my thanks go out to Gotthard Bechmann, Pasquale Femia, Andreas Fischer-Lescano, Roman Guski, Bertram Lomfeld and Anton Schütz. The texts by Rudolf Wiethölter are quoted/cited from the anthology, M. Amstutz and P. Zumbansen (eds.), *Recht in Recht-Fertigungen: Ausgewählte Schriften von Rudolf Wiethölter* (Berliner Wissenschafts-Verlag, 2014), as far as they are reprinted there, under the abbreviation *RW*, the title of the essay, the year of publication and the page, otherwise under their original publication.

[1] This is a generalisation of Blumenberg's famous thesis that in the Renaissance a reinterpretation of *curiositas* from a vice into a virtue took place, only by which did the modern institution of science become possible, H. Blumenberg, *The Legitimacy of the Modern Age* (MIT Press, 1986), 229 ff.

[2] T. Aquinas, *Summa Theologiae* (Eyre & Spottiswoode, 1964), Question 118.

[3] More on this in: N. Asfour, *The Cultural Perspective of Wrongful Enrichment Law: A Study in Comparative Poetics* (Hart, 2013), 56 ff, 60.

emperor.[4] Michelangelo's *concupiscentia oculorum*, his boundless 'lust of the eye', was no longer damning but revered. Meanwhile, he liberated autonomous art from its dependence on the Church. And finally, *contentio*, disagreement, and the desire to argue became the excellent rhetorical art of the jurist; meanwhile, it spread, following Accursius and his Bolognese colleagues, advancing into the autonomous system of law throughout Europe.

Thus began the (in)famous *take-off* of the West, which started in Italy during the Renaissance, to build its momentous dynamic: with this double transformation, with the re-interpretation of former mortal sins into individual virtues and – more importantly – with their social institutionalisation in the great autonomous universes of meaning, in science, art, politics, economy and law.[5] The basis for their productive forces to be unleashed in modern Europe was that each realised its particular rationality in exclusivity without considering other rationalities. This almost paradoxical multiple unifunctionality of autonomous spheres of action set the direction for Europe's unique path because it enabled cultural excellence in each of these action systems.[6]

But deadly sins remain deadly sins! In the late modern era, the destructive tendencies of the institutions built upon them can be experienced in all their severity. The excesses of *avaritia, superbia, contentio* and *curiositas* are mirrored in the excesses of modern functional systems. The systemic excesses of politics, the economy, law, science and technology and digitality appear internally in ruthless rationality maximisation and externally in colonising expansion. It becomes almost a collective addiction, that is, the repetition and multiplication of a self-damaging social behaviour despite the keen knowledge of its harmful effects.[7] And the global economisation, politicisation, scientification and juridification of society are driven simultaneously in divergent ways, with disastrous consequences for ecology in the broadest sense, that is, for the natural world, for society and for individuals.[8]

10.1.2 *System Crises*

For Rudolf Wiethölter, these self-damaging pressures of repetition and multiplication (*Steigerungszwänge*) in social systems has led to 'deadly "system crises"'.[9] He does not see its origin solely in the uncontrollable autonomy of the capitalist economy, as is the widespread view, but in the highly driven functional differentiation itself, which ends in an uncontrollable momentum of the various functional systems. This culminates in the battle over the glamour and misery of modernity. 'Social theories, as evolutionary theories, at any rate, agree that modern

4 The servitude of technology to theory, the almost symbolic rank of the telescope for the self-affirmation of theoretical curiosity, required a spiritual breakthrough from the boldness of the proclamation that Galileo was to carry out, see Blumenberg, *Legitimacy*, 229ff.

5 In his comment on this text, Anton Schütz argued that the concept of sin in its foundational role for autopoiesis is the most relevant pillar of modernity. It opens a new access to Luhmann's distinction of social and psychic systems: 'Psychic sins are social conditions for functioning systems'.

6 In-depth historical analysis of functional differentiation, N. Luhmann, *Gesellschaftsstruktur und Semantik I–IV* (Suhrkamp, 1980–96).

7 On collective addiction, G. Teubner, 'A Constitutional Moment? The Logics of "Hit the Bottom"', in P. F. Kjaer, G. Teubner and A. Febbrajo (eds.), *The Financial Crisis in Constitutional Perspective: The Dark Side of Functional Differentiation* (Hart, 2011), 4–42.

8 On the pressure of repetition and multiplication (*Steigerungszwang*) in functional systems, N. Luhmann, *Theory of Society* (Stanford University Press, 2013), vol. II, 95; R. Stichweh, 'Towards a General Theory of Function System Crisis', in P. F. Kjaer, G. Teubner and A. Febbrajo (eds.), *The Financial Crisis in Constitutional Perspective: The Dark Side of Functional Differentiation* (Hart, 2011), 54 ff; H. Rosa, 'The Speed of Global Flows and the Pace of Democratic Politics' (2005) 27 *New Political Science* 445.

9 *RW*, 'Arbeit und Bildung' [1989], 281 f.

developments are linked to system divisions, exclusions and differentiations. The extent and effect of such differentiations are the heart of the matter.'[10] For Wiethölter, the 'deadly system crises' are the most urgent constitutional problem of modernity. For the (ir-)rational differentiation of society's constitution generates the insight that 'with growing rationality in ever smaller and more distantly decentralised units, the irrationality of the "whole" grows all the more'. Yes, modernity suffers a 'historical curse' because the extreme differentiation of the social constitution has taken place historically in such a way that a synthesis of society as a whole, a 'reasonable identity for modern societies', can no longer be grasped.[11]

And precisely with this in mind, Wiethölter – beyond his analyses of constitutional history – lays out the blueprint for his constitutional utopia, designed to take up the struggle against modernity's mortal sins, against the self-destructive tendencies of social divisions.[12] Two distinct phases are discernible in Wiethölter's ideas about a future social constitution. In the first phase, in his 'political theory of law', he develops the programme of a material constitution, that is, an 'economic constitution as social constitution'. In the second phase, after his long march through the three dominant social theories of modernity, he turns toward a 'critical systems theory', which, however, he sharply positions against Niklas Luhmann's functionalist systems theory. Even if he is sceptical about overloaded expectations of critical systems theory,[13] he sympathises with it in his 'vision as productive utopia'. '*Selbstgerechtes Rechtsverfassungsrecht*' or 'self-justifying law of constitutional law' – this is how Wiethölter enigmatises his vision. Its two main elements of a novel 'reciprocity' and an 'impartial partiality' are no less enigmatic. How, if at all, can these enigmatic terms be deciphered? And what prospects do they open up to future work on such an ambitious constitutional programme?

10.2 POLITICAL THEORY OF LAW

Early Wiethölter's answer to the systemic crises described above was: a fundamental transformation of the much too narrowly conceived economic constitution of the Federal Republic of Germany – 'economic constitution I' – into a comprehensive societal constitution – 'economic constitution II':

> 'I, myself, am working on it under the heading of a "political theory of law". Such a political theory of law deals with a unity of labour, economic and social constitution as an object of interest in socio-historical development theories of the law'.[14]

Early Wiethölter sought such socio-historical development theories in the context of the Frankfurt school of critical theory as the basis for a renewed constitution of society, thus reacting to a precarious situation of post-Marxist legal theory he had so lucidly analysed. Especially in his radical critique of liberal law, he was always aware of the disaster of current Marxist legal theories, which urgently seemed to him in need of a comprehensive reorientation. If the result of historical transformations is not to abandon these theories, then the attempts of successor theories – such as critical theory, poststructuralism, critical legal studies, globalisation critique – to rethink the law would have to try a completely new construction.[15]

[10] RW, 'Wissenschaftskritische Ausbildungsreform' [1982], 544.
[11] RW, 'Sozialwissenschaftliche Modelle im Wirtschaftsrecht' [1985], 250.
[12] RW, 'Zur Argumentation im Recht' [1995], 172.
[13] R. Wiethölter, 'Der Reform-Planer', in D. Hart, F. Müntefering and F. Steinmeier (eds.), *Wissenschaft, Verwaltung und Politik als Beruf* (Nomos, 2015), 21.
[14] RW, 'Vom besonderen Allgemeinprivatrecht zum allgemeinen Sonderprivatrecht' [1983], 224.
[15] R. Wiethölter, 'Arbeit und Bildung', in R. Erd (ed.), *Kritische Theorie und Kultur* (Suhrkamp, 1989), 375.

But how? The early Wiethölter formulated a 'juridical negativism' that sought to critique the law in terms of its social conditionality by demythologising traditional jurisprudence.[16] For such a radical critique of law, Wiethölter sought to broaden law's relevant social basis drastically and to seek it not only in the economy but also in other social dynamics. His constitutional analysis focused on economic processes but, above all, it turned to underlying political conflicts to power struggles in politics and society. The critique of law then became essentially political criticism or criticism of social power asymmetries that have a lasting effect on the current constitution of the law.

For the early Wiethölter, the legal form, especially legal doctrine, which perceives itself as autonomous, was only a façade behind which the actually relevant politico-economic processes determine the dynamics. His brilliant 1968 ideological critique of the law garnered international recognition.[17] In fact, it isolated him in the German legal establishment, for he staged a merciless 'unmasking of a German idolatry', in which many cryptic formulations in law were nothing but 'closed loops, empty formulas, alibis, taboos, pathetic and ethical transfigurations, even artificial camouflages with which naked politics are covered up'. This is why he developed his 'political theory of law' that sought with sharp polemics to tear down the façades of the liberal legal doctrine, which consisted in 'gigantic, radiant empty formulas, mere tautologies, in short: fictitious justifications, in empty talk'. And in the name of political reason, Wiethölter called for an exit from self-inflicted faith in legal doctrine. The politicisation of private law ought to succeed, he recommended, through the law's 'connection to hypotheses and methodologies of social (more precisely: democratic) theory'.[18]

10.3 'ECONOMIC CONSTITUTION I, II'

This is the reason why Wiethölter was relentless in searching for the constitution behind the constitution. Neither philosophy nor the humanities could offer the compass, but only social theory. Sharply disputing prevailing jurisprudence, he advocated for a 'material theory of the constitution as a theory of society'.[19] From the outset, he theorised a strictly relational concept of the constitution. A material constitution cannot simply be understood as a corpus of higher-ranking legal norms but rather as a dynamic interaction between social relations and legal relations, more precisely as 'the transformation of social relations into legal relations via legal principles, norms, guidelines, programs'.[20] It is important to note: an active transformation, not a reflection, not a derivation, not a determination. Yet Wiethölter always emphasised the political economy's dominance, according to which constitutions are primarily temporary compromises in ongoing class struggles, historical group conflicts, and political power contestation. Only secondarily, a constitution is a corpus of higher-ranking legal rules. Without finally resolving the controversy between class theory and conflict sociology, Wiethölter identified historically

[16] The explicit self-description as juridical negativism can be found in R. Wiethölter, 'Recht und Politik: Bemerkungen zu Peter Schwerdtners Kritik' (1969) *Zeitschrift für Rechtspolitik* 155, 158.

[17] R. Wiethölter, *Rechtswissenschaft* (Fischer, 1968). For a debate in the English-speaking world: D. Kennedy, 'Comment on Rudolf Wiethölter's "Materialisation and Proceduralisation in Modern Law" and "Proceduralisation of the Category of Law"', in C. Joerges and D. M. Trubek (eds.), *Critical Legal Thought: An American–German Debate* (Nomos, 1989), 511–24.

[18] Wiethölter, *Rechtswissenschaft*, 9 f, 17 f, 26, 28 f.

[19] *RW*, 'Thesen zum Wirtschaftsverfassungsrecht' [1977], 49. For the recent debate on a material constitutional theory, which continues this tradition, see M. Goldoni, 'Introduction to the Material Study of Global Constitutional Law' (2018) 8 *Global Constitutionalism* 71.

[20] *RW*, 'Thesen zum Wirtschaftsverfassungsrecht' [1977], 48.

different class and group compromises that form the all-determining societal constitution behind the legal constitution. While in nineteenth-century constitutional monarchism, a compromise between the nobility (monarchy) and the bourgeoisie had founded the constitution of the German empire, the Weimar Constitution struck a compromise between different forces. Capital and labour negotiated the Stinnes-Legien Agreement, and the social democracy and the old elites of the empire produced the Ebert-Groener Pact.

And for the Federal Republic of Germany, he diagnosed a peculiar constitution behind the constitution,

> . . . a Basic Law of the Basic Law (Grundgesetz) . . . novel – nonbinding–binding – behavioural 'contracts' of institutionally and organisationally influential power representatives ('state' – 'enterprise' – 'trade unions' – 'Bundesbank' – 'antitrust office' etc.), less in the manner of concerted actions, planning councils, conversational rounds than in the manner of word-rich and silent mutual notifications of expectations and behaviour.[21]

Thus, it was not the formal rules of the democratic and social constitutional state that formed the Federal Constitution of Germany primarily. Instead, neo-corporatist power compromises between rival classes, social groups, strata, organised interests and collective actors dictated the constitution.

If constitutions have emerged as historical compromises of 'social power constellations' forming the interaction between social relations and legal relations, then it would no longer be plausible to restrict the constitution to the political state constitution. Yet, constitutional lawyers still emphatically advocate doing so today.[22] At the very least, the constitution of the economy would have to be recognised as independent of the state constitution – economic constitution I. What is more, Wiethölter considered it necessary to merge the latter into a more comprehensive 'unity of labour, economic and social constitution – economic constitution II'. Its task was to create a 'political obligation of the economy to act in the public interest'.[23] And in his commitment to the constitutions of science and higher education, it finally became apparent that Wiethölter presented a constitutional concept that refers to all sectors of society.[24] This applied both to his constitutional diagnoses and to his ideas of a future societal constitution. And for Wiethölter, as well as for his fellow campaigner Jürgen Habermas, the final goal was politicising and democratising society in all its sectors:

> Politicisation does not mean that we have to start from scratch this process in science and universities, but simply, that we bring the existing politicisation of science and universities . . . into their legitimate constitution. We need to succeed in this democratic constitutional project not only for universities, for example, but also for the economy, corporations, the press, etc., if we are to succeed in our main task, namely the constitutionalisation of political society as a whole.[25]

[21] Ibid., 49.

[22] D. Grimm, 'The Achievement of Constitutionalism and Its Prospects in a Changed World', in P. Dobner and M. Loughlin (eds.), *The Twilight of Constitutionalism?* (Oxford University Press, 2010); M. Loughlin, 'What Is Constitutionalisation?', in P. Dobner and M. Loughlin (eds.), *The Twilight of Constitutionalism?* (Oxford University Press, 2010).

[23] *RW*, 'Position des Wirtschaftsrechts im Sozialstaat' [1965], 298. Obviously, the background is the debate in the Weimar Republic on economic and labour constitutionalism. For an excellent analysis, R. Dukes, *The Labour Constitution: The Enduring Idea of Labour Law* (Oxford University Press, 2014).

[24] *RW*, 'Begriffs- oder Interessenjurisprudenz' [1977], 385 ff.

[25] *RW*, 'Anforderung an den Juristen heute' [1969], 535 f. On Wiethölter's assessment of the Bremen university experiment, Wiethölter, 'Der Reform-Planer', 22 ff.

10.4 CRITICAL SYSTEMS THEORY

From the 'social constitution', in which society determines the law, to the 'self-justifying constitutional law of the law' ('*selbstgerechtes Rechtsverfassungsrecht*'), in which law is condemned to radical autonomy – these are the changes in Wiethölter's later thinking about a material constitution in a nutshell. From the 'fateful year 1974', in which the conservative turn in the German government destroyed all his hopes for the reform of universities and legal education, Wiethölter retreats from activist political practice and reorients his focus toward constitutional theory. From this time on, he continuously exposed law to three major social theories: critical philosophy, systems sociology and institutional economics.

10.4.1 Social Theory Conflicts

Wiethölter avoids making a definitive decision regarding the conflict between these rival social theories. Instead, he practices 'transversality', a procedure developed in contemporary philosophy to deal with today's discourse plurality that followed the catastrophe of the *grands récits*.[26] For Wiethölter, the old European 'theory triunity against all intermediate ("societal") powers', that is, the unity of bourgeois political philosophy, political economy and political sociology, had collapsed. Therefore, a single universal theory of society can no longer exist under the new conditions of extreme social divisions. What remains is only the unsolvable conflict between several equally originary theories of society. They live in a contradictory coexistence based on the collisions of different social rationalities. Wiethölter fends off the claim to totality of each of the three theories. He accepts their intrinsic legitimacy, their conflicts, as well as their interdependence.

This conflict between social theories poses the real challenge for constitutional theory. Despite personal sympathies for Habermas' discourse theory, Wiethölter scrupulously maintains equal distance from all three. But the transversal approach does not at all amount to a non-binding, anything-goes relativism. Neither does Wiethölter lay claim to a super-theory that would eliminate the differences between the theories; instead, he marks a mysterious void within the triangle of social theories. Only such a suspension space, within which the validity claims of rival theories cancel each other out, creates the freedom to pose the question: 'Do we have the right to bring the law to trial?'[27] Upon re-entry of the three theories, there opens up an imaginary space for legal theory, which Wiethölter maximises to develop the law of constitutional law.

Wiethölter sets his hopes on mutual irritation, indeed on the reciprocal learning opportunities posed by the rival theories. But he does not allow this metaprocess to be determined one-sidedly by the logic of either rational discourse, autopoiesis or the market. His breathless to-and-fro translations of constitutional questions into the languages of discourse theory, systems theory and economic institutionalism are to be understood as such learning processes. The course of these translations ought to yield some normative surplus value that makes it possible to formulate constitutional principles which do justice to today's historical situation. And only for the time being, only on an experimental basis does he recommend searching for the initial distinction in

[26] W. Welsch, *Vernunft: Die zeitgenössische Vernunftkritik und das Konzept der transversalen Vernunft* (Suhrkamp, 1996).

[27] *RW*, 'Ist unserem Recht der Prozeß zu machen?' [1989], 55.

critical theory in order to connect it in its own light with the other theories, with systems theory and institutional economics, as consequential distinctions. Again and again, he emphasises the provisional nature of this decision when he sees the relationship between the theories in the fact that they mutually illuminate each other's blind spots.

10.4.2 *Reception and Critique of Systems Theory*

Critique of functionalist reason – this is the common struggle that Wiethölter and Jürgen Habermas wage against the destructive tendencies of modernity, against its legacy of deadly sins and at the same time against its apologists. Both authors have in common a theoretical programme in which they transplant diverse elements of functionalist systems theory into their concepts but then expose the adopted elements internally to an uncompromising critique from which they emerge radically transformed.

Wiethölter soon breaks free of Habermas' monumental theoretical architecture to pursue more experimental and daring trains of thought. Habermas incorporates systems theory in such a way that he always constructs two social worlds, each with a different action logic, and then opposes them to each other in an almost Manichaean style. The conflict of functionalist reason versus discourse normativity, Habermas submits, is historically realised in a dualism of system evolution. Functional imperatives collide in their evolution with normative developments. Parallel to functional differentiation, Habermas observes a movement from several normative levels of justification to discursive rationality. The dualism is repeated in the conflicts between system versus life-world and in the collisions of function systems of action with normative areas of life. The dualism reappears even within one system, namely the law, in the tension of law as institution versus law as medium.[28]

Wiethölter cannot accept such sharp territorial boundaries, with the help of which the normative world can shield itself from the functional imperatives of the systemic world, which in turn proves to be resistant to normative criticism. Especially for the economy, which Habermas no longer cares about, Wiethölter is looking for a constitution that proves normatively demanding. Critical potential must be uncovered, especially within the economy. Across all systems, functionalist reason ought to be pried apart from within. He is looking for opportunities for a social normativity that has a subversive effect under systemic conditions. A new possible legal order could only be an 'autopoietic non-system' that constantly breaks through the routinised self-fulfilment of autopoiesis. This will 'bring chaos into order'[29] – precisely in its deconstructive double meaning. This permanent nervous irritation of fixed legal concepts distinguishes Wiethölter's version of a critical systems theory from Habermas' rigorously constructed theory of communicative action. *Avaritia, superbia, contentio* – Habermas puts the functionalist mortal sins into deportation custody to protect the vulnerable discursive worlds. But Wiethölter puts up the 'good fight' against the deadly sins in all areas of society.

[28] J. Habermas, *The Theory of Communicative Action, Vol. 2: Lifeworld and System – A Critique of Functional Reason* (Beacon Press, 1987), 454 ff (on system/life world, evolution, separation of areas of action), 365 ff (on law as institution/medium).

[29] R. Wiethölter, 'Just-ifications of a Law of Society', in O. Perez and G. Teubner (eds.), *On Paradoxes and Inconsistencies in Law* (Hart, 2006), 72. Systems theory would emphasise that even after such an obstruction a new autopoietic system would always emerge, just as modern art has remained an autopoietic system after all obstructions.

10.5 THE LAW OF CONSTITUTIONAL LAW (*RECHTSVERFASSUNGSRECHT*)

10.5.1 *Law's Radical Autonomy*

Wiethölter now develops the idea of the law of constitutional law whose, as he says, '*pointe* it is to propose that systems theory be taken radically seriously as the leading theory of society'.[30] But why systems theory of all things? Wiethölter learned from Hegel, Marx and Bloch that utopias must not simply be good alternatives to bad reality. Instead, they must build on recognisable developmental trends in society and exploit the opportunities they present to draw up a realistic vision of the future and promote their realisation with thoughtful political strategies. And for Wiethölter, it is systems theory that provides the most advanced analyses of these development trends. At the same time, however, he wields the critical sting from within against functionalist systems theory in order to transform it into a critical systems theory from a normative perspective. Wherein exactly does the criticality of Wiethölter's version of a critical systems theory materialise in relation to Luhmann's functionalist systems theory? And how is it reflected in his concept of the constitution?

The enigmatic concept of a 'self-justifying law of constitutional law' marks the spectacular turn in Wiethölter's constitutional thinking. Whereas in the past he had clearly prioritised the constitution behind the constitution, that is, the social power compromises over constitutional norms, now, in his confrontation with social theories, he almost inversely emphasises the high autonomy of law, but nevertheless continues the search for a material constitution: 'Perhaps in the emancipation of such law from the law in the rival social theories, which probably does not (yet) seem outdated as "other than law" or "other law", lies a step towards the opportunity of realisation of an "other of the law", ...'. And then it comes out: '"Law" would then not be bowing to social theory designs, but itself be one, and therefore at any rate not "system", not "discourse", not an "undertaking".'[31] This astonishes friends and enemies alike. It is astonishing, for one, that Wiethölter now ascribes a high degree of autonomy to the operations of the law vis-à-vis its social correlates. Such autonomy is more radical than the mere 'relative autonomy' of law as critical social theory and uncritical legal sociology think alike. By no means should it be confused with the formalist autonomy of legal doctrine in the usual sense. Autonomy now means: The obstinacy of an area of social action whose identity is constituted not merely by norms, principles and doctrines, but rather foremost by its practice of dispute – by legal decisions, legislation, contract, judgement, academic controversies, political struggles – which generate a phenomenal inner world of the law.

Likewise, it is astonishing that Wiethölter no longer looks outside the law, in social theory or philosophy, for the all-determining guiding theory. While early Wiethölter used to argue passionately for integrating jurisprudence and doctrine into a comprehensive social science, he is now experimenting surprisingly with the opposite idea, namely that law itself produces an independent theory of society (*sic!*). Not just a theory of law, but a theory of society as a whole! To ensure that the law's own theory of society does not slide into the formalist self-sufficient legal doctrine, judicial ideology, and professional self-evidence, confrontation with the three major social theories is needed. These three external observers permanently provoke autonomous law

[30] RW, 'Zur Regelbildung in der Dogmatik des Zivilrechts' [1992], 152 (emphasis added). For the differences between Luhmann and Wiethölter: G. Teubner, 'Dealing with Paradoxes of Law: Derrida, Luhmann, Wiethölter', in O. Perez and G. Teubner (eds.), *On Paradoxes and Inconsistencies in Law* (Hart, 2006), 41–64.

[31] Wiethölter, 'Just-ifications', 73.

with incongruent perspectives. Legal doctrine, which has been captive to professional pressures, will thus gain the freedom to react to the irritations caused by the excess potential of the social theories. The effect is an opening to self-modification. In this confrontation, autonomous law itself becomes one of the noteworthy parts of society, whose potential for reflection is greater than that of society as a whole, as Gotthard Günther has described it.[32] Wiethölter's juridical utopia is developed out of the reflective potential of law itself and not from that of sociology or philosophy.

Such an enlightened, legally innate 'societal theory design' relies above all on an increased autonomy of law's operations and self-descriptions. Thus, the development of modern law is no longer to be understood as a mere epiphenomenon of more fundamental social processes. Instead, it is to be seen as an independent process of social autonomy – and simultaneously a process of alienation – within the framework of a capitalist society. Its course and its results are now to be understood primarily from the inherent logic of the law and only secondarily from its indirect but massive references to the intrinsic logic of the economy, politics, culture, etc.

10.5.2 *Critique of Juridical Functionalism*

So far, he is in consensus with systems theory. But the more Wiethölter emphasises the autonomy of law and, in strict parallel, the autonomy of other social systems, the more gravely he calls out their deadly sins. His critique of their ruthless rationality maximisation and of their equally ruthless expansion beyond their limits is fundamental. To the extent that 'law as law' has indeed 'emancipated itself radically towards self-determination and has uncoupled itself both from legal subjects and from (social) morals', he says, it commits a mortal sin when – as the current legal doctrine, especially in Germany, does – it bitterly resists new feedback with 'externality, normativity of socio-historical legitimations, structures, codes'. Wiethölter's prescription for a material constitution is the exact opposite: The law itself must now actively seek new, resilient ties back to society precisely because it has gained such a high degree of autonomy.[33]

The same applies to the relationship between law and other systems, especially the economy. The more they have decoupled themselves from social needs in their highly driven momentum, the more they would need external controls, particularly by law. When the law is confronting problems of world society – financialisation of social reproduction, ecological catastrophes, dangers of reproductive medicine, exclusion of entire population groups – all this as a result of worldwide functional differentiation, law acquires a new task in its relation to other autonomous social systems.

But it is precisely in confronting this major problem that the theory of autopoietic systems fails – this is Wiethölter's primary criticism of Luhmann. Almost cynically, Luhmann plays down the central problem of modernity, the urgently needed integration of an extremely divided society.[34] Worse still, according to Wiethölter, Luhmann wrongly denies even the possibility of an orientation toward the public good and accordingly the opportunities to contribute to the integration of an extremely divided society. Instead, he leaves it – and herein lies the scandal – to the economy of all things to secretly bring about society's integration. According to Wiethölter's devastating verdict, functionalist systems theory re-integrates the 'totality of differentiations into

[32] G. Günther, 'Cybernetic Ontology and Transjunctional Operations', in G. Günther (ed.), *Beiträge zur Grundlegung einer operationsfähigen Dialektik* (Meiner, 1976), 249–83.

[33] *RW*, 'Zur Argumentation im Recht' [1995], 169 f.

[34] Luhmann speaks of integration with irony as a 'concept of despair' whose overwhelming urgency he simply doubts. Instead, he describes modern society as 'over-integrated': Luhmann, *Theory of Society*, 16.

the "economy of society"'. It thus legitimises a highly questionable 'unity of "economy" and "law" to which systemic autonomy, positivity, self-reference as autopoiesis are accredited'.[35] But that would be nothing other than economic totalitarianism, which awards *avaritia* social primacy.

10.5.3 *Reciprocity/(Im-)partiality*

Wiethölter's normatively hotly charged vision of the material constitution is built up directly on Luhmann's cold, functional analysis because, as pointed out in Section 10.5.2, he sees it as the most advanced diagnostics of today's society. Wiethölter's two principles of the law of constitutional law – reciprocity and partial impartiality – are, therefore, a direct reaction to the functional differentiation of society. Simultaneously, though, they aim at the crucial common good, totally neglected by systems theory. Admittedly, both principles hardly have anything to do with their traditional meaning. An attempt to decipher them would no longer understand reciprocity as mutual balancing of two individual interests in the synallagmatic contract. Instead, it would imply the reciprocal productive and solidary interconnection of distant areas of social autonomy. Wanting to create contractual justice via singular judicial corrections, as lawyers with an alternative vision of private law entertain, then appears as an almost naive recourse to outdated concepts of a single, self-balanced legal relationship or of the autonomy of the bourgeois subject. That indeed would be the false utopia that suffers from a lack of social adequacy. Instead, what is sought in today's society is an adequate compensation of asymmetrical individual relations, which creates solidary relations via a long detour across several system boundaries. Obviously, Wiethölter thus goes far beyond Parsons' ideas of exchange relations between social systems and beyond Luhmann's analyses of their mutual complementarity and limitation.[36] He is concerned with normative reciprocity of the welfare state as a social equilibrium between partial autonomies, which links the autonomy of functional, large-scale systems and that of individuals, collectives, institutions and organisations in their mutual solidarity. As a thoroughly normative concept, such society-wide reciprocity is reminiscent of Durkheim's organic solidarity, which he had understood as a reaction to the social division of labour. In its normative charge, it distances itself from Luhmann's relatively pale concept of structural coupling.

Impartial partiality: Through this second, openly paradoxically formulated principle of the law of constitutional law, Wiethölter again concurs with systemic diagnoses of law in modern society but subsequently distances himself from systemic concepts of autonomy. '"Autonomy" was in fact never anywhere a guarantee of decentralised and sectoral "general good" but itself a party, to which one releases activities only at the cost of "objectively justified" criteria, venues kept open and fairness procedures kept to, in short, "relative impartiality" and the capacity for universalisation.'[37] If one wants to decipher this paradoxical (im-)partiality, one should see the role of the law against the deadly sin excesses of functional systems neither in directly intervening with their self-regulation nor in establishing a mere framework order. Instead, it should be the task of the law to aid in releasing the normativity potential already latent within the area of social autonomy – a kind of maieutic. In clear contrast to Luhmann's sociology, which in cool

[35] RW, 'Ist unserem Recht der Prozeß zu machen?' [1989], 64 f.

[36] On intersystemic relations: T. Parsons and N. J. Smelser, *Economy and Society: A Study in the Integration of Economic and Social Theory* (Routledge, 1956), 70 ff; Luhmann, *Theory of Society*, 6 ff.

[37] RW, 'Zum Fortbildungsrecht der (richterlichen) Rechtsfortbildung' [1988], 471.

indifference celebrates its supposedly impartial distance, Wiethölter's law of constitutional law consciously adopts the partiality perspective in the normative legal discourse. The impartial constitution would then be partial in a three-fold sense: Partial to the standards of normativity developed within the law, which impartially are applied to the social systems. But also partial toward the normative standards of the social systems themselves, for which law takes sides in conflict cases to solve disputes impartially. And finally, partial toward 'society as society', one of the strangest enigmas with which Wiethölter counterfactually holds on to the concept of society in modernity, although he explicitly insists on the destruction of this very concept in modernity.[38]

10.5.4 *Collisions of Constitutions*

10.5.4.1 Constitutional Pluralism

Luhmann's constitutional concept suffers a further critique when confronted with Wiethölter's 'society as society'. Luhmann's insistence on the constitutional monopoly of the state constitution is untenable in Wiethölter's eyes. As is well known, Luhmann argues against the extension of the political constitution to the whole society, against the horizontal effect of constitutional rights in non-state sectors, against the economic constitution and against societal constitutionalism, as represented by David Sciulli and Reinhart Koselleck. In addition, for Luhmann, a transnational equivalent for the national constitution as a coupling of politics and law does not exist.[39] Certainly, Wiethölter counters, one must accept systems theory's insight that the constitution must be conceived strictly relationally as structural coupling of law with non-legal processes. But to limit law's coupling exclusively to the political system of the nation-state, as Luhmann and the prevailing doctrine in constitutional law still do, is for Wiethölter an unacceptable reduction of the constitutional project. He opposes this with a material constitution, in his words, a 'society-as-society constitution': 'Society as society consists of ... not merely the "democratic" aggregation of human citizens but also a variety of "organised" institutionalisation for decisions, communication and educational processes.'[40] Should one then, like Reinhart Koselleck or Otfried Höffe, adopt a comprehensive constitution for society as a whole – or potentially even a world constitution – as a normative unity? Or should one opt for a diversity of constitutional sites? Wiethölter advocates, again in opposition to Luhmann, for the second option, for transnational societal constitutionalism in the 'struggle for the (international) social order as legal constitution'.[41] He opts for constitutional pluralism, for a multitude of social institutions to be legally constitutionalised. Indeed, he describes this as probably the 'most exciting prospect for hope' that a constitutional law of the law is beginning to develop 'conflict-of-laws principles for law versus morality, law versus politics, law versus the economy etc., or more exactly and more generally, law as a "structural coupling" of "life-world systems"'.[42] Thus, Wiethölter identifies not only the state constitution but also the economic constitution (national as well as international), the constitution of science and other function systems, as well as the constitution of multinational corporations, universities and other formal organisations and even the constitution of global supply chains[43] and other networks, each

[38] Ibid., 158; *RW*, 'Zur Argumentation im Recht' [1995], 183; Wiethölter, 'Just-ifications'.
[39] N. Luhmann, *Law as a Social System* (Oxford University Press, 2004), 487 f; Luhmann, *Theory of Society*, 430, fn. 356.
[40] *RW*, 'Zur Regelbildung in der Dogmatik des Zivilrechts' [1992], 158.
[41] *RW*, 'Begriffs- oder Interessenjurisprudenz' [1977], 374 ff.
[42] *RW*, 'Zur Argumentation im Recht' [1995], 185.
[43] *RW*, 'Begriffs- oder Interessenjurisprudenz' [1977], 374, 417 ff; *RW*, 'Anforderung an den Juristen heute' [1969], 535 f.

understood as a coupling of social institutions with the law. In Wiethölter's constitutionalism, the legal focus is now finally geared toward a radical pluralism of social autonomies. At odds with the obsolete dichotomy of private versus public law, multiple material constitutions, national as well as international in a meta-conflict law, regulate the relation of law to different social autonomies as a fusion of the law's global economic constitution with international private law.

10.5.4.2 Constitutional Governance of Social Autonomy

This may decipher a first dimension of the enigmatic 'self-justifying law of constitutional law' (*selbst-gerechtes Rechts-Verfassungs-Recht*).[44] It is obviously a concept with multiple layers of self-reflexivity. Its simultaneous use of *genitivus subjectivus* and *genitivus objectivus* brings law and constitution into multi-dimensional self-referential relations. They culminate in 'self-justifying praxis-games' (*selbstgerechte Praxisspiele*). In this first dimension, constitutional law decides whether the coupling relationship of each of the social sub-areas with the law meets the requirements of reciprocity and partial impartiality. This implies the relationship between the law and the autonomy of a social system and it entails the problem, 'if and how "autonomy" can be taken seriously as self-determination and, nevertheless, can become suitable as essential externalisation (control), not as external determination, but as a possible help in situations of impossible self-help, not unlike "counselling" help and "compatibility' therapy outside the law".[45] Thus, it is the task of the law to guarantee the autonomy of social processes in the first place through constitutive rules to exercise effective external control through limitative rules. This means at once protecting its integrity from false politicisation or economisation.

10.5.4.3 Collision Rules for Constitutions

Early Wiethölter already hinted at the second dimension of the law's constitutional law in speaking about the necessity of a meta-constitution as a constitution for the constitution. He later modified this under the conditions of constitutional pluralism more precisely as the meta-law of conflicting legal constitutions. Such a meta-constitutional law is supposed to offer a resolution of conflicts between the various constitutions of politics, economy, science and formal organisations.[46]

Here the typical Wiethölter way of thinking about conflict of laws comes into play. He extrapolates from private international law and tries to make it fruitful for other areas of law, especially for constitutional law. It is no longer only a matter of dealing with conflicts between national legal systems but also generalising conflict law thinking. Wiethölter applies it now in conflicts between other norm complexes, areas of law, legal institutions, state and social constitutions, but also for conflicts between the rationalities of different social systems and even between rival theories of society. With this double recourse to rich historical experiences of both international private law on the one hand and of massive social conflicts of rationality on the other, it is possible to prioritise such a generalised conflict of law in the juridical reconstruction of social contradictions. In Wiethölter's conflicts of law, however, the social contradictions

[44] Wiethölter, 'Just-ifications'.
[45] *RW*, 'Zum Fortbildungsrecht der (richterlichen) Rechtsfortbildung' [1988], 476.
[46] *RW*, 'Zur Argumentation im Recht' [1995], 185.

do not appear as such, but rather in a specifically juridical transformation. This complicated process translates society's real contradictions (*Realwidersprüche*) into conflicts of different constitutions. Social conflict dynamics are now exposed to the law's obligation to make decisions, which calls for suitable fora, procedures and criteria. Concepts of conflict sociology are translated into a doctrine of conflict law (connection, qualification, referral, *renvoi*, *ordre public*, alignment, internal and external decision-making harmony).

Therefore, the law of constitutional law must be understood in this second dimension as the law governing conflicts between constitutions. It adjudicates collisions between different national constitutions but, more importantly, conflicts between social rationalities, which articulate themselves legally as conflicts between different social constitutions – those of the economy, politics, science, education, information media. Here again, Wiethölter goes beyond his initial reception of a systems theory element – conflicts between functional systems – with its critical-normative transformation. The conflicts are not equanimously left to blind evolution, as Luhmann would see it, but instead transformed into a legal issue to be decided via suitable fora, procedures and criteria.

10.5.4.4 Ordre Public

Finally, a third dimension, hidden in Wiethölter's law of constitutional law, refers to the already mentioned 'society as society', which collides with the partial rationality of the diverse function systems. Wiethölter judges the mere compatibility of the function systems, as envisaged by Luhmann,[47] as entirely inadequate. Instead of compromising only between partial rationalities, a constitutional conflict law would have to seek its orientation toward an *ordre public* for society as a whole. Wiethölter's efforts are directed toward a material constitution of 'society as society', in the form of a constitutional theory which, as he says, works as 'a thorn in the flesh of socio-historical development'.[48]

For Wiethölter, 'society as society' should not be seen as a separate social sphere in contrast to the state, '... but rather as a space of cultural reproductions, of social identities, of successful socialisation. In society as society, it is not the "whole person" who is legally at home, but rather his participatory role, function, decision-making, education, which each constantly requires definition ...'.[49]

Wiethölter thus criticises functionalist systems theory because it dilutes the concept of society down to the mere sum of all communications that operate internally with the distinction between self-reference and other-reference. He contrasts it with a normatively highly charged concept of society. This accepts the systems theory division of the whole person initially into mutually closed off processes of consciousness and social communication. Under such radicalised conditions of alienation, however, the society-as-society constitution must stand all the more for liberation toward freedom against bondage, 'which speaks in the name of either the rule of objective reason, majority will, or liberal individual rights'.[50] 'Self-justifications of societal law'[51] produce a constitution of the whole of society, which, however, is not meant as a uniform constitution of world society but rather as a material meta-constitution for conflicts within constitutional pluralism.

[47] Luhmann, *Theory of Society*, 6 ff.
[48] RW, 'Franz Böhm (1895–1977)' [1989], 87.
[49] RW, 'Zur Regelbildung in der Dogmatik des Zivilrechts' [1992], 158.
[50] RW, 'Franz Böhm (1895–1977)' [1989], 81.
[51] Wiethölter, 'Just-ifications', 65.

10.5.4.5 A Culture of Conflict

'*Self-justifying* law of constitutional law'? The self-referential dynamics of object-norms and meta-norms unfolding in the three dimensions described in Section 10.5.4.4 culminate in a final self-referential loop. The ultimate formula of 'self-justification' (*Selbstgerechtigkeit*) cuts off the infinite regress of seeking ever higher norms and meta-norms, refusing Kelsen's *Grundnorm* as well as Luhmann's contingency formula. Wiethölter transfers the question of justice in the law of constitutional law to the manifold circular relationships of substantive norms and collision norms that are realised in the social practices (!) of the disputes over colliding norms. Such, as Wiethölter calls them, 'self-justifying praxis games' would be realised in a future 'law of conflict culture' as 'admission of different partial cultures, of course within limits'.[52] Such praxis games would have to transcend the narrow boundaries of the law, but not in the direction of religious transcendence of otherness, instead, in the direction of the immanence of a quasi-therapeutic relationship which is oriented more toward the healing normativity of medicine than toward juridical logic of injury and restoration.[53] Wiethölter openly admits to the question of what this search for an immanent transcendence of law could mean: '[That] is the numinosum, and each numinosum has a fascinosum and also a tremendum. That is what the theologians are saying'.[54]

10.6 CONTINUATION

But how, finally, can Wiethölter's work on the material constitution be further developed?

10.6.1 Various Pathways

In recent years, several attempts have been made to detach Wiethölter's concept of the law of constitutional law from its national context and to make it fruitful for the current transnational constitutionalisation.[55] In the future, the principles of society-wide reciprocity and partial impartiality will be a challenge for constitutionalist studies. The law of constitutional law can also provide an impetus for the recent debates on the digital constitution and ecological constitutionalism.[56] In other contexts, Wiethölter's ideas on conflict of laws have already set a precedent, revealing the deep structures of simple legal norm conflicts in a wide variety of areas and opening up possible solutions that leave the old conflict norms of *lex posterior*, *lex superior*, etc. far behind. And critical systems theory has experienced a clear resonance in both national and international debate. It has successfully broken open the hardened fronts of the Habermas/Luhmann controversy and found a connection to post-structuralist theories.[57]

52 RW, 'Politik und Aufklärung' [1988], 493.

53 Wiethölter, 'Just-ifications', 75.

54 RW, 'L'essentiel est invisible pour les yeux' [2013], 189.

55 A. Fischer-Lescano, 'Luhmanns Staat und der transnationale Konstitutionalismus', in M. Neves and R. Voigt (eds.), *Die Staaten der Weltgesellschaft: Luhmanns Staatstheorie* (Nomos, 2007), 99–113; D. Wielsch, 'Gesellschaftliche Transformation durch subjektive Rechte', in A. Fischer-Lescano, H. Franzki and J. Horst (eds.), *Gegenrechte: Recht jenseits des Subjekts* (Mohr Siebeck, 2018), 141–64.

56 On digital constitutionalism: E. Celeste, *Digital Constitutionalism: The Role of Internet Bills of Rights* (University College Dublin, 2020). On ecological constitutionalism: A. Cardesa-Salzmann and E. Cocciolo, 'Global Governance, Sustainability and the Earth System: Critical Reflections on the Role of Global Law' (2019) 8 *Transnational Environmental Law* 437.

57 A. Fischer-Lescano, 'Critical Systems Theory' (2012) 38 *Philosophy and Social Criticism* 3; A. Philippopoulos-Mihalopoulos, 'Critical Autopoiesis and the Materiality of Law' (2014) 27 *International Journal for the Semiotics of Law* 389.

10.6.2 *Real Contradiction in Law*

Another promising line of research seems to me to lie in Wiethölter's reinterpretation of one of Karl Marx's basic concepts. He claims that the fundamental real contradiction (*Realwiderspruch*) of law is between productive forces and relations of production – so far, so underwhelming, but here it comes! – not of the economy, but of the law itself. How's that? A legally innate 'dialectic of *legal* productive forces and *legal* relations of production'? Against Marx, with Marx and beyond Marx – here, the late Wiethölter pursues his approach of a radical autonomy of law and seeks to generalise the contradiction logic assumed by Marx only in the economy and to re-specify this logic within the law itself.

Wiethölter tries to identify a real contradiction between productive forces and relations of production that are innate to the law. Thus, he rejects Marx's thesis of law as a superstructure. Instead, he seeks to demonstrate that the contradictory dynamics, which Marx located exclusively in the economy, exist within the law itself. Then – in contrast to most critical legal theories – the legal form is no longer a mere façade that obscures relevant processes in the political economy. Instead, a fundamental contradiction immanent in the law itself drives a transformative dynamic independent of the economy. And the utopia of the law of constitutional law would have to build on the fundamental contradictions inherent in the law itself.

One obvious option would be to carry this idea further and to understand the innate relations of production as legal relations as well as to identify the legally relevant productive forces, possibly in the correlation of communication media and social norms. My proposal, however, goes in a different direction, namely to try an analogy to the economy in law, the analogy to the worst of all deadly sins, to *avaritia* – to the economic profit principle itself.

10.6.3 *Societal Surplus Values*

The critique of capitalist society is then no longer directed solely at the profit principle within the economy. Nor is it merely directed against the expansion, pushed by neo-liberal fanatics, of the economic profit principle into non-economic areas of society, threatening all social activities to produce a monetary profit or else be done away with altogether. Instead, it criticises a different kind of society-wide expansion of the capitalist logic. The very belonging to a function system forces every operation to generate a surplus value – but explicitly non-monetary – beyond its immediate production of meaning. In politics, non-monetary surplus value means that every policy decision needs to create a surplus of political power simultaneously. In science, successful research in the various subject areas, which is constrained by reputation maximisation, is only recognised as relevant if it generates a surplus of generalisable, applicable knowledge. In law, the courts are under the obligation to produce a normative surplus value, that is, norms that can be generalised for the future, over and above the concrete decision in a dispute. Legal acts need to reproduce and, if possible, to increase juridical normativity. This is the reason why in the famous parable 'Return of the Twelfth Camel', it is crucial that the khadi formulates his decision in such a way that the twelfth camel – the juridical normativity which guarantees acceptance – is not only used to resolve the concrete case but at the same time can be returned to the khadi.[58] And here, too, exploitation is at play – namely of those people who are actually interested merely in

[58] For an interpretation of the parable, see G. Teubner, 'Alienating Justice: On the Social Surplus Value of the Twelfth Camel', in D. Nelken and J. Přibáň (eds.), *Law's New Boundaries: Consequences of Legal Autopoiesis* (Ashgate, 2001), 21–44.

the success of their concrete legal dispute but who nevertheless have to muster the extra energy that generates the surplus values of new resources of normativity for future use that emerge from their dispute[59] and, more generally, that enables the law to reproduce and even increase its capacity to create acceptance in law and society.

In the language of systems theory: The orientation of a function system toward its societal surplus-value means constant pressure to co-produce a surplus of its mediality, beyond the actual production process, which only in the economy is monetary profit. The surplus of the system's own communication medium – money, power, law, knowledge – arises in the reflexive application of operations to further operations. In a reflexive process, not only are the usual follow-up operations made possible but, at the same time, each one's own ability to operate is restored or even increased.[60] If this is established as a criterion of self-regulation in various systems, then the surplus production becomes the driving dynamics of the expansion imperatives in modern society.[61] The production of societal surplus value, which serves to reproduce or even increase each system's own communication medium, is by no means simply to be confused with a constant increase in performance, with output maximisation, according to the motto 'Higher, further, faster'. Defining social surplus exclusively as strengthening the communication medium distinguishes a systemic concept of surplus from other attempts to describe all kinds of byproducts of production as social surplus.[62]

It is by no means immediately apparent why communication media, in particular, should be held responsible for the ubiquitously perceptible pressure of increase caused by function systems. The unique contribution of communication media in their area of application consists precisely in creating the *motives* (!) for the fact that communication expectations are also and especially accepted against resistance. They have the 'function of making the acceptance of a communication expectable in cases in which rejection is likely'.[63] The motivational power inherent in communication media thus proves to be the actual motor for the uncanny growth constraints, which each of the function systems develops endogenously out of itself. It is also the exclusive aim of surplus production to restore and increase communication media wherever possible.

The motivational power of communication media does not directly influence psychological states; instead, it twists social constructions that get by with the assumption of corresponding states of consciousness. Communication media, therefore, primarily shape the formation of social motives and, at best, have an indirect effect on individual intrapsychic decision-making. Here, then, lies the origin of the – understood in this way by media theory – will to power, to money, to law, to truth. Communication media force the individual from the outset in Max Weber's 'Housing of Future Bondage', which is understood here as the overwhelming motivational pressure created by each one-dimensionally oriented communication medium to produce added value. However, the individual is then subject not exclusively to the profit compulsion of the capitalist economy, which one usually has in mind as the cause of such dynamics, but also to other surplus constraints, that is, the power pressures of politics, the

59 N. Luhmann, 'The Unity of the Legal System', in G. Teubner (ed.), *Autopoietic Law: A New Approach to Law and Society* (de Gruyter, 1988), 12–35, 23.

60 This generalises Luhmann's theses on the profit principle of the economy for other function systems, idem, *Die Wirtschaft der Gesellschaft* (Suhrkamp, 1988), 55 ff.

61 The production of surplus value is indeed the object of desire for a collective addiction which is institutionalised in various function systems, see Teubner, 'A Constitutional Moment?'.

62 Usually associated with positive social policy ambitions, e.g., M. H. Moore, *Recognising Public Value* (Harvard University Press, 2013).

63 Luhmann, *Theory of Society*, II, IX.

knowledge pressures of science and technology, the novelty pressures of information media, the digitisation pressures of the online world and the standardisation pressures of law.

At the same time, it becomes possible to determine more precisely the different social forms of social surplus values than via the mere separation of economic, cultural and social phenomena (as in Bourdieu's capital concepts). Only when contributing to the function of the social system is 'generated' beyond the immediate activity and its meaning[64] does this count as a medial added value that acts as a criterion of self-regulation, as a recursive principle of the self-legitimation of systemic operations. This applies to payment operations of the economy no differently than it does to dispute decisions in law, policy decisions in politics, epistemic operations of science or curative interventions in medicine, possibly also for digital operations in cyberspace.

The society-wide pressure to produce surplus value does not aim at skimming off the surplus value for private use, as in the conventional understanding of profit. It is not at all about the antagonism between public production and private appropriation; on the contrary, it is precisely about a detachment from private motives. An orientation toward societal surplus makes it possible to detach oneself from the reciprocity of simple exchange relationships and instead establish reciprocity relationships throughout society. Pressure to make a profit generalised in this way is then in substance a system-immanent 'taxation' of every operation for the fulfilment of the system's function: monetary surplus in the economy for securing future needs, normative surplus of concrete dispute adjudication in law for norm production in society, power surplus of policies as generalised resources for future political decisions, surplus knowledge for the formation of theories in science and surplus medical value of individual operations for the development of the health sector.

10.6.4 *Societal Surplus Values as a Constitutional Problem*

At this point, at the latest, it becomes clear that massive pressures to produce various surplus values are a constitutional problem of the highest order. The surplus orientation is, after all, the actual driving *idée directrice* in both economic and non-economic institutions of a capitalist society, which is responsible for its productive dynamics, but especially for its destructive effects. It gives the respective system operations a formal goal that overlays, limits, dominates and ultimately falsifies their substantive goal. But how should the constitution deal with the excessive ambivalence of ubiquitous surplus production? Surplus restrictions? Changes to profit distribution? Collectivisation of the non-monetary generation of profit? Liberation from the societal pressure toward profit maximisation? If the compulsion to siphon off surplus value is structurally rooted everywhere throughout society, albeit in different forms, then it is obviously no longer sufficient to make a fundamental decision under economic constitutional law for or against a profit-driven economy. Hopes for the abolition of private property and the elimination of the monetary profit orientation are in vain because the destructive tendencies of non-monetary profit maximisation in other systems, especially in science, technology and, of course, politics, would remain completely unaffected.

The way constitutions deal with diverse societal surplus productions would have to be conceived more carefully than any simple prohibition strategy would do. One suggestion could be – *horribile dictu* – economic experiences with external societal pressures on commercial enterprises, which are currently being exerted in the direction of monetary profit generation.

[64] See N. Luhmann, 'Organisationen im Wirtschaftssystem', in N. Luhmann (ed.), *Soziologische Aufklärung 3: Soziales System, Gesellschaft, Organisation* (Westdeutscher Verlag, 1981), 390–414, 401 ff.

This is because the concrete design of surplus generation and distribution is not solely left up to the companies but instead imposed externally by a triad of surplus transfers: returns, taxes and employee wages. Various collective actors force the companies to achieve a monetary surplus beyond mere production and direct them how they distribute it to different beneficiaries: the state skimming off taxes, the trade unions fighting for wages and working conditions, the capital owners collecting the residual profits for their risk exposure, and the companies themselves reinvesting. And constitutional law plays a prominent role here because various social constitutions provide for the legal protection of such pressures: financial constitution, property constitution and labour constitution. Constitutional changes that influence the economic profit principle, such as state participation in companies, taxation for non-fiscal purposes or workers' co-determination, have arisen in the past quite regularly and are topical again for the future given the more recent criticism of capitalism. In view of new, increased inequalities, the task of politics and law to reduce 'parasitic' profit siphoning excesses, especially of the capital owners, is likely to come into sharp focus again. What will be seen as parasitic in these new attempts should be the surplus skimming that exceeds the required (!) motivation for generating surplus value.

Would it be worthwhile for a law of constitutional law, in the way Wiethölter formulates it, to learn from such experiences in the economic constitution? Can we free them from the tight corset of economic, monetary profit and make them fruitful in numerous areas of life for a political-legal direction of non-monetary surplus productions? Instead of direct interventions, the external pressures could indirectly work toward a changed – possibly ecological – orientation of the various societal surplus outputs in 'partial impartiality'. The role of law would be to institutionally promote a society-wide reflection on various societal surplus values, both their production and distribution, in 'society-wide reciprocity', including the normative surplus values of law itself. Left to their own devices, the systemic surplus productions will only follow their tunnel vision, focusing on maximising their own function. External pressures from civil society, from politics and law should induce them to become ecologically sensitive and to include the effects on nature, society and people in their decision-making. Would such pressures be the appropriate dealing with the modern equivalents of old mortal sins – *avaritia, superbia, contentio, concupiscentia oculorum*?

PART II

Challenges

11

The Material Constitution and Imperialism

Eva Nanopoulos[*]

In their pathbreaking article on the 'Material Constitution', the editors of the present volume called for constitutional theory to pay attention to the 'material conditions for the emergence and development of a constitutional order, and the material changes that prompt the suspension or modification of formal constitutional norms'.[1] Goldoni and Wilkinson defined the material context as the 'basic political and social conditions of possibility of constitutionalism and the dynamics of constitutional change'.[2] My aim in this chapter is to argue that those conditions and dynamics must be grounded in the genesis and development of capitalism and that this by necessity implies an engagement with imperialism or, to be more precise, of capitalist imperialism[3] defined as a global, Western-led, gendered and racialised system of domination and exploitation inherent to capitalism.

Such engagement both broadens and narrows the outlook of 'orthodox' approaches to constitutional law. Foregrounding imperialism moves us beyond the premise that constitutional forms are purely 'domestic' phenomena and hence expands the discipline's spatial coordinates. Yet, by breaking with a transhistorical reading of constitutionalism and constitutions – amenable to change to fit modern conditions but ultimately grounded in nature and reason – it also simultaneously restricts its temporal coordinates.

Redrawing the boundaries of the field through the lens of the material imperial constitution not only contributes 'new insights' to the discipline but also questions its own complicity in the emergence, development and contemporary reproduction of capitalist imperial relations. Elision of the international domain and of the historical context are part and parcel of a process of self-legitimation of liberal constitutionalism. Together, they form the bedrock of a 'constitutional mythology' that perpetuates the idea of the constitution as a great civilisational achievement and its spread as an ongoing march toward universal freedom and emancipation.

This complicity is not unique to constitutional law or indeed to law as such. Methodological nationalism and positivism pervade all fields of the humanities and the social sciences and have helped sever their connections to imperialism. But 'decolonial' efforts have been almost non-

[*] I would like to thank the editors not only for their insightful comments, but also for their patience in a difficult phase. I would also like to thank Tanzil Chowdhury for reading and commenting on an earlier draft, as well as Rob Knox, for the many lively (and endless!) discussions on race and capitalism.

[1] M. Goldoni and M. A. Wilkinson, 'The Material Constitution' (2018) 81 *Modern Law Review* 567, 568.

[2] Ibid.

[3] The notion of 'capitalist imperialism' acknowledges the fact that there existed previous forms of pre-capitalist imperialism, such as the Roman Empire. In this chapter, however, I use the term 'imperialism' as 'capitalist imperialism' and the term 'imperial constitution' as 'capitalist imperial constitution'.

existent in constitutional scholarship,[4] even as work in other areas – from political[5] and social[6] theory, to international relations[7] and international law[8] – has brought to light the imperial underpinnings of several key constitutional concepts.

At the same time, it is not sufficient merely to incorporate the 'external' or 'international' dimensions of constitutional law (i.e., to consider the ways in which the state engages with the outside world). Nor is it sufficient to uncover the imperial 'legacies' of constitutional ideas, concepts, law or practices in the hope of some historical redemption of the discipline. A materialist engagement with imperialism instead demands that we approach the material conditions that shaped the 'emergence and development of constitutional orders' as inherently transnational, binding people and places across territorial boundaries, and hence that we consider how the global imperial context shaped constitutional developments from within. And it also requires historical specificity, an attention to the multiple and changing forms that imperialism takes within constitutional law across time, up to the present day.

To illustrate some of the connections between constitutionalism, constitutional law and imperialism, I draw on select examples from British and French imperialism. The English and French revolutions (alongside the American) continue to provide the main reference points for constitutional history; the constitutional corpus that emerged from them continues to supply the core tenets of Western liberal constitutionalism; and their constitutional laws and practices offered models for constitution-building across the world.[9] In both cases, the dominant historiography has elided their relationship to imperialism, even as they were primary sites of capitalist development and, throughout their history, among the largest European empires. British history,[10] including constitutional history,[11] for example, continues to be told mainly as an 'island story', divorced from the history of the British Empire, while contemporary finance-based British imperialism remains under-investigated.[12]

These examples will be used to illuminate the imperial context in which 'modern' constitutional law emerged and developed (Section 11.1), the conceptual contradictions and material tensions that this created (Section 11.2) and the ways in which imperialism continues to structure contemporary constitutional orders (Section 11.3). Constraints of space, however, mean that certain topics could not be covered.

First, the analysis leaves out important aspects of the dialectical and co-constitutive relationship between constitutional law and imperialism whose erasure has been key to sustaining the 'constitutional mythology' and which any more systematic analysis of the imperial constitution would need to recover and theorise.

One such aspect is the connection between constitutional law and processes of internal colonisation. The chapter engages with the notion of 'imperial boomerang', that is, the effects

4 For exceptions see, e.g., J. Tully, 'Modern Constitutional Democracy and Imperialism' (2008) 46 *Osgoode Hall Law Journal* 46.
5 E.g., R. Shilliam, *Decolonizing Politics: An Introduction* (Polity Press, 2021).
6 E.g., G. Bhambra and J. Holmwood, *Colonialism and Modern Social Theory* (Polity Press, 2021).
7 E.g., A. Anievas and K. Nişancıoğlu, *How the West Came to Rule: The Geopolitical Origins of Capitalism* (Pluto Press, 2015).
8 E.g., A. Anghie, *Imperialism, Sovereignty and the Making of International Law* (Cambridge University Press, 2005).
9 M. Koskenniemi, 'Sovereignty, Property and Empire: Early Modern English Contexts Theoretical Inquiries in Law' (2017) 18 *Theoretical Inquiries in Law* 355, 356.
10 D. Armitage *The Ideological Origins of the British Empire* (Cambridge University Press, 2000).
11 T. Poole, *Reason of State: Law, Prerogative and Empire* (Cambridge University Press, 2015).
12 T. Norfield, *The City: London and the Global Power of Finance* (Verso, 2016).

'of imperialism upon the homeland'.[13] But it does not consider constitutional law's entanglements with settler colonialism[14] or various other forms of 'domestic colonies',[15] even if numerous former colonies went on to reproduce the colonial mindset and practices to rule over their indigenous populations. Neither do I systematically cover the influence of inter-imperial rivalries and wars, notwithstanding the considerable demands they often placed on constitutional structures.

Another is the crucial contribution of the colonised to the emergence and development of liberal constitutional law. Although I offer glimpses of how events in the colonies and resistance by colonial societies prompted key constitutional changes, I do not build a sustained critique of the 'Caliban' model, the assumption that, in their fight for emancipation, anti-colonial movements used ideas first developed in the metropolis, rather than directly contributed to what are today taken as purely Western constructs.[16] Neither do I consider the various constitutional experiments that emerged out of anti-colonial movements committed to an anti-imperial constitutionalism. Much of constitutional law's mythology is sustained by the writing of liberal constitutionalism as a universal, rather than distinctively European and particularistic, set of ideas. Yet, faced with the limits and contradictions of Western constitutionalism and constitutions produced by their entanglement with imperialism, beginning with Haiti,[17] non-Western revolutions produced ideas and documents that proposed far more radical visions of freedom, equality, and self-determination.

Second, the investigation will highlight some of the ways in which race structured the relationship between imperialism and constitutional law, looking at how different forms and processes of racialisation – of attributing social meaning to particular human characteristics that are deemed natural or fixed as a basis for differentiation and hierarchisation – and their attendant constitutional forms evolved at different stages in the evolution of capitalist imperialism, from its emergence as colonial capitalism, to nineteenth- and twentieth-century imperialism and to its contemporary global neoliberal form, playing different roles in the valorisation of capital[18] under each of these configurations. In doing so, it views race, like class, not as an epiphenomenal form, but as a material relation of expropriation, exploitation and domination which is built into capital's contradictory tendency to expand, universalise and homogenise, as much as to produce difference between people and territories, building on and transforming old patterns of stratification as well as creating new ones.[19] And I call the racial (imperial) constitution the set of constitutional laws, practices and discourses that constitute and reproduce the racialised differentiational basis of capitalist imperial relations. Yet, the question of the relationship between imperialism, racism and constitutionalism demands far greater theorisation and a fuller exposition of the connections between constitutional law and imperialism would also require an examination of gender, alongside race and class exploitation and oppression.[20]

[13] H. Arendt, *The Origins of Totalitarianism* (Harcourt, 1973), 155.

[14] A. Rana, *The Two Faces of American Freedom* (Harvard University Press, 2014).

[15] B. Arneil, *Domestic Colonies: The Turn Inward to Colony* (Oxford University Press, 2017).

[16] P. Gopal, *Insurgent Empire Anticolonial Resistance and British Dissent* (Verso, 2020).

[17] E.g., C. L. R. James, *The Black Jacobins: Toussaint l'Ouverture and the San Domingo Revolution* (Penguin, 2001).

[18] R. Knox, 'Valuing Race? Stretched Marxism and the Logic of Imperialism' (2016) 4 *London Review of International Law* 81.

[19] For a recent discussion, see N. Tzouvala, *Capitalism As Civilisation: A History of International Law* (Cambridge University Press, 2021).

[20] S. Federici, *The Caliban and the Witch: Women, the Body and Primitive Accumulation* (Penguin, 2021).

11.1 HISTORICAL CONNECTIONS: WELCOME TO THE DARK SIDE

11.1.1 *The Colonial Dawn of the Modern Constitution*

'The discovery of gold and silver in America', Marx famously wrote, 'the extirpation, enslavement, and entombment in mines of the indigenous population of that continent, the beginnings of the conquest and plunder of India, and the conversion of Africa into a preserve for the commercial hunting of black skins, are all things that characterize the dawn of the era of capitalist production'. These 'idyllic proceedings', he continued, were 'the chief moments of primitive accumulation'.[21] And so were they chief moments in the birth of modern constitutionalism and constitutions.

Marxist historiography has long pointed to the connections between the eighteenth-century revolutionary wars that led to the birth of the modern constitution and the development of bourgeois society.[22] In England, the revolution was precipitated by changes to property relations and the consolidation of a distinct bourgeoisie. In France, it played a crucial role in capitalist development, even if capitalist forms of labour already existed under the absolutist state.

Yet capitalist development was never a purely internal process. Historically, dispossession, colonialism, chattel slavery, the slave trade, merchant capital and imperialist wars all played key roles in the genesis of capitalism and the development of capitalist social relations. Theoretically, these were not archaic processes that kick started but otherwise lay 'outside' the logic of capital accumulation. Instead, they were embedded in circuits of commodity production and exchange[23] and were critical to the valorisation of capital. Their seeming opposition to capitalist social forms – economic compulsion, wage labour, formal equality – denoted a general characteristic of capital, whose expansionary logic, already highlighted by Marx and Engels in the *Communist Manifesto* and developed in later theories of imperialism, did not tend toward the universalisation of capitalist social relations, but toward the production of difference,[24] with racial distinctions playing a key role in value extraction in the colonies.[25] The de-valued labour of the black slave, for example, served to produce cheap commodities, whilst the triangular slave trade worked to channel profits back to Europe.

This global imperial context was crucial to capitalist development in both France and Britain. The colonisation of the Americas and the slave trade played key roles in the industrialisation of Britain.[26] Although France had lost several of its colonies to Britain after the Seven Years War, its colonial empire, particularly St Domingue and its thriving sugar production, remained crucial to its economic development.[27] Likewise, competitive pressures generated by British industrialisation and inter-imperial rivalries all contributed to creating the conditions for the revolutionary break with French absolutism. And it was crucial to the emergence of modern constitutionalism and constitutional law.

[21] K. Marx, *Capital Volume I*, B. Fowkes, trans. (Penguin, 1990), 915.
[22] e.g., N. Davidson, *How Revolutionary Were the Bourgeois Revolutions?* (Haymarket, 2012).
[23] Marx himself viewed slavery capitalism as a form of capitalism. See, e.g., J. B. Foster, H. Holleman and B. Clark, 'Marx and Slavery' (2020) 72 *Monthly Review* 3.
[24] F. Fanon, *The Wretched of the Earth* (Grove Press, 1963), 40.
[25] On the race form as a constitutive feature of the value form, see S. Salam, 'Limits of the Black Radical Tradition and the Value-form', PhD thesis, City University of New York (2019).
[26] E. Williams, *Capitalism and Slavery [1944]* (University of North Carolina Press, 1994).
[27] M. Covo, 'Race, Slavery, and Colonies in the French Revolution', in D. Andress (ed.), *Oxford Handbook of the French Revolution* (Oxford University Press, 2015), 292–93.

The social forces of the revolutionary process and the constitutional settlements which they reached were shaped as much by domestic class antagonisms as they were by imperial interests. In England, for example, support for the Crown included the old merchant elite 'associated with the East India Company, who depended on it for control of trading routes'[28] in the Levant. Numerous patents and charters were granted by the Crown using the royal prerogative between 1579 and 1732 for the purposes of establishing the colonial settlements of the Atlantic region. Capitalist support for Parliament, on the other hand, included a class of new merchants 'excluded from the state monopoly privileges and connected to the rising colonial trades in the Americas'.[29] The revolutionary period would eventually culminate in the constitutional primacy of Parliament. But this did not displace the power of the Crown, particularly over colonial matters, and the resulting division of labour between the Crown and Parliament, which lives on today, testified to the centrality of empire to British constitutionalism. Parliament took on an increasingly interventionist stance in matters of imperial trade, but colonies continued, in large part, to be established under the royal prerogative: the Crown ensured the expansion of the Empire, Parliament its exploitation.

The Enlightenment ideas on which these forces build and that would form the backbone of liberal constitutionalism – autonomy, liberty, equality, limited government, the rule of law and human rights – were born out of the colonial encounter. One example is Lockean constitutionalism. The purpose of government and constitutional law, for Locke, was the protection of natural property rights:[30] men entered society to enjoy 'their properties in peace and safety' and these were to be secured by a set of 'laws established in that society' and to 'govern even the legislative [power] itself'.[31] Locke's theory played a key role in England, where the primacy of Parliament marked the emergence of a constitutional order that tied political sovereignty to the protection of private property,[32] but also in the development of liberal constitutional ideas of limited government and the rule of law.

More than any of his contemporaries, Locke explicitly rooted his theories in capitalist principles of accumulation and competition.[33] Private property did not arise from mere use or occupation of the land (i.e., use value) but instead fell on those most able to improve the land and to extract, through money, the greatest profit from it (i.e., through the production and maximisation of exchange value). Nor did it need to be bestowed on the direct producer: it could accrue to the 'master' who put others' labour to productive use. Crucially, in Locke's theory, the appropriation of labour and the pursuit of profit do not appear as selfish or exploitative endeavours. To the contrary, by increasing the overall wealth of the community, private property and capital accumulation are the means through which to make the most of what God naturally and equally bestowed on all humans to the benefit of society as a whole. As such, they exercise a broader social function that justified protection through the law.[34]

Although concerns pertaining to the consolidation of bourgeois society in England were not irrelevant, Locke's theories were mainly designed to support the colonial project in North America. His understanding of property legitimised dispossession and settlement in conditions

[28] Anievas and Nişancıoğlu, *How the West Came to Rule*, 195.
[29] Ibid., 195.
[30] L. Ward, *The Politics of Liberty in England and Revolutionary America* (Cambridge University Press, 2004), 15.
[31] J. Locke, *Second Treatise of Government*, P. Laslett, ed. (Cambridge University Press, 1988), para 134.
[32] Koskenniemi, 'Sovereignty, Property and Empire'.
[33] E. M. Wood, *Empire of Capital* (Verso, 2003).
[34] See further on the specific function of law, S. Graf, *The Humanity of Universal Crime* (Oxford University Press, 2021), 66–72.

where land was already occupied by native populations. His emphasis on the improvement of land and the maximisation of exchange value allowed for a distribution of natural property rights based on a comparison between native use and imperial use according to capitalism's 'laws of nature', which essentially corresponded to the standards of the emerging English system of capitalist agrarian production. Judged to be 'wasteful' of the natural resources God vested in native lands, native occupation could not prevent colonial appropriation. In addition, Locke took the 'absence of monetisation' as evidence that the natives still lived in the state of nature[35] – 'in the beginning', said Locke, 'all the world was America, and more so than that is now; for no such thing as money was anywhere known'.[36] In the absence of authority securing private property rights, the British had a right, if not a duty, to assume political authority.

Both economic dispossession and political domination, moreover, built on assumptions about civilisation that gave expression to capital's logic of differentiation and would contribute to the development of distinctively capitalist ideas of 'racial superiority that rendered race contingent on specific forms of labour', property relations as well as political and legal organisation. As Bhandar shows, while biological conceptions of racism had yet to be fully developed, Locke equated capitalist British uses of land with civilised use and established legally protected private ownership of the kind emerging in Britain as a pre-condition for civilisation and hence for legal subjectivity: 'those who were not productive and industrious cultivators of land (or landowners, or engaged in commercial ventures of some kind) were deemed to be uncivilised and in need of improvement as much as their waste lands were'.[37] As Western domination consolidated, the connections between law, property and civilisation would lead to a more explicit mobilisation of Western constitutionalism as a tool of colonial domination. Collapsed with their Western iteration,[38] constitutional constraints were taken as markers of European superiority and their absence in the colonies as a sign of backwardness and a basis for denying indigenous sovereignty.

When imported back into the imperial metropolis and translated into constitutional practice, these ideas were not emptied of their colonial logic. The constitutional settlement that emerged out of the Glorious Revolution was based on the same assumptions about land use and subjecthood as those that shaped colonial social relations. These found their most salient expression in the enclosure movement of the eighteenth century, which dramatically accelerated the separation of the population from their means of subsistence. Here too, expropriation was premised on a distinction between productive and unproductive uses of land based on the logics of improvement and profit maximisation. Here too, it involved brutal methods. And here too, it was constructed around racialised understandings of land and personhood in which private ownership became a pre-condition for civilisation. The 'boomerang effect' extended well beyond processes of dispossession. Marx often spoke of the slave-like conditions of capitalist production and Losurdo extended the analogy to the political sphere. On condition that race is not understood 'in the purely ethnic sense', he writes, 'the society which emerged in England from the Glorious Revolution was configured as a sort of "master-race democracy"'. Liberties were so gravely infringed and inequalities so 'marked and insuperable that "each class assumes the aspect of a distinct race"'.[39] The parallels between the colonial and the domestic contexts

[35] O. Ulas Ince, *Colonial Capitalism and the Dilemmas of Liberalism* (Oxford University Press, 2018), 7.

[36] Locke, *Second Treatise of Government*, para. 49.

[37] B. Bhandar, *Colonial Lives of Property Law, Land, and Racial Regimes of Ownership* (Duke University Press, 2018), 47.

[38] See, e.g., Article 16 of the Virginia Declaration of Rights 1776: '[a]ny society in which the guarantee of rights is not assured nor the separation of powers determined has no form of constitution.'

[39] D. Losurdo, *Liberalism: A Counter-History* (Verso, 2011), 123–24.

would continue to shape capitalist development throughout its history, reaching its most dramatic expression with the European fascist state, which applied to the white man 'colonial procedures which until then had been reserved exclusively for the Arabs of Algeria, the coolies of India, and the blacks of Africa'.[40] In that sense, modern constitutionalism not only emerged out of the colonial experience and played a key role in constituting and justifying imperial social relations; the colonies also acted as a laboratory where its ideas and practices were developed, tested and re-imported into the imperial metropolis.

11.1.2 The Consolidation of the Imperial Constitution

As empires expanded and constitutionalism took a stronger hold on social and political life over the course of the nineteenth and twentieth centuries, the relationship between constitutional law and imperialism deepened. The emergence of finance capital and its relentless drive for new markets prompted dramatic levels of colonial expansion and inter-imperial rivalries. Their high point, the scramble for Africa, brought almost the entire African continent under Western rule. Materially, the shift from the export of commodities to the exportation of capital required further processes of dispossession and the destruction of native forms of subsistence and cultures. At the same time, in the colonies, various forms of coerced labour and slavery persisted, despite the latter's abolition. Ideologically, racism and liberal imperialism consolidated and support for Empire grew.[41] Imperial expansion, it was thought, fostered national glory, identity and unity, tempered social discontent and class antagonism, and helped to secure order and freedom in the imperial metropolis. Imperialism, in other words, became a political and cultural, as much as socio-economic, imperative.

This conjuncture left its imprint on the constitutional developments of the period. In the United Kingdom, the consolidation of a positivist and absolute conception of parliamentary sovereignty over conceptions of limited sovereignty rooted in natural law, was essential to imperial expansion and unity, particularly in conditions of increased territorial and personal differentiation. Parliament's exclusive ability to change and remake the law, Dicey stressed, enabled 'the easy incorporation of new territories, the adoption of varied political arrangements appropriate for the Empire's different peoples and rapid responses to internal or external threats'.[42] Similarly, the shift from a jurisdictional to a jurisprudential understanding of the common law as a 'rationally organized' body of principles and rules operating under the aegis of the rule of law rather than tied to the jurisdiction of the courts,[43] served as an important racialised justification for Empire and for thwarting rival imperial claims. England's 'spirit of legalism', unmatched, so it claimed, by any other European power, was evidence of the superiority of the Anglo-Saxon race and its rightful authority to extend its rule beyond its borders.[44]

In post-revolutionary France, imperialism was implicated in the continuous refashioning of the French Constitution and the French State. Between the eighteenth and twentieth centuries

[40] A. Cesaire, *Discourse on Colonialism* (Monthly Review Press, 1972).

[41] See J. Pitts, *A Turn to Empire: The Rise of Imperial Liberalism in Britain and France* (Princeton University Press, 2005); Alexis de Tocqueville, *Writings on Empire and Slavery*, J. Pitts, trans. and ed. (Johns Hopkins University Press, 2001).

[42] D. Lino, 'Albert Venn Dicey and the Constitutional Theory of Empire' (2016) 36 *Oxford Journal of Legal Studies* 751, 755.

[43] Poole, *Reason of State*, 11.

[44] D. Lino, 'The Rule of Law and the Rule of Empire: A. V. Dicey in Imperial Context' (2018) 81 *Modern Law Review* 739.

the Constitution was amended over 10 times and its form fluctuated between monarchism, republicanism and Bonapartism. Each corresponded to different phases and configurations of French imperialism. The dictatorial State and constitution – Bonapartism[45] – for example, was designed to enable dramatic territorial ambitions and/or expansion of the Empire, including within Europe, in contrast to other periods of contraction, of more informal forms of imperial domination or of colonial domination outside of Europe.[46] On the other hand, even during the Napoleonic eras, in France too the constitution was put to the service of Empire. Constitutional republican values were integrated in an ideology of French uniqueness according to which French imperialism was designed to export the French model across the world. The 'mission civilatrice' hardly reflected the violence of Empire on the ground. Yet not only did it justify Napoleon's expansionist policies, it also provided a basis to France's claim of an allegedly superior right of colonisation.

As is clear from these examples, the relationship between constitutional law and imperial ventures always took and will take different constitutional forms across time and space, even within the imperial core. These differences reflected both different constitutional traditions and differences in the nature and complexion of different imperial periods and projects. Britain's unwritten constitution generally allowed for greater flexibility and incremental development and its Empire was relatively more stable and continuous. In both cases, however, constitutional law played a key role in constituting and legitimising new forms of exploitation and domination and in securing them against claims by other imperial powers.

11.2 TENSIONS AND CONTRADICTIONS: IMPERIALISM AND THE RACIAL IMPERIAL CONSTITUTION

11.2.1 *The Racialisation of the Imperial Constitutional Order*

The imperial dimensions of constitutionalism and the constitutional processes that they informed, however, gave rise to tensions and contradictions. Chief amongst them was the disjuncture between the professed universalism of constitutional values and the particularism of the constitution's material reality of (racialised) difference and hierarchy.

This tension was central to the debates and struggles that shaped the various constitutions adopted in France from 1791 to 1795. The 'mulattos', an increasingly affluent class of free men of colour, and the black slaves demanded legal recognition, that is, that the imperial constitution live up to its promise of liberty and equality for all. It was not until Napoleon's counter-revolution and the death of Toussaint Louverture, the face of the Haitian revolution, that the black population realised the limits of this strategy and the necessity to break not only from slavery, but also from their imperial master. The white settlers, by contrast, demanded autonomy, including over matters of colonial trade and, crucially, the status of non-whites. One faction, in other words, fought for universalism, the other for differentiation. And these were divided along both class and racial lines.

In the early revolutionary phase, these contradictions were solved in favour of the colonists. The 1791 constitution made the colonies part of the French empire but excluded them from the

45 Although the term implies a somewhat mistaken analogy between the first and the second Napoleonic regimes and between the First and Second French Empires.

46 D. Todd, 'An Imperial Nation-State: France and its Empires', in P. F. Bang, C. A. Bayly and W. Scheidel (eds.), *The Oxford World History of Empires* (Oxford University Press, 2021), Vol. 2, 941–63.

scope of application of the constitution. This solution preserved the revolutionary 'project of constructing national legal and institutional uniformity',[47] thwarting settlers' demands for distinct laws and institutions. But the inapplicability of the French Declaration of the Rights of Man and of the Citizen enabled the continuation of the plantation system. The Declaration thus sanctioned not only social inequality in civil society, as Marx famously highlighted,[48] but also formal political inequality: the colonised were members but not citizens of the Imperial Republic.

This position changed in 1794, but the abolition of slavery hardly reflected a newfound commitment to the humanity and equality of the colonised. Even among the radical fringes of the revolution, imperial interests and rivalries prevailed. Prior to 1794, Robespierre had advocated for the legal recognition of the mulattos as equal citizens to preserve, rather than undermine, slavery and the Empire. The settlers argued recognition would weaken slaves' submission to their authority. Robespierre retorted that failure to do so would on the contrary unify people of colour against their white oppressor. His argument, as Aimé Césaire points out, effectively called for prioritising the class struggle over the racial struggle: the settlers had to abandon their racial prejudice – given their 'mixed' descent, one member of the national assembly had stressed, the mulattos shared after all some of the attributes of the white race[49] – and seek them out based on their common interests in slave production. And it was also a technique of divide and rule: a means to prevent insurrection. By 1794, however, the conditions had changed. Faced with the mounting slave revolt and the war with England, the defence of the Empire now mandated that slaves be recognised and enlisted to fight the English and that the slave trade, which was key to British dominance, be dismantled.

The prevalence of imperial interests found direct expression in law. By the time of the 1795 constitution, the differential basis of colonial capitalism had found a more specific articulation in the French legal order. References to slavery in legislation had disappeared. Slavery was formally abolished on the metropolitan territory and the maxim 'les lois se taisent' (the laws remain silent) reflected the revolutionaries' awareness that the institution of slavery contradicted both the letter and the spirit of the French Declaration and risked destabilising the foundations of the revolutionary project. Influenced by the growing prevalence of scientific racism, restrictions on the rights of black people began instead to be framed in terms of race rather than status.[50] Unsurprisingly, given those conditions, the 1795 constitution would become the exception in France's constitutional history: emancipation was among the first of the revolutionary gains to be reversed by the Bonapartist coup and no constitution ever wholly or unquestionably applied to the colonies.

For Aimé Césaire, the legal exclusion of the slave reflected the disjuncture between the emerging political and legal forms of metropolitan bourgeois society on the one hand, and those prevailing in the system of slave production in the colonies on the other. Capitalist production in the metropolis was evolving toward wage labour and assumed legal freedom and equality. Slave production positioned the slave as an object of production and assumed unfreedom and inequality. Its universal language notwithstanding, liberal freedom's symbiotic relation with capitalism confined its application to those parts of civil society that had been integrated in

[47] M. F. Spieler, 'The Structure of Colonial Rule during the French Revolution 1789–1802' (2009) 66 *The William and Mary Quarterly* 365, 365.

[48] K. Marx, 'On the Jewish Question' [1844], in. K. Marx, *Early Writings*, R. Livingstone and G. Benton trans. (Penguin, 1992), 211–41, although political equality was far from realised, even in the 'free State' of bourgeois society.

[49] A. Césaire, *Toussaint Louverture: La Révolution Française et le Problème Colonial* (Club Français du Livre, 1960), 103.

[50] S. Peabody, 'Race, Slavery, and the Law in Early Modern France' (1994) 66 *The Historian* 501.

capitalist social relations, to the exclusion of pre-capitalist social relations. But once we see slavery as an inherent part of the logic of capital, legal exclusion and differentiation appear not as archaic legal forms, but as constitutive features of modern constitutionalism. The 'double movement' of the French Enlightenment and constitutionalism – its tendency 'to incorporate and comprehend alongside' its tendency to 'cultural and ethical singularity or uniqueness',[51] in other words, found its material underpinnings in the development of capitalist imperialism with race, as a legal construct, emerging to constitute, rationalise and reproduce a system of valorisation based on difference.

Reading slavery as evidence of the exclusionary and discriminatory logic of modern (imperial) constitutionalism also brings nuance to existing accounts of its historical entanglement with Empire. In his important study, Fradera draws a distinction between what he calls 'imperial constitutions' and 'colonial constitutions'.[52] The first, which is illustrated by the 1795 constitution, emerged in the revolutionary period, and was characterised by universality and unity: nation-state and the empire were one, governed by a single constitutional order. The second gained ground after the Bonapartian Constitution of 1799 and was defined by separateness: nation-states and their empire were distinguished and governed by a dual constitutional order, one for the metropolis, another, if any, for the colonies. As we shall see, the nineteenth century did mark a shift in the legal technologies and ideology of Empires. But the handling of slavery in the French revolution warns against drawing any sharp divide between these two phases and models. The spirit of the 1795 constitution was never realised in the figure of the slave, whose subordination remained essential to the plantation regime. This disavowal may have been formally achieved by means other than the constitution (i.e., legislative or administrative measures) and it may have operated through the category of 'race' rather than 'slave'. But even from a purely positivist perspective, it was still regarded as a 'valid' interpretation of the constitution and thus compatible with its claims to equality. From that perspective, we could characterise Fradera's first phase of 'imperial constitutionalism' as a period marked by the gradual racialisation of the constitutional order, whereupon race, as a legal category, appeared in legislation to reconcile the unitary structure of the constitution with the particularism of its material basis and the second phase of 'colonial constitutionalism' as a period marked by the personal and geographical dislocation of the constitution, where racialised difference is constitutionalised, albeit not explicitly on racial grounds. In both cases, however, we have legal differentiation and, in that sense, both types of constitutions could be seen as racial imperial constitutions, that is to say as constitutional orders designed to operationalise and organise racialised social relations of exploitation and domination, even as they do so through different legal techniques.

11.2.2 *The Constitutionalisation of (Racialised) Difference*

Throughout the nineteenth and twentieth centuries, the contradictions at the heart of the imperial constitution deepened, leading to increased struggles. Colonies entered endless cycles of violence. The American and Haitian revolutions had stripped imperial powers of any illusion that the irrational native will submit to their will, fuelling increased repression, anti-colonial

[51] S. M. Agnani, *Hating Empire Properly: The Two Indies and the Limits of Enlightenment Anticolonialism* (Fordham University Press, 2013), 14.

[52] J. M. Fradera, *The Imperial Nation: Citizens and Subjects in the British, French, Spanish, and American Empires*, R. MacKay, trans. (Princeton University Press, 2018).

resistance and yet more brutal responses. In the metropolis, a growing labour movement not only criticised colonial excesses but began to formulate alternative non-bourgeois visions of internationalism that substituted cooperation for the exploitation and domination of capitalist imperialism. Its most radical fringes, such as the Communards, identified their own struggle with anti-colonial movements, from the Algerian fight against metropolitan France to the Indian and Irish revolts in the British Empire.[53] As other 'undesirables' before them, many were deported to the colonies and would come to face the reality of colonial violence directly.

These tensions fed into constitutional debates. Dicey, for example, became increasingly concerned with how to reconcile the principles of British constitutionalism with the goal of maintaining imperial unity. Parliamentary sovereignty and the wide discretionary powers of self-government conferred upon settler colonists were crucial to the imperial project. But they raised real prospects of abuse, which undermined the Empire's apparent commitment to the rule of law and fuelled resistance to imperial rule. In that sense, he concluded, 'British constitutional structures and principles could both help and hinder imperial unity'.[54]

New constitutional concepts, practices and institutions emerged to accommodate these contradictions, which, if anything, brought constitutionalism and the formal constitution closer to their imperial material underpinnings. One example is the development of emergency laws. Up until then, legal institutions associated with forms of 'extraordinary' legality – the dictatorship; martial law etc. – were either reserved for times of war or applied mainly to military personnel.[55] It is in the colonies, and in that period of colonial unrest, that more 'modern' versions of emergency, applicable in times of formal peace, were fashioned and developed. Another example is the consolidation of modern forms of citizenship based on an exclusionary bond tied to the territorial unit of the nation state by birth or filiation, which emerged out of the need to distinguish between coloniser and colonised.

These constitutional developments found their sources in a new consensus that the metropolis and the colonies could not be governed by the same set of laws. The settler colonial project required that the constitution be extended to the colonies: 'Settlers must encounter a "perfect image of their homeland" in Algeria', Tocqueville emphasised, 'or they would never stay'.[56] But, he was quick to add, the law must not be the same for all.[57] Algeria thus became a laboratory for the experimentation of differentiation. The 1848 constitution of the Second Republic made Algeria an integral part of France. But, in practice, a range of laws and administrative acts created both territorial and personal distinctions, resulting in dual juridical, political and administrative systems and a multiplicity of legal personhoods characterised by different attributes that departed from the principles and rights of the French Declaration.[58] At its heart was the distinction between French citizens and French subjects, which reached its climax with the adoption of the 1881 Code de l'Indigénat completing the process of emptying colonial personhood of any substance.[59] Similar developments shaped the evolution of the British Empire.[60]

53 K. Ross, *Communal Luxury: The Political Imaginary of the Paris Commune* (Verso, 2016), 57.
54 Lino, 'Albert Venn Dicey', 767.
55 M. Neocleous, 'From Martial Law to the War on Terror' (2007) 10 *New Criminal Law Review* 489.
56 Pitts, in de Tocqueville, *Writings on Empire*, xxiii.
57 O. Le Cour Grandmaison, 'L'Exception et la Règle: Sur le Droit Colonial Français' (2005/4) *Diogène* 42, 54.
58 O. Le Cour Grandmaison, *De l'Indigénat – Anatomie d'un 'Monstre' Juridique: le Droit Colonial en Algérie et dans l'Empire Français* (Zones, 2010).
59 Spieler, 'Structure of Colonial Rule', 368.
60 On emergency rule, see, e.g., N. Hussein, *The Jurisprudence of Emergency: Colonialism and the Rule of Law* (University of Michigan Press, 2004). On citizenship, see, e.g., N. El-Enany, *Bordering Britain: Law, Race and Empire* (Manchester University Press, 2020).

Initially, at least, different reasons were put forward to 'solve' the contradiction that differentiation produced for imperial ideology, which assumed colonial subjects could develop laws and institutions comparable to their enlightened rulers and that it was the imperial power's moral duty to see them through this civilising process. One was that colonial societies were not ready to benefit from the principles of civilisation and that repression and differentiation were a necessary, albeit transitory and temporary, step designed to pacify local populations and develop their capacity to embrace Western values and laws. On paper, for example, the régime de l'indigénat was originally limited to seven years.[61] Another was that colonial societies had to be treated differently because they differed in terms of their cultures, political practices and social and moral conventions. Civilisation, then, not only pre-supposed pacification, but the destruction of native culture, traditions and institutions, which acted as impediments to the development of the colonised. These two lines of argument sometimes operated together: it was because of racialised cultural and other differences that the native was not yet ready for successful assimilation.

With time, however, differentiation became entrenched. In the British Empire, indirect rule became far more widespread in non-white colonies, and by 1900, 'association' substituted 'assimilation' as the principle defining the relationship between the French Republic and its colonies. In both contexts, emergency rule became the norm and, as differentiation received more specific articulation in the ideology of Empire,[62] so did the racial assumptions on which it was based. Because of their inferior attributes, it was claimed, equality of treatment would be both detrimental to the native, who was incapable of exercising such rights, and unfair for society as a whole, as it would ignore natural differences in aptitude and talents.[63]

In many accounts, differentiation is legally captured as an 'anomalous legal zone', 'a permanent state of exception' or a 'monstrous derogatory regime'[64] which departed from the imperial constitution. Yet, not only do these characterisations underestimate the material basis of differentiation, but as we saw, legally, it had already received expression in the post-revolutionary settlement and emergency rule was never an exclusive attribute of the nineteenth century. Analytically, moreover, they might not do full justice to the distinctively legal character of differentiation. If we take seriously the fact that these states were never 'nation-states' who had 'empires' but 'imperial states',[65] perhaps a better analogy to other legal architectures and artefacts would be those of the settler colonial state. Constitutionally, differentiation would take the form of two different yet co-extensive legal regimes that do not oppose each other as 'norm' and 'exception' but that represent two different moments, two normal facets of the constitution that are part of its racialised basis and logic of differentiation. Indeed, it is telling that one of the most vocal proponents of separateness was Tocqueville, whose writings on Algeria essentially contain a blueprint of the settler colonial project. Although Le Cour Grand Maison remains within the frame of the exception, his notion of the Republican Imperial Constitution[66] captures this co-constitutive relation well: juridically, imperialism is not a departure from or in contradiction with the Republican Constitution but part of its constitutive logic.

[61] I. Merle, 'Retour sur le Régime de l'Indigénat: Genèse et Contradictions des Principes Répressifs dans l'Empire Français' (2002) 20 *French Politics, Culture & Society* 77.
[62] M. Mandani, *Citizen and Subject: Contemporary Africa and the Legacy of Late Colonialism* (Princeton University Press, 1996).
[63] Le Cour Grandmaison, *De l'Indigénat*.
[64] Ibid.
[65] Bhambra and Holmwood, *Colonialism and Modern Social Theory*, 34.
[66] O. Le Cour Grandmaison, *La République Impériale. Politique et Racisme d'État* (Fayard, 2009).

In that sense, we can indeed distinguish between a phase of unity and assimilation, and a phase of separateness and exclusion in the evolution of the (racial) imperial constitution. Materially, pressure on the formal constitution to cement differentiation increased as Empires expanded, racialised territorial and personal differentiation intensified and resistance to empire and cross-racial forms of solidarity based on the common experiences of exploitation and oppression grew. Ideologically, the constitutionalisation of colonial difference became far more acceptable as support for the Empire grew, as national identity solidified, as justifications for distinguishing between the races developed and as constitutional law matured, allowing for the emergence of constitutional forms capable of containing the contradictions of capitalist imperialism. Yet, constitutional assimilation and differentiation are not opposing facets of the modern constitution but different expressions of its material underpinnings of racialised difference at different historical conjunctures.

11.3 CONTEMPORARY MANIFESTATIONS: FROM COLONIAL LEGACY TO IMPERIAL PRESENT

Contemporary constitutions continue to carry the marks of their colonial past. The present account showed some of the processes and contexts through which constitutional concepts, laws and practices that linger in the present, from the doctrine of Parliamentary Sovereignty to the French Declaration, were shaped by the colonial encounter. Others have offered more comprehensive accounts of the colonial origins of other key constitutional categories[67] such as 'citizenship'[68] or 'reason of state'.[69] In some cases, the vestiges of Empire bear even more visible manifestations. The 14 British Overseas Territories and the French DOM-TOM are all territorial or administrative inheritances of Empire. Several are still listed as non-self-governing territories by the UN and their constitutional structures confirm the thesis of 'colonial continuity'. Notwithstanding important constitutional variations, for example, both the Crown and Parliament retain considerable executive and legislative powers over the BOTs.[70]

But the contemporary connections between constitutional law and imperialism can hardly be reduced to the old remembrances of Empire. As a social relation that operates both within and across national borders, capitalist imperialism can hardly be reduced to the colonial form. Already in Lenin, who developed one of the first Marxist theories of imperialism, we see that imperialism did not presuppose formal political and territorial control.[71] Finance capital may find it 'most "convenient"' and derive the 'greatest profit' from the establishment of colonies which 'alone gives the monopolies complete guarantee against all contingencies in the struggle against competitors'. But being 'such a great ... force in all economic and in all international relations', he continued, it was 'capable of subjecting ... to itself even states enjoying the fullest political independence'. Since then, political Marxism has placed even greater emphasis on market dependency as the distinguishing feature of capitalist imperialism when compared to other forms of empire, which instead depended on extra-economic force for the extraction of surplus value.[72] While violence and coercion remain central to capital accumulation, these

[67] P. F. Scott (ed.), The Constitutional Legacies of Empire (2021) 71(2) *Northern Ireland Legal Quarterly*.

[68] El-Enany, *Bordering Britain*.

[69] Poole, *Reason of State*.

[70] H. Yusuf and T. Chowdhury, 'The Persistence of Colonial Constitutionalism in British Overseas Territories' (2019) 8 *Global Constitutionalism* 157.

[71] V. Lenin, *Imperialism, the Highest Stage of Capitalism [1917]* (Penguin, 2010).

[72] Wood, *Empire of Capital*.

analyses make clear that colonialism was but one manifestation of capitalist imperialism and hence of the imperial constitution.

One difficulty in seeking out the constitutional manifestations of contemporary capitalist imperialism is that theories of imperialism vary in their understanding of (a) capital's 'laws of motion' (what is sometimes termed the 'logic of capital'); (b) the role of the state (what is sometimes termed the 'logic of territory')[73] and (c) the relationship between the two, including in terms of the relevance of national imperialisms and geopolitical rivalries, with significant implications for how we might broach contemporary constitutional developments. In addition, while the globalisation of capitalist imperialism has been accompanied by a globalisation of the imperial constitution, given the variety of constitutional arrangements in place across the globe, any investigation of the specific constitutional forms of contemporary imperialism will require far more empirical work into individual constitutional orders. Space prevents a full engagement with those questions, but two general and partly contradictory tendencies of the present phase of neoliberal capitalist imperialism and the imperial constitution can be highlighted that illustrate the enduring connections between constitutional law and imperialism, their impact on constitutional developments, as well as the tensions to which they give rise.

Under the dominance of finance capital, the imperatives of valorisation (i.e., the profit motive) and competition have led to a significant expansion of capitalism across space, social spheres and modes of being.[74] At the same time, capitalist expansion has not meant universalisation and homogenisation. On the contrary, deepening market fundamentalism and competition in the present phase of global neoliberal imperialism have produced increased levels and changing patterns of racialised differentiation and exclusion, along both old and new geographical and personal lines. Previous tendencies of capital concentration, uneven development, unequal divisions of labour both between and within countries, as well as the production of surplus populations and forms of un-waged labour have accelerated while new forms of 'accumulation by dispossession'[75] and over-exploitation have emerged, deepening racialised international and domestic inequalities. National imperialisms, moreover, persist, even if they are subject to the dominance of US capital. Imperial decline since the fall of Empire has not undermined the United Kingdom's position as a leading international actor in production, commerce, and particularly finance, which it uses, alongside its military power and intelligence capacity, to appropriate value and resources from dominated countries.[76] The concept of 'Franceafrique' similarly captures the endurance of French imperialism, with the FCA franc – the name for two currencies used in a number of former French colonies in West and Central Africa – and military interventions continuing to ensure economic exploitation and political domination. New forms of regional imperialism (e.g., the EU), moreover, have emerged, which have either complemented or produced tensions with pre-existing forms of imperialism, as the example of Brexit shows. All of these have produced their own dynamic of capitalist expansion and differentiation, further complicating the spatial and personal fault-lines of neoliberal imperialism.

These processes played a key role in contemporary constitutional developments. The globalisation of capitalist imperialism has gone hand in hand with the universalisation of the

[73] See, e.g., B. S. Chimni, *International Law and World Order: A Critique of Contemporary Approaches*, 2nd ed. (Cambridge University Press, 2017).

[74] R. Luxemburg, *The Accumulation of Capital* [1913] (Routledge, 2003). Luxemburg sees the need to realise surplus value and under-consumption as the key driver of imperial expansion.

[75] E.g., D. Harvey, *The New Imperialism* (Oxford University Press, 2003).

[76] Norfield, *City*, 23.

constitutional form and increased dominance of constitutional law over other political and social forms. Post-colonial societies following decolonisation all emerged as constitutional states and adopted written constitutions. Beginning in the 1990s, many of them, alongside post-communist states, underwent further processes of neoliberal constitution-building and reform. Everywhere, including in the imperial core, a legal constitutionalism foregrounding the rule of law and fundamental rights has overshadowed liberal values of democratic self-government. In the United Kingdom, for example, the absolute and positivist nature of parliamentary sovereignty has been increasingly challenged by a common law constitutionalism rooted in the rule of law and policed by the courts.[77]

Constitutionalisation and juridification were key to enabling the spread and deepening of imperial social relations, helping to open up new markets and to create the conditions for finance-led accumulation. Law and constitutional law have always been central to the constitution and reproduction of capitalist social relations[78] and classic Marxist theories of imperialism had already (implicitly) predicted that the export of capital prompted by finance capital would require the export of capitalist social relations and, hence, of constitutional structures. Law plays a particularly critical role in neoliberal ideology and practice[79] as a tool for creating the conditions of the competitive market order and for insulating economic power from political struggles.

At the same time, the growing cleavage between universalism and particularism produced increased tensions and struggles, drawing constitutional law ever more closely into the work of differentiation and exclusion. Constitutionalisation in the Global South has been both selective and coercive, leaving near to no control over the economy and departing from liberal constitutionalism's alleged commitment to democratic self-government. In the 'advanced' West, exclusionary conceptions of citizenship solidified and served to organise disparities between different forms of racialised labour. Everywhere, resistance to (imperial) neoliberalisation was met with the growing securitisation and militarisation of the state and the constitution. Emergency rule became the ordinary mode of governing surplus populations on the back of new constitutional categories such as 'national security'. The constitutional separateness and duality of earlier phases has been transformed into multiple spatial fault lines, with the border and the distinction between 'citizen', 'migrant' and 'illegal migrant' playing key roles in the ordering and reproduction of a racialised division of labour. Much like the 'slave' of the colonial period or the 'coolie' of nineteenth-century imperialism, migrants, particularly undocumented migrants, provide a source of de-valued cheap labour, which is critical to the valorisation of capital.

Some of these developments have resulted from membership in international organisations or various forms of international intervention and/or have tracked similar trends at the international level. The constitutional neoliberalisation of Iraq, for example, was achieved through military occupation, whilst constitutional reforms in the Global South and later the European periphery were orchestrated by international institutions under the aegis of the International Monetary Fund. But it would be a mistake to attribute them exclusively to international law. Constitutional law and international law have always played complementary and increasingly co-productive roles in the reproduction of imperial social relations, the transfer of powers to supra-national organisations being but one example of the ways in which constitutional law

[77] More generally on the empowerment of courts, see R. Hirschl, *Towards Juristocracy: The Origins and Consequences of the New Constitutionalism* (Harvard University Press, 2004).

[78] Wood, *Empire of Capital*, 16–17.

[79] E.g., H. Brabazon (eds.), *Neoliberal Legality: Understanding the Role of Law in the Neoliberal Project* (Routledge, 2017).

performs its functions of constituting, de-politicising and de-democratising imperial social relations. If anything, the persistence, if not revival, of the national constitutional form notwithstanding the globalisation of capital and the transnationalisation of the constitution points to its centrality to the reproduction of imperial social relations. Not only does the repressive apparatus of the national constitutional state have greater coercive means at its disposal to ensure the stability of imperial social relations, but it might also be better equipped to do imperialism's work of differentiation. While hierarchy and inequality are by no means alien to the international order,[80] international law formally at least aspires to universality. National constitutional orders, by contrast, are, by definition, 'bounded' and their constitutive categories – citizenship, national security, etc. – enable it to organise differential access to resources, rights and privileges, as well as guard against internal and external threats to transnational imperial relations.

As in earlier phases, racialised assumptions have underwritten differentiation and sought to contain the growing gap between the promise and practice of modern constitutionalism. The constitutional neoliberalisation of post-colonial societies built on old colonial justifications about the 'immaturity of the people and their lack of readiness for democracy', whilst the external imposition of the constitution and/or denial of substantive sovereignty echoed the premises of the civilising mission.[81] Similar assumptions migrated back to the West[82] as justification for the practices of the (racial) security state[83] and for limiting democratic participation. At the same time, neoliberal processes of racialisation have been far harder to discern. The language of civilisation has been superseded by a discourse of 'modernisation' and 'developmentalism', whilst the discrediting of scientific racism and the alleged colour-blindness of the market have produced new forms of 'neo-racism' structured around fixed essentialised understandings of culture, nationality or religion. The connection between culture and civilisation are clear in neoliberal thought, including in Hayek's writings, for whom the adoption of Western cultural values, by force if necessary, was a precondition for the market order.[84]

We might therefore begin to identify yet a new, and rather more complex, stage in the interrelationship between constitutionalism, constitutional law and imperialism,[85] although far more research would be needed to delineate its key characteristics. With decolonisation, the formal links between constitutional law and imperialism have, for the most part, been severed (or rather transferred to supra-national and international systems of law). This, however, has not marked the death of the 'imperial constitution'. On the contrary, the universalisation of the (neoliberal) constitutional form could be read as the universalisation of the racial 'imperial constitution' in the sense that all constitutions are materially shaped by imperial social relations. Formally, unity is maintained through the coordination and mediation of constitutional orders by international legal processes while the constitution continues to organise differentiation along both geographical and personal lines, which are defined by a number of variables, including the position of the state, groups and/or individual bodies in the global division of labour.

80 E.g., G. Simpson, *Great Powers and Outlaw States: Unequal Sovereigns in the International Legal Order* (Cambridge University Press, 2004).

81 N. Sultany, *Law and Revolution: Legitimacy and Constitutionalism After the Arab Spring* (Oxford University Press, 2017), 189.

82 J. Van Vossole, 'Framing PIGS: Patterns of Racism and Neocolonialism in the Euro Crisis' (2016) 50 *Patterns of Prejudice* 1.

83 A. Kundnani, 'The Racial Constitution of Neoliberalism' (2021) 63 *Race & Class* 51.

84 Ibid.

85 I deliberately avoided labelling this a 'third stage', as one could identify other intermediate stages between Fradera's second stage of imperial constitutionalism and the present phase of (imperial) neoliberal constitutionalism.

That stage, however, is precarious. The global neoliberal incarnation of the imperial racial constitution has intensified the contradictions at the heart of the constitution. Imperial neoliberalisation has not only deepened inequalities and eroded the social and political fabric: instead of securing unity, the colour-blind imperial constitution has also contributed to the polarisation of society along geographical, cultural and identity lines. As a result, in many places, constitutional struggles have morphed into a crisis, for many an existential crisis, of (neo)liberal constitutionalism. In some places, such as Iraq, such struggles descended into civil wars between sectarian groups and the breakdown of the state. Elsewhere in North Africa or the Middle East they led to revolutions.[86] In some of the 'advanced' 'civilised' Western countries, like Britain, they have led to constitutional rupture. Everywhere, liberal constitutionalism is in decline. With this crisis, the imperial boomerang has come full circle, returning to its point of origin, for, from the very inception of modern constitutionalism, its aims and practices were as much about deconstruction as they were about construction.

11.4 CONCLUSION

Orthodox Eurocentric accounts of constitutionalism and constitutional law see the birth of modern constitutions as the product of processes internal to Europe, whereupon an increasingly enlightened civil society broke with the shackles of feudalism, absolutism and their attendant legal forms. This chapter aimed to show how 'modern' liberal constitutionalism and constitutions were born out of the blood and violence of empire and how they continue to be implicated in the reproduction of racialised relations of domination and exploitation. If colonialism is the dark side of modernity, it is also always the dark side of constitutionalism, which has contributed as much to global inequality as it has to processes of liberation and emancipation. Much remains to be done to decolonise the field of constitutional law, theory and history and the introduction suggested some of the lines of inquiry that such an endeavour would require. Ultimately, however, this chapter argued that the answer is not merely to recover constitutional law's international dimensions or imperial legacies. Rather, it lies in a systematic materialist account of the historical and contemporary relationship between racial imperial capitalism and formal constitutions. And this is how such a project can make a distinct contribution to a 'decolonisation' of the field, one that goes beyond the work of deconstruction, critique and redemption toward an understanding of constitutional law with reconstructive and potentially transformative effects. The point, to borrow from Marx, is not merely to interpret the imperial racial constitution, the point is to change it.

86 Sultany, *Law and Revolution*.

12

The Material Constitution of Federations

Signe Rehling Larsen

One would be hard pressed to find anything written about the material constitutions of federations, at least explicitly in those terms. This entry, therefore, does not purport to provide an overview of any existing literature. Rather, it presents one way of thinking about the material constitution of federations. In *The Constitutional Theory of the Federation and the European Union*, I argue that the federation should be understood as a discrete form of political association on a par with, though distinct from, political modernity's two other significant forms of political association, namely, the *empire* and the *state*.[1] The federation is a political union of states founded on an interstate agreement of constitutional nature, a federal compact, that does not absorb the Member States into a new state. It is characterised by a double political existence and the internal absence, contestation or repression of sovereignty. A federal constitution, therefore, should not be understood as a 'form of government' comparable to, for example, a presidential or parliamentary system, nor is it a governing ideology, comparable to, for example, liberalism or republicanism. The federation, borrowing biological taxonomy, is not a 'species' of the state but a different 'genus' in the 'family' of political associations. The question for this chapter then is what it means to think about the material constitution of the federation as a discrete form of political association? What are the 'ordering forces'[2] of the federal constitution in a material sense? How are they different from those of the state?

12.1 THE FEDERATION AS A FORM OF POLITICAL ASSOCIATION

Within constitutional theory, it is relatively uncontroversial to argue that no constitution can be properly understood unless one goes beyond a mere formal analysis of the document called 'the Constitution'. Even the preeminent written constitution – the American Constitution – cannot meaningfully be reduced to the text of the Constitution and its formal amendments.[3] A constitution cannot be reduced to the sum of constitutional laws; even Hans Kelsen admitted as much.[4] This can be expressed in terms of the difference between the written constitution and

[1] S. R. Larsen, *The Constitutional Theory of the Federation and the European Union* (Oxford University Press, 2021).

[2] M. Goldoni and M. Wilkinson, 'The Material Constitution' (2018) 81 *Modern Law Review* 567, 569.

[3] B. Ackerman, 'The Living Constitution' (2007) 120 *Harvard Law Review* 1737.

[4] H. Kelsen, *General Theory of Law and State*, A. Wedberg, trans. (Harvard University Press, 1945), 124–25. H. Heller, 'The Nature and Structure of the State' (1996) 18 *Cardozo Law Review* 1139, 1212 expressed this succinctly: 'No written constitutional instrument contains all foundational norms, and every constitution also contains law which cannot count as foundational from the standpoint of a systematic political analysis.'

the 'real', 'substantive' or 'material' constitution. As this book bears witness to, there is no consensus on what it means to think about the constitution in this latter sense. Nevertheless, the importance of thinking of the constitution beyond a written document – in one way or other – is even more evident for the theory of the federation than the theory of the state. This is because the constitutional nature of the federation can only be discerned if one goes beyond a mere formal analysis. This has to do with the origins of federations.

A federation is a permanent union of two or more states that have come together in order to further their common goal of self-preservation. A federation is therefore founded on an inter-state agreement, a federal treaty or federal compact (*Bundesvertrag*).[5] From a formalistic perspective, therefore, the federation belongs to the world of international law. Nevertheless, the federal compact is not an ordinary international law treaty because it gives *birth* to new political order, the Union, and *transforms* the constitutions of the contracting states by giving them the new status of 'Member States'.[6] The federal compact is therefore also a constitutional contract or a constitutional treaty (*Verfassungsvertrag*) that relies for its authority on the will of the constituent powers of all the Member States.[7] Birth and transformation are two dynamic 'ordering forces' of the federal constitution. The federal compact is constitutional because it founds a new legal and political order to which the contracting states henceforth belong and subject themselves in a way, and to the degree, that they can no longer be described as fully 'sovereign'. The constitutional nature of the federation can thus only be discerned if a more political or material perspective on the constitution is applied.

12.2 BIRTH AND TRANSFORMATION

The federal compact is a special kind of contract, a 'status contract' in Carl Schmitt's terms, because it grants the contracting parties a fundamentally new status by integrating them in a new concrete order. A status contract differs from other contracts because it founds an 'enduring life relation' that integrates a person or a political entity into a total order that is not reduceable to concise individual relations and that cannot simply be terminated at will.[8] In a structurally similar manner to a more common status contract, namely marriage, a federation relies on a status contract between the federating states. This contract establishes a new comprehensive status and encompasses the states in their entirety and, beyond the merely individual, contractual obligations, alters them fundamentally by giving them a new status.[9] In this way, the federation establishes a constitution in a material sense, independently of whether there is any document known as the 'Federal Constitution'.[10]

[5] C. Schmitt, *Constitutional Theory*, J. Seitzer ed. (Duke University Press, 2008), 114; C. Schönberger, 'European Citizenship as Federal Citizenship: Some Citizenship Lessons of Comparative Federalism' (2007) 19 *European Review of Public Law* 112.

[6] O. Beaud, *Théorie de la fédération* (Presses universitaires de France, 2007), 132; Schmitt, *Constitutional Theory*, 398–99.

[7] Schmitt, *Constitutional Theory*, 114; Schönberger, 'European Citizenship as Federal Citizenship', 112.

[8] Schmitt, *Constitutional Theory*, 385.

[9] For a comparison of marriage as a status contract with the federal compact as a status contract, see C. Hughes, *Confederacies: An Inaugural Lecture Delivered in the University of Leicester 8 November 1962* (Leicester University Press, 1963), 12. Fittingly, Brexit has often been described as a 'divorce'. For example, the financial settlement in the Brexit withdrawal agreement was nicknamed the 'Divorce Bill' (formally the Agreement on the withdrawal of the United Kingdom of Great Britain and Northern Ireland from the European Union and the European Atomic Energy Community, OJ 2019 No. C384 I/01).

[10] For example, the German Confederation (1815–66) and the Swiss Confederation (1814–48) each relied on a federal compact (*Bundesvertrag*) and neither had any formal documents entitled 'the federal constitution'. Neither does the

Similarly, the constitutional transformation of the Member States will not necessarily manifest itself in a change of any constitutional laws. The constitutional change is to the *material* constitutions of the Member States, which might, or might not, be expressed in a formal constitutional amendment. Independently of whether any formal constitutional change takes place, the act of federating entails a transformation of what Schmitt called the constitutions of the Member States in the 'positive sense', namely 'the concrete content of the fundamental political decisions on the entire manner of the existence of the state'.[11] By federating, the states become members of another political community, the Union, that constitutes an autonomous source of law, which will have a direct effect in the Member States and, as a rule, take primacy over Member State law. After they have come together in a new Union, the Member States are no longer the same as they were before.

At the very minimum, this means that the material constitution of the Member States specifying 'the rules which regulate the creation of the general legal norms'[12], or the 'rule of recognition'[13], will be amended because the Union constitutes an additional source of domestic law. Whether this is guaranteed in a formal constitutional amendment or not, the federal constitution, in this way, is also a component of the individual constitutions of the Member States.[14] The Member States have to create a constitutional 'gateway' through which Union authority can be exercised and guarantee in constitutional terms that domestic law conforms with Union law. From a formal perspective, this can be done in the form of ordinary statute. Nevertheless, in a material sense, this will lead to a change in the constitutions of the Member States and 'open' their statehood to the Union.[15]

Beyond this 'legal' constitutional transformation of the Member States' material constitutions (a transformation of the norms regulating the production of general norms), becoming a Member State entails a more fundamental 'political' transformation because the dialectical relationship between governors and governed that lies at the heart of state sovereignty[16] is relativised.[17] The Member States' 'total political situation', in Herman Heller's words,[18] is transformed.

Federal citizenship provides a clear example of how the constitution of a federation leads to a transformation of the political relationship between governors and governed in the Member States.[19] When states come together in a federation, they will each have their own citizenship. By giving birth to the new Union, however, they create a new form of citizenship, Union citizenship, that does not supersede the citizenship of the Member States but exists in parallel to it. Federal citizenship is per definition dual citizenship, consisting of the citizenship of the

EU have a formal written constitution. Nevertheless, within EU law scholarship, it is relatively well established that the EU is constitutional even though it relies on a treaty.

11 Schmitt, *Constitutional Theory*, 384.

12 Kelsen, *General Theory of Law and State*, 124.

13 H. L. A. Hart, *The Concept of Law*, L. Green ed., 3rd ed. (Oxford University Press, 2015).

14 Schmitt, *Constitutional Theory*, 385.

15 It is, for example, no coincidence that the 1972 European Community Act was termed a 'constitutional statute' by the UK Supreme Court in R *(Miller)* v. *Secretary of State for Exiting the European Union* [2017] UKSC 5. Though formally an ordinary statute, in political and material sense, this act was part of the UK constitution until it was repealed as part of the Brexit process.

16 M. Loughlin, *The Idea of Public Law* (Oxford University Press, 2003), chapter 5.

17 In the context of the EU, this argument is made by C. J. Bickerton, *European Integration: From Nation-States to Member States* (Oxford University Press, 2012), chapter 2.

18 Heller, 'Nature and Structure of the State', 1195.

19 For a comprehensive theory on federal citizenship, see C. Schönberger, *Unionsbürger: Europas föderales Bürgerrecht in vergleichender Sicht* (Mohr Siebeck, 2005).

Member States and that of the Union. In young federations, Union citizenship might not be created as a formal status but the material rights inherent in Union citizenship will tend to be protected, most importantly the federal 'right to have rights'.[20] The citizens of a Member State will have the right to live in another Member State and be treated as a quasi-citizen of that Member State.

The core of Union citizenship is the rights of free movement and the right to non-discrimination on the basis of nationality.[21] This will be subject to some conditions, often that the mobile citizens are not an economic burden on the host Member State; and political rights will often be excluded. That being said, Union citizenship creates a new status for the citizens of a Member State that allow them to 'escape' their own state, if they so wish, and enjoy most of the rights of citizenship in another Member State.[22] Union citizenship, therefore, is a form of 'interstate citizenship' that displaces the binary of the state between national and alien with a tertiary distinction between citizen of a Member State, citizen of the Union and non-Union foreigner. Citizenship is a good example of the fundamental difference between the public law structure of a federation and that of a state. Union citizenship is derived from Member State citizenship, at least in young federations, and, as such, the dual citizenship statuses that exist alongside one another in a federation are interdependent.[23] Nevertheless, Union citizenship also represents the independent political existence of the Union as distinct from the political existence of its Member States. A federation leads to the constitution of a new institutionalised political relationship between the Union and *its citizens*, namely, the nascent federal nation.[24] In this way, a new relationship of political representation, a new 'imagined community', comes into existence and with it emerges a new source of political authority.[25]

When states come together in a federation, they give birth to a new political entity, the Union, which they then govern themselves through as Member States. The federation is a genuinely political community that, despite being a creation of the Member States, cannot be reduced to the sum of its parts. The limits of such an 'international' or 'intergovernmental' interpretation are clearly visible from the fact that even when federal decisions have to be made unanimously and all the Member States have a veto, they still differ from decisions made under international law. This is because the federal decision, as a rule, needs no ratification by the individual Member States. Exactly because the Member States have made the federal constitution a part of their own constitutions in the material sense, they are directly bound in public law terms by the

[20] H. Arendt, *The Origins of Totalitarianism*, A Harvest Book (Harcourt Inc, 1994), chapter 9.

[21] Schönberger, 'European Citizenship as Federal Citizenship'.

[22] This argument has been made in the context of the EU by F. De Witte, 'Emancipation through Law?', in L. Azoulai, E. Pataut and S. Barbou (eds.), *Constructing the Person in EU Law: Rights, Roles, Identities* (Hart, 2016). In the context of the United States, the same argument has been made by G. Gerstle, *Liberty and Coercion: The Paradox of American Government from the Founding to the Present* (Princeton University Press, 2018), 70: 'As long as one could choose one's state, one could live as one wished'.

[23] This is, for example, the case for EU citizenship and Swiss citizenship that to this day is derived from cantonal citizenship. In the United States, the derivative nature of federal citizenship was transformed with the 14th Amendment that ensured that anyone born in the US territory would be a citizen of the United States and that state citizenship could be derived from that status, see Schönberger, 'European Citizenship as Federal Citizenship'.

[24] Larsen, *Constitutional Theory of the Federation*, 116–17; O. Beaud, 'The Question of Nationality within a Federation: A Neglected Issue in Nationality Law', in R. Hansen and P. Weil (eds.), *Dual Nationality, Social Rights and Federal Citizenship in the U.S. and Europe: The Reinvention of Citizenship* (Berghahn Books, 2002), ch. 14.

[25] B. Anderson, *Imagined Communities: Reflections on the Origin and Spread of Nationalism* (Verso, 2006). A. de Tocqueville, *Democracy in America* (Penguin, 2003), 193, 'The government of the Union rests almost entirely upon legal fictions. The Union is an idealized nation which exists, as it were, only in men's imagination and whose scope and limitations are revealed by understanding alone'.

decision made by the Union.[26] The federal compact gives birth to an autonomous legal order and a new source of law. By coming together in a federation, the Member States constitute an autonomous public authority which is directly binding on them without further ratification.

After they have become Member States and for the duration of their membership, the federating states can no longer meaningfully be understood in accordance with the theory of the external and internal sovereignty of the state: 'Once they have come together in a federation, the Member States are no longer truly sovereign states, nor are they strangers to one another'.[27] The Member States of a federation do not relate to their fellow Member States (primarily) via public international law, but rather via the laws of the Union: federal public law. They cannot, for example, rely on international law mechanisms such as state retaliation to enforce the federal compact. A federation leads to the renunciation of self-help of the Member States vis-à-vis one another.[28] Nor will the Member States retain complete control of their internal affairs: 'in the interest of the security of the federation, a federation cannot ignore the domestic affairs of its Member States. Every federation leads to *interventions*'.[29] There are no internal affairs of the Member States, however sensitive, that cannot become a matter of common concern of the Union at large and subject to a federal intervention.[30] If the security of the Union as a whole is at risk, a federal intervention into the Member States' domestic affairs is always a possibility. In this way, the Union can act as a genuine political community in the interest of protecting its security and survival – ultimately even if this infringes upon the political self-determination of its Member States – in the name of the people of the Union.[31]

That the Union is a genuinely political community, however, does not mean that it is a new 'super-state' existing 'above' the Member States.[32] The Member States are not dependencies or administrative regions of the federation and the public authority of the Union is governed by fundamentally different forms of constitutional principles than the state. To understand the constitutional foundations and dynamics of power and authority of the Union, we need to examine the purposes for which it was created.

12.3 THE DOUBLE TELOS

Why do states federate? After all, as we have seen, being a Member State entails a constitutional transformation in a way and to the degree that Member States cannot be meaningfully understood to enjoy full sovereignty. If that is the case, why do states want to constitute a federal union among themselves? From a historical perspective, states have come together in federations because they have found it difficult to maintain their own political existence or autonomy.

26 Schmitt, *Constitutional Theory*, 401.

27 Beaud, *Théorie de la fédération*, 230 (my translation).

28 Schmitt, *Constitutional Theory*, 388.

29 Ibid., amended translation.

30 Larsen, *Constitutional Theory of the Federation*, chapter 5. See also E. R. Huber, 'Bundesexekution und Bundesintervention: Ein Beitrag zur Frage des Verfassungsschutzes im Deutschen Bund' (1953) 79 *Archiv des öffentlichen Rechts* 1.

31 Larsen, *Constitutional Theory of the Federation*, chapter 5. See also H. Lokdam, '"We Serve the People of Europe": Reimagining the ECB's Political Master in the Wake of Its Emergency Politics' (2020) 58 *Journal of Common Market Studies* 978.

32 The American Founding is a case in point. As pointed out by M. M. Edling, *Perfecting the Union: National and State Authority in the US Constitution* (Oxford University Press, 2020), 68, not even the revolutionary nationalists at the Constitutional Convention 'showed any interest in dissolving existing states (…) by 1787, all states, large and small, had become reified entities in the American political imagination. Citizens owed their primary allegiance to the state government and supported the union as a means to protect the independence and interests of their states'.

When a number of smaller states are under threat from a military or economic power, often a neighbouring empire, federations can come into existence between these states for their mutual welfare and/or security. They come together under the 'compulsion of defence and economic needs'.[33]

In substantive terms, the aims of the federation are welfare and/or warfare; two expressions of the general principle of 'salus populi'. At the most fundamental level, the federal telos is therefore to perpetuate the political existence of the Member States.[34] What this entails, however, changes historically and varies from federation to federation. As a consequence, all federal systems are unique. The federation, however, is not merely committed to maintaining the political existence of the Member States but also its own political autonomy and existence. When states federate, they express a will to live together and to treat each other as equal members of a new political community, the common Union. The federation is a genuine political community with an inside and an outside. It has a double telos planted in it with the federal founding: the will to preserve the states as autonomous and the will to live together in a common union.

This is grounded in the 'peculiar sentiment' that is at the origins of all federations: the wish to live together but without being one and the wish of remaining autonomous but without being completely separate from one another. In the words of Albert Venn Dicey, the inhabitants of the federating states 'must desire union, but must not desire unity'.[35] Dicey's argument is that if there is no desire for union, there is no basis for the constitution of a federation. However, on the other hand, if there is a desire not merely for union but for unity, this will be more adequately expressed in the creation of a unitary constitution, a unitary state. It is only in the case of the peculiar wish for union without unity that the proper political foundations for the creation of a federation pertain.

Because of the will to unite without unity, the federal telos is always characterised by an internal tension or contradiction between its two opposite ends. Martin Diamond expressed this internal contradiction between the 'federal ends' in the following terms: 'One end is always found in the reason why the member units do not simply consolidate themselves into one large unitary country; the other end is always found in the reason why the member units do not choose to remain simply small wholly autonomous countries.'[36] The federation is always committed simultaneously to unity and diversity, transformation and conservation, the past and the future. These are centripetal and centrifugal ordering forces that pull the federation in opposite directions. These contradictory political forces are at the heart of all federations precisely because the federation is a new political existence constituted in order to perpetuate the political existence of its constitutive parts.

The most fundamental constitutional question for the federation is thus how these contradictory forces can be stabilised. How can a constitutional balance between the Union and the Member States be protected? In *On Revolution*, Hannah Arendt describes the question of the political balance as the most important problem for the American founding fathers. The task of

[33] R. R. Bowie, 'The Process of Federating Europe', in A. W. MacMahon (ed.), *Federalism: Mature and Emergent* (Doubleday & Company, 1955), 493. See also C. F. Friedrich, 'Federal Constitutional Theory and Emergent Proposals', in A. W. MacMahon (ed.), *Federalism: Mature and Emergent* (Doubleday & Company, 1955); W. H. Riker, *Federalism: Origin, Operation, Significance* (Little, Brown and Company, 1964), 12 ff.

[34] This was a central argument advanced by the Federalist before the ratification of the 1787 Constitution of the United States, see C. D. Matson and P. S. Onuf, *A Union of Interests: Political and Economic Thought in Revolutionary America* (University Press of Kansas, 1990), 137 ff.

[35] A. V. Dicey, *Introduction to the Study of the Law of the Constitution* (Liberty Fund, 1982), 75–76.

[36] M. Diamond, 'The Ends of Federalism' (1973) 3 *Publius* 129, 130.

the constitution, she writes, was the 'erection of a system of powers that would check and balance in such a way that the power neither of the union nor its parts, the duly constituted states, would decrease or destroy one another'.[37] For the federation to persist, both kinds of political existence must continue next to each other. 'The mark of the federation', Christoph Schönberger writes 'is therefore a precarious condition of equilibrium, a *state of uncertainty*'.[38]

That the political balance between the Union and the Member States is at the very heart of all federations was acknowledged by Carl Schmitt who wrote: 'The Member States are not simply subordinated, subjects of the federation, nor is the federation subordinated to and subject to them. The federation exists only in this existential connection and in this balance.'[39] The question is how can the federal balance be maintained? How can the federal constitution allow for the coexistence of two forms of political existence, the Union and the Member States, without one destroying the other? How can the contradictory ordering forces of the federation – toward unity and diversity, transformation and conservation, the past and the future – be stabilised?

12.4 CONSTITUTIONAL BALANCE

The most prevalent answer to this question is good constitutional design. Is it not possible merely to solve the problem by creating a proper legal system with a prudent division of power between the Union and the Member States? As long as the Member States control 'sensitive issues' and the Union is merely concerned with accomplishing the 'mission' for which it was created, the federal telos, can the federal balance not be maintained? This is the alluring promise of an 'institutional fix' that characterises much of federal theory – as well as theories of European integration. The problem is that it is based on the flawed premise that the federation is a *static* rather than a *dynamic order*. The 'static interpretation' relies on the constitutional principle that a federation, in contrast to a state, cannot give itself a new constitutional purpose; it is not legally 'omnicompetent'.[40] Its powers are enumerated, and hence limited.[41] The power and authority of the Union is always bound to this foundational purpose, the *federal telos*. The aims of the federation are what justifies and limits the authority of the Union. The Union is only meant to have the authority granted to it by the Member States.

Nevertheless, exactly because of its teleological orientation, the federation is characterised by a dynamic form of constitutional ordering that tends to be expansive. The federal constitution is oriented toward the future and has as a core aim to bring something into existence: 'a more perfect union'[42] or an 'ever-closer union'.[43] On a more concrete level, federal constitutions that have an economic content, an 'economic federation', will tend to have as a federal aim the creation of a single internal federal market.[44] These 'limited' competences, such as the US

[37] H. Arendt, *On Revolution* (Penguin, 2006), 143.

[38] C. Schönberger, 'Die Europäische Union als Bund: Zugleich ein Beitrag zur Verabschiedung des Staatenbund-Bundesstaat-Schemas' (2004) 129 *Archiv des öffentlichen Rechts* 81, 105 (my translation, original emphasis).

[39] Amended translation of Schmitt, *Constitutional Theory*, 388.

[40] Beaud, *Théorie de la fédération*, 348.

[41] In the EU, this is expressed in terms of the principle of conferral, see Article 5 of the Consolidated version of the Treaty on European Union, OJ 2016 No. C202/13.

[42] Preamble to the 1787 American Constitution.

[43] Preambles to the Consolidated version of the Treaty on European Union, OJ 2016 No. C202/13 and the Consolidated version of the Treaty on the Functioning of the European Union, OJ 2016 No. C202/47.

[44] See especially M. Forsyth, *Union of States: The Theory and Practice of Confederations* (Leicester University Press, 1981); R. Schütze, *From International to Federal Market: The Changing Structure of European Law* (Oxford University Press, 2017).

'Commerce Clause' or the EU's internal market competence, can be relied on in order to expand the power and authority of the Union.[45] Moreover, the federation tends to be granted the powers necessary to achieve its constitutional aims.[46] This is sometimes known as the doctrine of 'implied powers'.[47]

Because of the dynamic constitutional ordering of the federation, the formal division of power might not reflect the material division of power between the Union and the Member States.[48] The material balance of power between the Union and the Member States in which the actual federal constitution resides might, and often will, shift significantly over time without the constitutional division of power necessarily being formally amended.[49] Such an expansion can be challenged as a matter of law by political or judicial scrutiny of whether the measures used in fact are 'necessary' and 'proper' or 'proportionate'.[50] Such challenges, however, tend to be relatively ineffective because the principle of necessity tends to be an enabler rather than a bulwark of political power as all necessity politics shows: 'he who wills the end, must also will the means'. Neither can the principle of 'proportionality' stem the exercise of governmental authority if the federation is faced with an existential crisis, which will render this principle meaningless. In questions of life and death, what means are deemed 'disproportionate'? This is not to say that constitutional design is unimportant but merely that it is not sufficient to protect the federal balance.

A response to this predicament is sometimes to attempt to institutionalise a 'neutral' guardian of the constitution, a federal supreme court, that can protect the constitutional balance between the Union and the Member States.[51] The problem with this response is that it assumes that the constitutional orders of the Union and the Member States are a part of one monist hierarchical system of legal norms. For Kelsen, as for many others, the only difference between the federation and the unitary state is the degree of centralisation.[52] This is a comforting assumption, because, if that were the case, it would suggest that the 'correct' balance can always be struck by a federal constitutional court on legal grounds.

45 R. Schütze, 'Limits to the Union's "Internal Market" Competence(s)', in L. Azoulai (ed.), *The Question of Competence in the European Union* (Oxford University Press, 2014), 215–33. For the expansion of the power and authority in the United States, see Gerstle, Liberty and Coercion; B. Ackerman, *We the People II: Transformations* (The Belknap Press of Harvard University Press, 1998).

46 An example is the 'Necessary and Proper Clause' of the American Constitution, Article I, Section 8. In the EU, this is stated in Article 6(4) of the TEU: 'The Union shall provide itself with the means necessary to attain its objectives and carry through its policies'.

47 In the United States, this was asserted in *McCulloch* v. *Maryland*, 17 US 316 (1819). The paradigmatic EU case is Case C-22/70, *Commission of the European Communities* v. *Council of the European Communities* [1971] ECR 263 (ERTA case).

48 See, e.g., Riker, *Federalism*, 81–84.

49 Heller, 'Nature and Structure of the State', 1184, made this point in regard to perpetual transformation of the internal power relations of the state in the production of 'the unit and order of the state as organization and constitution'. Given the material dynamic of the federation, the asymmetrical relations among the Member States may lead to imbalances or even relations of domination, as when a single state is dominant in a hegemonic federation, see M. Wilkinson, *Authoritarian Liberalism and the Transformation of Modern Europe* (Oxford University Press, 2021), 223–29.

50 In the EU, such a debate is currently taking place in the judicial confrontation between the German Constitutional Court and the European Court of Justice over the question of whether the ECB made an adequate proportionality assessment, see Case C-493/17, *Weiss and Others* [2018] ECLI:EU:C:2018:1000; BVerfG, Judgment of the Second Senate of 05 May 2020 – 2 BvR 859/15.

51 H. Kelsen, 'Kelsen on the Nature and Development of Constitutional Adjudication', in L. Vinx (ed.), *The Guardian of the Constitution: Hans Kelsen and Carl Schmitt on the Limits of Constitutional Law* (Cambridge University Press, 2015), 66, 72–75.

52 Kelsen, *General Theory of Law and State*, 316.

However, this misses a fundamental characteristic of the federation, namely that the federation is a pluralist not a monist legal order. It is characterised by multiple constitutional orders that stand in a heterarchical relationship to one another and enjoy a relative autonomy.[53] From the perspective of the Member States, the Union only has the powers that they have granted to it in the federal treaty. Its powers are enumerated and, hence, limited. This means that the Member States also have a valid claim to be the ultimate guardian of the constitution in order to police this limit and ensure that Union institutions do not act *ultra vires*.

This has to do with the ambiguous constitutional foundations of the federation in an interstate agreement of constitutional nature. The federation relies on a federal compact between the Member States. This compact or treaty, however, is also constitutional because it gives birth to a new constitutional order and transforms the Member States constitutionally. In a conflict between a Member State and the Union, a valid argument can be advanced either on behalf of the Member States stressing the foundations of the federation in a compact or *treaty* or on behalf of the Union stressing the foundations of the federation in a *constitution*. Today, such contestation takes place in the EU; however, it is by no means the first federation where this has happened. Contestation of federal authority is a feature of all (young) federations.[54]

In the antebellum United States, these arguments were put forward, respectively, by the seventh Vice President of the United States, John C. Calhoun and the Senator of Massachusetts, Daniel Webster. Calhoun argued that the United States was founded on a compact between sovereign states and the constitution was '*as a compact*, binding on them; – but only as such'.[55] Sovereignty, Calhoun argued, remained with the states and their peoples, rather than with the Union or the people of the United States: 'There is, indeed, no such community, *politically* speaking, as the people of the United States, regarded in the light of, and as constituting one people or nation', Calhoun declared.[56] The citizens of the United States, Calhoun argued, did for that reason owe their ultimate allegiance to the states rather than the Union. As part of their sovereignty, they had the right to judge on the constitutionality of federal law and, if necessary, to nullify it. In this way, the states had an effective veto power over federal legislation.[57] Daniel Webster, however, saw Calhoun's arguments as a dangerous threat to the unity and stability of the Union and its constitutional foundations: 'could anything', Webster declared, '[be] more preposterous, than to make a government for the whole Union, and yet leave its power subject, not to one interpretation, but to thirteen or twenty-four interpretations?'[58] Today, we are again faced by these questions in the constitutional confrontation between the European Court of Justice and the German Constitutional Court.[59]

53 In the EU, this view is held by constitutional pluralists. For an overview, see M. Avbelj and J. Komárek, *Constitutional Pluralism in the European Union and Beyond* (Hart Publishing, 2012).

54 L. Goldstein, *Constituting Federal Sovereignty: The European Union in Comparative Context* (Johns Hopkins University Press, 2001).

55 J. C. Calhoun, 'A Discourse on the Constitution and Government of the United States', in R. K. Crallé (ed.), *The Works of Calhoun Volume 1: A Disquisition on Government and a Discourse on the Constitution and Government of the United States* (Steam Power-Press, 1851), 129 (original emphasis).

56 Ibid., 162.

57 C. E. Merriam, 'The Political Theory of Calhoun' (1902) 7 *American Journal of Sociology* 577, 584–85.

58 Speech by Daniel Webster, as cited by T. C. Fischer, 'Federalism in the European Community and the United States: A Rose by Any Other Name' (1994) 17 *Fordham International Law Journal* 389, 431.

59 Case C-493/17, *Weiss and Others* [2018] ECLI:EU:C:2018:1000; BVerfG, Judgment of the Second Senate of 05 May 2020 – 2 BvR 859/15.

12.5 THE PRINCIPLE OF HOMOGENEITY

In *Democracy in America*, Alexis de Tocqueville maintained that a system of 'sound laws' would be incapable of pre-empting conflicts between the 'two sovereignties' that all federations brought face to face.[60] Constitutional engineering alone, he argued, would ultimately be incapable of diverting the peoples of the different Member States from war. But if the constitutional balance cannot be preserved solely by legal means, how then can it be protected?

Most federal theorists agree that the constitutional balance presupposes a relative *homogeneity* of all the Member States. In the *Spirit of the Laws*, for example, Montesquieu argued that a federal republic 'ought to be composed of states of the same nature'.[61] If there is an existential connection between the Member States, if they are of 'the same nature', then the necessary interference in the internal affairs of the Member States does not have to be experienced as 'foreign' in existential terms. If the will of one is the same as the will of all, it can remain a moot point who ultimately decides. Where there is an 'existential connection' between the Member States, Schmitt writes, a federation is legally and politically possible.[62]

The question, of course, is what does this mean? In what ways do the Member States need to be homogenous? Within federal theory, the answers range from the more 'essentialist' stress on the need for homogeneity with regard to 'civilisation' and nationality to more 'institutionalist' answers stressing homogeneity with regard to the Member States' form of government and their constitutional values.[63] In Schmitt's view, however, the *content* of the substantive homogeneity was insignificant: 'There can be a national, religious, cultural, social, class, or another type of homogeneity.'[64] What mattered was that, in existential terms, it was strong enough to preserve a political homogeneity between all the Member States.[65] A substantial similarity, Schmitt maintained, was 'the foundation for the conformity of the concrete mode of being of the Member States and ensures that the extreme case of conflict does not occur within the federation'.[66] If existential questions were raised, the Union and all Member States would not make conflicting political decisions.[67] If it came to war, they would not fight on opposite sides: 'the federation cannot have an enemy that would not at the same time be an enemy of every Member State'.[68] How the political identity of the Union and the Member States was *constructed* and how the political homogeneity was *maintained* was of little interest to Schmitt.

From a materialist constitutionalist perspective, a pure decisionist and existentialist account of political identity is unconvincing. The ambition of this volume on the material constitution is to go beyond both normativism and decisionism and open the 'black box' of the 'political' by enquiring into the material context of constitutional ordering. For example, in contrast to what American Founding Fathers like John Jay argued, it was not due to a blessing of 'providence'

[60] The legislators, de Tocqueville, *Democracy in America*, 192–93 argued, can make the interaction of 'these two sovereignties as simple and equal as possible and is to enclose both of them into their own carefully defined spheres of action. But he cannot meld them together into one single entity or prevent their bumping into each other at some point'.

[61] Montesquieu, *The Spirit of the Laws*, A. M. Cohler, B. C. Miller, and H. Stone, eds. (Cambridge University Press, 1989), bk. IX, chapter 2.

[62] Schmitt, *Constitutional Theory*, 395.

[63] For an overview, see Larsen, *Constitutional Theory of the Federation*, 112–26.

[64] Schmitt, *Constitutional Theory*, 392.

[65] Ibid., 394.

[66] C. Schmitt, *Verfassungslehre*, 10th ed. (Duncker & Humblot, 2010), 376 (my translation).

[67] Schmitt, *Constitutional Theory*, 394.

[68] Ibid.

that the United States was founded by white settlers only.[69] Rather it was a product of the exclusion of Native Americans and the enslaved black population from 'We the People' and hence the construction of political identity along racist lines.[70] In the antebellum Republic, this political decision on inclusion/exclusion was entrenched in the jurisprudence of the American Supreme Court, for example in the infamous 1856 *Dred Scott* case. A descendant of African slaves, the Supreme Court maintained, could not become a 'member of the political community formed and brought into existence by the Constitution of the United States'.[71] Only after the Civil War with the re-founding of the Republic during the Reconstruction was this decision overturned.[72]

Political identity and political homogeneity, in other words, is neither determined by a singular point in time nor is it something 'natural' or given. It is rather something that is continuously being constituted. The constitution of a political community is always both of and by the community as a collective self.[73] What sets the federation apart from the state with regard to the continual constitution of political identity is that it takes places at two interdependent levels. In a federation, nation-building takes place both at the centre and at the periphery.[74] Membership in both of these political communities, the Member States and the Union, is the product of the constitution of the political community as such; in neither is it something given. An important lesson from the writings of Herman Heller is to think of constitutional ordering in *dialectical* terms, as a productive relationship between law and politics, norm and decision, that is constantly developing.[75]

69 Federalist 2 (Jay), in *The Federalist Papers*, L. Goldman, ed. (Oxford University Press, 2008), 14–17.

70 During the 1787 Constitutional Convention, the infamous three-fifth compromise was struck between the slave holding southern states and the northern states on how the slave population would be counted for determining direct taxation and representation, see The Constitution of the United States, Article I, Section 2.

71 *Dred Scott* v. *Sanford*, 60 US 393 (1856). Important cases on the constitutional status of Native Americans are *Chereokee Nation* v. *Georgia*, 30 US 1 (1831) and *Worcester* v. *Georgia*, 31 US 514 (1832). See, also, B. Duthu, *Shadow Nations: Tribal Sovereignty and the Limits of Legal Pluralism* (Oxford University Press, 2013); S. Banner, *How the Indians Lost Their Land: Law and Power on the Frontier* (Harvard University Press, 2009).

72 Ackerman, *We the People II*.

73 H. Lindahl, 'Constituent Power and Reflexive Identity: Towards an Ontology of Collective Selfhood', in M. Loughlin and N. Walker (eds.), *The Paradox of Constitutionalism: Constituent Power and Constitutional Form* (Oxford University Press, 2008), 9–27.

74 M. Forsyth, 'The Relevance of Classical Approaches', in J. J. Hesse, V. Wright, and W. Hesse (eds.), *Federalizing Europe? The Costs, Benefits, and Preconditions of Federal Political Systems* (Oxford University Press, 1996); K. C. Wheare, 'Federalism and the Making of Nations', in A. W. MacMahon (ed.), *Federalism: Mature and Emergent* (Doubleday & Company, 1955).

75 Heller, 'Nature and Structure of the State', 1201.

13

The Materialist Turn in Constitutional Thought

Emilios Christodoulidis

13.1 THE INSTITUTIONAL AND THE MATERIAL: THE PROBLEMATIC VIS-À-VIS

It is remarkable, even if hardly ever raised as a problem, that in the discussion of the materiality of the legal order it is a *shortcut* that furnishes the perspective, in the form of a spatial *metaphor*; the shortcut organises access to the meaning of materiality, as *under*lying, *under*pinning, *under*girding. And because the metaphor is what grants access to the *layering* of the material and the institutional – observe how difficult it is to sidestep the *topology* of levels, of layers, of strata – the question becomes so difficult to ask: what does it *mean* to 'underlie'? But the question must be asked because materiality needs to be unfolded in the social, temporal and material dimensions of its meaning, beyond what is 'locked' in the *picture that keeps it captive* in its spatial positioning vis-à-vis the institutional.

The 'picture that keeps captive' is of course Wittgenstein's formulation from the *Philosophical Investigations*, and it is another one from the earlier *Tractatus* that runs usefully alongside it in this crosscurrent of metaphors. The latter is the metaphor of the 'ladder', that Wittgenstein deploys to talk about 'learning', and that he borrows from Kierkegaard.

> My propositions serve as elucidations in the following way: anyone who understands me eventually recognizes them as nonsensical, when he has used them – as steps – to climb beyond them. (He must, so to speak, throw away the ladder after he has climbed up it.) … He must transcend these propositions, and then he will see the world aright.[1]

This is intriguing when one considers that the philosophy presented in the *Tractatus* attempts to demonstrate just what the limits of language are – and *what it is to run up against them.* In the *Tractatus* these limits are unyielding. They set the contours of what can be meaningfully said, and what beyond them must be consigned to silence. Roughly speaking, what *can* be said for the early Wittgenstein – including questions of metaphysics – involves what would receive *precise* answers by reference to deep principles of sentence-construction. 'The theory of meaning must be started again from observation of language as it is',[2] determined in its precise and complex grammar, a 'solution' that as we now know was short-lived, abandoned in the later work.

[1] In what may be a deliberate reference to Søren Kierkegaard's *Concluding Unscientific Postscript to Philosophical Fragments* in the penultimate proposition of Wittgenstein's *Tractatus Logico-Philosophicus* (6.54).

[2] S. Hampshire, *Modern Writers and Other Essays* (Chatto & Windus, 1969), 125.

If metaphor makes so spectacular an appearance in Wittgenstein's later work it is perhaps to track that which eludes the careful architecture and orchestration of sense-making in the *Tractatus*, to track displacements and to open up vistas of meaning in the apparent untidiness of actual communication, the moving planes of signification. This is because metaphor strains at the deep structure of literal thought. 'One sees . . . how graphic and immediately responsive to his own needs [becomes] his style of writing', comments Stuart Hampshire in 1969; 'the free form, without conventions of exposition, did the work of a philosophical dialogue. Visual metaphors, natural to a designer and architect, . . . make his thought always accessible and vivid, never altogether abstract'. And Hampshire concludes: 'Sharply aware of a future public, he still needed to make no concession, to adopt no public and conciliatory manner, and he would follow only the connections that were significant to him, in a continual search, which was the way of life that he had chosen.'[3]

How to make 'accessible and vivid' the 'responsiveness' to the 'materiality question' at the heart of our concerns and to fashion the register on which it might be usefully asked? We will hold on to the insight that metaphor strains at the deep structure of literal thought because, to repeat, the 'materiality question' is one that is far from literally, self-evidently or readily graspable. And if the spatial 'layers', the 'strata', etc, are indeed steps of the ladder which serve only 'to climb beyond them' and 'so to speak, throw away the ladder after climbing it' what are we left with to explain the *relationship* between the material and the institutional? At this stage let us merely warn against a facile reading of the constitutional layer as supervenient on an underlying, *true*, materiality of practice, as well as the attribution to Marxism of this layering as standard departure. Instead, let us take up more *frontally* the methodological issue over the relationship between the legal order and the *underlying* materiality, with an emphasis on what 'underlying' denotes and the crucial – even constitutive – significance of *the vis-à-vis between the institutional and the material.*

I will argue that the significant insight that the materialist turn offers to constitutional thought turns on the question of how exactly to make sense of the 'vis-à-vis'. Against any notion that the material and institutional are 'coextensive', 'continuous' or coincident, that the latter 'supervenes' on the former, against any notion that there is an 'interplay' or 'dynamic relation' between the two, I will argue that the materialist 'corrective' turns on the possibility of locating antinomy and contradiction at their precarious juncture. For this reason, I will argue in Section 13.2, the materialist turn in constitutional thought cannot understand constitutional formation by relying on a governing *function*. Instead, by re-orienting constitutional thought to the material practices of the political economy to which they give (or withhold) expression, the constitutional question becomes a question over what material relations and needs are expressed, what are elided and what are silenced. A key step in this argument involves the difficulty of conceptualising the material constitution independently from its institutional expression. Such an 'extraction' away from its institutional accommodation is a condition of tracking the points of tension; it grants visibility to the contingency of the institutional arrangements and the possible fault lines, in other words also of the junctures at which political action might make a difference. The middle sections of the paper address these questions. I will conclude that a Hegelian–Marxist reading of the material constitution, one that pivots on the notion of *immanent critique*, allows both differentiation and traction between the formal and the material dimensions; moreover it sustains the critical import of its intervention in its insistence that the 'material' *not* fold into the 'institutional', that a moment of *negation* rather than affirmation hold the two moments

[3] Ibid., 135.

distinct and related, in a way that foregrounds a semantics of constitutional interpretation that opens up to democratic uses. At the level of constitutional semantics, the promise of the material constitution is to harness constitutional thought to disagreements and conflicts that might tap some of the deeper societal dynamics, typically by forcing re-interpretations of concepts that carry significant political import.

13.2 ON FUNCTIONAL DEFINITIONS

We are indebted to Marco Goldoni and Mike Wilkinson for suggesting a re-orientation of constitutional debate away from the endless dragging confrontations between 'political' constitutionalism and 'legal' constitutionalism, a distinction that for years now has served as something of a portal into constitutional debate. This is a tired debate, they rightly comment, it is 'suffering a certain fatigue', though perhaps more recently one might discern a certain re-vitalisation as the earlier clear lines of the stand-off begin to blur: the rise of right-wing populisms has sent 'political constitutionalists' to seek some degree of rights-protection to temper populist-democratic excess, while the rise and rise of free-wheeling proportionality has forced even hard-line exponents of 'juristocracy' to express some qualms about being ruled by judges. These developments in turn have led to a proliferation and further splintering of distinctions that serve to secure everyone some place or other in the meaningless cartography. The debate rages all the louder the more irrelevant it becomes, its fine distinctions supercoded to the operation of capitalism, to the barbarity of which both sides remain fully accommodating or, more precisely, as Goldoni and Wilkinson put it well, toward which they remain *mute*. The discussion of the material constitution, inaugurated in the fine paper of 2018,[4] moves the debate to more fertile democratic-theoretical ground and raises the stakes of constitutional debate considerably. Implicit in the discussion is a normative argument against eclipsing the materiality of practices and a suggestion about how the connection back might be reclaimed.

Here is their summary of the fascinating, important and urgent corrective that the *material turn* offers to the way that constitutionalism is customarily theorised:

> In short, political constitutionalism was insufficiently *material*. It remained mute in the face of renewed constitutional crises and political-economic crises of the state and the inter-state system, and impervious to the increasingly fraught nature of the social relations undergirding them. Political and legal constitutionalists alike neglected the material conditions for the emergence and development of a constitutional order, and the material changes that prompt the suspension or modification of formal constitutional norms. To understand these phenomena requires attention to the underlying material context, to the basic political and social conditions of possibility of constitutionalism and the dynamics of constitutional change. Otherwise constitutional theory will have little to say about the most important challenges to constitutional ordering, whether in the shape of the existential crisis of the Eurozone, the fracturing of the political unity of the modern state, or the return of anti-systemic political and social movements. (568)

The key difficulty the materialist corrective comes up against is how to make sense of the relationship between the 'formal/institutional' and the 'material' dimensions that, as stated in Section 13.1, set the 'political and social conditions of possibility' for it. And the reason why this is a conceptual difficulty is because the material terrain of what 'underlies' and 'conditions' the constitutional, requires (conceptually) that it precede it, and yet it cannot. With Alain Pottage

[4] All page references to M. Goldoni and M. Wilkinson, 'The Material Constitution' (2018) 81 *Modern Law Review* 567.

we might ask the disarming ontological question 'the materiality of what?',[5] or more specifically 'of what practices?', because it is not at all clear what field of human association is individuated as the '*undergirding*' (remember) factuality. What material practices count or qualify as (proto-) constitutional practices? All available answers (to what is individuated as material substratum) seem to borrow the leading perspective from the side of the 'institutional'. But this merely replicates at the conceptual level the material deficit of constitutionalism. Because while granting primacy to the institutional may of course allow us to circumvent the question-begging gesture, and thus give an adequate lead in delineating the constitution's 'substratum', it radically hedges in what the 'material' corrective is meant to correct. In any case the theory of the material constitution is, understandably, not prepared to concede such precedence: instead it is the institutional that must 'graft onto' the material, or 'embed' (569) itself in it, not vice versa. Following Mortati, 'the formal constitution is an instance of the material constitution' (593). Or, at the very least, its advocates insist, between the formal and the material there must be a 'dynamic relation'. In this appeal lies a stipulation of separate-and-related realms, one that presupposes and treats them as *coextensive*. But how exactly to understand the 'co-extensive'? We are not helped by the postulation that the two levels are 'internally and dynamically related' if our quandary is over what individuates each of the two, independently of each other, in the first place. The two realms have to be identified as separate in order for them to interface, graft, converge, embed or dis-embed, and yet this is a relation of co-implication or supervenience that appears forever conceptually to overdetermine the (materialist) corrective it promises to introduce.

It is the 'functional' definition of the constitution that, for the authors, breaks the impasse: the function of 'ordering' makes the levels coextensive by aligning the material and institutional 'forces'. In the way that Goldoni and Wilkinson put it, material conditions and relations are thus both constituted by and constitutive of politics: the dynamic is intrinsic to *constitutional ordering*, as the interface is underwritten by the fact that there is always an *internal* relationship between constitutional order and society.[6] The analysis goes on to identify 'four ordering forces of the material constitution' that systematise the 'conditions of constitutional formation and durability [that] include political economy, political culture, social relations, religion, as well as geopolitical factors, international relations and imperial forms of domination' (580). To the extent that these forces and processes 'combine to constitute order' they are not external to the constitution but 'intrinsic to constitutional ordering',[7] and form its material '*substratum*' (584 and passim); they constitute, remember, 'the [social and political] conditions of the possibility of constitutionalism' (568).

I want to stay with the methodology, rather than the content of the 'ordering forces', because the argument for the 'material constitution' is staked on the methodological move to re-orient

[5] A. Pottage 'The Materiality of What?' (2012) 39 *Journal of Law and Society* 167.

[6] I quote from the paper: 'These factors can be integrated into constitutional enquiry by placing their relation with the constitution at the centre of analysis. Taking this approach means, for constitutional scholars, to take as matters of *juristic* knowledge, geo-political, political, and social concepts which had previously been delegated – or relegated – to other disciplines, such as sociology, international relations, and political theory. Material conditions and relations are thus both constituted (by law and politics) and constitutive (of law and politics). The dynamic interactions among these elements are intrinsic to constitutional ordering' (580). 'Since there is always an *internal* relation between constitutional order and society, the constitution is conceived as a feature of political and social power. But power here is neither an insurgent mass nor a mere abstract relation. The formation, subsistence and reproduction of society always already entails constitutional ordering . . . But how is it ordered? And why might order turn to disorder? . . . We consider how to organise and conceptualise the process of constitutional ordering by offering four inter-linked building blocks of analysis: the ordering forces of the material constitution' (580).

[7] It is not just that the development of modern constitutions is shaped by these factors from the outside, as it were, as mere irritants to an already established order. It is that they combine to constitute order itself and to condition constitutional development through processes of re-ordering (and of *dis*ordering).

the constitutional gaze to the formative dimension of material practices. What achieves it is offered here in terms of a *functional definition* of the constitution. It is the function of ordering that aligns institutional and material factors, and that allows them to coalesce and cross-fertilise around the function of ordering, all the time engaging dialectically, both mutually enabling and limiting. The constitutional gaze finds its direction in function, that collects it as both constitutional *and* material.

But there are problems with *functional* definitions: The first problem with relying on function to define an institution is that it is undercut if there are functional equivalents. If one defines an institution through its function and other institutions perform it, then the definition cannot sustain the individuation of the institution. If 'ordering' is the defining function, and other institutions perform it – albeit the price mechanism, the Church, cultural institutions, or the police – then the specificity of the constitution is lost. In this context one does not need to impress how urgent it is not to lose the constitutional achievement to the market via the *ordering* function of *price*.[8]

The second problem is that it becomes very hard to thematise *dysfunctionalities* in the operation of institutions functionally defined. I am referring to the kind of dysfunctionalities that Goldoni and Wilkinson rightly worry that political constitutionalism, absent the material dimension, remain 'mute' about. The problem with dysfunctionalities is that they are precisely what functionally defined institutions are *constitutively poised to miss*. Because if one begins with functionality and uses function to define constitutionality in the way in which social 'ordering' allows formal and material forces to run alongside each other, it becomes problematic to locate and make sense of social forces that thwart, or potentially thwart, the smooth performance of the function. If, that is, at the material level there are blockages and dis*order* – expressed as conflicts over distributive allocations, over unmet social needs, over investment decisions, against the destruction of labour protection – how will the constitutional function, at once both institutional and material, make sense of them as constitutionally significant? Blockages, instead, become typically that which is *not* thematised due to a loss of concepts, signs of semantic deficit, sites of un-addressability. What is un-addressable is the main reason why a constitution remains 'mute'. And would it be far-fetched to suggest that the silence – the loss of concepts and the remaining mute because of it – was not in fact *perfectly functional* to the ordering/governing function, both at national and at supranational level? Remaining with the Eurozone for a minute and with the functional definition of the constitution: did the semantic deficit and consequent un-addressability[9] not allow an unprecedented level of extraction of surplus value out of the devastated states of the periphery, and therefore was it not perfectly compatible with the governance of the Eurozone? Was the crisis not productive to the operation? The distribution of constitutional 'silence' – the rendering 'mute' – becomes the sinister side of constitutional management, and perfectly *functional* for that reason.

13.3 THE MATERIALIST CORRECTIVE; SCOPE, LIMITS, LEVERAGE

If these objections have any value, then we may have to concede the conceptual problem with functional definitions; in the end, perhaps functional definitions sit uneasily with critical theory

[8] I have made this argument in E. Christodoulidis, *The Redress of Law: Globalisation, Constitutionalism and Market Capture* (Cambridge University Press, 2021).

[9] I am thinking here specifically of the 'constitutionality' of the intervention of the ECB in the sovereign debt crisis of Greece, the denying of liquidity and of 'quantitative easing', the un-addressability of that denial, of its ersatz constitutionality.

and the impetus to harness 'dysfunctionality' to the attempt to make our societies more *humanly* functional. What alternatives (to functional definitions of materiality) present themselves?

To answer the question, we need to return to the *kind* of methodological innovation that the 'material constitution' presents to us. The way that the question is posed shifts onto centre ground a different set of distinctions, key to which is that between constitutional semantics and the material structures to which they give expression. And the promise that the material constitution holds is to lend visibility to that which is ordinarily missed in the way in which constitutional reason closes itself off from political dynamics, contestation and conflict and immunises itself against it. The material constitution aims to challenge the form of closure that underwrites that immunity. The conceptual gain of the material constitution is measured on this turn toward the interface between constitutional form and semantic on the one hand, and the materialities that underlie them on the other.

The reason why the challenge is so steep is because, while the constitution straddles both law and politics, it is ultimately the *reduction* of political dynamics to legal representations that constitutes its achievement, *not* their dynamic interplay or any commitment to keeping both sides alive in that interplay. The materiality of political practices, in civil society, in associations and movements, in the workplace, will receive a semantic content in constitutional law in terms of an economy of representation that, while of course holding the promise of some variation of structure, nonetheless imposes itself as a highly *redundant* order. 'Redundancy' in its systems-theoretical meaning, contrasts with 'variety' and denotes a closing down of options and contingencies. Redundancy sets the limits of openness to the processes that constitutional law is capable of addressing. This limited openness is justified in the name of stabilising societal expectations and underwrites no less than the Rule of Law ideal. And with this we are back to function: function that provides the justification for foreclosure, for controlled exposure to the materialities of society, for controlled openness to contingency, and for the stemming of destabilising dynamics.

If the terms 'redundancy' and 'variety', function, foreclosure and immunity lean this discussion too far in the direction of systems theory, these methodological objections are certainly not the exclusive domain of systems theory. From a radically different theoretical perspective, the same set of problems is encountered in Marxism in terms of some of the more intractable problems of theory-construction. The authors are keenly aware of the pitfalls of 'orthodox' Marxism and steer clear of the reductive readings that posit the material base as defining of the institutional superstructure. There have been of course suggestions about how to temper that uni-directionality, in the arguments about the 'relative autonomy' of the institutions of the superstructure, and the economy being definitive only *in the last instance*, but these still do not adequately capture the dialectical dynamic of the material- and the formal-constitutional. Because of course Marx was insistent that the materiality of social reproduction could not occur or be thought of independently of the constitutional function of property title and economic rights. On these institutions depended the institutionalisation of scarcity, the reproduction of the relations of production and the creation of profit margins. But for another reason too. The notion of 'formal subsumption', so central to Marx's argument in *Capital*, in fact reverses the direction and begins with the institutional – supervening – layer as definitional of what underlies it. Formal subsumption names the process whereby property title and economic freedoms, as constitutionally guaranteed, take hold of labour power under capitalist valorisation. Formal subsumption names the form of capture that allows the (commodity) *form* to pass itself as the truth of the thing it subsumes; and the same logic carries over to the institutional form of property right. Under these circumstances the predication 'material' of the material constitution is doing no independent work. It is simply what is projected, from the institutional point of view, as necessary (external) reference for the operation of the institution.

This is a form of capture that takes hold of social and political relations and embeds so deep that it remains immune to the materialist corrective. Marx's analysis of the fetish-phenomenon associated with the commodity form is exemplary of this kind of capture. It is a form of institutional capture that cannot be stepped behind in order that the materiality of practice might be retrieved or that the smooth operation of the language of property and freedoms might be tempered or disturbed, because there is no 'behind' to step back to. The constitution of value incurs and is exhausted at the level of its signification by the order of capital; labour is what capital calls forth as labour, and the collective position of labour similarly is called forth according to what capital demands and what work it makes available. *Value* production is only ever recognised at the site where it is *already* appropriated as the exchange value of labour; collective labour *identities* are formed in a field where the availability of labour is controlled by capital, with *its* investment decisions, shifts in the forms of production, use of technologies to instil precariousness, etc. This is as blatant now as it was back then, endlessly instrumentalised, forever renewed. What matters for our discussion is that it impacts constitutively on the kinds of material practices and identities that can be conceived of as 'underlying' institutional practices. At the limit point the capture is comprehensive, making the supervening level of constitutional formation decisive to the point where the constitutional level always-already substitutes for the material, and fully overdetermines the 'layering' as such.

This is the danger that confronts the material constitution, where the institutional level is what gives form and calls the material level into line, to the point where it cannot perform an independent corrective function. Marx does not go as far as stating this indictment and his concern is only incidentally with the constitution. But the fundamental problem of the fetish-phenomenon and the invisibility it inflicts, once posed by Marx, is then picked up and restated emphatically in relation to *law* by Evgeny Pashukanis, whose profound insight of the relation of form to content is that content is eclipsed by the form of law. Crucially, for Pashukanis, this erasure is constitutive of law as a formal system. *It is by absenting the underlying content, the material relations of production, that law attains to its form* in a broadly similar way that in Kelsen the validity of the law collects the objective meaning of the underlying facticity into what is formally law and what underlies its 'purity'. What becomes meaningful *as* law is what is given objective meaning at the level of legal semantics, and the underlying materiality, the givenness of brute fact, does not impact nor does it 'intertwine' with legal meaning. In this, *the very gesture that organises law is the one that excludes its material base.* This of course would be the very negation of the 'material' constitution. For Pashukanis, law's exclusionary function is founded on nothing but its own ongoing articulation, immunising what may count as a possible evolution of its thematics from any challenge that might have emerged from the material reproduction of social life or in terms of alternative configurations of individual and collective identity. The content of the law (the ensemble of relations of production and their effects) is eclipsed by the formalism of the law, at both ordinary and constitutional levels: and this erasure (of material content) is integral to the constitution of the law *qua* formal system. The effacement of content by form is drawn out in striking parallel by the two theorists, in Kelsen as a function of the purity of legal thought, in Pashukanis as a function of immunisation of bourgeois law from the contradiction-laden terrain of social reproduction.

Of course, this radical moment of erasure of the 'material constitution' should not be generalised across the whole spectrum of Marxism(s) nor of course beyond them. But already the question of supervenience has been dealt a serious blow, as has the whole notion of the overlaying of the institutional on the material, such that the movements of the latter are felt and its energies transfer to the former, or such that 'the animating movement of the material constitution, with its cascading effects on institutions, is enabled' (595) and, following Lassalle, the 'distance between constitutional form and constitutional material' (593) somehow crossed. How we might venture that 'enablement' and that improbable crossing from within Marxist thought is something that we will return to in Section 13.4.

For now, let us stay a little longer with the materialist readings of conflicts, movements and dynamics that remain pivotal to the invocation of the material constitution. If it is difficult to discern what critical purchase materiality might provide for these more structural varieties of Marxism that we have visited in this section, although arguably there still inheres in them a conviction that the capture *will* be reversed and that the labour of the proletariat will not remain domesticated in the form in which it becomes facilitative of the reproduction of capitalist structures. Here is Marx in a famous extract from the first chapter of *Capital*: 'The labour time necessary for production asserts itself like an over-riding law of nature. The law of gravity thus asserts itself when a house falls about our ears'.[10] Marx here is expressing the faith that 'like a law of nature' material forces in the form of labour power will 'over-ride' because, ultimately, labour power, the 'living, form-giving fire' of the *Grundrisse*, will break free of its capture and institutional containment and ride the tide of history, forcing the demolition of the house 'about our ears'. The problem with this formulation, as Stephen Connelly points out,[11] is that the law of gravity of course asserts itself also when the house does *not* fall down. That we perceive it as 'over-riding' in the collapse does not mean that it was not operating all along during the stable state. Similarly, with the constitution that 'houses' the material practices, conflicts and identity-forming processes of civil society: it is just as much the realisation of bourgeois society as it is its potential undermining. The material constitution does not, not yet, not as such, manifest the over-riding force; the invocation of the material constitution does not *as such* expose the contingency of the institutional arrangements that accommodate it or realise it. It manifests neither the junctures at which political action might make a difference, nor the points of foreclosure on which the unity of the formal constitutional order depends. Instead the accommodation might be water-tight, with no visibility of the 'remainder', however insistently that visibility is invoked. And yet the dislodging of the material constitution from its institutional accommodation is a condition – even a first step in the direction – of tracking the points of tension; it introduces a gap or 'distance'[12]; it grants visibility to the contingency of the institutional arrangements and the possible fault lines, in other words also of the junctures at which political action might make a difference. It is to this reconstruction, and defence of the material constitution that we turn in Section 13.4, with the emphasis on what critical leverage it provides, on what it means to create an aperture in the constitutional situation. And for this we will follow a semiotic route, away from the 'structuralist' Marx and in the direction of his earlier philosophical work.

[10] K. Marx, *Capital* (Penguin, 1991), Book 1, Ch. 1, s. 4.

[11] Connelly writes: 'What determines the delay in the point of destruction is the ability of the house, like the system of exchange relations, not just to defy gravity, but use it to its advantage.' S. Connelly, *Spinoza, Right and Absolute Freedom* (Routledge, 2015), 138.

[12] As Goldoni and Wilkinson put it, 'the distance between constitutional form and constitutional material'. Goldoni and Wilkinson, 'The Material Constitution', 593.

13.4 IMMANENT CRITIQUE AND THE CONSTITUTIONAL SITUATION

One of the most fundamental insights that Hegelian Marxism has bequeathed us is that the categories at our disposal – the thwarted, historically poised, always provisional knowledge-set that furnishes the reflexivity of the age, *any* age – do not quite give us the semantic reach that we crave and that emancipation requires. They come in a language – of right, of identity, of freedom – that already carries the deficit that we deploy them to overcome. It is this deficit of the language of the formal constitution that the material corrective aims to redress. Along this semiotic route, the materialist turn requires that the language of communication and contestation carve out a space that disturbs the smooth deployment of the signifiers (right, identity, freedom, etc.) as mobilised at the institutional level. Much is staked on this notion of 'disturbance'. This is because signification must retain traction while at the same time re-negotiating the incidence of the terms, two operations that are reciprocally at odds with each other. At the one end of the spectrum, losing traction would turn key constitutional terms into 'empty signifiers', floating them across expanses of equivalence where they would name everything and nothing at all! Look at the extension of the language of human rights agency to corporations, or the proliferation of the language of stake-holding as *democratic* governance, for obvious examples of this type of implosion of constitutional language. At the other end of the spectrum a certain rigidity descends to curtail the open texture of constitutional language, policing the use and confining it to prescribed uses, to the extent, of course, that such functions can be secured. Against both extremes, at the level of constitutional semantics, the promise of the material constitution is to harness constitutional thought to sematic disagreements that might tap some of the deeper societal dynamics, typically by forcing re-interpretations of concepts that carry significant political import. A politics of constitutional interpretation can then carry the energies of the material constitution, not as a matter of course (as 'over-riding law') but to the extent that political-strategic uses might be mobilised, with all the risks and the lack of warrant that accompany such deployments.

A politics of constitutional interpretation fastens on to 'the relative indeterminacy of the material order'. Such 'indeterminacy' becomes manifest during 'critical or conjunctural periods, where material forces push in antagonistic directions and open up alternative paths for constitutional change' (593). A gap is prised open as the 'distance between constitutional form and constitutional material'. But it is 'misleading', argue Goldoni and Wilkinson, 'to suggest a dichotomy' at this point of breach; instead 'the relationship between the formal constitution and the material constitution is better characterised as internal'. Now (and while this is not the authors' idiom) the more customary philosophical rendering of this 'internal relationship' reserves the term *particular* for instantiations in *material* contexts and holds the *universal* at the level of *formal* stipulation. And if we assume that any *felicitous* particular instantiation of a universal concept involves a clean subsumption of the former to the latter,[13] the difference emerges on those 'critical or conjunctural' occasions when the smooth process of subsumption is upset. On these occasions a gap opens as internal to the order of the constitution, between 'form' and 'material': a gap between the language of accommodation and that which remains incongruous to it. It is an asymmetry that it introduced and that persists between that which appears as constitutional and that which appears as an imperfect instantiation, and remains resistant, too, to the sealing over. How to understand the resistance? Only by linking it to the experiential

[13] This clean subsumption is what Georg Lukacs criticised in the 'pure reflection' of the 'speculative' philosophy of Kant and the stillness of its categories: a *stasis* that, for him, is the hallmark of bourgeois thought.

dimension of the material practices that engage people in their social and political lives. I would suggest that this 'gap', 'distance' or disrupted subsumption of the material to the formal constitution is best understood and thematised in terms of *immanent critique*.

With Hegel the relationship between 'concrete' particular and universal is understood in terms of a *process* that brings the two into *relation*. Which means that the universal is mediating and mediated by its relation to particulars. It is as mediation rather than subsumption that it enters Marx's thought too. The coincidence between formal and material levels is broken, a certain 'slack' comes into play. A discrepancy enters where there was mere subsumption, a discrepancy that inserts itself between material and formal levels, that can, in 'critical or conjunctural' moments, tap a contradictory dynamic. The unifying formulae of constitutional representation – and the linkages and distinctions that allow them to organise the institutional world of law – are found wanting at these moments. Subsumption loosens its hold as the constitutional vocabulary comes adrift. The loosening and the disconnect are felt by those engaged in constitutional practice as antinomies: the formal-constitutional signifier 'popular sovereignty' comes to be experienced in material contexts as powerlessness; the constitution promises dignity and delivers indignities in people's public and working lives; the formal signifier 'people' elides national, social and class antagonisms in which concrete collective identities are forged; the signifier 'freedoms' stands for freedom to sell one's labour at any price, if not freedom to starve; the formal signifier 'citizenship' carries anaemic political capacity; etc. Contradiction arises between the level of formal signification and what comes to be experienced as its meaning at the level of material life. In all this the experiential-affective dimension is crucial. Immanent critique, the experience of the discrepancy, mobilises people to act where these contradictions acquire traction in the constitutional semantic, as thwarted constitutional promise and imaginary, as the discrepancy between the normative language of the constitution and the reality of powerlessness. The function of negation lies at the heart of these deployments that generate productive blockages. These are cleavages in the language of constitutional formation that lay the constitutional open – as the terrain of contradiction – to some appropriation. That, I would argue and would endorse, as the principal promise of the material constitution.

I have attempted to address the methodological question at the heart of the *material* constitution, where its designation as 'underlying' the *formal* constitution, pivots on the crucial – even constitutive – significance of *the vis-à-vis between the institutional and the material.* Discussions of constitutionalism remain largely inattentive to the 'social relations' and 'political objectives' that underlie it, withdrawing the theorisation of the constitutional system from the material contexts which inform it and in which it plays out. Against the reliance on function to introduce the materialist 'corrective' through the language of 'ordering', as that which brings the two layers into relation and aligns them in a way that supposedly tracks both coincidence and discrepancy, I have argued that functional definitions typically remain 'mute' regarding dysfunctionalities that they are programmed to immunise from. Marxism bequeaths an ambivalent legacy to the material constitution. In its more structural varieties, it becomes nearly impossible to extricate the material from the formal or insert any distance between the two that might allow us to address 'gaps', discrepancies or elisions. A different, Hegelian-Marxist, reading, on the other hand, might allow both differentiation and traction between the formal and the material conceptions and foreground a semantics of constitutional interpretation that opens up to democratic uses, harnessing the semantic reach of constitutional concepts to material forces of ordering *and* of disruption. The materialist turn in constitutional thought suggests that constitutional formation is not principally understood as the governing function 'from above';

instead by re-orienting constitutional thought to the material practices of the political economy, constitutional formation attaches to changing dynamics in the relations of production. This is not necessarily the portal through which the ever-expanding field of 'constitutionalisms from below' can enter the scene; the theory of the material constitution may offer opportunities to this line of theorisation but provides it with no warrant. The dynamics of concept formation, the immunising forces that buttress constitutional reflexivity, raise steep barriers to such assumed passage. I have argued instead that it is primarily *antinomy* and contradiction in the tradition of *immanent critique* that give expression to the constitutional practice that is envisaged and invoked by the turn to the 'material constitution'.

14

Three Registers of the Material Constitution

Neil Walker

14.1 INTRODUCTION

The notion of the material constitution has undoubtedly played an important part in the explanation and critique of constitutional law and practice at various points in the history of political modernity. This is most notably so in the Europe of the first half of the twentieth century, but in the decades that have followed the material constitution has remained a present and sometimes prominent feature of our intellectual vocabulary. In a broader perspective, our understanding of how the development of constitutional thought has been informed by constitutional practice would be quite incomplete if we did not acknowledge the role that the material constitution has played as one of a cluster of cognate concepts, including 'economic constitution' and 'political constitution',[1] typically invoked and refined in a certain type of debate. These debates arise or intensify at key historical conjunctures when the course or significance of constitutional development is unclear or contested and they frequently involve actors who have a political stake as well as a theoretical interest in the outcome. Paying attention to how, when and why the material constitution and similar terms are deployed should also remind us of – and caution us against – an enduring and problematic feature of our conventional understandings of the nature of constitutional ordering, as relevant and as instructive today as at any point in the past. On the one hand, as such attention reveals, a purely 'legal-normative'[2] understanding of the constitution is quite inadequate – neither a reliable nor a resilient indicator of the balance, pattern and direction of power within society – the normative structure of the constitution instead dependent on the deeper play of economic, political and cultural forces of the society in question; on the other hand, despite this body of evidence, the legocentric

[1] See, e.g., P. Minkinnen, 'Political Constitutionalism vs. Political Constitutional Theory: Law, Power and Politics (2015) 11 *International Journal of Constitutional Law* 585; N. Walker, 'Where's the "E" in Constitution? A European Puzzle' (2020) University of Edinburgh School of Law Research Paper Series No 2020/14.

[2] I use the term 'legal-normative' as the capsule opposite of 'material' in recognition of the limitations of various other candidates. The term 'normative constitution' is inappropriate here as it is often used in an evaluative or prescriptive sense to refer to a normatively attractive constitution. See, e.g., A. Menéndez, *Three Conceptions of the European Constitution* (Arena Working Paper, 2003), 8. The term 'legal' constitution is open-ended as to the range and type of legal phenomena it may refer to, including institutional features (courts, police, etc.) that fall within certain definitions of the material constitution. The term legal-normative is preferred as a clearly descriptive rather than evaluative or prescriptive deployment of the 'normative' and as limiting its reference to the 'legal' to the basic normative framework of the law. As we shall see in Section 14.2, 'legal-normative' nevertheless remains capable of embracing a number of sub-variants.

inclinations of many constitutional scholars means that they nevertheless remain tempted to stick with or revert to exclusively or predominantly normative understandings of our object of study.

All this, I would suggest, is fairly obvious and should be uncontentious. It is already sufficient justification for our continuing to take the idea of the material constitution seriously, therefore, that the insights this promises are an important aspect of any well-rounded historical sociology of the conditions and outcomes of constitutional knowledge, and also that such an approach offers a useful corrective to the narrowly law-centred *déformation professionelle* of some sections of our intellectual trade. How useful the notion of the material constitution is beyond these general benefits, however, is less clear. For it is deployed in such a range of different and sometimes incompatible ways, and it stands in such a diverse and complex set of relations to the idea of the 'legal-normative' constitution, that it is not easy to find common ground on which to build discussion and insight. Yet that very diversity of endorsement is also tribute to how widely shared is the intuition that this is the kind of concept that ought to form an important part of our common discourse.

In what follows, I will try to account for the reasons why the material constitution offers up such a diverse, complicated and somewhat conflicted menu. That account is based upon the idea that the concept occurs in three different registers of thought, each of which allows much scope for internal variation and contestation. An exploration of these registers, and of the relationship between them, cannot offer a definitive answer to the question of just how useful the continuing exploration of the concept might be, or how much intellectual effort should be expended in that direction. But it can at least point to some of the benefits and difficulties involved for those of us who seek to continue the journey.

14.2 THREE REGISTERS OF THE MATERIAL CONSTITUTION

A first and most basic register, in the sense of tending to be closely allied to certain political-ideological concerns of the constitutional analyst, places the material constitution in a relationship of *rhetorical contrast* with the legal-normative constitution. In the second place, typically alongside its rhetorical invocation, the material constitution functions for some authors as a *theoretical fulcrum* – as a way of gaining deep explanatory purchase on the question of the salient features of constitutional order and its relationship to other forms of order in social life. Thirdly, the material constitution can figure more broadly – and more loosely – as a *methodological orientation*; as a kind of general focusing device, a signal to attend to a certain type and range of factors and a certain modality of explanation in seeking to account for the constitutional order.

Importantly, the first of these registers, that of a politico-ideologically inflected rhetorical contrast with the notion of a legal-normative constitution, retains a particular framing significance for the other two registers. Indeed, the very term the 'material constitution', we might argue, would not have been coined if it were not for its ideological function as a way of highlighting and dramatising its distinction from the juridical form and face of the constitution – a distinction and division that might be fleshed out as a contrast, or as an opposition, or, perhaps, as a relationship of cause and effect, or even of absorbing and absorbed. And in turn, the two structuring features of that framing distinction; namely the *division* of material and non-material realms, and the *continuity of the idea of a 'constitution'* across these material and non-material realms, continues to inform and in some ways constrain how we think about the material constitution within the other two registers, theoretical and methodological.

14.3 RHETORICAL CONTRAST

The best-known early instance of the rhetorical invocation of the material constitution concept in a context of ideological disputation is supplied by Ferdinand Lasalle, the Prussian socialist and acquaintance of Marx. In contemplation of his own title question in an 1862 lecture – 'What is a Constitution?', Lasalle responded polemically: 'The army, that is the constitution. The police, that is the constitution. The bankers, that is the constitution', and so on.[3] His general point was that constitution-talk should lead us toward rather than deflect us away from the material base of the constitutional order, which he views as nothing other than 'the actual relations of force existing in a given society'. Lasalle's purpose in drawing the rhetorical contrast between material and non-material was simple but direct; to show how a textual constitution, even one with certain formally democratic features, could be no more than a legitimating façade for the authoritarian institutions of the Prussian regime.

Yet this is just one way in which the rhetorical contrast can be drawn for critical ideological purposes. Costantino Mortati, writing in the context of the fascist transformation of the inter-war Italian state, defended the material constitution as a stable background of control mechanisms securing the hegemony of the ruling political bloc against the transience of popular democratic will.[4] Herman Heller, writing in the same period in Weimar Germany against the radical top-down extra-constitutional political decisionism of Carl Schmitt, also made much of the material/normative contrast and how it translated into the efficacy/validity distinction. But in his case the emphasis was on the mutual dependence and articulation of the two elements in the production of the 'real constitution'.[5] Constitutional stability in the context of the new age of social democracy was viewed as a function of the vital but precarious social homogeneity of a community formed through the operation of a broader 'law of democracy', for which the materiality of (relatively equal) socio-economic relations supplied indispensable grounding.

Other commentators on interwar Germany developed the material/normative contrast in much more critical vein to indict the Nazi dictatorship that overthrew the Weimar Republic in 1933. Writing from American exile, Franz Neumann deployed a materialist analysis of National Socialism as a totalitarian form of monopoly capitalism which had reduced the state and its law to the arbitrary instrument of domination of the party.[6] His fellow German Jewish political scientist and American exile, Ernst Fraenkel, developed a more subtle account of our key contrast, introducing the highly suggestive rhetorical device of the dual state (*der Doppelstaat*) as the label for the entity that he claimed to have replaced the *Rechtsstaat*.[7] Under the Nazi regime, he argued, the state did not disappear but split into two elements: namely, the prerogative state (*Maßnahmenstaat*), a set of measures and activities fashioned solely to meet the purposes of party rule, and the normative state (*Normenstaat*), a system regulated through statutes and judicial decisions. In tandem, these two elements spoke to the two material foundations of power – political and economic. By removing restraints on the police, reducing judicial overview and making the party the key legislative and executive authority, the prerogative state consolidated party domination of the political sphere. But the normative state remained an indispensable part of the whole. It supplied a regime of predictable private law rules through

[3] F. Lasalle, 'On the Essence of Constitutions', E. O'Callagan, trans. (1942) 3 *Fourth International* 25.
[4] See, e.g., Chapter 5, by Lucia Rubinelli.
[5] See, e.g., H. Heller, 'Nature and Function of the State' (1996) 8 *Cardozo Law Review* 1213.
[6] F. Neumann, *Behemoth: The Structure and Practice of National Socialism* (Gollancz, 1942).
[7] E. Fraenkel, *The Dual State: A Contribution to the Theory of Dictatorship*, E. A. Shils, trans. (Oxford University Press, 1941). See, further, Chapter 6, by Lars Vinx.

which activity at the economic core of the order could be regulated, including relations between government and business. For, in order to sustain and stabilise its arbitrary political power, the Nazi regime needed to retain a sufficient core of non-arbitrary rules of the economic game to allow capitalism to flourish and the state coffers to fill.

So, where Mortati saw the material constitution as fixed, Heller's sense of the product of the material constitution was instead more fragile and responsive to shifting political circumstances and fluid democratic possibilities. In both cases, however, the priority in the last instance of the material constitution over the legal-normative constitution is clear,[8] just as it was for Lasalle, Neumann and Frankel. In the case of this latter group, however, their different politico-ideological point of departure dictates that the dominant influence of the material constitution, at least in the form that they encounter it, is a matter to be regretted rather than welcomed.

Yet the differing ideological predilections of different authors means that even the basic commonality of an approach asserting material primacy should not be assumed from the mere endorsement of the rhetoric of binary division. Hans Kelsen offers a case in point. In the Weimar debate over the nature and justification of the final power of the constitution, Kelsen was as much Heller's critical target on the normativist side of the argument as Schmitt was on the opposite political decisionist side. Kelsen also made use of the distinction between the material and the non-material constitution, but in his case, the purpose of the distinction was to close down rather than open up inquiry into any deeper non-positive roots of constitutional order. For Kelsen's material constitution was thin gruel, comprising merely the fundamental legal norms that authorise law-making, law-interpreting and law-applying powers.[9] The function of the material constitution, so narrowly understood, was only to secure the effectiveness of the formal legal-normative constitution and so guarantee the 'pure' internal logic of legal validity of the *stufenbau*. Within this positivist framework, therefore, the point of invoking the material constitution is precisely *not* to expose and refer back the posited legal-normative constitution to its socially and economically generative forces. Rather, it serves the double objective of indicating the necessary jural glue offered by second order legal or meta-legal norms in service of the formal legal-normative constitution, while sealing off consideration of the influence of wider social and material factors.

14.4 THEORETICAL FULCRUM

In these various approaches we can see how what is introduced as one side of a rhetorical opposition can also come to serve as a theoretical fulcrum. Indeed, even thinkers working on as expansive an intellectual canvas as Mortati and Heller come to rely upon the notion of the material constitution as one of the key supports of their theoretical scheme. Yet it remains doubtful how much weight the concept can actually bear for these purposes. For far from offering the stable foundation of a coherent and cumulative project of explanation and appraisal, the material constitution is a concept of highly contested meaning and evaluative implications.

The diversity of evaluative implications is already clear from our survey of the differing intents behind the invocation of the material/legal-normative contrast. Indeed, the former may be seen as flowing quite directly from the latter – the very rhetorical purpose of the claim being to lend

8 In many approaches, indeed, the material constitution not only has priority over the formal constitution but is understood to contain and absorb the latter. For a thorough discussion of the different modes of dominance of the material over the formal constitution, see J. Colón-Ríos, *Constituent Power and the Law* (Oxford University Press, 2020), chapter 8.

9 H. Kelsen, *General Theory of Law and State* (Harvard University Press, 1945), 124–25.

TABLE 14.1. *The binary division of material and non-material realms: three candidates*

Material		Legal-Normative
informal	←	Formal (formative properties)
substantive	←	Formal (abstract forms)
material	→	*Ideal*

weight to a particular value judgement. Some, such as Lasalle and the critics of the Nazi order, come to warn of the material constitution. Others, like Mortati, come to endorse it or, like Heller, come to value it as a worthwhile yet fragile and elusive accomplishment or, like Kelsen, come to bury it back into the folds of the formal constitution. In all cases the original rhetorical impulse looms large over the ultimate normative conclusion. Yet even if we put the various and quite diverse politico-contextual motivations and rhetorical strategies to one side and proceed to explore the ways in which the schemes that are developed may exhibit a degree of explanatory autonomy, the material constitution seems fated to generate a high degree of indeterminacy and contestation. This is so because it is a concept that invites confusion over the very shape and extent of its referential field.

That potential for confusion is closely bound up with the first of the two key structuring effects of the framing distinction mentioned in Section 14.2; namely, its association with a strictly *binary division* of constitutional order into material and non-material dimensions. The splitting of the constitutional domain into just two dimensions patently places an enormous explanatory burden on the precise terms of the divide. So far, we have discussed the non-material side of that divide under the general heading of 'legal-normative' – simply as a way of indicating that its broad domain of reference is that of the legal order itself. Yet this can cover a variety of different specific possibilities. Often in the literature this general legal-normative domain goes instead under the label of 'formal'. But, as set out in simplified and stylised form in Table 14.1,[10] it is both the case that 'formal' itself can mean different things, covering more than one specification of the general legal-normative domain, and that even these different variations of 'formal' do not exhaust what may be covered under the general legal-normative domain. And given that the definition of the material constitution emerges from and relies upon its contradistinction with the legal-normative domain, then, depending upon what version of the legal-normative domain is emphasised, what counts as the essential properties of the material constitution will differ.

A first specification of the formal constitution resonates with the understanding of law associated with legal formalism.[11] It does so by focusing on the particular properties we associate with the legal form. The relevant properties of the legal form are rules and other law-specific normative standards such as legal principles, and so the formal constitution is the constitution as defined by and restricted to these formal legal properties. If this line is taken, then the material

[10] This stylisation is intended to demonstrate the in-principle unavoidability of confusion based on an ordinary language analysis of the relevant terms, but in fact it *understates* the actual variety and complexity of forms of usage and the attendant scope for confusion. In some cases, the adherence of authors to any of the positions set out in Table 14.1 is merely implicit rather than explicit or may be only partial or inconsistent. For example, both Mortati and Heller at points refer to the written or codified constitution as the formal constitution, and it is this that supplies the contrast to the material constitution. In my scheme the written constitution would figure as just one of the abstract or detached legal forms under the second formal/substantive distinction, and so would supply only a sub-category of the second sense of 'formal'.

[11] Understood as a commitment to 'autonomous conceptualism' in judicial and broader legal decision-making. See, e.g., P. Cox, 'An Interpretation (and Partial Defense) of Legal Formalism' (2003) 36 *Indiana Law Review* 56, 59.

constitution refers to matters constitutional that do not possess these formal legal properties. In other words, the material constitution becomes synonymous with the 'informal' constitution.

If 'formal' under this first heading refers to these elemental features that are deemed constitutive of the very 'form' of law, 'formal' under a second heading refers instead to the general 'forms' that we associate with law and the wider legal system; put more concisely, the second heading refers to what is 'formed' rather than, as in the first heading, what is 'formative'. And so the emphasis falls more expansively on the forms typically taken by or produced through law, including both those general devices and structures we identify and organise within legal doctrine (e.g., tort, contract, property and their various sub-categories) and the catalogue of general juridical and governmental institutions. So understood in this second sense, 'formal' speaks to the quality of abstraction and detachment from the concrete instantiated features of whatever is presupposed by or produced according to law's 'formal' (in the first sense) properties. If this line is taken, the material constitution becomes synonymous with these concrete features – the opposite of 'formal' becomes 'substantive'.

Whether or not our definition of the 'material' of material constitutionalism follows the formal/informal distinction or the formal/substantive distinction is significant, even if this deeper choice of binaries rarely seems to be consciously acknowledged in the relevant conceptual analyses. Under the formal/informal distinction, just because the formal side is itself so strictly defined the emphasis on the informal side is more likely to remain on what some writers have understood as 'the legal understanding of the material constitution'.[12] That is to say, a narrow emphasis on legal form highlights by way of material contrast that which does not meet the strict criteria of legal form. Yet such contrasting 'informal' factors are more likely to remain legal phenomena *in senso lato*, whether deep jurisgenerative norms, as with Kelsen's version of the material constitution, or 'living' features of the legal system such as the operative processes and outcomes of courts, executives and legislatures, including the evolved canons and conventions of constitutionality applied by these bodies.[13] Under the formal/substantive distinction, where the emphasis is instead on the abstract/concrete divide, just as the formal and abstract side is more expansively defined to include 'informal' legal features such as general institutions of the legal governmental system, there is, correspondingly, more scope on the material and concrete side to penetrate the deeper political motivations and economic underpinnings of the constitution, so moving beyond even the most generously informal understanding of the world of law and legal system.[14]

Consideration of the more expansive understanding of the material constitution produced by this second opposition between abstract form and concrete substance also serves to highlight one further opposition, and one further associated uncertainty, that challenges theory-building under this sign. For, in revealing a deeper 'non-legal' sense of the possibilities associated with the material constitution, it points us to a further binary that, in contrast to the first two binary oppositions, is predicated upon and governed by the material signifier rather than the legal-normative signifier; namely the contrast between 'material' and 'ideal' – between that which strictly belongs to the world of matter and of material influences upon our life-chances and that which belongs to the world of ideas and of cultural influences on social relations. Both sides of

[12] A. Menéndez, *Three Conceptions of the European Constitution* (Arena Working Paper, 2003), 7.

[13] For Menéndez this produces a further subdivision between the 'structural' and the 'substantial' elements of the legal understanding of the material constitution; Menéndez, *Three Conceptions*, 7–8.

[14] Heller distinguishes between material constitution in the strict sense (fundamental content) and in the wide sense (including legal culture) in acknowledgment of the slipperiness of the concept and its dependence on the particular opposition invoked. Heller, 'Nature and Function'.

this contrast – not only the narrowly material but also those aspects of the ideational that reflect embedded social relations of domination – can and in some analyses do form part of the deep structure that we call the material constitution in the more expansive understanding available under the formal/substantive framework.

But this third candidate meaning, in which 'material' is much further removed from the legal-normative domain than under the formal/informal distinction while being more narrowly conceived than under the formal/substantive distinction, merely underlines the fragility of our key terms as weight-bearing theoretical concepts. And in so doing, it only underscores the scope for competition and confusion between different renderings of the underlying binary. Indeed, since the attitudes and strategies attendant upon deeply embedded positions of social and political power stand in most theoretical imaginaries toward the more concrete and so non-formal end of the abstract/concrete spectrum, there is an ironic tendency for the more expansive understandings of the material constitution *qua* substantive, just on account of their broad reach across the socio-political domain, to expose themselves to the criticism that, at least in terms of the strict material/ideal distinction, they 'remain insufficiently materialist'.[15]

14.5 METHODOLOGICAL ORIENTATION

If the concept of the material constitution lacks the common focus and stability of reference to offer the basis of a shared theoretical project, does it nevertheless retain value as a general methodological signal of and commitment to the importance of looking beyond text and immediate context when investigating constitutional constraints and possibilities? In a basic sense, that is undeniable. As noted in the introduction to this chapter, reviewing the historical debates over the material constitution offers a salutary reminder of the importance of deeper investigation into the social and economic conditions and consequences of any and all constitutional settlements. Beyond this basic reminder function, however, the methodological defence of the idea of the material constitution meets a sceptical challenge. It must either be able to offer a persuasive argument as to why a materially informed methodology of constitutional analysis needs to work with the specific idea of the 'material constitution'; or, at the very least, it ought to be able to show that operating in these specific terms is not detrimental to any general programme of research.

In addressing this concern, I turn to the second of the structural effects of the legal-normative/material framing distinction; namely the *continuity of the idea of a 'constitution'* across the divide. The legal-normative/material pairing is a good example of what Balkin calls a 'nested opposition'.[16] That is an opposition where the two terms bear a relationship of conceptual dependence or similarity as well as conceptual difference or distinction. Each term contains some element in common with the other, which common element provides the conceptual background on the basis of which the foreground distinction can be drawn. And, in the present case, it is the notion of a 'constitution' that supplies the common and continuous conceptual background upon which the legal-normative/material distinction rests.

But what, if anything, does continuity entail? By making 'constitution' the noun to which we attach the term 'material', what structuring effect follows, and why should we be concerned about possible distortions? To explore this sceptical possibility, we may borrow from David

[15] As Goldoni and Wilkinson remark of both Heller and Mortati; M. Goldoni and M. Wilkinson, 'The Material Constitution' (2018) 81 *Modern Law Review* 567, 579.

[16] J. Balkin, 'Nested Oppositions' (1990) 99 *Yale Law Journal* 1669.

Kennedy's analyses of various biases he claims as recurrent features of constitutional thought and practice.[17] Kennedy talks of a purposive bias, an institutional bias and a settlement bias, amongst others.[18] The purposive bias refers to the tendency for constitutional method to conceive of the social and material world as something that can be the subject of intentional design, set purpose and progressive planning. The institutional bias refers to the faith that constitutional method places in particular resilient institutions of government as the shapers and drivers of the social whole. The settlement bias refers to the sense that constitutional method offers full and once-and-for-all solutions to the problems of social order that it confronts. In a nutshell, constitutional method is seen as at once teleological, institutionally embedded and conclusive in its assumptions and predilections.

Kennedy's analysis is directly concerned only with formal constitutional structures, yet it also appears to respond to a deeper logic of constitution. The purposive bias arises from the assumption, implicit in the very notion of constitution, that 'things do add up, one way or the other'.[19] The institutional bias is related to an idea of structural self-containment. Etymologically, the notion of constitution originated with reference to the constitution and integrity of discrete bodies in the physical world, and was then extended to the 'body politic' with the same kinds of assumptions carried over about the joined-up coherence and resilience of the relevant political structures or 'institutions'.[20] The settlement bias is linked to the idea, again implicit in the basic idea of constitution, of an achievement, a successful construction, a now resolved state of affairs.

Each of these deeper assumptions in turn is linked to the idea of the constitution as noun rather than adjective, as an identifiable entity rather than a mobile quality that describes and attaches to other entities. And it is this analogous 'thingness' that allows us to see the possibility of a structuring effect and, therefore, a transfer of bias between the legal-normative and the deeper material constitution. Without putting it any higher, it is possible to imagine how articulating an inquiry into the underlying material dynamics of constitutional law and practice as an investigation into something called the 'material constitution' might encourage the writing over from the method associated with legal-normative constitutionalism of various assumptions about the purposive, institutionalised and stable quality of a discrete object.

What arguments can be raised against this sceptical line? In what is probably the most rigorous case yet put for the general methodological benefits of an orientation toward the material constitution that stands independently of any particular explanatory pay-off, Goldoni and Wilkinson have made persuasive points on the credit side of the ledger.[21] In so doing, while it is no part of their explicit remit to confront the Kennedy challenge, they meet some of his main objections.

Their point of departure involves distancing themselves not only from legocentric constitutionalism, but also from various other approaches that seek to take constitutional analysis beyond the confines of the legal-normative constitution. They see many of these as unduly one-dimensional. Political constitutionalism tends to concentrate too narrowly on questions of

[17] D. Kennedy, 'The Mystery of Global Governance', in J. Dunoff and J. Trachman (eds.), *Ruling the World?* (Cambridge University Press, 2009), 62–65.

[18] Kennedy also talks of a proceduralist bias – the disguising of substantive biases behind apparently neutral legal procedures. While pertinent to the study of the legal-normative constitution, there is no counterpoint in the material constitution for the translation and reception of this particular framing bias.

[19] Kennedy, 'Mystery of Global Governance', 62.

[20] See, e.g., N. Walker; 'Reframing EU Constitutionalism', in J. Dunoff and J. Trachoma (eds.) *Ruling the World?* (Cambridge University Press, 2009), 149–65.

[21] Goldoni and Wilkinson, 'Material Constitution'.

institutional efficacy (e.g., Parliaments versus Courts)[22] while economic constitutionalism, including its Marxist or Marxisant variants, tends to make the economic base deterministic of all other levels.[23] Their own approach is more capacious and more ecumenical. They specify four layers or 'ordering forces'[24] of the material constitution; the formation and sustenance of political unity, the operation of governmental and non-governmental institutions, the wider pattern of economically inflected social relations and the fundamental political *telos* of the polity in question. The intersection of the layers, however, reveals no unidirectional causal logic. Rather, Goldoni and Wilkinson see all four layers in a continuous state of mutual influence both *inter se* and with the formal constitutional carapace. Against the charge of purposive bias, therefore, they could argue that the fundamental political *telos* of the polity possesses no general causal primacy, and against the charge of institutional bias they could answer in the same terms about the influence of governmental and non-governmental organs.

Moreover, through a deep reading of constitutional ordering, they claim, 'the concept of the material constitution captures the internal relation between constitutional order and society without, however, eliding its conflictual and evolving nature'.[25] Indeed, conflict plays a central role in constitutional ordering so conceived, though the authors want to draw a distinction between two types.[26] On the one hand, much conflict can be diverted and managed through the complex legal operations of the constitution in ways that consolidate the underlying material order. On the other hand, conflict can threaten and undermine the dominant social and economic forces situated at the material base where the agents of these forces lose the capacity to exert sustained effects through the constitutionally coded political system. The multi-dimensionality of the material constitution, therefore, produces a mixed picture; an account that treats the legal-normative aspect of the constitutional order neither as a regular resource of radical challenge to underlying societal power structures nor as a guarantor of the *status quo ante*, but as a vehicle than can accommodate either tendency at different times and places. And so, the charge of settlement bias can also be answered in the negative without conceding the basic resilience of the material constitution.

It might be argued that it is precisely the use of constitution as a noun rather than an adjective that allows Goldoni and Wilkinson to avoid Kennedy's various biases. For it is through according primacy to the overall material constitution considered as a distinct, holistically conceived object that they are able to provide the stable and robust framework within which an ecumenical multi-causal understanding of the whole becomes possible. Far from being detrimental, therefore, it could be contended that the structuring effects of the continuity of the idea of the constitution in nominal rather than adjectival terms from legal-normative to material domains is in fact beneficial in terms of a general capacity to supply methodological enlightenment. Before drawing that conclusion, however, we should consider one final tendency, and one final possible bias, that may be associated with looking at the interconnected world of legal political and economic forces in the 'constitutional' round; namely the singularity bias.

Let us probe further the way in which, by analogy with entities in the physical world, the idea of a constitution, and by further extension the idea of a material constitution, describes a

[22] Ibid., 568.
[23] Ibid., 587; see also M. Goldoni, 'Introduction to the Material Constitution: Traditions and Constitutive Elements' *Legal Form Blog*; February 9, 2018; available at: https://legalform.blog/2018/02/09/introduction-to-the-material-constitution-traditions-and-constitutive-elements-marco-goldoni/, last accessed 1 August 2022.
[24] Goldoni and Wilkinson, 'Material Constitution', 597.
[25] Ibid., 597.
[26] Ibid., 595–96.

complex unity. It is a complex unity that is singular in a double sense; both internally, in the integrity of its inner structure, and externally, in its separateness from the material constitution of other polities. Positing the material constitution as an object of explanation, therefore, involves a gambit that we have identified the combination of a depth of analysis – embracing all material factors – and a level and site of analysis – that of the discrete polity – that is uniquely or at least most appropriate for 'constitutional' explanation. And so, while it is true that treating the material constitution as our object of analysis is in a significant sense methodologically expansive, allowing us to cast our explanatory gaze well beyond the terrain of the legal-normative constitution, it also imposes its own particular methodological limits – its own assumptions about what constitutional analysis should focus on and where it should end. Granted, to repeat a point, if we focus on the expansiveness rather than its limits, then, as Goldoni and Wilkinson would attest, that is precisely what allows the space for a multi-causal and multidirectional model of the kind they advocate that is not trapped in rigid orthodoxies of causal primacy. Yet can the argument not be made that, just because it ties the material constitution to a singular object that is, in turn, intimately connected to the singular object of the legal-normative constitution, there is a risk that their own framework may contain its own rigidities – its own blind spots and restricted pathways? In the final analysis does the important search for a deeper explanation of surface constitutional product end up limiting its own range and focus of analysis by assuming that the object of the deeper explanation should possess the same discrete and self-contained form as the surface?

Goldoni and Wilkinson's treatment of the content and internal dynamics of the material constitution is so carefully measured and closely qualified that any broad-brush critical observation risks doing it an injustice. Yet there are some indications of how their singular approach takes the analysis in certain directions at the expense of others. Perhaps most obviously there is a degree of state-centredness in their approach. For them, for all the variations in polity form that emerge from time to time, 'in [the] process of constitutional ordering the modern European nation-state remains paradigmatic'.[27] It is consolidated as a political unity – the first of their four ordering forces – through the 'establishment of a bounded community of belonging'.[28] Behind this political unity lie material factors. The development of the state involves the assertion of a certain conception of political space, one that involves an appropriation and consolidation of territory, underscored by a long-term process of 'transformation of social and geopolitical relations through the *commodification of land, labour and money* based on the logic of capital accumulation'.[29] Importantly, however, the time-frame with which we are primarily concerned is constitutional time. Constitutional ordering, and indeed the expansive modern conception of political unity itself, begin with the emergence of the idea of the authorising claim of an independent constituent power. Through this we find asserted the autonomy of the political, which has specific roots in religious disenchantment as well as general roots in the longer pattern of economic transformation. And today, that 'relatively autonomous mode of political authority'[30] remains, albeit the political unity and formal equality it promises stands in constant tension with the material relations of inequality within civil society. That assertion of the relative autonomy of the political then, reinforced by the ordering forces supplied by the hegemonic settlement of fundamental political objectives and the conflict-mediating work of political

[27] Ibid., 581.
[28] Ibid.
[29] Ibid., 583.
[30] Ibid., 584.

institutions, stands alongside and as a close complement to state-centredness as a fixed feature of the authors' singular view of the material constitution.

How can we fault this approach? To the extent that it draws on certain in-built methodological assumptions about the typical form and discrete quality of the polity to which the material constitution refers, who would disagree? Certainly there are versions of the economic constitution, in particular those driven by ordoliberal or neo-liberal assumptions about the actual – and also preferred – shaping of global social and political order, that might take issue with this line.[31] But as we have already noted, Goldoni and Wilkinson can reasonably retort that such a criticism, by treating the economic dimension as axiomatically prior, comes from a less rounded methodological position than their own. Nevertheless, it is possible to construct a position that, while much more critical of the dominant underlying economic forces than some of the proponents of economic constitutionalism with ordoliberal or neo-liberal sympathies and, in explanatory terms, not wedded to the automatic priority of economic causes, is nevertheless more questioning of state-centredness and less influenced by the constitutional self-expression of the autonomy of the political than the Goldoni and Wilkinson approach.

That alternative position begins from the observation – hardly novel – that the constitutional state of high modernity, equipped for the first time with a systematic, expansive and impersonal plan of government expressed by a settled normative code, declares and promotes a monopolistic sense of its own jurisdiction-bound authority. Done in the name of sovereignty – increasingly a self-determining popular sovereignty – its assertion of constituent power necessarily precludes rival or complementary claims to power in the public domain. In the constitution's own terms all other forms of authority, *including the forms of economic and social power*, are effectively relegated to the private domain. Their position is one of subordination. They remain within the implicit gift of the constituent power to break or remake and so have only secondary and 'derivative' standing.[32]

It is precisely the prominence of the derivative model of economic constitutionalism – a prominence due to the prior and all-pervading quality of the new constitutional state's claim to political authority, that accounts for the relative inattention to the economic domain in the classical tradition of modern legal-normative constitutional thought and practice. If constitutional authority trumps everything else, and if it provides the generative source upon which the formation and fate of all other capacities depend, then its formal authority over the economic domain is implicit and does not demand textual specification, still less detailed elaboration. Constitutional authority, therefore, could traditionally be somewhat 'indifferent'[33] toward economic power and, indeed, could in principle accommodate any sort of economic model, whether or not capitalist. There need, therefore, be no explicit reference to the 'e' word in the constitutional text. Instead, what are foregrounded are the constitution's own meta-political values which, as the constitutional state consolidated over the late nineteenth and twentieth century, can be summarised as the 'trinity' of democracy, human rights and the rule of law.[34]

Clearly, Goldoni and Wilkinson do not buy this legocentric story of monopolistic authority. The question remains, however, whether their version of state-level political unity and the 'relative autonomy' of the political more generally may nevertheless allow this constitutional

[31] See, e.g., Q. Slobodian, *Globalists: The End of Empire and the Birth of Neoliberalism* (Harvard University Press, 2018), 184–93.

[32] Walker, 'Where's the "E" in Constitution?', 4, 7.

[33] G. Gerapetritis, *New Economic Constitutionalism in Europe* (Hart, 2019), 6.

[34] See, e.g., J. Tully, J. Dunoff, A. Lang Jr., M. Kumm and A. Winer, 'Editorial: Introducing Global Integral Constitutionalism' (2016) 5 *Global Constitutionalism* 1, 3.

orthodoxy more influence than is merited. As Tully and his colleagues have argued, the modelling of economic power as merely secondary and derivative supplies but a partial perspective – one directly challenged by what has been called the paradigm of 'progressive development'.[35] In setting out the development paradigm, they draw, more insistently than do Goldoni and Wilkinson,[36] on Polanyi's thesis as to the three forms of commodification that underpin modern constitutionalism.[37] First, there is the generation of natural resources through the privatisation and commodification of the earth itself. Second, there is the generation of human resources through the commodification of human productive capacities. And, third, there is the generation of fiscal resources through the commodification of money. For Polanyi, it is these deeper economic processes and institutions that are primordially constitutive. Recast within a legal-normative register, it is the mechanisms of private law – property, contract, etc., that give juridical shape to the increasingly commodified social world from which public constitutional law emerges and to which it responds. The new commodified forms, according to the development paradigm, are placed under the control of private corporations, their global spread facilitated by profit-driven competition among corporations as well as military and financial competition among states during and after empire. Over time, the more advanced states and corporations establish hegemonic forms of governance of the capitalist economy, and only once that primary 'economic constitution' is established does the stabilisation of the secondary constitutional qualities of human rights, democracy and the pervasive rule of law become possible.

In a nutshell, this deeper economic perspective posits the existence of two complexes of constitutive power rather than just one. Previous and indispensable to the much heralded constitutive – or constituent – power of the people we have the much less heralded constitutive power of the three processes of commodification of natural resources, labour and capital. The political agency available to the constituting people is no mirage; but it is conditioned and often deeply compromised by these prior underlying economic forces. And because the argument of Tully, and of proponents of the 'new constitutionalism' more generally,[38] tends to be concerned not only with origins but also with the *longue durée* of the spread of modern capitalism, as that extended evolution draws to the present we can see just how compromising these economic forces have become. Various contemporary 'sustainability crises'[39] are seen to flow directly from the basic development paradigm. Global inequality, militarism, mass migration and, most urgently of all, environmental degradation are viewed as the pathological accompaniments of advanced capitalism. And from this perspective, the neo-liberal turn in late modern constitutional politics is viewed as the latest and most aggressive iteration of commitment to a model of unencumbered growth that can only accelerate these crises.

In the last analysis there may be little substantive disagreement between this approach and that of Goldoni and Wilkinson. Yet it might nevertheless struggle to be accommodated within a methodological framework with such an emphasis on a primarily state-centred political unity. Political unity from the Tully perspective is but one of two equiprimordial sources of constituent

[35] Ibid., 3.

[36] Goldoni and Wilkinson, 'Material Constitution', 587.

[37] K. Polanyi, *The Great Transformation: The Political and Economic Origins of Our Time [1944]* (Beacon Press, 2004). Discussed in the broader context of global constitutionalism by Tully et al., 'Introducing Global Integral Constitutionalism'.

[38] See, e.g., S. Gill, *Power and Resistance in the New World Order*, 2nd ed. (Palgrave, 2003); G. Anderson, 'Beyond "Constitutionalism beyond the State"' (2012) 39 *Journal of Law and Society* 359.

[39] See, e.g., Tully et al., 'Introducing Global Integral Constitutionalism', 5–7.

power alongside the deep sources and processes of commodification. These both work to an earlier and deeper time scale and to a different spatial logic than the self-standing constitutionally endowed polity. They possess a structuring power that is distinct from state sovereignty, albeit also influenced over time by the operation of sovereignty. And it is a power that today contributes to a series of crises demanding responses which go well beyond any individual state and its local political capacity.

14.6 CONCLUSION

To the extent that I am a critic of the idea of a material constitution, I am very much a sympathetic critic. The rhetorical roots and the narrower theoretical understandings of the concept can leave it mired in disagreement – and even confusion, but as a general methodological framework it holds much more promise. It is in many ways a compellingly attractive container of the message of the need to go beyond legal-normative constitutionalism, especially if that container is filled with a suitably multi-directional explanatory structure. Perhaps though, that same message could be conveyed in a more flexible if less conceptually arresting manner, by adjective rather than by noun; through insisting on material factors as a prominent and pervasive feature of constitutional explanation without tying these factors to the bespoke material constitutions of particular polities with their singular histories and prospects.

15

What Matter(s)? A Processual View of the Material Constitution

Mariano Croce

The notion of material constitution conjures up the idea of matter, that is, a substance that gives form because of specific contents of its own. As the story goes, the constitution cannot be considered as if it were a mere set of fundamental procedures and binding provisions. Nor is it enough to conceive of this substance as a set of fundamental rights that delimit the power of the state over the individual and get entrenched in a written-down document.[1] Rather, the matter of the constitution emerges out of an underlying material reality comprising sedimented social practices, informal institutional mechanisms, and concrete societal ends. A constitutional document is nothing other than the transposition of an ongoing societal project that only needs verbalising to ensure survival and persistence. On this account, the material is believed to possess *nomic force*, that is, a normativity that not only provides guidance for conduct but also moulds people's understanding of the social world. Importantly, the material constitution carries out this job from within, well before a process of verbalisation puts it into words.

One major consequence of this conception bears relevance for the task of jurisprudence, as this is believed to be the particular type of science that delves deep into the material, mostly unspoken constitution to make it speakable. In this sense, jurisprudence is not only a cognitive enterprise because cognition of the material constitution affects the process whereby its contents get formalised. Not only does jurisprudence unearth the contents of the material as they are to be made explicit; it also helps to understand when the formal constitution dries out in that it no longer reflects the material one. It is in the light of this conception that Carl Schmitt stated: 'Jurisprudence is itself the true source of law'.[2] This task is political through and through. Much more than representative politics, which is always exposed to contingency, jurisprudence cuts deeper into the core elements of a society – those elements that need protection against the caprice of the political will. In short, jurisprudence voices and protects the nomic force of the material substance that makes a society what it is.

The present essay makes a case against this *substantive understanding* of the material constitution. I will centre on Schmitt's concrete-order thinking as a telling exemplification of a theory that attaches priority to the material over the formal and yet fails to explain where matter comes from. Materiality turns out to be a shorthand for the social, while what the social is remains mostly underdeveloped. The social is taken for granted and claimed to shore up the formal

[1] For this understanding of the material constitution, see L. Vinx, 'Hans Kelsen and the Material Constitution of Democracy' (2021) 12 *Jurisprudence* 466–90.

[2] C. Schmitt, 'The Plight of European Jurisprudence' (1990) 83 *Telos* 35, 57.

constitutional order, although, as I will contend, the idea of the social finds no grounds other than Schmitt's own ideological conviction that a community should be rooted in a limited and durable set of core principles and values. I will continue by arguing that this critique of the material does not necessarily lapse back into its opposite, which merely regards the material constitution as the formal constitution considered from a sociological perspective. By drawing from Santi Romano's and Karl Llewellyn's institutional theories, I will dig out an alternative notion of the material that makes no reference to an underlying substantive reality. The constitution is an institution in the sense of a set of organisational practices as practices, not the sedimented outcome of these practices, such as behavioural standards, normative values or fundamental principles that are selected by the political power to get enshrined into constitutional provisions. Unlike substantive conceptions, this *processual understanding* of the material constitution that conceives the material as a set of ongoing activities accounts for how a collective can make room for change of its substantive contents while it preserves its identity as a collective.

15.1 THE SUBSTANTIALIST UNDERSTANDING OF THE MATERIAL CONSTITUTION

Although Italian jurist Costantino Mortati is certainly the scholar who tied his name to the idea of the material constitution as based on the hegemony of a ruling political block and the fundamental political aims it imposes,[3] Mortati himself stressed that Schmitt's institutional theory was the cradle of a compelling notion of materiality.[4] In this section, though, I will not concern myself as much with Schmitt's theorising in itself as with his second thoughts whereby he came to realise that the constitution is first and foremost material. For whether or not Schmitt made a genuine institutional turn between the early 1920s and the early 1930s,[5] it is beyond any doubt that he significantly revised the conception of the legal order that he had provided in *Political Theology* (1922), where the law was made to depend on the decision of the sovereign – and he did so precisely to bring to surface the material element of the constitutional order. In 1922, the normality of everyday life – where legal norms and judicial measures effectively do their job of governing conduct – was entirely contingent on the inception of the legal order on the part of a sovereign decider. Normality is a by-product that can get a foothold only once the sovereign has established the conditions for stability. In Schmitt's graphic formula: 'The rule proves nothing; the exception proves everything'[6] – meaning that if one wants to understand what the law is, one should turn one's eye from the everyday working of legal rules and focus on

[3] See M. Goldoni and M. Wilkinson, 'The Material Constitution' (2018) 81 *Modern Law Review* 569; Chapter 5, by Lucia Rubinelli.

[4] See C. Mortati, 'Brevi note sul rapporto fra costituzione e politica nel pensiero di Carl Schmitt', in *La teoria del potere costituente* (Quodlibet, 2020), 131–52.

[5] Andrea Salvatore and I put emphasis on Schmitt's revision of preceding themes that effected a break with his theory of the early 1920s and shed new light on his interests in the 1910s (see M. Croce and A. Salvatore, *The Legal Theory of Carl Schmitt* (Routledge, 2013)). Other interpreters adopt a 'continuist' view such that he was always interested in the issue of institutions and made his approach more and more conservative as he espoused the Nazi ideology (see J. Meierhenrich, 'Fearing the Disorder of Things: The Development of Carl Schmitt's Institutional Theory, 1919–1942', in J. Meierhenrich and O. Simons (eds.) *The Oxford Handbook of Carl Schmitt* (Oxford University Press, 2016)). Though I do not think this continuist conception is entirely mistaken, Salvatore and I provide a critique of it in M. Croce and A. Salvatore, *Carl Schmitt's Institutional Theory: The Political Power of Normality* (Cambridge University Press, 2022).

[6] C. Schmitt, *Political Theology: Four Chapters on the Concept of Sovereignty*, G. Schwab, trans. (University of Chicago Press, 2005), 15.

the original conditions in which the legal order was established. In this light, Schmitt is significant for my purpose in this chapter insofar as he came to realise that the constitution is primarily material and that he had mistakenly neglected its relation to social life.

To cut a long story short, *Political Theology* made the claim that for one to know what the legal order is, one must know who is able to suspend it.[7] The gist of Schmitt's view at this stage was that an effective legal order always depends on there being a sovereign who determines the conditions under which the order is in force or not. Therefore, the ordinary, daily working of legal rules and procedures fails to tell one what the valid legal order is. One should then turn one's attention to the person whose decision can suspend the law and re-establish it as the appropriate circumstances arise – only this type of inquiry reveals what the valid legal order is. In this frame, legal normality is demoted to a negligible aspect in the life of the law. However, toward the end of the 1920s, Schmitt changed his mind about what is foundational to there being a law. He eliminated any reference to a sovereign decider who establishes legal normality through a decision as he realised that normality is nothing anybody can produce out of nothingness. In other words, Schmitt brought himself to acknowledge the constitutive role of the social practices within which normative standards are produced *before* the law makes them binding. The inner normativity of these standards is not contingent on there being a legal order, but the other way around.

This change of mind looks particularly conspicuous in his conception of the *institutional guarantees*. In *Constitutional Theory* (1928), Schmitt had already revised his understanding of the sovereign decision as the keystone of the legal order and came to advocate a plebiscitary, identity-based idea of the constitutional order pivoted on the people's power to generate a positive constitution. In that context, he insisted on the constitution being that which gives form to and protects an already existing substance, a concrete form of life. He thereby began to lay emphasis on institutions as socio-historically produced forms that make up the social and attached some importance to so-called institutional guarantees as constitutional provisions granting 'particular institutions special protection' so as to prevent their elimination 'by way of simple legislation'.[8] However, in *Constitutional Theory* institutional guarantees are still part of the more comprehensive set of constitutional guarantees. Soon after 1928, Schmitt tried to put more flesh on the bones of this material 'substance' and broadened the notion of institutional guarantees. With respect to basic rights (such as freedom of person, privacy of the home, freedom of speech, secrecy of mail and telephone, freedom of association, and the right to property), institutional guarantees have a higher legal status because they can only be changed with a two-thirds majority rather than a simple majority. Schmitt then concluded that basic rights should be subsumed under institutional guarantees.

In the essay *Freiheitsrechte und institutionelle Garantien der Reichsverfassung* (The Rights of Liberty and Institutional Guarantees of the Reich Constitution) (1931), he made this case by distinguishing more clearly between *individual rights*, which he called 'rights of freedom' (*Freiheitsrechte*), and the *guarantees* (*Sicherungen*). The latter have legal priority over individual rights, as they represent more comprehensive and reliable guarantees for the freedom of individuals.[9] He then introduced a further distinction between institutional guarantees

[7] This is the crux of the 'jurisprudential reading' of *Political Theology* that Andrea Salvatore and I put forward in Croce and Salvatore, *Carl Schmitt's Institutional Theory*.

[8] C. Schmitt, *Constitutional Theory*, J. Seitzer, trans. (Duke University Press, 2008), 209.

[9] We analysed Schmitt's revision of the notion of institutional guarantees in Croce and Salvatore, *Legal Theory of Carl Schmitt*, 26–29. See also B. Schupmann, *Carl Schmitt's Constitutional and State Theory: A Critical Analysis* (Oxford University Press, 2017), 185–89.

(*institutionelle Garantien*), which are guarantees of public law nature, and guarantees of institutions (*Institutsgarantien*), which are of a private law nature. Institutional guarantees are prior to the guarantees of institutions in that every institution presupposes organisational forms of a public nature. Institutional guarantees belong to public law and are understood as constitutional guarantees of any institution with public relevance, whereas institutional guarantees are private in nature and are defined as constitutional guarantees of legal institutions, understood as a set of sedimented norms and legal relations. With respect to the latter, therefore, institutional guarantees apply to pre-existing institutions, already up and running and organised in traditional forms of their own. The constitution is required to protect these forms against the legislative power that could put them in jeopardy via ordinary statutory law.

Doubtless, this makes a substantive understanding of the constitution in a strong sense, for the legal order recognises the internal life of (some) institutions and subsumes under its laws the kinds of relations that are constructed therein. Basic rights turn out to be conditional upon, or even to derive from, individuals' being members of institutions. While rights are entrenched into institutional guarantees, protected institutions provide the formal constitution with a substance. On this account, the constitution does not bring anything about; it recognises, absorbs and makes binding the normative substance that institutions furnish. This explains why, in 1933, in the new preface to the second edition of *Political Theology*, Schmitt highlighted the link between the rejection of his previous decisionism and his theory of institutional guarantees: 'I now distinguish not two but *three* types of legal thinking; in addition to the normativist and the decisionist types there is the institutional one. I have come to this conclusion as a result of discussions of my notion of 'institutional guarantees' in German jurisprudence.'[10] In 1934, in *On the Three Types of Juristic Thought*, he offered a full-fledged picture of this material understanding of law as he developed his *konkrete Ordnungs- und Gestaltungsdenken* (concrete order and formation thinking).[11] The legal order incorporates a concrete order, namely, sedimented institutional practices that are the pillar of the German historical tradition and, by doing so, the law gives a unitary, homogeneous form (*Gestaltung*) to the social. Within historical institutions (such as marriage, the Church, the army, the bureaucracy), models of conduct and prototypical figures unfold through the centuries, so much so that they come to make the basic substance of the community that it behoves the constitution to protect and nurture as party to a homogeneous tradition.

While it is interesting to understand how Schmitt revised his previous position and how his revisions did remedy a few shortcomings of his view in the 1920s, it is not altogether clear how this material substance comes to life. At face value, there are two interpretative options. First, some social institutions are selected based on the arbitrary will of the prevailing political power that takes it upon itself to determine what counts as an acceptable social institution and what, on the contrary, jeopardises the social fabric. On this first option, the selection is a matter of power based on *de facto* prevailing social forces. This does not look Schmittian, for he was averse to all reductionist theories that claimed legal normativity to be ultimately based on bare power. The alternative option is that the political power does the job of selecting, but the latter is based on the political ruler's (presumed) ability to read and interpret the whole history of the German society. On this second option, the selection depends on the (presumed) intrinsic value of the selected institutions as they are taken to be (by the ruling power) that which makes the German society what it is. This looks more Schmittian. For it is a conservative, traditionalist

[10] Schmitt, *Political Theology*, 2.

[11] C. Schmitt, *On the Three Types of Juristic Thought*, J. W. Bendersky, trans. (Praeger, 2004).

understanding of power as the protector of deep-seated practices that are valuable because time-tested. However, this second interpretative line leaves a question unanswered: Based on what can one be sure that the prevailing political power is the best interpreter of that historical tradition?

Regrettably, Schmitt never addressed this problem. In 1933–34 – quite an unfortunate historical juncture – he clearly presumed the Leader to be the genuine interpreter of the German tradition who could provide his loyal subordinates with a wise design to be realised in all the various sites of the social. He put little effort into offering a robust theory of practices, identifying the source of their normative value, discussing the intrinsic normativity of history and justifying the special role of the Leader. He held two highly resilient ideological commitments that he never justified. First, in order that a community may not be riven by conflict, it is to be as homogeneous as possible – not only as to habits and traditions, but also in ethical and ethnic terms. Second, social change is intrinsically dangerous, as the models and standards that ensure the survival of the social are century-old institutions such as marriage, the family, the army – exactly in the form Luther or Hegel had under their eyes. Such two commitments certainly warrant some sort of justification. And yet the lack of justification is not the only flaw of Schmitt's concrete-order thinking. For his theory also begs the question: Was it the material constitution that called for the formal constitutional setting Schmitt advocated? Or was it the formal constitutional setting Schmitt thought desirable that called for the specific theory of the social he offered? On this point, he was far from clear. He never cared to discuss either the nature of institutions in general or the specific contribution of the few institutions he listed. Nor did he expand on the relation between social normativity and legal normativity and especially the conditions under which legal normativity is legitimised to cut out those institutions that do not fit the project drawn up by the Leader.

What looks much clearer, on the contrary, is that, for Schmitt, the material substance is unable to give itself a form. Though institutions provide the law with material contents, a jurisprudential activity is needed to shape these contents and turn them into manageable constitutional material. This is why from the 1930s onward Schmitt insisted more and more on the unique contribution of the jurists.[12] Jurisprudence is not a mere method to make sense of the unity of the legal order and its validity; let alone a mere sociological inquiry into law's social working. Much more than this, as Mortati nicely put it, jurists are tasked with identifying and correctly interpreting 'the "normative facts" that must be investigated as possessing the characteristic of regularity' in the light of which one can 'presume that they are fit to play the function of criteria for the assessment of social relationships'.[13] In other words, both Schmitt and Mortati believed legal science is the knowledge that identifies the social standards that are fit to become legal standards. Contrary to purely descriptive jurisprudential paradigms, legal science is required to look beyond the legal system to investigate social reality and to identify those pre-existing social standards that need legal recognition. Unlike the sociology of law, legal science is claimed to be normative because it plays a primary role in converting the unverbalised substance of the concrete order into valid legal standards. Mortati's conclusion is telling: 'From this point

[12] Schmitt somewhat revived his 1910s interest in the legal practice. See L. Vinx and S. G. Zeitlin, 'Introduction: Carl Schmitt and the Problem of the Realization of Law', in L. Vinx and S. G. Zeitlin (eds.), *Carl Schmitt's Early Legal-Theoretical Writings* (Cambridge University Press, 2021), 1–36. However, while in the 1910s he primarily focused on judicial activity, from the 1930s on he conceived jurisprudence as a site of knowledge which included, but was not confined to, the activity of the judges.

[13] C. Mortati, *Istituzioni di diritto pubblico* (CEDAM, 1967), vol. I, 9.

of view, the two terms of the factual "normality" and of "normativity" come to overlap'.[14] As the concrete order is made speakable through the jurists' activity, normality is turned into normativity. Needless to say, it is not the spontaneous normality that social life produces freely; rather, it is the normality that makes it through a process of selection, whereas alternative normalities are left out or even eradicated.

15.2 THE PROCESSUAL UNDERSTANDING OF THE MATERIAL CONSTITUTION

Evidently, Schmitt's is a fairly thick conception of the material and the role of jurisprudence – one that should be grounded on a much more robust theory of social normativity and its relation to law. It then comes as no surprise that scholars who tried to cut deeper into the relation between social and legal normativity steered clear of Schmitt's oversimplifications.[15] In this section, I would like to briefly concentrate on Romano's and Llewellyn's models as they emphasise the material side of the constitution but avoid the substantialist pitfall. Though their theories are different under many respects, Romano and Llewellyn share an idea of the material as an *ongoing activity*, an *organisational process*. To put it otherwise, the material is processual, in the sense of a work that gets carried on for a group to remain a group. Both authors pointed out that constitutions – here understood as the basic law of a collective – do not only appertain to state-based political communities but are present in all groups that persist through time. The constitution of groups is nothing other than their organisation, namely, the set of techniques and measures that are deployed to make sure that the group continues to exist as a group.[16]

Before I briefly summarise Romano's and Llewellyn's take on this issue, let me begin with an illustrative example from Llewellyn's 'The Constitution as an Institution' – one that, interestingly enough, is redolent with a patriarchal culture:

> Mr. Hubb goes out to work and provides for payment of the bills. When he rises, his breakfast has been attended to; and the bathroom has been left free for his shaving. He, and no other, reads the newspaper while he eats. Before he leaves for his train, he fixes the furnace; and he receives certain instructions as to the things to be brought back on his return. There is no need to go on. It is obvious that Mr Hubb's patterns of behavior are not those of Mrs. Hubb, nor those of the maid, nor those of little Lorna. But it is equally obvious that the patterns of all four intercog like the wheels of a clock, and make a *whole* go round which we choose to call 'a family,' and which is more than and different from the constituent parts. It is obvious, moreover, that Mr. Hubb's behavior lies in good part in patterns, expected and reckoned with by the others. And normatized. If he should fail to come home to dinner, or should forget the ordered purchases, or should gamble away his pay-check at the poker-game, Mrs. Hubb would not only be upset in her cooperation, but would *feel* aggrieved. Meanwhile, each other

[14] Ibid., 9.

[15] Here I have to leave aside Mortati's theory, which should be examined in some detail to determine if it is amenable to the same type of criticism, as I believe.

[16] The *locus classicus* of Romano's theory is S. Romano, *The Legal Order* (Routledge, 2017). Sketches of Llewellyn's less systematic theory of institution can be found in K. N. Llewellyn, 'Behind the Law of Divorce: I' (1932) 32 *Columbia Law Review* 1281; K. N. Llewellyn, 'The Constitution As an Institution' (1934) 34 *Columbia Law Review* 1; K. N. Llewellyn, 'The Normative, the Legal, and the Law-Jobs: The Problem of Juristic Method' (1949) 49 *The Yale Law Journal* 1355; K. N. Llewellyn, 'Law and the Social Sciences: Especially Sociology' (1949) 62 *Harvard Law Review* 1286.

> member of the family contributes her own quite diverse patterns in the interlocking whole that goes on *as* a whole.[17]

This example is relevant under many respects. First, it tells us that all groups, however small they are, possess a constitution – the latter being more or less complex according to the complexity, not necessarily the size, of the relevant group. In this sense, a constitution is the inner order of a group, of *any* group. Second, this constitution is not a set of written rules (that which Llewellyn called 'the Document'), but lies in an interwoven set of patterned, mostly unverbalised activities that are routinised and become constitutive of the group. Third, what counts for the group being a group, and remaining a group, is this nested set of doings, not the context-dependent values, norms, and principles they are working on. This is why I noted that the patriarchal residue that taints Llewellyn's portrayal of the Hubb family makes the example even more interesting. The description of the family as comprising a breadwinner and a housewife today is a far less dominant model than in the 1940s, though the institution of family can hardly be said to be extinct. At present there are families in the sense specified by Llewellyn, although the values, norms and principles underlying them are different than those underpinning familyhood in the 1940s. If we piece these three points together, we can say that the constitution (as an institution) is a set of organisational activities that makes a group go places. It is material because it is an organised process that needs performing, not because it produces context-bound values and models. Accordingly, what allows us to say that a family of the 1940s and a present-day family are both families – and not two different practices bearing the same label – is the organisational process that integrates the activities of family members – so much so that, say, a family not based on conjugality or coupledom today could well qualify as a family in the light of the organisational job it carries out.[18]

What distinguishes Romano's and Llewellyn's models from Schmitt's is the insistence on the notion of organisation as the core feature of the institution, and this makes a significant difference when it comes to understanding the legal phenomenon.[19] Their more accurate conceptualisation of social normativity vis-à-vis the legal phenomenon led Romano and Llewellyn to espouse a pluralist conception of the law and the constitution. For Schmitt, the gulf separating the social from the legal cannot be bridged but through the jurisprudential activity that selects the standards of some institutions and helps them make it to the official body of state law. No legal order is conceivable other than state legal order – for Schmitt, political modernity essentially depends on the state monopoly on law, to the extent that the state as a political form would collapse should it lose this monopoly.[20] Quite the reverse, Romano and Llewellyn believed that all organised groups have an inner legal ordering.[21] As the excerpt on the

[17] Llewellyn, 'Constitution As an Institution', 18.

[18] On the various reasons why nonconventional kinship configurations could/should be considered as families by family law, see F. Swennen, 'Un-Coupling Family Law: The Legal Recognition and Protection of Adult Unions Outside of Conjugal Coupledom' (2020) 28 *Feminist Legal Studies* 39, and N. Palazzo, *Legal Recognition of Non-Conjugal Families. New Frontiers in Family Law in the US, Canada and Europe* (Hart, 2021).

[19] Because of this, such terms as 'constitution', 'institution', 'order', and 'law' come to signify the same organisational process. I will then use them interchangeably when referring to Romano's and Llewellyn's theorising.

[20] This is the core argument advanced in C. Schmitt, *The Concept of the Political*, G. Schwab, trans. (University of Chicago Press, 2007) and C. Schmitt, 'State Ethics and the Pluralist State', in A. Jacobson and B. Schlink (eds.), *Weimar: A Jurisprudence of Crisis* (University of California Press, 2000), 300.

[21] Romano was categorical when he stated that institution is synonymous with legal order, while Llewellyn distinguished between 'the law' and the 'The Law' – but this difference is negligible for the present purposes.

Hubb family illustrates, the law comprised interlocked patterns of behaviour that assign roles and distribute tasks according to the role members play.

However, unverbalised patterned behaviour is not enough to make an ordering. In different ways, Romano and Llewellyn highlighted that the behavioural aspect is only part of the story – or else, a normative ordering would not be distinguishable from complex habits. Either of them assigned a key role to the jurisprudential activity, although they did not construe it, as Schmitt and Mortati did, as the passage from (formless) social normativity to (formed) legal normativity. Rather, in every stable group there is an oscillation between unspoken interlocked behavioural patterns and a reflective attitude that makes them speakable. Therefore, the inner law of all groups is a combination of behaviour and reflective knowledge about behaviour – though the reflective attitude can be more or less prominent depending on the characteristics of the group. But just as knowledge is required to there being a law, so is there in all groups a sub-unit who take upon themselves to develop knowledge about the activities of the group.

Romano openly took up this issue in his last book, *Frammenti di un dizionario giuridico* (Fragments of a legal dictionary).[22] Here he insisted that the spontaneous, unspoken organised behaviour – what he calls *ius involuntarium* (involuntary law) – that governs the inner life of institutions is just as much law as the law issued by state agencies. Therefore, the organised behavioural aspect, though unverbalised, possesses a legal value of its own. However, when a circumstance arises in which a group needs to specify what is legal from what is not, Romano thought a jurisprudential process is required. Here the role of the specialists comes to the surface and starts to seep out. For the jurist is one who 'must have an eye capable of dominating and scrutinising in the smallest detail an almost boundless horizon', one that covers 'the whole of social life, which is so varied and protean'. The jurist should not neglect any 'relation or phenomenon [. . .] since those that are relevant to the law are in reality fused and mixed with others that have no legal relevance'. The 'jurist's preliminary task is to isolate and separate the former from the latter, distinguishing them and dissolving their amalgam'.[23] Evidently, Romano thought that the law – the inner law of institutions – can be spontaneous and unspoken, and yet a jurisprudential inquiry is needed to make it speakable when it is necessary, and especially when one needs to know what in an institution is legal and what is lawful or illegal.

However, Romano was not entirely clear on who the jurists are. For his theory to be self-consistent, it should be framed in such a way that patterns of behaviour plus reflective attitude are present in every institution, and that all institutions have their 'jurists', that is, specialists who do the job of selecting what is relevant to the inner law. Romano unfortunately never got to clarify the role of legal knowledge or legal specialists within nonstate institutions. On this point, Llewellyn was clearer. Famously, he broke the legal process down into a set of 'law-jobs'[24] that are to be carried out in all groups and also insisted that almost all groups comprise smaller groups and are contained into broader groups. He wrote that it should be made

[22] S. Romano, *Frammenti di un dizionario giuridico* (Quodlibet, 2019).

[23] Ibid., 145.

[24] Llewellyn listed five main law-jobs: (1) Adjustment of the trouble case; (2) Preventive channelling of conduct and expectations; (3) Allocation of authority and procedures for its exercise; (4) Provision of direction and incentive within the group; (5) The juristic method. The most extensive discussion of each of these law-jobs is to be found in Llewellyn, 'The Normative, the Legal, and the Law-jobs'. For a most instructive analysis of the law-jobs theory, see W. Twining, 'The Idea of Juristic Method: A Tribute to Karl Llewellyn' (1993) 48 *University of Miami Law Review* 119.

> unmistakeable that the law-jobs hold, as basic functions, for *every* human group, from a group of two persons on up. They are implicit in the concept of 'groupness'. In any community or society which may be taken as a larger unit, the law-jobs therefore appear at least doubly: once for the big unit, and again for every sub-unit within the big one; and again, of course, for every sub-sub-unit within a sub-unit, 'etc. ad inf.' This requires to be made explicit, because the 'Law'-concept of modern thought goes only to that great unit called the State or to such other *political* whole as may come in question.

Consistently with this vision of the legal phenomenon, Llewellyn claimed that legal specialists are not only the official personnel of the modern state, in that all groups at some point specialise to the extent that specialists are needed. He explained that knowledge about behaviour is produced in the management of 'trouble-cases' (dispute, grievance, offense), that is, conflict-laden situations that must be settled lest the group be split into hostile factions. Legal knowledge is that type of knowledge that not only handles these problematic cases, but also provides standards for future behaviour as it performs this basic task. For, as the case is settled, a normative generalisation is to be extracted from this settlement. This is a job that needs expertise and techniques and that grants authority to those who supervise it. Here the legal and the political merge, in that those who solve conflicts and oversee the production of normative generalisations attach their authority to their unique capacity to pull the group together, especially in the most difficult conditions:

> Political authority must be concerned with the interest of the whole, and so of peace, and so of guiding adjustment, even by the aggrieved, into channels which reduce the chance of counter-grievance. Indeed, if the specialization of personnel into this law-job of the trouble-case take any of the alternative roads – that over the wise old man, the peace-maker, or over the judge, or over the priest, or over the Ifugao combination of advocate and mediator, or over the sorcerer – then such personnel must in turn be regarded as carrying latent germs of ultimate political power.

It is not for this chapter to go into the details of this intriguing hypothesis. What counts here is the idea that all groups develop internal, legally binding patterns of behaviour, go through potentially dangerous crises, have these crises managed by specialists and in so doing undergo processes of internal specialisation. This is an utterly processual view of the material constitution, where the material is couched as the *concrete process of specialisation carried out by concrete people*. Such concreteness is evidently miles away from the concreteness of Schmitt's concrete order. For the material side does not concern the actual norms, expectations, values, and principles that the process yields. Rather, material is the process itself – so much so that norms, expectations, values, and principles can change over time by means of that very process.

15.3 CONCLUDING REMARKS

This chapter aimed to lay out a conception of the constitution that places emphasis on the material aspect but does not identify it with specific norms, values or principles. With substantialist views, the processual paradigm shares the rejection of normativism as the latter claims that the material viewpoint simply complements the purely legal perspective on the proper workings of a constitution. The analysis of the legal order should dispense with the separation of sociology and jurisprudence in that the latter is normative is a strong sense: jurisprudence plays a vital role in the process that turns some social standards into legal standards. Yet, substantialist and processual views part ways when it comes to who plays this role and in what circumstances. Conceiving the material as a process, and not as a substance, means conceiving the law as a set of organisational activities that take place in every group.[25] Importantly, this activity is exactly what allows a group to make more or less extensive revisions to norms, values or principles without ceasing to be that group. Accordingly, the material constitution is what enables a group to oversee change and to preserve its identity as its substantive characteristics morph. As Romano put it:

> When the law is assigned the function of stabilizing, normalizing, fixing certain aspects and movements in social life – a function that could be called conservative – this must be understood in a sense that excludes any reference to conservative tendencies in the sense in which the term characterizes policy frameworks that are so qualified. A legal order, unless it is poorly constructed, on the one hand plays that function; yet, on the other hand, it can always renovate itself and even make room for radical and extensive changes to its structure and workings. If this were not the case, it would not be vital.[26]

In conclusion, if the main virtue of a materialist approach is that it 'captures the internal relation between constitutional order and society without, however, eliding its conflictual and evolving nature',[27] one should certainly privilege a processual view as it does not sacrifice either conflicts or change for the preservation of substantive contents. The processual view is an invitation to draw attention to how substantive contents are adapted, rethought and amended in many sites of social life as social agents struggle to keep their many practices alive and how state law could/should accommodate change as it is produced in those sites.

[25] This view can certainly be charged with overstretching the label 'law' and missing out on a few specific aspects of nonlegal phenomena that are foisted upon a character that does not belong to them and thus are misconstrued. On this criticism, see S. Roberts, 'After Government? On Representing Law without the State' (2005) 68 *The Modern Law Review* 1. Though I cannot tackle this criticism here, my take is that the risk of misinterpreting a normative practice is not necessarily entailed by one's sticking to a label, provided that one is fully aware of the performative power of using labels.

[26] Romano, *Frammenti di un dizionario giuridico*, 113–14.

[27] Goldoni and Wilkinson, 'Material Constitution', 597.

16

The Material Constitution and the Rule of Recognition

Francesco Bilancia and Stefano Civitarese Matteucci

16.1 INTRODUCTION: THE MATERIAL CONSTITUTION AS THE SUPREME SOURCE OF THE LEGAL SYSTEM

The idea of the material constitution is generally traced to an institutionalist approach to law. By institutionalist approach to law, we mean different theories – whose prominent representatives are thinkers such as Maurice Hauriou, Santi Romano and Carl Schmitt – that purport that legal orders are best explained as organisations rather than normative systems.[1] For a strand of institutionalism, the distinctive feature of a legal system is the pre-existence within a social group of an organisation capable of shaping and maintaining order.[2] Indeed, the material constitution has recently been depicted as a theory about the ordering forces (political, economic, geopolitical) that underpin the constitution.[3] It aims to take to the surface 'the deeper societal context in which formal constitutional development is embedded'.[4] Along this line, the material constitution is regarded as an analytical device, the *explanans* of an explanatory relation, whose *explanandum* is the constitutional order. The 'relation between the organisation of the social order and the form of the constitution' is what the material constitution explains.[5]

We do not engage here with this more sophisticated use of the ideas at the root of the notion. We stick with the account that the constitution in the material sense, rather than being an analytical construct, is the 'original constitution' that is the 'supreme source of the legal system [. . .]. An independent source, which thereby does not exhaust itself into the posited legal sources and does not exclusively operate through them, but it also operates immediately and directly'.[6] This is what Costantino Mortati claimed about eight decades ago in possibly the most ambitious study of the material constitution. This 'original' constitution was made of two elements: a

[1] For a broader and more precise account, see A. Pintore, *'Institutionalism in Law'*, *Routledge Encyclopedia of Philosophy* (Taylor & Francis, 1998). Available at: www.rep.routledge.com/articles/thematic/institutionalism-in-law/v-1, last accessed 29 July 2022.

[2] In C. Schmitt, *Constitutional Theory [1928]* (Duke University Press, 2008), 75, one finds a statement about legal constitutional scholarship that is archetypical of institutionalism: 'considered juristically, what exists as political power has value because it exists'.

[3] Other meanings of the expression can be found in the literature. For example, for J. Colón-Ríos, *Constituent Power and the Law* (Oxford University Press, 2020), 186, the material constitution is 'generally understood as including the norms that establish the basic structure of the state and that regulate the legal relations between state and citizens'.

[4] M. Goldoni and M. Wilkinson, 'The Material Constitution' (2018) 81 *Modern Law Review* 567, 580.

[5] M. Goldoni, 'The Material Constitution', in R. Bellamy and J. King (eds.), *The Cambridge Handbook of Constitutional Theory* (Cambridge University Press, forthcoming).

[6] C. Mortati, *La Costituzione in senso materiale* (Giuffré, 1940), 121 (our translation).

fundamental goal and a political party to achieve it.[7] For Mortati, the Constitution's function is precisely to trace every legal source to one principle, in a way that – as Mortati writes – they appear as springing from one thought.[8] This 'unity' of the legal order was only possible by recognising the constitutional predominance of the (fascist) party as the bearer of the fundamental political goal of the state. The goal had to be as comprehensive as to include in unity the various interests which the state contemplates. In Mortati's view, this 'material' constitution was not the sociological basis of the formal constitution; it was as legal as the latter, for it constituted the determinant that transmitted legal energy to any other act by which the system worked. From this standpoint, the approach shares with many others over the period between the two wars the claim – *contra* Kelsen – legal status can be assigned to facts other than norms. The curious thing is that the polemic against Kelsen, carried out from a 'realistic' point of view,[9] ends up contending that efficacy can be the ultimate criterion of justification of a legal/normative order.

On the contrary, Mortati theorised that a 'social organisation' and the existing power relationship are legal. Unfortunately, it remained obscure how this could be so. Mortati did not separate between the Constitution either in the material or formal sense and the legal system. His endeavour – to look for the 'first constitution' – seems to be directed indistinctly toward both such notions.

The problem of not clarifying whether one is speaking of the constitution, the legal order, or the constitution as a proxy for the legal order often affects theoretical constitutional law scholarship. The 'constitution' is a political and social construct, primarily. It is barely possible to frame a discourse on such a concept and related terms without using political science's epistemology and vocabulary. In other words, it is hopeless to think that one can grasp the political arrangement (the constitution) of the state from a legal perspective only. Consequently, by looking at the (material) constitution from the viewpoint of a legal system, we attain a partial knowledge of it. It is fitting to note that, by this, we are not in any way suggesting that a jurist or a legal scholar should not use in their work – that inevitably involves a normative stance – any political, economic, moral perspective as they deem fit. The only constraint is that they do not overcome the limits constituted by the concept of law and the rule of recognition shared by the relevant group (see Section 16.3). Otherwise, they risk being seen as playing a game other than law.

Be that as it may, within the exemplary of Mortati's perspective, the material constitution links the political forces that make up a group into a state/legal order with a set of 'purposive norms, which can take, among others, the form of principles, aims or values'.[10]

In this chapter, we take on two questions: first, whether and to what extent such a perspective is compatible with a normative, legal positivistic approach; second and foremost, whether a concept of the rule of recognition (RoR) of a legal system can help cast light on the 'ordering forces' of a Constitution. We do not mainly deal with how the material constitution can operate or be operated. However, there are at least two circumstances in which the material constitution may come to the fore: when there is disagreement regarding what the written constitution prescribes and when the legislator wants to amend the written constitution in a way that conflicts with the material constitution. We shall say something about that in Section 16.5. In presenting our argument, we have in mind jurisdictions with a codified constitution, in which it is easier to

7 C. Pinelli, 'Costituzione formale-costituzione materiale' (Treccani online entry, 2010). Available at: www.treccani.it/enciclopedia/costituzione-formale-costituzione-materiale_%28Dizionario-di-Storia%29/, last accessed 29 July 2022.

8 Mortati, *La Costituzione in senso materiale*, 130.

9 Time and time again, Mortati uses terms such as 'real' constitution, 'real' sources.

10 Goldoni and Wilkinson, 'Material Constitution', 580.

conceptualise the relationship between the material and the formal (codified) constitution.[11] We also confine our argument to societies adopting a form of representative democracy.

16.2 LAW AND THE RULE OF RECOGNITION

Given that the rule of recognition is often depicted as a convention,[12] it is fitting to clarify at the outset that the material constitution is not the same as the constitutional conventions. They are either a practice operating within the gaps of written constitutions or the constitution itself for the political notion that part of the British scholarship uses for the British constitution.

Another distinction that cuts across the idea of the material constitution is between the traditional and modern concepts of the constitution. While the latter deals with the office of government and separates it from society, the former indicates the 'real' constitution of the state based on manners, culture and customs of people.[13] This idea of a 'real' constitution reflecting changes in the political culture seems to chime with the notion of the material constitution sketched in Section 16.1. There are two fundamental differences. In our stipulation, the material constitution is a 'reality' within the legal domain. It is not 'real' in the sense of factual. As such, it does not necessarily play out against the written constitution. On the contrary, it usually upholds the latter, even against future change.

A sketch as comprehensive as possible of a positivist approach to law or at least one on which many legal positivists could agree seems equally apposite.[14] We mean that law is a collective practice of social control[15] of the dominant political power through normative and coercive mechanisms.[16] According to the so-called social thesis or source thesis, law is a social phenomenon and, therefore, the discussion about the nature of law is essentially a question of complex social facts.[17] Such social facts are social rules determining what law is and how the law is identified, created and modified. The relevant social fact, then, is what ultimately explains the existence of a legal system and constitutes it as a social artefact. This implies a more fundamental – metaphysical – thesis, that a set of conditions for a norm to count as law in any conceivable legal order must be identified. As Hart called it in *The Concept of Law*, such conditions are

[11] We assume that what we shall say is valid in British-like situations as well. However, we eschew from engaging with the issue. Another contentious field about the existence of a (material) constitution is the European Union. On the latter, see F. Bilancia and S. Civitarese Matteucci, 'The Material Constitution Arrangement of the European Union', in M. Belov (ed.), *Peace, Discontent and Constitutional Law: Challenges to Constitutional Order and Democracy* (Routledge, 2021), 53–73.

[12] An exponent of such a thesis seems to be N. MacCormick, 'Institutional Morality and the Constitution', in N. MacCormick and O. Weinberger (eds.), *An Institutional Theory of Law: New Approaches to Legal Positivism* (Springer, 1986), 184. He claims that 'a constitutional order depends upon custom: that is, on the custom of referring all legal issues ultimately to being governed by and under the provisions set out in the constitutional instrument'. Carlo Esposito, one of the most prominent Italian constitutional scholars of the last century, had spoken of a custom of recognition of the sources of law, shared by political parties and officials, since 1962, building on his previous theory on the validity of the law. See C. Esposito, *La validità delle leggi* (CEDAM, 1934), 238; C. Esposito, 'La consuetudine costituzionale' [1962], in C. Esposito, *Diritto costituzionale vivente: Capo dello Stato e altri saggi* (Giuffrè, 1992), 302, 306; F. Bilancia, *La crisi dell'ordinamento giuridico dello Stato rappresentativo* (CEDAM, 2000), 311.

[13] M. Loughlin, *The British Constitution: A Very Short Introduction* (Oxford University Press, 2013), 20.

[14] See S. Civitarese Matteucci, 'Is Legal Positivism as Worthless as Many Italian Scholars of Public Law Depict It?' (2010) 23 *Ratio Juris* 505.

[15] H. Kelsen, *Pure Theory of Law* (University of California Press, 1967), 15.

[16] Even though the conceptual and/or practical necessity of coercion has often been questioned in the post-Hartian discussion in the Anglo-American area, we believe that it is indeed as much a fundamental part of Hart's account of law as of Kelsen's.

[17] E. Bulygin, 'Objectivity of Law in View of Legal Positivism' (2004) *Analisi e diritto* 219.

ultimately spelt out in a rule of recognition (RoR).[18] For Hart, law is a system of primary and secondary rules. While primary rules are norms of conduct, secondary rules are meta-norms that confer powers of change and adjudication. The RoR is the most crucial type of secondary rule, by which all the others can be recognised as belonging to the same legal order.

To undertake that function assigned to such a social practice, another feature of a positivist concept of law is the claim for legitimate practical authority as part of the nature of law.[19] This means that any normative order that aspires to be legal should be able to possess authority. This is, in turn, path-dependent on the social efficacy of the law. The acceptance of its rules as guidance for behaviour is a feature we will discuss further in Section 16.3.

16.3 THE RULE OF RECOGNITION AND THE (MATERIAL) CONSTITUTION

The Kelsenian version of the material constitution seems to be an obvious candidate for one legal positivist notion. Moreover, that Kelsen acknowledges the notion of a material constitution might be all we need to claim that legal positivism is compatible with the material constitution. In his Pure Theory, Kelsen explains that

> The Constitution represents the highest level of positive law. 'Constitution' is understood here in its material sense; that is, we understand by Constitution the positive norm or norms which regulate the creation of general legal norms. The Constitution may be created by custom or by specific act performed by one or several individuals, that is, by a legislative act. In the latter case, it is always formulated in a document and hence called a 'written' constitution, in contradistinction to the 'unwritten' Constitution brought about by custom. The material constitution may consist partly of norms of written and partly of unwritten law. The unwritten norms of the Constitution may be codified; and if this codification is the work of a law creating organ and therefore acquires binding force, it becomes a written constitution.[20]

As has been noted, what makes the material constitution material, in this account, is its function, not any content.[21] A different but related question is whether the material constitution must have procedural content only. Kelsen is particularly interested in the mechanism through which the rules governing legislation receive a specific formal constitutional form and, besides, a device for a constitutional amendment is entrenched. In this way, and very significantly, the formal constitution underpins and stabilises the material constitution, not the reverse. It has been observed that by adopting Kelsen's perspective, one cannot claim that the material constitution may also have substantive 'political' content. Since 'he rejects any account of the political or social relations behind these norms or the state as a politico-juristic or sociological entity',[22] the underlying material order of the constitution remains hidden from sight. We do not need to take up this specific point except for noting that there are no logical hurdles that the 'norms which regulate the creation of general legal norms' include substantive rules. It is so for any other piece of law created through the combined operating of the static and dynamic principles.[23]

[18] H. L. A. Hart, *The Concept of Law*, 3rd ed. (Oxford University Press, 1994), chapters 4 and 5.
[19] K. H. Himma, 'The Instantiation Thesis and Raz's Critique of Inclusive Positivism' (2001) 20 *Law and Philosophy* 61.
[20] Kelsen, *Pure Theory of Law*, 222.
[21] L. Vinx, *Hans Kelsen's Pure Theory of Law* (Oxford University Press, 2007), 158.
[22] Goldoni and Wilkinson, 'Material Constitution', 569–70.
[23] Kelsen, *Pure Theory of Law*, 195.

A better explanation of this issue is offered by the notion of the RoR, based on social practice. As we mentioned, for Hart, the RoR must be efficacious, namely sustained by the social practice of law, at least as shared by officials. There is overwhelming literature on the flaws and problems that Hart's notion of the RoR would incur, mainly from the same positivist camp.[24] While, in our view, the kernel of the theory remains unchallenged, we think it apposite for this chapter's sake to discuss a few of them.

The marrow of the social thesis is that the concept of law depends on something external to it. Both Kelsen and legal institutionalism erred in building it on an abstract principle of reason or institutional forces internal to law . The inestimable contribution of Hart's theory is that it reveals that the concept of law is fundamentally rooted in common sense and ordinary language. Building on that insight, Mario Jori has explained that both the *identification* of law (in general) and the *individuation* of the law in space-time depend on (imprecise) intuitions shared between all the participants in the social practice we call law.[25] Such intuitions regard the essential features that the practice must possess and that people must recognise. They amount to those situations in which organised coercion and power management through norms are at stake. Such an awareness (that Harts notoriously calls 'acceptance') is triggered by clues that 'mark' specific facts as the law. They are hints – intermeshed with past experiences, traditions, all embedded in ordinary language – that guide us with reasonable (not incontrovertible) certainty to believe that we are asked to act in a certain way or that a person is not capable of producing a legal act.[26] For example, we understand that a self-proclaimed traffic cop is not an authentic (or valid) traffic cop because she is not wearing the relevant uniform.

The problem with Hart is that he does not clearly and sufficiently separate between the operations regarding, respectively, the individuation and *determination* of the law.[27] Officials undertake the more sophisticated (technical) operation of determining what the law is through the rule of recognition, which allows them to build the normative chains to assess the validity of a legal rule. Nonetheless, the first stage common sense individuation of the law is shared by laypeople and officials.[28] It is precisely this first step that gives conceptual and pragmatic foundation to a legal order not dependent on such ephemeral entities as forces, generic effectiveness, an ideal presupposed *grundnorm*.

Moreover, this partial reformulation of Hart's theory helps overcome one of the most puzzling characters of the recognition by officials of the 'master rule': its circularity.

[24] See, for example, J. Coleman (ed.), *Hart's Postscript: Essays on the Postscript to 'The Concept of Law'* (Oxford University Press, 2001).

[25] M. Jori, *Il diritto inesistente* (ETS, 2010), 21–40.

[26] As Jori (ibid., 34, 40) conveniently emphasises, fragmentary and episodic knowledge is at the same time sufficient and necessary. Without this indeterminacy, people could not understand and make normative judgements in their everyday life. Indeterminacy is not a flaw, but a crucial feature of ordinary language to manage complex social interactions. This mechanism works on normal situations, that is when there is only one possible candidate as the legal system (ibid., 62). When there is uncertainty on this point, for example after a state coup, a legal crisis looms.

[27] Nonetheless, there are passages in which he mentions 'private persons' together with 'courts' and 'officials' as the users of the 'ultimate rule of recognition': Hart, *Concept of Law*, 107.

[28] Jori, *Il diritto inesistente*, 63–64. A. Marmor, 'Legal Conventionalism', in J. Coleman (ed.), *Hart's Postscript: Essays on the Postscript to 'The Concept of Law'* (Oxford University Press, 2001), 209–10, makes a similar point by referring to a kind of division of labour between a 'core of practitioners', who share the technical meaning of the rule of recognition (the rules constitutive of the practice) and 'further groups of people in the outer circles'.

> After all, the officials are only 'officials' because there is a rule of recognition that validates the rules declaring them to be officials; and the rule of recognition, in turn, is only the rule of recognition because they (the officials) treat it as such. So, they are only 'officials' from their point of view, not from the point of view of the citizens who do not accept the officials' rule of recognition.[29]

However, both laypeople and clerics accept the same law.

Following Hart,[30] we can colour such an approach as conventionalist in the minimalistic meaning of a practice shared by persons thanks to certain characters of social reality and the language that expresses it.[31] It refers to the internal aspect of the acceptance of law, consisting of the group members converging on a critical reflective attitude that constitutes the social rule as normative in that deviations from that rule are appropriately criticised.[32]

We can now come back to the problem regarding the content of the material constitution left behind by Kelsen's idea of positive norms regulating the creation of general legal norms. For Hart, in a modern legal system characterised by a variety of sources of law, the RoR is

[29] L. Alexander and F. Schauer, 'Rules of Recognition, Constitutional Controversies, and the Dizzying Dependence of Law on Acceptance', in M. Adler and K. E. Himma (eds.), *The Rule of Recognition and the U.S. Constitution* (Oxford University Press, 2009), 178.

[30] Hart, *Concept of Law*, 256.

[31] Spurred by Dworkin's critique, Hart described in the Postscript the RoR as a conventional rule, meaning that 'the general conformity of a group ... is part of the reasons which its individual members have for acceptance'. Hart, *Concept of Law*, 255. From this proposition, an entire body of literature conceiving the RoR as a conventional rule flourished. John Gardner has criticised this scholarship as excessively technical and focusing on 'only those rules that serve coordinating social functions'. J. Gardner, 'Some Types of Law', in D. E. Edlin (ed.), *Common Law Theory* (Cambridge University Press, 2007), 23. David Lewis's *Convention: A Philosophical Study* (Basil Blackwell, 1969) spun out the debate on social conventions. It argued, contra Quine, that conventions are not agreements, as claimed by Dworkin, but rules that emerge as practical solutions to coordination problems. Such rules have two fundamental connected features. They are arbitrary and generally followed within a group.

Arbitrariness refers to the availability of more than one course of action. The choice to follow the conventional rule depends precisely on that other people follow it as well. Such an account of social rules does not fit in with Hart's RoR, however. On the one hand, to define it as arbitrary is implausible unless one qualifies this arbitrariness as not implying indifference to the rule's rationale. On the other hand, reducing the rationale of a RoR to solving coordination problems is improper. Although many primary legal rules do solve coordination problems (such as righthand drive), secondary rules which deal with power arrangement have a broader and more complex scope. Indeed, their primary function is to create the same social practice to which they refer. They belong to another class of conventions, called constitutive conventions, whose usual token is the game's rules, where the game exists only thanks to its rules. Even though the reasons for following constitutive conventions may be more complex and varied than coordination conventions, they share that they only exist if they are practised.

Most controversy arises around whether judges (and the general public) must abide by the RoR of a legal system. Such a supposed obligation does not stem from any property of constitutive rules. So, the question should be answered by resorting to other sources, such as ethics. Nonetheless, if we decide to play a game, we usually accept to play by the rules. Otherwise, we do not play that game. When we deal with hugely more complex realms than games, such as law, uniformity as a typical foundational character of conventional rules comes forward. After all, a social rule exists – for historical rather than functionalist reasons – in the first place as a custom of people that follow it. If other people who follow the rule – implicitly asking for conformity – is not a sufficient reason for action in a non-coordination convention, it still puts pressure on the participants in the practice.

See A. Marmor, *Social Conventions: From Language to Law* (Princeton University Press, 2009).

[32] A weak formulation of Hart's acceptance, as officials' acceptance alone, fails to account for the normative and collective aspect of social norms according to M. Wilkinson, 'Is Law Morally Risky? Alienation, Acceptance and Hart's Concept of Law' (2010) 30 *Oxford Journal of Legal Studies* 441, 456, who pursues a stronger notion of acceptance as a critical reflective attitude. It entails 'an obligation on others' and 'involves *understanding of law's social aspect*' (original emphasis).

correspondingly more complex: the criteria for identifying the law are multiple. 'They commonly include a written constitution, enactment by a legislature, and judicial precedents'.[33] He distinguishes the RoR as ultimate – for it does not depend on the existence of any other rule in the system – from the supremacy of one of the criteria to which the RoR refers over the others. Thereby, there is a criterion that is 'supreme', for it points to those legal rules which are not trumped by any other possible rule.[34] Given that the RoR, as Hart explicitly states, is usually unwritten, so the supreme criteria can be unwritten as well as written. Think of the unwritten rule about 'the authority of judicial precedents' in the United Kingdom and United States. If the material constitution amounts to the 'ordering forces' of a legal system, we assume that the former coincides with the supreme criterion. For example, in the United States, a supreme criterion is that constitutional amendments made in accordance with Article V trump earlier constitutional provisions.[35] Then, under the said assumption, the RoR and the material constitution are not coextensive concepts. The material constitution is the supreme criterion to which the RoR, as a social rule, points. The material constitution is thus divested of some of its crucial features, such as a necessary arrangement of political power and socio-economic relationships. However, the RoR can well incorporate purposive norms. Hart famously states in the 'Postscript' 'that in some systems of law, as in the United States, the ultimate criteria of legal validity might explicitly incorporate besides pedigree, principle of justice or substantive moral values, and these may form the content of legal, constitutional restraints'.[36] The ultimate difference between a legal positivist and institutionalist approach to the material constitution is that the former considers the incorporation of purposive norms only contingent upon the specific social rules on which the legal order is built. It still holds that the RoR is content independent, whereas, for the other conception, a set of goals – unified around a political actor – is necessarily the generating factor of the constitution.

The gist of our understanding of the relationship between the RoR and the material constitution is that they are not coextensive. While the RoR points to those 'external' (to the legal order) criteria that allow us to identify the law, the material constitution amounts to those supreme rules (within the legal order) that make the legal order function. We acknowledge that a fully-fledged notion of the material constitution is an endeavour of institutionalist accounts of law. However, institutionalism cannot explain how organisations, facts, et similia count as law in a group.

The above descriptive sketch of a possible legal positivist account of the material constitution may appear a rarefied concept. The risk in these cases is to engage in dispute about terminology. We think, though, that the idea of the material constitution, under the perspective of the RoR, still captures something valuable for making sense of the complex interplay between written and unwritten rules in constitutional law practices. Moreover, a more robust function of the material constitution within that frame can be grasped by shifting the discourse from descriptive to normative grounds. Hence, in Section 16.4 we will conceptualise the material constitution as a political construct rooted in people's attitudes rather than factual determinants.

[33] Hart, *Concept of Law*, 101.

[34] Ibid., 105.

[35] S. J. Shapiro, 'What is the Rule of Recognition (and Does It Exist)?', in M. Adler and K. E. Himma (eds.), *The Rule of Recognition and the U.S. Constitution* (Oxford University Press, 2009), 254.

[36] Hart, *Concept of Law*, 247.

16.4 FROM A DESCRIPTIVE TO A PRESCRIPTIVE ACCOUNT OF THE MATERIAL CONSTITUTION

It is fitting to look back at the assumption that common sense and ordinary language are foundational both of law and the RoR as determined by officials. Regarding the Constitution, this linkage can be interpreted either in a weak or strong form. The weak form is that identification and individuation of (the) law are necessary for determining a legal order. Within this view, the Constitution is not usually part of this process, other than in a very shallow sense, such as that a country has a republican or monarchic form.[37] The strong form is that the Constitution, as the fundamental rule about the exercise of political power, is part of the common sense individuation of the law. The strong linkage between the individuation of the law by laypeople and the existence of a constitutional order is what we call the normative core of the constitution in a material sense. Although the strong form of linkage is hard to demonstrate empirically, it seems reasonable to fathom that it exists in at least some contemporary jurisdictions with a documentary constitution.[38] However, we do not need to assume this linkage as existent either. Our point is that a legal positivist should commit to a concept of law in which people understand society's fundamental constitutional structure as law. This requires articulating further the notion of rules' acceptance.

As seen in Section 16.3, the technical operation of 'determining' the RoR is what officials do. Nevertheless, the acceptance (individuation) of the RoR as a social rule pertains to ordinary citizens too, 'for, in the absence of general obedience, the legal system would not exist'.[39] According to Michael Wilkinson, this acceptance must be of a strong (reflective) type for a legal system to 'flourish' as a 'legal system qua social order'. A legal system can exist under conditions of unreflective acquiescence, but it causes alienation from its subjects.[40] The archetypical form of strong acceptance is found in modern constitutionalism, where 'constitutional popularity' (we, the people) is proclaimed 'in the form of the implicit normative claims of a social order'.[41]

A consequence of the strong linkage between the individuation of the law by laypeople and the existence of a constitutional order is that the material constitution is so thanks to a specific normative legitimacy within a legal order. In what follows, we limit ourselves to probing this scheme regarding the constitutionalisation of democratic principles.

The legitimacy of a given political order – and the socio-economic relations embedded in it – is primarily a political, philosophical problem.[42] We can formulate this problem too in terms of an obligation, namely, why the commands of holders of a specific type of power should be obeyed.[43] Leaving aside any attempt to deal with a discussion that has been going on for centuries, we presuppose that legitimate political authority cannot depend, particularly in contemporary pluralistic societies, on the adherence to the specific goal of the state (or the

[37] We owe this specification to the comments made by Mario Jori on a first draft of this chapter.

[38] See note 12.

[39] Wilkinson, 'Is Law Morally Risky?', 461

[40] Ibid., 462.

[41] Ibid., 461.

[42] The principle that upholds a legal order is external to it, but it cannot dissolve into the mere legal order's efficacy from the internal point of view. Only a legitimising normative principle can 'convince' people to accept a normative order. Furthermore, such an acceptance is fundamentally a political choice. U. Scarpelli, *Cos'è il positivismo giuridico* (ESI, 1997), 126–42, has provided, as far as we know, the best explanation of this point.

[43] See N. Bobbio, *Democracy and Dictatorship* (University of Minnesota Press, 1989), 81. The kind of answer that a conception of the material constitution à la Mortati would provide to such a question is that the justification of the coercive power of the state resides in it being the bearer of political unity through unifying substantive goals.

dominant parties), whatever that may be.[44] Within a normative approach, contractarian conceptions, seeing the state founded on a common accord of all those who will henceforth be subject to it, defend the cause of ascending as against descending power. In other words, the underlying principle is that power moves from bottom to top and not vice versa: 'in a word, it means establishing democracy to counteract autocracy'.[45]

If one considers Weber's descriptive approach to political legitimacy, one notes that legal power stands at the opposite pole of charismatic power. According to Norberto Bobbio, this is because the latter is the embodiment of the rule of men, the former of the rule of law.[46] For Weber, the belief in legality, 'the compliance with enactments which are *formally* correct and which have been made in the accustomed manner', was the 'most common form of legitimacy'.[47] The legal-rational rule must entail a recognition mechanism dependent on compliance with general valid rules enacted through legal institutionalised procedures to function as a legitimating factor. This recognition is independent of the adherence to the rule content. In conventional (social rules) terms, that recognition can be translated into a convergence (or collective intentionality) on the legitimating role of legality and, namely, procedural legality.[48] Along this line, we advance three correlated claims. First, that the 'material constitution', as a legal artefact, can incorporate the principle of legitimacy based on the convergence on the belief in procedural legality; second, that the same principle has been incorporated, historically, in many an individual legal order; third, that, thereby, the material constitution is a legitimising factor of political authority.[49] In normative parlance, an account of the material constitution should be based as much as possible on procedural grounds rather than substantive goals. Political struggle is not a matter of legal battles in court. This is not to deny that political principles penetrate the constitution,[50] but their legitimacy depends primarily on procedural devices.[51]

In this guise, the material constitution – that can include and often includes purposive norms – must necessarily set the organising principles about political authority. In turn, a normative commitment toward democracy rather than the assumption of political dominance can (and ought to) be part of it. After all, 'what is democracy other than a set of rules (the so-called rules of the game) for the solution of conflicts without bloodshed? Furthermore, what constitutes good democratic government if not rigorous respect for these rules?'[52] Thereby, an active normative attitude toward democracy and the rule of law demands cultivating a shared

[44] A different matter is that the 'constitutional order' can incorporate values, such as equality, justice and dignity that 'operate irrespective of the political forces that alternate each other at government, and which correspond to widespread values within the same civil society': A. Barbera, 'Ordinamento costituzionale e carte costituzionali' (2010) 30 *Quaderni costituzionali* 319.

[45] N. Bobbio, *The Future of Democracy: A Defence of the Rules of the Game* (University of Minnesota Press, 1987), 133.

[46] Ibid., 155.

[47] M. Weber, *Economy and Society [1922]* (University of California Press, 1978), 37.

[48] In this regard, what Wilkinson, 'Is Law Morally Risky?', 465, observes regarding 'input legitimacy' as the level of engagement with the 'authority structure' is apposite: 'This involves consideration of the manner in which our norms are constructed, interpreted and applied rather than their substantive results alone. It means that we need to consider the system that is responsible for our norms as a whole.'

[49] According to Weber, *Economy and Society*, 217, legitimacy is a condition for validity.

[50] G. Ferrara, *La Costituzione. Dal pensiero politico alla norma giuridica* (Feltrinelli, 2006), 242 ss. – one of the most fervent advocates of a normative, counterfactual role of the Constitution – thought there is an overarching political principle that the Constitution sets to law.

[51] It should be added that the discourses of jurists and scholars contribute to shape the common sense understanding of the law. A posture inclined to favour the primacy of a 'material' constitution based on democracy and deliberation contributes to make the constitution evolve toward it or maintain it.

[52] Bobbio, *Future of Democracy*, 156.

belief in the Constitution's authority and the value of deliberative democracy. The latter, of course, is not a requirement of every conceivable 'order'. Instead, it is the insertion of a material supreme (constitutional) rule within the fabric of the legal system.

It is fitting to spell out in some more detail the relationship between the rule of law and the democratic principle to articulate the kernel of the material constitution in a democratic society. The most fundamental procedural mechanism to let every citizen participate in the governing system and being heard is the right to vote. And particularly to deliberate. In a way, deliberative rules are even more fundamental than the right to elect people's representatives because they regard how to make collective decisions in the interest of everyone, irrespective of whether applied in a representative or direct democratic system. It is radically different from the 'market model' of democracy as the former does not utilise 'voting only in a context of ongoing deliberation in which preferences are taken as given, fixed inputs, but change and develop in the process of seeking agreement'.[53] Indeed, a discussion usually occurs over the relevant processes; parties and groups introduce and debate different proposals to influence each other about a course of action. Through bargaining, such players may get to compromise. This mechanism is a crucial legitimising factor, for, in a democratic system, the most basic cog is the majority rule.[54] Without such a set of rules that all the players must respect, democracy is lame. Gianni Ferrara thus used to define voting rules as the most important triggers of constitutional agency.[55]

Some other conditions are necessary for the system to work, once again relating to the attitude (acceptance) toward the rules of the game. While participating in the voting procedure, everyone ought to acknowledge the authority of the outcome, irrespective of one's personal interest and goal. Correlative to this commitment is the mutual trust in the legality and fairness of the deliberating process, whose outcome is accepted irrespective of the decision's content.

Given the inescapability of the majority rule, the most notable feature of a democratic system is the effective and concrete opportunity for minorities and idiosyncratic positions to be involved in the decision-making process. This is a matter of genuine concern that can affect constitutional ordering and the constitution in a material sense. The failure to recognise the game's rules by the said groups and the community may lead to the fall of the political system's legitimacy. When, therefore, democratic legality collapses as the ruling principle, in other words, if the society at large gets detached from the rule of recognition as shared by the officials,[56] then a breakdown may occur that tampers the 'external statement of fact that a legal system exists'.[57] One can detect such a situation when sizeable societal sectors continuously look for alternative means of reaction and polemic participation. Revolutionary events are possible outcomes. An example of potential threats to the material ordering of democratic power through the rule of law is to be found in contemporary populist movements.

16.5 THE FORMAL CONSTITUTION ENTRENCHES THE MATERIAL

As noted in Section 16.3, the material ordering factors that constitute the Constitution's kernel become truly 'constitutional' through their entrenchment into the documentary (formal)

[53] T. Campbell, *Prescriptive Legal Positivism: Law Rights and Democracy* (UCL Press, 2004), 259.
[54] Bobbio, *Future of Democracy*, 63.
[55] G. Ferrara, *Gli atti costituzionali* (Giappichelli, 2000), 5.
[56] Hart, *Concept of Law*, 118, who envisages the case that 'there is no longer general obedience to the rule which are valid according to the criteria of validity in use in the courts'.
[57] Ibid.

constitution. The material constitution is indeed strengthened and stabilised by becoming public and potentially enforceable. This tenet is consistent with the framework sketched in Section 16.4. A highly ranked written document is ordinarily necessary for having a (formal) constitution. However, it does not suffice. The documentary constitution must have codified the constitutional order. In other words, sufficient social pressure (collective acceptance) on the criteria of which the RoR consists is necessary. Conversely, without such a codification, the material constitution cannot acquire those characters of certainty and stability beside limitations on the holders of the highest powers of government, which are typical of law in modern societies. When the phenomenon of strengthening the material constitution by the formal does not occur, we could speak of 'non-constitutionalist or minimally constitutionalist constitutions ... made for ideological reasons and sometimes primarily for external consumption'.[58]

However, if the material constitution has normative traction, one must be able to build normative propositions upon it. This area regards the practical (judicial) application of the material constitution. We enter this area when a conflict between the material and the documentary constitution arises. In other words, we face the disputed issue of constitutional change.

Recent theorists of the material constitution tend to use it as an 'analytical tool' to capture 'constitutional reality when the form of the constitution is deceptive'.[59] We can easily translate this language into a normative one. For example, Kelsen argued that dictatorship rather than democracy was the Soviet Union's form of government according to the 'real constitution' as against the letter of the 1936 Constitution.[60]

Along the spectrum, one meets the vexed and unresolved dispute concerning constitutional continuity and amendments. One implication of the theory is that the material constitution embodies the non-amendable core of the constitution. Namely, it is immune to changes enacted through the procedure appositely laid down in the constitutional text. In Italy, for example, with decision n. 1146 of 1988, the Constitutional Court has set up a doctrine of unwritten limits to constitutional amendments.[61] It has done so by a non-originalist interpretation of article 139 of the Constitution, which prohibits changing the republican form of the state. The Court ruled that, besides the latter written limit, principles that belong to the 'core of the supreme values' on which the Italian Constitution is founded cannot be subject to the amendment process. The Court did not say what such principles are. Since the judgement revolved around equality, equality must be among them. Afterward, part of the literature has interpreted this doctrine as ruling that the republican form must contain some material elements that found the community's political structure, such as democracy, equality, freedom, whereby substantive norms can trump (formal) secondary rules of change and bind political power.

Moreover, the Court can use these supreme constitutional principles to strike down legislation if they find the latter in conflict with the former. We limit ourselves to noting that, within the frame of a democratic material constitution, such a very sensitive issue requires much

[58] A. Arato, *The Adventures of the Constituent Power: Beyond Revolutions?* (Cambridge University Press, 2017), 6.

[59] Goldoni, 'Material Constitution'.

[60] H. Kelsen, *The Political Theory of Bolshevism: A Critical Analysis* (University of California Press, 1948), 52.

[61] R. Albert, *Constitutional Amendments: Making, Breaking, and Changing Constitutions* (Oxford University Press, 2019), 151, defines this practice 'the basic structure doctrine' as an instance of 'interpretive unamendability'. He traces this doctrine to various cases decided by the Supreme Court of India, then followed by the Constitutional Courts of Colombia and Taiwan. The comparative constitutional law literature has vastly discussed such cases, while the Italian case is almost entirely neglected.

self-restraint when establishing the non-amendable core. For example, the Constitution's text should always be the starting point and the frame to look for such unamendable core principles, the first of which is democracy itself.

This point borders the equally busy battleground of constitutional interpretation. Should the courts use the material constitution as an interpretive argument to decide hard cases, in other words, balance constitutional goals, principles, and rights? Most constitutional norms are vague and they often provide only weak guidance for ruling institutions and judges. Under contemporary constitutional settlements, the many tensions that suffuse pluralistic societies cannot be solved once and for all by an authoritative text. However, the temptation to think that the 'study' of the material constitution can ordinarily illuminate something more profound than the codified constitution must be treated cautiously. An analytical, apparently detached approach can quickly turn into subjective – unchallenged – normative claims. Such a subjectivism overtly runs against an account of the RoR, pointing to a shared belief in democracy as the ruling principle.

From the perspective of political (or critical) legal positivism,[62] the most crucial precept regarding the use of 'facts' as interpretive devices is a commitment toward a weak form of objectivity amounting to intersubjectivity. The latter entails a theory of discretion based on the awareness about the inevitable exercise of power whenever a general directive is to apply.[63] The only antidote to such a situation is a form of sincerity. The commitment not to hide one's choices behind 'facts' or 'objective values'.[64] This is why a political-legal positivist, on the one hand, prefers that the constitutional ordering factors are spelt out as much as possible in the codified Constitution; on the other hand, she recommends that, in applying the law, officials try to understand what the law means in the first place. Nonetheless, she is aware that often the outcome is not the result of the legal provision only – as every official claims. Their beliefs, opinions and interests influence the upshot.

Finally, a political-legal positivist is wary of judicial activism. A master rule based on democracy, primarily expressed in deliberative processes, tends to defer to judicial discretion only as a last resort means when legislative institutions fail to reach any agreement. It is manifest that, by coupling principles with expectations about rights, contemporary constitutions confer resolution powers to the courts, particularly when legislators remain silent. Nonetheless, too much judicial power may be another clue of a breakdown of the RoR having the outline presented here.

The operation we have tried in this chapter is, above all, conceptual cleanliness about the relationship between the RoR and the material constitution. While the RoR concerns the ultimate criteria to identify the law, we can term as material constitution those of such criteria (rules) that are supreme within a legal order. By understanding, instead, the material constitution as the 'original constitution', an independent source stemming from institutional facts to derive the legal order, one cannot explain how such facts count as law for a social group. Albeit downsized, this notion of the material constitution as a facet of the RoR remains helpful in illuminating the complex interplay between written and unwritten constitutional rules. Moreover, by adhering to the idea of the internal statement about the existence of the law as critical acceptance by ordinary citizens (not only officials) – as opposed to detecting objective ordering forces – we have sketched the contours of a material constitution based on a normative

[62] Campbell, *Prescriptive Legal Positivism*; Scarpelli, *Cos'è il positivismo giuridico*, 151–57.

[63] Jori, *Il diritto inesistente*, 120–21.

[64] It is plausible to argue that political legal positivism requires the adherence to a non-cognitivist ethics. See R. M. Hare, *The Language of Morals* (Clarendon Press, 1952).

political conception of the RoR. The normative presupposition of such a conception is a strong linkage between the individuation/acceptance of the law by laypeople and the existence of a given constitutional order. A consequence of such a strong linkage is that the material constitution, as a legal notion, is so thanks to a specific normative legitimacy within a legal order (again, not any factual determinants). In our view, in pluralistic contemporary societies, such legitimacy hinges fundamentally on democratic/procedural principles rather than substantive goals.

17

Constitutional Matter and Form

An Exploration of Constitutional Language

Denis Baranger

The ambition of what follows is exclusively to clarify the meaning of two words in the context of constitutional law: 'matter' and 'form'. This inquiry should, we believe, be conducted before passing judgement (or taking sides) on the controversy between supporters of a material constitution and 'formalists' who take the view that the constitution resides only in positive legal sources. Our intuition (and starting point here) is that the vocabulary of matter and form brings about serious theoretical difficulties *per se*. A conceptual enquiry is therefore in order.

In legal parlance, a 'form' refers to 'any action or manner of proceeding which presides to the making of a legal act (contract, will, judgment, decision, . . .)' and is strongly related to a theory of the formation of law through acts of volition. The word 'form' is connected to several cognate terms such as 'formality'. Formalism, in turn, appears to refer to the 'tendency (. . .) to multiply formalities during the making of the act'.[1] Legal forms give rise not only to such procedures and constraints but also to a mode of reasoning, also called 'formalism'.[2] A formal reason is 'a legally authoritative reason on which judges and others are empowered or required to make a decision' as there appears to be 'a valid legal rule'.[3] A substantive reason, conversely, points to 'a moral, economic, political, institutional, or other social consideration' that comes into play at different moments in the life of the law, but particularly in its formative period. They 'serve as the primary ingredients of most constitution, statutes, precedents, . . .'.[4]

Form and substance are frequently united in such a conceptual couple. The alliance of 'form' *with* (or disjunction *from*) 'matter' is less frequent in modern law. Yet it appears in the idea of a 'material' constitution. The idea of a material constitution has found its way into constitutional law for at least two reasons. The first reason consists in the absence of coincidence between the scope of the rules of the formal or written constitution and the wider field of constitutional rules. This lack of coincidence may be rejected dogmatically by those who consider that the only existing constitutional rules are those to be found in the formal constitution. This view generally coexists with the position according to which there is no specific constitutional matter: any norm in the constitution is constitutional. What is or is not constitutional is not defined by a certain

[1] I translate freely from G. Cornu, *Vocabulaire Juridique* (Presse Universitaire de France, 1997), 395.

[2] Most of the discussions about 'formalism' in contemporary legal theory point to a wider concept of formalism as adherence to literal meaning in the course of legal interpretation. See F. Schauer, 'Formalism' (1988) 97 *Yale Law Journal* 509. We will not refer to this sense of formalism here.

[3] P. S. Atiyah and R. Summers, *Form and Substance in Anglo-American Law: A Comparative Study of Legal Reasoning, Legal Theory and Legal Institutions* (Clarendon Press, 1989), 2.

[4] Ibid., 5.

content, but by the form of its enactment, that is, the constitutional form. Yet this claim clashes with a great deal of empirical evidence. In France, the formal constitution has long ceased to be the only repository of constitutional norms. Since at least 1971[5] the French Constitutional Council (our constitutional court) takes the view that the constitutional norms against which it assesses the compatibility of statutes stretch beyond the formal constitution and extend to the Declaration of the rights of man and citizen (1789), the Preamble to the 1946 Constitution and, since 2005, the 'Environment Charter'. In the United Kingdom, where there is no formal constitution because of the principle of the sovereignty of Parliament, case law has identified a body of 'constitutional statutes'.[6] In the United States, it is widely acknowledged that certain 'superstatutes', such as the Administrative Procedure Act (1946),[7] contain quasi-constitutional rules. There are many more borderline cases of this kind, as we shall see.

Second, the idea of a material constitution also comes into play for doctrinal reasons. Some authors will define the constitution by a specific content or 'matter'. This is emphatically the case of the main proponent of the idea, the Italian jurist Costantino Mortati.[8] The purpose becomes to demonstrate that the constitution is not contained – or even defined – by a certain enactment, but in a certain set of concepts and subject-matter. Despite the variety of approaches and their relative lack of clarity – for instance the identification of 'matter' with 'content' is far from self-evident – the idea of a material constitution is based on the notion that the formal conception is insufficient and possibly a denaturation. Asserting the material constitution as the 'real' or 'proper' one raises questions of its own. The formal dimension of constitutional law is hard to ignore. The very project of constitutionalism has a formal dimension attached to it. Written constitutions – and even to a large extent unwritten ones – are by definition set into form, formulas, formalism(s) and formalities. Thinking in terms of a constitutional matter runs the risk of promoting the archaic vision in which matter is equated with disorder, chaos and potentially – as in neoplatonism – *evil*. This may help us understand why the idea of a material constitution is often the object of outright rejection. Law as such is supposed to be form and form is supposed to bring orderliness (and therefore goodness) to politics. In French orthodox constitutional doctrine, from Georges Vedel to Louis Favoreu, this is how law is always opposed to politics as form is opposed to substance.

17.1 THE UNDETERMINED PROVINCE OF CONSTITUTIONAL LAW

17.1.1 *Normativism and the Rejection of the Material Definition*

From the viewpoint of a formalist, constitutional law cannot be conceived materially. To take Kelsen's normativist point of view, the so-called material unconstitutionality will ultimately boil down to a formal unconstitutionality, as a so-called unconstitutional law would become constitutional if it were enacted in the constitutional form (a new rigid constitution or a valid constitutional amendment).[9] This approach is not illogical. The formal argument against the material constitution is always *formally* correct, in the sense that it always prevails where formal reasons are held to be conclusive. You can't beat the argument that the constituent power can

[5] Decision n°71-44 DC of 16 July 1971 '*Liberté d'association*'.

[6] *Thoburn* v. *Sunderland City Council* [2003] QB 151; [2002] 3 WLR 247.

[7] 11 June 1946, chap. 234, 60 stat. 237. Cf. W. N. Eskridge and P. Frickey, 'Quasi-Constitutional Law: Clear Statement Rules as Constitutional Lawmaking' (1992) 45 *Vanderbilt Law Review* 593.

[8] C. Mortati, *La Costituzione in senso Materiale* (Giuffré Editore, 1998).

[9] H. Kelsen, 'la garantie constitutionnelle de la Constitution' (1928) 45 *Revue de droit public* 206.

validly incorporate or set aside any given legal proposition in the entrenched constitution. And the same can be said of the amending power if it follows the proper amending procedure. As a result, whatever content is (or not) embodied in the validly enacted constitution will be held to prevail and, conversely, any 'constitutional material' lacking a proper pedigree will be cast aside. Yet – as is often the case with Kelsen – it amounts to a *reconfiguration* of the existing positive material. What positive law views *de prima facie* as a certain 'matter' (distinguishable from the mere legal form of enactment) is requalified as boiling down to a mere question of procedure. This reconfiguration seems to ignore the fact that law requires a great deal of substantive reasoning and also that different subject-matter involves different formal treatments. For instance, the case could be made that human rights are norms of an entirely different kind than, say, rules of legislative procedure. In that case, a different matter or substance requires a different legal formalism. Human rights law arguably requires much more complex modes of legal reasoning than simply the question of an adequate enactment procedure.

The formalist view of the constitution reduces the constitution to a norm whose only specificity is its normativity. Yet the causation has in fact to be reversed. The normativity of the constitution as 'supreme' or 'higher' law is only a result.of its specific nature and function. The specificity of the constitution is found in its relationship with politics. The forms and modes of reasoning that obtain in constitutional law are not identical to other forms and modes of reasoning extant in other branches of the law. One of the weaknesses of formalism so understood is that it overlooks the peculiar formal characters of the positive constitution. Ignorance of the substantive content of the constitution leads to a lack of understanding of its forms. Formalism thus fails to explain constitutional forms.

Conversely, the strategy that purports to separate 'matter' from form in constitutional law has difficulties of its own. It might be that constitutional content can be severed from form. This idea has been defended in particular by Carl Schmitt, for whom the actual constitution is the constitutional decision about the political form of the state, while the constitutional act or 'formal constitution' is only a manner to bring into application this decision. As a result, for Schmitt, the content of the constitutional enactment can be merely fortuitous. This is for instance the case, says Schmitt, of the (temporary) prohibition of alcohol by the eighteenth amendment to the Constitution of the United States (1917–19, repealed in 1933). Schmitt also draws attention to the variety of 'eclectic clauses' contained in the second part of the German Constitution of 1919 ('Weimar Constitution').[10] These 'fortuitous' clauses had only been entrenched in order to shield them from changes by way of ordinary legislation. 'Without a written constitution as a stabilizing force, there is a risk that (issues needing settlement) will remain excessively uncertain'.[11]

This interpretation runs up against two difficulties. First, any constitutional clause can be of significance, despite its apparently trivial nature. The struggle against alcoholism could appear as a policy goal or a higher moral value as legitimate as any other. The same thing could be said about the decision to amend the French Third Republic constitution in 1926 in order to enshrine the independence of the State's debt repayment fund (*Caisse d'amortissement de la dette publique*). Serious reasons of general interest – such as stabilising public finances – could be adduced for this amendment. Closer to us, it was understandable that the 1997 Constitution

[10] C. Schmitt, 'Das Reichsgericht als Hüter der Verfassung' (1929). I quote from the French translation: *Le Tribunal du Reich comme Gardien de la Constitution* (Dalloz, 2017), 72.

[11] F. Schauer and L. Alexander, 'On Extrajudicial Constitutional Interpretation' (1997) 110 *Harvard Law Review* 1359, 1376.

of the post-apartheid Republic of South Africa[12] should contain extremely detailed provisions about arbitrary arrest which 'resemble a detailed code of criminal procedure'.[13] The incorporation of large chunks of criminal law into the Constitution was explained by the recourse of the Apartheid regime to arbitrary arrests in the recent past.

17.1.2 *Borderline Cases*

Ideally, all constitutional matter should be contained in the formal constitution. The perfect constitution, to be, as philosophers would have it, 'in keeping with its concept' (*conforme à son concept*) should achieve this perfect fit. For many reasons, it does not. In contemporary constitutional law 'a norm can be constitutionalized in several ways, its inclusion in the "Big C" constitution [ie the entrenched constitution] being only one of them. Other methods include judicial interpretation, quasi-constitutional statutes, and constitutional conventions.'[14] The same disjunction between form and matter is also caused by the developing role of international law. There is a growing sense that international law, especially treaties, contain norms of a 'constitutionally' relevant nature. To be convinced that this is the case, it would be enough to point to the number of constitutional revisions that took place in Europe – and notably in France – to enable the ratification of certain major international treaties.

This distribution of legal material between several sources is neither stable nor final. Clauses, types of rules or entire subject-matters are moving to and from between the written constitution and other formal sources. As a result, at certain key moments in constitutional history, certain matters are 'constitutionalised' or 'de-constitutionalised'. A certain subject-matter is incorporated into the formal constitution or conversely it is set aside from it. In the case of 'de-constitutionalisation' the 'receiving' source (or so to speak) consists mostly in legislation. This nearly constant process of constitutional content moving between different sources is apparent in the transformation of the French law of legislative delegation during the Third (1875–1940) and the Fourth (1946–58) French Republics. An increasing number of Third Republic parliamentary statutes delegated regulatory competences to the executive. There has been a long debate about whether it was the statutory competence that was delegated as such or the subject-matter (a certain scope) itself. The second solution has been generally held as correct, as Parliament was, since 1946, barred by article 13 of the Constitution from delegating legislative power. Moreover, the regulations made on the basis of such delegations were subject to judicial review by French administrative courts and thus retained the nature of executive regulations, not of legislative acts. In any case, this mechanism was thus raised by case law to the level of a constitutional principle. It was declared constitutional, under certain restrictions, by the Council of State in an advisory statement of 6 February 1953.[15] This statement about the law as it then stood acknowledged that certain subject-matters were 'legislative by nature' and thus could not be delegated to the executive rulemaking power. This distribution of 'subject-matters' as such was ultimately incorporated into the written Constitution in 1958. It is now governed by article 34 (legislative subject-matters) and article 37 ('residual' regulatory subject-matters). Article 38 of the Constitution now regulates a mechanism of 'ordinances' (delegated or secondary legislation by way of executive orders).

[12] SA Act n°200.
[13] Ibid., p. 1376, fn. n°73.
[14] T. Khaitan, 'Balancing Accountability and Effectiveness: A Case for Moderated Parliamentarism' (2021) 7 *Canadian Journal of Comparative and Contemporary Law* 81.
[15] N° 260.497.

In other cases, certain subject-matters are shared between the constitution and other legal sources. In France, the law of elections – which appears to deal with a core constitutional problem, that of political representation – is split between statutes, administrative regulations and a few very general constitutional clauses. Another striking example is parliamentary law. It used to be practically the monopoly of each House's Standing Order. Since 1958, however, the Constitution has incorporated many rules regarding the legislative process, with a view to tipping the balance of power in favour of the executive. This type of constitutional drafting has been called 'rationalised parliamentarism'. What used to be the province of the standing order is now regulated by the formal constitution. This also results in a normative change. The standing orders are held to be of inferior normative force than the formal constitution. Article 61-1 of the 1958 Constitution subjects any amendment to these standing orders to a mandatory judicial review by the *Conseil constitutionnel*. While the subject-matter has been transferred, its content has also radically been altered. The new procedures incorporated in the Constitution strictly limit the freedom of the Houses of Parliament.

Conversely, the formal constitution does not always suffice to cover the entire span of constitutional topics. This was emphatically the case with the three constitutional statutes of 1875 in France. Their material paucity was often bemoaned by contemporaries. Raymond Carré de Malberg, a major public lawyer of the time, called it 'too short to be rigid'. It only contained 'procedural rules, with no interest for litigation by private parties'. Nowhere did it provide 'a substantive content with regard to individual rights'.[16] As a result, the formal constitution had to be supplemented in several ways. Key articles of the Declaration of 1789, itself not a part of positive law, were thus informally incorporated into judicial review of administrative action by way of unwritten 'general principles of law'.[17] This often raised a discussion about the constitutional or sometimes 'supraconstitutional' nature of the Declaration of 1789.

17.2 POLITICAL MATTER AND LEGAL FORM

17.2.1 *Politics as the Matter of Constitutional Law*

The matter of constitutional law is *politics*. The form of constitutional law is *law*. Politics, however, is the exact contrary of an inert material. It reflects the constant self-concern and self-moulding of society. We face the same difficulties defining politics as when it comes to defining society: 'there is not a single phenomenon of the social'[18] and neither is there a single phenomenon of the political. We tend to see 'society' and 'politics' as shapeless and formless, because 'politics' and 'society' refer to an infinite variety of processes nevertheless building a whole. As a result, politics is not a mere set of facts or events that law can frame. Politics, for one thing, is an intrinsically normative process. It generates evaluations of different kinds: moral ones (this is good or bad) as well as intrinsically political ones (we want this collectively; we reject this collectively). This intrinsically normative nature of politics bridges a gap between politics and law. Politics cannot be just a raw material that law takes hold of and gives shape to. Politics is a relatively autonomous and creative form of social activity. So is law. Both politics and law, as

16 The *Commissaire du Gouvernement* Latournerie in his pre-judgement brief (*conclusions*) on the '*Arrighi and Dame Coudert*' cases, Sirey, 1936. 3. This was a landmark case in which the Conseil d'Etat refused to act as a constitutional court.

17 That was especially the case of the principle of equality.

18 P. Kahn, *Origins of Order: Project and System in American Legal Imagination* (Yale University Press, 2019) 183.

social processes, create themselves and build up outer social realities. This reciprocal autonomy generates complex interactions in which law shapes politics as much as politics gives birth to law.

17.2.2 *Law as the Form of the Constitution*

Constitutional law is a *relatively* autonomous branch of the law. Its forms, while drawn from the general body of legal forms, are nevertheless attuned to politics. The word 'form' should not mislead us here. Law is not only made of forms. The elaborate legal theories at play in any given legal system make room for another dichotomy between law and substance or substantive reasons[19]. Yet the very substance of law is conveyed through forms. When law comes up in a substantive fashion, it must be clothed in a legal form (a precedent, a statute, a constitutional amendment, . . .). The discussion is therefore made somehow murkier by the fact that, in this process, legal substance is as relevant as legal form. Speaking of a 'material constitution' therefore muddles the issue as, first, the true matter of the constitution is politics and, second, constitutional law deals with politics by way of both its form and its substance.

What we know today as constitutional law is merely one of the last major attempts of law to hold sway over politics. Constitutional law is the child of several 'formative' projects defined by a certain vision of the mutual arrangement of law and politics. One such important formal project is the institutional approach to the constitution, as expressed classically by Montesquieu. The constitution is a 'disposition of things', an institutional framework rather than a set of norms. Yet, because it shapes politics and guides behaviours, there is no reason not to call it legal. It generates institutions which, in turn, generate legal norms, although this was not the vocabulary Montesquieu would have used. Modern constitutionalism insisted on the written form as central to its own political project. Yet it was not born at the precise date when the Philadelphia draft was ratified by the newly independent American states or when the French National Assembly put together (in a rather piecemeal fashion) the Constitution of 1791. Constitutional law emerged through the numerous historical processes in which political power has been envisaged by law. As we have tried to show elsewhere,[20] constitutional law begins where a certain approach to power becomes embedded into law. We have called this approach the 'syllogism of liberty' and it consists in a logical pattern which is the same in the early English Charters of liberty, the great English cases of the seventeenth century (*Five knights Case*[21]) and eighteenth century (*Entick* v. *Carrington*[22]). It was then replicated, with some evident modifications, into the American Constitution. This logical structure can be summarised in this way: a wrongful infringement of liberty has taken place; this calls for the affirmation (or reaffirmation) of certain propositions of law; finally, a remedy is granted. What is important here is that raw political power is approached by way of a fact pattern, an apprehension of power as simply *taking place* and being potentially conducive to abuses. Constitutional law then appears in the form of a set of remedies against such abuses. Yet in the same tradition, abuse of power is viewed not only through the lens of harm caused to the subjects, but also as the violation of a pre-existing legal ordering. Whether this is mythical or not is irrelevant. What counts is that the form–matter relation is productive of power as well as curative of its abuses. Power is generated by public law

19 Atiyah and Summers, *Form and Substance*.

20 D. Baranger, 'Law, Liberty and Entick v Carrington', in A. Tomkins and P. Scott (eds.), *Entick v Carrington. 250 Years of the Rule of Law* (Hart Publishing, 2015), 185–206.

21 (1627) 3 How St Tr 1.

22 [1765] 95 ER 807.

as well as it is caught in the toils of the law.[23] The English and American – and to a lesser extent French – Revolutions are based on this pattern. The syllogism of liberty is apparent on the face of the 1628 Petition of Right, the 1689 Bill of Rights, and the 1776 Declaration of Independence, to quote just those major constitutional documents. They all stood as the background and foundation for a new constitutional settlement.

The syllogism of liberty is only one of the possible relationships between legal form and political matter. Law is the prominent form of institutionalised politics. It mediates our access to politics. We acquire no intelligibility of political matter outside legal and institutional forms and formats. Constitutional law aims at conferring legal forms on political activity. There has evolved a specific body of constitutional legal forms (entrenched constitutions, amendment procedures, modes of constituent power, constitutional judicial review, ...). However, law as such – a concept and also a catalogue of forms, formulas, formalities, ... – stays in the background as a resource for new developments. In that case, it is not easy to distinguish the concept of form from other cognate notions. Law itself is held to be the mould into which power and more generally political activity has to fit. But it should be noted that law as such is a form of a very elusive kind. Any attempt at restricting law to 'pedigreeable' sources[24] will prove unable to capture the broader dynamics of legal reasoning. The Constitution is never fully self-contained. It is immersed in the larger body of the law. This is the obvious conclusion which one can draw from the understanding of the British Constitution as a 'common law constitution'. The same thing is true, however, about written constitutions. The interpretation of their relatively vague words will require an enquiry into other aspects of the law. A member of the first Supreme Court had proudly said that 'the constitution would be the only fountain from which [he] draw[s]'. One of his nineteenth century successors would instead refer to the common law – a 'fountain of justice' – as a guide to the interpretation of the fourteenth amendment.[25]

17.3 THE DYNAMICS OF MATTER AND FORM

17.3.1 *Constituent Power*

There is a tendency for the constitution to become increasingly legalised and for legal formats to become more specific when they come into contact with the phenomenon of political power. This distinctiveness of constitutional forms is a topic far too wide to be covered here. Yet one can suggest that all constitutional forms can be reduced to certain patterns. Constituent power is the first such mode under which legal form and political matter are articulated. The political 'matter' consists of a certain community (generally called a society) which is the locus of a certain ongoing political activity and to which certain political intentions can be ascribed. This is more or less the raw material with which the constituent power will set out to work. Constituent power is the name (and the form) attributed to this political art of making and unmaking constitutions. This art takes an 'artist'. In seventeenth-century parlance, this person is the 'artificer'. The word evokes an individual at work (or *artifex*) and the offspring of his undertaking (the artifice). It also evokes a certain competence, or ability, to mould the materials into an adequate form: an *art*. This art is also generative: pre-existing matter has been moulded into, or possibly inserted into, a certain form. Contrary to the claims of the founding fathers of

[23] This is one of the core ideas of M. Loughlin's *Foundations of Public Law* (Oxford University Press, 2010).

[24] The word has been coined by Frederick Schauer; Schauer, 'Formalism' ('pedigreeability').

[25] *Hurtado* v. *California*, 110 US 516 (1884) (per Matthews J).

constitutionalism – notably Sieyès – constituent power is not inherently devoid of form. A new constitutional order is frequently set up before the definitive constitutional enactment. Yet those provisional or temporary enactments – or pre-constitutions – bear many resemblances with an actual constitution. They often take the form of a fully-fledged constitutional statute which could be applicable indefinitely were it not for the 'definitive' constitution to come into force. This was the case, for instance, of the French 'small constitution' (*petite constitution*) of 2 November 1945. Other such pre-constitutions, such as the statute of 3 June 1958, do not aim at setting up governmental powers. Yet the content of the statute of 3 June 1958 is indisputably constitutional. First, it sets up the procedure for the enactment of the new constitution. Second, it establishes several substantive principles that the Constitution has to respect (representative nature of government, political accountability, separation of powers, . . .). If anything, the statute of 3 June 1958 would have had to be seen, by a rigid legal logician, as supra-constitutional, as it was supposed to be obeyed by the constituent power. But in any case, whatever its normative value – which is secondary in that case – it is evidently constitutional.

17.3.2 *The Constitution and Social Change*

Formalism can only provide a very basic, unsophisticated, account of constitutional activity. Restricting oneself to this formal recording amounts more or less to referring to a mere accounting book in order to get acquainted with the actual functioning of a business undertaking. Formally, the items that can be recorded in the legal equivalent to such an accounting book are very limited indeed: norms are made and unmade, become valid or invalid. Some are enacted, maybe even entrenched. Then, in the course of judicial review, the validity of these norms can be controlled. This can result in these norms being discarded or set aside. The accounting book only records the coming and going of the merchandise, not its content. This cannot be satisfactory. As a matter of fact, this accounts for the systematically self-defeating nature of formalistic accounts of constitutional law: they never remain formal. At one moment or another they have to incorporate some material content.

Conversely, one could at least hope that the material constitution would provide an understanding of the dynamics of constitutional law in terms of its relationships with a living social fabric. The original constitution is generally set in a specific historic and social context, not to mention its economic infrastructure.[26] The politics of a certain era provide certain ideas, representations, prejudices about the scope of state intervention, the desirable social and moral arrangements, etc. Constituent power results not so much in a 'pre-commitment' to these values, ideas or representations, as in an original setting for institutionalised political activity. The main quality of the setting is its relative stability and ability to adjust to 'people of fundamentally differing views'.[27] The dismissive view of politics often held by lawyers has no other cause. The prejudices of lawyers against politics could be expressed as follows: law is objective and settled once and for all; politics is stained by interests and power-grabbing, as well as unstable. None of these prejudices stand up to scrutiny. Politics involves the formulation of higher, relatively stable principles. Conversely, law is neither inherently neutral, nor inherently stable or capable of stabilising social life. The indeterminate nature of constitutional rules (such as the 'general words' contained in the fifth and fourteenth amendments of the Constitution of the United States), however, is such that their wording can only generate an open-ended consensus about

[26] See M. Goldoni and M. Wilkinson, 'The Material Constitution' (2018) 81 *Modern Law Review* 567.

[27] *Lochner* v. *New York*, 198 US 45 (1905) (dissenting opinion by Oliver Wendell Holmes, Jr.).

political justice and the moral good. Who can disagree with such an abstract requirement as that of the maintenance of a 'due process of law'? Yet such constitutional standards relate to a web of socio-political values and social arrangements with a long history and a robust pedigree. This is just one example of how the abstract universalism of classical constitutionalism paved the way for the progressive inclusion of new modes of social activity. Human action evolves and constitutional law has to adapt in consequence. In other terms: the material content of social life which cries out for certain constitutional settlements (the 'Atlantic revolutions' themselves, or to take only examples drawn from American constitutional history, the reconstruction amendments or the civil rights struggle, . . .) also generates new constitutional paradigms, when and where this is possible. As a result, the confrontation with new socio-political 'matter' generates new legal forms and structures. Constitutional law, as such, is one such larger structure, made necessary by the larger changes in European and American society during the nineteenth century. Once established, constitutional law provided new legalistic methods of entrenchment, constitutional drafting and eventually judicial review. All these formal changes have been triggered by large scale 'material' changes such as capitalism, democratisation, the concern for human rights and possibly now the concern for climate change.[28]

This dynamic explains the apparition of new subject-matters in the constitutional sphere. Law must prove it is able to tackle social problems as they arise. A very clear example is the taking up of the matter of education in American constitutional law since *Brown* v. *Board of Education* (1954).[29] This moment when a new subject-matter *becomes* constitutional seems to be encapsulated in the famous sentence to be found in the majority opinion: 'We must look instead to the effect of segregation itself on public education'.[30] From this moment on, education has become a central constitutional topic and a gateway for the larger topic of racial segregation. In this new context, the previous constitutional thinking in terms of 'social vs. political rights' spelled out in *Plessy* v. *Ferguson* (1896)[31] suddenly appeared as inconsistent, which it was, in all likelihood since 'the day it was decided'. The fourteenth amendment has operated over time as a filter through which an almost infinite variety of social problems could be subjected to a process of 'constitutional translation'. *Brown* 'reasoned about the constitutionality of segregation in context-dependent terms'.[32] This was unavoidable. Constitutional law always emerges out of a given political context. It is always situated and contextualised. This contextualisation of constitutional law is a force as well as an inherent limitation. *Brown* 'left unresolved the constitutionality of segregation in contexts less fundamental than education – that is, most areas of life'.[33] It took a series of other precedents to extend desegregation to other social areas (sports clubs, public transportation, . . .).

17.3.3 *Form and Substance*

The inclusion of education in the field of constitutional subject-matters was predicated upon the capacity of all the parties – from civil rights activists to the Supreme Court – to apply the general

[28] This is not to say, however, that constitutional law is a mere superstructure of these social or economic changes. Law is autonomous in the sense that it is neither entirely conditioned by social fact nor neutral or transparent. Within the legal world, as we shall see, constitutional law is itself an autonomous field.

[29] 347 US 483 (1954).

[30] Ibid., 493.

[31] 63 US 537 (1896).

[32] R. Siegel, 'Equality Talk: Antisubordination and Anticlassification Values in Constitutional Struggles over Brown' (2004) 117 *Harvard Law Review* 1470, 1480.

[33] See M. J. Klarman, 'An Interpretive History of Modern Equal Protection' (1991) 90 *Michigan Law Review* 213.

words of the Fourteenth Amendment to the problem of school segregation. What has mattered, thus, is more the capacity of legal substance to be adjusted to social and political issues than a question of legal form or formal reasoning. As far as our topic is concerned, this example points to a momentous conceptual problem. The discussion on the material constitution is made murkier by the fact that, in the process of giving shape to politics, legal substance is as relevant as legal form. This may not be the case of all the scholars who adhere to the idea of a material constitution, yet the very dichotomy between form and matter runs the risk of falling victim to what one may call a conceptual Manicheism. Form would appear to be one dimension of constitutional reality, while matter would be another such dimension. Yet legal form is always impregnated by a substantive project or purpose. While the idea of a material constitution has the virtue of pointing to aspects of constitutional reality that are not of a legally normative nature (facts, institutions, non-legal norms), it runs the risk of ignoring that constitutional matter always needs to be conveyed by some sort of form, formality or formalism. As the American desegregation cases show, constitutional law deals with politics by way of both its form and its substance.

In the life of the law, form and substance are ultimately indistinguishable. The fence is constantly straddled. In order to embrace political realities, legal thinking has to extend beyond mere forms: formal reasons (legally authoritative reasons on which judges and others are empowered or required to base a decision or action[34]) are rarely sufficient to solve major political issues and 'hard cases'. Despite the dominantly deductive and formalist orientation of many western legal cultures, the legal mind stands out by its tendency to ignore the form/substance divide. This appears in the development of the doctrine of substantive due process of law in the United States. The history of the due process clauses of the Fifth and Fourteenth amendments to the American constitutions is paved with implicit or explicit[35] Magna Charta-style references to political power as something to be 'guaranteed against'. Yet the idea of due process has had a singular propensity to develop as simply an analytical exploration of the wider idea of 'law' as such. 'Increasingly, judges came to believe that using the due process clause to review the substance of state regulation (. . .) could be confined by boundaries derived from common law categories.'[36] Very rapidly – as soon as the *Dred Scott* case (1857)[37] and possibly before[38] – process and content, form and substance, became indistinguishable in the interpretation of the due process clause. The term 'law' has absorbed all the other preceding terms ('due', 'process') in the clause. Its interpretation has extended to substance as well as process, matter as well as form. The judicial history of the due process clause, and even the sub-history of the 'substantive due process' case law, is evidence that invoking the general words of 'due', 'process' and 'law' itself also meant letting many other genies – 'substance', 'spirit' – out of the legal bottle. At the end of the day it is 'every quality of the law'[39] that was required of legislation reviewed under the due process clause.

17.4 CONCLUSION: THE 'GOOD ENOUGH' CONSTITUTION

This chapter has aimed at clarifying the uses of the reference to a constitutional matter by exploring the form versus matter conceptual couple in constitutional law. The core of our case

34 Atiyah and Summers, *Form and Substance*, 2.
35 See *Hurtado* v. *California*.
36 L. Tribe, *American Constitutional Law* (Foundation Press, 1999) vol. I, 1341.
37 60 US 393 (1857).
38 See, for instance, *Trustees of Dartmouth College* v. *Woodward*, 17 US 518 (1819).
39 *Hurtado* v. *California*, 529.

can be summed up as follows: *the form of the constitution is law; the matter of the constitution is politics*. Politics, as a social activity, influences law as much as law, in turn, can govern political action to a certain degree. This is a trite, yet generally overlooked, conclusion. Constitutional formalism is unable to account for the law-politics relationship. What happens in the constitutional sphere stretches beyond the region of the formal constitution. At the same time, reasoning in terms of a material constitution runs the risk, not only of moral subjectivism or political activism but of disregarding the actual interactions between law and politics and, within law, between form and substance. What counts in this regard is a relative degree of fitness between political activity (or matter) and law (in which form and substance are mostly indistinguishable). Not all constitutional formats are capable of accommodating this kind of mutually generative relationship between law and politics. What we should aim at, therefore, is a 'good enough' constitution, not an ideal or perfect one. A 'good enough' constitution is one that allows for political activity to be ultimately generative of institutional power. In return, institutionalised power is expected to shape society in keeping with basic constitutionalist values and principles. It is submitted that such a constitution can be defined as *a principled instrument of self-government*.

The 'written' or 'formal' constitution is – and has to be – an *instrument of self-government*. A constitution ought to be 'a charter for the governance of generations to come'.[40] 'A constitution combines moral and political theory (...) with an assertion of self-government (...) It combines reason and will (...) the fecundity of our commitment to self-government arises out of the diverse accounts we deploy to explain ourselves.'[41] The formal constitution is a document (*instrumentum*) creating a frame of government. The written form – where it exists – matters significantly. There is serious argument and experience supporting the view that a written constitution is preferable to a customary one. Yet form is not self-sufficient. The frame of government ought to have a certain political quality. It ought to be conducive to political autonomy, in the sense of the people being collectively autonomous. Otherwise, it may be a perfectly adequate legal enactment. But it will not be a Constitution. Many such documents around the world bear the title of 'constitution' but do not pass the test of self-government. This accounts for their lack of real authority: they become 'paper constitutions' for this or that kind of authoritarian regime. As a frame of self-government, the constitution 'licenses you to act as you do' and to do so *consciously*: the actor abiding by the constitution, whatever that involves, does so when '[his] all things considered judgments are guided by constitutional principles'.[42] The Constitution expresses the autonomy of the collective body of citizens that has enacted it, or on whose behalf it has been enacted.

A constitution that stifles political activity, therefore, strays from the ideal of the good enough constitution, as it tends to dissociate political matter from legal form. This is of course the case of the so-called constitutions of despotic regimes. But any constitution is at risk of losing track of the ongoing forms of political activity taking place within its confines. In the nineteenth century, representative government appeared to be the best 'fit' between politics and law. Today, this is less clear. The ability of constitutional forms to adjust to new types of social activity and new levels of political involvement on the part of citizens is being put to the test. The fitness between legal form and political matter is a constant challenge for existing constitutions. Where and when this fitness is impaired, institutions lose contact with society. In contemporary France, for instance, there is significant evidence that this is the case. Polls show a severely diminished

40 A. Bickel, *The Least Dangerous Branch: The Supreme Court and the Bar of Politics* (Yale University Press, 1986) 102.
41 Kahn, *Origins of Order*, xiii–xiv.
42 M. Tushnet, *Taking the Constitution Away from the Courts* (Princeton University Press, 1999) 51.

confidence of citizens into institutions and even the democratic principle. Social unrest – as in the case of the *Gilets Jaunes* in France or the storming of the Capitole building on 6 January 2021 in the United States – targets the political regime and its alleged elitism and lack of legitimacy. Institutional solutions such as participative democracy are devised to meet this challenge but they are slow in the making and not always used in good faith. Most countries are faced with a similar phenomenon of the decoupling of social and political activity and the Constitution. This is inevitable. The matter of constitutional law is and will always be politics. New political events and new political representations will always call for 'an unrestricted flow of practical reasoning' as well as for law's capacity to 'proceed by positing a system of rules (...) sealed off from [that] unrestricted flow'.[43] The good (enough) constitution, as a principled instrument of self-government, has to adjust both its form and substance to this protean 'material' reality. Constitutional law stands exactly at the crossroads between society's never-ending debating and quarrel on how it is governed and law's more or less clumsy attempts to impart a form to social reality. Both make for what we call 'self-government'.

[43] These citations are drawn from John Finnis, *Natural Law and Natural Rights*, 2nd ed. (Oxford University Press, 2011), 355. I adhere to the twin ideas of the existence in society of a continuous process of practical reasoning and of law as a 'sealing off' of that process through 'rules of stipulation' (ibid.). But, unlike Finnis, I would not reject 'originating acts and circumstances' as the trigger and the necessary situational content of this process of practical reasoning as well as its legal output (ibid., 350). As I have tried to show in the first part of this essay, our constitutional 'instruments' (written constitutions, bills of rights, constitutional precedents, etc.) have arisen out of certain specific circumstances. It took those political situations for adequate constitutional form and substance to emerge. Our constitutional 'originating acts' have expressed a valuable practical reasoning when confronted by these 'originating circumstances'.

PART III

Analyses

18

A Material Understanding of Constitutional Changes

Revisiting 'Constitutional Maintenance' Doctrines

Graziella Romeo

18.1 THE MATERIAL CONSTITUTION AND CONSTITUTIONAL AMENDMENT PROCEDURES

Mortati's seminal work on the material constitution begins by expressing the need to reformulate the problem of determining the content of the constitution.[1] At the time of his writing, continental European scholarship had long framed this issue as a dispute over the identification of which part or parts of the constitution could be changed only according to a special amendment procedure. The prevailing conceptualisation of constitutional supremacy was indeed quite formalistic and mostly grounded on the theory of the sources of law. As a consequence, the problem of the content of the constitution was inexistent when (a) a constitutional text could not be identified, (b) the principle of parliamentary sovereignty made it impossible to discern which part of the text deserved special treatment or (c) the written constitution was interpreted as capable of conditioning the validity of any other law because of its supremacy. In all those cases, the identification of the constitution was unnecessary either because a constitution was non-existent or because it coincided with a constitutional master text.

According to Mortati, such a frame was based on a flawed reasoning, whereby the content of the constitution was derived from the rigidity of its particular legal transposition.[2] After all, the dominant formalistic logic conceived of the constitution in terms of the nature of its norms, qualified by their peculiar source of validity, whether a constituent power or a presupposed external *Grundnorm*. In either case, the constitution was uncannily unravelling from an a-juridical world. Mortati detected at least two theoretical incongruences in such a conceptual frame. The first one was the artificial creation of legal norms from non-legal realities, a trap from which even Schmitt's theory of the fundamental political decision did not escape.[3] The second, and more significant, incongruence was the identification of the constitution with the existence of a given regulation of facts and relationships that were assumed to be relevant for the life of a certain state by an historically situated constituent power.

Mortati's dissatisfaction with such a conclusion stemmed from his rejection of any formalistic reading of the term 'constitution' as well as from his need to pursue a theory of the constitution that would transcend the circumstances of a particular legal regime. From his perspective, then, the content of the constitution cannot be qualified by the amending procedure necessary to

[1] C. Mortati, *La costituzione in senso materiale* (Giuffrè, 1940), 13–14.

[2] Ibid., 77.

[3] G. Zagrebelsky, 'Premessa', foreword in C. Mortati, *La costituzione in senso materiale* (Giuffrè, 1998), XV.

modify it; rather, resistance to amendment is a characteristic belonging to the constitution as an entity to be isolated through a substantial reading of the moment in which the political decision became law. The material constitution can be traced back to that moment, which coincides with the implementation of conducts designed to establish rules of political relevance. Those rules, deduced from the general ends of a given state, govern the political sphere. Since the material constitution is established by the enforcement of norms of political relevance, Mortati calls it the 'original constitution'. The use of the term 'original' helps him in underlying that the material constitution originates when the dominant class is capable of juridifying, through effective and consistent implementation, its political decision to establish that particular set of values and priorities of political action.[4]

The identification of the material constitution thus unearths the identity of the state or, as Mortati would say, the *form* of the State, a term that continental scholarship uses, to this day, to distinguish and classify a particular arrangement of the relationship between state and citizenry, as connected to the general ends of the state legal order.

Mortati's intellectual effort to identify the material constitution was functional, among other things, to securing state ends through changes that over time affect particular subsets of rules or influence political courses of action in a certain direction. Those changes and political decisions, irrespective of their formalisation, can leave the material constitution untouched or can even attain its broad aims and ends.

In the theory of the material constitution, then, the logical *prius* was the identification problem; once solved, constitutional amendments could be understood by comparing the material constitution and changes in rules or political directions observed in the legal order. Such a theory was precisely designed to shield the essential content of the constitution from the instability (or even capriciousness) of political bodies.[5] But when the practice of writing constitutions, equipped with special amending procedures, became widespread in continental Europe in the years following Mortati's work, the concept of a material constitution was interpreted as a threat to the normativity of the formal document. In continental Europe, constitutional theory was more comfortable theorising constitutional rigidity as the result of the *pouvoir constituant*'s accomplishment of its historical role.

A large part of the scholarly debate on constitutional amendments remained completely indifferent to suggestions coming from the theory of the material constitution until the latter re-emerged to help navigate the slippery territory of informal constitutional amendments. The experience of states equipped with written constitutions is, indeed, one in which constitutional changes frequently take place outside the rules set forth to amend the master text. Against this backdrop, the concept of a material constitution is at times used to understand (a) whether changes have indeed occurred in the essential elements of the constitution and (b) whether these changes are still consistent with the formal (and untouched) written constitution.

This chapter contributes to studies of material constitutions precisely by applying Mortati's concept of the material constitution to theories of constitutional change. In particular, it focuses on 'constitutional maintenance' doctrines elaborated in continental Europe to explain cases of

[4] In *La costituzione in senso materiale*, the term 'original constitution' appears as a synonym for 'material constitution'. In other works, Mortati clarified why the material constitution is also original. In particular, he explained that the material constitution can be seen as a normative fact, meaning that the factual establishment of rules of political relevance as well as the stabilisation of those rules by the ruling classes creates the constitution, which then continues existing thanks to those ruling classes that have originally established it: C. Mortati, *Studi sul potere costituente e sulla riforma costituzionale dello Stato. Raccolta di scritti* (Giuffré, 1972), vol. I, 13.

[5] Morati, *La costituzione*, 20–21.

limited and/or substantively guided constitutional changes that generally elude formal amendment procedures. It argues that, while constitutional maintenance doctrines capture one of the functions of the theory of the material constitution, namely, to guide constitutional changes, they fall into a logical contradiction by identifying the material constitution with some parts of the written constitutional text protected by special amending procedures. As a consequence, those doctrines (a) observe constitutional changes on the basis of mismatches between constitutional practice and the master-text constitution and (b) support the need to minimise those mismatches. It further argues that one reason for such a misuse is the scepticism surrounding the notion of a material constitution in those legal systems equipped with a written text. The argument is preceded by an analysis of doctrinal debates on constitutional change in selected jurisdictions (para. 2). It is then developed by unpacking the material constitution theory in two logical steps. In particular, it focuses on the problem of the identification of the constitution (para. 3) and on the related need to reduce the substantive distance between the formal and the material constitution (para. 4). Finally, the chapter offers conclusions on how material constitutionalism can contribute to studies of constitutional change.

18.2 CONSTITUTIONAL MAINTENANCE: AN ALTERNATIVE READING OF UNCLASSIFIABLE CHANGES TO THE CONSTITUTIONAL TEXT

Constitutional rigidity, defined by the existence of special amending procedures, is linked to the need to protect constitutional values from political capriciousness. It also expresses constitutions' desire for 'immortality', to remain in place no matter how much political circumstances change over time. Constitutional rigidity has proved to be a challenging characteristic of written constitutions. The experience of constitutional states is studded with political parties claiming the need to change constitutional rules so as to improve the functioning of political institutions.[6] Reforms have also been framed as necessary to update the text according to societal transformations.[7] In a significant number of cases, constitutional reforms fail because either the political or the popular consensus required to amend procedures is difficult to achieve.[8] Therefore, under some circumstances, constitutions have been substantially changed through the judicial elaboration of constitutional doctrines, the adoption of ordinary laws or the development of constitutional praxis. These phenomena are evidence of informal constitutional changes, that is of transformation of the constitution without affecting the master text. As a result, scholarship devoted to analysing informal constitutional changes developed in the field of constitutional law. The research question scholars were keen to answer was: How might we identify what counts as a valid constitutional amendment when the formal procedure to change the text has been eluded? Answers vary. In countries with a tradition of unwritten constitutional law, such as

[6] The failed 2016 reform of the Italian Constitution is an example. Proponents of the reform pointed to the need to speed up legislative procedures and advance the efficiency of the whole system of government: S. Bolgherini, 'Crisis-driven Reforms and Local Discretion: An Assessment of Italy and Spain' (2016) 46 *Italian Political Science Review* 71, arguing that the need for reform had been prompted by the global financial crisis, which forced governments to pursue efficiency and fast-track normative procedures. See also M. Morelli and M. Osnabrügge, 'Some Neglected Reasons to Eliminate Perfect Bicameralism: The Italian Constitutional Reform and Legislative Efficiency' (2016) *Vox* 26 November 2016, available at: http://voxeu.org/article/italian-constitutional-reform-and-legislative-efficiency, last accessed 1 August 2022.

[7] T. Donnelly, 'Popular Constitutional Argument' (2020) 73 *Vanderbilt Law Review* 73, 90 also discusses informal changes driven by societal developments.

[8] Italy has a long history of failed constitutional reforms: C. Fusaro and D. Bull, 'Yet Another Failed Attempt to Reform the Italian Constitution' (2017) 32 *Italian Politics* 111.

Canada, the identification problem is fairly recent, as the stratification of uncodified or even undocumented constitutional norms was part of the ordinary development of constitutional law. Scholars there have labelled constitutional changes that escape formalisation 'quasi-constitutional amendments'.[9] They are conceived as 'subconstitutional alteration[s] to the operation of a set of existing norms in the constitution'.[10] Interestingly enough, the formula looks at the constitutional consequences (or effects) of norms introduced in the legal system at a subconstitutional level. The ability of those norms to substantially and durably affect the functioning of the master-text constitution defines their legal status.[11] In the United States, the same phenomena have been branded 'supra-constitutional statutes',[12] while in Australia they go by the name 'constitutional statutes'.[13] The same label has been employed by the UK Supreme Court to describe statutes that resist normal rules of abrogation because they contribute to the delineation of the uncodified British constitution.[14]

The substantively constitutional nature of these statutes is generally not disputed by this line of scholarship. The 'constitutional' qualification is linked to two different features of statutes: (1) they affect the functioning of constitutional institutions, for example by impacting the legislative process and (2) they regulate relationships between the state and its citizens by recognising fundamental rights.

Once the identification problem has been solved, the question turns to the problem of establishing the constitutional legality of these statutes. One can frame the issue along these lines: Can these statutes be subjected to judicial scrutiny, and, if yes, can they resist judicial overview? Many authors have focused their attention on the desirability of constitutional adjudication in constitutional changes, taking for granted that a constitutional change exists any time a clear mismatch between constitutional praxis and the written text is observable.[15]

The Canadian Supreme Court touched upon this issue in the *Senate Reference*.[16] The question under scrutiny was whether Parliament, acting outside the amending procedure, could have reformed the Senate by creating consultative elections to select senatorial nominees endorsed by the populations of provinces and territories.[17]

The Court maintained that Parliament was fundamentally altering the structure of the Constitution, even though the reform would have left untouched the process for appointing individuals to the Senate, which consists of the governor general selecting appointees on the advice of the prime minister.[18] In the Court's view the reform was substantially an informal constitutional change because the Constitution expressly requires the amendment procedure for changes concerning the 'method of selecting senators'. The sentence was interpreted as including procedures impacting how a senator is chosen for the final appointment. The reform was then classified as unconstitutional. The Court argued that to decide otherwise would have

[9] R. Albert, 'Quasi-Constitutional Amendments' (2017) 65 *Buffalo Law Review* 739.
[10] Ibid., 739.
[11] Ibid., 740, citing as an example the Canadian Bill of Rights of 1960.
[12] W. N. Eskridge and J. Ferejohn, 'Super-Statutes' (2001) 50 *Duke Law Journal* 1215, 1216.
[13] S. Stephenson, 'The Rise and Recognition of Constitutional Statutes', in R. Albert and J. I. Colón Ríos (eds.), *Quasi-Constitutionality and Constitutional Statutes* (Routledge, 2019), 27.
[14] F. Ahmed and A. Perry, 'Constitutional Statutes' (2017) 37 *Oxford Journal of Legal Studies* 461, 471.
[15] Albert, 'Quasi-Constitutional Amendments', 763; R. Dixon, 'Partial Constitutional Amendments' (2011) 13 *University of Pennsylvania Journal of Constitutional Law* 643. See also R. Hirschl, 'The Judicialization of Mega-Politics and the Rise of Political Courts' (2008) 11 *Annual Review of Political Science* 93, 97, who observes that courts' adjudication of constitutional amendments is an example of judges' progressive occupation of the political arena.
[16] *Reference re Senate Reform* [2014] 1 S.C.R., para. 62 (Can.).
[17] Ibid., para. 49.
[18] Constitution Act 1867.

meant performing a narrowly formalistic reading of the Constitution. Eventually, the material change happened despite the Court's resistance. As some scholars have pointed out, a political escamotage was put in place to substantially achieve the goal of establishing a different procedure for selecting senators.[19] In particular, now the Advisory Board to the Prime Minister advises him or her about the selection of senators, who are then appointed by the governor general. What is relevant to note here is that the Court identified the constitution with its texts and refused to look into the factual transformations already driven and accepted by political forces.

In continental Europe, scholars and constitutional judges frame the problem in partially different ways. The growth of constitutional law outside the text of constitutions is even less acceptable within legal cultures in which the master-text constitution tends to overlap with constitutional law as such. In some cases, notably Germany, this may depend on a certain conceptualisation of constitutional supremacy, whereby it is defined thanks to a theoretical criterion organising sources of law and conditioning their validity. In such a context, the absence of formalisation is perceived as a deviation of political reality from the constitutional text that expresses the highest political will, even when only fictitiously attributed to the people.[20] This is not to say that material readings are extraneous to German constitutional culture. Quite the contrary. The classical reference is Schmitt's notion of the 'fundamental political decision', a concept synthesising the political will identifying a people and uniting them under a constitution.[21] The notion echoes Mortati's material constitution to a certain extent. In particular, Schmitt and Mortati agree on the unifying function of the constitution created by an act of political will, historically situated. Assonances, though, end here, because for Mortati that political will can only be expressed by a portion of 'the people'; that portion that is politically active and capable of overcoming competing social forces.

Traces of material understanding of the constitutional state can be found in other authors writing in the years of the Weimar Republic. Indeed, in that period, the legal literature discussing the meanings and limits of constitutional change, whether realised or not through formal amending procedures, looked at material transformations of the legal order. Jacobi used the term '*Verfassungsdurchbrechung*' for an alteration of the constitution substantively determined by a presidential decision that leaves the constitutional text untouched and yet breaches the constitution.[22] And Heller's distinction between *Rechtsgrundsätze* (founding juridical values) and *Rechtssätze* (established rules)[23] resonates with Mortati's argument about the juridical value of the original constitution from which the written constitution derives. Nevertheless, if one looks at contemporary constitutional scholarship, the dominant position is that the written fundamental law is (and should be) coextensive with the German polity.[24] The constitutional text supports this conclusion by stating, in Art. 79, that the Basic Law can be modified only by a law, to be adopted with a special procedure, amending or expressly integrating the text of the

19 Albert, 'Quasi-Constitutional Amendments', 763.

20 As is the case for the Basic law of 1949: see D. Grimm, 'Constituent Power and Limits of Constitutional Amendments' (2016) 2 *Nomos* 2.

21 C. Schmitt, *Constitutional Theory* (Duke University Press, 2008).

22 E. Jacobi, Die Diktatur des Reichspräsidenten nach art. 48 der Reichsverfassung (1924) 1 *VVdDStRL* 1, 109. The classification of constitutional changes has been developed by E. W. Böckenförde, *Staat, Verfassung, Demokratie. Studien zur Verfassungstheorie und zum Verfassungsrecht* [I quote from the Italian translation, *Stato, costituzione, democrazia. Studi di teoria della costituzione e di diritto costituzionale*] (Giuffrè, 2006), 603.

23 H. Heller, *Staatslehre* (Sijthoff, 1934), 175.

24 D. P. Kommers and R. A. Miller, *The Constitutional Jurisprudence of the Federal Republic of Germany* (Durham University Press, 2012), 47.

Basic Law.[25] To this extent, any material reading of the constitution, which is not functional to its amendment, would endanger the body of values and principles that a particular Basic Law entrusted political powers to enforce.[26]

An alternative framework of analysis of constitutional changes is the one offered by 'constitutional maintenance' doctrines. A version has been theorised in Italy, where constitutional amending procedures rarely succeed, and para-constitutional techniques and practices have been pursued to achieve constitutional changes. Alessandro Pizzorusso coined the expression 'constitutional maintenance' to indicate modifications, updates and corrections to the existing constitutional text incorporating factual or normative changes developed after its entry into force.[27] Truth be told, Pizzorusso did not intend to build a normative theory of constitutional changes, rather he described what he thought was a way to circumvent the Constitution and its normativity: adopting rules with a clear constitutional impact that were justified as necessary to keep formal constitutional rules in good shape or even to realise constitutional imperatives. Later, Italian scholars developed the doctrine, which also put forward a partially different understanding of what is involved in constitutional maintenance. This concept is now also used to label constitutional changes entailing formal revisions and consisting of minor (*revisione minima*) or strictly focused changes (*revisione mirata*) to the constitutional text.[28] These changes affect the functioning of the legal order without altering the essential values that the Constitution has established.

The idea of constitutional maintenance draws from the theory of the material constitution. In fact, it incorporates the core intuition behind Mortati's original notion of the material constitution: the dominant political force's (or forces') understanding of the essential values and ends of the state does not only define the original constitution, it also drives constitutional changes. The material constitution unfolds beyond the formal constitution in the daily life of the legal order. Therefore, the identification of the material constitution becomes the theoretical tool used to distinguish between those changes that, albeit informally achieved, are still within constitutional boundaries and those modifications that alter the essential values and ends of the formal constitution. These latter modifications can even be performed according to amending procedures and still represent a substantive violation of the Constitution. The Italian Constitutional Court partially agreed to this idea when it stated that the Constitution expresses supreme principles not encapsulated by explicit limitations to amending power. These 'supreme principles of the constitutional order' on the one hand cannot be altered, even by resorting to the special amending procedure, and on the other represent the parameters that are used to assess the validity of constitutional amendments.[29]

The paradigm of constitutional maintenance, albeit with some relevant alterations, has circulated beyond Italy. In Portugal, it was used to explain reforms that, although approved through the formal amending procedure, went beyond a constitutional revision by implying a complete change of the constitutional paradigm, which was closer to an exercise of constituent power. In fact, the 1976 socialist constitution was converted into a liberal-democratic one via

[25] See Art. 79, German Grundgesetz.

[26] J. Limbach, 'The Concept of the Supremacy of the Constitution' (2001) 64 *Modern Law Review* 1, 7 argues that the job of the Federal Constitutional Court 'is to tie policy to law, and subordinate it to law'.

[27] A. Pizzorusso, *La costituzione ferita* (Laterza, 1999), 47, and A. Pizzorusso, 'Le riforme costituzionali: una transizione per destinazione sconosciuta' (2005) 128 *Il Foro Italiano* 217.

[28] F. Palermo, 'La "manutenzione costituzionale": alla ricerca di una funzione', in F. Palermo (ed.), *La Manutenzione Costituzionale* (CEDAM, 2007), 4.

[29] Italian Constitutional Court dec. no. 1146 of 1988, para. 2.1.

progressive transformations of the original master text, which started shortly after the establishment of the first democratic government. In particular, while the 1976 Constitution declared Portugal to be in transition to the socialist form of state, the Partido Social Democrata, a right-wing party which led the government from 1978 to 1983 after the fall of the coalition government led by the Socialist Party, modified the master-text to reduce ideological references to the socialist state.[30] When the Socialist Party lost the 1985 elections, the right wing coalition introduced a new constitutional revision in 1989 which completed the transformation of the economic model of the Constitution by eliminating any residual reference to the socialist state and by supressing the principle of irreversibility of nationalisations predating 25 April 1974, the date of the revolution overthrowing the authoritarian regime.[31]

When the process of suppression of the socialist paradigm was completed, some scholars labelled this phenomenon an 'ideological neutralization of the Constitution'.[32] Interestingly enough, other scholars, including those who participated as members of the 1976 Constituent Assembly, did not interpret those changes as a political act of instauration of a new regime. Instead, they read constitutional reforms, at least the ones affecting the frame of government, as the mere formalisation of constitutional practices that had been accepted since 1976.[33] Moreover, according to this line of scholarship, the 1976 Constitution lived on through constitutional reforms because the latter only represented a progressive dilution of the revolutionary constituent act that ended the dictatorship, along with its 1933 Constitution. In fact, the master text can be subjected to changes to develop the principles of the 1976 Constitution itself, without altering the essential values and organisational principles, as inferable by the master text.

To support their argument, those scholars pointed to the substantive limits to constitutional revision, included in Art. 290 of the Portuguese Constitution (Art. 288 of the Constitution now in force). Those limits would delineate the material constitution (or the state's fundamental identity) by describing, if taken all together, a democratic and rule-of-law-based state (*Estado de direito democrático*).[34] That notion in turn defines the Portuguese material constitution.[35]

Notably, Art. 290 itself was amended in 1989 to remove ideological references to socialism.[36] In particular, the principle of collective appropriation of means of production was reformulated into that of coexistence of public, private, cooperative and social property of means of production. Moreover, the principle of democratic economic planning was replaced by the principle according to which economic planning is established within the framework of a mixed economic system. Still, the argument concerning the continuity of the constitution throughout these transformations withstood. According to Portuguese scholars, the choice to abandon the socialist project was compatible with the material constitution, being a particular development of its content and a dilution of ideological premises that was not questioning the fundamental option for a democratic and rule-of-law-based state.[37] In other words, the formal constitution was subjected to maintenance to preserve consistency with the evolution of the material one.

30 Lei Constitucional n. 1/82, Diário da República n. 227/1982, Série I de 1982-09-30, 3135–206.

31 The revisions are summarised by J. Miranda, 'A originalidade e as principais características da Constituição Portuguesa' (2007) 16 *Cuestiones constitucionales* 270.

32 A. De Sousa Franco and G. D'Oliveira Martins, *A constituição económica portuguesa. Ensaio interpretativo* (Almedina, 1993), 147.

33 J. Miranda, *Manual de Direito Constitucional*, 3rd ed. (Almedina, 1991), vol. II, 182 and J. J. G. Canotilho and V. Moreira, *Constituição da República portuguesa anotada* (Almedina, 1993), 1062.

34 Miranda, *Manual de Direito Constitucional*, 184.

35 Miranda, 'A originalidade e as principais características da Constituição Portuguesa', 279.

36 Art. 191, Lei Constitucional n.1/89, Diário da República n. 155/1989, Suplemento n. 1, Série I de 1989-07-08.

37 Miranda, 'A originalidade e as principais características da Constituição Portuguesa', 280.

Mortati's view resonates in the argument put forward by Portuguese constitutional maintenance scholarship. At the same time, however, those theories reverse the relationship between the formal and the material constitution. To explain this point, let us come back to Mortati's theory.

Along with Mortati, Portuguese scholars single out the original constitution, identified with a number of principles, to be secured from political instability. This creates a distinction from the master-text constitution formed by rules that encapsulate a provisional arrangement of relationships, which are in turn exposed to changes according to the particular directions determined by dominant political forces. Portuguese scholars, however, pushed the argument, going so far as to maintain the continuity of the original constitution even through changes that profoundly reshaped the economic constitution, realising the transition from a socialist paradigm to a full-fledged free market economy. Being the material constitution identified with the principle of the democratic and rule-of-law-based state, the option for either a socialist or mixed economy system was understood as equivalent to a particular specification of that form of state. Thus, a radical change in the formal constitution became a development of the ordinary life of the 1976 Constitution. The formalisation of new principles concerning the regulation of economic activities was deemed to be a step in the process of settlement of the material constitution. The logical premise is that the material (real) constitution is not entirely encapsulated in the master text; the consequence is the need to update the formal constitution so as to secure the endurance of the material one.

On a more general level, the constitutional maintenance doctrine employs Mortati's idea of the irreducibility of the material constitution to the formal one to explain the practice of constitutional changes. In his work, Mortati clarified that the constitution is there to give stability to the form of the state it has created. Therefore, on the one hand, the identification of the material constitution is decisive in detecting the continuity of the legal order through changes it will inevitably face; on the other, the constitution contemplates transformations because it has an intrinsic planning (or forward-looking) capacity that does not end with the formalisation of (some) rules. If the material constitution is a source of constitutional rules, however, it does not need to be formalised to express its authority. Rather, constitutional rules, codified or not, should always conform with the material constitution in the sense that, when conformity is lost, the material constitution ends its life. This event, in turn, signals a crisis of dominant political forces or even the exhaustion of their ruling power.

From Mortati's notion of the material constitution, constitutional maintenance doctrines deduce that transformations fulfilled by means of judicial interpretation, ordinary laws or substantively constitutional statutes are entitled to complete the formal constitution. By the same coin, according to those doctrines, constitutional amendments can be justified by the need to codify these transformations. In fact, the latter already belong to the constitutional order in two complementary senses. First of all, these transformations have been accepted by the ruling political class and integrated into the ordinary life of the legal order. Secondly, these changes are consistent with the material constitution, understood as the body of substantive values and organisational conceptions largely accepted and capable of producing rules of constitutional relevance by also granting their coherent application.

However, while constitutional maintenance doctrines draw from the theory of the material constitution the need to identify the original constitution beyond both the master text and constitutional law, understood as the body of rules surrounding the functioning of the constitutional order, these doctrines tend to detect changes by measuring constitutional practice against the backdrop of the master text for then pushing for formalising changes in constitutional rules. That is why some scholars go further, maintaining that the formal constitution must continuously keep up with the material one by including any change that signals that a substantial transformation has taken place within the legal order. Examined closely, these conclusions reveal that constitutional maintenance doctrines misunderstand the logic of the material constitution. In order to explore this misunderstanding, the following paragraphs are dedicated to analysing, separately, (a) the problem of identifying the constitution and its changes and (b) the argument for realising an almost complete overlap between the formal and the material constitution.

18.3 THE PROBLEM OF IDENTIFYING THE CONSTITUTION AND ITS CHANGES

Theories of constitutional change, including maintenance doctrines, build on the need to conceptualise constitutional transformations that do not comply, either substantially or formally, with prescribed amending procedures. These theories share a certain methodological approach: A constitutional change is always measured against the backdrop of the constitutional text or of its prevalent interpretations. Constitutional maintenance doctrines are no exception. According to such doctrines, constitutional transformations, which can take different forms, represent deviations from the master text. The distinguishing trait of constitutional maintenance theory is that a deviation is considered to fall within the boundaries of what is constitutionally permissible if it corresponds to the material constitution. Constitutional maintenance doctrine, therefore, draws from Mortati's material constitutional reading only to a limited extent. Indeed, Mortati's theory of the material constitution moves from the premise that the master text is not coextensive with the 'constitution'. His intellectual project places itself within a legal culture that rejects positivism's radical attempt to force the whole juridical experience into formalised imperatives.[38] At the same time, Mortati does not discard positivism *tout court*. Rather, he uses methodological positivism to argue that the material constitution is juridical *par excellence* because the social forces establishing it also guarantee its enforcement. In other words, the material constitution exists – and it can be studied – as a juridical norm. The material constitution, therefore, is an authoritative 'ought to be' shaping the course of political action as well as the essential functioning of the legal order. If the material constitution is juridical, it creates norms operating without the mediation of the formal constitution. At the same time, the material constitution contains the potential for its own development. In fact, its nature rests on its ability to impose rules as well as to impress a political direction on the legal order. As a consequence, constitutional changes in the sense of transformations of the original constitution do not happen until there is an observable shift in the values and practices of the dominant political force.

If one takes Mortati's viewpoint, theories of constitutional change suffer from what can be labelled as a 'legal positivist bias'. The problem such theories intend to solve is one of tracing constitutional transformations that escape formal amending procedures back to some sort of legal positivist logic. They do this either by defending the need to adjudicate those transformations against the backdrop of the master-text constitution or by arguing for the need to formalise those parts of the material constitution that have not yet been translated into positive law. In either case, the problem of constitutional change is framed by the assumption that the master-text constitution expresses a higher form of legality than the material constitution. To put it differently, theories of constitutional change do not escape the normativist approach when they

[38] Mortati, *La costituzione*, 227–28.

identify the constitution with one or more legal documents to which a constitutional value is substantially or formally attached. Interestingly enough, this is the case even in those legal cultures in which constitutions, being the result of a long series of transformations and arrangements, cannot be entirely identified with constitutional texts. An example is Canada where the written constitutional text coexists with customary constitutional law and yet scholars would feel the need to discuss constitutional changes by looking at deviation between constitutional practice and the master text.[39]

Against this backdrop, what a material reading of the constitution suggests is to reset the methodological framing by addressing the preliminary problem of identifying the constitution. This is something that theories of constitutional change do not seem interested in doing. In the English-speaking world, the problem is apparently solved by resorting to the common law understanding of the term constitution. By valuing the development of the constitution through history and political transformations,[40] these theories assume that the mutability of the constitution is not so much an issue of the alteration of a given, settled, arrangement of powers and relationships as a progressive, historical development. The more intriguing constitutional issue becomes understanding the limits of judicial adjudication in the case of constitutional transformations.[41]

On the contrary, for scholars analysing legal cultures in which a constitutional text has been adopted following a formal constituent phase, the task of identifying the constitution cannot be conceptually separated from the problem of ensuring the full normativity of the written text.[42] If the constitution is the political decision encapsulated in the master text, it should be enforced in all its particulars.[43] At the same time, any attempt to enlarge the range of what counts as the constitutional norm is generally disfavoured by scholarship and courts on account of the risk of undermining the normativity of the written constitution.[44] When observed from this perspective, constitutional maintenance doctrines try to address a conceptual conundrum: making sense of the existence of substantive constitutional norms while protecting the normativity of the written text. They do so by suggesting that informal changes fall within the constitutional umbrella so long as they represent transformations accepted and enforced by those social and political forces supporting the formal constitution. Such a doctrine adopts the methodology of constitutional materialism without fully embracing its premise, that is the dismissal of the conceptual framework of constitutional rigidity as linked to special amending requirements. At least in Mortati's version of constitutional materialism, the constitution is flexible in terms of its ability to shape the legal order beyond the original act of establishing a written text. Rules, having the same force as constitutional provisions, can be directly derived from the material constitution. Therefore, the fundamental setting of the legal order, as defined and enforced by the political forces

[39] Albert, 'Quasi-Constitutional Amendments'.

[40] S. Gardbaum, 'The Place of Constitutional Law in the Legal System', in M. Rosenfeld and A. Saj´o (eds.), *Oxford Handbook of Comparative Constitutional Law* (Oxford University Press, 2013), 167.

[41] Y. Rosnai, *Unconstitutional Constitutional Amendments* (Oxford University Press, 2017). See in particular the chapter on implicit constitutional unamendability.

[42] M. Luciani, 'Costituzionalismo irenico e costituzionalismo polemico' (2006) 4 *Giurisprudenza costituzionale* 1643.

[43] M. Kumm, 'Who's Afraid of the Total Constitution? Constitutional Rights as Principles and the Constitutionalization of Private Law' (2006) 7 *German Law Journal* 341.

[44] M. Dogliani, 'Costituzione in senso formale, materiale, strutturale e funzionale. A proposito di una riflessione di Günther Teubner sulle tendenze autodistruttive dei sistemi sociali' (2009) 15 *Diritto pubblico* 295; S. Fois, *Costituzione legale e costituzione materiale, La costituzione materiale. Percorsi culturali e attualità di un'idea* (Giuffrè, 2001), 36. There is no shortage of scholars who insist on the importance of not reducing constitutional law to the master-text constitution: A. Barbera, 'Ordinamento costituzionale e carte costituzionali' (2010) 30 *Quaderni costituzionali* 311.

endorsing the formal constitution, is translated in formal constitutional provisions and legislative acts as well as in constitutional practice.[45] As a consequence, amending procedures merely describe how to modify the master-text constitution; they do not contribute to the definition of what counts as constitutional norms. This is possible because the original constitution is not entirely included in the formal constitution; therefore, the special amending procedure does not operate as a criterion to distinguish what can be classified as constitutional and what cannot possibly claim such a nature.

A material account of constitutional practice is based on the identification of an original constitution which, at the same time, founds the legal order and outlines the trajectories of constitutional courses of political action. This original constitution may or may not contemplate some changes to the specific arrangement made by the master text. Variances are measurable by looking at the original constitution, while the mere fact that a parliament passes a law of substantively constitutional significance should not provoke alarm in the political community. The theoretical risk of using a material constitutional frame to justify constitutional changes as a matter of accepted practice without clarity on the identity of the constitution is one of confusing the logic of the material constitution with that of customary constitutional law, where constitutional rules are the result of a series of historical developments that contribute to shaping a political regime, while they do not intend to prescribe future evolutions. This is not to say that in evolutionary systems, such as those with no documented constitution (UK) or with a flexible constitution (New Zealand), a material constitution cannot be identified. Rather, the logic of identification is different. Under a customary constitutional law framework, the constitution is identified as a structure built over time and ordered according to a rationalising principle, that is, that of parliamentary sovereignty.[46] In a material constitution frame, the constitution is identified by detecting the juridification of a political foundational decision. The practical threat of using a material constitutional frame to justify constitutional changes is one of legitimising political capriciousness: Precisely what a material understanding of the constitution intends to avoid by insisting on the identification of the founding traits of the constitutional order.

18.4 IS THERE A NEED TO MATCH THE MATERIAL CONSTITUTION WITH THE FORMAL ONE?

Theories of constitutional change develop from the observation of mismatches between the formal constitution and the functioning of institutions and/or the organisation of constitutionally relevant legal relationships, as realised through praxis, judicial interpretations or legislative reforms. They work on the assumption that mismatches are anomalies in the life of a written constitution. Moreover, these theories generally call for the minimisation of misalliances between the formal and the substantial constitution because misalliances threaten the normativity of the master text. Constitutional maintenance doctrines reason along the same lines when they support constitutional reforms on the basis of the need to align constitutional texts to transformations already taking place within the political community. In Italy, for example, promoters of the failed 2016 constitutional reform faced harsh criticism from scholars claiming that the proposed constitutional change went beyond the substantive limits to the amending power. They responded by invoking the need to incorporate into the master text those

[45] Barbera, 'Ordinamento costituzionale e carte costituzionali', 313, argues for replacing the material constitution formula with the concept of a 'constitutional order'.

[46] G. Gee and G. Webber, 'Rationalism in Public Law' (2013) 76 *Modern Law Review* 708, 724.

transformations already taking place in Italian constitutional practice without touching the essential identity of the Italian Constitution.[47] Portuguese constitutional reforms profoundly changing the economic constitution were justified by resorting to similar arguments.[48]

Arguments of such a kind overlook a pivotal element of Mortati's material constitutionalism. The material reading of constitutionalism does not just unveil the political decision that lies at the origin of any constitution, it attributes to that political decision a juridical value, making it a driving force for both the establishment *and* the development of the legal order. In materialist accounts, there is no necessary factual overlap between the formal and the material constitution, nor is such an overlap required or even desirable. The political forces establishing the original constitution safeguard the continuity of their legal order by making sure that the constitution unfolds in the changing circumstances of the life of any political community. This is the reason why the material constitution cannot be entirely absorbed by the formal one.

The utility of the notion of the material constitution, then, is one of providing the legal order with an instrument to identify its founding norms. Those norms drive constitutional changes and assist interpreters and legal practitioners in navigating those transformations of the political community that neither alter the original constitution, nor find in the master text their sole source of legitimisation. Material constitutionalism readings are not interested in pursuing the co-extensivity between the formal constitution and the political community, that is the overlap between the master-text constitution and the reality of relationships of constitutional relevance, a co-extensivity that a large part of European continental scholarship deems to be indispensable to guarantee the normativity of the (written) constitution.[49] The all-powerfulness of the master-text constitution, when it comes to regulating relationships of constitutional relevance, is a problem that material readings of the constitution do not intend to solve for two distinctive, though related, reasons. First, the master-text constitution stems from the original constitution, being one peculiar manifestation of founding norms. As a consequence, there are portions of the original constitution not captured by the text that are still equipped with normative power. From a material constitutionalist standpoint, then, there is no logical necessity to conclude that the written text should absorb the material constitution, whose normativity is even stronger than that of the formal constitution or master text.[50] This means that any account justifying the need to change the constitution in order to include those constitutional practices that exist without being codified misreads the logic of material constitutionalism.

Second, the material constitution is dynamic in the sense that the political forces that established it also intend to keep it alive through the life and vicissitudes of the legal order. The preservation of constitutional founding values and norms allows dominant political forces to modify secondary or marginal elements without endangering the original constitution. This is not equivalent to maintaining that the constitution is inherently flexible or open to all possible legislative changes. Rather, the dynamism of the original constitution rests in its ability to determine political courses of action that fulfil the same state ends as those the dominant political forces connected to the establishment of the original constitution. Although the constitution is dynamic, there are limitations to its ability to change. Its founding values and

[47] See the foreword to a volume supporting the reform written by the former Minister for Constitutional Reforms: M. E. Boschi, 'Prefazione', in C. Fusaro et al. (eds.), *Perchè sì* (Laterza, 2016), 5–8.

[48] Italian Constitutional Court dec. no. 1146 of 1988, para. 2.1.

[49] Luciani, 'Costituzionalismo irenico', 1665.

[50] A constitution to the nth degree, in Mortati's words: Mortati, *La costituzione*, 136.

norms cannot be altered without resulting in a constitutional breach and the end of the ruling political forces' power to enforce their original constitution.[51]

Therefore, from a materialist standpoint, the problem of constitutional change is one of detecting whether the original constitution defining both fundamental values and aims that drive political actions, supported by dominant political forces, still stands. To shift the focus from the original constitution to the master text is a substantial rejection of the basic assumption behind Mortati's theory of the material constitution.

18.5 CONCLUSIONS

This chapter suggests that constitutional maintenance doctrines misuse Mortati's theory of the material constitution when they adapt its logic to a concept of constitutional rigidity that is defined by the existence of special amending procedures. One reason for such a misuse is the scepticism surrounding the notion of a material constitution in those legal systems equipped with a written text. In particular, scholars often suspect the material constitution to compete with or even to replace the formal one, thus exposing the constitutional order to political arbitrariness or even legitimising authoritarian drifts.[52]

Mortati did not intend the material constitution to oppose the formal one. In fact, he believed in consistency between the two; where consistency was lost, it was because the dominant political forces had lost their ability to enforce the rules on which the fulfilment of their ends depended. Yet his critique of legal positivism can easily be misinterpreted as an attack on the normativity of the written text. This may be because rationalist epistemology supports the practice of writing down constitutions so as to completely conform the reality to an act of political will, a practice that is fundamentally extraneous to Mortati's notion of the material constitution. It is also extraneous to material understandings more generally because material constitutionalism suggests reading the legal order through a constitutional matrix that is irreducible to the written text. Therefore, it is difficult to reconcile material constitutional readings with an idea of constitutional rigidity that is linked to the existence of a special procedure to amend the master-text constitution. That special procedure is a formal safeguard for only a portion of constitutional reality, precisely that portion that has been captured by the written constitution.

Mortati's version of material constitutionalism cannot provide theories of constitutional change with an account of constitutional transformations that seek to detect modifications and assess their legitimacy against the backdrop of a written text. The whole theory is built on a different premise, namely the existence of an original constitution that is the expression of a constitutional super-legality. Similarly, it cannot help in legitimising *ex post* constitutional changes on the assumption that they are rooted in and accepted by dominant political forces. Doing so would imply equating material constitutionalism and customary constitutional law, diluting the independent juridical value of the original constitution to the verification of constitutional practice in particular circumstances.

Contributions that material constitutionalism can offer to theories of constitutional change have something to do with how we frame the problem of constitutional change from a methodological standpoint. First of all, material constitutionalism argues for an interpretation of notions such as constitutional rigidity or flexibility that is disconnected from formalist

[51] Mortati, *La costituzione*, 20.

[52] Luciani, 'Costituzionalismo irenico', 1663.

accounts. It excludes the proceduralisation, and thus formalisation, of constitutional changes as a criterion to prove the rigidity of a given constitution. Therefore, material constitutionalism can help to classify changes through the analysis of constitutional reality as the combination of text, interpretation, institutional praxis and political action.

Second, material constitutionalism separates the problem of constitutional change from that of identifying the constituent power and the correlative constituted power. The notion of the material constitution distinguishes itself from that of constituent power because the former does not realise itself in the founding of the written constitution. On the contrary, it intends to direct the future development of both the constitution and the constitutional order. At the same time, the material constitution is not a permanent constituent power because it contains its own limitations, namely the values and the principles that the dominant political forces deem to be indispensable to realising their ideology or vision of the state. By not relying on the notion of constituent power, material constitutionalism offers explanations of constitutional practice that are not bound by a binary choice between legitimising constitutional changes accepted by the political community, as constitutional maintenance doctrines tend to do, and claiming constitutional discontinuities or ruptures any time a significant change affects the constitutional order.

Finally, the notion of the material constitution elucidates the founding values and norms of a constitutional order so as to identify the essential limits of constitutional amendment. It is therefore relevant for interpretative practices, whether instrumental or not, to assess the validity of constitutional changes.

19

The Material Constitution in Latin American Courts

Mariana Velasco-Rivera and Joel Colón-Ríos

The notion of the constitution in the material sense, or the material constitution, is not so popular among lawyers. To the extent that it points toward a series of non-specified norms relating to the basic structure of government and to the relationship between citizens and the state, it lacks a key feature associated with legal rules: its susceptibility to be identified by reference to some rule of recognition. There may even be aspects of the material constitution (e.g., unwritten conventions) that, although easily identifiable, are not constitutional *law*, and others that can only be found in judgments that determine the scope and limits of fundamental rights. The constitution in the formal sense, in contrast, would seem to allow lawyers to identify the relevant constitutional content with the precision of a natural scientist. All norms that, by virtue of being included in a specific document, are protected from the ordinary law-making process (through their subjection to a special amendment rule) can be easily categorised as part of the formal constitution. Nonetheless, the material constitution has often played important legal functions. In this chapter, we will focus on two judgments of Latin American constitutional courts where, by relying on a specific conception of the material constitution, judges sought to define the competence of the amending authority and justify or reject the imposition of implicit limits to the power of constitutional reform.

We will proceed in the following way. Section 19.1 highlights the relationship between the notion of the constitution in the material sense and the doctrine of the historical (or the internal) constitution. The doctrine of the historical constitution, we will argue, should be understood as an early formulation of the more recent idea of the constitution in the material sense. In fact, the historical and the material constitution are in most ways indistinguishable from each other even though, as we will see, the former (unlike the latter) involves a rejection of the theory of constituent power. In Section 19.2, we consider two instances of judicial engagement with the notion of the material constitution. The most obvious role that one would expect the material constitution to assume in a judicial context is that of serving to justify the imposition of limits to the amending authority. That is to say, that every constitution is characterised by a 'material' content that cannot be the subject of a constitutional amendment. The first judgment to be considered, issued by the Constitutional Tribunal of Peru, provides an example of this phenomenon, even though, interestingly, it was the 'historical' constitution which became the key operating concept.

The second judgment is a dissenting opinion issued by Justice Humberto Sierra Porto at the Constitutional Court of Colombia. The dissent explicitly engaged with the concept of the material constitution to criticise the majority's adoption of the doctrine of unconstitutional

constitutional amendments. For the dissenting judge, that doctrine allows a non-elected entity to identify the content of the material constitution and then place it outside of the scope of the amending authority of democratically elected institutions. These two judgments exemplify how, perhaps because of its non-specificity, the concept of the material constitution can be deployed by jurists to defend opposite positions about the limits of constitutional reform. One key difference between the approaches presented in these two cases is their understating of the way fundamental constitutional content should be created or re-created. For the Peruvian Constitutional Tribunal, that content should be ultimately determined by the people; under the approach advanced by Justice Sierra Porto, it would be in the hands of the ordinary amendment authority. The chapter ends with a brief reflection about the uses of the concept of the material constitution in Latin American courts, and about its relation to principles developed at the level of international law.

19.1 FROM THE HISTORICAL TO THE MATERIAL CONSTITUTION

The conceptual origins of the notion of the constitution in the material sense are to be found in the doctrine of the historical constitution.[1] This doctrine was influential in several jurisdictions during the eighteenth and nineteenth centuries, particularly Spain. It continues to be relevant in different countries,[2] even though the concept of the constitution in the material sense has largely replaced the idea expressed by it. According to the doctrine of the historical constitution, each society is governed by a set of fundamental norms that develop through history and that reflect the way of being of the community in question. In Spain, its main proponent was Gaspar Melchor de Jovellanos, who died shortly before the country adopted its first written constitution in 1812.[3] 'What is a constitution', Jovellanos wrote, but the 'fundamental laws that fix the rights of the sovereign and the subjects, and the healthy means of preserving both?'[4] These fundamental laws, which he called the 'effective or historical' constitution, were to be found in 'our old codes, in our ancient chronicles, in our depreciated manuscripts and dusty archives'.[5] Since the historical constitution was formed slowly through the ages, '[t]o think that a constitution can be made just in the same way that someone creates a play or a novel is a great insanity'.[6] Jovellanos insisted that not even the nation had the right to 'alter the form and the essence' of that 'received constitution'.[7]

[1] This view was held by Luis Sánchez Agesta who, noting the similarities between the historical/internal constitution and the material one, maintained that 'the *internal* constitution is a fact that is prior to any formal juridical declaration; it is what we would today call the *material* constitution, using the unhappy term with which we have replaced the suggestive one invented by the Spaniards of the 19th century': L. Sánchez Agesta, 'Los Principios del Constitucionalismo Español: Soberanía Nacional y Constitución Interna', in *Archivo de Derecho Público* (Universidad de Granada, 1953), 29.

[2] See, for example, Article R(3) of the Constitution of Hungary (2011): 'The provisions of the Fundamental Law shall be interpreted in accordance with their purposes, the National Avowal and the achievements of our historical constitution'. For a discussion, see F. Hörcher, 'Is the Historical Constitution of Hungary Still a Living Tradition? A Proposal for Reinterpretation', in A. Górnisiewicz & B. Szlachta (eds.), *The Concept of Constitution in the History of Political Thought* (De Gruyter, 2017), 89–112.

[3] Not counting the French-imposed *Estatuto de Bayona*.

[4] G. M. de Jovellanos, 'Memoria sobre Educación Pública, o sea Tratado Teórico Práctico de Enseñanza', in C. Nocedal (ed.), *Obras Públicas e Inéditas* (Biblioteca de Autores Españoles, 1858), vol. II, 39.

[5] G. M. de Jovellanos, 'Carta a Antonio Fernández de Prado' (Gijón, 7 December 1795), in C. Nocedal (ed.), *Obras Públicas e Inéditas* (Biblioteca de Autores Españoles, 1858), vol. III, 179–80.

[6] 'Diarios Inéditos de Jovellanos', cited in J. Somoza, *Las Amarguras de Jovellanos* (Auseva, 1989), 178.

[7] Jovellanos, 'Memoria', vol. IV, 585.

The doctrine can be summarised as follows. First, there are certain parts of a country's constitution, normally related to the structure of government (for instance, the sovereignty of the Crown-in-Parliament), that cannot be modified. In this context, saying that certain norms 'cannot be modified' does not simply mean that their modification would be illegal (in fact, it may be perfectly legal) but that the very idea of 'modifying' them made no sense: the fundamental laws that regulate the structure of government are simply inseparable from the relevant society. If there is a written constitution, it must reflect those fundamental laws and, if it fails to do so, it would be impossible for it to guarantee social stability; it would not even work as a constitution.[8] Second, the doctrine of the historical constitution radically negated the theory of constituent power. The idea of 'creating' a constitution was, for proponents of the historical constitution like Jovellanos, a ridiculous notion.[9] Constitutions were a product of history, not of the momentary will of an assembly or group of individuals. In this respect, a constitution-making episode was always a potential repudiation of this doctrine. In the Spanish Constitution of 1812, that repudiation was explicit: 'Sovereignty resides essentially in the Nation, and for this reason it has the exclusive right of establishing its fundamental rights'.[10]

19.1.1 *The Material Constitution*

The constitution in the material sense shares the key element of the doctrine of the historical constitution: the view that there are certain precepts that are so fundamental that they form part of a country's constitution even if they do not find expression in a written constitutional text, that is, in the constitution in the formal sense. Nevertheless, as we will see in this section, it does not necessarily involve the rejection of the theory of constituent power. The precepts that comprise the material constitution have been generally associated to the form of government (as in the doctrine of the historical constitution) and with the protection of certain rights. In constitutional theory, one finds two main conceptions of the material constitution: a descriptive and a normative one.[11] Hans Kelsen, for example, had a descriptive conception. For him, the material constitution referred to the rules that established the procedures for the creation of the law.[12] Kelsen's conception is descriptive because no special juridical consequences derive from it: the rules that are part of the material constitution can be modified in the same way as any other norm, provided that the relevant procedure is followed. Accordingly, it is an approach that would be of limited use to courts attempting to review the substance of the norms adopted through the established amendment procedure.

Carl Schmitt, on the contrary, developed a normative conception of the material constitution (which he called 'the constitution in the positive sense').[13] The material constitution, for him, referred to the fundamental decision of the constituent subject about its mode of political existence. Schmitt's conception points to the same kind of content captured by Kelsen's as well as by the doctrine of the historical constitution: the norms related to the form of government and

8 See, for example, F. Mellado, *Tratado Elemental de Derecho Político* (Madrid, 1891), 360.

9 Perhaps for a similar reason, Burke ridiculed Sieyes' multiple constitutional proposals: 'Abbé Sieyes has whole nests of pigeon-holes full of constitutions readymade, ticketed, sorted, and numbered; suited to every season and every fancy': E. Burke, *Further Reflections on the French Revolution* (Liberty Fund, 1992), 317.

10 Constitution of 1812 (Spain), Article 3.

11 This argument is developed further in J. Colón-Ríos, *Constituent Power and the Law* (Oxford University Press, 2020).

12 H. Kelsen, 'The Function of a Constitution', in R. Tur & W. Twining (eds.), *Essays on Kelsen* (Clarendon Press, 1986), 114.

13 C. Schmitt, *Constitutional Theory* (Duke University Press, 2008), 75.

the rules regulating the basic relationship between citizens and the state.[14] However, for Schmitt, since those norms have been the result of a decision of the constituent subject, they are out of the scope of the ordinary amendment process. The normative conception of the material constitution, in this respect, invites judges to determine whether the ordinary amending power is being used to alter or replace the fundamental laws posited by the constituent people. In contemporary times, this is exemplified in the judicial embracement of the doctrine of unconstitutional constitutional amendments. But the cases that apply that doctrine do not present the fundamental content of the constitution (i.e., the material constitution) as unchangeable: it can always be altered by the people acting through an extra-ordinary mechanism.

Given the close relationship between the concepts of the material and the historical constitution, we may say that the doctrine of unconstitutional constitutional amendments, rather than being a novel development, is a return to a previous status quo: a situation where a society's fundamental laws were not subject to change. In fact, during the nineteenth century, when the doctrine of the historical constitution was still highly influential, it was not uncommon for written constitutions to even lack an amendment rule.[15] A mechanism for altering the constitutional text was by no means seen as a necessary component of a written constitution, so, when amendment rules became a standard feature of constitutions, the notion that some provisions should be out of the scope of the amending power would have seemed entirely natural.

The cases that are discussed in Sections 19.2.1 and 19.2.2 exemplify the ways in which some Latin American judges have engaged with the concept of the material constitution. Perhaps surprisingly, we have found no instances where it played a key role in the judicial application of the doctrine of unconstitutional constitutional amendments. In fact, as we will see, judges have applied the concept of the material constitution in order to argue *against* the doctrine of unconstitutional constitutional amendments and, in other cases, it is the doctrine of the historical constitution which has done the work of limiting the legislature's amending authority.

19.2 JUDGES AND THE MATERIAL CONSTITUTION

The concept of the material constitution, despite its arguable vagueness, is at first sight well suited for judicial development and application. Whenever courts have a need to place certain constitutional norms above others, to argue that there is a hierarchy of constitutional principles or provisions, the material constitution provides a seemingly easy way out: every norm contained in the constitutional text is formally constitutional, but only some norms are materially so. In that context, the phrase 'materially constitutional' would not be merely describing the 'constitutional' subject matter of the relevant norm; it would rather point to their character as *fundamental* norms. The main example of that type of situation is the doctrine of unconstitutional constitutional amendments. When applying that doctrine, judges could say that the amending authority cannot touch the material constitution. 'Material constitution', in that respect, would play the same role that 'basic structure' has played in the jurisprudence that

[14] These kinds of views were challenged by Hermann Heller who, in addition to the distinction between the constitution in the formal and the material sense, examined the concept of constitution from what he called a sociological perspective. H. Heller, *Teoría del Estado*, L. Tobío, trans. (Fondo de Cultura Económica, 2012), 347. Following Ferdinand Lassalle, he described the 'real constitution' as referring neither to the norms contained in a particular document nor to those (written or unwritten) norms regulating the fundamental structure of the state, its relations to citizens, etc., but to the actual 'relations of power present in a country': ibid., 317.

[15] See, e.g., the French Charter of 1830 and the Spanish Constitution of 1837.

has emerged since the famous decisions of the Indian Supreme Court.[16] However, at least in Latin America, we have not found any cases were the concept of the material constitution is explicitly deployed with those objectives.[17] However, its precursor, the doctrine of the historical constitution, played that role in an important judgment of the Peruvian Constitutional Tribunal, discussed in Section 19.2.1.

19.2.1 *Peru's Historical Constitution as a Limit to Constitutional Replacement*

Peru's current constitution was adopted by a Constituent Congress called by Alberto Fujimori's government after the 'self-coup' of September 1992. The coup involved a purge of the judiciary, the dissolution of Congress, the suspension of the Constitution of 1979, the establishment of an authoritarian government and the adoption of a new constitution in 1993 through a highly controversial process.[18] In 2001, and shortly after the fall of Fujimori's regime, the Peruvian Congress passed a law that (among other things) vested a congressional commission with the task of drafting a new constitutional text.[19] Importantly, the law established:

> The Comisión de Constitución, Reglamento y Acusasiones Constitucionales will propose a draft for the *total reform* of the Constitution, taking into account the *historical constitution of Perú* and in particular the text of the Constitution of 1979. After approval by Congress, the draft will be subject to referendum. If the draft is approved [by the electors], the Constitution of 1993 would be abrogated. (emphasis added)[20]

The law was challenged in the Constitutional Tribunal and, in its judgment, the court discussed at some length the limits of the ordinary power of constitutional reform and the meaning of the legal mandate to respect Peru's historical constitution.

The claimant argued that the amendment rule of the Constitution of 1993 (Article 206)[21] could not be used for the 'total reform' of the constitution: such an action involved the

[16] See, e.g., *Kesavananda Bharati Sripadagalvaru & Ors.* v. *State of Kerala & Anr*, 4 SCC 225 (1973).

[17] Although the idea of 'material limits' to the power of constitutional reform is frequently used by Latin American courts, the notion of the 'material constitution' or the 'constitution in the material sense' is less common in judgments discussing the existence of limits to the amending power. For example, in an appeal decision where the Supreme Court of Mexico decided on the admissibility of challenges against constitutional amendments, the court adopted a theory of formal and 'material' implicit limits to the amendment power. Regarding the latter, the court maintained 'the political principle of popular sovereignty necessarily entails implicit material limits which justification and development should be deducted from … the material values based on which the idea of the constitutional state rests upon' (*see* SCJN, Pleno, Amparo en Revisión 186/2008, at 22). The term 'constitution in the material sense' makes a rare appearance in a dissenting opinion in a case where the court decided that the amending power could not be subject to any type of limits (procedural or substantive), where the dissenting judges maintained that 'fundamental rights provisions …[as well as] constitutional supremacy … belong to the constitution in the material sense' (SCJN, Pleno, Controversia Constitucional 82/2001, at 644–45). However, this part of the dissent was not central to the reasoning of their disagreement with the majority. Interestingly, we found that in Mexico, claimants often use the concept of 'material constitution' to articulate their claims (see, e.g., SCJN, Pleno, Amparo en Revisión 1477/2004, 15 May 2006 at 66; SCJN, Segunda Sala, Amparo en Revisión 1378/2005, 18 Nov 2005, at 40; SCJN, Primera Sala, Amparo en Revisión 528/2016, 9 Oct 2019, at 14), but did not find cases in which the court uses the concept as part of its reasoning.

[18] See 'Mensaje a la Nación del Presidente del Perú, Ingeniero Alberto Fujimori' (5 April 1992) and Decree Law No. 25418 (6 April 1992).

[19] Law no 27600 (14 December 2001).

[20] Ibid., Article 2.

[21] Article 206, Constitution of Peru (1993): 'Any initiative of constitutional reform must be adopted by Congress through an absolute majority of the legal number of its members and must be ratified by a referendum. The referendum may be exempted when the consent of Congress is obtained in two successive regular sessions, with a favourable vote of greater than two-thirds of the legal number of congressmen in each case.'

replacement of the existing constitutional text and thus required an exercise of the 'original constituent power' and the convocation of a Constituent Assembly. In response, the Congress' legal representative maintained that a 'total reform' of the constitution did not require an extra-constitutional exercise of constituent authority. Counsel pointed toward Article 32 of the Constitution of 1993, which referred to 'total and partial reforms of the Constitution' as one of the matters that could be submitted to a referendum.[22] That provision, it was claimed, necessarily implied that the amendment process contained in Article 206 could be used to replace the existing constitution. The fact that Article 32 also stated that 'the suppression or the reduction of the fundamental rights of the person cannot be submitted to referendum' meant that such rights 'constitute a personal and moral identity core that neither the political process nor the juridical norms are ethically authorized to ignore and that are internationally recognized', not that the total reform of the constitution lies outside of the jurisdiction of the amendment power.

The court maintained that the power of constitutional reform, as a constituted power, was subject to formal and materials limits.[23] The formal limits are the procedural requirements contained in the amendment rule and the material ones establish 'parameters of constitutional identity or essence, immune to any possibility of reform'.[24] The latter type of limits could be explicit or implicit. That is to say, they could take the form of eternity clauses or be derived from principles implicit in the constitutional text. According to the court, those principles included 'human dignity, popular sovereignty, the democratic state of law, the republican form of government and, in general, the political regime and the form of the State'.[25] Reforming those limits would entail the 'destruction of the Constitution' and would be 'illegitimate in constitutional terms'.[26] The court expressly associated this view with the conception of constitutional reform developed in Schmitt's *Constitutional Theory*, noting that from that perspective, a change 'that involves the integral substitution of the Charter, including the clause that regulates the amending power, would imply an act of revolution and would therefore be anti-juridical'.[27]

The court nonetheless noted that there are constitutions which do vest the amending organ with the authority to replace the established constitutional text. The question was whether the Constitution of 1993 was one of those constitutions. If one follows some scholarly discussions on the subject, the fact that Article 206 did not explicitly authorise the amending authority to replace the constitution in its entirety (to engage in a 'total reform' of the constitution) would seem to point toward the conclusion that the amending organ only had a limited power that could not be used to replace the constitutional text.[28] However, as noted by the respondent, Article 32 referred to the possibility of a 'total reform'. For the court, that provision (in combination with Article 206), 'constitutionalise[d] the constituent function', following the tradition of the French Constitution of 1793.[29] The constitutionalisation of the constituent function should not be taken to mean that the legislative branch of government, as a constituted power, becomes the constituent authority. However, 'as an organ of the representation of the

[22] Article 32, Constitution of Peru (1993): 'A referendum may be held on the following: (1) Partial or total reform of the Constitution ... The abolition or abridgement of the fundamental rights of the person may not be submitted to a referendum, neither may tax and budget rules nor international treaties in force.'

[23] Part V, sec. 5.

[24] Ibid., para. 72.

[25] Ibid., para. 76.

[26] Ibid.

[27] Ibid., para. 80

[28] Ibid.

[29] Part VIII, para. 104.

general will, there is no reason why Congress cannot propose a constitutional draft, so that the Constituent Power, as the original fountain of power, decides to accept or reject it'.[30]

Such a mode of proceeding could involve a Constituent Assembly whose acts are ratified in a referendum or one that not only drafts but adopts the new constitution. In the former case, the court expressed, the Constituent Assembly would only be playing a constituent 'function', with the actual constituent 'decision' remaining in the hands of the electorate.[31] However, it would also be entirely appropriate to place that constituent function in Congress itself, leaving the final constituent act to the 'decision of the sovereign, through the referendum', the 'only way in which the Constituent Power can be expressed directly'.[32] A decision of the sovereign would be required any time a 'total reform' takes place. The question then becomes what counts as such a major constitutional change. For the court, when considering whether a particular change amounts to a 'total reform' of the constitution, the number of provisions altered is not the determining factor.[33] What must be looked at is whether 'the essential content of the established Constitution remains or is changed ... [I]f this constitutional "hard core" – or the historical Constitution, as stated in the challenged law – changes, a total reform would have taken place, even if not all constitutional provisions are altered'.[34]

What comprises Peru's historical constitution? And what is the relationship between it and the more general principles (e.g., human dignity and the democratic state of law) that the court also presented as limits to the power of constitutional reform? The principles that comprise the historical constitution, the judges stated, started to emerge in the *Bases de la Constitución* de 1822 and in the Constitution of 1823.[35] The *Bases* were adopted by a Constituent Congress convened at a time when the war of independence was still ongoing and sought to identify the essential content of a future constitution. For example, the *Bases* stated that the new constitution must recognise 'that sovereignty resides essentially in the Nation, which is independent of the Spanish Monarchy, of any foreign domination, and cannot belong to any person or family', that the government would be 'popular and representative', that the separation of powers would be respected and that a series of individual rights (including, for example, the freedom of the press) were to be respected.[36] Those principles served as a limit to the process of constitutional change that had been triggered by Congress, and were reflected in the many constitutions adopted in Peru, even though they were not respected during the authoritarian regime that adopted the Constitution of 1993.

The court thus maintained that the law challenged by the plaintiffs, although referring to the 'total reform' of the constitution, only mandated its *partial* reform, as it required the constitution-maker to respect the 'historical Constitution and the Constitution of 1979'. Accordingly, the draft constitution to be prepared by the constitutional commission, the judges determined, 'shall be based on the historical Constitution of the country, and thus implicitly re-establish the principles and values of the Constitution of 1979. Such a process must end in a referendum in which the draft constitution would be approved or rejected'.[37] In this sense, although Congress could

[30] Ibid., para. 109.
[31] Ibid.
[32] Ibid., 113.
[33] Part IX, para 122.
[34] Ibid.
[35] Part V, para 37.
[36] *Bases de la Constitución Política de la República Peruana* (16 December 1822). The *Bases* also stated that the new constitution should recognise that the nation's religion was Catholicism ('to the exclusion of the exercise of [any other religion]').
[37] Part XI, para 131.

trigger a process leading toward the 'total reform' of the Constitution of 1993, that is, one that went beyond the scope of the ordinary amending power, the proposed changes in any case would not have that effect. Those changes would find as their ultimate frontier Peru's historical constitution and, presumably, would also be within the boundaries of the implicit material limits that always apply to the amending authority. However, from the Constitutional Tribunal's judgment, it is not entirely clear what is the relationship between those implicit limits and Peru's historical constitution.

At times, it seems the material limits that always apply to the amending power are already comprised by the notion of the historical constitution. But the court also stated that a 'total reform' would take place if the 'basic principles and basic presuppositions of the political, economic, and social organization that serve as the basis of the hard core of the Constitution of 1993 are modified'.[38] It could also be argued that the Constitution of 1993, and its basic principles and presuppositions, could be replaced (i.e., through a total reform *via* Articles 206 and 32) while at the same time respecting the historical constitution of Peru. That is to say, to replace the Constitution of 1993 in order to return to a constitutional past in which the principles that were first formulated in 1822 are fully recognised and respected. In the end, the Constitutional Tribunal dismissed the challenge against the 2001 law, opening the way for the desired changes. A draft constitution was prepared by the commission and initially approved by Congress in its first reading, but it was eventually taken off the legislative agenda among fears that it would be rejected by the electorate. Be that as it may, there are two additional points worth making about the court's conception of the historical constitution and its views on what constitutes a total reform.

First, note that the court's conception of the historical constitution does not reject, but rather embraces, the theory of constituent power. In fact, it is the electorate who in the end would ultimately decide whether the draft constitution submitted to it reflected the historical constitution of Peru. From that perspective, the court's approach to the historical constitution appears indistinguishable from the notion of the constitution in the material sense (as noted in Section 19.1.1, the main difference between these two concepts is that the former involved a rejection of the theory of constituent power). Second, note that, according to the court, modifications to 'the economic and social organization' of the country would involve a violation of the material (and implicit) limits to the amending power. Here we see actual 'material' factors (i.e., economic and social ones) playing a role in limiting political authority.[39] A similar notion was briefly considered (and not rejected) by the Supreme Court of Justice of Colombia in a 1978 case which referred to those who saw the 'real factors of powers' not in the law but in the economy.[40] However, as we will see in Section 19.2.2, it was a juridical (as opposed to economic or social) notion of the material constitution that was deployed by a dissent at the Constitutional Court of Colombia as part of an objection against the court's assumption of the power to declare constitutional amendments unconstitutional.

[38] Ibid., para 123.

[39] These were the kind of factors identified by Ferdinand Lasalle in his famous essay, F. Lasalle, 'On the Essence of Constitutions' [1862] (1942) 3 *Fourth International* 25. For Lasalle, 'the material constitution as nothing else but the actual relation of forces existing in a given society'. See also M. Goldoni and M. Wilkinson, 'The Material Constitution' (2018) 81 *Modern Law Review* 567; C. Mortati, *La Constitución en el Sentido Material* (Centro de Estudios Constitucionales, 2000).

[40] Judgment No. 2397, Supreme Court of Justice (5 May 1978), 105–6.

19.2.2 The Material Constitution and Judicial Discretion in Colombia

One of the most famous judgments of the Colombian Constitutional Court was rendered in 2005. In that case, the court considered the constitutionality of an amendment proposal that would allow President Álvaro Uribe to run as a presidential candidate for a second time.[41] The court dismissed the action, but reaffirmed its jurisdiction to review proposed constitutional changes in order to determine if they fell outside of the scope of the amending authority.[42] For the court, the limits of the amending authority were to be found in the notion of constitutional replacement: an amendment could alter the constitutional text, but not in ways so fundamental that really amount to the creation of a new constitution. In this particular case, the court concluded that the proposed change was constitutional since it would not involve the replacement of the constitutional order. One of the main obstacles confronted by the Colombian Constitutional Court's adoption of the doctrine of unconstitutional constitutional amendments was the text of the Constitution of 1991. Not only did it not include any eternity clauses, but its Article 241 stated that the court's power to review the validity of constitutional amendments was limited to 'procedural errors in their formation' (*vicios de procedimiento en su formación*).

In a series of judgments, the court nonetheless determined that in order to decide whether the amendment procedure has been correctly followed (as required by Article 241), it was first necessary to inquire into the competence of the amending organ. That is to say, for the court, 'competence' was a key element of any procedure and the competence of the amending organ did not include the constituent power to create new constitutional orders, only the legally regulated faculty of *amending* a constitution that would continue to exist after the relevant change. Such an analysis would be 'limited to study if the reforming authority has replaced (*sustituido*) the constitution, which does not entail a material control of the relevant act ... In a replacement judgment, there is no comparison between the reform and the Constitution that seeks to determine if the content of the first contradicts the content of the second'.[43] The concept of replacement was in turn defined by the court in the following way: '[A] transformation of such magnitude and transcendence that [makes] the Constitution existing before the reform [...] integrally different from the one that emerged after it, to the point that they result incompatible with each other'.[44]

Justice Humberto Sierra Porto dissented from that approach in the 2005 case. What is interesting about that dissent, from the perspective of this chapter, is that it is largely based in an opposition between the formal and the material constitution. The judge began by discussing, and rejecting, Schmitt's critique of the notion of the constitution in the formal sense. As is well known, for Schmitt, such an understanding was incapable of distinguishing between fundamental and non-fundamental norms that have nonetheless been included as part of a constitutional text.[45] For Sierra Porto, such a relativisation was not a problem as long as the formal constitution was seen as superior to ordinary laws and could only be altered through an adequate amendment

[41] Judgment no 1040/05, Corte Constitucional de Colombia.

[42] The doctrine of unconstitutional constitutional amendments had already been adopted by the Constitutional Court. See Judgment no 551/03.

[43] Judgment no 1040/05, para 7.10.2.

[44] Ibid.

[45] Schmitt, *Constitutional Theory*, 67. In other words, the constitution in the formal sense failed to see the constitution as expressing the fundamental decisions of the constituent power.

rule.[46] Sierra Porto maintained that the approach adopted by the court, like Schmitt's, rejected the formal concept of a constitution. Despite being presented as a 'procedural' one, such an approach 'would inevitably involve a material control of constitutional changes, which would have at its basis a material conception of the constitution, one that was expressly recognised by the court in its C-971 judgment of 2004,[47] when it expressed "… the Constitution is, by definition and in its material sense, a normative body that defines the essential structure of the State, its principles and fundamental values".'[48]

The constitution, the dissenting judge continued, would thus be accompanied by an 'absolute unchangeability comprised by its essential part, what Mortati called the "constant element" or the "absolute limit of the Constitution"'.[49] Under that perspective, 'a change in the material Constitution would involve the fall of the State and of its fundamental principles'.[50] Sierra Porto considered this approach unacceptable, as it moved the court's jurisprudence 'toward the concept of the material constitution', a development that contradicted 'the textual or literal content' of Article 241 and of other constitutional provisions.[51] According to the view adopted by the court, the 'constitution' would not only be comprised by the set of rules that regulate the creation of norms by the organs or the state (a view we earlier associated with Kelsen's 'descriptive' conception of the material constitution) and it would not be a norm with special formal characteristics (i.e., a norm subject to a special rule of change).[52] Rather, norms would only be part of the constitution 'if they guarantee certain values, that is, those values allegedly embraced by the constituent power in 1991'.[53] This was described by the dissenting judge as a 'normative conception [*concepción valorativa*] of the Constitution … according to which a norm is only legal if it guarantees values that are believed true and are shared by society'.[54]

The material conception of the constitution adopted by the court was thus based on an erroneous premise: that whether a norm belongs in a constitution depends on its political or juridical importance. The notion of the constitution in the material sense, the judge stated, 'does not allow one to identify norms as constitutional regardless of time and place; their constitutional character would depend' on how the juridical order is conceived in a specific moment. A key problem with that approach is that, in 'determining the defining elements of the Constitution' (i.e., one of the steps that the majority of the judges identified as part of the judicial method in constitutional replacement cases), the court would find itself expounding its very content.[55] Put differently, 'the identification of the material Constitution would every time depend on the composition of the Constitutional Court and of its internal majorities', such that

46 Justice Humberto Sierra Porto, Dissent, Judgment 1040/05, para 7.

47 This is one of the few cases involving the doctrine of unconstitutional constitutional amendments where the notion of the material constitution makes an appearance, even if it did not play a key role in the court's reasoning. The relevant passage states: 'One cannot forget, however, that the power of constitutional reform responds to the need of accommodating the Constitution to new political realities, social requirements, and collective consensus. Accordingly, the concept of constitutional replacement cannot deprive the power of constitutional reform of content. If the Constitution is, by definition and in its material sense, a normative body that defines the essential structure of the State, its principles and fundamental values, the relations between the State and society, rights and duties, it is clear that the power to reform the Constitution can touch those elements.'

48 Ibid.

49 Ibid.

50 Ibid.

51 Ibid., para 1.

52 Ibid., para 7.

53 Ibid.

54 Ibid.

55 Ibid.

the act of reforming the constitution would partly take place in the court itself, that is, inside the organ that is supposed to control the amending authority.[56] Moreover, for the dissenting judge, the material concept of the constitution transformed the constitutional regime into a 'closed order', that is, one that forever fixes a particular set of values.[57] The idea of a 'closed order', Sierra Porto maintained, contrasted with the notion of an 'open constitution', a concept that described the type of order established in 1991.

For Sierra Porto, an open constitution included three main ideas: (1) the possibility of defending, according to established legal means, values that are contrary to those considered fundamental; (2) the possibility of modifying those fundamental values legally and (3) the possibility of developing the most diverse political views without the need of constitutional reform.[58] This kind of view, he maintained, was reflected in the debates of the Constituent Assembly that drafted the Constitution of 1991 and in its very composition (from members of traditional political parties to members of previously armed revolutionary groups), as well as in the fact that the text lacked any eternity clauses. In giving itself the task of identifying the 'defining elements' of the Constitution of 1991 – elements that would act as material limits to the power of constitutional reform – the court had transformed the constitutional system into a closed one. That is, one that excludes the modification of the values and principles that at some point a majority of the constitutional judges determines to be part of an unmodifiable core.[59] The adoption of a material conception of the constitution, Justice Sierra Porto concluded, may have the unintended effect of encouraging extra-legal attempts of transforming the constitutional order.

This dissent exemplifies one of the main reasons why the notion of the constitution in the material sense has been largely absent from some constitutional circles. As Georges Vedel once noted, the material concept of the constitution is characterised by 'boundary problems'.[60] Its ability to be filled with any content means that, whoever can authoritatively determine what constitutional norms and principles are part of it, becomes, from a certain perspective, the constituent power. For Justice Sierra Porto, this was the necessary implication of the court's adoption of the doctrine of unconstitutional constitutional amendments: the embracement of a material conception of the constitution gives too much power to judges. But Justice Sierra Porto's approach may result in a different problem: the reliance on a formal conception of the constitution would give too much power to the legislature, that is, to the organ authorised to alter the constitutional text through the ordinary amendment rule. This is why the solution given by the Peruvian Constitutional Tribunal may be a more attractive one. That is to say, neither the judges nor the legislature have the last word on the constitution's material (or historical) content; this authority belongs to the people acting through participatory processes, which should, in our view, not be limited to a mere referendum.

19.3 FINAL THOUGHTS

We have seen that the constitution in the material sense – as well as its precursor, the doctrine of the historical constitution – has made its way from constitutional theory to some Latin American courts. The juridical notions of the material and the historical constitution, in pointing toward

[56] Ibid.
[57] Ibid., para. 8.
[58] Ibid.
[59] Ibid.
[60] G. Vedel, *Manuel Élémentaire de Droit Constitutionnel* (Dalloz, 2002), 112.

certain fundamental content, are intrinsically conservative: they are about protecting some norms from whoever would normally have the power to change them. In this respect, one would expect these notions to become most relevant whenever there is an attempt of creating a hierarchy between formally indistinguishable norms. Just as Lord Laws attempted to distinguish between formally equal statutes by classifying some as 'constitutional' and others as 'ordinary' in order to narrow the scope of the doctrine of implied repeal,[61] judges may appeal to the notions of the material or the historical constitution in an attempt to distinguish between formally equal constitutional provisions. That kind of distinction would be especially useful in the context of judicial efforts directed at limiting the amending power.

Despite the relevance of the notion of the material constitution to questions related to constitutional change and its limits, we don't want to give the impression that that is the extent of its possible and actual roles in judicial reasoning. For example, the Bolivian Plurinational Tribunal has relied on the concept of the material constitution not to justify its jurisdiction to review constitutional amendments, but to defend a particular interpretation of the constitutional text. This was exemplified in a 2010 criminal appeal process, where the court analysed the scope of the right to counsel and the role of public defenders in the realisation of such right. The court maintained that Article 119.II, the constitutional provision regulating the state's duty to provide a public defender to those defendants in economic need, aimed at 'bridging the gap between the formal constitution ... and the material constitution ... [T]herefore, in light of the principle of the progressive realisation of rights, [Article 119.II] cannot be restrictively interpreted in the sense that the state is bound to provide a public defender only to those defendants that cannot afford private counsel ...'.[62] Importantly, the court understood the material constitution as not only including domestic constitutional law, but also principles recognised by the international community, such as the previously mentioned principle of the progressive realisation of rights.

In our view, this is an interesting development that illustrates the possibility of adding a supranational dimension to the notion of the material constitution. This development would be consistent with the material constitution's conceptual predecessor, the doctrine of the historical constitution. Naturally, Jovellanos and other early proponents of that doctrine could not have predicted the rise of the post-Westphalian order. Yet, since they saw a constitution as the product of history and as reflecting the way of being of the community in question, the inclusion of principles of international human rights law could be understood as a natural addition to those elements that form part of a country's historical constitution. The idea of considering international human rights law as part of the interpretative framework for judicial review is indeed central to the doctrine of the 'constitutional block' [*bloque de constitucionalidad*],[63] through which Latin American apex courts have granted constitutional hierarchy to international human rights instruments.[64]

Like the doctrine of the historical constitution, the notion of the 'constitutional block' originated in Europe (the term was coined by Claude Emeri in 1970, but the concept was further developed and disseminated by Louis Favoreau through a discussion of Decision 71-44

[61] *Thoburn* v. *Sunderland City Council* [2003] QB 151; [2002] 3 WLR 247, para. 63.

[62] Judgment 1614-2011-R, 11 October 2011, Tribunal Constitucional Plurinacional, p. 8.

[63] F. Rubio Llorente, 'El Bloque de Constitucionalidad' (1989) *Revista Española de Derecho Constitucional* 9.

[64] M. Góngora Mera, 'La difusión del bloque de constitucionalidad en la jurisprudencia latinoamericana y su potencial en la construcción del ius constitutionale commune latinoamericano', in A. Von Bogdandy, H. Fix-Fierro and M. Morales (eds.), *Ius constitutionale commune en América Latina. Rasgos, Potencialidades y Desafíos* (IIJ/UNAM e Instituto Max Planck de Derecho Público Comparado y Derecho Internacional, 2014), 308.

DC of the *Conseil Constitutionnel*)[65] and has been influential in Latin American constitutionalism (it has been mainly embraced by apex courts through remission clauses or *clausulas de apertura*). However, the Latin American version of the doctrine, which found one of its earliest expressions in a judgment of the Colombian Constitutional Court,[66] includes international instruments as opposed to only domestic legislation.[67] Bolivia not only followed Colombia through its jurisprudence between 2005 and 2006,[68] but it seems to be the only country that explicitly refers to the term 'constitutional block' in its constitutional text.[69] Article 410.II of the Bolivian Constitution states: 'The constitution is the supreme law of the Bolivian legal order and enjoys supremacy before any other normative disposition. The constitutional block is comprised by the Human Rights international Treaties and Covenants and the norms of Communitarian Law that have been ratified by the country ...'.

Although not articulated specifically in terms of the material constitution, the use of principles and instruments of international human rights law reflects the receptivity of courts to historical changes in the world order that may be understood as being a fundamental part of their own constitutional system. The idea of considering international human rights law as part of the interpretative framework of domestic judicial review is also found in the European context. For example, it has been suggested that international human rights law may serve as a material constraint on the amendment power.[70] In this same vein, it would not be surprising if, at some point in the near future, domestic discussions of the material constitution become fully intertwined with notions of international human rights law, such that the consideration of any argument about implicit limits to the amendment authority would ultimately remit domestic judges to the international legal system. When that happens, the question would be whether, as in the decision of the Peruvian Constitutional Tribunal, the material constitution would still be considered subject to the will of the constituent people.

65 For a discussion, see, M. E. Carpio, 'Bloque de Constitucionalidad y Proceso de Inconstitucionalidad de Las Leyes' (2005) 7 *Revista Iberoamericana de Derecho Procesal Constitucional* 79, 81–83.

66 Sentencia C-225/1995, Corte Constitucional de Colombia.

67 M. Gongora Mera, 'Bloque', 307–8.

68 Ibid., 314–15.

69 See constituteproject.org [search term: 'bloque de constitucionalidad']. The constituteproject.org's English translation of Article 411.II of the constitution of Bolivia translated the term 'bloque de constitucionalidad' into 'the components of constitutional law'. There is a possibility of inaccuracy in the figure reported here regarding those constitutions that are not originally in Spanish, that adopt the concept of 'bloque de constitucionalidad' and which might have gotten lost in translation. Even though 'constitutional block' is a literal translation, we think that in this case it would be the most accurate.

70 L. Garlicki and Z. A. Garlicka, 'External Review of Constitutional Amendments? International Law as a Norm of Reference' (2011) 44 *Israel Law Review* 343.

20

A Materialist Analysis of the Indian Constitution

Sandipto Dasgupta

The nearly two decade-long dissolution of European empires led to the formal political independence of nearly one third of the world's population. In the place of empires emerged a host of nation states, all of which adopted a written constitution to create and organise the new post-colonial regime. It was, by a stretch, the most productive period in the history of constitution making. However, such a momentous endeavour has been analysed primarily through a derivative lens. It was implicitly assumed that the basic norms, features, and formal structure of a modern constitution were already forged in Europe and America. The work of post-colonial constitution-makers was primarily that of adaptation; their 'successes' and 'failures' to be measured by how well or poorly they managed to incorporate a script that had already been written. Post-colonial constitutions are therefore to be viewed as a derived instantiation of a 'globally shared mode of organizing socio-political formations'.[1] That assumption erases the socio-historical specificity of the post-colonial transitional moment and the political creativity of the regime formation. It also shares a particular view of constitutions – as a set of widely shared norms, whose validity is independent of their specific socio-historical context, and one which necessarily bestows legitimacy on any political regime. The tradition of the material constitution stands as a critique of that assumption, which is precisely why it is a significant intellectual standpoint from which to interrogate the specificities of post-colonial constitutional experiences.

The absence of material constitutional analysis from the post-colonial scene was not just a scholarly oversight. As Chris Thornhill points out, during the Cold War era the intellectual momentum in both constitutional theory and constitutional practice was toward a more formal, normative, view of constitutions.[2] Certain features were prescribed in order for constitutions to be considered a part of the liberal democratic world.[3] With the eventual triumph of the US-led global order, this view became globally hegemonic, especially during the constitution-making era that coincided with the wave of democratisation in Central and East European countries. Constitutions, at least in their prescriptive form, became globalised and standardised.[4] This was particularly true for the post-colonial countries. With the demise of Third Worldist projects of

[1] J. Go, 'A Globalizing Constitutionalism? Views from the Postcolony, 1945–2000' (2003) 18 *International Sociology* 72.

[2] C. Thornhill, *A Sociology of Constitutions* (Cambridge University Press, 2011), 3–4.

[3] A. Rana, *The Two Faces of American Freedom* (Harvard University Press, 2010); M. Tushnet, '"Our Perfect Constitution" Revisited', in P. Berkowitz (ed.), *Terrorism, the Laws of War, and the Constitution: Debating Enemy Combatant Cases* (Hoover Institution Press, 2005), 131–58.

[4] H. Klug, *Constituting Democracy: Law, Globalism and South Africa's Political Reconstruction* (Cambridge University Press, 2000).

economic sovereignty and developmentalism, and under the compulsion of sovereign debt crises, countries in the global periphery were unable to assert their ideational or economic autonomy. In the heady days of unipolar globalisation, international organisations and constitutional experts advocated homogenous constitutional forms. The contextual, materialist type of constitutional analysis found little political favour.

A material analysis of the post-colonial constitutional form is therefore also a recovery of a historical moment. Decolonisation was not just a time of formal political freedom to be then baptized by the adoption of certain idealised juridical norms. It was an attempt at shaping a distinctive post-colonial future through autonomy from the circuit of imperial capital. In the condition of a weak and dependent bourgeoisie under colonialism, post-colonial countries tried pursuing autonomy through projects of planned development, state-led industrialisation, and social transformation. These projects demanded the primacy of sovereignty over property – as witnessed in the various attempts at nationalisation and land reform in the first decade after decolonisation. The constitution of the post-colony therefore sought to differentiate itself from the borrowed norms of the metropole privileging property rights and constraints on state intervention.

However, any study of the material constitution of the post-colony has to also contend with the eventual decline and exhaustion of that initial project and to consider how the initial constitutional vision and practice changed or struggled on its own terms. Rather than a simplistic judgement about success or failure to achieve some idealised version of 'liberal constitutionalism', it has to account for constitutional change in terms of shifting social bases.

In this chapter, I will explore some of the main elements of that experience through a material analysis of the Indian Constitution. India is in many ways exceptional amongst its post-colonial peers. The most significant colony of the British Empire, it gained independence through the largest and most popular anti-colonial movement in the world. Its constitution was drafted without any interference from or influence by its former colonial rulers. That constitution has survived over seven decades without any coups or foreign interventions – a rarity amongst its post-colonial peers. However, these exceptional elements make India a particularly suitable case to investigate the material constitution of the post-colony on its own terms. It showcases some of the central terms and problematics of the material constitution of the post-colony.

The persistent danger posed by the 'social question' in conditions of under-development and inequality was the central challenge for the post-colonial regime builders. The solution, across much of the post-colonial world, was a project of state led social transformation, known as development planning. The post-colonial constitution, I would argue, was designed to facilitate and realise this central goal. It was a constitution by and for administrators and planners. Setting up the terms of the foundational constitutional design in these terms then allows us to track its shifting coordinates over the next decades. In the subsequent parts of the chapter, I will explore how lawyers and judges supplanted administrators as the primary custodians of the post-colonial constitution as the fortunes of development planning declined and the Third World became 'liberalised'; concluding with some reflections on the fate of the original post-colonial ambitions of social transformation through the constitution.

20.1 THE PROBLEM OF HEGEMONY

The anti-colonial movement that brought independence to India was the largest mass movement of its kind anywhere in the world. After the First World War, Gandhi emerged on the Indian political scene and transformed the Indian National Congress – till then a party of urban professionals petitioning the colonial government for various remedies – into a mass party with an organisational structure spread across every district in the country. When independence from colonial rule happened, Congress became the ruling party with little doubt about its claim to be the legitimate representative of the hitherto colonised population. The scale and the success of the Congress and the anti-colonial movement that it led gave rise to the view of a constitution of the post-colonial regime based on consensual and high minded principles.[5] This picture held sway until the 1970s, when irrevocable tensions between different organs of the state and factions within the party led to a full-blown constitutional crisis.

Scholars at the time questioned the earlier model of consensual post-colonial transition to highlight the various conflicts and contradictions that lay at the heart of the post-colonial regime. They utilised the work of Antonio Gramsci to make the argument that the post-colonial ruling elite faced a crisis of hegemony.[6] Despite Gandhi, the Indian elite were not successful in fully overcoming their distance from the peasant masses – remaining unable to create a new common *Weltanschauung*. The alliance between the elites and the masses that led to a genuinely popular anti-colonial movement under the umbrella of the Congress was contingent on fighting a common enemy, and did not necessarily translate into a widespread 'common sense' about the new order that was to follow.

The absence of an ethico-political hegemony gave special urgency to the social question borne by two major problems: under-development and inequality. A highly uneven distribution of landholding, backed by the colonial system of *zamindari* (landlordism), subjected the rural masses to deep-rooted hierarchy and oppression. Although facilitated by the colonial regime, the sources of much of these quotidian experiences of hierarchy and oppression were indigenous landlords and money lenders. With the departure of a common enemy, there was a very real danger that the resistive energy turn inwards against the indigenous sources of social power. At the same time, colonial economic policy, domination of British capital and persistent under-investment meant relatively low levels of industrialisation, indigenous capital formation, and economic growth. Taken together these manifested in widely prevailing poverty and scarcity. Added to a population politically mobilised through the anti-colonial movement, such conditions portended very real dangers of social upheaval. The social question was an unavoidable one for the nascent post-colonial regime.

The lack of hegemony and threat of social upheaval led the Indian elites to a 'passive revolution' in the Gramscian sense, that is, a deliberate project of 'revolution without revolution'.[7] The post-colonial ruling elites realised that their rule depended upon addressing the social question in a deliberate, gradual, and controlled fashion. They needed to intervene in and transform society without risking a tumultuous and extra-institutional revolutionary upheaval. The Constitution, rather than a formal impedimentum of political sovereignty or a set of treasured and widely accepted norms, was a carefully designed institutional structure for that project.

The lack of hegemony and the potential for social conflict provided the need and the rationale for managing the social transformation through the Constitution. The particular

[5] R. Kothari, 'The Congress "System" in India' (1964) 4 *Asian Survey* 1161; M. Weiner, *Party Building in a New Nation: The Indian National Congress* (Chicago University Press, 1967); R. Kothari, *Politics in India* (Little and Brown, 1970); I. Lloyd and S. H. Rudolph, *In Pursuit of Lakshmi: The Political Economy of the Indian State* (Chicago University Press, 1987).

[6] R. Guha, *Dominance without Hegemony: History and Power in Colonial India* (Oxford University Press, 1998); P. Chatterjee, *Nationalist Thought and the Colonial World: A Derivative Discourse?* (Oxford University Press, 1986); S. Kaviraj, *The Imaginary Institution of India: Politics and Ideas* (Permanent Black, 2010).

[7] A. Gramsci, *Selections from the Prison Notebooks*, Q. Hoare and G. N. Smith, trans. (International Publishers, 1971), 58.

dynamic of formulating the constitution was further conditioned by two related sets of conflicts. The first was a credible threat of popular unrest, and the second was the conflict and negotiations between the different groups that comprised the post-colonial ruling elite.

20.2 THE PARTY, THE PEOPLE AND THE STATE

For the Indian constitution-makers, the challenge was how to manage a revolution (through the Constitution) in order to avoid a revolution (in the streets). 'If the Constitution holds up, blocks, the future progress of our country', warned a member of the Constituent Assembly, 'I dare say that the progress which has been thus retarded will be achieved by a violent revolution: revolution will take the place of evolution.'[8] This threat was a result of the events that were playing out outside the Assembly during the four years it took to draft the Constitution. The decade preceding the Constituent Assembly was one of increasing radicalisation of peasant and labour politics which, while never challenging Congress' dominance of the political landscape, did constitute a cause for concern. In 1946, the year the Constituent Assembly convened, major militant (and at times armed) peasant movements broke out in Bengal, Maharashtra, Travancore, and elsewhere.[9] During the years of drafting the Constitution successful strikes took place in textile mills, ports, railways, mines and postal services.[10] One can add to this the threat posed by the Communists given the global prominence of the Communist movement and the revolution in neighbouring China. As Chairman of the Drafting Committee B. R. Ambedkar noted in the Constituent Assembly 'this urge for self-realization in the down-trodden classes must not be allowed to devolve into a class struggle or class war [. . .] That would indeed be a day of disaster'.[11]

The anxiety about the radical energy of the popular movements was based in the nature of the Congress as a party. It was not a revolutionary party organised under the banner of a coherent ideology, with a committed army of cadres. Nor did the radical sentiments on the ground find a relatively unmediated path through the party. By the 1920s, the anti-colonial movement had become a genuinely popular struggle. Mass movements have an inherent tendency to radicalise and exceed the scope and focus of their leaders. By the end of the 1930s, the majority of the Congress leadership made a deliberate choice – over the protest of the left-wing faction within the party – to contest elections and enter provincial government under the colonial constitutional act called the Government of India Act of 1935. This transformed it from the party of anti-colonial mass movement to a government in waiting.[12] Its primary habitus shifted from the streets to the government buildings.

The ordering principles for the post-colonial polity would therefore not be drawn for the organisational structure of the anti-colonial mass movement. There remained an almost uninterrupted continuity between the institutions, norms and personnel of the late colonial state into the post-colonial regime. The very same bureaucracy, police and army that was used to suppress the anti-colonial movement transitioned seamlessly to administering the new post-colonial regime.[13] Given India's centrality to the British empire, the colonial state machinery was the

[8] H. V. Kamath, *Constituent Assembly Debates*, 17 September 1949.

[9] S. Sarkar, *Modern India: 1885–1947* (Macmillan, 1983).

[10] R. Chandavarkar, *Origins of Industrial Capitalism in India: Business Strategies and the Working Classes in Bombay, 1900–1940* (Cambridge University Press, 1994); M. D. Morris, *The Emergence of Industrial Labor Force in India: A Study of Bombay Cotton Mills, 1854–1947* (University of California Press, 1965).

[11] B. R. Ambedkar, *Constituent Assembly Debates*, 4 November 1948.

[12] Sarkar, *Modern India*.

[13] A. Burra, 'The Indian Civil Service and the Nationalist Movement: Neutrality, Politics, and Continuity' (2010) 48 *Journal of Commonwealth and Comparative Politics* 404.

most developed version of its kind. Now, the new rulers sought to use it, with only minor modifications, for the purpose of post-colonial governance and transformation.[14] The state in other words, preceded the Constitution, which in turn was built around the existing infrastructure of the state.

20.3 THE DOMINANT CLASSES AND THE CONSTITUTION

Hegemony, however, is not just a question of political common sense. A necessary, though not sufficient, condition is supplied by the political economy of post-colonial transition. In a capitalist system investment decisions are private and, since governments in power depend on continued investments both for electoral gains and political stability, they are generally not willing to extend their redistributive agenda beyond a point that would – in Gramsci's phrase – 'touch the essential'.[15] In such a condition of dependence, the present material interest of the capitalist (i.e., profit) appears as the future universal interest of the whole society (growth).[16] Through two centuries of colonial rule, the developmental trajectory of Indian industrial capital was heavily determined by the needs and policies of the metropolitan economy. For most of colonial history, the focus was on the export of cheap raw materials and trade controlled by British capital. Development of indigenous capital under this condition remained weak, sporadic and informal.[17] Therefore, capital in India was not in a position where its interests could appear, simply by virtue of its place in the economy, as the universal interest of the nation. Instead, capital was crucially dependent on the state for its growth and reproduction.[18]

The economist Pranab Bardhan developed the notion of a 'coalitional model of domination' whereby he argued that in India the capitalist class, due to its historic weakness, had to share power with other dominant classes.[19] This coalition consisted of three groups – industrial capitalists, rural landowning elites and professional elites. Independent dominance of any one of these classes was never a concrete historical possibility. Hence the coalition was not an incidental fact or an accident, it was the very condition of elite dominance, which would otherwise be destabilised. This provided a centripetal constraint on the coalition, but not a frictionless unity of purpose. As independence drew near, the general goal of winning freedom from colonial rule gave way to intense negotiation among these classes for determining the structure of new political institutions and the allocation of resources.[20] The process of drafting the Constitution was similarly marked by intra-coalition negotiation between the dominant classes. That negotiation was constrained by the aforementioned inability of any group to claim independent dominance. In terms of constitution-making this implied an inability to propose a separate system of rule, from the one being hammered out inside the Assembly. In other words, neither group had the ability, and hence the desire, to lead either a revolution or a coup. This was the material basis that created the condition for, and maintained the stability of, an electoral democracy in India.

[14] S. Dasgupta, 'A Language that is Foreign to Us: Continuities and Anxieties in the Making of the Indian Constitution' (2014) 34 *Comparative Studies of South Asia, Africa, and the Middle East* 228.

[15] Gramsci, *Prison Notebooks*, 161.

[16] A. Przeworski, *Capitalism and Social Democracy* (Cambridge University Press, 1985).

[17] A. K. Bagchi, *Private Investment in India* (Cambridge University Press, 1972); A. Kohli, *Imperialism and the Developing World* (Princeton University Press, 2020).

[18] F. R. Frankel, *India's Political Economy, 1947–2004: The Gradual Revolution* (Oxford University Press, 2005); P. Chatterjee, *The Nation and Its Fragments: Colonial and Postcolonial Histories* (Princeton University Press, 1993).

[19] P. Bardhan, *The Political Economy of Development in India* (Blackwell, 1984).

[20] S. Kaviraj, 'A Critique of the Passive Revolution' (1988) 23 *Economic and Political Weekly* 2429.

Although shaped by the dynamics of this coalition, one amongst these three groups exercised overwhelming influence in formulating the Constitution: the professional elites. The reason for their prominence was the corresponding weakness of the other two dominant classes when it came to constitution-making. While the industrial capitalist class did have a plausible vision of 'national interest' shaped in its own image and borrowed from the annals of the advanced capitalist countries, it lacked either the political or the economic position required for its vision to become hegemonic. Its dependence on the state manifested itself in its acquiescence in developmental planning, where the state was to play the primary role in the economy.

The situation of the rural land-owning elites was in a sense the opposite. Their control over land and agrarian labour – the vast majority of the labour force – gave them substantial power. Much of the Congress organisation in the rural areas was dominated by this group.[21] However, what limited the influence of the rural elites in the Constitution-making process was the fact that, unlike the other two groups, they lacked an 'alternate coherent vision' which they could posit as a vision of 'national interest'.[22] Added to this was the fact that their influence and organisation was local and internally differentiated due to the vast diversity in land holding patterns across India. Furthermore, they did not possess the necessary technical skill or language with which to control the levers of the state. The most they could do was act as a 'persistent undertow' to the dominant developmental vision. The centralised architecture of the Constitution, with more power allocated to the national as opposed to the provisional governments (where the landowning elites had more influence), was a mark of their relative weakness regarding the constitutional project.

The group that supplied much of the vision, the language and the terms of public justification for the Constitution was the professional elites. The professional elites did not constitute a class by virtue of their control of the production process or material resources. Rather, their position was derived from their role in managing the state institutions and their mastery of forms of knowledge and skills suited for that task. The colonial regime created limited opportunities for westernised education for a section of the indigenous elites. Although a miniscule proportion of the population, this class consisted of a substantial number who went into professional services like law, bureaucracy or academia. The nature and interest of the colonial state – the professional sphere of activity for this class – was related only minimally, if at all, to the interests of Indian capital. As a result, this class developed a distinct sphere of its own, without 'much of a direct stake in the fortunes of private capital'.[23]

20.4 THE ADMINISTRATOR AS THE AUTHOR OF THE CONSTITUTION

What made the class of professional elites prominent was both the nature of the post-colonial transition and the complexity of post-colonial regime formation. The fact that the transition did not happen through a disruptive revolutionary process and hence left the infrastructures of the state nearly intact meant that the task of building and maintaining the nascent post-colonial regime fell primarily to this group. Specialised knowledge of the workings of state institutions was highly prized, as evidenced by the overwhelming presence and influence of the members of this class in the Constituent Assembly. Beyond the affairs of managing the state, the professional

[21] E. Stokes, 'Agrarian Relations: Northern and Central India', in D. Kumar and M. Desai (eds.), *Cambridge Economic History of India, Vol. 2, c. 1757–c. 1970* (Cambridge University Press, 1983); P. R. Brass, *Fractional Politics in an Indian State* (University of California Press, 1965).

[22] S. Kaviraj, 'A Critique of the Passive Revolution' (1988) 23 *Economic and Political Weekly* 2429, 2431.

[23] P. Bardhan, *The Political Economy of Development in India* (Blackwell, 1984), 52.

class was crucial to the strategy of gradual and controlled social transformation. Development planning, the mode in which that transformation was to be achieved, was the terrain where the specific attributes of this class was most valued. The 'scarcity value of education' made the knowledge and expertise offered by the professional class an especially prized asset. Apart from the fact that India had nearly 85 per cent illiteracy at the time of independence, there was no sufficiently developed intellectual apparatus of the peasantry or the working class that could propose and execute an alternative vision of transformation. This lack of alternatives from below, nearly as important as the corresponding weakness of the capitalist class, made the professional elites crucial for the realisation of a planned development.

As freedom came to be defined not just in political but also economic terms, modernisation and productivity increase through planning and the consequent eradication of material deprivation was the basis on which the post-colonial rulers appealed for the continuing support of the masses. They claimed authority not on the basis of force but of knowledge. Colonial rule had deprived India of a sufficient base of engineers and scientists, but it did leave behind an enormous corps of trained administrators. While they had to adjust to a very different set of instruments and language by which to perform their task – from coordinators of coercion to impresarios of democratic order – their basic skill set was critical to the construction and legitimacy of the nascent regime. In India, the pre-eminent constituent subject was the administrator.

This explains a couple of curious facts about the Indian Constitution. The first is that nearly two-thirds of the Constitution was almost a verbatim reproduction of the colonial Government of India Act of 1935. Like all putative constitutional acts of the colonial government this Act was primarily an administrative manual: a comprehensive rule-book for operating the complex and vast machineries of the colonial state and ensuring its functional coherence. The professional elites had been trained in that manual for operating the state machinery. Its language and grammar, levers and pulleys, were familiar to them from experience. So when the time came for them to devise their own institutional architecture, they drew heavily from the text they knew well.[24]

Second, it also explained the extraordinary length of the Constitution, which made it the longest national constitution in the world. This was due to the inclusion of exhaustive details about administrative arrangements, apportionment of various governmental duties, lengthy schedules and so on. These are things that one would not expect to find in a constitution but in less celebrated public law iteration of administrative acts. Ambedkar acknowledged in the Assembly that normally such 'administrative details' would 'have no place in the Constitution'. But, the 'necessities' of the Indian condition 'justifies their inclusion'.[25]

Beyond these particularities, the administrative authors of the Constitution adopted what Martin Loughlin calls a 'functionalist' view of public law.[26] They challenged the view that law could be understood as a set of norms that transcend the particularities of its social context and stipulate ideal standards. The functionalist view situated public law within an objective matrix informed by the basic function of the state. In the context of post-colonial India, this was primarily development and planned social transformation. Both the formulation and interpretation of public law had to be purposive. This framing could be contrasted with a rights-based

[24] S. Dasgupta, 'A Language that is Foreign to Us: Continuities and Anxieties in the Making of the Indian Constitution' (2014) 34 *Comparative Studies of South Asia, Africa, and the Middle East* 228.

[25] B. R. Ambedkar, *Constituent Assembly Debates*, 25 November 1949.

[26] M. Loughlin, 'The Functionalist Style in Public Law' (2005) 55 *Toronto Law Journal* 361.

framing, which focussed on the constraints on the actions of the state. After emerging in the mid-nineteenth century (primarily in continental Europe), by the early twentieth century the functionalist style was a globally influential current.[27] It was coeval with the rise of the administrative state and consequently administrative law.

In India, in the condition of a revolution without revolution, there did not exist a widely shared common political vision that could override or transcend the divisions and fractures of social existence. The unity of the Indian territory was an administrative legacy held together by the force of colonial arms. The creation of a genuine post-colonial unity therefore had to be constituted at the level of the state, as an administrative task. These were the men, the technicians of the state, who sought to construct the architecture of public law in India: one that sought to functionally analyse and perform the task of making a whole out of this fractured society.

'We have bigger decisions to take, graver choices before us, than those of lawyers' making', Jawaharlal Nehru, the First Prime Minister of India, reminded his colleagues in the Constituent Assembly.[28] Public law had to be imagined outside the orthodoxies of legal thought. Not as general rules standing above society, but as precise mechanisms based on analysis of particular social condition. To control and manage this complex condition, one had to anticipate the possible ways the transformational project could unfold in practice – the various authorities that might be involved, the cohesiveness of their actions, the potential interpretations of the text and probable obstacles. This required a calculation of mechanics, techniques and scenarios. Indian constitution-makers studied recent constitutional experiences across the world – searching for precise parts of the machine and seeking insights into how they operated in practice.[29] The aim of this impressive comparative analysis was to analyse the particular problems that develop through constitutional practice, especially the possible meanings phrases can assume, and to identify provisions that could fit India's needs. There was an explicit focus in these studies on technical solutions and phrasings – that is functions – rather than any general principles or abstract ideals. Global constitutional practices were analysed from the point of view of an expert administrator.

20.5 THE PARLIAMENT AND THE PLANNERS

The Indian constitution-makers chose to have a parliamentary, as opposed to a presidential, system of government. Parliament was envisaged as a mediating institutional mechanism for the two most significant, and potentially destabilising, elements of the new order – deliberate state-led socio-economic transformation (i.e., development planning) and universal adult franchise. There is an analytically trivial explanation for this choice. Most post-colonial countries, at least initially, adopted the institutions of their former colonial rulers.[30] Though several former British colonies would later shift from a parliamentary to a presidential system, almost none went the other way. But a story of institutional legacy is complicated by the fact that the state that the post-colonial rulers inherited, namely the colonial state, was a model of unfettered executive authority.

[27] M. Loughlin, *Public Law and Political Theory* (Clarendon Press, 1992).
[28] J. Nehru, *Constituent Assembly Debates*, 21 July 1947.
[29] G. Austin, *The Indian Constitution: Cornerstone of a Nation* (Oxford University Press, 1972).
[30] A. Przeworski, *Democracy and the Limits of Self Government* (Cambridge University Press, 2010); Go, 'A Globalizing Constitutionalism?', 71.

There was a further reason why India could have moved toward an empowered executive-driven presidential model, as many of its post-colonial peers. The inherent institutional unity of the presidential system was far better equipped to handle the complex task of managing a planned transformation. From Bismarck's Germany to Stalin's Soviet Union to Meiji Japan, all the late developing economies followed such a path, as did India's Third World contemporaries like Nasser's Egypt or Sukarno's Indonesia. The choice of parliamentarism was far from an obvious or standard choice.

For the Indian constitution-makers, however, the problem was a specific one: how to pursue a planned transformation under conditions of mass democracy. In the transitional moment of decolonisation, there was no immediate definable crisis, nor a plan of action to be enforced post-haste. Rather, mass electoral democracy meant the situation in India was 'dynamic and fluid' (to use Nehru's words), with yet unforeseen demands and coalitions that could arise requiring a constant process of calculation and relatively swift adjustments.[31] A parliamentary system with inbuilt mechanisms for negotiations, coalition building, and deliberations was much better suited for such a task than a presidential system. Most importantly these mechanisms were available for use almost continuously and were suitably low key, not requiring the mobilisation of nation-wide elections to achieve their aims. They could act as the node for a two-way process: allowing members of parliament to voice the demands of their constituents, thereby creating an efficient feedback mechanism for development planners and administrators; and on the other hand the parliamentarians with a local base could act as the spokespersons of the state and its developmental agenda, thereby generating legitimacy and stability for it.[32] In its ideal version, the parliament could serve as the mediating plain between the developmental administration and popular political expression. There is a familiar critique of the presidential/executive driven social transformation project in say Egypt or Latin America whereby the rulers were more willing to make expansive social policy statements than to give popular politics any real voice in the affairs of the state.[33] The parliamentary model in India therefore had the potential to be a more democratic form of post-colonial developmentalism.

This ideal was not fully realised, however. The assumption that a robust democratic process that would successfully translate popular aspiration at the level of the state could be achieved merely through institutional arrangements, proved to be wrong. In the absence of a party that was willing to actively engage in popular mobilisation and organisation around the social question, the kind of active feedback mechanism imagined never came to fruition. Any organisation or mobilisation was purely electoral. Consequently, democracy in this context came to stand in purely for electoral competition rather than any expansive sense of popular participation in the developmental agenda. And without that mediating link, parliament's role soon became just one of garnering enough votes to capture the executive This trend was formalised by the rise of Indira Gandhi in the 1970s as a plebiscitary executive standing above both the party and the parliament and one that has been reproduced with even more favourable institutional balance by the current regime.[34]

[31] J. Nehru, *Constituent Assembly Debates*, 10 September 1949.

[32] S. Dasgupta, 'Parliamentarism, Not Presidentialism: Development and Democracy in India' (2018) 53 *Economic and Political Weekly* 43.

[33] J. Beinin, *Workers and Peasants in the Modern Middle East* (Cambridge University Press, 2001); R. Gargarella, *Latin American Constitutionalism 1810–2010* (Oxford University Press, 2013).

[34] S. Kaviraj, 'Indira Gandhi and Indian Politics' (1986) 21 *Economic and Political Weekly* 1697.

20.6 LAWYERS AND SOCIAL TRANSFORMATION

The decline in the prominence of the parliament opened up space for the third branch of government to play a role that was not initially envisaged by the constitution-makers. The drafters were well aware that one potential obstacle to a constitutional path to social transformation was the judiciary. It was not the familiar concern about the counter-majoritarian power of judicial review that worried them. Unlike in the United States, they explicitly incorporated that power into the Constitution. Rather, what was at stake was the different kinds of expertise and judgement that planner administrators and judges were trained in, and how the former were much better suited to the task of planned social intervention and transformation. Technocrats and administrators, mediated by parliamentary deliberations, had both the necessary knowledge and expertise as well as the proper method for deciding on the various issues that could arise in the course of post-colonial social transformation. Judges, trained in the specialised body of rules and precedents, lacked both that knowledge and the expertise. Second, the very nature of the common law tradition in which all Indian lawyers and judges were raised – an obedience to past norms and precedents – ran counter to the future-oriented project of social transformation that the post-colonial regime was committed to. Finally, judges viewed matters through the lens of specific litigations. The framing of a litigation was fundamentally different from the way the transformational project was meant to be framed. The technocrats and administrators situated individual problems within a larger whole, in a purposive manner. Litigation on the other hand could potentially frame complex issues of social transformation through the lens of the conflict between two parties and their contending rights.[35] The resolution of this conflict had to be found not in the most appropriate solution for advancing the goals of the transformative plan, but in the correct set of legal doctrines and methods of interpretation. True to their functionalist orientation, the constitution makers sought to set up a 'division of labour' between the executive/legislature and the judiciary.[36] The executive/legislature was to act on complex social and economic questions facing the country. The judiciary was to act as a watchdog to ensure that such acts never become capricious or arbitrary, instead of judging them on their substance or merits. As Nehru stated in the Assembly regarding the transformational project: 'The law should do it. Parliament should do it. There is no reference in this to any judiciary coming into the picture.'[37]

There are three prominent examples in the Constitution of this deliberate attempt to keep the judiciary away from substantive questions of social transformation. First was the list of enumerated rights. Each article declaring the right (say, a right to free speech) was followed by a set of clarifications called 'permissible limits' that listed carefully crafted exceptions for actions that would otherwise be construed as a violation of that right (for example, 'security of the state' or 'public order'). Normally, such exceptions to rights are carved out through judicial decisions. The constitution-makers felt that the task of such 'balancing' should be left to the legislative and administrative branches rather than the judiciary, given they were better suited to striking the

[35] E. Pashukanis, *General Theory of Law and Marxism* (Pluto Press, 2001).

[36] U. Baxi, 'The Little Done, The Vast Undone: Some Reflections on Reading Glanville Austin's The Indian Constitution' (1967) 9 *Journal of the Indian Law Institute* 323.

[37] J. Nehru, *Constituent Assembly Debates*, 10 September 1949.

balance between particular instances of individual rights and the project of planned development.[38]

The second example was the deliberate absence of the phrase 'due process' from the property clause of the Constitution. During their comparative constitutional study, the constitution-makers heard from the New Deal justice Felix Frankfurter, who warned that the phrase 'due process' opened up the possibility of judges examining the substantive aspects of legislation rather than just its procedural fairness.[39] Worried that this would lead to a pathway for the judiciary to sit in judgement over aspects of the social transformational agenda, the constitution-makers removed the phrase from the draft.

Finally, there was the example of the 'Directive Principles of State Policy': a part of the Constitution that included a host of goals for the post-colonial regime – from social welfare to labour conditions, education to women's empowerment. The reason these were not drafted as social 'rights' was to keep them outside the purview of judicial determination. Rather they were framed as explicitly non-justiciable aspirational goals, whose realisation and temporal horizon was to be determined by the administrators and legislatures as they moved along with the transformational project, unencumbered by interference from the judiciary.

The divide between the administrative and judicial power was not simply a matter of abstract institutional analysis. Its social basis lay in a prominent division within the class of the professional elites: lawyers versus administrators. Under colonial rule, while the administrators were tasked with the stability and functioning of the colonial state machinery, the lawyers represented individual interests to, and often against, the state. As a result, the lawyerly standpoint tended to emphasise decolonisation more in terms of the 'rule of law'. This required some forms of general norms and abstract rights, not just 'lessons of experience'. Due to the role they played under colonial rule as the most prominent intermediaries between the otherwise estranged colonial rulers and the colonised subjects, the lawyers enjoyed a significant social base and prominence. If the claim to authority of the experts and managers rested on their knowledge and the future progress it could help bring about, the lawyer's authority was built through a more quotidian experience of mediating disputes between (predominantly upper and middle class) individuals and the state. This social base meant their viewpoint was a counterpoint to the administration – which explains the anxiety about the potential actions of the judiciary. Their relative absence from the life of the subaltern masses – who faced the coercive violence of the colonial state with little mediation or recourse to law – on the other hand underlined the need for more effective administrative interventions. Despite the differences between them, the professional elites in general shared a wariness towards popular mobilisation and class conflict. The administrative viewpoint, with its self-assured confidence that technocratic solutions could successfully rise above the conflict of interests and classes, initially made it more suited for the transitional project. But as that project stalled, the lawyers and their institutional expression – the judiciary – sought to play a larger role in constitutional life.

Constitutional development in India for the first seven decades of the republic can be plotted along the lines of a conflict between lawyers and administrators for the custody of the constitution. As the developmental aspirations of the transitional moment seemed exhausted by the beginning of the 1970s – both in terms of achieving its stated goals and as a result in terms of its

[38] D. Kennedy, 'The Critique of Rights in Critical Legal Studies', in W. Brown, & J. Halley (eds.), *Left Legalism/Left Critique* (Duke University Press, 2002), 178–229.

[39] G. Austin, *The Indian Constitution: Cornerstone of a Nation* (Oxford University Press, 1972).

political legitimacy – the Supreme Court began playing a more assertive role in claiming the final say over all matters constitutional and by extension most forms of social intervention. Within the professional elites, the administrators and planners had lost their initial prominence to the rural landowning classes due to the latter's ability to successfully capture the electoral machine. They then successfully mobilised that power to frustrate major transformational projects like land reform.[40] At the same time, international developments like sovereign debt and economic dependencies lessened the developmental aspirations and ability of the post-colonial state. While the prestige of the administrative elites diminished and the initial aspirations of the parliament to act as a mediator of popular aspirations was frustrated, the courtroom became the primary site for voicing demands for social policy, and lawyers once again became the primary conveyors of middle class voices to the state. As a result the Supreme Court began adjudicating complex matters of social policy through the vehicle of 'Public Interest Litigation' – in keeping with trends in other post-colonial countries especially in Latin America and Africa.[41] There has been no prominent social movement in the last three decades – whether it be for education, housing, or the environment – that has not filed a case before the Supreme Court to meet its demands. The judicial custodianship of the Constitution was complete when, in a judgement unprecedented in the annals of constitutional law, the Supreme Court asserted that they could exercise power of judicial review even over constitutional amendments. As the material basis of the project of 'social transformation through constitution' shifted, lawyers rather than administrators emerged as the principle post-colonial constituent subjects.

20.7 CONCLUSION

Lawyers replacing administrators as the custodians of the Constitution was not just a change in style – from functionalist to legalist. It was the result of a major change in the social basis of the transformational project and, by extension, the Constitution. The decline in prominence of the administrator was conditioned by the corresponding rise of the other two dominant classes: first the landowning classes through their control of the electoral machine; and subsequently of the capitalist class as the country was integrated into the global market. These were, in their respective ways, a signal of the decline of the developmental project that was shared by so much of the Third World. It is only after its passing that the project of transformation through constitution moves from the parliament and planning commission to the courtroom. This shift of location was also a shift of scope. While the original transformational ambitions envisaged projects like land reform and nationalisation of resources, the best that the Courts could offer were targeted rights claims for the remedy of specific misfortunes. The increasing dependence of progressive political actors on the Courts – in India as elsewhere – over the last few decades is in a sense as much a sign of a defeat and a retreat from much more expansive ambitions of the past.

As frustrations with the transformational project grew, the domain of extra-constitutional agitation again resurfaced as part of the repertoire of political action for making material or welfare claims on the state. It is now a common feature of Indian political life to witness blockades of roads or symbolic attacks on government properties to demand better infrastructure, entitlements or jobs. This is what Partha Chatterjee has influentially termed the domain of

[40] A. Kohli, *The State and Poverty in India: The Politics of Reform* (Cambridge University Press, 1987); F. R. Frankel, *India's Political Economy, 1947–2004: The Gradual Revolution* (Oxford University Press, 2005).

[41] A. Bhuwania, *Courting the People: Public Interest Litigation in Post Emergency India* (Cambridge University Press, 2017).

'political society', conducted entirely in extra-legal terms, rather than through any formal constitutional paths.[42] On the other hand, the Courts increasingly sought to embody the deliberative transformational domain, instituting social policies, forming expert committees and pronouncing broad developmental plans in the nominal guise of rights claim – from education to electrification. Unsurprisingly, this produced no broad transformational vision but rather a patchwork of committee reports and judgements, focused on particular disputes, often unimplementable. As both these paths show, the constitution makers were correct in their foresight that the social question would remain the central issue of Indian political life. Yet, the conflicts over that question are now fought precisely on the terms that they sought to avoid.

[42] P. Chatterjee, *Politics of the Governed: Reflections on Popular Politics in Most of the World* (Columbia University Press, 2004).

21

China's Material Constitution

Ngoc Son Bui

China is particularly relevant to the theoretical conversations on the material constitution[1] due to ideational, historical, and institutional reasons:

First, dialectical materialism is the key methodology of Marxism–Leninism, the official ideology of the Communist Party of China – the ruling party in the country.[2] This methodology focuses on the real social and economic conditions of institutional development, including those of law and constitution.

Second, China's socialist constitutional history is shaped by social and political conditions. The founding of the People's Republic of China in 1949 after a communist revolution created the political condition for the new socialist constitutional order, part of which is the 1954 Constitution. The Cultural Revolution led to the promulgation of the 1975 Constitution. The need to institutionalise Four Modernizations (modernising agriculture, industry, national defence and society and technology) animated the enactment of the 1978 Constitution. China's current Constitution was enacted in 1982 to institutionalise and facilitate the 'Open Door' economic policy. The 1982 Constitution was amended several times (in 1998, 1993, 1999, 2004 and 2018) to respond to domestic socioeconomic reform and China's increasingly important role in the international political order. The mutual interactions between formal constitutional development and societal conditions are well captured in Qianfan Zhang's contextual account of China's constitution.[3]

Third, China lacks a judicial institution for constitutional review. The state's Constitution vests the constitutional interpretation power to the Standing Committee of the National People's Congress – the permanent body of the national legislature – and courts are not allowed to review the constitutionality of governmental actions.[4] Without judicial constitutional review, China's actual constitutional development is shaped by social, political dynamics rather than by legal arguments in courtrooms.

[1] M. Goldoni and M. Wilkinson, 'The Material Constitution' (2018) 81 *Modern Law Review* 569.

[2] China's Constitution, Preamble (amended 2018).

[3] Q. Zhang, *The Constitution of China: A Contextual Analysis* (Hart, 2012).

[4] Q. Zhang, 'Establishing Judicial Review in China: Impediments and Prospects', in A. H. Y. Chen and A. Harding (eds.), *Constitutional Courts in Asia: A Comparative Perspective* (Cambridge University Press, 2018), 311.

This chapter explores the material constitution of the socialist state in mainland China.[5] It first reviews the material accounts of China's constitution. These accounts are not explicitly self-identified as 'material', but touch on contextual aspects of China's constitutional system, which echoes the main concerns of material constitutionalists. This chapter then considers how the material constitution is manifested in China. China's material constitution refers to both Chinese party-state constitutional order and its social-economic conditions. They are inter-related: the constitutional order both shapes and is shaped by the social-economic conditions. The chapter concludes by considering the relation of the material constitution and the formal Constitution.[6]

21.1 MATERIAL ACCOUNTS OF CHINA'S CONSTITUTION

A body of English-language scholarship explores various societal aspects of China's constitutional order, which resonates with the material accounts of the constitution. These include the inquiries into China's ancient constitution, unwritten constitution, dual constitution and political constitutionalism.

Consider first the study on the ancient constitution in China by Su Li (Zhu Suli), a scholar of sociology of law at Peking University Law School.[7] Following Aristotle, he uses the term 'constitution' to refer to both the action of constituting and to the fundamental institution.[8] On that basis, constitution in ancient China means the action of constituting China's dynastic state and its fundamental institutions.

> Some of these institutions and practices are laws; some of them, however, are perhaps principles or norms that direct executive or judicial decisions, but most of them in the actual practice of political and legal activity in historical China have impregnated Chinese society and people's everyday life, working in a hidden and silent way to make these people Chinese as well as shaping and forming China. They form an effective constitution.[9]

That 'effective' constitution emerged in the Qin-Han period and continued to develop in the subsequent dynasties in China.[10]

Like the accounts on the material constitution, Su Li's account of the 'effective constitution' in ancient China deals with the formation of a unified state ('a common political body'), the actual working of fundamental dynastic institutions, the social institutions (the rural villages), the common goals of organisational structure ('how to form and maintain this huge political, economic, and cultural body, how to shape and constitute this common body from the political, economic, and cultural angles').[11] Su Li also discusses the geophysical factors (the Yellow River and agriculture) of the constitution in ancient China. These are the material conditions of constituting China.

[5] For contextual, historical accounts of other jurisdictions of Greater China, see J. Buhi, *Global Constitutional Narratives of Autonomous Regions: The Constitutional History of Macau* (Routledge, 2021); R. Cullen, *Hong Kong Constitutionalism: The British Legacy and the Chinese Future* (Routledge, 2020); J. Yeh, *The Constitution of Taiwan: A Contextual Analysis* (Hart, 2016).

[6] In this chapter, the small-c 'constitution' refers to China's material constitution or the constitutional order, while the big-C 'Constitution' denotes its formal Constitution or the constitutional text.

[7] S. Li, *The Constitution of Ancient China*, Y. Zhang and D. A. Bell, eds. (Princeton University Press, 2018).

[8] Ibid., 19.

[9] Ibid.

[10] Ibid., 28.

[11] Ibid., 22, 27.

Su Li's work explores the actual institutional formation and development in ancient China. The difficulty with this account is it may collapse into the study of the formation and institutional development of the Chinese ancient state.[12] However, Su Li's study has implications for comparative study of the material constitution in the ancient world. For example, it is possible to compare the constitution of the city-states in ancient Greece with the constitution in ancient China.

Other accounts of the socialist constitutional order in modern China also deal with its material conditions. One of them is the study of the 'unwritten constitution' in socialist China by Jiang Shigong, another law professor at Peking University Law School.[13] Criticising formalism in Chinese constitutional studies, he focuses on 'political reality' and adopts 'historical and sociological methods to explore "what the real constitution is in political life", or "what the effective constitution is"'.[14] On that methodological assumption, Jiang Shigong argues that the Chinese constitutional order includes both the written formal Constitution and unwritten constitution. He focuses on important issues of Chinese constitutional politics, namely: the relationship between the Communist Party of China and the National People's Congress; the position of state chairman; central–local relations; and the 'one country two systems' arrangement. He demonstrates that these issues are, respectively, shaped by four sources of unwritten constitutional norms: party's constitution, constitutional conventions of 'trinity system of rule' (one person heading the party, the military and the state), the constitutional doctrine called Initiatives from Two Sources (reform deriving from both central and local government), and constitutional statutes (the Hong Kong Basic Law).[15]

Other accounts on the 'dual constitution' in China particularly focus on the relation of the party Constitution to the state Constitution. The Party Constitution sets down its political goals, membership, organisational structure, officials, and discipline.[16] Cuban-American constitutional law scholar Larry Catá Backer argues that party-state constitutional order in China includes both the party Constitution regulating the political power and the state Constitution regulating the administrative power of the state, with the former as the source for the latter.[17] This view is adopted in Jiang Shigong's study.[18] Xin He also discusses the party leadership as a living constitution in China.[19] In the same vein, Shucheng Wang provides a detailed account of the evolution of the dual constitution in China, including the dual congresses (the party congress and the state's legislature), dual judiciaries (the party discipline institutions and the state courts), the dual executive systems (the Government and the Party's parallel departments).[20]

[12] For unification and development of a bureaucratic empire under the state of Qin in 221 BCE and the subsequent institutional developments of the dynastic states in China, see D. Zhao, *The Confucian–Legalist State: A New Theory of Chinese History* (Oxford University Press, 2015).

[13] J. Shigong, 'Written and Unwritten Constitutions: A New Approach to the Study of Constitutional Government in China' (2010) 36 *Modern China* 12.

[14] Ibid., 15.

[15] Ibid., 23–40.

[16] Constitution of the Communist Party of China, revised and adopted at the 19th National Congress of the Communist Party of China on 24 October 2017, available at: www.xinhuanet.com//english/download/Constitution_of_the_Communist_Party_of_China.pdf, last accessed 9 August 2022.

[17] L. C. Backer, 'Party, People, Government, and State: On Constitutional Values and the Legitimacy of the Chinese State-Party Rule of Law System' (2012) 30 *Boston University International Law Journal* 343.

[18] J. Shigong, 'Chinese-Style Constitutionalism: On Backer's Chinese Party-State Constitutionalism' (2014) 40 *Modern China* 133.

[19] X. He, 'The Party's Leadership As a Living Constitution in China', in T. Ginsburg and A. Simpser (eds.), *Constitutions in Authoritarian Regimes* (Cambridge University Press, 2013), 245.

[20] S. Wang, 'Emergence of a Dual Constitution in Transitional China' (2015) 45 *Hong Kong Law Journal* 819, 841–47.

Another approach to China's constitution is political constitutionalism.[21] Echoing the UK story, Chinese political constitutionalism emerged since 2008 as an antithesis to legal constitutionalism, the mainstream scholarly trend toward the judicialisation of China's Constitution, which has been influenced by American constitutional law.[22] Chinese political constitutionalists include Chen Duanhong, Gao Quanxi and Zhai Xiaobo, among others. Some argue that Chinese political constitutionalism was inspired by the 'reflexive wave' of political constitutionalism in the UK discourse.[23] The reflexive accounts focus on the context and condition of the political constitution and what the political is.[24] Similarly, Chinese political constitutionalists discuss the political conditions and constitutional events (such as constitution making and the use of constituent power and constitutional moment) and the actual working of the political institutions.[25]

The accounts of the 'unwritten constitution', 'dual constitution' and 'political constitutionalism' in China resonate with the material approach to constitution as it aims to understand the reality of the Chinese constitutional order. These studies, however, focus on the actual working of political institutions and have not yet substantively explored the broader social and economic context of Chinese constitutional ordering.[26]

21.2 ELEMENTS OF CHINA'S MATERIAL CONSTITUTION

China's material constitution refers to the party-state constitutional order and its socio-economic conditions. It includes three elements: the party-state, the economy and the society. In China's constitutional ordering, the party-state both shapes and is shaped by the social and economic conditions.

21.2.1 *The Party-State*

The political unity for the material constitution is Chinese modern state. David Shambaugh observes:

> The modern Chinese state has undergone several macro transitions: from imperial to republican to revolutionary communist to modernizing socialist and, in Taiwan, to democratic phases. While radically different in its basic ethos and organizational structure in each phase (monarchical–republican–Leninist–liberal), the Chinese state on the mainland has had three enduring missions: modernization of the economy, transformation of society, and defense of the nation against foreign aggression.[27]

[21] B. Su, 'Political but Incontestable: A Review of "Political Constitutionalism" in China' (2021) 10 *Global Constitutionalism* 10; L. Brang, 'The Dilemmas of Self-Assertion: Chinese Political Constitutionalism in a Globalized World' (2022) 48 *Modern China* 498; A. H. Y. Chen, 'The Discourse of Political Constitutionalism in Contemporary China: Gao Quanxi's Studies on China's Political Constitution' (2014) 14 *China Review* 183.

[22] H. Liu, 'Regime-Centered and Court-Centered Understandings: The Reception of American Constitutional Law in Contemporary China' (2020) 68 *The American Journal of Comparative Law* 95.

[23] Su, 'Political but Incontestable', 20.

[24] M. Goldoni and C. McCorkindale, 'Three Waves of Political Constitutionalism' (2019) 30 *King's Law Journal* 74, 84.

[25] For more details about the 'political registers' in Chinese political constitutionalism, see Su, 'Political but Incontestable', 20–27.

[26] For the exploration of the social and economic conditions of constitutional system in China, see R. Peerenboom, 'Social Foundations of China's Living Constitution', in T. Ginsburg (ed.), *Comparative Constitutional Design* (Cambridge University Press, 2012), 138.

[27] D. Shambaugh, 'Introduction: The Evolving and Eclectic Modern Chinese State', in D. Shambaugh (ed.), *The Modern Chinese State* (Cambridge University Press, 2000), 1.

Due to limited space, this chapter focuses on the Chinese modernising socialist state in the mainland as the political unity for the country's material constitution. Economic reform, social transformation and national defence to build 'socialism with Chinese characteristics' are the fundamental political objectives of the state. The Chinese socialist state is the party-state. The material accounts of China's constitution indicate that the Communist Party of China is an integral part of Chinese constitutional order, not an electoral party as in liberal democracy. Throughout its history, the Party has transformed from a revolutionary party (the party leading radical political revolution) into a ruling party (the party leading social and economic reform).[28] The Party's leadership is mandated in Article 1 of the state's formal Constitution through the 2018 amendments. China's party-state constitutional order is constituted by actual political institutions, their operation, and their relations. The political institutions include party institutions and state institutions.

The party's institutions include the National Congress, the Central Committee, Political Bureau, specific institutions (such as Central Commission for Discipline Inspection and Central Military Commission) and numerous party cells at the local level. As an inherent part of China's material constitution, the Party influences teleological and institutional aspects of the constitutional order. The Party sets down fundamental objectives for the development of the socialist state. Institutionally, since 1993, the positions of the General Secretary and President of State 'have always been held by the same person'.[29] This can be considered a constitutional convention of China's material constitution. Through its institutions, the Party decides directions for the institutional development of the state and party members to hold key state posts.[30]

The legitimacy of the Party's leading role in the constitutional order is shaped by change in the material conditions. The Party first came to power by leading a revolution resulting in the founding of the People's Republic of China on 1 October 1949. Therefore, its legitimacy originally depended on the revolutionary source. Since 1989, when China began to reform, the Party's legitimacy has depended on its actual performance in leading economic development and social transformation. In the last four decades, economic development and the improvement of living standards confer performance-based legitimacy on the Party's rule.[31]

The state institutions include bureaucracy, the legislature and the judiciary. China has created a strong administrative system capable of macroeconomic management and proving basic goods like public security, national defence, legal enforcement and infrastructure. Francis Fukuyama argues that the new bureaucracy emerged in China since the beginning of the reforms in 1978 corresponded to 'the massive shift from the centrally planned economy to a more open and marketized one'.[32] The administrative government in today's China now 'is centralized, massive, and extraordinary complex'.[33] However, corruption in the administrative system is pervasive, which has challenged the legitimacy of the political leadership. Political leaders are aware of the gravity of the situation and initiated forceful anti-corruption campaigns.[34] The recent formal constitutionalisation of the anti-corruption agency (the State

[28] Peerenboom, 'Social Foundations of China's Living Constitution', 144.

[29] T. Zhang and T. Ginsburg, 'China's Turn Toward Law' (2019) 59 *Virginia Journal of International Law* 306, 353.

[30] For more details on the Party's influence on the state's institutions, see He, 'The Party's Leadership As a Living Constitution in China', 248–57.

[31] J. Ci, *Democracy in China: The Coming Crisis* (Harvard University Press, 2020), 19.

[32] F. Fukuyama, *Political Order and Political Decay: From the Industrial Revolution to the Globalization of Democracy* (Farrar, Straus and Giroux, 2015), 371.

[33] Ibid., 374.

[34] Ibid., 380.

Supervision Commission) through the 2018 amendment signals the regime's perception of anticorruption as an issue fundamental to the regime's resilience.

Also, China has created a legislature capable of making a huge amount of law corresponding to the socio-economic transformation in the last three decades. This body is called National People's Congress (NPC) and periodically elected by the people every five years according to the state's Constitution. In practice, popular elections are the main mechanism to create the legislature, albeit under the political control of the Party with various levels. The NPC is unicameral, comprising of a standing committee and special bodies responsible to specific national affairs. The departmentalisation of the legislative structure is instrumental to enhancing law-making capacity. The development of the legislative institution in China is closely connected to economic development. Economic reforms require new laws to regulate new social and economic relations, which puts pressure on enhancing legislative institutional capacity. In turn, legislative development facilitates further economic development by offering the legal framework for economic transactions.[35]

Scholars discuss the role of the legislature in Chinese constitutional order. Yan Lin and Tom Ginsburg argued that China's legislature is the mechanism to interpret the formal Constitution, which redistributes governmental power, defines citizens' rights and adjusts the economic structure.[36] Yan Lin additionally demonstrates that: 'Through statute-making, both the National People's Congress and its Standing Committee have enriched and changed the definition of both vertical and horizontal governmental relations, as well as created new rules and principles for inter-regional relations. As a result, the overall state power structure has become more decentralized, diverse and balanced.'[37]Michael W. Dowdle even considers the legislature as the locus of Chinese variant of constitutionalism as this institution was able to veto draft bills submitted by the other political actors and 'discipline other political actors through the use of parliamentary investigations'.[38] He argues that the growing of distinct social interests incentivised the political elite and the emerging civil society to shift the locus of their dialogue out of the Party and into a constitutional apparatus, like the National People's Congress.[39]

China has also created a sophisticated judicial system in the last three decades capable of resolving a variety of legal disputes. The judicial institution is complex, consisting of thousands of district-level basic people's courts staffed by 46,000 judges, hundreds of prefecture-level intermediate people's courts staffed by 36,000 judges, 31 provincial level high people's courts staffed by 7,000 judges, and the Supreme People's Court (SPC) at the central level staffed by more than 500 judges, in addition to specialist courts, such as military courts and maritime courts.[40] The Chinese courts are capable of resolving a vast number of legal disputes.

35 For the reform of the legislature in China, see K. J. O'Brien, *Reform without Liberalization: China's National People's Congress and the Politics of Institutional Change* (Cambridge University Press, 1990); M. W. Dowdle, 'The Constitutional Development and Operations of the National People's Congress' (1997) 11 *Columbia Journal of Asian Law* 1.

36 Y. Lin and T. Ginsburg, 'Constitutional Interpretation in Lawmaking: China's Invisible Constitutional Enforcement Mechanism' (2015) 63 *American Journal of Comparative Law* 467, 472.

37 L. Yan, 'Constitutional Evolution through Legislation: The Quiet Transformation of China's Constitution' (2015) 13 *International Journal of Constitutional Law* 61.

38 M. W. Dowdle, 'Of Parliaments, Pragmatism, and the Dynamics of Constitutional Development: The Curious Case of China' (2002) 35 *NYU Journal of International Law and Politics* 1, 3–4.

39 Ibid., 53.

40 W. Gu, 'Courts in China: Judiciary in the Economic and Societal Transitions', in J. Yeh and W. Chang (eds.), *Asian Courts in Context* (Cambridge University Press, 2015), 489–92.

To illustrate, from January to September 2014, the SPC handled 10,929,314 cases.[41] Lower courts have decided millions of cases annually. Weixia Gu observes that, among different types of cases, 'civil and commercial cases far outnumbered', 'because in the course of deepening marketization, Chinese courts have more and more been expected to serve as impartial arbiters of civil and commercial disputes among citizens and market entities'.[42] The party-state has initiated a comprehensive program for judicial reform. In China, since 1999, the SPC has initiated three five-year judicial reform plans, 1999–2003, 2004–8 and 2009–13.[43] The Chinese Communist Party also issued its *Opinions on Deepening the Reform of the Judicial System and Its Working Mechanisms*.[44] The judicial reform programs cover many issues, like the quality of judges, depoliticisation of the judge election system, professionalism, judicial integrity, judicial anti-corruption and reducing local protectionism, among others.[45]

Judicial reform in China has been undertaken due to the economic reform. Economic growth has engendered social complexity which in turn creates more economic and civil disputes. The conventional informal dispute resolution mechanisms like mediations and social negotiations may still be employed but are insufficient to resolve new disputes. The court system has therefore been reformed to meet with new demands generated by socioeconomic development, although it does not replace the conventional informal mechanisms. But, whether and how judicial reform contributes to economic development in China require empirical investigation. Some empirical survey reveals the judicial institution is less relevant to socioeconomic development than the regulatory environment.[46] One of the reasons may concern the political control of the court system. The courts in China are politically controlled,[47] which limit their independence and efficiency, and this may make social and economic actors turn to alternative dispute solutions.[48]

However, court in China has different functions in commercial and political fields. Yuhua Wang argues that Chinese rulers have incentives to promote partial rule of law and judicial fairness in the commercial realm but impose 'constraints on citizens' political and civil rights to use the court to challenge the state'.[49] One consequence of the latter is that Chinese courts are not formally vested with the power to review the constitutionality of political actions. The absence of judicial constitutional review, however, does not dismiss the court from the material constitution. The court is a part of China's broader constitutional order due to its institutional relations with the Party and state institutions.[50] The Party need courts to implement its political objectives. The legislative and executive institutions also need to rely on courts to resolve daily legal disputes.

[41] 'Cases Tried by People's Court Jan - Sept 2014', *The Supreme People's Court of The People's Republic of China*. Available at: Cases Tried by People's Court Jan–Sept 2014.

[42] Gu, 'Courts in China', 495.

[43] Ibid., 515–17.

[44] Ibid., 517.

[45] Ibid., 515–17.

[46] C. Wei, 'Does Judicial Independence Matter? A Study of the Determinants of Administrative Litigation in an Authoritarian Regime' (2017) 38 *University of Pennsylvania Journal of International Law* 941.

[47] L. Ling, 'The Chinese Communist Party and People's Courts: Judicial Dependence in China' (2016) 64 *American Journal of Comparative Law* 37.

[48] C. F. Minzner, 'China's Turn against Law' (2011) 59 *American Journal of Comparative Law* 935.

[49] Y. Wang, *Tying the Autocrat's Hands: The Rise of The Rule of Law in China* (Cambridge University Press, 2014), 13–14.

[50] F. Hualing, 'Autonomy, Courts and The Politico-Legal Order in Contemporary China', in L. Cao, I. Y. Sun and B. Hebenton (eds.), *The Routledge Handbook of Chinese Criminology* (Routledge, 2013), 76–88.

21.2.2 The Economy

The party-state plays a leading role in the transformation and operation of the socialist market economy in China. The party-state initiated and implemented the program to reform the economy. The China's *Gǎigé kāifàng* ('Reform & Opening up') program in 1978 concentrated on economic reforms toward the model called 'socialist market economy'. The party-state plays a leading role in implementation of these market reforms, which lead to the transformation of the national economy from the planned into market-oriented one.

Several scholars have argued that China is an example of developmental state.[51] The Chinese experience of developmental state is often situated within the East Asian model of developmental state in Japan, South Korea and Singapore.[52] One scholar, for example, argues that Chinese law and development experience is consistent with the model of (East) Asian developmental state, stating that 'Modern Chinese law, like law in the 1960s Asian developmental states, is an instrumentalist mix of borrowings and pragmatic adaptations from both east and west which has grown into an autochthonous construct that serves specific local concepts of development'. Similar 'localist' statutes and institutions have been evident in the newly industrialised nations in Asia, which have been dubbed the Asian developmental states, tigers and miracles. Their laws were designed to serve the developmental purposes of the Asian societies in which they are fostered.[53]

It is true that the Chinese party-state has adopted legal instrumentalism to foster economic development. However, it is misleading to conceptualise China within the East Asian model of developmental state. Scholars who believe that China is within the model of East Asian developmental state tend to focus on legal reforms in the area of private law and overlook the constitutional law and political aspects in Chinese law and development experience. One of the key distinctive features of these two stories is that legal instrumentalism is employed mainly by the party rather than by the government. China is differentiated from other East Asian developmental states by the dominant single communist party. One may argue that law has also been used by other Asian authoritarian states to foster economic development. However, the party-model of authoritarianism in China is different from the models of authoritarianism in other Asian developmental states in the 1960s. The communist party in China is not a private political organisation but the essential component of the polity, inseparable from the state and, hence, the so-called party-state.[54] Law in China is, therefore, instrumental to institutionalising the party's socialist-oriented developmental policies.

In addition, other aspects regarding the legal origins, bureaucracy, the courts, legal education and legal profession in China are considerably divergent from the East Asian model of developmental state. For example, the modern legal system in China has its roots in the Soviet socialist legal tradition, which includes many features different from those of legal systems of other East Asian developmental states which are rooted in western civil law tradition (Japan, South Korea and Taiwan) or common law tradition (Singapore). The difference of legal origins defines the differences in the bureaucracy, the courts, legal education and legal profession. To illustrate, the

[51] J. B. Knight, 'China as a Developmental State' (2014) 37 *The World Economy* 1335; T. Heberer, 'The Chinese "Developmental State 3.0" and the Resilience of Authoritarianism' (2016) 1 *Journal of Chinese Governance* 611.

[52] W. Chen and S. Keng, 'The Chinese Developmental State in Transition: In Light of The East Asian Experiences' (2017) 2 *Journal of Chinese Governance* 209.

[53] C. Carter, 'The Success of Law and Development in China: Is China the Latest Asian Developmental State?', in E. P. McAlinn and C. Pejovic (eds.), *Law and Development in Asia* (Routledge, 2012), 89.

[54] Backer, 'Party, People, Government, and State', 331.

bureaucracy and the judiciary in East Asian developmental states enjoy more independence than their counterparts in China. This is because the Asian developmental states operate within the separation of power scheme while the structure of the Chinese party-state is defined by the Marxist doctrine of 'democratic centralism' which favours concentration of power. In China, the party and the centralised government are the forces that lead and implement development projects.

The role of the party-state in development China is better conceptualised as the 'socialist developmental state'. *The socialist developmental state is a party-state that plays an active role in promoting economic development to achieve socialism within the transformative institutional and legal framework informed by socialist legal concepts and institutions.* The socialist developmental state presents a complex combination of both developmental and socialist properties. The socialist developmental state is *developmental* in the sense that this state, like any developmental state, plays an active role and uses law in promoting economic development. However, the socialist developmental state is *socialist* in two senses. First, the developmental projects are directed toward achieving the paradise of socialism. Second, developmental projects are pursued within the socialist constitutional framework. This framework is transformative as a response to the imperative of economic development, but still retains the core features of socialist constitutional and legal concepts (e.g., party vanguardism, democratic centralism and socialist legality) and the corresponding institutions. These socialist features differentiate the socialist developmental state from other developmental states in East Asia and elsewhere.

21.2.3 *Society*

China lacks mature institutions to limit the government's power. Elections are dominated by the single communist party as a tool to legitimatise the party's monopoly rather than hold the party accountable.[55] Constitutional review, the separation of power and other major institutions of checks and balances are absent. However, China has some other social mechanisms to hold the government and the party accountable, which is animated by socio-economic development. Socio-economic developments in the last three decades have created new social groups and diversified the social interests, which put pressure on creating mechanisms to address the diversified interests of the increasingly pluralised society. New social groups, especially the middle class, demand and mobilise for a government accountable to the public. Domestic socio-economic dynamics and globalisation have also resulted in the dissemination of new ideas about the constitutional legitimacy (such as constituent power, judicial review, the separation of power, limited government) which have challenged the existing arrangement rooted in the Soviet constitutional tradition.[56] This has begun to put pressure on the initial practice of accountable government.

Without a judicial review system, social mobilisation is the social mechanism for the society to protect individual rights and check the abuse of the public power. This is evident in the Chinese *weiquan* movement, 'a comprehensive movement involving all social strata throughout the country and covering every aspect of human rights'.[57] As Feng Chongyi documents:

[55] E. Malesky and P. Schuler, 'Star Search: Do Elections Help Nondemocratic Regimes Identify New Leaders?' (2013) 13 *Journal of East Asian Studies* 35.

[56] R. Creemers, 'China's Constitutionalism Debate: Content, Context and Implications' (2015) 74 *The China Journal* 91.

[57] F. Chongyi, 'The Threat of Charter 08', in J. Beja, E. Pils and H. Fu (eds.), *Liu Xiaobo, Charter 08 and the Challenges of Political Reform in China* (Hong Kong University Press, 2012), 129.

> Most cases of this right defense movement aim to protect economic and social rights, including protests by peasants against excessive taxes, levies, and forced seizes of farmland; strikes by workers against low pay, arrears of pay, and poor working conditions; protests by laid-off unban workers against unfair dismissal by their employers; protests by homeowners against forced eviction by government and developers; protests by residents against forced relocations; campaigns by citizens against unpaid social entitlements; campaigns for the rights of women and children; and protests by affected residents against environmental pollution.[58]

Social actors have mobilised for constitutional change. For example, in 2008, 303 Chinese dissident intellectuals and human rights activists released a manifesto called Charter 08, which was then signed by more than 10,000 people inside and outside China. The charter called for amending the formal Constitution and changes to the broader constitutional order, including separation of power, legislative democracy, judicial independence and basic political freedoms, among others.[59] Ordinary citizens also deployed constitutional arguments as an advocacy strategy to influence policy change.[60] Society's constitutional mobilisation is the dynamics of Chinese's constitutional ordering.

To summarise, the logics of the interaction of the party-state, the economy and society in constitutional ordering in China in the last four decades involves two aspects. The party-state constitutional order both *shapes* and *is shaped* by social and economic changes. At the very beginning of the new development path, the party-state initiated the programmes to reform the economy according to which the state-owned enterprises play the dominant role while private sectors are allowed to develop. The implementation of these programmes has resulted in economic development and social change, which in turn have instigated the needs for both formal and material constitutional development. So, economic development precedes constitutional development. But later constitutional development is coupled with economic development, which in turn has engendered the rise of the new middle class, the social force that is equipped with new ideas and engaged in social mobilisation for further constitutional development. These socio-economic developments are putting pressure on curbing administrative corruption, constraining the public power, effectuating the legislature, ensuring judicial independence and fostering government accountability.

21.3 THE MATERIAL AND THE FORMAL CONSTITUTION

The distinction between the formal and the material constitution in China is important. The replacement of the formal Constitution does not equate to the replacement of the material constitution. Socialist China enacted five constitutions, but core principles (e.g., party leadership, centralised state power, the socialist economy) of the party-state constitutional order largely remain intact. However, formal constitutional replacement reflects and facilitates material constitutional amendments: the actual modification of the party-state's institutional structure, ideological commitments, and social and economic policy.

Formal amendments to China's Constitution in the last decades are shaped by political, social, and economic conditions. Changes in political leadership and the party's policy normally lead to formal constitutional change. Social and economic development and the rise of China

58 Ibid., 129–30.

59 See, generally, J. Beja, E. Pils and H. Fu (eds.), *Liu Xiaobo, Charter 08 and the Challenges of Political Reform in China* (Hong Kong University Press, 2012).

60 M. Jia, 'China's Constitutional Entrepreneurs' (2016) 64 *The American Journal of Comparative Law* 619.

in the global political and economic order also animate formal constitutional amendments. The amendment power formally belongs to the legislature, but the amendment process is functionally placed under the party's leadership. Everything in the Constitution is formally amendable as the document does not have an eternity clause, but substantive cores of the party-state constitutional order (such as party leadership, democratic centralism and the commitment to socialism) are politically unamendable. These are amendable principles because changes to them may lead to a constitutional revolution. The Party may impose informal, implicit, political limits to ensure that the legislature will not change the Constitution in a way that alters the constitutional cores of the socialist regime in China.[61]

China's formal Constitution is a part of the broader constitutional order. It has four functions: teleological, institutional, economic and social. First, the Constitution sets down fundamental political objectives to achieve 'socialist modernization along the road of socialism with Chinese characteristics', such as 'to uphold the people's democratic dictatorship, stay on the socialist road, carry out reform and opening up, steadily improve the socialist institutions, develop the socialist market economy and socialist democracy . . .' (preamble). Second, the Constitution provides a framework for the structure and operation of institutions of the party-state. The teleological, institutional functions are politically relevant. Scholars argued China's formal Constitution carries political weight in the sense that political leaders adhere to it, as evident in the constitutionalisation of the party's leadership, removal of term limits, 'Xi Jinping Thought' and anti-corruption agency through the 2018 formal amendments.[62] Third, the Constitution establishes basic principles of the economy, such as 'socialist public ownership of the means of production' (article 6), diverse forms of ownership (article 6), the leading force of state economic sector in the economy (article 7) and the protection of private property (article 13). These principles both reflect and facilitate economic reform in the last decades.[63] Fourth, the Constitution provides vocabularies for ordinary citizens to voice their concerns about the existing constitutional order and demand for change. In practice, citizens actually use the Constitution to frame their constitutional arguments in their demand for policy change. For example, in 2003, Sun Zhigang, a migrant worker in Guangzhou, died while being detained under China's custody and repatriation system. The incident provoked great public attention. Chinese scholars questioned the constitutionality of China's custody and repatriation system, which, along with other factors, led to the abolition of the system.[64]

The prospective dynamics of China's constitutional order is animated by the 'disharmony'[65] between the formal Constitution and the material constitution. To illustrate, in the public debate on constitutionalism in 2013, liberal intellectuals called for implementing the 1982 Constitution's provisions on fundamental rights and government structure.[66] The gap between formal constitutional commitments and the constitutional practices creates the space for the

61 I explain these in detail in B. N. Son, *Constitutional Change in the Contemporary Socialist World* (Oxford University Press, 2020), 278–84.

62 Zhang and Ginsburg, 'China's Turn Toward Law', 346–47.

63 Z. Wang and Y. Tao, 'Achieving Development through Innovative Constitutionalism: A China Story' (2013) 4 *The World Bank Legal Review* 201, 202

64 For detailed treatment on the case, see K. J. Hand, 'Using Law for a Righteous Purpose: The Sun Zhigang Incident and Evolving Forms of Citizen Action in the People's Republic of China' (2006) 45 *Columbia Journal of Transnational Law* 114.

65 For the idea of constitutional disharmony, see G. J. Jacobsohn, *Constitutional Identity* (Harvard University Press, 2010), 15.

66 See, for example, Z. Qianfan, *The Implementation of the Constitution and Long-Term Governance* (China Copyright and Media, 22 August 2013), available at: https://chinacopyrightandmedia.wordpress.com/2013/08/22/the-implementation-of-the-constitution-and-long-term-governance/, last accessed 9 August 2022.

social actors to struggle through discourse or social mobilisation for constitutional realisation. The gap between the formal and material constitution renders China's formal Constitution to have four social, discursive functions: assertive, expressive, interpretative, and normative. First, through public discourse, citizens may claim their constitutional rights which are not sufficiently materialised. Second, through public discourse, the citizens can express their critical concerns about constitutional and social problems animated by the formal and material constitutional gaps. Third, the citizens, through public discourse, may provide informal interpretations on unmaterialised constitutional commitments which may be very different from formal interpretations. Finally, through public discourse, the citizens may advance new norms and proposals to bridge the gap between the constitutional text and reality.

22

The Material Constitution and Extractive Political Economy

Lessons from Mongolia

Jennifer Lander

22.1 INTRODUCTION

The political economy of natural resource extraction has attracted virtually no interest from constitutional scholars. In this chapter, I explain why this is a grave oversight and how the material constitution can be usefully deployed as an analytical framework in this context. Drawing on a recent socio-legal study of Mongolia's mining economy,[1] I will demonstrate the explanatory acuity of material constitutionalism regarding the political economy of resource extraction and its intrinsic relationship with the transformation of state law and institutions. Section 22.2 sets out the framework of material constitutionalism that will be used to explain legal and political phenomena associated with Mongolia's mining boom in the second – and main – part of the chapter.

22.2 MATERIAL CONSTITUTIONALISM AND EXTRACTIVE POLITICAL ECONOMY

As evidenced by the variety of approaches adopted in this Handbook, there are clearly multiple angles on the theory and method of the material constitution. Consequently, it seems sensible to begin by setting out in broad brushstrokes the approach taken in this chapter. Because of the widely held associations with the term 'materialism', it is important to say right off the bat that I do not adopt a mechanical materialist approach which treats the constitutional order of states as a 'mask'[2] for economic relations of production. From this so-called 'Marxist' perspective, the political and legal domains of the state become a unilinear superstructure crudely determined by its economic base,[3] a type of theorising associated with early twentieth-century state socialist experiments in the Soviet Union and its satellites, including Mongolia.

My approach generally follows the tracks of constitutional materialism represented in the vein of scholarship influenced by Costantino Mortati, among others, where the constitutional order (including the formal constitution) is conceptualised as part of a wider process of societal

[1] J. Lander, *Transnational Law and State Transformation: The Case of Extractive Development in Mongolia* (Routledge, 2020).

[2] A. Shinar, 'The Ideologies of Global Constitutionalism' (2019) 8 *Global Constitutionalism* 22.

[3] I put Marxist in quotation marks because, as Ellen Meiksins Wood astutely points out, Marx himself only ever used the 'base-superstructure metaphor ... in the most aphoristic and allusive formulations'. See E. Meiksins Wood, *Democracy against Capitalism: Renewing Historical Materialism* (Verso, 1995), 49.

organisation.[4] As Goldoni and Wilkinson observe, a core feature of Mortati's approach is its commitment to theorising the role of governing – both legal and political aspects – in constituting society itself: 'Mortati presents society as something that has to be organised, rather than a given.'[5] From this perspective, constitutionalism can never simply be a normative task of identifying ideal-type norms for what the state – and law – *should* be. Rather, it is always an historical task, even if part of its object is to identify what ideals have become normative within a constitutional order. In this sense, the formal, normative constitution does not compete with the material constitution, but is inevitably entangled with it. The material constitution is not unconcerned with norms, jurisprudence or legal doctrine, but contextualises them 'in the deeper societal context in which formal constitutional development is embedded (or, as the case may be, dis-embedded)'.[6]

Material constitutionalism, for it to be worthy of the name, must re-centre history, power and social struggle in its analysis of constitutional norms and forms, which distinguishes it both from traditional 'black letter' approaches to constitutionalism as well as the popular trends of global constitutionalism and sociological constitutionalism.[7] Where doctrinal approaches err on the side of abstraction, turning constitutions into hermetically sealed spaces of law, new varieties of constitutionalism suffer from a tendency to treat contemporary processes of constitutional ordering as radically untethered from the national state and the *transnational* structures of political economy which continue to depend upon territorial jurisdictions. These poles in the wide field of constitutional scholarship miss the messy way in which state constitutions emerge over time, under the influence of a kaleidoscope of 'interdisciplinary' factors, path dependencies and the continual dialectic of ideology and practice.

There is a strong sense that constitutionalism must retain a relatively monist character if it is to be worthy of the description, given that we are speaking of political and legal relations that acquire a hegemonic force in ordering societies. Constitutional orders are by their nature the product of social struggles over which certain norms, procedures, actors and institutions become dominant in ordering society and there is very little ordering of society that happens without negotiating with the received territorial, legal and political jurisdiction of national states, even as 'key enablers and enactors of the global scale'.[8] Consequently, I argue that while plural forms of legal ordering may exist both 'outside' and 'within' the state, they are arguably only constitutional insofar as they supplant or become embedded within a 'higher level of authoritative ordering which frames the breadth and width of claims for recognition and redistribution within the jurisdiction of the state'.[9] There is good reason to continue to think of hegemony in the singular, rather than the more recent turn in legal studies that conceptualises hegemony as something which only occurs at 'discrete and disconnected sites'.[10] Law, particularly constitutional law, is not simply recapitulated as a crude tool of power in this context, but becomes a critical locus of

[4] Shinar, 'Ideologies of Global Constitutionalism', 22.

[5] M. Goldoni and M. Wilkinson, 'The Material Constitution' (2018) 81 *The Modern Law Review* 575.

[6] Ibid., 569.

[7] See A. Slaughter, A *New World Order* (Princeton University Press, 2005); A. Peters, 'The Merits of Global Constitutionalism' (2009) 16 *Indiana Journal of Global Legal Studies* 397; G. Teubner, *Constitutional Fragments: Societal Constitutionalism and Globalisation* (Oxford University Press, 2012); C. Thornhill, A *Sociology of Constitutions: Constitutions and State Legitimacy in Historical-Sociological Perspective* (Cambridge University Press, 2011).

[8] S. Sassen, *Territory, Authority, Rights: From Medieval to Global Assemblage* (Princeton University Press, 2006), 3.

[9] Lander, *Transnational Law and State Transformation*, 24.

[10] D. Litowitz, 'Gramsci, Hegemony and the Law' (2000) 2 *BYU Law Review* 515.

hegemony and, therefore, of resistance.[11] Material constitutionalism as an analytical approach not only identifies and explains how specific legal and institutional patterns become hegemonic, but also helps to explain why and how counter-hegemonic efforts succeed, fail or settle somewhere in between.

One of the most under-recognised inputs in the material constitution, due no doubt to the blind spots of public lawyers who continue to operate along the public/private dichotomy, is that of political economy. Taking Wood's point that 'the economic sphere rests firmly on the political'[12] seriously opens the question of how political, legal and economic relations are co-constituted in different places and times and across different scales. This co-constitutive approach avoids determinism by demanding concrete, historical analysis of how particular constitutional arrangements become hegemonic, attending to the role of agency and contingency in perpetuating, undermining or transforming structural tendencies in these social relations.[13] Importantly, viewing political economy as a relevant source of constitutional law and politics is not deterministic or even contrary to normative analyses of the constitution. Political economy is crucially enabled and shaped by legal processes and norms, as well as social values, so attending to political economy is not antithetical to more normative readings of constitutional development, but rather complementary to them.

As a theoretical framework which views constitutional arrangements as historically contingent, material constitutionalism can help us to conceptualise how transnational economic 'actors, norms and processes'[14] – operating across local, national, regional and global scales – shape the normative and institutional character of states. Transnational economic processes can have constitutional effects when the economic incentive structure is powerful enough to limit legislative or regulatory options and challenge or change constitutional relations or norms. In general, a precondition for national integration in the global economy is the state's adoption of specific constitutional configurations where the state either withdraws from the economic sphere through privatisation – achieved institutionally and legally – to attract foreign investment or, more rarely, when states make the logic of market competition the foundation of their 'political' logic (i.e., as in Chinese state capitalism).[15] Frontier and emerging economies in the Global South, in most instances, pursue the former strategy, lacking the public capital base to compete in the global economy. By privatising or deregulating former 'political' domains, such as price-setting and measures against nationalisation, the 'law of the market' often becomes a *grundnorm* for future constitutional development.[16]

The volatility of natural resource extraction makes this economic sector particularly constitutionally charged. As I have argued elsewhere, states 'practically mediate and absorb profound transnational tensions between public and private interests over resource extraction at significant

[11] See M. Lazarus-Black and S. F. Hirsch, *Contested States: Law, Hegemony and Resistance* (Routledge, 1994).

[12] Lander, *Transnational Law and State Transformation*, 30.

[13] For a similar approach in politics, see N. Pratt, 'Bringing Politics Back in: Examining the Link between Globalisation and Democratisation' (2004) 11 *Review of International Political Economy* 311.

[14] P. Zumbansen, 'Defining the Space of Transnational Law: Legal Theory, Global Governance and Legal Pluralism' (2012) 21 *Transnational Law and Contemporary Problems* 308.

[15] L. Xing and T. M. Shaw, 'The Political Economy of Chinese State Capitalism' (2013) 1 *Journal of China and International Relations* 88–113.

[16] S. Frerichs, 'The Rule of the Market', in P. Blokker and C. Thornhill (eds.), *Sociological Constitutionalism* (Cambridge University Press, 2017), 241. See also C. May, 'The Rule of Law As the Grundnorm of the New Constitutionalism,', in S. Gill and C. Cutler (eds.), *New Constitutionalism and World Order* (Cambridge University Press, 2014), 63–76; Lander, *Transnational Law and State Transformation*, 226–29.

sites of constitution formation'.[17] Extractive economies provoke deep social conflict about socio-environmental impacts, taxation and resource distribution at the national level, as well as transnational conflicts about the terms and benefits of investment. These conflicts are commonly played out at constitutional 'pressure-points', as new struggles for hegemony pressurise established constitutional balances between government institutions (e.g., legislative, judicial and executive), central and sub-national levels of administration and the governance of civil society and citizenship.[18] The pressure on national governments to resolve the tension between the varying interests of local, national and global stakeholders in natural resource extraction is heightened by the fragility and crisis-prone nature of global commodity markets.

The structural volatility of the extractives sector – both nationally and globally – invites unprecedented levels of legal and institutional change within national states, largely driven by international perceptions of economic, political and legal risk, particularly when the state depends upon attracting risk-averse foreign investment to catalyse market competitiveness in extractives. Transnational legal norms which prioritise the ease and security of investment (e.g., non-discrimination, anti-expropriation and sanctity of contract) have become authoritative as a legal *order* that cuts across national borders,[19] transmitted through international investment contracts, treaties and project financing instruments.[20] The normative effects of transnational legal ordering in extractive economies deepens material constitutional change alongside the structural effects of natural resource markets, impacting 'baseline patterns and processes of "rule, redistribution and recognition"'[21] as well as formal constitutional commitments. While every state negotiates these constitutional pressures in different ways, there is an *intrinsic* linkage between extractive economy and material constitutional change,[22] as shall be discussed through the Mongolian case study.

22.3 RECONCEPTUALISING MONGOLIA'S MINING BOOM AND BUST AS MATERIAL CONSTITUTIONAL CHANGE

Mongolia emerged from the wake of the collapsing Soviet Union with a crashed economy but a huge amount of optimism about its future as an independent democracy aligned with the West. Mongolian state formation has always occurred between the Scylla and Charybdis of its geopolitical situation, sandwiched between Russia and China, a context that is only becoming more complex as Mongolia pursues competitiveness in natural resources. In the early 1990s Mongolia surprised the international community with the fervency of its commitment to liberal democracy and market economy. Despite the crushing impact of the Soviet Union's withdrawal of investment and trade with its former satellite and the consequences of 'shock therapy' experiments conducted by international financial institutions (IFIs), Mongolia embraced a new constitutional trajectory. The 1992 Constitution reformed the former socialist government

[17] J. Lander, 'Shifting States: The Constitutional Risks of Extractive Development' (2022) 43(1) *Canadian Journal of Development Studies* 59, 63.

[18] Ibid., 60.

[19] A helpful definition of transnational legal order is '*a collection of formalised legal norms and associated organisations and actors that authoritatively order the understanding and practice of law across national jurisdictions*' See T. C. Halliday and G. Shaffer, *Transnational Legal Orders* (Cambridge University Press, 2015), 475 (original emphasis).

[20] K. Bhatt, *Concessionaires, Financiers and Communities: Implementing Indigenous Peoples' Rights to Land in Transnational Development Projects* (Cambridge University Press, 2020).

[21] Lander, *Transnational Law and State Transformation*, 23, citing M. Goldoni, 'Introduction to the Material Study of Global Constitutional Law' (2019) 8 *Global Constitutionalism* 86.

[22] For an in-depth discussion of this general argument, see Lander, 'Shifting States'.

by instantiating the separation of powers, constitutional democracy and the rule of law, thereby establishing the institutional preconditions for the marketisation of the economy.

Democratic Mongolia is a unitary state characterised by multi-party elections, a unique parliamentary system and a civil law jurisdiction. The 1992 Constitution established that the unicameral legislature has the constitutional status as the 'supreme organ of state power' (Article 22), which means that the Mongolian constitution is characterised by 'virtually unlimited legislative power'.[23] Governments, led by the Prime Minister, are formed through parliamentary elections every four years and a President with specific responsibilities as head of state is directly elected every six years. Like many other parliamentary systems with first-past-the-post electoral systems, the legislature in Mongolia is easily dominated by the government, with very low quorum rules for passing legislation. All matters of constitutional oversight and accountability are referred to a specific constitutional court that exists independently from the rest of the judicial system – the *Tsets* – and exercises concentrated powers of judicial review. Judicial review remedies are not readily available through the general court system, and the *Tsets* does not review the decisions of the Supreme Court. The *Tsets* exerts limited control over Parliament – and governments with a strong Parliamentary majority – because the constitution provides that the decisions of the *Tsets* are subject to Parliamentary approval (Article 66). The ambiguities of the constitution about the role and function of the *Tsets*, the accountability of Parliament and the role of the President has regularly led to institutional gridlock since 1992. Mongolia's constitutional trend following reforms in 2019, like many other post-socialist countries, is characterised by the consolidation of strong executive powers enabled by clear Parliamentary majorities, with limited judicial oversight.

In terms of economic reforms, Mongolia embraced financial liberalisation, the privatisation of extensive state assets and deregulation of the pastoral economy,[24] which had been a prominent economic sector under the socialist regime. Without Soviet support or trading partnerships, Mongolia's textile and manufacturing industries collapsed. Decades of economic planning and diversified industrial development were effectively washed down the drain. Through the lending policies of the IFIs and its own post-socialist constitutional commitments, Mongolia became receptive in the 1990s not only to transnational private capital investment but also the transnational legal cultures, norms and instruments which enable global trade and transactions. While Mongolia's traumatic post-socialist experience was not unique, its remarkably pro-Western geopolitical approach and fulsome embrace of liberal democratic institutions make it a particularly clear case study of how global economic and legal processes become entangled with the material constitutions of national states. Its relatively open democracy and willingness to engage with international institutions has made the effects of global economic integration remarkably visible, as opposed to other semi-authoritarian states which can disguise them more easily. Consequently, as I have argued elsewhere, Mongolia's recent history warrants close attention by scholars who want to unpick the constitutional implications of shifts in political economy and vice versa.[25]

[23] Ch. Enkhbaatar, D. Solongo, P. Amarjargal and T. Ginsburg. *The Role of the Constitution of Mongolia in Consolidating Democracy: An Analysis.* (UNDP, Ulaanbaatar, 2015), 26. Available at: www.mn.undp.org/content/mongolia/en/home/library/democratic_governance/RoleoftheConstitutionofMongoliaInConsolidatingDemocracy.html, last accessed 26 November 2021.

[24] Pastoralism is a form of agriculture based on animal husbandry, involving the grazing of animals over large pastures, traditionally herded by groups of people who move nomadically with their herds. Semi-nomadic livestock herding (sheep, goats, horses and camels) has been the historic basis of the economy in what is now Mongolia for millennia and continues to play an important economic role today.

[25] Lander, *Transnational Law and State Transformation*, 244.

22.3.1 A Brief History of Mongolia's Emergence as a Mineral-Exporting Economy

The twentieth century was a time of rapid constitutional change for Mongolia, change consistently wrapped up with questions of land use. Mongolia's 1992 constitution committed to protecting all forms of public and private property to promote economic development, accounting for both 'universal trends of world economic development and national specifics' (Article 5.1). This ambiguity seemed on face value to balance pastoralists' ongoing interests in accessing use rights for common land, as well as the new government's commitment to marketisation. The privatisation of the pastoralist collectives in the early 1990s and the deregulation of the agricultural sector did not make land any less relevant to Mongolia's constitutional transition but created the conditions for conflict over its use by those with interests in different kinds of property rights. Thus, while the formal constitution written in 1992 purported to 'balance' property rights between global and national requirements, the written text pre-figured a social conflict that would mark the material constitution in the years to come as that balance was tested by an unprecedented wave of foreign investment in mining in the late 1990s.

With the pastoral collectives and manufacturing industries having been demolished by the economic collapse and structural adjustment policies, the only real basis to resuscitate the economy was cashmere and mining. Constitutional reform in the early 1990s made it possible for Parliament to pass legislation allowing private foreign investment in the Mongolian economy. Mongolia's unique global selling point, from the point of view of its global financial advisors, was its status as a 'final frontier' of greenfield mining. While some exploration and exploitation had been conducted during the socialist period through Soviet–Mongolian joint ventures, the majority of Mongolia's minerals remained unmapped and untapped. With a mineral base believed to be worth at least 1.3 trillion US dollars, with substantial reserves of high-quality coking coal, copper, gold, fluorspar and iron ore, among others,[26] Mongolia had a product that domestic political elites and international financiers thought was worth selling on the global market.

In 1997, Parliament passed a new Minerals Law to make the sector more attractive to foreign investors. With significant input from the World Bank, Mongolian legislators passed 'the most investor-friendly and enabling law in Asia'[27] which crucially removed the distinction between domestic and international investors (Article 10.1) and gave licence holders the right to sell products at market rates (Article 16.3).[28] The 1997 Minerals Law significantly lowered tax and royalty rates and provided for tax stability agreements for large investments, as well as rights to transfer licenses without government pre-approval. Alongside these easing measures for investment, the role of the state in mining changed. The law banned the government from participating directly in mining projects and restricted the role of Parliament with regard to mining permissions and access to land. It also removed the requirement for feasibility studies, only required environmental impact assessments when a license had already been granted and decentralised environmental regulation to sub-national administrations.

The 1997 Minerals Law marked a profound change in the relationship between the state and the market and put Mongolia's new constitutional order to the test. Prior to the 1997 Minerals Law, the seeds for Mongolia's transition to a market economy had been planted, largely by stripping away the socialist legacy of economic control, but the fruit had yet to be tasted. From

[26] National Development Agency, *Your Guide to Invest in Mongolia* (National Development Agency, 2019), 14.
[27] C. Husband and V. Songwe, 'Mongolia Mining Sector: Managing the Future' (2004) 1 *World Bank* 52.
[28] Lander, *Transnational Law and State Transformation*, 109–10.

1997, Mongolia's new constitutional commitments to liberal political and legal institutions moved from paper to practice, with these institutional frameworks enabling the government to actively facilitate a new market economy in minerals through concrete legislative and policy changes. By 2004, over a quarter of Mongolian land was licensed for exploration and extraction, with 50 per cent of licenses held by seven companies, the majority of which were foreign invested entities.[29] By 2009, over 45 per cent of Mongolian land was licensed for extractive activities.[30]

The influx of private capital investment in extraction in rural areas, particularly led by foreign companies, catalysed unprecedented social conflict over access to land and water between pastoralists, illegal gold miners and mining companies. These conflicts were underpinned by conflicting expectations of the state in relation to property rights; pastoralists expected sub-national administrations to be able to protect their land use rights, as had been the case during the socialist era, whilst miners held centrally-issued permits which routinely trumped pastoralists' customary entitlements.[31] These conflicts about property also raised new questions about subsidiarity and central-sub-national relations under the new constitution, and the balance between constitutional principles of 'self-governance and state management'[32] in the context of the governance of land. It was at this time that the deregulation of the pastoralist sector and land administration more generally began to be acutely felt by rural inhabitants, leading to the emergence of Mongolia's first rural environmental movements.[33] The River Movements took a leading role in mobilising rural and urban social discontent about the regulation of mining.

Alongside rural socio-environmental conflicts and urban protests about foreign investment and lack of public benefits from mining, a new struggle for hegemony began to play out in central political and legislative institutions in Ulaanbaatar over the balance between national and global control of natural resources. The discovery of the Oyu Tolgoi copper and gold deposits in 2001 by Canadian Ivanhoe Mines prompted a national stock-take of the 1997 Minerals Law and the open terms of access for foreign investment in contrast with ongoing restrictions for the government to participate directly in mining projects. The 1997 Minerals Law was replaced in 2006 with a new minerals law that allowed minority government participation in nationally strategic projects and reinstituted a role for Parliament in approving large-scale investment agreements.[34] Alongside the 2006 Minerals Law, the government introduced a controversial Windfall Profits Tax – the highest in the world – which taxed copper and gold ore and concentrate at 68 per cent when market prices exceeded certain limits.[35] These measures, particularly the Windfall Profits Tax, prompted intense criticism from foreign investors, although investment interest in Mongolia continued to increase as global commodity markets began to pick up.

[29] Husband and Songwe, 'Mongolia Mining Sector', 7.

[30] Y. Suzuki, 'Conflict between Mining Development and Nomadism in Mongolia', in N. Yamamura, N. Fujita and A. Maekawa (eds.), *The Mongolian Eco-System Network: Environmental Issues under Climate and Social Changes* (Springer, 2013), 277.

[31] E. Endicott, *A History of Land Use in Mongolia: The Thirteenth Century to the Present* (Palgrave Macmillan, 2012), 97.

[32] A. Lkhagvadorj, 'Fiscal Federalism and Decentralisation in Mongolia' (2010) MPRA Paper 28758, University Library of Munich, 79.

[33] D. Byambajav, 'The River Movements' Struggle in Mongolia' (2015) 14 *Social Movement Studies: Journal of Social, Cultural and Political Protest* 92.

[34] Lander, *Transnational Law and State Transformation*, 116.

[35] S. Sukhbaatar, 'Law and Development, FDI and the Rule of Law in Post-Soviet Central Asia', in G. P. McAlinn and C. Pejovic (eds.), *Law and Development in Asia* (Routledge, 2012), 142.

By 2007, the Oyu Tolgoi project had already pushed Mongolia into the category of mineral dependence, with the sector's share growing from 10 per cent of GDP in 2002 to 33 per cent in 2007.[36] Mongolia's state of natural resource dependency only grew from 2009, when the Mongolian government signed a landmark investment agreement for the Oyu Tolgoi project, with Rio Tinto holding a managing share and the government a minority share of 33 per cent. The signing of the investment agreement and the repealing of the Windfall Profits tax seemed to settle the issue of balance between national and global interests. However, this agreement ushered in a huge tide of foreign investment – 4.6 billion USD – which overshadowed the entirety of the Mongolian economy (GDP of 4.2 billion USD in 2009).[37] In 2011, Mongolia was dubbed as a 'Global Growth Generator', with the world's highest GDP growth at 17.5 per cent,[38] although this high rate of growth, driven by one sector, should have signalled economic precarity rather than strength, as the country's public and private capital assets were now dangerously locked into mining.

The 'darling of international risk-takers'[39] began to falter in 2012, as global commodity prices started to decline and the Mongolian government recognised the extent of its vulnerability. This vulnerability was both macro-economic in nature – due to lack of diversification and ballooning levels of debt to fund infrastructure projects – as well as geo-economic: by 2012, China controlled 90 per cent of Mongolia's minerals export market.[40] The anti-discrimination provisions in both the 1997 and 2006 Minerals Laws had allowed Chinese state-owned enterprises (SOEs) to hold unlimited numbers of mining licenses, given on a first-come-first-served basis and transferable to other parties. Mongolia's embrace of international economic legal norms had led to a situation where China was effectively able to dictate the market price for mineral exports, particularly coal, where its SOEs held the exploitation rights and where the products were destined for the Chinese market.

To prevent effective takeover of its coal market, the Mongolian government introduced a new investment law in 2012 – the Strategic Entities Foreign Investment Law (SEFIL) – which gave Parliament significant oversight in screening large investments, particularly where these came through state-owned enterprises. Shortly thereafter, the government sought to renegotiate the Oyu Tolgoi investment agreement under the provisions of SEFIL, aiming to amend the tax stabilisation measures which had been incorporated into the agreement in 2009 which prevented the government from maximising tax revenue during the global commodity boom.[41] Mongolia's ballooning public and external debt was a major factor for this attempted renegotiation, with the government having issued its first bonds on international debt markets around the same time. These new debts, acquired to fund the Mongolian government's share in the Oyu Tolgoi project and develop infrastructure, amounted to over 2 billion USD and doubled Mongolia's debt burden between 2011 and 2012.[42]

36 S. Combellick-Bidney, 'Mongolia's Mining Controversies and the Politics of Place', in J. Dierkes (ed.), *Change in Democratic Mongolia: Social Relations, Health, Mobile Pastoralism and Mining* (Brill, 2012), 273.

37 A. Isakova, A. Plekhanov and J. Zettelmeyer, 'Managing Mongolia's Resource Boom' (2012) 138 *EBRD Working Paper* 1.

38 World Bank, *Mongolia Economic Update* (World Bank, 2013), 3.

39 J. Manthorpe, 'Mongolia Struggles with the Complexity of Resource Development', Business in Vancouver, 29 September 2013.

40 T. Edwards, 'Mongolia to Ease Conditions on Private Foreign Investors', *Reuters*, 23 April 2013.

41 Lander, *Transnational Law and State Transformation*, 123.

42 World Bank, 'Mongolia Economic Update', 24.

The introduction of SEFIL and the attempted renegotiation of the Oyu Tolgoi investment agreement sparked widespread criticism from foreign investors, mining companies, credit ratings agencies and IFIs. Once praised for its embrace of market economy and its liberal investment climate, Mongolia quickly became the pariah of the international finance media, with loud allegations from impacted corporations and shareholders about Mongolia's 'resource nationalism' and lack of respect for the rule of law.[43] While the Oyu Tolgoi project was the most high-profile project in Mongolia, other foreign mining companies complained of similar woes.[44] The ensuing crisis of international confidence in Mongolia's investment environment caused a steep and rapid decline in foreign direct investment (FDI). Between 2012 and 2014, FDI spiralled from 4.45 billion to 508 million USD, which promptly sent Mongolia into an unprecedented debt crisis and led to one of the largest bailout packages from the International Monetary Fund in history.[45]

22.4 ECONOMIC CRISIS AS A 'CONSTITUTIONAL CRUCIBLE'[46]

It is at this low point in Mongolia's recent economic history that we can begin to see the effects of extractive political economy upon the Mongolian constitutional order, particularly the ways in which market actors, norms and processes began to dominate institutional relations, legislative and political horizons, the scope of civil society and the substance of citizenship. One of the first manifestations of material constitutional change arising from Mongolia's turbulent encounter firstly with post-socialist constitutionalism and then market-based extractivism has been the articulation of a firm limit on national legislative sovereignty and the strengthening of executive power in the Mongolian constitution. While global commodity booms give momentary political and policy space for the government to flirt with nationalisation, the concrete effects of FDI withdrawal and the discourse of declining investor confidence has a powerful disciplinary effect on the legislative options on the table.

As soon as FDI really began to spiral in 2013, the government scrapped SEFIL and introduced another investment law, with significant input from the International Finance Corporation (IFC) of the World Bank Group, which returned Mongolia's investment framework to a similar standard of liberal commitment as the 1997 Minerals Law. Under the new investment law, the government removed screening measures for private foreign investment, provided new tax and non-tax incentives to investors and provided a general right of recourse to international arbitration.[47] A new State Policy on Minerals accompanied these general legislative measures in 2014 'to establish a stable investment environment . . . and to strengthen competitiveness in the global

[43] For an excellent critique of the use of 'pejorative labels' such as resource nationalism to discursively undermine the laws and policies of the Mongolian state, see D. Bumochir, 'Nationalist Sentiments Obscured by "Pejorative Labels"' (2019) 21 *Inner Asia* 162.

[44] For example, in 2011, a prominent Canadian mining company – Khan Resources – initiated international arbitration proceedings against the government for the deregistration and non-renewal of its uranium mining license following the implementation of a new nuclear energy law. Hundreds of licenses were cancelled around the same period (2011–13). The implementation of a controversial environmental law strongly supported by rural social movements led to the cancellation of licenses for over 200 mining projects in 2011 and a corruption scandal in the Mineral Resources Agency led to the swift cancellation of 106 licences in 2013. See Lander, *Transnational Law and State Transformation*, 125.

[45] In 2017, the IMF approved an external financing package of 5.5 billion USD to prevent Mongolia from defaulting on its debt, notably – and remarkably – reliant on the involvement of China to provide USD 2.19 billion in currency swap lines to maintain Mongolia's financial liquidity. See Lander, *Transnational Law and State Transformation*, 133.

[46] Ibid., 208.

[47] Ibid., 127.

market'[48] by promoting 'private-sector led development' and reducing the direct role of the state in the mining economy. The new State Policy reformed the mining licencing process to the deregulated standard of the 1997 Minerals Law. As a signal of 'remorse' for damaging its international investment credibility, the government agreed to pay an 80 million USD arbitration award to Khan Resources in 2015 and concluded an international agreement ('the Dubai Agreement') to settle the tax dispute between Rio Tinto and the Mongolian government with regard to the Oyu Tolgoi Investment Agreement.

Alongside specific legislative and policy measures, significant changes in the distribution of regulatory power between central and sub-national government institutions were instigated and legitimised to resuscitate investment confidence. As I discuss in detail in *Transnational Law and State Transformation*, Parliament had garnered a reputation among investors and mining companies as a key source of political risk between 2006 and 2012, with its propensity to introduce more stringent or 'discriminatory' legislation and attempts to re-negotiate large-scale investment agreements.[49] The 2013 Investment Law and the 2014 State Policy on Minerals shifted the balance of institutional power in relation to the mining economy away from Parliament toward the executive, through unusually high quorum measures to prevent legislative reform. These legislative initiatives were complemented by the establishment of executive policy councils and agencies which managed investor-state relations exclusively through the Ministry of Mining,[50] in close cooperation with the Fiscal Revenue Division of the Ministry of Finance and the Central Bank. Alongside the increasing domination of the legislature's function by the economic priorities of the executive, the role of the Central Bank has also increased to enforce fiscal discipline and constrain Parliament's budgetary function.

Alongside efforts to purge 'nationalist' politics from central institutions and resuscitate investment flows, the Ministry of Mining sought to limit the role of representative institutions at the sub-national level from 'politicising' the local investment environment. Sub-national governments had become key sources of corporate and investor ire in the early 2000s, by making demands upon mining companies for local contributions and attempting to protect pastoralists' land rights against mining licenses. The 2014 amendments to the Minerals Law, following the new State Policy, mandated compulsory local development agreements to be negotiated between the Governor's office – an unelected position in the executive branch of local government – and mining companies in order to financially align their interests and manage expectations. In addition to amendments to the national budget law, these changes meant that sub-national governments who supported mining in their localities would substantially benefit, thereby incentivising their cooperation (or co-optation).[51] Bringing sub-national administrations into 'line' with the central government pro-extractive agenda has been a critical aspect of consolidating a material constitutional settlement around the regulatory role of government in relation to mining projects.

Around the same time, the government convicted high profile leaders of the famous River Movements on trumped-up charges of 'environmental terrorism'. These criminal convictions and the government's new anti-political policies and rhetoric have had a significant impact on

[48] Article 1.2, State Policy on Minerals (2014–2025), cited in Lander, *Transnational Law and State Transformation*, 129.

[49] Lander, *Transnational Law and State Transformation*, 146.

[50] For example, the 2013 Investment Law is uniquely protected from 'political' legislative reform by a two-thirds quorum measure.

[51] J. Lander, 'Community Development Agreements and the State's Extractive Strategy in Mongolia: Participatory Governance or Governance Participation?', in S. Adelman and A. Paliwala (eds.), *The Limits of Law and Development: Neoliberalism, Governance and Social Justice* (Routledge, 2021), 218–20.

Mongolia's growing environmental civil society and the extent to which small organisations are willing to engage in overtly conflictual terms. A marked trend towards authoritarianism has intensified over the past decade, with new legislation passed by Parliament in 2021 which bans civic activity impacting the reputation of business interests. This gradual chilling effect on civil society has been starkly born out in recent months by the government's criminal investigation of a high profile environmental advocate on charges of "sabotage" of large-scale development projects.

Within this broader shift towards 'collaborative' modes of civic engagement, local populations impacted by mining increasingly interface with non-state mechanisms of redress. These may be available through corporate social responsibility (CSR), investment safeguards in project finance or international development donors seeking to bridge community–corporate relations. These programmes generally reposition Mongolian citizens as 'impacted stakeholders' in relation to mining projects, with no reference to their constitutional rights.[52] While it is positive that impacted populations are able to make some gains through these varying CSR programmes and non-state grievance mechanisms, they effectively become part of the insulating bulwark for foreign investment that privatises issues of widespread public concern about the social and environmental impacts of mining in Mongolia and prevents them from becoming 'politicised'.[53] Furthermore, there is high risk of uneven access to justice through these non-state mechanisms because of the significant variability of CSR standards and investment safeguards across the range of mining projects occurring within Mongolia.

While these legislative, political and policy shifts at the central and subnational levels may seem disconnected, they form a cohesive picture of change *across* critical axes of the national state. Mongolia's embrace of a market-based mining economy and its associated legal politics has shaped the distribution of regulatory and political power within central government institutions and between central and sub-national administrations in a pro-extractive, executive direction, with tangible impacts for civil society and the substance of citizenship. While there are sputters of so-called 'nationalist' sentiment from the platforms of political parties and politicians about taking back Mongolia's mining sector and challenging the terms of foreign investment when market prices begin to recover, the rhetoric does not match Mongolia's FDI-dependent reality.[54] Overall, the election of new governments has done little to substantially change the terms of Mongolia's mining investment regime, which speaks to the constitutional quality of global economic integration in natural resources for Mongolia.[55] Where in the 1990s it was possible to locate the two main political parties along a traditional left–right political spectrum, particularly on economic issues, today there is no tangible difference between them. While the FDI crisis was initially managed by the Democratic Party, since 2016 the Mongolian

[52] Lander, *Transnational Law and State Transformation*, 168–204 deals with this issue in greater depth than the scope of this chapter allows.

[53] P. Hatcher and J. Lander, 'Searching for New Political Spaces: Negotiating Citizenship and Transnational Identities on Mongolia's Mining Frontier' (2022) Vol. ahead-of-print *Journal of Contemporary Asia*, 1–24.

[54] Even the current government's tenacity in wrangling with Rio Tinto over missing tax revenues between 2016–18 has little hope of challenging the new status quo. With Rio Tinto having initiated international arbitration proceedings in 2020, Mongolia's position will be narrowly interpreted through the narrow parameters of international investment norms and, unless the arbitration tribunal upholds the government's counterclaim, the government will be in the unhappy situation of having to capitulate again on tax revenues or make good on its thread to void the Oyu Tolgoi Investment Agreement. In either case, Mongolia faces deepening dependence on foreign investment on Western international terms or on China's, with profound material constitutional ramifications in terms of legislative and geo-economic sovereignty.

[55] D. Schneiderman, *Constitutionalising Economic Globalisation: Investment Rules and Democracy's Promise* (Cambridge University Press, 2008), 4.

People's Party has 'maintained the commitments and virtually identical institutional frameworks of its predecessor',[56] despite its populist rhetoric.

22.5 CONCLUSION: ECONOMIC HISTORY AS CONSTITUTIONAL HISTORY

Mongolia is not a case study of a weak state 'versus' global capital but shows how constitutional features of states can be materially transformed by transnational processes of legal and economic ordering. Critical aspects of Mongolia's constitutional democracy have been weakened by its pursuit of FDI in extractives, particularly in terms of limiting any deliberative role of Parliament as a safeguard on foreign investment and the sensitivity of local governments to the demands of local populations. While civil society in Mongolia remains vibrant, outspoken organisations which seek to hold the government accountable for infringements of citizens' rights are under increasing political and financial pressure. However, other institutional features of the state have been strengthened, notably bureaucratic, technocratic and executive institutions and norms. This simultaneous weakening and strengthening of different aspects of the state strongly suggests that a new hegemonic order has become dominant within the national constitution, an order which is underscored by new dependencies on foreign capital investment and transnational processes of legitimation, which invite new economic constituents to shape the trajectory of public law and policy. Because these changes in the material constitution have occurred through economic laws and policies, the courts have played no supervisory function.

Material constitutionalism invites re-conceptualisation of what counts as constitutionally significant and which actors drive constitutional processes. The Mongolian case study suggests that it is a great loss to our understanding to overlook non-traditional actors (e.g., Parliaments, sub-national governments, civil society organisations, investors, corporations, arbitration tribunals and IFIs), norms (e.g., those derived from international investment law) and processes (e.g., FDI and global market cycles) in contributing to constitutional change. If we take as our point of departure the co-constitutive relationship between law, economy and political systems – in the sense of 'creating conditions for the possibility of each other'[57] – then it is only common sense to begin to pay closer attention to political economy as a relevant source of constitutional change, particularly in the case of extractivism which generates such significant tensions within national states. This is not to suggest that all economic, institutional or legal change counts as constitutional, or we drain the term of its meaning. However, when an 'economic' transformation such as that witnessed in Mongolia has such profound implications for law-making, administrative relations, domestic politics and civil society – with a widening gap between the formal constitution and its practice – it seems like a good time to check our constitutional blind spots.

56 Lander, *Transnational Law and State Transformation*, 236.
57 Ibid., 23.

23

The Military in the Material Constitution of Turkey

Tarik Olcay

23.1 INTRODUCTION: ACCOUNTING FOR THE MILITARY IN MATERIAL CONSTITUTIONAL ENQUIRY

The rediscovery of the concept of material constitution[1] offers many avenues to study the operation of particular constitutional orders. The material study of constitutions opens up lines of enquiry that legal constitutionalism and political constitutionalism struggle to register,[2] and helps to provide an explanation, if not justification, of political practice that the formal constitution fails to capture or simplistically labels 'unconstitutional'. It helps to look beyond the formal constitution in a systematic way to understand and explain why particular constitutional orders are created in the way they are and why they operate in the way they do. It calls for a focus on the institutions in society that condition – or precondition – the constitutional order that the formal constitution may not fully account for. Above all, it is an enquiry that is curious to understand and interested in explaining why some seemingly unconstitutional or extra-constitutional political values or practices can have a central place in a given constitutional order.

What is material to a constitutional order is not always captured in formal constitutional arrangements. This may be due to oversight or poor design, but it can also be the result of negotiation, concealment, manipulation or deferment in formal constitution-making. The exclusion of aspects of the material constitution in the formal constitution can have a profound impact on the constitutional order over time, either by the constitutional form moulding the materiality of the constitutional order or the formal constitution amounting to a sham constitution,[3] but, in any case, constitutional analysis is poorer when the material forces that condition the constitutional order are not taken into account only because they are absent from the formal constitution.

The material study of the constitution captures what underpins the formal constitutional values and structures and helps to explain how a constitution operates beyond its formal confines, providing tools for constitutional explanation and prediction, in addition to its significant epistemic value. The identification of how the constitution operates within a polity through a study of the ordering forces that permeate the constitutional order is a more holistic enterprise

[1] M. Goldoni and M. Wilkinson, 'The Material Constitution' (2018) 81 *Modern Law Review* 567.

[2] M. Goldoni and T. Olcay, 'The Material Study of Constitutional Change', in X. Contiades and A. Fotiadou (eds.), *Routledge Handbook of Comparative Constitutional Change* (Routledge, 2020), 262–68.

[3] D. S. Law and M. Versteeg, 'Sham Constitutions' (2013) 101 *California Law Review* 863.

of recognising loci of constitutional power compared to not only formal enquiries but also enquiries that centre around constituent power, which tend to focus on the extraneous shaping of constitutional orders.

There are many places one can look to understand the material constitution of Turkey. Indeed, some of the chapters in this handbook, which apply the conceptual framework of the material constitution to other constitutional orders, show the relevant places to look at in particular constitutional orders. These may include, broadly, political economy, political culture, social structure, religion, geopolitics, international relations, and imperial factors.[4]

Specifically with regard to the Turkish constitution, the role of religion in public life as well as the role of the state in organising religion,[5] including the current religious–corporatist structure of bureaucracy,[6] the independence of the Central Bank,[7] the 'deep state'[8] and the rise of alternative – and conservative – business elites, especially in the past few decades,[9] may be relevant to a material study. This chapter aims to offer a modest starting point for an enquiry into the material constitution of Turkey by looking at perhaps the most obvious aspect of the Turkish Constitution beyond its formal boundaries: the military. Although some constitutional powers are given to senior military officials in Turkey, no other central aspect of the Turkish constitutional order is more understated in the formal constitution than the military. There has been an overbearing presence of the military on Turkish politics, ranging from explicit institutional expectations to a constant threat of a coup d'état. Against this background, the aim of this chapter is to introduce the military as an ordering force in the Turkish Constitution, through an examination of its role in the making and re-making of the 1961 and 1982 Constitutions. The chapter explains the military's constituent and ongoing authority over the constitutional order and its role in guaranteeing the fundamental political objectives of the constitutional order. What this reveals is that, although recognition of its constitution-making role is limited in the formal constitution, the military is a defining constitutional actor in Turkey. Only through accounting for the constitutional role of the military can the materiality of the Turkish Constitution be grasped and a more accurate description of the Turkish constitutional order be provided.

Whilst the chapter will argue that the military's role has been central in shaping Turkey's constitutional order, it is worth noting that its involvement has not been confined to a founding moment in Turkish constitutional history. The military has been part of a wider web of institutional ordering forces, albeit with a central role, but it has been tasked within this wider web to provide security for the top-down secularist and nationalist reforms made during the founding era of the Turkish Republic in the 1920s and 1930s, and has been designed to have tutelage over democratic politics.[10] The motivation behind this role has not been to provide for a protracted military rule, but to protect the secular order and the state apparatus;[11] and the Turkish military has been a crucial institutional guarantor of the constitutional principles of secularism and

4 Goldoni and Wilkinson, 'The Material Constitution', 580.

5 A. Kuru, *Secularism and State Policies toward Religion: The United States, France, and Turkey* (Cambridge University Press, 2009), 161–235.

6 D. Coşan and C. Uğur, 'Cults in Turkey on the Move to Replace Gülen Community', Birgün Daily, 29 October 2016.

7 S. B. Şahin, 'Central Bank Independence in Turkey: A Neo-Gramscian Analysis' (2012) 47 *Cooperation and Conflict* 106.

8 M. Soyler, *The Turkish Deep State: State Consolidation, Civil–Military Relations and Democracy* (Routledge, 2015).

9 D. Kenner, 'The Happy Story of the Anatolian Tigers', Foreign Policy, 19 March 2010.

10 A. T. Kuru, 'The Rise and Fall of Military Tutelage in Turkey: Fears of Islamism, Kurdism, and Communism' (2012) 14 *Insight Turkey* 37.

11 Z. Sarigil, 'The Turkish Military: Principal or Agent?' (2014) 40 *Armed Forces & Society* 168, 169.

nationalism, which have been protected by unamendability clauses in both the former 1961 Constitution and the current 1982 Constitution.

23.2 THE PLACE OF THE MILITARY IN TURKEY

Looking at the role of the military in constitution-making in Turkey is an obvious starting point for a material study of the Turkish constitution. The involvement of the military in Turkish constitutional politics pre-dates the Republic of Turkey, which was founded in 1923, but the chapter will focus specifically on the 1961 and the current 1982 Constitutions, both of which were made following coups d'état and under strict military control. Not only was the current 1982 Constitution drafted by military generals who carried out the 1980 coup d'état, but the previous 1961 Constitution was also drafted under the control of the military junta responsible for the 1960 coup d'état. In addition to such direct involvement in constitution-making, the military has also had an indirect, yet defining, influence on constitutional change in Turkey from the time the 1982 Constitution has been in force to this day. The military's failure in the 2016 coup attempt, for instance, inversely reshaped the constitutional order by paving the way for the constitutional changes that created an autocratic system of presidential government.[12]

The central role of military is not simply about the threat of physical power it may exert but also the place and perception of the military in Turkish society more generally. Turks consider themselves a military-nation, as evident in the adage 'every Turk is born a soldier'.[13] Turkey has a considerably large military force, having the highest number of military personnel in NATO after the United States,[14] military service is compulsory for every male Turkish citizen,[15] and a mandatory national security curriculum has been taught in high schools by active servicemen until recently.[16] The military also has long been the institution enjoying the highest levels of public confidence in Turkey.[17] It is therefore a socially and materially very powerful institution that retains its influence on the daily lives of the citizens of Turkey.

The Turkish constitutional order is embedded within the civil law tradition with an apparent commitment to legalist formalism. A conscious choice was made to adopt this legal tradition in the formative years of the Turkish Republic, where public law was heavily based on the French tradition.[18] Coupled with a tradition of a 'strong state',[19] this resulted in a legalist approach to law

[12] Z. Yilmaz, 'Erdoğan's Presidential Regime and Strategic Legalism: Turkish Democracy in the Twilight Zone' (2020) 20 *Southeast European and Black Sea Studies* 265.

[13] A. G. Altinay, *The Myth of the Military-Nation* (Palgrave Macmillan, 2004), 13–32.

[14] 'International Comparisons of Defence Expenditure and Military Personnel' (2021) 121 *The Military Balance* 517.

[15] 1982 Constitution of Turkey, Article 72.

[16] A. G. Altinay, 'Human Rights or Militarist Ideals? Teaching National Security in High Schools', in D. T. Ceylan and G. Irzik (eds.), *Human Rights Issues in Textbooks: The Turkish Case* (Tarih Vakfi Yurt, 2004), 76–90.

[17] M. Aydin, M. Çelikpala, E. Yeldan, M. Güvenç, O. Z. Zaim, B. B. Hawks, E. C. Sokullu, Ö. Şenyuva, O. Yılmaz and S. D. Tığlı, *Kantitatif Araştırma Raporu: Türkiye Siyasal Sosyal Eğilimler Araştırması* [Quantitative Research Report: Turkey Political Social Leanings Research] 2020, İstanbul, Kadir Has Üniversitesi, Türkiye Çalışmaları Grubu, Akademetre ve Global Akademi, 7 January 2021, available at: www.khas.edu.tr/sites/khas.edu.tr/files/inline-files/TEA2020_Tur_WEBRAPOR_1.pdf, last accessed 3 June 2021.

[18] For example, see K. Gözler, 'Türk Belediye Sistemi Üzerinde Fransız Etkisi: 3 Nisan 1930 Tarihli Belediye Kanunu Fransa'dan mı İktibas Edilmiştir?' (2019) 28 *Çağdaş Yerel Yönetimler* 1 (arguing that the Turkish municipality regime is inspired by the French one) or K. Gözler, 'Osmanlı/Türk Köy İdaresi Sistemi Üzerinde Fransız Etkisi: 1864 ve 1871 Osmanlı Nizamnamelerinin Köylere İlişkin Hükümleri ve 1924 Köy Kanunu Fransa'dan mı İktibas edilmiştir?' (2019) 68 *Ankara Üniversitesi Hukuk Fakültesi Dergisi* 413 (arguing that the Turkish village regime is inspired by the French one).

[19] M. Heper, 'The Strong State as a Problem for the Consolidation of Democracy: Turkey and Germany Compared' (1992) 25 *Comparative Political Studies* 169.

whereby a gargantuan body of administrative law has been legislated. This, in turn, created a formalist public law culture that mainly dealt with a detailed body of public law, focussing its enquiry on the forms that the constitution and other administrative laws create.

The influence of legalist formalism has resulted in the concealment of certain aspects of the legal and constitutional order from view. While, on the face of it, Turkey has had a formally advanced constitutional and administrative law with established administrative judiciary and administrative traditions, the body of public law remained insufficient to account for certain phenomena within the constitutional-legal order. The history of modern Turkey is rife with constitutional crises, where certain political issues could not be resolved within the operation of the formal constitutional mechanisms or the major political actors feel that way, resorting to (formal) constitutional amendment[20] or simply (at least temporarily) setting the formal constitution aside.[21] Whilst the former also tells an important story as to the place of the formal constitutional text and whether it is truly *constitutional* if it is amended at every critical political juncture,[22] the focus of this chapter is on the latter, as that is where the role of the military has been most significant in constitution-making.

Considering its key role in shaping the Turkish constitutional order, the place of the military in the formal constitution seems modest. The main constitutional provision that gives the military an important albeit rather limited constitutional role is the one creating the National Security Council.[23] This body was created by the 1961 Constitution and was tasked to 'communicate' its views on national security policy to the Cabinet until the 1971 constitutional amendment that gave it the power to make 'recommendations' to the Cabinet.[24] According to the amended 1982 Constitution, the National Security Council currently consists of the President, deputies of the President, Ministers of Justice, National Defence, Internal Affairs and Foreign Affairs, the Chief of the General Staff and the commanders of the Land, Naval and Air Forces.[25] While this formal arrangement gives the military a central role in shaping the national security policy, it does not do justice to the actual constitutional power it is capable of exerting.

Both the 1961 and 1982 Constitutions were adopted in the aftermath of military coups d'état and under military junta rule. Throughout the period they have been in force they have undergone several major reforms and experienced further military intervention. As mentioned, the Turkish military has enjoyed high public confidence, especially in comparison with the political elite, and it was therefore able to intervene in constitutional politics with no significant backlash from the general population. Although it has suffered major setbacks since the 2007 Presidential election,[26] including the *Ergenekon* and *Balyoz* trials of active and retired military officials[27] and the 2016 coup attempt and its aftermath,[28] on the whole, but not necessarily in all sectors of the society, it remains a powerful and trusted institution in Turkey.[29]

20 As of 2021, the current 1982 Constitution has been amended 19 times, including several major omnibus amendments.
21 The governmental system was arguably changed unconstitutionally with a *de facto* amendment. See T. Olcay, 'The Turkish Constitution as a Disrespected Idol', *IACL-AIDC Blog*, 14 January 2021, available at: https://blog-iacl-aidc.org/cili/2021/1/14/the-turkish-constitution-as-a-disrespected-idol, last accessed 3 June 2021.
22 Ibid.
23 1982 Constitution of Turkey, Article 118.
24 1961 Constitution of Turkey, Article 111.
25 1982 Constitution of Turkey, Article 118/1.
26 R. Karakaya Polat, 'The 2007 Parliamentary Elections in Turkey: Between Securitisation and Desecuritisation' (2009) 62 *Parliamentary Affairs* 129.
27 E. Aydinli, 'Ergenekon, New Pacts, and the Decline of the Turkish "Inner State"' (2011) 12 *Turkish Studies* 227.
28 L. Haugom, 'The Turkish Armed Forces and Civil–Military Relations in Turkey after the 15 July 2016 Coup Attempt' (2019) 2 *Scandinavian Journal of Military Studies* 1.
29 Altinay, 'Human Rights or Militarist Ideals?'

23.3 MILITARY INVOLVEMENT IN CONSTITUTION-MAKING

The military has had a double function in the Turkish constitutional order. First, it played various direct and indirect roles in creating the conditions for major constitutional changes as well as in constitution-making processes. Second, through its involvement in constitution-making it placed itself as one of the guardians of secularism and nationalism, the fundamental constitutional principles of the Republic of Turkey. Due to the abrupt end to the multi-national and Islamic Ottoman Empire and the top-down nature of the Kemalist revolution, the Republican political elite, itself originating from the Ottoman military, designed the Turkish military as a central constitutional actor having the power to wield physical force whenever secularism or nationalism are considered to be under threat in domestic politics.

Direct military involvement in constitution-making has occurred since the first constitution of Turkey during the Ottoman Empire. Two of the 28 members of the committee that drafted the 1876 Constitution, which was the first step towards a constitutional monarchy, were military officials.[30] The Committee of Union and Progress, which carried out the Young Turk Revolution in 1908 that led to the Second Constitutional Era of the Empire, had infiltrated the Ottoman military and the Republic was founded in 1923 under the leadership of Mustafa Kemal Atatürk, a field marshal. The more focussed and direct involvement in constitution-making, however, came following Turkey's transition from a one-party state to a multi-party state in 1945 and the eventual rise of the Democrat Party, which broadly represented the conservative masses against the secularist–nationalist elites of the Republic. In 1960, a group of middle-ranked officers in the Turkish military overthrew the Democrat Party government and set up a military regime with a view to 'ending the increasingly oppressive Democrat Party regime'.[31] This coup d'état has been looked on favourably by many constitutional scholars due to its claims of reorienting the country toward 'Atatürk's path' and away from 'religious manipulation'.[32] The 1960 coup was recently even reconceptualised as a 'democratic coup d'état'.[33]

The National Unity Committee (NUC), the military junta that took power after its overthrow of the democratic government in 1960, commissioned a group of legal academics to draft a new constitution. The draft produced by the commission received wide criticism for weakening the principle of universal suffrage by creating a second chamber with a corporatist character, as well as excessively limiting the executive power for the benefit of various autonomous institutions it proposed, such as a State Council, a National Security Council, a National Economy Council, a National Bank of Turkey and universities.[34] The NUC then created a constituent assembly that consisted of two chambers: (i) the NUC itself and (ii) the House of Representatives. Despite what its name may suggest, the latter chamber was not elected; rather, it consisted of members appointed by the head of the state (10 members), the NUC (18), provinces (75), the Republican People's Party (49), the Republican Villagers Nation Party (25), bar associations (6), press (12), the Veterans' Association (2), small businesses (6), youth (1), trade unions (6), chambers of commerce (10), teachers' unions (6), agricultural unions (6), universities (12) and the judiciary (12).[35] The Democrat Party, which had received 48.6 per cent of the votes in the 1957 general

[30] B. Tanör, *Osmanlı-Türk Anayasal Gelişmeleri*, 17th ed. (YKY, 2008), 133.
[31] Ibid., 365–66.
[32] Ibid., 365.
[33] O. O. Varol, 'The Democratic Coup d'État' (2012) 53 *Harvard International Law Journal* 291, 323–28.
[34] K. Gözler, *Türk Anayasa Hukuku*, 2nd ed. (Ekin, 2018), 105.
[35] Tanör, *Osmanlı-Türk Anayasal Gelişmeleri*, 369–70.

election and had been overthrown in the 1960 coup d'état, was not represented in the Constituent Assembly.

To draft the new constitution, a Constitution Committee was established in the House of Representatives, consisting of 20 members. The process designed regarding the approval of the draft of the Committee gave similar powers to each chamber of the constituent assembly, which is significant especially when contrasted to the system adopted in the making of the 1982 Constitution that is completely deferent to the military wing, as explained in the following paragraphs. Still, given the considerable control of the NUC over the House of Representatives and the complete absence of the Democrat Party which represented almost half of the electorate before the coup d'état, it would be difficult to imagine that the substantive demands of the military were not catered for in the drafting of the constitution in the process.

Following the approval of the final constitutional text in a referendum by 61.5 per cent of the votes on 9 July 1961, the NUC forced the leaders of the political parties to sign a joint declaration that, among others things, recognised the legitimacy of the 1960 coup d'état and denounced the Democrat Party ideology as well as 'partisanship' generally.[36] The military elite also ensured that the Justice Party, a descendant of the Democrat Party, did not put forward a presidential candidate so that Cemal Gürsel, the leader of the NUC, could be elected President.[37]

The 1961 Constitution is commonly regarded as a constitution that prioritised the individual over the state, rather than the other way around.[38] This is especially the case when it is contrasted with the 1982 Constitution, which is – or at least in its original form was – a more authoritarian constitution with a state-centric approach to rights and freedoms. That said, the 1961 Constitution contained many provisions that demonstrate a serious distrust in democratic politics and provide for bureaucratic mechanisms to keep it under control.[39] For instance, the members of the NUC were made Senators for life in the Senate of the Republic, the second parliamentary chamber created by the 1961 Constitution.[40] The Constitution also gave the President the power to directly appoint another 15 Senators.[41] This was designed to ensure that the interests of the military bureaucracy were sufficiently present in the legislature to keep democratic politics in check. The 1961 Constitution also entrenched the military judiciary and the Military Court of Cassation as constitutional authorities.[42] More importantly, it created the National Security Council for the first time, with a view to creating a mechanism that would liaise the Cabinet with the military bureaucracy, placing it hierarchically at the same level as the Cabinet in the Constitution.[43]

The next direct military involvement in constitution-making came on 12 March 1971, this time in the form of a memorandum with an ultimatum to end 'social and economic unrest' in response to the political violence between rightist and leftist groups,[44] and form a 'strong and credible government'. The generals signed the memorandum as 'members of the National Security Council',[45] demonstrative of the intended uses of the creation of the National Security

[36] Ibid., 376–77.
[37] Ibid., 377.
[38] B. Tanör, *Iki Anayasa: 1961–1982*, 5th ed. (XII Levha, 2013), 17.
[39] E. Özbudun, *Türk Anayasa Hukuku*, 11th ed. (Yetkin, 2010), 45–46; Tanör *Osmanlı-Türk Anayasal Gelişmeleri*, 399–401.
[40] 1961 Constitution of Turkey, Art. 70.
[41] 1961 Constitution of Turkey, Art. 70.
[42] 1961 Constitution of Turkey, Art. 141.
[43] Tanör, *Osmanlı-Türk Anayasal Gelişmeleri*, 400.
[44] E. J. Zürcher, *Turkey: A Modern History*, 3rd ed. (I. B. Tauris, 2004), 253–58.
[45] Tanör, *Osmanlı-Türk Anayasal Gelişmeleri*, 411.

Council. Following the 1971 memorandum, martial law was declared and this lasted over two years, during which three constitutional amendments were made to the 1961 Constitution. These amendments extended the scope of the military courts in a way that allowed certain civil matters to be tried before them due to martial law, strengthened the National Security Council by giving it recommendatory powers, and strengthened the executive to the detriment of the legislature.[46]

The military once again stepped in as political violence spread during the late 1970s, claiming the lives of not only left- and right-wing militants but also of public figures, including a former prime minister.[47] On 12 September 1980, the military announced that it had taken over political power claiming that the state organs had stopped functioning, and dissolved the Turkish Parliament. The military made it clear that it intended to hand back political power, but not before significant reforms had been made to the political system. The junta set up the National Security Council (not to be confused with the constitutional organ with the same name), which consisted of the Chief of the General Staff, the three Commanders of the Land, Naval and Air Forces and the General Commander of the Gendarmerie. Whilst the National Security Council delegated day-to-day government business to an unelected civil cabinet, it dictated the government programme.[48]

The National Security Council bestowed upon itself constitutional reform powers.[49] In 1981, it established a constituent assembly that consisted of (i) the National Security Council and (ii) an Advisory Assembly.[50] The Advisory Assembly was not elected and its members were not affiliated to any political party, all of which had already been dissolved. One hundred and twenty of the 160 members of the Advisory Assembly were recommended by unelected governors in each province and appointed by the National Security Council, and the remaining 40 members were appointed directly by the National Security Council. Ensuring its complete control over the constitution-making process, the National Security Council also empowered itself to approve or amend and approve the draft constitution passed by the Advisory Assembly.[51] The 1982 Constitution was drafted under these conditions and the draft finalised by the National Security Council was approved in a plebiscite by 91.37 per cent of the votes on 7 November 1982, with a 91.3 per cent turnout. It is worth noting that the National Security Council officially banned criticism of the National Security Council's campaign for the draft constitution and strongly implied that if the draft constitution was rejected, military rule would continue for the foreseeable future,[52] prompting voters to vote for the lesser of two evils.

The resultant 1982 Constitution created a more authoritarian constitutional order as well as strengthening the military's constitutional position in several respects. It provided that the number of civil members would not exceed the number of military members of the National Security Council (the constitutional organ) and further escalated the role of this Council in a way that forced the government to prioritise the Council's decisions. It expanded the scope of national security to bring social and political conflicts into the constitutional remit of the military. It also gave even more powers to the executive branch than the 1971 amendments, including an easier process for the President to dissolve the parliament. It provided extensive

[46] Tanör, *Iki Anayasa: 1961–1982*, 217–22.
[47] Zürcher, *Turkey*, 264.
[48] Özbudun, *Türk Anayasa Hukuku*, 52.
[49] Law on the Constitutional Order, No. 2324, dated 27 October 1980, Art. 6.
[50] Law on Constituent Assembly, No. 2485, 29 June 1981, Art. 1.
[51] Law on Constituent Assembly, No. 2485, 29 June 1981, Art. 26.
[52] Özbudun, *Türk Anayasa Hukuku*, 56.

Presidential powers to appoint members of the senior judiciary and placed several restrictions on the activities of political parties. It also made it easier to place limitations on all fundamental rights and freedoms on general grounds such as national security, public order, public utility and public morality.

As the approval of the referendum on the 1982 Constitution also automatically elected Kenan Evren, the Chief of General Staff and the leader of the National Security Council (the organ of the military junta), as President for a seven-year term as per Provisional Article 1 of the Constitution, the junta had direct control over democratic politics until the late 1980s. Following the end of Evren's presidential term, Turkish politics became more plural and eventually the Welfare Party, an Islamist political party and the political ascendant of the Justice and Development Party (AKP), came to power in 1996, leading a coalition government with two centre-right political parties. This government only lasted for a year, after the military issued a memorandum on 28 February 1997 to force out the government due to activities it regarded as a threat to secularism. The Welfare Party was eventually banned by the Constitutional Court in 1998 as it had become a 'focal point' of activities against secularism, which is an unamendable principle of the Turkish Constitution.[53] This military intervention is widely known as the 'post-modern coup' as it forced a government out through a memorandum with a thinly veiled threat of an actual military coup by the National Security Council, yet it did not dissolve the parliament as in previous interventions.

In 2007, the military provoked an unintended constitutional change. Reflecting on its historical practices, it made its discontent with the prospect of Abdullah Gül's presidential election clear through what has come to be known as the 'e-memorandum' of 2007. Abdullah Gül was the candidate put forward by the AKP and was likely to be elected President by the Turkish Parliament. The fact that he came from a religious background and that his wife wore the Islamic headscarf became an issue with the secularist parts of society.[54] The military weighed in on the matter by publishing a statement on its website, signalling that it will 'act' if secularism comes under attack within the context of the presidential election. The government refused to succumb to this pressure and pressed on with Gül's candidacy, only to find itself unable to achieve quorum in the Turkish Parliament after a move by the parliamentary opposition to innovate a new rule on quorum requiring that the number of votes required in the first round of election (367) is also the number for the session to be quorate. Although the AKP had enough MPs to elect Gül in the second round, where 276 votes were sufficient, the Constitutional Court ruled in favour of the opposition regarding the quorum rule.[55] A general election was called in response to this and the AKP, although losing some of its seats, were able to achieve quorum because the Nationalist Movement Party gained enough seats in the Turkish Parliament to make up the 367 required for quorum. After the election, Gül was elected President and the AKP introduced a significant constitutional amendment that provided for a popularly elected President, as well as clarifying the rule on quorum. This amendment was approved in the 2007 referendum by 68.95 per cent of the voters.

Especially since the 1990s, there has been a constant debate regarding the democratic legitimacy of the 1982 Constitution and the need to adopt a 'civil' constitution to replace the current 'military' constitution.[56] This discourse has ranged from simple calls to formally remake

[53] Constitutional Court, E. 1997/1 (Political Party Closure), K. 1998/1, 16 January 1998.

[54] Ş. Dinçşahin, 'A Symptomatic Analysis of the Justice and Development Party's Populism in Turkey, 2007–2010' (2012) 47 *Government and Opposition* 618, 627–30.

[55] Constitutional Court, E. 2007/45, K. 2007/54, 1 May 2007.

[56] Z. Arslan, 'Turkey's Bid for the New Constitution' (2007) 9 *Insight Turkey* 7.

the constitution by a civil body and rescue it from its military underpinnings to substantially reform it and rid it of mechanisms that maintain the tutelage of the military over democratic politics. Whilst much of the authoritarian foundations and language of the Constitution remains intact, reforms made in line with Turkey's process of accession to the European Union in late 1990s and 2000s created, at least nominally, a less restrictive constitutional framework for the protection of fundamental rights and freedoms as well as allowing more space for democratic politics.[57]

Turkey witnessed another coup attempt in 2016. This was striking for many reasons, but especially for demonstrating the ongoing relevance of the military in shaping the Turkish constitutional order. Since the early 2010s, many observers considered that military tutelage over democratic politics in Turkey was over and that the military had lost its purchase within society, at least when it came to shaping domestic politics.[58] Especially after what was considered to be the AKP's victories over the military, such as the 2007 presidential election and constitutional amendment referendum, and the *Ergenekon* and *Balyoz* trials, the predominant view was that the 'era of coups' was over. The 2016 coup attempt and its aftermath are a testament to the continuing central relevance of the military to constitutional ordering in Turkey.

23.4 CONCLUSION: THE EFFECTS OF MILITARY INVOLVEMENT AND THE MATERIAL CONSTITUTION

The formal constitution of Turkey equips the military with significant powers, including a pivotal role in making and executing national security policy. As the making of the last two constitutions and several military interventions at critical constitutional junctures demonstrate, the military has a defining constitutional role, more than simply informing about the work of the executive in Turkey. It is clear that there is a strong lingering presence of the military within the Turkish constitutional order, providing a checks and balances mechanism, not necessarily to curb excessive use of governmental power, but to keep democratic politics in check when it feels that political unity or the fundamental political objectives that make up the particular constitutional order are at stake. It is telling that the national security policy document, the 'red book', is known as the 'secret constitution' of Turkey and a former Chief of General Staff called it 'the god of all policies, the mother of all laws: it is unthinkable to act against it'.[59]

The Turkish Constitution has been shaped by the military more than by any other institution. Some effects of the military involvement in constitution-making in Turkey are self-evident. The current constitution itself was drafted under military control and to this day the people of Turkey are constantly reminded of its military origins. That said, enquiries into the Turkish constitution rarely take the ongoing constitutional role of the military into account. This is not to say that the military is not treated in the constitutional law scholarship as having exercised 'constituent power', but rather to emphasise that the formal constitution fails to acknowledge how much influence the military has consistently had over constitutional actors and not only during coups d'état or the transitional periods following them. A mere focus on the act of founding with regard

[57] E. Özbudun and Ö. F. Gençkaya, *Democratization and the Politics of Constitution-Making in Turkey* (Central European University Press, 2009), 43–72.

[58] Y. Cilliler, 'Popular Determinant on Civil–Military Relations in Turkey' (2016) 38 *Arab Studies Quarterly* 500. Cilliler notes strong popular support for the government in the civil and political society as well as by major economic interest groups, the power of the pro-government media and the change in political opposition's approach to a more cautious stance toward the political involvement of the military as some of the reasons for the fading influence of the military over domestic politics.

[59] K. Akkoyunlu, 'Chapter Two: Turkey' (2007) 47 *The Adelphi Papers* 21, 37.

to the military's involvement in constitution-making in Turkey conceals the fact that the constitutional relevance of the military is reinforced by the success of the military-made constitutions.

The aforementioned legitimacy deficit of the 1982 Constitution due to its military origins may be overstated as well. There was a serious constitution-making attempt between 2011 and 2013, bringing together the four major political parties representing 95 per cent of the voters in an *ad hoc* constitution-making committee in the Turkish Parliament with equal representation. The idea was to replace the 'authoritarian' constitution made by the military with a 'civil' one based on the protection of human rights. This attempt failed miserably as the threshold for agreement was set too high with consensus required among the four political parties involved in the process and three of the four political parties' reluctance to compromise on their 'red lines' – presidentialism for the Justice and Development Party (AKP), secularism for the Republican People's Party (CHP) and nationalism for the Nationalist Movement Party (MHP). This led the way to a rapid eradication of political goodwill and an increasing authoritarianism until this day.[60] The failure of the process may be explained away as being unfortunate, but the political parties knew it would mean the 1982 Constitution living on. This may be, therefore, a legitimacy crisis only in name; perhaps the 1982 Constitution, at least the basic framework it sets up, caters well to the needs of the Turkish polity. This is not to praise the 1982 Constitution but rather to point out that its framework is amenable to speak to the material constitution of Turkey. This can also be observed in constitution-making debates, including the 2011–13 constitution-making process,[61] where there are two fault lines: (i) nationalism and the unitary character of the state and (ii) secularism. These are the essential characteristics of Turkey's material constitution, conditioned by military tutelage.[62] The main political forces in the country, represented by the AKP, the CHP and the MHP, do not wish to move away from these fundamental political objectives. The perceived legitimacy deficit, therefore, seems to be a shallow and formalistic pre-occupation with the fact that it was the military that oversaw the making of Turkey's constitutions, rather than one of profound disagreement with the essence of the 'military' constitution.

This chapter has sought to show the constitutional role of the military in the Turkish constitutional order beyond its formal constitutional powers and its direct interventions to democratic politics roughly once every decade. The role of the military is ongoing and it conditions the constitutional order, protecting its fundamental political objectives and shaping the behaviour of constitutional actors. The material enquiry of the constitution promises to help to pinpoint the forces responsible for such ordering. Further studies on the material constitution of Turkey may enquire into the political interests or factions that make up the military.[63] What happened in the aftermath of the 2016 coup attempt, muddled as it may be, has exposed the presence of an organised political interest group inside the military, seeking to exert political power within the military and beyond. It would be naïve to assume that the rest of the military is not organised as such and does not consist of other interest groups that have political influence. Studying the corporatist nature of the military can yield useful data regarding the type and extent of the current constitutional relevance of the Turkish military.

60 F. Petersen and Z. Yanaşmayan (eds.), *The Failure of Popular Constitution Making in Turkey: Regressing towards Constitutional Autocracy* (Cambridge University Press, 2020).

61 F. Petersen and Z. Yanaşmayan, 'Explaining the Failure of Popular Constitution Making in Turkey', in F. Petersen and Z. Yanaşmayan (eds.), *The Failure of Popular Constitution Making in Turkey*, 49–56.

62 See Kuru, 'Rise and Fall of Military Tutelage in Turkey'.

63 See, e.g., B. Esen, 'Praetorian Army in Action: A Critical Assessment of Civil–Military Relations in Turkey' (2021) 47 *Armed Forces & Society* 201.

24

The Material Constitution of International Investment Law

Jessica Lawrence and Tom Flynn

24.1 INTRODUCTION

When an owner of capital invests this capital in the state of their citizenship or nationality, this 'domestic' investment is governed by the ordinary rules of national law. But when an investor *exports* their capital, investing it in a state in which they are legally a foreigner, a whole extra body of law supplements, and in some cases supplants, these domestic arrangements. This is international investment law (IIL): the vast and ever-growing body of international investment agreements (IIAs), decisions of arbitral tribunals and other forms of law – formal and informal, 'hard' and 'soft' – that seek to protect the rights of foreign investors against the actions of 'host' states.

Whether the investor invests their capital at home or exports it abroad, we are concerned in this chapter with the interplay between the actions of an investor (someone with capital who wishes to make a profit) and the actions of a state (a body which, in democratic theory, claims to be the legal avatar of 'the people'). The legal relations between these actors – contractual, tortious, constitutional, etc. – cannot be understood in purely formal terms. Rather, following Goldoni and Wilkinson,[1] we argue that it is only through a materialist analysis (and in the broadest legal context a material constitutionalist analysis), emphasising the role of power and political economy, that we can unpack the ways in which the constitutional order shapes and is in turn shaped by the figure of the (international) investor.

We argue in this chapter that investment law must be understood in the context of struggles between capital exporters and states, where investors seek to protect their individual property rights against the actions of political authorities. At the domestic level, the 'legitimacy' and 'proportionality' of state action are frequently key to determining whether or not a particular intervention that impacts an investor's property will be deemed legal and/or compensable, and to what degree. IIL, on the other hand, is more agnostic about the 'public good', frequently requiring compensation in cases where state actions are in some way justifiable with reference to non-economic or communitarian values, and at levels set without regard to the impact on the public purse and the ability of the state to fulfil its broader social responsibilities. In this, IIL differs from the practice of both domestic constitutional law and international human rights law, where not every interference with a right is necessarily a violation of that right and where the

[1] Marco Goldoni and Michael A. Wilkinson, 'The Material Constitution' (2018) 81 *Modern Law Review* 567.

legitimacy of the aim of the interference, its means and its extent are all relevant in determining whether a right has been violated and, if it has, the amount of compensation due to the victim.[2]

In effect, IIL internationalises the protection of property and contract rights over and above other competing rights and obligations of the state and prioritises the protection of investors over and above that of ordinary citizens. IIL does this in part by drawing on and relying on formal constitutional concepts such as equality, non-discrimination and the rule of law, but uses these concepts differently to how they are used within national constitutional orders. This comes as no surprise, once we acknowledge the very different material context within which IIL has been created, developed, practiced, enforced and re-created.

These tensions between IIL and public policy have not gone unnoticed. Indeed, IIL is currently undergoing something of a 'constitutional crisis', as states in both the global North and South bristle against the restrictions they have imposed on themselves and on each other in the hope of attracting investment and stimulating economic growth. Extensive criticism of the inconsistent decisions of arbitral tribunals; the perceived bias and conflicts of interest of arbiters; broad interpretations of investor protections and consequent limitations of policy space; increasingly massive awards; and a lack of evidence regarding the benefits of the system have created a backlash and spurred a number of different reform efforts. Much of the discussion has focused on substantive and procedural tweaks to the formal constitutional order of IIL, in order to make it more consistent, less biased and more attentive to states' 'right to regulate' and investors' obligations to their host states.

However, in this chapter, we argue that we cannot simply rearrange the legal formalities and expect meaningful systemic change. Rather, an analysis of the material constitution of IIL reveals that it is an order bound up in fundamental ways with the history of imperialist expansion; the inscription of the particular rights of the investor class as general and international; and a desire to protect capital and markets from state interference. Section 24.2 briefly maps the *formal* constitution of IIL: its origins, its development; its texts; and its institutions. In Section 24.3, we adopt Goldoni and Wilkinson's four ordering forces of *material* constitutionalism – political unity, institutions, social relations and fundamental political objectives – to draw attention to the distinct ordering principles of this international regime. In doing so, we demonstrate the impact of an international legal order that self-consciously uses the language of constitutionalism to introject political objectives and a conception of social relations at odds with a substantive conception of democracy; that re-casts a set of rules and institutions designed to further the interests of capital-exporters as international rights claims; that does so on behalf of an investor-subject afforded protection purely as a function of its transnational economic activity; and that is produced and reinforced by means of institutions of meagre democratic legitimacy in a political unity that, unlike the state, does not consist of a physical territory, but precisely of a non-physical 'international' space, outwith the borders and beyond the control of governments. We conclude that though the various calls for reform may well improve certain serious flaws in the formal system of IIL, material constitutionalist analysis reveals inherent features of the system that cannot be reformed without a fundamental reconfiguration of the material relations between international capital and state constitutional orders.

[2] The European Court of Human Rights, for example, takes the position that it will not interfere with a state's decision regarding the level of compensation to be paid in the event of an expropriation unless it is 'manifestly without reasonable foundation.' *Lithgow* v. *United Kingdom* (1986) 8 EHRR 329, 373. Likewise, the Court's general view is that the level of compensation should be relative to the public purpose of the measure. *James* v. *United Kingdom* (1986) 5 EHRR 35, 147.

24.2 THE FORMAL CONSTITUTION OF INTERNATIONAL INVESTMENT LAW

The question of whether, to what extent and in what context it is appropriate to use the language of constitutionalism to describe and engage with non-state legal orders is not settled. Though widely accepted in some international contexts (such as in that of the European Union), the 'project'[3] of transplanting constitutionalism from the statist frame to other global frames has met with more resistance. For the present purposes, the 'global constitutionalism' debate of the 2000s and 2010s[4] is not important: IIL is certainly not a constitutional legal order such as that of a state in the formal sense. It is not autochthonous or self-standing and it is so partial in its sectoral coverage that it lacks the breadth and overarching nature associated with constitutionalism proper. Nevertheless, the concept of constitutionalism and its vocabulary are used here as a discursive framework that throws some important issues of formal law into sharper relief than would be the case without constitution-talk: democratic legitimacy, equality before the law, institutional independence and much else besides. We are not alone in using constitutional tools to assess IIL: by specifically adopting methods, norms, processes and language commonly associated with constitutionalism, the architects and practitioners of IIL themselves have been actively trying to constitutionalise the IIL regime for years; just as critical scholars have been deploying those same tools to contest its power and legitimacy.[5]

24.2.1 *Sources of the Constitution*

Having clarified this context, we can now turn to setting out the three main sources of the formal constitution of IIL.

First, there are around 3,000 IIAs currently in force,[6] most notably including Bilateral Investment Treaties (BITs) and treaties that contain provisions or chapters covering investment, such as some modern Free Trade Agreements (FTAs). There are also sectoral agreements, such as the Energy Charter Treaty, which protect investors' rights in particular economic fields; as well as other treaties that contain certain protections for the rights of investors, though this may not be their central function and they may or may not contain the 'common core' of rights generally found in IIAs. Examples of this latter sort of treaty are the WTO's General Agreement on Trade in Services (GATS) (in particular mode 3 commitments regarding commercial presence) and Agreement on Trade-Related Investment Measures (TRIMS); the EU Treaties insofar as they concern the free movement of capital and the right of establishment; and regional human rights treaties such as the European Convention on Human Rights (ECHR) insofar as they concern the protection of property rights.

Second, IIL is to be found in the procedural rules, institutions and treaties governing international investment arbitration. The International Centre for the Settlement of Investment Disputes (ICSID) Convention (also called the Washington Convention) and the

[3] D. Kennedy, 'The Mystery of Global Governance', in J. L. Dunoff and J. P. Trachtman (eds.), *Ruling the World? Constitutionalism and Global Governance* (Cambridge University Press, 2009), 40.

[4] See, e.g., J. L. Dunoff and J. P. Trachtman, 'A Functional Approach to International Constitutionalization', in in J. L. Dunoff and J. P. Trachtman (eds.), *Ruling the World? Constitutionalism and Global Governance* (Cambridge University Press, 2009), 3–37.

[5] See, e.g., D. Schneiderman, *Constitutionalizing Economic Globalization: Investment Rules and Democracy's Promise* (Cambridge University Press, 2008).

[6] A regularly updated database can be found at: https://investmentpolicy.unctad.org/international-investment-agreements, last accessed 10 August 2022.

New York Conventions lay down much of the legal framework in this respect, supplemented by the provisions of individual IIAs; and institutions such as ICSID and the UN Commission on International Trade Law (UNCITRAL), amongst others, provide significant forums, personnel, and expertise for arbitration. The vast majority of IIL disputes are brought by private actors, empowered to make claims against national governments through investor-state dispute settlement (ISDS) provisions in IIAs. Such claims are heard by ad hoc investment tribunals modelled after private commercial arbitration mechanisms, staffed with a mix of lawyers, arbitrators and academics. Arbitration takes place outside the jurisdiction of the state and its courts, which – importantly – are *presumed* to be potentially biased against foreign investors and subject to pressure from national actors, in contrast to 'de-politicised' and 'neutral' international forums.[7]

Third, the vast and varied jurisprudence of arbitration tribunals constitutes a source of law in its own right. While the decisions of these tribunals have no formal precedential value or binding effect beyond the parties themselves, they can be influential, and well-crafted decisions can have persuasive value. Around 700 such decisions are known; however, the real figure may be much higher, as not all are made public.[8]

To these three major sources of the formal constitution of IIL, we can add a range of supplementary sources, including customary international law (e.g., rules regarding the protection of aliens, rules of treaty interpretation); national legal practices and rules; investor–state contracts; and related areas of international law such as international tax agreements; finance and debt arrangements; ILO and OECD codes of conduct; and many others.

24.2.2 *Rules and Principles of the Constitution and Their Malleability*

In terms of their substance, while IIAs vary greatly in terms of their precise content, they generally follow a common format, typically including rules regarding non-discrimination on grounds of nationality; prohibition of expropriation without compensation; and 'fair and equitable treatment' (FET). Other protections may be added to the mix as well – capital transfer rights and protection against breach of contract through 'umbrella clauses', for example, are also common. These protections are frequently cast in the language of *rights* and are sometimes analogised to protections found in human rights law: denial of justice, the right to a fair trial, the right to property, due process and non-discrimination are deployed by both the IIL and human rights regimes to defend natural and legal persons against the actions of the state.[9] However, the terms of the protections afforded by IIAs are vague, leaving wide latitude for arbitrators to interpret their meaning and making arbitral decisions notoriously unpredictable.[10]

To provide just one example, the prohibition of expropriation or nationalisation without compensation includes not only 'direct' expropriation (the mandatory legal transfer of property or outright physical seizure), but also 'indirect' expropriation (measures 'tantamount to' or 'equivalent to' expropriation, where the investor is deprived of the use and enjoyment of their

[7] See S. Puig, 'No Right without a Remedy: Foundations of Investor-State Arbitration (2013–14) 35 *University of Pennsylvania Journal of International Law* 829.

[8] For a current list of known disputes, see: https://investmentpolicy.unctad.org/investment-dispute-settlement, last accessed 10 August 2022.

[9] See M. Paparinskis, 'Analogies and Other Regimes of International Law', in Z. Douglas, J. Pauwelyn and J. E Viñuales (eds.), *The Foundations of International Investment Law: Bringing Theory into Practice* (Oxford University Press, 2014), 73–107.

[10] This has long been discussed as a problem undermining the legitimacy of tribunals. See, e.g., S. D Franck, 'The Legitimacy Crisis in Investment Treaty Arbitration: Privatizing Public International Law through Inconsistent Decisions' (2005) 75 *Fordham Law Review* 1521.

property while retaining formal ownership). This latter category has, at its most expansive, been interpreted as including any action 'depriving the owner, in whole or in significant part, of the use or reasonably to be expected economic benefit of property even if not necessarily to the obvious benefit of the host State',[11] a sweeping definition that could cover nearly *any* state action that diminished the value of the investment. Most tribunals have not gone quite so far, requiring a 'substantial deprivation' of property to have taken place before a measure will be found expropriatory.[12] However, the uncertainty that is built into the ad hoc arbitration system means that it is difficult to predict *ex ante* where a particular tribunal will stand on such questions, leaving open the possibility for investors to threaten suits in order to dissuade governments from taking actions contrary to the investors' interests.[13]

Such strong-arm tactics are particularly concerning given that the category of 'indirect expropriation' has sometimes been interpreted to cover so-called regulatory takings. As the tribunal stated in *Santa Elena* v. *Costa Rica*, in the context of a challenge by a tourism resort developer to a decision by the state to convert the resort's intended location into a coastal wildlife reserve:[14] 'Expropriatory environmental measures – no matter how laudable and beneficial to society as a whole – are, in this respect, similar to any other expropriatory measures that a state may take in order to implement its policies: where property is expropriated, even for environmental purposes, whether domestic or international, the state's obligation to pay compensation remains.'[15] But here too there is contrary practice from other tribunals. Consider the following, from *Methanex*:[16] '[N]on-discriminatory regulation for a public purpose, which is enacted in accordance with due process, and which affects, *inter alios*, a foreign investment, is not deemed expropriatory and compensable unless specific commitments had been given by the regulating government to refrain from such regulation.'[17] Subsequent decisions have not resolved this issue: the line between a compensable expropriation and a 'legitimate' regulation which does not give rise to a claim for compensation remains unclear.

Even murkier is the interpretation of the nebulous and frequently litigated FET standard, and the extent to which compensation should be paid when governments undermine the 'legitimate expectations' of a foreign investor. Tribunals reading this standard broadly have found compensable harms in situations including a state's refusal to issue or renew a permit required for a business to operate, the regulatory phase-out of an environmentally harmful business and the withdrawal of a tax exemption. They have even – at their most extreme – read the standard as implying an obligation to maintain 'regulatory stability',[18] thus clearly limiting the possibility of domestic actions that undermine the interests of international investors. Others have read the obligation more narrowly, as protecting only 'legitimate' and 'reasonable' expectations, such as where specific representations were made to the investor to induce the investment.[19]

[11] *Metalclad* v. *Mexico*, 5 ICSID Reports 209, Award, 30 August 2000, para. 103.

[12] *Pope & Talbot, Inc.* v. *Government of Canada*, UNCITRAL Award, 26 January 2000.

[13] The notion of 'regulatory chill' is widely discussed in the literature.

[14] *Compañia del Desarrollo de Santa Elena S.A.* v. *Republic of Costa Rica*, ICSID Case No. ARB/96/1, Award, 17 February 2000.

[15] Ibid., para. 72.

[16] *Methanex Corporation* v. *United States of America*, UNCITRAL Final Award, 3 August 2005.

[17] Ibid., at Part IV, para. 7

[18] *Tecmed* v. *Mexico*, ICSID Case No ARB (AF)/00/2, Award, 29 May 2003.

[19] *Duke Energy Electroquil Partners and Electroquil SA* v. *Ecuador*, ICSID Case No ARB/04/19, Award, 18 August 2008; *Masdar Solar & Wind Cooperatief U.A.* v. *Kingdom of Spain*, ICSID Case No ARB/14/1, Award, 16 May 2018.

Tribunals taking the narrower approach have sometimes noted the need to balance investors' expectations against the legitimate regulatory activities of host countries.[20] This importation of 'proportionality'[21] or 'reasonableness'[22] analysis into IIL has been advocated by some scholars as a way of addressing legitimacy concerns and in light of the growing list of clashes between IIL and domestic regulation over issues relating to, for example, environmental protection and public health.[23] However, many scholars continue to view IIL through the traditional lens of private commercial law, arguing that its 'public' character is overstated[24] and that these disputes remain, at their heart, commercial ones. To date, use of proportionality analysis by tribunals remains inconsistent and of variable quality, raising further questions about its value as a means of imbuing IIL with legitimacy.[25]

The stakes of these *constitutional* debates in IIL are made much higher by the eye-watering awards that can come with successful ISDS claims. Bonnitcha and Brewin have found more than 50 cases in which compensation exceeded USD 100 million, the largest of which was an award of $40 billion in a case involving the nationalisation of Russian oil company Yukos.[26] Awards of this nature seriously impact national budgets and affect the ability of states to take action for the benefit of their citizens.

Illustrative of the potential pitfalls is the case of *Tethyan Copper* v. *Pakistan*,[27] in which an Australian mining company filed a successful ICSID arbitration against Pakistan regarding the denial of an expected mining license. The tribunal ultimately found that Tethyan had a legitimate expectation that the mining license would be granted and that due process was not followed: the denial therefore violated the rights of the investor. It awarded Tethyan $4 billion plus interest in compensation, taking into account the *future* income the investment *would have* earned (or, rather, *might have* earned) over its 50-year operating cycle if it had in fact been built (even though the investor's original outlay was only $150 million).[28] This award was nearly as large as the $6 billion bailout package that the IMF and Pakistan had agreed a few months earlier:[29] the perverse result is that two thirds of the bailout went straight into the pockets of an Australian mining company.

[20] *Saluka Investments BV (The Netherlands)* v. *Czech Republic*. UNCITRAL Rules, Partial Award, 17 March 2006; *EDF International S.A., SAUR International S.A. and León Participaciones Argentinas S.A.* v. *Romania*, ICSID Case No. ARB/05/13, Award, 8 October 2009.

[21] B. Kingsbury and S. W. Schill, 'Investor-State Arbitration As Governance: Fair and Equitable Treatment, Proportionality and the Emerging Global Administrative Law' (2011) 2 *Transnational Dispute Management*; C. Henckels, *Proportionality and Deference in Investor-State Arbitration: Balancing Investment Protection and Regulatory Autonomy* (Cambridge University Press, 2015).

[22] V. Vadi, *Proportionality, Reasonableness and Standards of Review in International Investment Law and Arbitration* (Edward Elgar, 2018).

[23] See, e.g., A. M. Daza-Clark, *International Investment Law and Water Resources Management* (Brill, 2016); V. Vadi, *Public Health in International Investment Law and Arbitration* (Routledge, 2012); J. E. Viñuales, *Foreign Investment and the Environment in International Law* (Cambridge University Press, 2012).

[24] J. E. Alvarez, 'Is Investor-State Arbitration Public?' (2016) 7 *Journal of International Dispute Settlement* 534.

[25] See, e.g., D. Schneiderman, 'Global Constitutionalism and Its Legitimacy Problems: Human Rights, Proportionality, and International Investment Law' (2018) 12 *The Law & Ethics of Human Rights* 251; G. Bücheler, *Proportionality in Investor–State Arbitration* (Oxford University Press, 2015).

[26] J. Bonnitcha and S. Brewin, *Compensation under Investment Treaties* (International Institute for Sustainable Development, 2020).

[27] *Tethyan Copper Company Pty Limited* v. *Islamic Republic of Pakistan*, ICSID Case No. ARB/12/1, Award, 12 July 2019.

[28] The use of the so-called discounted cash flow (DCF) method to calculate an investment's expected future income over its entire life cycle is frequently used as a basis for awarding compensation. See Bonnitcha and Brewin, *Compensation under Investment Treaties*.

[29] IMF, Press Release No. 19/264, 'IMF Executive Board Approves US$6 billion 39-Month EFF Arrangement for Pakistan', 3 July 2019, available at: www.imf.org/en/News/Articles/2019/07/03/pr19264-pakistan-imf-executive-board-approves-39-month-eff-arrangement, last accessed 10 August 2022.

In an effort to reign in the potentially broad scope and unpredictable interpretation of IIL protections, some states have begun to include preambles, exceptions and carve-outs that seek to protect non-economic interests and the right to regulate in new generation IIAs. Others have begun to exit the system, terminating IIAs and withdrawing from ICSID. The EU has sought to move away from ad hoc arbitration and toward a more formalised Investment Court System or potentially even a Multilateral Investment Court. Even UNCITRAL is currently debating ISDS reform.[30]

But such reform efforts can, at best, improve the perceived legitimacy of IIL's doctrinal and institutional architecture. To understand the structural limitations of such formal constitutional change, we must look to the material forces at work in the undergrowth of IIL that created this legal world and which these institutions and constitutional debates reflect and reproduce.

24.3 MAPPING THE MATERIAL CONSTITUTION OF INTERNATIONAL INVESTMENT LAW

24.3.1 *Political Unity*

24.3.1.1 Development

IIL's history is a long one and is deeply embedded in the imperialist expansion of European commercial interests beginning in the seventeenth century.[31] Early treatments of the (European) law of nations held that foreign traders, once admitted to a state's territory, should be treated no worse than nationals.[32] Friendship, Commerce and Navigation (FCN) treaties built on this foundation, establishing networks of treaty-based protections for the property of expatriates, sometimes reciprocal, but often – especially in non-European contexts – on the basis of 'enforced compliance' and unequal treaties.[33] International customary law developed an 'international minimum standard' for the treatment of aliens that prohibited bad faith and 'outrageous' conduct by the state,[34] as well as a rule prohibiting the expropriation of alien property except when for a public purpose, where not arbitrary and where 'prompt, adequate, and effective' compensation would be paid (the so-called Hull formula).[35] Failure to uphold these standards triggered international responsibility and the home states of sufficiently powerful and

[30] UNCITRAL, 'Working Group III: Investor-State Dispute Settlement Reform', available at: https://uncitral.un.org/en/working_groups/3/investor-state, last accessed 10 August 2022.

[31] K. Miles, *The Origins of International Investment Law: Empire, Environment and the Safeguarding of Capital* (Cambridge University Press, 2013).

[32] The idea that there is a freedom to trade on a non-discriminatory basis can be found back as far as de Vitoria, Grotius and de Vattel. F. de Vitoria, *De Indis et De Iure Belli: Relectiones* (orig. 1532, E. Nys, ed. 1964), Part 2; H. Grotius, *De Jure Belli Ac Pacis Libri Tres* (orig. 1625, J. B. Scott, ed., F. W. Kelsey, trans., 1925), Book II, Chapter II, XXII; E. de Vattel, *Law of Nations* (orig. 1798, J. Chitty, trans.), Book II, Chapter VIII, s108–9.

[33] Miles, *Origins of International Investment Law*, 25 et seq. See also Antony Anghie, *Imperialism, Sovereignty and the Making of International Law* (Cambridge University Press, 2012).

[34] *Neer Claim*, 1926 4 RIAA 60.

[35] C. Hull, Letter, 'The Secretary of State to the Mexican Ambassador (Castillo Nájera)' Washington, 21 July 1938, available at: https://history.state.gov/historicaldocuments/frus1938v05/d662, last accessed 10 August 2022.

well-connected investors might choose to espouse the claims of wronged nationals, leading to arbitration between the capital-exporting and -importing states, or, if this failed, to so-called gunboat diplomacy or outright military intervention, a tactic eventually outlawed by the Drago–Porter Convention in 1907.[36]

This gradual spread of international property rules did not go uncontested. Beginning in the 1860s, Latin American states began to resist the 'diplomatic protection' system used to enforce the rights of investors in their territories and presented an alternate theory of what the 'fair treatment' of investors and their property should entail. Under this new 'national treatment' standard, known as the Calvo doctrine,[37] investors were to be treated no worse but also no better than the nationals of the host state. This position was unattractive to capital-exporters because it meant that if the state were to treat its own investors in a disagreeable manner, it could treat foreign investors in this manner too: indeed, the Soviet Union relied on the Calvo doctrine to justify its refusal to compensate a gold mining venture expropriated in 1917.[38]

This history of imperialism and resistance sits at the heart of the modern system of investment law. The rise of IIAs must be understood in significant part as a reaction to post-colonial, socialist and other state interventions that put international property rights in jeopardy. Decolonisation in particular created risks for investors, as property acquired and rights established under colonial regimes were challenged by new governments seeking to redistribute wealth, re-assert sovereignty over natural resources and exercise national control over their economies. Nationalisations and the retraction of concessions were important tools for these newly-independent governments: one study found 875 recorded expropriations across 62 countries between 1960 and 1974.[39]

Socialist and post-colonial states made several attempts to assert what they saw as their economic rights and to create a new international standard for the protection of investments. The 1962 UN General Assembly Resolution on Permanent Sovereignty over Natural Resources recognised the right of the state to expropriate private interests on payment of 'appropriate compensation, in accordance with the rules in force in the State taking such measures in the exercise of its sovereignty and in accordance with international law'[40] – a far more flexible standard than the Hull formula favoured by capital-exporters. The 1974 Declaration on the New International Economic Order[41] recognised the right to expropriate without paying fair market value and stated that '[n]o State may be subjected to economic, political, or any other type of coercion to prevent the free and full exercise of this inalienable right'.[42] Similarly, the 1974 Charter of Economic Rights and Duties of States attempted to abolish the 'minimum standard' on the expropriation of alien property and replace it with domestic law, in accordance with the Calvo doctrine.[43]

36 Hague Convention II – Limitation of Employment of Force for Recovery of Contract Debts (Drago-Porter Convention), 18 October 1907, art. 1(1).

37 C. Calvo, *Derecho internacional teórico y práctico* (Amyot, 1868).

38 V. V. Veeder, 'The Lena Goldfields Arbitration: The Historical Roots of Three Ideas' (1998) 47 *International and Comparative Law Quarterly* 747.

39 O. T. Johnson Jr. and J. Gimblett, 'From Gunboats to BITs: The Evolution of Modern International Investment Law', in K. P. Sauvant (ed.), *Yearbook on International Investment Law & Policy 2010-2011* (Oxford University Press, 2012), 675 (quoting Permanent Sovereignty Over Natural Resources Report of the Secretary General, UN Doc. A/9716 (1974)).

40 G. A. Res. 1803 (XVII), reprinted in (1963) 2 *International Legal Materials* 223.

41 Resolution 3201 (S-VI).

42 Ibid., para 4(e).

43 G. A. Res. 3281, U. N. GAOR, 29th Sess., Supp. No. 31, at 50, UN Doc. A/9631, 15 January 1974, reprinted in 14 I.L.M. 251 (1975).

Capital-exporting states, spurred by the efforts of 'norm entrepreneurs' from the banking, business and legal sectors,[44] responded by creating the modern system of international investment law. Following several failed attempts to create a multilateral investment law framework,[45] which fell apart due to disagreements between capital-exporting and capital-importing states over investor protection standards, individual capital-exporting states instead divided and conquered, turning to bilateral negotiations and laying the foundations for modern IIL. The first BIT was signed between Germany and Pakistan in 1959.[46] ICSID was established as part of the World Bank Group in 1966 to provide a set of rules and a de-localised forum for hearing investment disputes and the web of treaties slowly began to build. It was not until 1989, however, that IIL really began to blossom. The fall of the Soviet Union brought with it the need for states around the world (post-Soviet and otherwise) to attract capital and the end of the Cold War led to a decline in foreign aid budgets. At the same time, the debt crisis of the 1980s reduced the availability of private lending; export-led growth strategies in Asia seemed to demonstrate the successes of liberal economic policies; and the general climate of 'end of history' thinking in political and intellectual circles was evident in the Washington Consensus, which regarded 'a restrictive attitude limiting the entry for foreign direct investment' as 'foolish' behaviour motivated by 'economic nationalism'.[47]

These ideas were pushed in particular by capital-exporting states and international financial institutions, including via conditionality mechanisms,[48] but were also taken up enthusiastically by capital-importing states convinced of the promise of economic growth; convinced of the perceived need to compete for scarce investment capital; and eager to reap the benefits.[49] From the democratic perspective, it is notable that this flurry of treaty-making and institution-building in the 1990s took place 'virtually unnoticed', with mid-level government officials negotiating and concluding the agreements largely without scrutiny by parliaments, the media or the public[50] and with little attention to the potential consequences of the commitments being made, aside from the promised increases in international investment.[51]

44 N. M. Perrone, *Investment Treaties and the Legal Imagination: How Foreign Investors Play by Their Own Rules* (Oxford University Press, 2021).

45 See, e.g., Havana Charter for an International Trade Organization (1948), UN Conference on Trade and Employment, UN Doc. E/CONF.2/78; International Chamber of Commerce, International Code of Fair Treatment of Foreign Investment (1948); International Law Association, Draft Statute of the Arbitral Tribunal for Foreign Investment and the Foreign Investment Court (1948); Abs and Shawcross, Draft Convention on Investments Abroad (1959); OECD, Draft Convention on the Protection of Foreign Property (1967).

46 Treaty between the Federal Republic of Germany and Pakistan for the Promotion and Protection of Investments, signed 25 November 1959 (1963) 457 UNTS 23 (entered into force 28 April 1962).

47 J. Williams, 'What Washington Means with Policy Reform', in J. Williamson (ed.), *Latin American Adjustment: How Much Has Happened?* (Institute for International Economics, 1990), 7–20.

48 A. Kaushal, 'Revisiting History: How the Past Matters for the Present Backlash against the Foreign Investment Regime' (2009) 50 *Harvard International Law Journal* 491.

49 Andrew Guzman suggests that poorer states face a prisoners' dilemma 'in which it is optimal for them, as a group, to reject the [adequate, effective, and prompt compensation rule], but in which each individual LDC is better off "defecting" from the group by signing a BIT that gives it an advantage over other LDCs in the competition to attract foreign investors'. A. T. Guzman, 'Why LDCs Sign Treaties that Hurt Them: Explaining the Popularity of Bilateral Investment Treaties' (1998) 38 *Virginia Journal of International Law* 639, 666–67.

50 J. Bonnitcha, L. N. Skovgaard Poulsen and M. Waibel, *The Political Economy of the Investment Treaty Regime* (Oxford University Press, 2017), quoting Daniel C. Etsy.

51 A recent survey of government officials from 13 developing countries, for example, found that 'all officials, including stakeholders, noted that they had been unaware of the far-reaching scope and implications of BITs during the 1990s, when the treaties proliferated'. L. N. Skovgaard Poulsen and E. Aisbett, 'When the Claims Hit: Bilateral Investment Treaties and Bounded Rational Learning' (2013) 65 *World Politics* 273, 281–82.

It is from this history of conflict over the extent to which capital markets should be shielded from state intervention that the political unity of the material constitution of IIL has come into being.

24.3.1.2 Territory

Goldoni and Wilkinson write that '[a] constitutional order . . . represents a certain conception of political space (which, in the political form of the modern state, is conceived as a territory)'.[52] But the material constitution of IIL specifically and deliberately does *not* conceive of its political space as a physical territory: on the contrary, it conceives of it in *opposition* to physical territory, precisely because IIL is the means by which capital exporters can escape from the jurisdiction of the state while still maintaining an emplaced physical or legal presence within the state. Such escape is to an imagined non-physical, liminal space of internationality, outwith and beyond the direct control of states. Here, disputes regarding physical assets, legal rights or agreements with foreign investors are removed to the metaphysical plane of IIL (this is all despite the fact that the actual panels themselves are physically located within the very real territory of seats of international economic power, such as London, Geneva, Paris and Washington, DC). The deterritorialisation of international law and the shift from 'territoriality' to 'functionality' as 'an organizing principle for regulatory authority'[53] are fully on display in this context, as are the associated questions of democratic legitimacy and control. Deterritorialised IIL therefore presents acute problems of 'social dis-embeddedness',[54] as it regulates conflicts between 'legality and market rationality, competition and solidarity, and between opposing political and social [and economic] forces'[55] in a jurisprudential context far removed from democratic norms as developed within the territorial state.

However, as Arcuri and Violi rightly emphasise, territoriality and the territorial state remain key to the (oppositional) spatiality of IIL.[56] This is true in the prosaic sense that IIAs define their scope in terms of territorial limits, but more importantly through IIL's reliance on the apparatus of the state for the enforcement of judgements. It is also true in the sense that states are ultimately the source of IIL's legality and legitimacy. Though we have emphasised that IIL is a means by which capital exporters can remove themselves from state law and jurisdiction, it must also be noted that IIL is not only a creation of a capital-owning class imposed on innocent and unwitting states, but is also a creation of states themselves – and not only capital-exporting states. As David Schneiderman notes, 'states paradoxically are conceding space to the rules and institutions of transnational economic law . . . authoring the very rules and institutions that bind them well into the future'.[57] Note, here, the dualistic element at work: IIL relies on the (constitutionally-derived) authority of the state for its creation, operation, enforcement,

[52] Goldoni and Wilkinson, 'Material Constitution', 581.

[53] C. M. Brölmann, 'Deterritorialization in International Law: Moving Away from the Divide between National and International Law', in A. Nollkaemper and J. E. Nijman (eds.), *New Perspectives on the Divide between National and International Law* (Oxford University Press, 2007), 84, 87.

[54] Goldoni and Wilkinson, 'Material Constitution', 586.

[55] Ibid.

[56] A. Arcuri and F. Violi, 'Reconfiguring Territoriality in International Economic Law', in M. Kuijer and W. Werner (eds.), *Netherlands Yearbook of International law 2016: The Changing Nature of Territoriality in International Law* (The Hague: Asser Press, 2017), 175.

[57] D. Schneiderman, 'Global Constitutionalism and International Economic Law: The Case of International Investment Law', in M. Bungenberg, C. Herrmann and M. Krajewski (eds.), *European Yearbook of International Economic Law 2016* (Springer, 2016), 29.

perpetuation and expansion; while simultaneously impeding the (constitutionally-derived) mandate of the state to act. In this sense, it is not so much that IIL constrains the state, but rather that it is a means by which the state constrains *itself*, exercising its authority to reduce its authority and to fundamentally alter the conditions under which democracy is supposed to operate at the national level. It is through this sleight of hand that transnational IIL defends its democratic credentials, relying on the political voluntarism of treaty-making as grounding for its legitimacy.

24.3.1.3 Collectivity

If 'the formation of political unity requires a material process of political integration ... of a collectivity',[58] the collectivity in question here is a diverse and sometimes unselfconscious one, consisting of three broad and sometimes overlapping categories of actor: *states* (capital-exporting and capital-importing), *investors* and those whom we will call here *practitioners*. We can begin by noting that the two categories of *state* in the collectivity overlap: while we can distinguish in a general sense between countries that export capital and countries that import it, all countries are recipients of inward investment flows and even the poorest countries may also be home to (sometimes very) rich individuals and firms that engage in capital export.[59] By *investors* we mean natural and (especially) legal persons with the means and the desire to engage in international investment. By *practitioners* we mean the disparate network (sometimes tight-knit, sometimes very loose) of national and international politicians, industrialists, lobbyists, lawyers, intellectuals, bureaucrats and others who actually *run* and *sustain* and *develop* the system.[60] This is the epistemic community that provides the political impetus for IIAs, that staffs arbitral institutions and that engages in the IIL discourse of 'rights', 'justice', 'fairness' and 'equality'. This is, in the Gramscian sense, the hegemonic class who obtain the consent of the dominated by projecting their own particular interests as general interests.[61]

IIL is one means by which this loose collectivity organises economic and social relations in accordance with its (perceived) interests, insulating the economic from political interference. IIL uses the mechanism of investor rights to constrain state power, claiming that states are free to regulate the economy as they see fit *within the confines of the rule of law*.[62] The 'rule of law' here is given a particular and contingent interpretation, as part of the project of introjecting a set of investor- and property-friendly values into the pre-existing discourse of constitutionalism.

24.3.1.4 Constitutionalisation and Entrenchment

IIAs make domestic policy decisions regarding investments difficult (read: expensive) to reverse in future, essentially attempting to insulate them from democratic control. It is important to note

58 Goldoni and Wilkinson, 'Material Constitution', 581.

59 B. S. Chimni, 'Capitalism, Imperialism, and International Law in the Twenty-First Century' (2012) 14 *Oregon Review of International Law* 17.

60 Compare Leslie Sklair's transnational capitalist class (TCC), which she describes as including '[transnational corporation] executives and their local affiliates (corporate fraction); globalizing state and inter-state bureaucrats and politicians (state fraction); globalizing professionals (technical fraction); and merchants and media (consumerist fraction)'. Leslie Sklair, *Globalization: Capitalism and its Alternatives* (Oxford University Press, 2002), 99.

61 A. Gramsci, *Selection from the Prison Notebooks* (International Publishers, 1971).

62 See S. W. Schill, 'International Investment Law and the Rule of Law', in J. Lowell, J. C. Thomas and J. van Zyl Smit (eds.), *Rule of Law Symposium 2014: The Importance of the Rule of Law in Promoting Development* (Academy Publishing, 2015), 81; P.-T. Stoll, 'International Investment Law and the Rule of Law' (2018) 9 *Goettingen Journal of International Law* 267.

that this is exactly what national constitutions try to do when they entrench fundamental norms. In some cases constitutions attempt to make certain norms entirely permanent and unamendable,[63] but more usually the amendment or repeal of constitutional rules is made subject not to the procedure for ordinary law-making outlined in the constitution (whatever that may be) but to a special procedure for constitutional amendment (often one requiring a parliamentary supermajority).[64] Constitutions vary widely in their degree of entrenchment and in which parts of themselves, if any, they designate as fundamental and thus part of some unalterable core. IIL has successfully transposed this logic of entrenchment from the field of national constitutionalism to that of the regulation of international capital flows, placing property rights and investor protections 'beyond (ordinary) politics' and successfully generalising this logic across a broad range of states. The intention here was explicit: the elevation of managerialism and technocracy to the status of constitutional modes and norms of governance was described by the World Bank as a process of 'locking in good policies',[65] whereby constitutional, legal and political inflexibility are deliberately chosen and perpetuated in order to achieve long-term economic goals.[66]

It is therefore through the historical, political and material processes outlined here that the collective subjects of IIL have created a loose but powerful form of political unity. The organisation of this unity gravitates around the distinction between centre and periphery (crudely, between North and South, between West and the rest), but it also oscillates between these two rough poles: it is increasingly the case that the capital-exporting states of the global North and West are beginning to chafe under the rigours of a system they played a major role in designing, which suited them only for so long as it did not unduly restrain them. Moreover, there is also oscillation within states and not just between them, such as when we see discontent and disaffection within less-privileged parts of the citizenries of rich states, blamed in part on exactly the processes of globalisation and neoliberalisation that form the fundamental aims of IIL.

24.3.2 *Institutions*

As with national political unity, the material order of IIL depends on the work of formal and informal institutions. The formal system is comprised of the range of international institutions, treaties and tribunals, described in Section 24.2, that perform the substantive legwork of creating and recreating the norms of IIL and of embedding them ever further within national and international systems of law.

However, IIL does not only play out at the international level. Under the ICSID and New York Conventions, if a state refuses to pay compensation following an investment award, the investor can bring actions for enforcement before the courts of any other member state and have any commercial assets of the state in that jurisdiction seized and attached to the judgement. We see here the quite fundamental – indeed, parasitic – way in which IIL depends on states: as described, it is states that negotiate and sign IIAs, it is the institutions of states that enforce these treaties and the arbitration systems set out thereunder, and it is states that legitimise the system of IIL by injecting it with an element of democratic authorisation (the system of IIL having been

63 E.g., Art 79(3) of the German *Grundgesetz*.
64 See R. Albert, *Constitutional Amendments: Making, Breaking, and Changing Constitutions* (Oxford University Press, 2019).
65 World Bank, *World Development Report 1997: The State in a Changing World* (Oxford University Press, 1997), 50–52.
66 S. Gill, 'New Constitutionalism, Democratisation, and Global Political Economy' (1998) 10 *Pacifica Review: Peace, Security & Global Change* 23, 34

'freely' entered into by states), even as IIL reduces the scope of state action. For this reason, David Schneiderman argues that IIL is essentially ordoliberal, assigning the state 'a special role to play in the structuration of free markets by laying down the rules of the game via an economic order'.[67] Observing this 'special role', Wolfgang Streeck notes the 'drama of democratic states being turned into debt-collecting agencies on behalf of a global oligarchy of investors'.[68]

This relationship between IIL and domestic legal orders is an interactive one, with national norms (such as doctrines of US constitutional law[69]) filtering upstream to the IIL level and norms of IIL filtering downstream to the national level. The transformation of host state legal systems and institutions is a specific goal of IIL; as Stephen Schill writes: 'investment treaties aim at binding states into a legal framework that gives them an incentive and a yardstick for transforming their legal systems into ones that are conducive to market-based investment activities and provide the institutions necessary for the functioning of such markets'.[70] Proponents of IIL see this as a significant benefit, arguing that IIL promotes the rule of law and 'good governance' domestically and thus not only protects investors, but also creates 'spill over' effects that improve state administrative practices to the good of national citizens as well.[71] However, as Mavluda Sattorova has shown, this 'spill over' does not seem to play out on the ground: IIL appears to have had little impact in terms of promoting *ex ante* compliance with 'good governance' standards, with domestic responses instead tending toward the ambiguous, reactive and bureaucratic.[72]

Informal processes are also at work here, encouraging not only the spread of IIL, but also the narrative of IIL as necessary for development, as a tool for promoting the rule of law and good governance and as essential for protecting the rights of investors against abuses by the state (and thus as a sibling regime to human rights law). Of particular importance to this diffusion of norms and discourses are the networks through which investors, capital-exporting states and practitioners co-ordinate their actions and frame their interests as general rather than sectoral: chambers of commerce, industry lobbying groups, political party funding and so forth; but also law schools, professional networks and scholarship that adopt and reproduce the language and assumptions of IIL.[73] Moreover, the Venn diagram of the personnel involved is a complex one, as lawyers become arbitrators become lawyers become judges become academics. These individuals, already defined as part of the 'practitioner' constituency of the collectivity of IIL, play a crucial role, as the adjudicative moment is at the core of the system. The whole array of norms and institutions of IIL are mere paper tigers until they show their non-paper teeth and it is precisely at the moment of adjudication, when awards are handed down and made legally binding, that IIL demonstrates its credentials as a truly *legal* order and not as a mere instance of institutionalised diplomacy or international politics.

67 D. Schneiderman, 'Global Constitutionalism and International Economic Law: The Case of International Investment Law', in M. Bungenberg, C. Herrmann and M. Krajewski (eds.), *European Yearbook of International Economic Law 2016* (Springer, 2016), 31.

68 W. Streeck, 'The Crises of Democratic Capitalism' (2011) 71 *New Left Review* 5, 28.

69 D. Schneiderman, 'NAFTA's Takings Rule: American Constitutionalism Comes to Canada' (1994) 46 *University of Toronto Law Journal* 499; Gill, 'New Constitutionalism', 34.

70 S. Schill, *The Multilateralization of International Investment Law* (Cambridge University Press, 2009), 377.

71 R. Echandi, 'What Do Developing Countries Expect from the International Investment Regime?', in J. E. Alvarez and K. Suavant (eds.), *The Evolving International Investment Regime: Expectations, Realities, Options* (Oxford: University Press, 2011), 13.

72 M. Sattorova, *The Impact of Investment Treaty Law on Host States: Enabling Good Governance?* (Hart, 2018).

73 Perrone, Investment Treaties and the Legal Imagination.

IIL is therefore a sophisticated system of norm-diffusion, whereby concepts, practices and ideas from one legal order or physical territory can be transplanted to others by the rotation of personnel and their acculturation to an international habitus that regards the system of IIL as not merely legally sound and economically useful but as a moral good.

24.3.3 *Social Relations*

IIL embodies and reproduces a very specific and particular vision of social relations and as such enacts particular processes of subjectivation.[74] The subject, as constituted by IIL, is a *homo economicus* in the purest sense, existing only insofar as it is economically active, with no inherent value beyond this material calculus.[75] Rights are afforded to the investor-subject as a function of its economic status – if it ceases to 'invest', it is once again rendered invisible to IIL. Likewise, the investor is a specifically *international* subject and is protected only insofar as it acts as such. Citizens (whether legal or natural) of a state cannot use IIL to protect their rights unless and until they reconstitute themselves as transnational economic actors; it is through the transfer of capital across state borders that the investor-subject is made legible to and gains the protection of IIL.[76]

If IIL is a 'constitutional' order, it is one that exists for the benefit of these investor-subjects. As a collective, the investor class is imagined by IIL to be disempowered, vulnerable and subject to the whims of powerful host state governments, who may at any time expropriate their property, discriminate against them or act arbitrarily against their interests. The rights extended to investors provide protection against these threats, placing them on an equal footing with states, and the institutional system of IIL is deployed to ensure that investors are granted *ex post* compensation in the event of any harm. Note that while the rights of investor-subjects are analogous to those provided by human rights law, IIL provides these protections only to the economic actor *as* economic actor. The result of a violation is monetary damages – IIL does not deal in specific performance, cannot force domestic legal change and provides no relief to anyone other than the complainant. Whereas a national constitutional court may (or may not) be able to strike down a statute that breaches constitutional rights or may compel a government department to adopt or reverse a particular decision or policy (and thus have legal effects that ripple outward from the complainant to the citizenry as a whole), IIL sees only the bottom line. In this way, IIL also subjectivises the state itself as an economic actor, relying on the calculus of rational cost-benefit maximisation to *incentivise* (rather than to legally *compel*) governments to act without prejudice to investors' interests. Non-investors (such as citizens of the host state who may be impacted by investment activity) are largely invisible to IIL, except insofar as they are imagined as the general beneficiaries of economic development, good governance and the rule of law.

Excluded from this world are any other subjectivities an investor may inhabit (as, for example, a human being), any other subjectivities the state may inhabit (as, for example, a democratic institution) and other ways of conceiving the relationship between them.

74 Goldoni and Wilkinson, 'Material Constitution', 587.

75 See R. Urueña, *No Citizens Here: Global Subjects and Participation in International Law* (Martinus Nijhoff, 2012), 53.

76 In many cases this is true whether or not the internationalisation is 'real' or a legal fiction. For example, in *Tokios Tokelés* v. *Ukraine*, an investment Tribunal found that a company incorporated in Lithuania could make use of the Lithuania–Ukraine BIT to bring a claim against Ukraine, despite the fact that it was controlled and 99 per cent owned by Ukrainian nationals. *Tokios Tokelés* v. *Ukraine*, Case No. ARB/02/18, 29 April 2004.

24.3.4 *Fundamental Political Objectives*

In the words of the World Bank:

> [A] greater flow of foreign direct investment brings substantial benefits to bear on the world economy and on the economies of developing countries in particular, in terms of improving the long term efficiency of the host country through greater competition, transfer of capital, technology and managerial skills and enhancement of market access and in terms of the expansion of international trade.[77]

The explicit teloi of IIL are therefore two-fold: protecting investors and encouraging and accelerating economic growth. The standard story sees these two teloi as intertwined: investment leads to economic development (both immediately and in the longer term by promoting 'good governance'); and, in order to get investment, (developing) states need to prioritise property rights so that investors will feel secure. Countries make such commitments via IIAs, which, through ISDS, raise the cost of discriminating against an investor or acting in ways that would damage the value of their investment. This, then, is the grand bargain by which IIAs claim to provide benefits both for investors and their home states and for host states and their people.

While the first objective – protecting the rights of investors – has been a 'success' of IIL, the second objective – contributing to economic development – is open to question. To begin with, the basic link between strong IIAs and attracting investment has not been borne out by empirical studies: the evidence for whether IIAs and ISDS really do promote investment is mixed at best, with most studies finding either no effect or limited effects.[78] To take but one example, Brazil has long refused to include ISDS in its Cooperation and Investment Facilitation Agreements and yet was the sixth largest global destination for foreign direct investment in 2019.[79] The link between IIAs and 'good governance' has also been challenged, with studies finding little impact on domestic administrative practices and the biggest impacts coming in terms of restricting domestic policy space and national budgets.[80]

In keeping with its lopsided focus on protecting the interests of investors, IIL spreads a particular vision of the proper relationship between state and market. IIL has embraced a vision of protecting investors, investments and markets from political interference and of preventing 'populist democracy', corruption, 'bad governance' or simple change of heart from undermining individual property rights. In this sense, IIL is a key instrument in the service of market expansion and the process David Harvey has called 'accumulation by dispossession', by which new spaces and assets are opened for exploitation and profit through commodification, privatisation and the management of public and private debt.[81] IIL provides legal security for this process, ensuring that privatised assets cannot be re-nationalised without significant cost, preventing countries from enacting capital controls or other mechanisms that would undermine the value of investors' property rights and generally dissuading public authorities from changing the regulatory environment to the detriment of international investors. B. S. Chimni makes explicit the way that these processes of accumulation by dispossession manifest the integral links

77 World Bank Group, 'Guidelines on the Treatment of Foreign Direct Investment', in *Legal Framework for the Treatment of Foreign Investment*, Volume 2: *Guidelines* (World Bank Group, 1992), 35–44 (preamble).

78 L. E. Skovgaard Pousen, *Bounded Rationality and Economic Diplomacy* (Cambridge University Press, 2015).

79 UNCTAD, 'Foreign direct investment', available at: https://stats.unctad.org/handbook/EconomicTrends/Fdi.html, last accessed 10 August 2022.

80 Sattorova, *Impact of Investment Treaty Law*.

81 D. Harvey, *The New Imperialism* (Oxford University Press, 2003).

between capitalism and imperialism and specifically the new 'global imperialism' that characterises the era of globalisation.[82] IIL drives the 'internationalization of property rights' and contributes to the 'loss of economic sovereignty' that are key components of global imperialism.[83] It inscribes a protective barrier around the market activities of its investor-subjects in part through its adoption and co-option of the grammar of constitutionalism and human rights and thereby serves to benefit 'those segments of the capitalist class in the advanced capitalist economies and emerging economies that gain from the globalization process at the expense of the subaltern classes in both the First and Third Worlds'.[84] This is also how IIL has come to be a double-edged sword for capital-exporting states and has in recent years also begun to render states of the global North and West vulnerable to the reduced regulatory space that results: a case not so much of the empire striking back as of the empire backfiring.

24.4 CONCLUSION

All four ordering forces of the material constitution – political unity; institutions; social relations; and telos – can be seen at work in the ongoing controversy over the legitimacy of IIL in general and ISDS in particular. The formal constitution of IIL could be revised to encompass the kind of proportionality, reasonableness or balancing rules that national and international courts might follow. IIAs could be amended to impose obligations on investors. Appellate systems could be set up to correct for inconsistent ISDS decisions and the more general problem of variable quality in terms of tribunal reasoning. Such reforms would no doubt counter some of the criticisms of IIL – specifically by injecting into it concepts and structures drawn from administrative and public law contexts.

Reforming this formal constitutional structure, however, will not alter the underlying material commitments of IIL: its logic of market expansion; projection of market subjectivities; constitutionalisation and entrenchment of property and contract rights; and inscription of a strong and – ideally – irreversible constitutional line between the political and economic spheres. Understanding IIL in terms of material – rather than formal – constitutionalism reveals it is a para-constitutional system designed to entrench permanent constraints on governments' ability to intervene in the market and to privilege the needs of transnational business above democratic choice. Material constitutionalist analysis provides an opening through which we can at least begin to subject this constitutional order for transnational capital to democratic scrutiny.

[82] Chimni, *Capitalism, Imperialism, and International Law*.
[83] Ibid., 28–31.
[84] Ibid., 19.

25

The 'Terrible' Functional Constitution of the European Union

'Sound' Money, Economic Freedom(s) and 'Free' Competition

Agustín José Menéndez

the crime of that unhappy section of men to whom the perhaps 'terrible' and 'unnecessary' right to property has allowed nothing but a bare existence.

Cesare Beccaria, *Of Crimes and Punishments*

25.1 INTRODUCTION

This chapter reconstructs the key norms and practices that constitute and structure public power in the European Union (hereafter, EU). At the core of what may be labelled the 'functional' constitution of the EU we find three fundamental principles: 'sound' money, economic freedom(s) and 'free' competition (Section 25.2). The force of this trio stems from two main sources. First, 'sound' money, economic freedom(s) and 'free' competition are the key parameters ('the yardstick') by reference to which the validity and soundness of all national norms and policies is determined by supranational institutional actors. This entails that those national norms and policies which are found to be in conflict with the trio of principles may be derogated, set aside or eventually declared void by the just mentioned actors (Section 25.3). Second, the division of labour between supranational decision-making processes is so structured that it is far easier to approve European regulations and directives which aim at further realising 'sound money', economic freedom(s) and 'free' competition than to make part of EU law norms or decisions that limit the scope of such principles, for example through the redistribution of economic resources across and within borders (Section 25.4). In addition, it should be noted that, while representative institutions are formally placed at the core of the EU decision-making processes, actual practice results in the empowerment of (some) private actors, (some) technocratic institutional actors and (some) national governments to define the substantive content of European norms (Section 25.5). The result is a peculiar blend of authoritarian legalism which places a radical conception of private property at the very heart of the functional constitution of the EU, therefore disciplining, enervating and fragmenting (national) public power (Section 25.6).

25.2 *THE TRIO*: 'SOUND' MONEY, ECONOMIC FREEDOM(S) AND 'FREE' COMPETITION, THE BEATING HEART OF THE FUNCTIONAL CONSTITUTION OF THE EUROZONE

In this first section, I describe the key components of the constitution and organisation public power in the EU: 'sound' money, economic freedom(s) and 'free' competition.

25.2.1 'Sound' Money

The 'soundness' of money refers to the preservation of its capacity to command goods or services. 'Sound' money is money that can serve as the store of value, thereby creating the conditions for capital accumulation and the preservation of the value of the capital already accumulated.[1]

The 'soundness' of European money is guaranteed by means of a specific discipline of monetary and economic policy. In particular, by (a) affirming that monetary stability is the paramount goal of monetary policy; (b) ensuring that fiscal policy is also oriented toward the realisation of 'sound' money (entailing what may be referred to as 'monetary' dominance); and (c) making public institutions responsible for the preservation of liquidity in financial markets, a goal generally referred to as the achievement of financial stability.

25.2.1.1 Monetary Stability as the Paramount Goal of Monetary Policy

Price stability is the paramount goal of monetary policy in the Eurozone.

The principle emerged and became entrenched as a quasi-necessary consequence of the monetary arrangements predating European Monetary Union (hereafter, EMU), in particular the European Monetary System (hereafter, EMS). Under the latter, states were required to keep their currencies within established fluctuation ranges (tied to a 'peg'). Given how the EMS was run, this created the conditions under which all states had massive incentives to follow the policy lead of the German central bank, the Bundesbank, which assigned huge importance to the achievement of price stability, to the point of the latter trumping other socio-economic goals.[2]

Monetary stability became 'codified' as the paramount objective of monetary policy in the Treaty of Maastricht, and is now enshrined in Article 119.2 TFEU, in which we read that: 'the primary objective of [monetary policy] shall be to maintain price stability and, without prejudice to this objective, to support the general economic policies in the Union, in accordance with the principle of an open market economy with "free" competition' (emphasis added).

It should be noted, however, that price stability is defined by reference to 'consumption' prices, something which places outside the observation focus of the ECB the prices of financial assets,[3] a far from irrelevant or for that matter neutral choice, to which we will return in Section 25.6.

The primacy of monetary stability so defined has been further confirmed since the beginning of the financial, economic and fiscal crises in 2007. Not only because policies aimed at overcoming the crises which might have resulted in higher inflation were not even considered, but also because of the emergence of practices and conventions aimed at ensuring the full value of public debt (an asset that is key, in direct and indirect ways, to the preservation of the value of cumulated capital). Two developments in this latter regard are especially relevant. First, Eurozone states seem to be precluded from deciding the unilateral default of their public debt. At the final stages of the fiscal crisis of the Greek state in the spring of 2015, a convention emerged according to which unilateral default would result in the defaulting state being

[1] I consider the distributive implications of 'sound' money and the other fundamental principles in Section 25.6.

[2] See A. J. Menéndez, 'The Sleep of Numbers Produces Monsters: The Case of "Numerical Rules"', in C. Caruso and M. Morvillo (eds.), *Il governo dei numeri* (Il Mulino, 2020), 95–120, 101–2.

[3] See ECB, A Stability-Oriented Monetary Policy for the ECSD, 11 October 1998, available at: www.ecb.europa.eu/press/pr/date/1998/html/pr981013_1.en.html, last accessed 8 August 2022.

expelled from the Eurozone.[4] Second, explicit norms have been introduced ensuring the absolute priority of the repayment of principal and interest of public debt over any other public expenditure. In some cases the priority has been enshrined into the Constitution (cf. article 135.3 of the Spanish Constitution); in other instances, a similar result has been achieved by means of subjecting the issuing of debt to laws other than those of the country of issuance, characterised by their emphatic protection of creditors (typically England before Brexit, Luxembourg afterwards).[5]

25.2.1.2 'Sound' Public Finances and Economic Policies through Monetary Dominance

We have just seen that price stability is the paramount goal of monetary policy in the Eurozone. But it is much more than that. European norms and practices ensure that monetary stability is a precondition for the pursuit of any other socio-economic goal through any other economic policy. The *dominance* of the goals of monetary policy all across the policy board results in 'sound' money projecting itself into 'sound' public finances, 'sound' labour policies, a 'sound' tax system and so on. In such a way, the preservation of the store value of capital becomes a prerequisite for any conceivable socio-economic policy.

Beyond the formal proclamation (Article 119.3 TFEU), this is ensured to a large extent by solving the asymmetries built into EMU by 'mainstreaming' the goals of monetary policy. In particular, the coherence between a single and centralised monetary policy (run by the European Central Bank, hereafter ECB) and a plurality of national fiscal and economic policies (decided by national parliaments and national governments) is guaranteed by a number of limits to the latter, not the former. This accounts for the most conspicuous components of the 'sound budgetary' canon, the fiscal rules setting ceilings to the stocks of public debt (60% GDP) and to public deficits (3% GDP).[6] In the wake of the 2010 fiscal crisis, new fiscal rules have been added to the set constraining national fiscal policy, from tighter limits to the 'structural' deficit of Member States,[7] to those fixing trajectories of deficit and debt reduction,[8] closely associated to a peculiar form of automatic stabilisers in reverse, the automatic expenditure cuts.[9] The room for discretionary fiscal policy is further constrained by the panoply of indicators of macroeconomic imbalances, which reach into the four corners of economic policy.[10] These rules substantiate the ideal of 'sound' budgetary policy and are rendered effective through a complex set of procedures (now referred as the European Semester), formally aimed at the coordination of fiscal policy in

[4] The German Chancellor of the Exchequer rendered explicit what was until then an implicit rule. See P. Inman, 'Greece's debt can be written off – whatever Wolfgang Schäuble says', *The Guardian*, 17 July 2015. The fact that, despite the results of the referendum held literally some days before, the Greek state accepted an agreement which did not contain any concrete debt write off seems to confirm that the view of Schäuble prevailed.

[5] At the same time, however, Eurozone states have been required to insert collective action clauses in their debt issuances (Art. 12(3) of the ESM Treaty of 2 February 2012, consolidated version available at: www.esm.europa.eu/legal-documents/esm-treaty, last accessed 8 August 2022), something which seems to raise the eventuality of non-payment. However, it should be kept in mind that the very point and purpose of such clauses is to prevent the full default on the debt and thereby to facilitate that creditors are repaid as much as possible.

[6] Article 1 of Protocol No. 12 to the Treaty on the Functioning of the European Union of 13 December 2007, OJ 2012 No. C326/279 ('TFEU').

[7] Article 2a and Article 9(1), first paragraph of Council Regulation 1466/97, OJ 1997 No. L209/1, as amended by Council Regulation 1055/2005, OJ 2005 No. L174/1 and Council Regulation 1175/2011, OJ 2011 No. L306/12 ('consolidated text of Regulation 1466/97').

[8] Article 5(1), second paragraph and Article 9(1), second paragraph of the consolidated text of Regulation 1466/97; Article 5(1) of the consolidated text of Regulation 1466/97; Article 1(1) of the consolidated text of Regulation 1467/97.

[9] Fiscal Compact, Article 3.1. e.

[10] Article 2 of Regulation 1176/2011, OJ 2011 No. L306/28.

the European Union, but which have acquired an increasingly hierarchical and disciplinary character. In particular, the Commission has acquired a growing power to shape and mould national economic policy through the issuance of 'recommendations'. The persuasive power of the Commission was always linked to the fact that lack of compliance may at the end of the day result in sanctions being imposed upon the delinquent Member State (Article 126.11 in conjunction with Articles 11 to 16 of Regulation 1467/97). Since the reform of the Growth and Stability Pact in 2011 and, very especially, since the ratification of the Fiscal Compact, the powers of the Commission have been scaled up, not least because sanctioning has become easier, as the European executive only needs to be supported by a qualified *minority* of Member States (cf. Articles 4.2 and 5.2 of Regulation 1173/2011 and Article 7 of the Fiscal Compact; Article 17.3 of Regulation 241/2021 establishing the Recovery and Resilience Facility confirms the transformation of the recommendations issued by the Commission to Members States in the context of the European Semester into de facto binding norms.)

Private actors are also expected to contribute to the fostering of 'sound' economic policies through the pressure they have been rendered structurally capable of exerting over Member States. Their structural power results from the combination of the prohibition of the financing of deficits by the ECB (Article 123.1 TFEU),[11] which forces states to seek funding in financial markets, and the scope of free movement of capital, which applies not only within the Eurozone but all over the world (Article 63.1 TFEU). As a result, states running a deficit are obliged to seek funding in financial markets, while actors in financial markets are free to invest or not in the public debt of a state (they can indeed pick and choose *which* public debt to buy). Under such conditions, a reduced number of powerful actors in financial markets may become the arbiters of the financial fortunes of states, 'voting' with their capital, so to say.[12] Not by chance, the European Court of Justice (hereafter, ECJ) has characterised the structural dependence of states on financial markets as key to ensure the implementation of 'sound budgetary policies'.[13]

It could be argued that the suspension of all fiscal rules in the spring of 2020,[14] combined with the virtually unconditional funding of (huge) state deficits by the ECB (through the ad hoc PEPP programme)[15] may result in a radical reversal of the relationship between the goals of monetary and fiscal policy, eventually putting an end to monetary dominance and, consequently, creating the political space into which the appropriateness of 'sound' budgetary policies may be reconsidered. At the time of writing, however, European institutions remain committed to reapply the fiscal rules as soon as the crisis has been 'resolved'.[16] Indeed, it may be argued that whatever the *intentions* of policymakers, the 'emergency' actions taken by the ECB (and other leading central banks) have prevented the fiscal collapse of Eurozone states (and of the world economy), but perhaps at the price of further increasing wealth inequalities.[17] That is an empirical question that requires further research, but it is telling that financial markets boomed as 'real' economies entered into unprecedented peace-time recessions.

[11] Resort to compulsory loans from financial institutions is precluded by Article 124 TFEU.

[12] W. Streeck, 'Markets and Peoples: Democratic Capitalism and European Integration' (2012) 73 *New Left Review* 63.

[13] See C-370/12, *Pringle* [2012] ECR I-0000, para. 135.

[14] Communication from the Commission to the Council on the activation of the general escape clause of the Stability and Growth Pact, of 20 March 2020, COM(2020) 123 final; Statement of EU ministers of finance on the Stability and Growth Pact in light of the COVID-19 crisis, of 23 March 2020, available at: www.consilium.europa.eu/en/press/press-releases/2020/03/23/statement-of-eu-ministers-of-finance-on-the-stability-and-growth-pact-in-light-of-the-covid-19-crisis/, last accessed 3 August 2022.

[15] See Decision (EU) 2020/440 of the European Central Bank of 24 March 2020, OJ 2020 No. L91/1-4.

[16] There is, though, a vivid academic debate on the need of reforming European economic governance, led by O. Blanchard, Á. Leandro and J. Zettelmeyer, 'Ditch the EU's Fiscal Rules; Develop Fiscal Standards Instead', *Vox EU*, 22 April 2021, available at: https://voxeu.org/article/ditch-eu-s-fiscal-rules-develop-fiscal-standards-instead, last accessed 8 August 2022.

[17] Along such lines, see A. Tooze, *Shutdown: How Covid Shook the World's Economy* (Allan Lane, 2021).

25.2.1.3 Financial Stability

Supranational and national public institutions are expected to play a major role in preserving the stability of the financial system as a whole, something that may well require state intervention to underpin the value of financial assets when there is a serious risk (now labelled a 'systemic risk') that the market will undermine itself, threatening the stability of the economy as a whole.

While the role of the state as a lender of last resort to financial institutions is far from being a new one, the breadth and scope of the responsibilities of public institutions has expanded geometrically under EMU, most clearly since 2007. If before that date it was assumed that markets were capable of stabilising themselves,[18] provided that the consumer prices were contained by the central bank, in the aftermath of the financial crisis the active prevention of the build-up of 'excessive' risks not only became a fundamental task of public institutions, but the ECB was given a mandate to play the leading role in that regard.

As a result, the ECB has become the lender of last resort of financial institutions, either fully or partially substituting financial markets as a source of credit, or, more modestly but not less decisively, stabilising the conditions under which financial markets operate (acting as a 'market maker'). As a result, allocation of capital in the European Union has been constantly mediated by the ECB, through massive refinancing operations (from which, it should be said *en passant*, financial institutions have constantly profited). The intense mediation of capital markets by the ECB seems to contradict the requirement that capital be allocated through markets (Article 127 TFEU).[19]

The value of capital has not only been protected by assigning new powers to the ECB. Individual states and the Eurozone as a whole have played a significant role as guarantors of last resort. In particular, a convention has emerged that allocates responsibility for cross-border financial loans to the state where the debtor is established or resides (*debtor state as guarantor of last resort*). This emerged with great force during the Irish financial crisis (2008) and was confirmed by the terms of the programmes of financial assistance to Eurozone states from 2010. At the same time, the Eurozone and the European Union as a whole have equipped themselves with the financial means to underwrite debtor states through the provision of *conditional* financial assistance. That was rendered possible by baroque legal structures such as the European Financial Stability Facility,[20] and then with the reform of Article 136 TFEU,[21] by a European equivalent of the IMF, the European Stability Mechanism, the legal discipline of which hangs however uneasily between public international law and European Union law.[22]

[18] The so-called efficient markets hypothesis.

[19] See K. Tuori, 'Has Euro Area Monetary Policy Become Redistribution by Monetary Means? "Unconventional" Monetary Policy As a Hidden Transfer Mechanism' (2016) 11 *European Law Journal* 838. Of course, it could be discussed whether the requirement imposed by Article 127 TFEU is sensible or, indeed, whether it is at all feasible. That, however, does not detract from the fact that the provision is not being complied with.

[20] The state of Luxembourg created on 7 June 2010 a 'société anonyme', which was technically speaking a 'special purpose vehicle'. Immediately afterwards, Eurozone states became shareholders and, once and at the same time, signed a framework agreement with the European Financial Stability Facility itself. The original text of the Framework Agreement can be consulted at www.irishstatutebook.ie/eli/2010/act/16/enacted/en/pdf, last accessed 8 August 2022.

[21] European Council Decision 2011/199/EU of 25 March 2011 amending Article 136 of the Treaty on the Functioning of the European Union with regard to a stability mechanism for Member States whose currency is the euro, OJ 2011 No. L91/1.

[22] Treaty establishing the European Stability Mechanism, 2 February 2012, available at: www.esm.europa.eu/legal-documents/esm-treaty, last accessed 8 August 2022.

Finally, a convention has been developed concerning the obligation of states to underpin systemic financial institutions, in particular ruling out the imposition of losses on the shareholders and the creditors of such institutions (in technical jargon, favouring bail-outs and disfavouring bail-ins). This was clearly the practice followed during the 2007–8 financial crisis. The so-called bail-in directive[23] is supposed to result in a radical shift of paradigm, in particular ensuring that losses are suffered by private shareholders. As a matter of fact, however, its actual effects confirm the consolidation of the 'bail-out' convention. To avoid the 'severe disruption of the functioning of financial markets', article 27.5c of Regulation 806/2014[24] codifies the different treatment to be granted to 'systemic' banks. While the shareholders and creditors of ordinary banks should be the first to suffer losses, the same is not the case when the bank is a systemic one. Then public money can be used to bail out the financial institution so as to avoid 'contagion' to the financial system.[25] This entails codifying the unequal treatment of shareholders depending on the size of financial institutions.

25.2.1.4 A Caveat: 'Sound' Money and Non-Eurozone Member States

Does 'sound' money apply with equal force across the European Union? The answer seems to be complicated by the 'variable geometry' of EMU. Nineteen Member States are part of the Eurozone, eight are not. One may think that the latter are not subject to the full disciplining force of 'sound' money, at least not with the same intensity as Eurozone states that have actually transferred their monetary policy to the institution mandated to ensure the 'soundness' of money, the ECB (on the basis of the 'derogating' provisions of Article 139 TFEU). However, Denmark, Bulgaria and Croatia are de facto within the gravitational space of the Eurozone, as members of the 'Exchange Rate Mechanism II', which 'anchors' their currency to the euro.[26] This results in a powerful economic constraint subjecting them to the same actual constraints as Eurozone Member States, at least as long as they remain within ERM-II. The five remaining Member States (Sweden, Hungary, Czech Republic, Poland and Romania) are in principle in a position to implement an 'autonomous' monetary policy. But could it be oriented to realise goals other than securing the 'soundness' of money? While it is clear that these five countries have a margin of autonomy which can be expressed in a different inflation target (as in the case of Poland), it is relevant to notice that the general discipline enshrined in the Treaty on the Functioning of the European Union applies unless it is expressly derogated by Article 139 TFEU. No derogation is foreseen from article 131, which requires the 'independence' of the

[23] Directive 2014/59/EU of the European Parliament and of the Council of 15 May 2014 establishing a framework for the recovery and resolution of credit institutions and investment firms and amending Council Directive 82/891/EEC and Directives 2001/24/EC, 2002/47/EC, 2004/25/EC, 2005/56/EC, 2007/36/EC, 2011/35/EU, 2012/30/EU and 2013/36/EU and Regulations (EU) No 1093/2010 and (EU) No 648/2012 of the European Parliament and of the Council Text with EEA relevance, OJ 2014 No. L173/190.

[24] Regulation 806/2014 of 15 July 2014 establishing uniform rules and a uniform procedure for the resolution of credit institutions and certain investment firms in the framework of a Single Resolution Mechanism and a Single Resolution Fund and amending Regulation (EU) No 1093/2010, OJ 2014 L225/1.

[25] The different standards applied to big and small banks can be illustrated by comparing the bail-in of a cluster of small Italian savings banks in 2015 and the bail-out of the much larger Monte dei Paschi di Siena in 2017. The latter decision was taken despite the fact that ECB inspectors had serious doubts about the solvency of Monte dei Paschi. See E. Martinuzzi, 'What the ECB Didn't Say about Monte Paschi's Bailout', Bloomberg.com, 30 June 2019, available at: www.bloomberg.com/graphics/2019-opinion-monte-paschi/, last accessed 8 August 2022.

[26] See Agreement of 16 March 2006 between the European Central Bank and the national central banks of the Member States outside the euro area laying down the operating procedures for an exchange rate mechanism in stage three of Economic and Monetary Union, OJ 2006 No. C73/1.

national central bank, or from 119.3, which affirms not only price stability, but also sound public finances, sound monetary conditions and a sustainable balance of payments as objectives to be pursued by the economic policy of *all* Member States. Were any of the 'autonomous' five to pursue an 'alternative' monetary policy, it is more than probable that Eurozone states would exert pressure for that policy to be rectified, in the name of not altering 'the levelled playing field' within the 'open market economy'. Quite tellingly, when confronted with a major financial, economic, and fiscal crisis in 2008, Hungary and Romania preferred the harsh terms of conditional financial assistance from the EU, which entailed an internal devaluation that preserved the value of capital) rather than exploring the limits of their fiscal and monetary autonomy.[27]

25.3 ECONOMIC FREEDOM(S)

The literal tenor and the structure of the provisions of the Treaty establishing the European Economic Community defining the 'four' economic freedoms (Article 30 TEC – elimination of quantitative restrictions; Article 48 TEC – free movement of workers; Article 52 TEC – right of establishment; Article 59 TEC – freedom to provide services; and Article 67 TFEU – elimination of (some) limits to the movement of capital) were ambivalent. This reflected the lack of a consensus among the drafters on the point and purpose of European integration. Was the European Economic Community to be an *external enabler* of national Democratic and Social states, rendering possible their consolidation through the expansion of external trade, but without constraining the power of states to steer socio-economic activity? Or rather, was the EEC to serve as an external constraint setting limits to national socio-economic powers in view of realising the liberal ideal of economic freedom? This ambivalence has marked the evolution of European institutions, oscillating between the paradigm of the 'common' market proper of the external enabler vision, to that of the 'single' market, in which the EU comes closer to an external constraint.

From the late 1950s to the early 1970s, the constellation of political forces at the national and supranational levels favoured the building of an internal market gravitating around the freedom to trade goods and the right to cross borders to pursue gainful employment, at the very same time that all economic freedoms were to a considerable extent socially, politically and culturally 'embedded' through national (and supranational) regulation.[28]

From the mid and late 1970s onward, the political and economic constellations radically changed, giving way to a balance of forces in which economic freedoms came to be understood as actionable subjective rights, largely emancipated from national law and politics into a 'single market'. The odd combination of economic stagnation and high inflation eroded the intellectual and political consensus around the Democratic and Social State, resulting in the decline of political parties as a constitutional force, and the parallel rise of courts and central banks, promoted as actors that could solve an alleged 'governability' crisis (caused by the 'excesses' of democracy).[29] Non-financial corporations and financial institutions, largely subdued during the '*treinte glorieuses*' regained, slowly but steadily, the political and legal means to translate their economic power into political might. The Commission and the ECJ were key actors in these

[27] Financial assistance was jointly offered by the EU and the IMF with the support of the World Bank.

[28] The extremely difficult act of squaring liberalisation with the consolidation and development of social states was to a large extent rendered possible by an exceptional political and economic climate, which was not deprived of its dark elements, from the resilience of patriarchy to the realpolitik of the Cold War.

[29] M. J. Crozier, S. P. Huntington and J. Watanuki, *The Crisis of Democracy* (New York University Press, 1975).

transformations and saw their decisions partially codified with the deep reforms to the literal tenor of the Treaties, with economic freedoms strengthened and articulated as general subjective rights.[30]

This radical transformation has deeply marked the prevalent construction of economic freedoms.[31] Not only they are characterised as subjective rights, but each of them is regarded as a manifestation of a wider and encompassing 'economic freedom', that, as we will see in Section 25.6, is closely related to a specific conception of private property. And at the heart of such wider economic freedom, we find the right to fully command one's own capital. At one time understood as the (relatively modest) freedom to make payments corresponding to non-financial transactions (Articles 67.2 and 67.1 TEEC), free movement of capital was first turned into a fully-fledged subjective right by Directive 88/361[32] and then into the most fundamental of the economic freedoms by the Treaty of Maastricht. This primacy of free movement of capital is reflected in its legal force. Not only is it the only freedom that applies '*erga omnes*', beyond the territory of the European Union (Article 63 TFEU), but it may eventually defeat conflicting Treaty provisions, including article 345 TFEU. In particular, the Court of Justice has concluded that the full realisation of free movement of capital may require a narrow construction of the national power to define property regimes.[33] That reveals, as we will see in Section 25.6, that beyond the economic freedom(s) (and indeed of the whole trio of principles at the heart of the fundamental European norms) lurks a radically strong conception of private property.

25.3.1 *'Free' Competition*

The principle of 'free' competition prescribes that the allocation of goods and services must take place through 'competitive' markets, so that the welfare of the consumer is maximised.[34]

While the principle was originally interpreted as empowering the Commission to monitor and eventually constrain private activity that could undermine the effectiveness of economic freedoms,[35] the centre of gravity of the principle shifted in the 1980s, leading to its transformation into a yardstick that determines the validity of public regulation of economic activity and, above all, the direct public engagement in the provision of goods and services (for example, through public ownership of corporations).[36] At the same time, the rise of 'consumer welfare maximisation' (and not sheer economic size and power) as the criterion by reference to which the legality or illegality of corporate structures and practices is determined has favoured the concentration of economic power, fuelling the further oligopolisation of the European economy. The de facto

[30] See the referred provisions with Articles 28, 45, 49, 56, 63 TFEU.

[31] This transformation was led by the ECJ, which first 'decoupled' free movement of goods from non-discrimination on the basis of nationality (case 120/78, *Cassis de Dijon* [1979] ECR 00649) and then sidestepped the very structure of the Treaties to regard all four economic freedoms as making up a single normative block, on the basis of which projected the new understanding of free movement of goods to the other economic freedoms. See the rulings in C-76/90, *Säger*, ECLI:EU:C:1991:331; C-55/94 *Gebhard*, ECLI:EU:C:1995:411; C-415/93 *Bosman*, ECLI:EU:C:1995:463 and C-163/94, *Sanz de Lera*, ECLI:EU:C:1995:451.

[32] Council Directive 88/361/EEC of 24 June 1988 for the implementation of Article 67 of the Treaty, OJ 1988 No. L178/5.

[33] C-367/98, Golden Shares, ECLI:EU:C:2002:326.

[34] H. Hovenkamp, *The Antitrust Enterprise: Principle and Execution* (Harvard University Press, 2006).

[35] For example, through the abuse of market power that rendered difficult access to different national markets European Court of Justice. See rulings in cases 56 and 58/64, Consten Grundig, ECLI:EU:C:1966:41; 6/72 *Continental Can*, ECLI:EU:C:1973:22; 85/76, *Hoffmann*, ECLI:EU:C:1979:36; 322/81, *Michelin*, ECLI:EU:C:1983:313; *Ford vs. Commission*, ECLI:EU:C:1985:340.

[36] See rulings in cases 18/88, *Régie des télégraphes et des téléphones*, ECLI:EU:C:1991:474; C-41/90, *Höfner*, ECLI:EU:C:1991:161; C-218/00, *Inail*, ECLI:EU:C:2002:36; C-399 and 401/10, *Bouygues*, ECLI:EU:C:2013:175; and T-296/97, *Alitalia*, ECLI:EU:T:2000:289.

suspension of competition law in the aftermath of the financial crisis in 2008 and of the coronavirus crisis in 2020 proves the malleability of the principle of 'free' competition when constructed in the image and semblance of consumer welfare maximisation. In both cases, national Treasuries have been deployed to inject massive amounts of capital in 'ailing' companies (financial institutions in 2008–9, all kinds of corporations in 2020). Actual practice, thus, seems to diverge radically from the theoretical ideal models which inspired the drafting of Article 119.1 TFEU ('open market economy with free competition') and to basically point to a discipline of state intervention, which should not meddle with private control over the investment of capital. Quite tellingly, even nationalisations ceased to be a taboo during the coronavirus crisis, provided, however, they were temporary, and private ownership and control remained the rule and the goal.

25.4 THE 'TRIO' AS YARDSTICK OF THE VALIDITY AND SOUNDNESS OF NATIONAL NORMS

'Sound' money, economic freedom(s) and 'free' competition constitute the key parameter by reference to which the validity of all national legal norms and decisions is determined by supranational institutions. In other words, European institutions claim that to be valid, national statutes, regulations, decrees, administrative decisions and judicial rulings must comply with the substantive requirements stemming from the full recognition of 'sound money', economic freedom(s) and 'free' competition.

'Sound' public finances (the second limb of the principle of 'sound' money) has become the yardstick by reference to which the European Commission and the Eurogroup assess national fiscal, social and tax policies through the European Semester. It is also the principle which guides the review of national economic policies when states are subject to forms of 'conditionality' under programmes of financial assistance and is indeed expected to play the same role under the recovery programmes to be implemented from 2021 onward.[37] There are clear indications that the activation of the role of the ECB as a conditional buyer of last resort of public debt is indeed subject to the requirement that states follow not only 'sound' fiscal policies, but more widely 'sound' economic policies.[38]

Economic freedom (s) and 'free' competition have become the key yardsticks by reference to which the ECJ determines the validity of all national socio-economic norms, independently of whether the point and purpose of such national norms is at all related to cross-border economic activity (as we saw in Section 25.3). The key administrative powers assigned to the European Commission on what concerns competition law make it a key additional enforcer of 'free' competition as a parameter of the validity of national law.

It is pertinent to consider why 'sound' money, economic freedom(s) and 'free' competition are the only components of the yardstick of European validity and soundness. In particular, it is necessary to consider why fundamental rights (as enshrined, for example, in the Charter of

[37] See Article 17(3) of Regulation 2021/241 of the European Parliament and of the Council of 12 February 2021, establishing the Recovery and Resilience Facility, OJ 2021 No. L57/17.

[38] See the letter sent by the ECB to the Italian government on 5 August 2011, rendered public by *Il Corriere della Sera* some weeks afterwards. See 'C'è l'esigenza di misure significative per accrescere il potenziale di crescita', *Corriere della Sera*, 29 September 2011, available at: www.corriere.it/economia/11_settembre_29/trichet_draghi_italiano_405e2be2-ea59-11e0-ae06-4da866778017.shtml, last accessed 8 August 2022. A similar letter was sent the same day to the Spanish government. See now the Transmission Policy Instrument of the ECB, which aims at containing bonds spreads. Eligibility is dependent on "sound" budgetary policy. See 'The Transmission Protection Instrument, 21 July 2022, available at: www.ecb.europa.eu/press/pr/date/2022/html/ecb.pr220721~973e6e7273.en.html.

Fundamental Rights of the EU) are not part of such yardstick. First, competences matter. The original text of the Treaties mentioned economic freedom(s) and 'free' competition, but not fundamental rights (with the sole exception of the different dimensions of the right to non-discrimination on the basis of nationality and sex). True, the Court of Justice made the principle of fundamental rights protection an integral part of unwritten EU law and the Charter of Fundamental Rights was made part and parcel of the primary law of the Union when the Treaty of Lisbon entered into force in 2010. Still, rights standards have been consistently deemed as applicable to supranational law and decisions only, while not to national laws and decisions, unless the latter are 'implementing' Union law (see now Article 51.1 of the Charter). Article 51.2 of the Charter renders explicit that the provisions of that text do not and cannot result in the accrual of new competences to the EU. Second, European institutions, most notably the ECJ, have subordinated fundamental rights to the trio, by characterising fundamental rights as potential exceptions to the full application of, mainly, economic freedom(s). This has resulted not so much in a rebalancing of the substantive core of European law, but in the construction of fundamental rights in the mould of economic freedoms, that is, as subjective rights, neglecting their fundamental relational character, and the key role played by collective rights and collective goods in that regard.[39] The following sections (Sections 25.5 and 25.6, perhaps especially 25.6.3) go a long way to explain why not even the crises have shocked the EU strongly enough as to veer it off the path it has travelled in the last decades.

25.5 IN-BUILT BIAS IN SUPRANATIONAL DECISION-MAKING

The progressive empowerment of the European Parliament as (co)legislator is frequently said to have created the conditions under which EU law would not only enjoy direct democratic legitimacy, but also become instrumental in rebalancing the substantive content of European law away from the primacy of 'sound' money, economic freedom(s) and 'free' competition. By shifting the last legislative word from intergovernmental to supranational procedures, the direct representatives of citizens (the Euro-parliamentarians) would gain power, something which would be likely to shift the emphasis from 'market-making' to the 'political' government of markets.

Such a line of reasoning fails to take seriously the extent to which the division of labour between the different procedures of supranational law-making results in a bias in favour of the trio of principles, rendering improbable the referred 'rebalancing'. To become aware of this inbuilt bias it is necessary to reflect on the fact that Treaty reforms have not resulted in the primacy of co-decision so much as in the emergence of a peculiar division of labour between co-decision and intergovernmental procedures of law-making. It follows that the chances of a regulation or directive being adopted depend, to a considerable extent, on the procedure through which it has to be discussed and voted. While co-decision increases the chances of adoption, unanimous agreement in the Council diminishes them.[40] Quite obviously, it is more difficult to make all national ministers agree than, as co-decision requires, forge a qualified

[39] A. J. Menéndez, 'The Unencumbered European Taxpayer As the Product of the Transformation of Personal Taxes by the Judicial Empowerment of Market Forces', in R. Letelier and A. J. Menéndez (eds.), *The Sinews of European Peace* (University of Oslo, 2009), 157–268.

[40] In some cases (paradigmatically, the Own Resources Decision, ex Article 311 third paragraph) agreement in the Council is not enough, and there is a need for national parliaments to express their consent.

majority in the Council and a simple majority in the European Parliament.[41] What turns the imbalance into a substantive bias is the fact that this division of labour is far from random. Market-making norms, amplifying the breadth and scope of 'sound' money, economic freedoms and 'free' competition are decided through co-decision; while market-correcting bills, fleshing out socio-economic rights and collective goods, have to be adopted through unanimity, and are, consequently less likely to be transformed into regulations and directives (the case of capital income taxation is very telling, discussed next).

This shows how the fundamental norms organising supranational decision-making tend to prevent European institutions from redressing the imbalance between on the one hand private property and entrepreneurial freedom and on the other hand other socio-economic goals.

It is important to keep in mind that this is so not only because measures reflecting alternative socio-economic views are much less likely to be adopted, but because the division of labour between decision-making procedures fosters the artificial splitting of issues. Questions that used to be regarded as so inextricably intertwined as to require simultaneous legislation (e.g., capital taxation and the discipline of free movement of capital) have been turned into separate questions by the division of labour between supranational decision-making processes, likely to be settled in different pieces of legislation and at different points in time (if at all). Unsurprisingly, the full liberalisation of the movement of capital was decided in 1988,[42] once the Single European Act had subjected that decision to the qualified majority, while the harmonisation of the norms on capital income taxation failed to materialise until 2002[43] and was manifestly insufficient.[44] The result is not only the legal primacy of free movement of capital, but the *de facto* facilitation of large-scale tax avoidance.

25.6 PRE-EMPTING SUPRANATIONAL DEMOCRATIC LAW- AND DECISION-MAKING

The chances that the bias described in Section 25.5 is rectified by the forging of a strong democratic will at the supranational level are very limited. While the European Union identifies itself as a democratic polity (Article 2 TEU) and while the supranational law-making procedures are formally structured so as to ensure democratic representativeness,[45] the fact of the matter is that supranational law- and decision-making is dispersed in a wealth of procedures, something which not only limits the democratic legitimacy of European legal norms but also reduces the chances of a coherent democratic impulse underpinning European legislation.

In fact, the democratic legitimacy of co-decision is undermined by the empowerment of (some) private actors (Section 25.6.1), (some) technocratic actors (Section 25.6.2) and (some) national executives (Section 25.6.3) to define the content of common norms and practices.

[41] The chances of a unanimous agreement in the Council of Ministers have declined given the successive enlargements of EU membership and the ensuring larger social and economic heterogeneity among states.

[42] See Council Directive 88/361/EEC of 24 June 1988 for the implementation of Article 67 of the Treaty, OJ 1988 No. L178/5.

[43] See Council Directive 2003/48/EC of 3 June 2003 on taxation of savings income in the form of interest payments, OJ 2003 No. L157/38.

[44] See G. Zucman, *The Hidden Wealth of Nations* (Chicago University Press, 2015).

[45] The decisive role played by the Council of Ministers contributes *indirect democratic legitimacy*, to the extent that ministers are appointed by prime ministers or presidents, themselves chosen by the direct representatives of the national people; while the European Parliament, being directly elected by European citizens, contributes *direct democratic legitimacy*.

To this should be added the emerging tendency to depart from majoritarian decision-making (Section 25.6.4).

25.6.1 *The De Facto Delegation of Law-Making Powers to Actors Repeatedly Mobilising Their Economic Freedoms*

The characterisation of economic freedoms as full-blown subjective rights has turned such freedoms into legal instruments which can be used by private actors to challenge the validity of national legal norms and policies that allegedly set obstacles to the full enjoyment of the rights stemming from EU law. It should now be added that, when economic freedoms are repeatedly used as battering rams with which to attack national legislation, it becomes possible to shape to a considerable degree the set of (national and supranational) regulatory frameworks, to the point of rendering supranational regulation unnecessary.

It is important to observe that, while the normative effect of the unleashing of private actors through economic freedoms is usually described as leading to a 'mutual recognition' of regulatory standards,[46] in dynamic terms it triggers a process of regulatory competition, which serves as a functional substitute of politically mediated harmonising legislation. The substitution has massive social, economic and political consequences. Political representative institutions get weakened, while owners and managers of capital, especially mobile capital, acquire a meaningful power to influence the choice of the ultimately preferred collective decision. As is well known, 'repeat players' before the ECJ are not infrequently economic actors routinely operating across borders (i.e., multinationals), which have adapted their institutional and operational structures to maximise the chances of profiting from the empowering of private actors brought about by EU law.

25.6.2 *Epistocracy and Empowered Technocrats*

A good deal of the powers that have been Europeanised in the last 30 years has been assigned to institutions whose legitimacy stems from the 'expert knowledge' held by officials.

The European Central Bank is the paradigmatic instance of such an epistocratic institution. As we already pointed out, the ECB plays a formidable role in the government of the Eurozone and in general of the EU. The Frankfurt institution defines and implements the monetary policy of the Eurozone, as foreseen in Article 127.2 TFEU. Since 2007 it has been granted decisive powers concerning the macro and micro prudential supervision of financial institutions,[47] as well as assigned a central role in the monitoring of financial assistance (as part of the so-called troika). Even more decisively, the ECB has acquired quasi-sovereign powers as a lender of last resort to financial institutions and as a (conditional) buyer of last resort of public debt.[48] To this it should be further added that the sheer impossibility of drawing a clear line between the breadth of monetary and fiscal policy has resulted in the ECB actually shaping general economic policy

[46] Communication from the *Commission* concerning the consequences of the judgement given by the Court of Justice on 20 February 1979 in Case 120/78 ('*Cassis de Dijon*'), OJ 1980 No. C256/2.

[47] Regulation 1092/2010 of the European Parliament and of the Council of 24 November 2010 on European Union macro-prudential oversight of the financial system and establishing a European Systemic Risk Board, OJ 2010 No. L331/1 and Council Regulation 1024/2013 of 15 October 2013 conferring specific tasks on the European Central Bank concerning policies relating to the prudential supervision of credit institutions, OJ 2013 No. L287/63.

[48] True, the ECB plays such a role through the convoluted and expensive mediation of financial institutions, so as to keep the appearance of compliance with Article 123 TFUE.

through what is labelled its 'non-conventional' monetary policy. This practice has been justified by the ECJ, which has concluded that the remit of monetary policy should be deemed as wide as necessary to achieve the *goals* of monetary policy, rather independently of the (narrow) legitimacy basis of the ECB.[49] Among many other things, this implies that the ECB can decide on the shape of its monetary policy independently of whether or not this affects the conduct of national fiscal policies, while the reverse does not hold. While the Federal German Constitutional Court in *Weiss*[50] threw further doubts on the extent to which such an interpretation was compatible with democratic constitutional law, it failed to translate its concerns into any operative constraint.[51]

The ECB is far from being the only non-representative institution which has acquired important powers in the last decades. Independent fiscal authorities have been created in all Member States and have become part of a wider European network.[52] Such authorities do not only produce the key figures on the basis of which national fiscal plans are elaborated, but also produce influential reports assessing the fiscal costs of alternative policy options. There are plans to create 'competitiveness' authorities, with an even broader mandate, extending to the analysis of policy options to 'strengthen' national economies.[53] By the same token, the IMF has become one of the key players in the processes of granting financial assistance to Eurozone states undergoing fiscal crises and of monitoring compliance with the economic programmes to which the said assistance was conditioned.

25.6.3 *The Recurrence of Emergencies and the Empowering of Asymmetric Executive-like Institutions and of Creditor States*

Supranational decision-making is cumbersome because there are quite a number of veto points. This results in the EU being not slow to react, but in some occasions incapable of doing so, entangled as it is in a 'joint decision trap'.[54] Not only is the problem compounded when extraordinary circumstances require prompt decisions, but the slow path at which the EU decides results in challenges deteriorating into crises, thus making emergencies recurrent. When confronted with major challenges, the EU follows a cycle of procrastination and ineffective action, leading to emergency decision-making in the absence of any declaration of emergency.

On such a basis, it is perhaps only a trifle exaggerated to argue that the EU has developed an addiction to emergencies, while largely lacking specific provisions governing them. As long as 'ordinary decision-making' is close to impossible because of its cumbersomeness, emergencies are bound to be regarded as the only way out of the *impasse*, so decision-makers start to internalise a new identity as emergency decision-makers.

49 Conclusions of AG Cruz in case Case 62/14, Gauweiler, ECLI:EU:C:2015:7, para. 111; ruling of the Court, ECLI:EU:C:2015:400, cf. para. 52 ff.

50 BVerfG, Judgement of the Second Senate of 5 May 2020 – 2 BvR 859/15, ECLI:DE:BVerfG:2020:rs20200505.2bvr085915.

51 Cf. M. Dani, E. Chiti, J. Mendes, A. J. Menéndez, H. Schepel and M. Wilkinson, '"It's the Political Economy . . .!" A Moment of Truth for the Eurozone and the EU' (2021) 19 *International Journal of Constitutional Law* 309–27.

52 See www.euifis.eu/, last accessed 8 August 2022.

53 'Five Presidents' Report', available at: https://ec.europa.eu/commission/sites/beta-political/files/5-presidents-report_en.pdf, last accessed 8 August 2022.

54 F. Scharpf, 'The Joint-Decision Trap: Lessons from German Federalism and European Integration' (1988) 66 *Public Administration* 239.

An obvious danger is that the recurrence of undeclared emergencies results in the selective and arbitrary breach of legal norms and, consequently, in the slow but steady erosion of the capacity of EU law to integrate European society. At any rate, emergencies lead to a further encroachment of ordinary, 'representative' supranational decision-making procedures. Cycles of emergencies favour the empowerment of those institutions that are structurally capable of deciding swiftly and quickly (i.e., basically executives or executive-like institutions). By the same token, emergencies favour the aggravation of pre-existing power imbalances, which not infrequently project themselves beyond the emergency in the legal norms written under it. Such tendencies seem to be confirmed by the institutional and procedural developments in the wake of the financial and fiscal crises: the central role of the Euro Summit and the Eurogroup and, within them, the heightening of power asymmetries in favour of 'creditor' states and to the detriment of 'debtor states'.

25.6.4 *Minoritarian Government*

Finally, we can observe both formal and informal tendencies to divorce the forging of a European general will from the democratic formation of a majoritarian will.

First, the reform of the procedures through which national fiscal policies are formally coordinated, and in actual practice monitored and controlled, has resulted in a move from majoritarian decision-making (a 'qualified' majority in the Council of Ministers or the Eurogroup) to minoritarian decision-making (the Commission concurring with a 'qualified' minority of the members of the Council of Ministers or the Eurogroup). It should be noticed that such change affects fundamental decisions, including the imposition of sanctions in the case of a persistent breach of the fiscal rules mentioned in Section 25.2.

Second, the empowerment of the European Parliament as co-legislator has resulted in the addition of quite a number of additional steps in the law-making process. That has created a serious risk that the gains in democratic legitimacy compromise the capacity to take effective and prompt decisions. This has favoured the 'informal' simplification of the law-making process through the creation of mixed institutional structures (the so-called trilogues) in which the main institutions with legislative responsibilities, the Council of Ministers, the Parliament and the Commission iron out their differences and strive to reach an agreement.[55] Now, what has been gained in efficiency has been lost in democratic legitimacy. Minority groups tend to be underrepresented in 'trilogues', while some parliamentarians emerge as repeat players. Furthermore, the 'trilogues' proceed behind closed doors, undermining the achievements of the increased transparency of the workings of Parliament and Council.

25.7 PRIVATE PROPERTY AS THE SUPREME VALUE OF EUROPEAN LAW

The legal and economic force of the trio of 'sound' money, economic freedom(s) and 'free' competition has turned the EU into a most powerful *external constraint* that champions a radical conception of private property. European law has released European property owners from many of the limits and constraints imposed by the post-war Democratic and Social State in pursuit of its vision of socialised and temporary property rights.[56] At the very same time, European law fosters fiscal and monetary policies that preserve the value of accumulated capital

[55] A. E. Stie, *Democratic Decision-Making in the EU: Technocracy in Disguise?* (Routledge, 2012).

[56] T. Piketty, *Capital et Ideologie* (Seuil, 2019), chapter 11.

and ensure the means for the future and indefinite accumulation of capital. As a result, while national public power has been enervated and fragmented, supranational public power remains essentially *disciplinary* and regulatory, capable of preventing and channelling action but ill-equipped to undertake positive action. In other words, the powers that states have lost have not been transferred to the supranational level but have either been dispersed or have resulted in a stronger position of the owners of capital.

This peculiar organisation of public power relies very heavily on the authority of European law, in particular on its pretence to be the supreme law of the land.[57] The bite of the claim to substantive supremacy of private property depends on the success of the structural claim to supremacy of EU law over national law (otherwise, states will be free to make social concerns prevail over private property). It should be said, however, that the claim to supremacy of EU law has not gone uncontested. As is well-known, national constitutional and supreme courts, following the leads of the German Federal Constitutional Court and the Italian Constitutional Court, have insisted on national constitutions remaining the ultimate source of validity and legitimacy of the law within each state. From that claim follow a number of limits to the structural supremacy of EU law, which come hand in hand with limits to the supremacy of private property. However, higher national courts have refrained so far from considering the substantive tensions lurking behind structural conflicts. They have actually limited themselves to insist on the structural primacy of national constitutions, while accepting, at the end of the day, the substantive choices of EU law. Thus, the much debated case law of the German and the Italian constitutional courts setting 'counter-limits' to the force of EU law has had very limited (if any) substantive implications.[58] National courts seem to be worried about the allocation of competences and not so much about the substantive content of the law.

Whether the present organisation of power is stable remains an open question. What can be said is that the supremacy of a radical conception of private property, guaranteed by the trio of principles referred in the title of this chapter, seems to have contributed to the growth of income and wealth inequalities in the European Union in the last 40 years. National policies aimed at countering such trends have been either dismantled or pre-empted by arguing that they breached economic freedom(s), distorted 'free' competition or led to 'unsound' public finances. Supranational equivalents did not materialise (most of the time they were not even proposed) given the many veto points in-built in the asymmetric supranational law-making process.

25.8 IS IT PERTINENT TO SPEAK OF A 'EUROPEAN CONSTITUTION' OR OF EUROPEAN CONSTITUTIONAL LAW?

The euro and Frontex are powerful reminders of the fact that the EU has acquired state-like traits and that European law, consequently, engages with the most politically sensitive questions. Should we then extend rather freely the constitutional language to the European Union? Should we speak of the 'European constitution' and of 'European constitutional law'?

The answer cannot but be nuanced. In descriptive, 'sociological' terms, there is no doubt that the European Union has a constitution, for sure in 'functional terms', perhaps even in the 'material' terms referred to in this handbook. And the study of such a constitution requires, as

[57] On the evolution of the structural principle of supremacy, see M. Dani and A. J. Menéndez, 'European Constitutional Imagination: A Whig Interpretation of the Process of European Integration?', I-Courts Working Papers, 243/2021.

[58] A. J. Menéndez, '"False Friends" costituzionali: l'irresistibile ascesa dei conflitti fondamentali tra il diritto europeo e quello nazionale' (2019) *Diritto pubblico comparato ed europeo* 887.

I have tried to do in this chapter, going beyond the 'law in the books' and considering the relevant socially enforced conventions and practices, but also keeping at least one eye on the way in which power is actually wielded. By the same token, we need to reconnect the study of political agency with that of the content of the fundamental legal norms and to do so without the many blinders that the mythology and dogmas of European law imposes upon us. Although Mortati's concept of the material constitution remains problematic, not least on account of its origins (or to be more precise, its role model), the 'research agenda' that comes hand in hand with such a concept is in itself a powerful reminder of the importance of agency even in processes which are deeply mediated by heavy structural forces, such as the transformation of European Union law in the recent past. It should constitute, among other things, a powerful warning against naïve formalism and an incentive to bring into the scope of our analysis the key institutions through which power is actually exerted.

Still, there are many serious doubts as to whether such a functional constitution can be regarded as legitimate in democratic terms, so as to be considered on a par with the national democratic constitutions of the Member States. Freely characterising European fundamental norms as constitutional may result in, ingeniously or disingenuously, cloaking in plain sight the profound substantive mutation that the European Union has experienced in the last four decades, bordering on a regime change. By a too generous application of the term 'constitution' to EU law, we run a serious risk of projecting into it qualities that it does not have, connotations that it does not deserve. Above all, we may end up devaluing the currency of democratic constitutional law, concluding that European law and national constitutional law are part of a continuum, an assumption that cannot but end up in conceptual and normative confusion.

Index